Encyclopedia of the
AMERICAN
JUDICIAL
SYSTEM

Encyclopedia of the
AMERICAN JUDICIAL SYSTEM

*Studies of the Principal
Institutions and Processes of Law*

Robert J. Janosik, *EDITOR*
Occidental College

Volume I

CHARLES SCRIBNER'S SONS · NEW YORK

Copyright © 1987 Charles Scribner's Sons

Encyclopedia of the American judicial system.

Includes bibliographies and index.
1. Law—United States—Dictionaries. 2. Justice,
Administration of—United States—Dictionaries.
3. United States—Constitutional law—Dictionaries.
I. Janosik, Robert J. (Robert Joseph)
KF154.E53   1987   349.73′0321   87–4742
ISBN 0-684-17807-9 Set   347.300321
ISBN 0-684-18858-9 Volume I
ISBN 0-684-18859-7 Volume II
ISBN 0-684-18860-0 Volume III

Published simultaneously in Canada
by Collier Macmillan Canada, Inc.

1 3 5 7 9 11 13 15 17 19 V/C 20 18 16 14 12 10 8 6 4 2

Printed in the United States of America.

The paper in this book meets the guidelines for permanence and
durability of the Committee on Production Guidelines for Book Longevity
of the Council on Library Resources.

Editorial Staff

Advisory Board

PREFACE

IN the 1930s, a group of critics of the legal profession upbraided lawyers and judges for their habit of obscuring the nature of their professional work. Jerome Frank, one of these critics, spoke of the "cult of the robe" and of the gloss on the law created by trial lawyers that hides the dynamics and chanciness of the enterprise from the public. Another, Karl Llewellyn, concurred and called lawyers the shamans of the modern world. Whatever the merit of these criticisms, it is certainly clear that the voluminous literature on the law is often inaccessible to the layperson, university student, and academic researcher not trained in the ways of the law library.

The *Encyclopedia of the American Judicial System* is an effort to remedy this problem. Like the three reference works which preceded it in the Scribner's American Civilization Series—the *Encyclopedia of American Political History,* the *Encyclopedia of American Economic History* and the *Encyclopedia of American Foreign Policy*—these three volumes bring together current scholarship on a variety of topics. This *Encyclopedia* encompasses both the substance of American law and the process that produces and utilizes legal precepts. Although some of the subjects discussed are by their very nature technical and difficult, the essays included here were written as self-contained units, providing enough information to guide the reader without legal training. Thus, these essays are accessible to a wide audience and serve as introductory studies of subjects that previously may have been difficult to approach or explore.

The initial selection of the topics in this collection was a simple process. In consultation with a group of teachers, we sought to identify and include essays of interest to students and scholars doing basic research on the American legal system. Hoping to reflect our efforts to produce a series that attends both to the substance and process of the law, we organized the work into six categories across the three volumes.

It seemed necessary to consider major topics in Constitutional law and to add a list of topics that surveyed non-Constitutional, substantive areas of the law. We also wanted to include a set of entries describing and detailing the structures of the judicial system as well as selections about the personnel who inhabit and use those institutions. The behavioral revolution in the social sciences instructed us in the need to include essays on the actual operations of these institutions, whatever their formal configurations; hence, the topics concerning the processes of American legal institutions. To reflect a developmental perspective we commissioned essays concerning topics which consider the activities of the judiciary, especially the Supreme Court of the United States. And, finally, under the catch-all rubric "Methodology," we have included essays on the historiography of American law, jurisprudence and behavioral studies of the legal system.

Authors were not given a specific format. Discussions were held to reach agreement on the appropriate content for an essay, but the products of these discussions illustrate a wide range of techniques for approaching any broad topic. The essays covering Supreme Court history, for example, vary considerably. Some authors employ detailed case analysis. Others emphasize the social

vii

PREFACE

context of a historical period and the impact of such events on the judiciary. Still others develop the topic from the point of view of intra-court blocs and pressures. This variation is an asset rather than a liability; it allows the student of court behavior to experience the many ways scholars have productively investigated the broad topic of judicial history. In the same spirit, the editorial staff did not impose a particular critical perspective on authors. Indeed, in commissioning authors, an effort was made to identify a variety of points of view concerning the American legal system. Authors were asked to express a personal voice in their essay, a feature warranted by the length of the entries. We are confident that the authors provide readers with sufficient information to understand the various dimensions of a controversy, thereby permitting them to reach informed conclusions about such topics. The perceptive reader will find in these essays a range of postures concerning American law and the legal system. Criticism of important aspects of American legal practice is well represented; so, too, are voices that find the system to be strong and astonishingly resilient.

A number of individuals contributed their support and enthusiasm over the period during which these volumes were conceived and assembled. The editorial board proved to be essential in identifying the authors who contributed essays. Judge Marvin E. Frankel, Professors Sheldon Goldman, Thomas M. Franck, and C. Herman Pritchett, and Mr. David Kairys, Esq. offered interesting and helpful suggestions. I also owe a debt of gratitude to the three managing editors at Charles Scribner's Sons who have seen this project through. Mr. David William Voorhees, there at the outset, lent his professional experience and wide-ranging knowledge. His successor, Mr. Steven Sayre, brought efficiency and humor to the project during the long commissioning phase and the early editorial work. Mr. Jonathan Aretakis added new, much-needed energy as the editorial process was completed and the manuscripts went to press. I would also like to thank the fine editorial staff who reviewed manuscripts—Martha Cooley, Kathleen Erickson, Joan Field, and Leland Lowther. And my special thanks to Ann Manning, the secretary in the Department of Political Science at Occidental. Her help and good cheer throughout have been greatly appreciated.

Robert J. Janosik

CONTENTS

ix

CONTENTS

CONTENTS

xi

CONTENTS

Encyclopedia of the
AMERICAN
JUDICIAL
SYSTEM

Part I
LEGAL
HISTORY

COLONIAL LAW AND JUSTICE

Stephen Botein

THE history of early American law some-times seems forbiddingly complex because it lacks a focal institution at the center, such as a Supreme Court resolving urgent public issues by reference to a written national statement of constitutional principles. The ingredients of law in colonial America were variously combined and recombined in numerous jurisdictions. Nevertheless, its history has a certain thematic unity. Colonial law was responsive to broad configurations of social power, as revealed in military strength, population growth, and trade. The rules of early American law, even when formulated and applied inconsistently, had the effect of recognizing or maintaining the priority of some group interests over others and of strengthening or weakening different patterns of social organization.

Although government in the American colonies normally conducted its business at minimal expense, without large-scale programs imple-mented bureaucratically, it was far from light-handed in its efforts to realize public goals. It tried to act through everyday regulation of activity that in later times would be regarded as essen-tially private. By so intervening to guide the be-havior and the belief of individuals, the public authorities in colonial America significantly al-tered the lives of ordinary men and women.

RACE AND ETHNICITY

Two hundred and seventy-five years after John Cabot first saw the coast of Newfoundland, an English population of approximately 1.5 mil-lion occupied the seaboard region of northeast-ern America, from Penobscot Bay to Georgia. Inevitably, law had been developed both to jus-tify control by this one people of territory in which others claimed rights and to define the status of those who stayed or came to live there under English sovereignty.

Despite frequent citation of Cabot's voyage as the basis of English title in the New World, it was often acknowledged that "visual apprehension" of territory was legally insufficient for such a claim. The essence of the English position was phrased in terms that reflected domestic land law. Actual possession was what established title. In disregard of papal grants to Spain and Portu-gal, the English government was free to autho-rize settlement of land uninhabited by other Europeans.

When English colonization of North America finally got under way, there were only the broad-est of legal guidelines. Two clauses were re-peated in most patents and charters. According to one, English colonists would remain English subjects, and their children born overseas would be English by birthright. The other clause granted the power to frame governmental regu-lations, stipulating that they conform as far as possible to the laws and policies of the mother country.

It was generally agreed that English royal au-thority could be asserted over the native "hea-then" of America by reason of conquest in a "just war." This convenient doctrine skirted the issue of Native American rights. The simplest ratio-nale for dispossession of Native Americans was to cite the fundamental right of self-defense against "barbarians" said to be capable of grue-some atrocities. Possibly it was disappointing to some impatient settlers that their first contacts with Indians were peaceful.

In Virginia, the devastating native attack of 1622 put an end to white restraint. Without such

1

a violent incident to create legitimacy in other colonies, Englishmen buttressed proclamations of sovereignty by legal devices or argumentation that purported to establish their property rights in particular North American lands. Most English efforts to acquire territory from native leaders were temporary expedients, usually undertaken to rebut claims to title by other Englishmen or by rival European interests. Deceit might well be involved—presentations of trinkets along with rum, accompanying promises misrecorded or later broken at will. In New England, Puritan ideologues brusquely and inaccurately dismissed the Indians as nomadic hunters and foragers who should no more be allowed to "usurp" the land than wild beasts of the forest.

Even when the English dealt with the Indians in good faith, they ignored alternative conceptions of property that prevailed among the woodland tribes of the Northeast. Land was thought to have been transmitted by descent from ancestors who had lived and died and been buried in the same area; it belonged to each Indian nation as a whole, not to individuals. A chief might agree to transfer territory to other Indians or to Europeans, but this was regarded as a free gift, perhaps to promote a fraternal alliance. Merchandise received during such a voluntary transfer was understood to be a form of ceremonial reciprocity, not payment as part of a mutual bargain. European gifts might then be distributed within a tribe as a means of recording what had taken place. To the bewilderment of most English leaders, their native counterparts preferred to rely on oral tradition for agreements rather than on written documents.

During the decades that Englishmen were removing one alien race from their new American territories, they were beginning to import another and to lay the legal groundwork for its enslavement. Despite the rapid expansion of black chattel slavery in the British West Indies, it took the mainland tobacco colonies in the Chesapeake region almost half a century to write such a labor system into law. One reason for this delay was that Englishmen needed that much experience to appreciate how enslaving Africans was a way to avoid the worst consequences of restricting the freedom of their own countrymen.

For most of the seventeenth century, the great majority of field hands in the Chesapeake tobacco fields were white indentured servants from the mother country. Many were young and poor. If they had signed their indentures in England, in exchange for ocean passage under miserably crowded and unsanitary conditions, they would then be sold on arrival for the period of service specified in their contracts—anywhere from one or two years to seven years or more. At the end they could set out on their own, with some clothing and tools as "freedom dues" and perhaps an official grant of acreage. Indentured servants were unable to vote, engage in trade, or marry without the consent of their masters. Most important, their obligation of service was transferable without their consent.

Indentured service was effective in moving people to the New World to meet a growing demand for labor, especially in the Chesapeake colonies. But how could English settlers hope to prosper if they continued systematically to reduce their own people to a condition that would have been intolerable in the mother country? This situation led to an effort to distinguish and degrade the status of black labor.

Before the middle of the seventeenth century, there were evidently some African slaves in the Chesapeake region who served for life, with the same obligation passing to their children; other Africans worked with and on the same terms as white servants or were free. Gradually, the position of blacks deteriorated. Over several decades following 1660, statutes appeared on the books in Maryland and Virginia confirming the formula that all blacks and no whites would be slaves for life. Baptism would no longer imply a possibility of freedom; miscegenation was banned. A slave was just another asset, attachable for debts and part of the owner's taxable property. In 1705 Virginia declared slaves to be the equivalent of real estate and therefore subject to the usual rules of inheritance. Nothing comparable to slavery was to be found in the legal system of the mother country.

Because English law suited a population that was more or less homogeneous, there was also difficulty dealing with some of the non-English white groups that populated the mainland American colonies south of New England. For example, New York's Dutch inhabitants posed problems. England had never recognized Dutch sovereignty there and could readily justify royal transformation of the New Netherlands after 1664 by right of conquest; but this took time to achieve. For several decades, in the interest of conciliating a sullen local majority, English courts allowed Dutch residents to retain their own customs concerning inheritance and to settle contracts made before 1664 according to Roman civil usages observed in the New Netherlands. Subsequently, as English settlers poured into the colony, it became feasible to suppress most Dutch forms, but not without stubborn Dutch resistance, which continued through the eighteenth century.

Some whites entering the colonies in the eighteenth century seemed nearly ungovernable. Immigrants from Ulster in Northern Ireland, the Presbyterian Scotch-Irish, streamed through the backcountry of the middle and southern colonies quite indifferent to jurisdictional boundaries and English legal conventions, squatting on whatever vacant land appealed to them. Large numbers of German-speaking immigrants also spread out through the same backcountry. They included numerous pietistic sects—Mennonites, Dunkers, Schwenkfelders, Moravians—espousing various degrees of nonaccommodation with civil government. Further, coming as they did from the Continent, their legal status as subjects or citizens was unclear. In theory, they could be declared citizens of the realm either by a royal patent of denization or by a parliamentary naturalization act, but these were expensive, individualized procedures. Some colonial governors and assemblies devised less costly and intricate means of conferring a rather dubious kind of local citizenship on the new arrivals.

In 1740, trying to clarify the situation, Parliament passed a general act that allowed foreign settlers in the colonies to acquire certificates of naturalization, valid in all parts of the empire, after seven years of residence. Brief absences were permitted by this legislation, the costs of application were minimal, and there were some exemptions from its requirement of avowed Protestantism. In the next three decades, however, fewer than seven thousand colonists were naturalized accordingly. Seven years could be an inconveniently long time to have to be classified as an alien, whose land would revert to the government in case of death.

In the course of the eighteenth century, English law proved less than adequate for regulation of an increasingly diversified white population on the colonial mainland. Meanwhile, the number of black slaves in the colonies was growing prodigiously. One result, particularly in areas where whites were not numerous enough to feel safe, was an immense volume of legislation to keep blacks in order. Special courts were erected to try slaves accused of committing felonies, according to rules of evidence that differed from those of English law; special patrols were authorized to protect the countryside, sometimes with extraordinary powers of search and seizure in slave quarters; special punishments were decreed for slaves; and special regulations governed their movements.

Finally, there were more Indians to contend with, not along the coast but toward the interior —where large and well-organized tribes could resist white encroachment by adept maneuvers with rival European nations. This political reality, in turn, vastly complicated official handling of legal disputes within the colonies which involved long-dormant Indian claims to land.

The difficult task of determining what English law applied in America was magnified by the presence of non-English peoples. A century and a half after the founding of Jamestown, it appeared that the laws of the mother country and those of her mainland colonies could not be harmonized as easily as proponents of unitary English nationhood had once assumed.

RELIGION AND THE STATE

Within the legal environment that English settlers established in northeastern America, the most troublesome ideological source of disharmony was religion. At the extremes of the colonial Protestant spectrum were strict advocates of the Church of England as a state religion and radical dissenters espousing pure voluntarism. What developed eventually was a pattern of localistic deviation from English norms. The precarious role of the Church of England in colonial America was symptomatic of underlying weaknesses in the structure of transatlantic empire.

There is no reason to think that the Puritans monopolized official religiosity during the seventeenth century. In Virginia, it was taken for granted from the start that public authority had a major function to perform in collaborating with the church to supervise moral conduct throughout the territorial boundaries of its jurisdiction and to maintain uniformity of belief. Even in the brutal early years at Jamestown, Virginians were governed by "Divine" and "Moral" in addition to "Martial" regulations. Twice a day, by drumbeat, they marched to prayers; severe penalties were prescribed for nonattendance and profanity. In 1619 the first colonial assembly passed a series of laws against gaming, drunkenness, swearing, and other moral offenses. In 1705 the legislature in Virginia was still busy seeking to enforce observance of the Sabbath. Maryland, in 1678, drew up laws to curb the "licentiousness" of its inhabitants. In New York, the same concerns underlay an "Act for Suppressing Immorality" passed by the General Assembly in 1708.

Although the colonies south of New England followed traditional Elizabethan theory in writing laws to criminalize sin and encourage righteousness, they failed to replicate the Anglican ecclesiastical system that had been largely responsible for such legal regulation in the mother country. The case of Virginia is most revealing. Like colonial Anglicans everywhere, lay members of the Church of England in Virginia self-consciously declined to erect a system of ecclesiastical courts, preferring to retain the system of moral regulation that had been developed in a series of statutes about midcentury. Local vestrymen would choose churchwardens, who twice a year reported to their county court on the morals of the parish. In cases of delinquency, the vestry itself might hear evidence and take depositions, but prosecutions—sometimes managed by a churchwarden—would be brought before the county justices. Their judgments, which commonly involved fines or whippings or public confessions in church, might be executed by either a sheriff or a churchwarden. Such procedures, characteristic of Maryland and New York as well, jumbled civil and ecclesiastical government, but they firmly established the laity's authority to oversee morals.

The net effect was irregular enforcement, because the local leaders who dominated both vestries and courts appear to have been reluctant to look closely into the sins of their neighbors. Informants were discouraged from coming forward because they were liable for court costs in the event of acquittal. Evidently it was the laissez-faire temper of planters in the Chesapeake region, rather than skepticism regarding the occult, which accounted for the tendency of Chesapeake courts to treat charges of witchcraft as actionable slander without bothering to try the accused. A similar pattern of prudent inattention characterized the response of local officialdom to the arrival of Quakers in seventeenth-century Virginia. Despite threats and passage of penal statutes, there was much de facto tolerance of Quakers at the county level.

Established state religion in Virginia declined further during the eighteenth century. While prosecutions for swearing and like offenses might be numerous in some counties, a statute of 1727 imposing fines on householders who neglected to report bastards born in their homes was a sign that legal enforcement of morality had languished in others. So had legal enforcement of religious uniformity. To promote settlement along the frontier, the House of Burgesses passed miscellaneous acts exempting foreign Protestants from parish levies. After 1740, as the religious fervor of the Great Awakening swept through the colony, dissenting itinerants preached to enthusiastic crowds in defiance of restrictive regulations. Appearing in the 1750s, Baptist spokesmen were sharply critical of lapses in virtue by local justices of the peace and by the established clergy.

In 1755, when Anglican ministers in the colony petitioned for higher salaries, the House of Burgesses was almost unanimous in rejecting their request; instead, Virginia's Two Penny Act fixed the ratio of tobacco to currency in such a way as to reduce clerical income drastically. Another such Two Penny Act, passed in 1758, was eventually disallowed by the Privy Council in London. Here was the setting for the celebrated Parson's Cause of 1763, in which the twenty-three-year-old Patrick Henry persuaded a jury to award only nominal damages to a minister suing for the back pay due him. Henry's argument, radical in its constitutional implications, questioned whether the crown government could legitimately place the welfare of the clergy over legislation in the public interest. It was clear that the English model of official state religion had not prevailed in Virginia.

The English model certainly had influenced other colonies no more, and usually less. Such eighteenth-century Anglican jurisdictions as South Carolina, Maryland, and New York included so many dissenters of English as well as other ethnic origins that it would have been foolhardy to try to compel adherence to a state church. Two other colonies, Pennsylvania and Rhode Island, were committed to religious tolerance by the ideology of their founders. In the former, Quaker hopes for moral reformation were to be realized not through the state but in the voluntary discipline of local and monthly meetings. Eventually, this utopian system proved less workable than the ·ordinary processes of civil justice; but the experimental operation of Quaker moral law for several decades testified to the strength of a radical religious vision that acknowledged the necessity of the state as a basis of external social control but looked elsewhere for enhancement of the inner life. A similar ideal led Roger Williams to separate strictly church and state in Rhode Island.

This achievement met with favor among many English dissenters, but most Puritans in New England were intent on staking out a middle way. Theirs was an ambiguous theory, susceptible to different readings and applications. Although government and organized religion might properly collaborate, somehow this had to be done without either meddling in the affairs of the other. New England's Puritans provided for congregational discipline of members who transgressed scriptural laws against such offenses as drunkenness, unchastity, cheating, and heresy. A Puritan church might appoint a standing committee to prepare cases; decisions were made by majority vote and proclaimed by the minister. The disciplinary verdicts of a congregation had no civil consequences, however, and most colonial Puritans thought the deterrents of secular law could help persuade men and women to turn from sin to righteousness. As in seventeenth-century Virginia, in most of Puritan New England morality was an important component of statutory law. But there were significant differences. The Puritans were careful to distinguish formally congregational discipline from the operations of secular courts, and they sought to implement Hebraic standards of justice peculiarly appropriate to their self-image as a "second Israel."

Except for Rhode Island, where English law was said to apply in the absence of local enactments, the ideal polity of early Puritan New England was thought to comprehend divine intentions as revealed in Mosaic law. Sometimes this meant only that legal precepts found in the Old Testament might serve as general guidelines for policy. But there was no mistaking the specific biblical sources of some statutory law in Massachusetts. Although ministers could not act as public officials there, they advised lawmakers from time to time. In 1636 John Cotton drew up a code known as "Moses His Judicials." This was not adopted, but some of its Hebraic content resurfaced in the Massachusetts Body of Liberties, formulated in 1641 by another minister, Nathaniel Ward, who had also been trained as a lawyer in the mother country. Technically, it seems, Ward's code was never enacted, in order to avoid the appearance of disharmony with English law. Many of its provisions were recycled into *The Book of General Lawes and Libertyes* of 1648, however, which influenced legislation in Connecticut, New Hampshire, and to a lesser extent New York, New Jersey, and Pennsylvania. Especially in the text of Massachusetts' notorious capital laws, which prescribed death for such offenses as adultery and the cursing or smiting of parents, scriptural citations appeared by way of authoritative explanation.

Although no one was ever actually sentenced to death for abuse of a parent, Puritans generally emulated the example of Calvinists in Geneva by following through on charges against minor as well as serious offenders, seeking full substantiation and then prosecuting to reach a verdict and a sentence. High rates of conviction were typical of courts in Puritan communities.

Seventeenth-century Massachusetts was also appreciably stricter than Virginia in controlling ecclesiastical life. In addition to standard laws that associated political rights with church membership, imposed fines for absence from services without reason, and punished contemptuous behavior toward the clergy, the public authorities were quick to frame legislation suppressing such deviant religious groups as Anne Hutchinson and her followers in the 1630s and the Quakers who invaded the region in the 1650s. They were relentless, too, in their endeavor to root out witchcraft.

Gradually, the Puritan identity of early New England eroded. A new royal charter issued in 1691 forced Massachusetts to abandon much of the idiosyncratic biblicism and intolerance that had informed its previous laws. Blasphemy and sexual offenses continued to bulk large among the crimes for which New Englanders were punished, but for the latter category the trend by the middle of the eighteenth century was to concentrate on instances where bastard children threatened local taxpayers with the burden of public maintenance. If the state no longer banished dissidents, it still made an effort to support religious uniformity by public taxation for the support of orthodox clergymen. By bringing political pressure to bear from London, however, Anglicans as well as Quakers and Baptists in Massachusetts and Connecticut extracted statutory concessions that earmarked their tax money for their own ministers.

Hard-liners had to yield the least in Connecticut, which had managed to retain its independent corporate charter. The Saybrook Platform was adopted there in 1708 to facilitate cooperation between church councils and the state in supervising individual congregations. During 1742 and 1743, after the revivalistic uproar of the Great Awakening, Connecticut passed a group of statutes known as the Intolerant Acts. Aimed at Separatists who dared to criticize the colony's clerical establishment, this detailed legislation regulated the comings and goings of preachers, disallowed marriages and baptisms that they had performed, and removed their sympathizers from civil office.

It was ironic that state-sponsored churches were most powerful in an old Puritan stronghold such as Connecticut. Soon enough, Anglicans in New England would launch an aggressive campaign to propagandize the region and increase their numbers. One consequence was a counteroffensive by leading Congregational clergymen in Massachusetts, who called for full disestablishment of the British Empire. Here, just before the crisis that led to American independence, was a challenge to the Church of England as sweeping as that voiced in Virginia by Patrick Henry. Anglicanism was under attack almost everywhere. This pattern of conflict had come about slowly within a context shaped by the novel and irregular features of colonial American society.

COMMUNITY

The development of early American law reflected narrowly localized social experience in colonies that had been formed without steady direction from the mother country. Particularly in the small towns of New England, the result was a consensual mode of lawmaking that survived under stress into the eighteenth century. Elsewhere, law tended to become an instrument by which the gentry class could attempt to exploit people who had little or no access to political power.

Although some early Puritan leaders resisted, settlers entering Massachusetts in the 1630s moved purposefully to decentralize authority. All legislators and executives were subject to annual election; the governor had virtually no independent role; a major part of governance devolved to the level of the town meeting. The shaky constitutional foundation of these arrangements was a charter organizing a commercial company, which the Puritans tacitly misinterpreted as a blueprint for their commonwealth. To limit further the powers of officialdom, the colony's later statutory compilations of 1641 and 1648 guaranteed many of the traditional liberties of Englishmen, such as trial by jury.

In seventeenth-century Massachusetts, the boldest dreams of legal reformers in the mother country became fact. There was a unitary court system in the Bible commonwealth rather than the multiplicity of specialized tribunals through which Englishmen had to navigate. County courts handled the bulk of civil business as well as most routine crimes; they also assumed administrative responsibility for churches, schools, roads, mills, and the like. At the town level, magistrates might resolve minor civil disputes, perform marriages, and attempt to suppress drunkenness. Appeals ran to the Colonial General Court, which was also the legislature, or to a Court of Assistants composed of the governor, deputy governor, and magistrates, which also asserted trial jurisdiction over serious crimes.

For a time Massachusetts prohibited anyone from taking a fee to represent someone else in court. Not until 1673 was there formal recognition of the right to practice law in the colony, and then fees were strictly regulated. The few men who took up this invitation before the end of the century were poorly trained and lacked enough clients for full-time legal work. Predictably, in these circumstances, there was little of the technical precision insisted upon in the royal courts of the mother country. The only official language of the courts in Massachusetts was English; it was unnecessary to master obscure medieval terminology. Untrained judges joined juries in mixing matters of law with matters of fact, relying on just those basics of doctrine and procedure that could be learned by a lay court clerk from a manual. In the absence of professional lawyers, there was no one to maintain orthodoxy and no great reason to do so; simplified procedure was less costly to litigants.

The distinctive pattern of lawmaking that emerged in seventeenth-century New England was suitable for Puritans hoping to achieve personal and social reformation. It was suitable, too, for small-scale farmers dwelling in tightly knit communities where marked disparities of social and economic position were unusual. It may be that some New Englanders were consciously trying to create a system based on social covenant, by which individuals gathered and consented to the rule of law. Many communities in the region came into existence by virtue of collective written promises—the most famous being those recorded in Plymouth's Mayflower Compact. Such compacts had been conceptualized by political philosophers, but they had never before been put in practice. Along with some other legal features of early New England, this habit of covenanting may have reflected the shadowy influence of customary law in the English manors and boroughs from which many settlers had emigrated. It seems to have expressed spontaneous folk feeling for a localistic society consisting of compatible and participating citizens.

It was natural enough that similar results were reached in other colonies, such as Connecticut and Pennsylvania, founded by religious idealists. Elsewhere, too, distaste for legal formalism and its practitioners was widespread, although the motives involved might have been less than visionary. In Virginia, for example, early settlers were contemptuous of lawyers representing the interests of a distant commercial company. Later in the century, planters fearful of executive patronage power repeatedly frustrated initiatives by the governor to professionalize legal practice in the colony by a system of licensing.

Because early Chesapeake society had not formed around compact agricultural communities, the legal environment of both Virginia and Maryland in the seventeenth century differed significantly from that of New England. With settlements dispersed as a consequence of runaway tobacco production, judicial and administrative authority barely existed below the county level. Chesapeake justice had a frontier look rougher than what was usual in the mother country—and rarely to be found in New England. Judges in oversized counties were chronically reluctant to leave the comforts of home and travel in bad weather; absenteeism was a feature of many courts. Until late in the century, when most counties constructed modest courthouses, judicial proceedings were often held in taverns, where all concerned were likely to grow abusive. Criminals might be lodged in the same place as well, for lack of prison facilities.

It was not only the forms of early American law that differed according to local social circumstances. Substance varied too. Even laws that were uniformly worded could take on divergent social meanings from one colonial jurisdiction to another.

Statutes in New England, for example, accorded with one in Virginia providing that an owner of horses or cattle would not be liable for damage they might cause in a neighbor's field if the neighbor had failed to make a reasonable effort to guard against such a possibility. Here the colonies deviated from English law, which held the owner of animals liable whether or not the neighbor's land was fenced. Everywhere the colonial rule reflected the importance of encouraging settlers to import and breed livestock, and perhaps, too, the relative availability of timber. But other factors were in play as well. In the average town of early New England, where differences in wealth were apt to be inconsiderable and cattle might be distributed approximately in proportion to acreage, the costs of such a public policy were shared rather equitably. In Virginia, however, fencing laws provoked hostility. Large-scale planters were far less vulnerable to mischievous animals than were subsistence farmers cultivating small plots. Moreover, it was the large-scale planters who kept horses, which were the worst troublemakers.

In some respects, seventeenth-century Chesapeake conditions resembled those of a poor rural area in England. Probably no behavior occupied the Maryland authorities more than hog stealing. Every effort was made to record the markings on stock; punishments prescribed by statute included branding on the shoulder with an "H" for a second offense and death for a third! Both

Maryland and Virginia retained much of England's harsh criminal law protecting small as well as large amounts of property. As in the mother country, pardons and commutations softened the law's rigor, sometimes only after a bizarre ritual in which the condemned man would not be told of his reprieve until the rope was about his neck.

To the north, both the Puritans and the Quakers chose to rely much less on fear of execution to prevent crimes against property, although within a few decades Pennsylvania began to revert to a grim deterrent policy by increasing the number of capital laws. In many cases of minor theft that were capital crimes by English law, the usual Puritan penalty was a whipping and double or triple restitution to the victim. This was a model of pragmatic penal legislation in a society largely free of unsettling conflict between the very rich and the very poor.

Seventeenth-century New England was composed mainly of small landowners enjoying security of title. At least in theory, most acreage elsewhere in the colonies was subject to demands for annual rent by the crown or a proprietor. Puritan colonists were proud that their charters had eliminated such feudal features. For the sake of secure title, all transfers of houses and acreage in New England had to be publicly recorded; a registered deed normally prevailed over any other claim to the same property. Although most colonies south of New England made similar arrangements, there was seldom as much of a public commitment to the process. Maryland, for example, did not respect the priority of a registered deed.

To keep their towns intact and peaceful, New Englanders depended on effective family organization of property rights. The legal framework of the early New England family was less patriarchal than English law allowed. Women gained at least some status within the local legal system. In 1650 Massachusetts made it a crime for either spouse to strike the other. A court might well void a husband's will if it left a worthy widow with an inadequate share of his estate. It was easier in New England for married women to assert some degree of legal personality, instead of having their decision-making powers submerged under those of their husbands according to the formulas of the royal courts in the mother country. A Massachusetts woman might well contract before marriage for the freedom afterward to dis-

pose of specified property, regardless of her husband's wishes.

Intergenerational family affairs usually seem to have been managed in such a way as to emphasize mutuality of interest. With land abundant, New England differed from England in having few estates that were "entailed" so as to restrict the right of descendants to sell off acreage. It was expected that each generation would stake the next in the same locality. Outside Rhode Island, where law followed English precedent, New Englanders abandoned the traditional rule of "primogeniture," by which the eldest son succeeded to the entire estate of a man who died without making a will. Instead, all children got equal portions except for the eldest male, who by Mosaic precept received a double share. This was also a rule that New Englanders tended to observe voluntarily when they took the common precaution of drawing up wills.

Pennsylvania followed New England in its laws of inheritance; New York, Maryland, Virginia, and the Carolinas retained the English doctrine of primogeniture and, on paper, were less permissive in allowing descendants to undo entailed estates. Everywhere south of New England, women benefited to some extent from the informality of legal procedure. In the Chesapeake region for much of the seventeenth century, however, the family unit of parents and children could not function as a stabilizing force. Women were scarce and the life expectancy of males dismally low. These conditions prompted Chesapeake legislators to set up orphans' courts with broad supervisory authority to prevent exploitation of a child's estate or labor. As mortality rates became less severe, planters evolved a legal framework for family affairs that mixed Old World forms with regional custom. The great majority of eighteenth-century Chesapeake men who drew up wills made provision for younger children, but the eldest son generally inherited the home plantation. The diffusion of family life in the region showed up in the practice of making numerous secondary bequests to siblings, cousins, nephews, and unrelated friends.

For servants and slaves, Chesapeake law could be vicious. Whereas in New England a servant without sufficient clothing might successfully bring a complaint in court, evidence of outrageous brutality was often required to persuade justices of the peace in Maryland or Virginia to intervene. The law of the region did little to restrain an intemperate master or mistress. What it did do was to whip runaways and extend their terms of service by a rate of as many as ten days for every one in absence. Female servants bearing children might also have to put in extra time.

Of course black slaves fared the worst in the colonial system of justice. A master could count on immunity from prosecution if his slave died as a result of "moderate" correction. The unpleasant logic of tender treatment for such a master was that no man would premeditatedly destroy his own property. Implicit here was a massive irony in the legal system of slavery. Masters could not always be trusted to enforce the laws against people whom they owned, lest the value of their investment be diminished. Unlike white servants, black slaves could not be threatened with longer terms. Several jurisdictions in the eighteenth century promised public compensation not only to owners of slaves who were executed but also to owners of those who died during capture. If a slave escaped, all whites in the area would be unleashed in his pursuit, with license to kill. In such a situation, which lawfully invited poor citizens to destroy the property of their social superiors, the deepest contradictions within white society might become luridly apparent.

To the north, especially in the major port towns, other contradictions were becoming visible by the middle of the eighteenth century. Poverty was a growing problem in New York City, for example, and executions of criminals there increased sharply in the decades before independence. Even in New England, communal life was disconcertingly less resilient than before. Boston teemed with harbor vice and unattached people, many of whom took to the roads in search of work; at each stop, lest their poverty impose a burden on the town's taxpayers, they were likely to be "warned out" of the vicinity. Meanwhile, as the population of the older New England towns swelled, there was frequently not enough land left for younger sons, who then might emigrate to the frontier or hope to be established in trades. Widows found it ever more difficult to subsist on property subject to competing claims by different children. Indebtedness was widespread. Some New Englanders worried publicly that the entire class of middling freehold farmers would one day disappear.

Nowhere were communal traditions under more stress, in the years before the Revolution,

than on the great manorial estates that lay along the Hudson River in New York. These huge tracts of land were cultivated by tenants according to leases varying in length from a short specified period to perpetuity. Rents were modest, but the small farmers of the area—many of them former New Englanders—had grievances. To transfer a lease, a tenant might have to pay his landlord a fee equal to as much as one-fourth the market value of his farm. He might have to take his grain to a proprietary mill and pay whatever excessive price was asked there. In 1765, the heirs to the Philipse Highland patent in Dutchess County began to evict settlers near the Connecticut border. Soon the entire region was in turmoil.

The spectacle of colonial farmers rioting on behalf of secure title was ominous, coming as it did in the middle of the Stamp Act crisis. These were not lawless people by habit. Colonial conditions had rarely given them occasion to sustain the traditional forms of crowd violence and dissent that were so familiar in the mother country. But their behavior suggested that in some circumstances, violations of the norms of communal welfare by external authority could incite revolutionary activity.

EMPIRE

Overlaying the localized development of early American law from the late seventeenth century onward was an expanding program of imperial administration directed from London. The legal focus of this program was the structure of the colonial judiciary. Colonial courts were to be reorganized in conformity with the centralized model of royal justice in the mother country.

Efforts along these lines in New York had dated almost from the beginning of English rule. In 1691 New York's Act for Establishing Courts of Judicature completed the reforms of previous decades by consolidating local justice within a county court system and setting that system under the authority of a Supreme Court. In cases involving more than £100, appeals were allowed to the governor and council; where more than £300 was at stake, it was possible to proceed to the Privy Council in England. Elsewhere, about and after the turn of the century, the trend was much the same. Although provincial legislators sometimes were balky, the Privy Council made clear that it would disallow colonial statutes designed to keep control of legal decision-making in local hands. Closer imperial supervision of colonial courts would strengthen officials charged with enforcing unpopular parliamentary legislation. It would also help to protect the interests of English merchants who extended credit to the colonies.

English administrators originally intended that the Privy Council would function as the supreme appellate court of the empire. Unfortunately, the deliberations of the Privy Council were usually prolonged and haphazard. Councilors often had neither legal training nor acquaintance with colonial affairs, so it was difficult to know in advance what they would do—or afterward what they had done, as their main instrument of decision was an oral order that was seldom printed or even circulated in manuscript. Few colonists valued this appellate forum. More cases went to the Privy Council from Rhode Island than from any other mainland colony, but the rate of appeal there was still only about one per year. By the 1760s, some colonists and English administrators alike were toying with proposals for construction of a new appeals court to serve the continental colonies.

According to orthodox English doctrine, the power of creating courts was the prerogative of the crown. If that power was too distant when exercised from London, it was far too immediate when institutionalized under the auspices of royal governors representing the king. Not only did they appoint most judges but they also appointed them without life tenure; the guarantee of independence from executive control, which Parliament had enacted for the mother country in 1701, did not extend to the colonies. This was understandable because colonial legislatures would otherwise have dominated the judiciary by refusing to appropriate permanent salaries. Local politicians naturally objected, and the issue often had to be resolved by informal compromise. In 1761, the Privy Council restricted such maneuvers with an order prohibiting the issuance of judicial commissions unless they specified tenure upon the "pleasure" of the crown.

Royal governors selected other judges who more dependably eluded legislative influence. Vice-admiralty courts, authorized by act of Parliament in 1696, were convenient forums for the adjudication of maritime disputes over prizes, wrecks, insurance, contracts, and wages. These were single-judge courts that sat without juries, however, and their jurisdiction in the colonies ranged beyond routine maritime law to include enforcement of imperial trade regulations. Judicial compensation consisted not of salaries voted by local assemblies but of fixed fees and percentage payments on the goods that they condemned.

Even more controversial was another kind of gubernatorial court. Over time, England's High Court of Chancery had come to oversee the jurisprudence known as "equity," which dealt with problems not easily recognized by the formalistic "common law" dispensed in the older royal system of justice. Throughout the seventeenth century, most colonial judges had been inattentive to rules of common law and so in practice had been supplying equity without realizing what it was. After 1700, colonial governors south of New England gradually tried to establish their own chancery courts on the basis of their authority as representatives of the king. Many colonists fought back strenuously to prevent the introduction of a juryless system in which a governor would sit alone or with his council. Proceedings were apt to be costly, there was no appeal except to the mother country, and it was the unusual governor who had legal training.

After 1750, in most places, the furor over chancery courts died down. One good reason for growing acceptance of this parallel jurisdiction was its greater utility, as practice in the older colonial courts became markedly more technical. Colonial libraries expanded to make room for specialized treatises as well as elementary manuals. Particularly in the southern colonies, the forms of legal action were more likely to imitate esoteric English prototypes.

This tendency toward formalism in law, evident from colony to colony, was due not only to resident imperial officialdom but also to an emerging legal profession. That profession was a creation of commerce and empire. Up and down the coast, it was apparent that opportunities for successful legal careers were multiplying, as mercantile activity became more complex and predictable rules were needed to resolve disputes within court systems remodeled along English lines. On behalf of merchants overseas as well as those in the major port towns, lawyers pressed suits deep into some inland areas in order to recover money due on different instruments of credit. The most enterprising practitioners aimed for a share of vice-admiralty litigation, where the value of ships and cargoes in question determined counsel's fees (disproportionately high compared with the schedules established by provincial assemblies).

Imperial officials promoted professionalism in law. During the first two decades of the eighteenth century, for instance, royal governors of Massachusetts used their powers of appointment to improve the caliber of provincial judges, who in turn demanded greater precision of lawyers practicing in their courtrooms. In Virginia, toward the beginning of the 1730s, the attorney general introduced a law that prohibited anyone from pleading another person's cause without first having been examined in Williamsburg and licensed by the governor. After midcentury, imperial officials urged colonial lawyers to adopt the ceremonial trappings of the profession in the mother country, including robes and gowns.

It soon became clear to sons of the colonial gentry that a career in law, which might produce an income exceeding £1,000 annually, was not incompatible with elevated social rank. The infiltration of American-born gentlemen into the profession enhanced its status for others of like background. Some, most often from the southern colonies, traveled to London for the prestige of training at the Inns of Court, but most entered through the route of colonial apprenticeship. Much like the royal officials around whom they were inclined to congregate, leading colonial lawyers, eager to promote their credentials as members of a learned profession, were quick to deride the crudities of local justice. Distinguishing themselves ostentatiously from the mass of poorly trained practitioners, they championed the cause of legal reform. Proposals abounded in the various colonies to improve the educational qualifications of lawyers and judges. Leading lawyers organized themselves into associations that sought to regulate admission to the bar, reduce inefficiency in the courts, and prevent competitive fee-cutting.

But the colonial social environment hindered fulfillment of the highest professional aspirations in law. Even where the titles designating the superior and inferior ranks of the English legal profession were in use, there was insuffi-

cient legal business in the colonies to support functional divisions of practice according to the model of the mother country. The formal training of a colonial "barrister" might not differ from that of a colonial "attorney" or "solicitor." The most prominent colonial lawyers had to engage in precisely the same routine work—such as debt collection—that occupied inferior practitioners in England.

Almost everywhere in colonial America, about and after midcentury, lawyers were entering politics in significant numbers. Here it was that the ambiguities of their professional situation became most troublesome. Some could hope to move in and out of different crown offices, but the apparatus and patronage of empire remained too underdeveloped to entice most into signing up loyally as friends of prerogative power. Many drifted into the opposite political camp; a few made reputations displaying their oratorical talents in the cause of "liberty." For professional lawyers to make a go of being popular politicians might call for delicate footwork, however, because much of their everyday legal business consisted of dunning debtors and tenants.

This was the setting for the tumultuous events of the revolutionary decade. Some prominent lawyers, many quite young, joined a movement threatening to destroy the empire that had sustained their professional identity. Others, generally somewhat older and likely to be on the imperial payroll, held back or openly backed the Tory side. Most of those who became revolutionaries did so with unease. Trained to respect legal forms, they were reluctant to endorse radical demands that judges do business as usual in flagrant violation of the Stamp Act, although the alternative—closing down the courts—sharply reduced their professional incomes. And they agonized over the weaknesses of their shifting constitutional position, which contradicted orthodox principles of English public law.

By 1775 there was no turning back, and legal ideologues of the revolutionary movement had finally formulated the constitutional theory that would justify independence. The first settlers had not simply carried their legal birthright to America, it was argued, but had founded separate new societies outside the realm. They had then voluntarily reassociated with the king. If the king and his ministers violated the terms of agreement by which this reunion had supposedly been achieved, the Americans were free to leave the realm again.

However professionalized, lawyers making the ultimate case for revolution adopted a constitutional vocabulary that resonated with popular traditions. In its historical and metaphorical content, this was primarily the theory of New Englanders, who knew what it meant to leave the realm because they understood the very history of Protestantism as a drama of repeated separations or withdrawals. A constitutional argument based on compact and attuned to the religious idealism of an earlier age could appeal in New England as nowhere else.

What would happen afterward was another matter. The challenge of creating a national republic would test the relevance and staying power of New England's traditions, and determine their influence within the evolving constitutional system of the United States of America.

BIBLIOGRAPHY

Essays collected in George A. Billias, ed., *Law and Authority in Colonial America* (1965), make basic reading. Elaboration and documentation of this essay are found in Stephen Botein, *Early American Law and Society* (1983). Another kind of overview is George Dargo, *Roots of the Republic: A New Perspective on Early American Constitutionalism* (1974). An excellent if somewhat dated survey is provided in David H. Flaherty, "An Introduction to Early American Legal History," in David H. Flaherty, ed., *Essays in the History of Early American Law* (1969). The other essays in this book make basic reading.

Lawrence M. Friedman, *A History of American Law* (1973; rev. 1986), is also very helpful. There is a lengthy bibliography, extending to all the colonies, in Herbert A. Johnson, *Essays on New York Colonial Legal History* (1981). The best historiographical article on the subject is Stanley N. Katz, "The Problem of a Colonial Legal History," in Jack P. Greene and J. R. Pole, eds., *Colonial British America: Essays in the New History of the Early Modern Era* (1984). Richard B. Morris, *Studies in the History of American Law with Special Reference to the Seventeenth and Eighteenth Centuries* (1930), remains impressive for its originality and breadth.

The following specialized studies might offer the most useful points of departure: Douglas Greenberg, *Crime and Law Enforcement in the Colony of New York, 1691–1776* (1976); James H. Kettner, *The Development of American Citizenship, 1608–1870* (1978); David Thomas Konig, *Law and Society in Puritan Massachusetts: Essex County, 1629–1692* (1979); William E. Nelson, *The Americanization of the Common Law: The Impact of Legal Change of Massachusetts Society, 1760–1830* (1975); A. G. Roeber, *Faithful Magistrates and Republican Lawyers: Creators of Virginia Legal Culture, 1680–1810* (1981).

[*See also* ARTICLES OF CONFEDERATION.]

THE ARTICLES OF CONFEDERATION

Henry J. Bourguignon

B Y the end of the 1760s, the furor over the British Stamp Act had died down in the thirteen American colonies. Although Parliament had repealed the Stamp Act, it had ominously proclaimed its general power to legislate for the colonies in the Declaratory Act. The Townshend Acts had imposed duties on colonial trade, but these also had generally been repealed in the face of American opposition.

The radicals who had led the opposition to these forms of parliamentary taxation discovered in the early 1770s that they no longer had a cause which could rouse a following. They had developed an organization, the Sons of Liberty, especially powerful in Massachusetts, and had created close ties with other radical organizations. Without a stirring issue, however, these radicals lost much of their support. Radicals, who proclaimed the tyranny of parliamentary taxation without colonial representation, had already made colonial independence their ultimate goal.

In the fall of 1773, Lord North's ministry decided to assist the financially troubled East India Company. The company was allowed to ship its tea directly to the American colonies without paying the ordinary duties in England. This policy seemed completely reasonable to the British government. The company would be strengthened, and the American tea drinkers would pay less for their tea, even less than they paid for smuggled Dutch tea. The Tea Act of 1773, however, looked quite different from America. Americans would now be tempted to buy taxed rather than untaxed tea because of its lower price. The radicals determined that none of the tea should be landed, so they again raised the cry of monopoly and taxation without representation. City after city in America refused to accept the cargoes of this monopoly-privileged tea. When the royal governor, Thomas Hutchinson, of Massachusetts refused to issue the necessary papers to allow the tea to be shipped back to England, the radicals took action. On 16 December a band of men disguised as Indians boarded the tea vessels and dumped the cargo into Boston harbor.

The British government could not be expected to ignore this destruction of private property, which symbolically challenged all British authority in America. Early in 1774, Parliament, in response to the Boston Tea Party, enacted the Coercion Acts, which American radicals called the Intolerable Acts. This series of acts was intended to bring Massachusetts to its knees and thereby deter similar acts of rebellion in the other colonies by revealing the price of insubordination. Thus, Parliament closed the port of Boston to all commerce; reconstituted the government in Massachusetts to assure a more dominant role for the royal authority; protected British officials and soldiers accused of crimes by allowing a change of venue to distant Nova Scotia or England, far from the Massachusetts juries; and provided for the quartering of British troops within Boston.

The radicals at last had their cause. If the colonists submitted to these "intolerable" acts, the radicals proclaimed, then the British government could tax their property at will, destroy their right to jury trials, and reduce them to a state of slavery. The spirit of resistance to British rule was increased not only in Boston but throughout the colonies. The Massachusetts assembly, encouraged by the expressions of support and outrage from other colonies, invited all the colonies to send delegates to a general American congress to be held in Philadelphia.

13

THE ARTICLES OF CONFEDERATION

With this call for the First Continental Congress, the opposition to British policies and ultimately to British rule shifted from scattered, partially coordinated radical groups within the various colonies to a central body that, though shaky and anemic, would become the first government of the United States.

When the delegates, who in many ways resembled ambassadors from different countries, met at Carpenters' Hall in Philadelphia early in September 1774, the gathering was hardly unanimous in considering how it should respond to the Intolerable Acts and other acts of British dominance. As is evident from the debates, practically all the delegates shared a similar political philosophy. They often argued from the same general principles and relied on the same sources. Nonetheless, the First Continental Congress was clearly divided between the radicals, who were determined to resist the forceful assertion of British authority over the colonies, and the conservatives, who insisted on reconciliation between Britain and the colonies. The radicals, who by and large spoke for their own local, agrarian interests, had already denied all British authority to rule the colonies. Through the next year and a half the thrust of their arguments and their actions led inexorably to the independence of the American colonies. The conservative delegates to the Continental Congress had more cosmopolitan and commercial interests. They sought some formula for accord between the mother country and the colonies that would allow an acceptable level of home rule for the colonies. Though they often agreed that British actions had been wrong and ill advised, they opposed or sought to delay independence.

The radicals ultimately dominated the First Continental Congress. All the delegates agreed that the Congress must seek effective means to redress colonial grievances. The conservatives preferred words while the radicals insisted on actions. The petitions and resolutions favored by the conservatives were not sufficient for the majority of the delegates. The Congress, therefore, on 24 September 1774, agreed to cut off all importations of goods from Britain by December 1774 and to cease exporting colonial goods to Britain or its West Indian colonies after 10 September 1775. The radical policy of nonintercourse implicitly denied Parliament's authority over the colonies. Local committees

in each colony were instructed to use various forms of coercion to assure uniform compliance with these nonintercourse agreements. The Congress also adopted a statement of fundamental rights derived from the laws of nature, the principles of the English constitution, and the colonial charters. Before adjourning, the delegates decided that the colonies should select delegates to a second congress to meet the following May.

Before Congress reassembled, hostilities had broken out in the bloody skirmishes at Lexington and Concord in April 1775. The British government had made the fateful decision to use armed force rather than compromise to guarantee compliance with Parliament's laws. The Second Continental Congress, therefore, convened in an atmosphere of military ardor. Its first order of business was no longer to seek redress of grievances but to prepare an adequate military response to the British use of force. Military reinforcements were promised to the thin line of undisciplined troops outside Boston, and George Washington was named commander in chief. Congress urged the colonies to prepare their militias for military action and to provide armed vessels to protect their harbors and coasts. Massachusetts, Rhode Island, Connecticut, Pennsylvania, and South Carolina, in the fall of 1775, began building their own naval forces to oppose British attacks. While Congress continued to debate possible compromise solutions to the increasingly tense situation, it in fact was already fighting a war. Long before the Congress formally declared the independence of the American colonies in July 1776, it had authorized the use of military force against the British troops, opened American ports to non-British trade, encouraged the use of armed vessels to capture British ships carrying military supplies, and taken the first steps toward establishing a small naval force for the defense of all the colonies. The Americans were fighting for independence before they had formally declared their independence to the whole world.

DRAFTING AND RATIFICATION OF THE ARTICLES

Richard Henry Lee, on 7 June 1776, made the following motion in Congress:

THE ARTICLES OF CONFEDERATION

These United Colonies are, and of right ought to be, free and independent States, that they are absolved from all allegiance to the British Crown, and that all political connection between them and the State of Great Britain is, and ought to be, totally dissolved. That it is expedient forthwith to take the most effectual measures for forming foreign Alliances. That a plan of confederation be prepared and transmitted to the respective Colonies for their consideration and approbation.

This decisive resolution, which led to the drafting and promulgation of the Declaration of Independence the next month, also led to the drafting of the Articles of Confederation.

An effective form of government to unite the thirteen newly independent states was necessary not only to fight a successful war against Britain and to gain desperately needed support from foreign allies but also to prevent any hostilities between states. Land was the primary source of contention between the states, which created a serious danger of civil war. Many states had ill-defined or unlimited boundaries, which led to rival claims for land. Connecticut had some of its citizens in the Wyoming Valley, which was also claimed by Pennsylvania. Virginia and Pennsylvania, as well as Virginia and Maryland, had unsettled rival claims to land. New York's northern boundary was challenged. An effective form of government for the newly born United States was therefore essential.

All the delegates agreed that some union was necessary, at least a limited form of central government which had authority to deal with matters that affected all the new states, such as the way to conduct the war, the maintenance of an army and navy, the quest for foreign alliances and financial support, and the supervision of Indian affairs. Of course, the states would retain power over all questions of purely local concern. Beyond agreement on these vague generalities, the members of Congress were once again divided into conservative and radical factions.

The conservatives, who favored a strong, effective central government, dominated the committee that had been appointed to draft articles for the confederation of the states. The most prominent member of this drafting committee was John Dickinson of Pennsylvania, and thus the draft of the articles submitted to Congress in July 1776 has been called the Dickinson draft.

This first draft began with noncontroversial articles naming the confederacy the United States of America and declaring that the sovereign states were thereby entering into a firm league of friendship with each other for their common defense and to secure their liberties. According to this draft the states, however, would retain only so much of their present law, rights, and customs and their legislative power over local matters ("Government of its internal police") as would not interfere with the Articles of Confederation. Though vast governmental power might be implied in their retained powers, the states were to enjoy these powers only to the extent that they did not interfere with the powers granted by the Articles to Congress.

The strong centralizing thrust of the Dickinson draft can best be appreciated by considering the broad powers granted to Congress. The United States, through Congress, was granted the sole and exclusive power to determine war and peace, to establish legal rules governing the capture of enemy property on land or sea, to grant commissions to privately armed vessels to make captures of enemy property at sea, to appoint courts for the trial of crimes committed on the high seas, to establish courts of appeals to determine finally all cases of capture, to send and receive ambassadors, to enter into treaties and alliances, to settle all boundary disputes between states, to coin money, to regulate trade and control Indian affairs, to impose limited boundaries for those states which had open-ended boundaries under their colonial charters, to establish new states and dispose of—through sale, trade, or incorporation—the land within any territory acquired by the United States, to establish post offices, to regulate the army and navy, and to appoint a "Council of State" and other government officials who would conduct the business of the United States, especially when Congress was not in session. Congress furthermore had the broad authority to provide for the defense and welfare of the United States, to determine the amount of money to be spent, to borrow money on the credit of the United States, to raise a navy, and to determine the quotas for each state to contribute to the army. The central government would not only have broadly stated legislative powers but would also have the beginnings of an executive department in the Council of State, as well as a limited national judicial power over crimes committed at sea and over captures of enemy property.

The Dickinson draft also contained other controversial provisions. Each state had one vote in Congress, and no proposal could be approved unless seven states voted for it. Taxes would be apportioned among the states according to the total population of the states, not counting Indians.

For the next year and a half Congress debated the draft when it had the time free from more pressing business. The Articles submitted to the states for ratification in November 1777 turned the Dickinson draft inside-out. The states, not the Congress, became the dominant partners in this form of confederation. Although Congress considered and modified many provisions of the Dickinson draft, the debate focused primarily on three issues: the large states opposed equal representation of all the states; the slave states opposed the apportionment of the financial burden according to the entire population, since this would include slaves; and the states with unlimited charter claims to western lands opposed congressional control of state boundaries.

After considerable debate in which the large states had tried to assure for themselves greater influence in Congress, the states ultimately approved the mode of voting included in the Dickinson draft, one vote in Congress for each state. The financial contributions to the central government, as the Articles were finally determined, would be based on the estimated value of real estate in each state instead of being based on total population.

Congressional control over the vast western lands claimed by some states became the most heated issue in the debates on the Dickinson draft. Some states, especially Virginia, had colonial charters that extended their territory in the west to the "South Seas." Obviously these unlimited western boundaries resulted from the mistaken geographical knowledge of the seventeenth century. As a result of these charters from the British government, some landed states had boundless claims to western lands, and others, the landless states, had clearly defined western boundaries. In the debates over the Dickinson draft, the states with vast western land claims opposed any power in Congress that could deprive them of these lands by redefining their western boundaries. The landed states prevailed

in Congress. The Articles as submitted to the states gave Congress no power to fix western boundaries. On the contrary, the Articles guaranteed that no state would be deprived of territory for the benefit of the United States. This victory for the landed states, however, turned out to be meaningless, since one state, Maryland, held out with fierce determination and refused to ratify the Articles of Confederation until Congress was given power over the western lands. As a result the Articles were not ratified until 1781, but ultimately Congress was given vast western lands that it could dispose of and that could become new states.

Under the Dickinson draft, Congress had broad powers expressly granted that were interpreted to imply even broader power for the central government. The states retained only the limited power to legislate over local matters and only to the extent the states' powers did not interfere with congressional power. In the debates on the Dickinson draft, this strong centralizing force of the Articles was reversed. The states retained their full sovereign power, and Congress received only those powers expressly delegated. The second article, in its final form, read, "Each State retains its sovereignty, freedom and independence, and every power, jurisdiction, and right which is not by this confederation expressly delegated to the United States, in Congress assembled." The strong central form of government envisioned by the Dickinson draft did not survive. Other amendments of the draft articles likewise generally weakened the central government.

The debate was completed and the Articles were ready for the states to ratify by November 1777. The delegates felt such urgency in having the states promptly adopt the Articles that they agreed that the states should act within four months. Three and a half long years were to pass before all the states ratified, three and a half years during which Congress had to continue directing a war, finding financial support for the army, seeking foreign alliances, and governing the nation—all without the constitutional authority that would have come from the Articles. Under the circumstances, the congressional achievements were truly amazing.

Some states ratified the Articles with qualification, while others proposed numerous amendments. By the date Congress had set for ratification by all the states, only one state, Virginia, had ratified without conditions or qualifications. Gradually other states ratified, but Maryland made it clear that it would not ratify until Congress had the power to set limits to the western boundaries of those states with unlimited territorial claims.

Finally, as a result of military necessity as well as a belief that its territory was too large to be well governed, Virginia agreed to cede its lands northwest of the Ohio River to the United States. New York had previously agreed to cede its western lands to the United States. Maryland, prompted by its vulnerability to the advancing British army and its hope for military help from Congress or from the French, ratified the Articles. On 1 March 1781, Congress formalized the ratification of the Articles. Throughout most of the years of the war for independence, Congress had of necessity acted as if it were constitutionally authorized to do so. At long last the first Constitution of the United States was ratified in time to complete the war, plan for the peace ahead, and make some wise and farsighted laws for the western lands.

THE COURT FOR THE DETERMINATION OF LAND DISPUTES

It has been thought that no organized society can long survive without some formal, peaceful method of resolving at least the disputes most likely to cause social disorder. That courts are better than bloodshed has for centuries been suggested as the justification for judicial systems. The United States, under the Articles of Confederation, had a skeletal judicial system, inadequate in nearly every way, to resolve the heated controversies over rival land claims, yet even this judiciary played a role in preventing interstate conflicts.

Serious disputes existed between the states when they first declared their independence. The boundaries of the states, as defined in their colonial charters, had been based on inaccurate maps and charts, not on precise survey. A long-simmering dispute divided New York and what ultimately became Vermont, concerning the New Hampshire land grants. New York's eastern boundary also was challenged by Massachusetts. The Pittsburgh area remained a source of dispute between Pennsylvania and Virginia. The Wyoming Valley lands had been claimed by settlers from Connecticut as well as by Pennsylvania.

One of the concerns in the debates over the Articles had been the realistic fear of bloody interstate battles over land. Some conservatives before the war worried that without Britain's authority over the colonies, mutual obstinacy over territorial claims would lead to hostilities between the states. They thought that, even if the United States survived its war with Britain intact, it would be torn apart subsequently by interstate wars over land.

Congress fully understood the need for a peaceful mode of resolution for rival land claim disputes. Article IX contained a lengthy and cumbersome procedure for settling such disputes. Congress therein assumed the power to be "the last resort on appeal in all disputes and differences . . . between two or more states concerning boundary, jurisdiction or any other cause whatever." Since there existed no court of first instance from which to appeal, it is not at all clear why Congress used the phrase "the last resort on appeal." Obviously no interstate dispute over boundaries could be tried in any state immediately involved. Only Congress could provide a neutral forum remotely comparable to the British Privy Council, to which boundary dispute petitions had been carried during the colonial days. Since Congress had a strong interest in acquiring title to land from the landed states, even its neutrality was questionable, so it provided for a separate judicial body to resolve land disputes.

Article IX provided that when any state petitioned Congress for a hearing on a dispute, Congress would give notice to the other state involved and set a date for the states to have their lawful agents appear. These agents would, by mutual consent, appoint judges or commissioners to constitute a court to hear and determine the dispute in question. If these lawful agents failed to agree on a panel of judges to hear the case, Congress would name three persons from each of the thirteen states, and the agents of the two states would alternately strike names from this list until the list contained only thirteen names. From this list of remaining names, apparently those so utterly unknown or noncontroversial that neither party had sufficient incentive to remove them, Congress would draw not fewer than seven and not more than nine names. Any five of those drawn by lot would be the "commissioners or judges to hear and finally determine the controversy." A majority of these judges would be sufficient to decide the dispute. Congress also provided in detail for the situation where one state might not appear and also set out the oath that the judges were to take before hearing the case.

Since Congress nowhere provided, nor did it have the authority to provide, for an assured mode of execution of the decrees of this ad hoc body of commissioners, it is difficult to consider it a court at all. Without some coercive power behind their decrees, these commissioners could do little more than arbitrate a dispute and recommend a fair and mutually acceptable solution. If either state should ignore the final decree, it would merely demonstrate what had become apparent in so many other situations—that Congress was in fact impotent if the states did not voluntarily comply.

The clumsy procedures of Article IX were tested by only one land dispute. Pennsylvania's boundaries were clearly defined in its colonial charter. The ambiguity of its boundary with Maryland had in 1769 been removed when the British government had confirmed the Mason-Dixon line. With the coming of independence, however, these boundaries, based on colonial charters, appeared less sacred. Since Pennsylvania had not settled some regions of the state, its claims rested exclusively on its charter. Land speculators and settlers from Virginia had begun arriving prior to independence in the Pittsburgh area of the state and from Connecticut in the Wyoming Valley. Without any Pennsylvania magistrates to enforce the state's laws and without any Pennsylvania settlers in the areas, the state had little hope of exercising its jurisdiction over the settlers. When independence did come, many of those Pennsylvanians with strong interests in the disputed areas became Loyalists and lost any influence in the new state. Furthermore the new state's ultrarepublican constitution emphasized the need for consent of the governed as a basis of legitimate government. Since the Connecticut and Virginia settlers had little intention of consenting to be governed by Pennsylvania, the state's clear charter claim to the two areas became more questionable. The Pennsylvania

claim to these lands appeared to many a mere paper right when compared with the human rights of those who had settled the undeveloped land.

In 1779, prior to invoking congressional authority, Pennsylvania and Virginia had agreed, without the aid of any Article IX judicial body, to settle their boundary dispute. The Mason-Dixon line was continued west five degrees of longitude, and a line was drawn north from the end of that line. Pennsylvania accepted the Virginia demand that Virginia settlers would be secure in their rights to the land they had settled. It was only after this successful bilateral negotiation with Virginia and after the Articles of Confederation had finally been ratified that Pennsylvania turned to Congress and Article IX for help in determining its dispute with Connecticut over the Wyoming Valley lands.

Proceedings under Article IX began in November 1781 with Pennsylvania's petition to Congress. Connecticut was notified, and the first Monday of June 1782 set as the date for both states to appear as represented by their legal agents. When only one of Connecticut's agents appeared in June, attempts were made to postpone the proceeding until the war was completed, since necessary papers were in England. Congress postponed consideration of this motion. When Pennsylvania authorized new agents to represent it, Connecticut objected that the new agents had not been properly authorized by the state. After ignoring these dilatory tactics, Congress told the agents of the two states to name the commissioners. The agents, without the use of the elaborate machinery provided in Article IX for alternate striking of names, agreed on seven commissioners. Congress was then confronted with the embarrassing question of who would pay the commissioners. Finally the parties agreed to divide the per diem expenses of the commissioners if Congress would merely appoint them.

The commissioners met in Trenton in November 1782. Two of those selected declined to serve. As a result, four of the five commissioners came from states, like Pennsylvania, with defined western boundaries, and only one from a state, like Connecticut, that claimed a western boundary extending to the South Seas. If such considerations prejudiced the issue, then Connecticut began the hearings with a decided disadvantage.

18

The court of commissioners denied various motions that would only have delayed further the proceedings and for twelve days heard testimony and legal arguments on the petition. Finally, on 30 December, after a weekend of deliberation, the commissioners, without stating their reasons, decreed that Connecticut had no right to the Wyoming Valley lands in question but that Pennsylvania did.

Such, in brief, is the entire story of the court Congress envisaged under Article IX to settle disputes between states over rival land claims. No other case ever used these procedures, which were elaborate, time-consuming, and ultimately unsatisfactory.

Even in the single dispute that was heard, the decree of the commissioners did not end all conflicting claims. The Connecticut settlers in the Wyoming Valley were so disconcerted by the decree that they threatened to petition for a new Article IX commission to hear their claims to the land. Pennsylvania eventually learned that the commission's decree confirming its jurisdiction over the land in dispute did nothing to decide whether the settlers in the area would acquiesce in becoming Pennsylvania citizens. The settlers, a Pennsylvania official reported, appeared sullen and discontented, like a conquered nation. It took Pennsylvania's suffering through five years of continued resentment and organized opposition by the Wyoming settlers to realize that only by securing the land titles of all bona fide claimants could the state win the settlers' allegiance.

Yet the existence of this Article IX court to settle interstate land conflicts, though no model of an effective judiciary, may not have been totally futile. In spite of their heated disputes over rival land claims, the states did not go to war with each other to vindicate their claims. The United States, during the years Congress struggled to have the Articles ratified and the years it limped along under the Articles, had just enough authority to induce the states to avoid violent conflicts with each other. The mere fact that an appeal to an Article IX adjudication was possible perhaps encouraged states to negotiate rather than engage in hostilities with each other. The states, of course, had few resources and little enthusiasm to go to war among themselves. Their war with Britain was exhausting enough.

It seems clear that the experience of long-standing interstate rivalries over land led some Americans in the end to appreciate the need for a more effective government with a judicial power sufficient to determine with finality all land disputes between the states. In 1787 when the convention met in Philadelphia to consider a new constitution, ten states were involved in serious disputes over boundaries, lands, and river rights. It is not surprising that the drafters provided in Article III, Section 2, that the federal judicial power would extend "to Controversies between two or more States." The Supreme Court of the United States was given jurisdiction to hear all these disputes. The limited experience with the extremely restricted and virtually powerless Article IX court demonstrated the need for effective federal judicial power.

THE APPELLATE PRIZE COURT OF CONGRESS

Congress, even before the Declaration of Independence, discovered the need for some judicial authority to resolve another type of dispute. Congress had authorized the capture of British ships and cargoes. Unfortunately the capturing vessels often made mistakes. They sometimes captured a neutral vessel or an American vessel from some other state. Occasionally more than one vessel claimed to have made the capture. In these situations, Congress soon realized that some judicial body would have to determine whether the capture was legal in the first place and who had made the capture. Without ultimate authority to determine such questions of prize law, Congress learned that it could become involved in serious disputes with a friendly foreign power or that a new source of interstate tensions could arise.

Today prize law is a rare and exotic area of legal scholarship. At least until the time of World War I, prize law remained a vital part of the international law of war. A "prize" is property lawfully captured from the enemy during war. Generally the term applied to captures made at sea, the capture of enemy ships or cargoes. Prize law was the body of procedural and substantive law limiting and regulating the capture of enemy property in time of war.

In the seventeenth and eighteenth centuries, when few nations had an adequate navy, much of maritime warfare was carried on by privateers.

These private vessels were armed at the expense of their owners, who had received from their own government a commission, or letter of marque, authorizing them to capture the ships and cargoes of the enemy. When the captured property had been brought to a home port, the captors had to bring it before an admiralty court that had been given special jurisdiction to determine questions of prize. It was through the judgments of these prize courts and the writings of authorities on the law of nations (the eighteenth-century term for international law) that the body of prize law evolved.

When the Second Continental Congress met in Philadelphia in the spring of 1775, the shot heard around the world had already been fired. Congress, in response to the British use of military force, began urging the colonies to prepare for hostilities. In July 1775, Congress encouraged the states to start building their own naval forces, and in the fall at least five states did just that. General George Washington soon saw the desirability of capturing British vessels that carried much-needed military supplies. By September 1775, Washington had several armed vessels at sea. In October, Congress informed Washington that two British ships were carrying a cargo of military supplies to Quebec without a convoy and urged him to intercept them. By November, Congress had taken the first steps toward establishing a United States navy.

Long before the United States had declared its independence, Congress had started learning about prize courts. In November 1775, Washington urged Congress to set up proper courts to decide on the legality of the captures of enemy property. Apparently he had been approached to decide such questions, and he told Congress that a court was necessary, "otherwise I may be involved in inextricable difficulties." Washington clearly had in mind some summary form of procedure that would spare him the trouble of determining the legality of the captures but also assure that the few vessels that had been armed at congressional expense would be promptly back at sea making more captures.

On 25 November 1775, Congress passed a series of resolves that would remain the basis of its appellate prize jurisdiction throughout most of the war. Citing various warlike acts of the British navy and thinking of the ancient right of reprisal, Congress passed eight resolves. It authorized the capture of British naval vessels, military transports, and cargoes of military supplies, but these captures could be made only by vessels commissioned by the Congress. Congress further recommended that each colony (for they had not yet declared themselves to be independent states) set up courts to determine cases of capture. All trials should be by jury, a clearly radical break from centuries of practice in admiralty courts, where the prize trials were never before a jury. Congress then added "that in all cases an appeal shall be allowed to the Congress, or such person or persons as they shall appoint for the trial of appeals." Congress set time limits for bringing appeals and decided what shares of each prize should belong to the owners and crew of the capturing vessel, depending on whether the vessel had been fitted out at the expense of the United States or of a private party.

These resolves display a wisdom that was greater than Congress at the time could have been expected to possess. In the first place, Congress had insisted on the exclusive right to issue commissions for privateers and thereby maintained some hope of controlling their often piratical activity. Second, Congress had asserted, even before the Articles had been drafted, much less ratified, that some court under its authority must have the final say as to the legality of maritime captures. Only with the brutal experience of the years ahead could Congress fully appreciate the wisdom of these resolves.

Congress had recommended that each colony should set up some court to try the legality of any captures brought within its jurisdiction. The colonies, many before becoming independent states in July 1776, complied with this congressional request, but each in its own way and with its own peculiar restrictions. For instance, Massachusetts and New Hampshire allowed appeals to the congressional appellate court only if the capture had been made by a ship fitted out and commissioned by Congress. Later these two states agreed to allow appeals to Congress if any neutral party was involved in the case. Rhode Island and Connecticut granted appeals in all cases unless the party seeking the appeal came from a state that had limited the right of appeal to Congress. Pennsylvania restricted appeals to questions of law. All questions of fact were to be determined finally by the jury. Pennsylvania's restriction led to a most serious confrontation between this state and Congress and in the end convinced Congress that the entire structure of its appellate prize court needed repairs. The states had shown that they were just as independent of Congress as they were of Britain. With such a confusing array of state restrictions, it is surprising that the congressional court ever functioned effectively at all.

When Congress first started receiving petitions for review of state court decrees in prize cases, it was, as always, preoccupied with far more pressing issues. Congress therefore appointed a separate, ad hoc committee for each prize appeal. Even in the earliest appeals—for example, the first eight—Congress generally appointed members with some legal experience. A committee reviewed the records of the trial courts and the jury verdicts that had been sent forward for the appeal. It allowed new evidence, in the form of depositions, to be introduced for the appeal. It also heard oral argument by counsel for the parties to the appeal.

The committees at first showed some doubts about their role in hearing and determining the appeals. They wrote reports, similar to legislative committee reports, and submitted them to Congress. Soon, however, the committees began issuing decrees which showed that they already considered themselves somewhat independent judicial bodies. They affirmed or reversed the judgment of the lower court without reporting to Congress.

As early as October, Congress showed that it was not satisfied with this case-by-case handling of prize appeals. In January 1777, Congress appointed a permanent, standing committee to hear and determine appeals from the judgments of state admiralty courts in cases of captures. Congress began by appointing five members to this committee and would have to replace members from time to time, but at least this standing committee promised more continuity than the ad hoc approach it had first employed. Knowing the recurring problem of extended absence of its members, Congress decided that any three of the five members appointed to this committee on prize appeals should have the authority to act. Congress also showed its intention to transform this legislative committee into a clearly judicial institution by declaring that the committee should conform its decisions to the various resolves of Congress on the subject and by authorizing the appointment of a registrar (like a clerk of court) to serve the committee.

Congress soon felt the heat of wounded neutral sensitivities when an American privateer, the *Phoenix,* in 1778 captured a Portuguese vessel, *Our Lady of Mount Carmel and St. Anthony.* The unauthorized capture was doubly embarrassing to Congress since one of its members, Robert Morris, was part-owner of the *Phoenix.* The Massachusetts admiralty court did the right thing in decreeing that this was not a lawful capture and restoring the ship and its valuable cargo to its owners. The American privateer, violating accepted international practice, had not brought the master of the Portuguese ship to Massachusetts to act in defense of the ship. When the ship was to be restored to the owners, there was therefore no representative of the owners to receive the ship and cargo. Morris, hoping to extricate himself and the other owners of the *Phoenix* from possible liability for damages, urged Congress to have the Portuguese ship and cargo sold and the proceeds of the sale invested for the owners until they would come to claim it. Congress allowed the sale of the *Our Lady of Mount Carmel* and its cargo, and invested the money in public funds of the United States and notified the Portuguese owners through the American commissioners in Paris.

Unfortunately for Congress, when John Garcia Duarti appeared to claim the funds for the owners, he objected to being paid in American money, which was useless to the owners. Furthermore, he objected to the substantial amount that had been deducted from the proceeds as commissions for the sale. Duarti asked for some £6,000 sterling, which would have been an enormous sum for the virtually bankrupt Congress to pay. The negotiations dragged on until January 1781, three years after the capture, when Duarti was finally given a substantial settlement and took the first ship for Cadiz. When Congress tried to show its good faith to neutral nations by asking Virginia to prosecute the master of the *Phoenix* and its principal owner for this illegal capture, Virginia's attorney general replied that the state's admiralty court lacked jurisdiction over criminal offenses committed on the high seas.

Heated conflicts with friendly foreign powers were not the only problems Congress found inherent in its weak handling of prize cases. Congressional impotence in the face of a state's adamant opposition to a decree of the Committee on Appeals also demonstrated the inadequacy of the entire structure of its appellate prize court. This issue came to a head in the case of the sloop *Active*. Gideon Olmsted and three other Connecticut sailors had been captured at sea by the British and impressed to serve on the sloop *Active*, which was carrying supplies from Jamaica to New York. In September 1778 they took control of the *Active* and made prisoners of the English sailors and the irate English captain. Despite the captain's efforts from below deck to frustrate their navigation, Olmsted and the other Americans managed to sail the ship toward New Jersey. On the morning of 8 September land was in sight. Just at that time two American privateers from Pennsylvania came in sight, hailed the *Active*, boarded it, and took control of it.

When the Pennsylvania privateers brought the *Active* before the Pennsylvania admiralty court for adjudication, Olmsted and his companions claimed to be the true captors of this British property, since they had effective control of the vessel before Pennsylvania privateers boarded. The Pennsylvania jury held that all the captors shared in taking the prize and gave Olmsted and his companions only one-fourth of the value of the *Active* and its cargo. The admiralty judge decreed that the prize should be divided as the jury had indicated, one-fourth to the Olmsted claimants and three-fourths to the two Pennsylvania privateers. Olmsted and his companions turned to the congressional Committee on Appeals.

When Congress' appellate prize court heard the case of the *Active* in December 1778, it reversed the Pennsylvania court and decreed that Olmsted and the Connecticut sailors should receive the entire proceeds from the sale of the *Active* and its cargo. The Pennsylvania admiralty court refused to execute this decree, contending that under state law the facts in a prize case were to be established by the jury without reexamination or appeal to any court. Since the jury had determined that the Olmsted claimants were merely joint captors with the two privateers, that verdict must stand.

When the members of the Committee on Appeals heard of this standoff, they issued an injunction commanding the marshal of the Pennsylvania admiralty court to retain custody of the money from the sale of the *Active*. The Pennsylvania executive council, however, directed the marshal to turn the money over to the admiralty court.

The Committee on Appeals momentarily considered holding the admiralty court's marshal in contempt, the usual course of an effective court whose injunction is disregarded. Instead, it merely recorded that its injunction had been ignored and its order flouted. It reported to Congress that it would proceed no further with any prize appeals until its authority had been settled and its decrees given full effect. Congress, as it always did when it faced a problem it lacked the power to solve, appointed a committee to examine the report of the Committee on Appeals.

This specially appointed committee reported to Congress on 6 March 1779 that the United States alone possessed the power to determine war and peace. Therefore, only the federal government could determine finally the legality of captures on the high seas, since such cases must be decided according to the law of nations, which the federal government alone had authority to apply. Brave words, indeed! The report detailed the danger to international relations if juries, sitting in the different states, could decide questions involving the rights of neutrals. The special committee therefore concluded that Pennsylvania ought to carry into effect the decree of the Committee on Appeals.

Pennsylvania, in the months ahead, made it clear that its admiralty court would never abide by the decree of the Committee on Appeals. It reminded Congress that it had recommended the use of juries for prize trials, contrary to international practice. Pennsylvania insisted it was merely upholding the integrity of the jury system by not allowing any appellate court to reopen the factual determination of a jury.

Unable to persuade Pennsylvania to comply with the decree of the Committee on Appeals, Congress looked at the committee itself and decided that a court of appeals for prize cases should be established, independent of Congress, rather than as a committee of Congress. Perhaps such an independent court would command greater respect from the states.

Article IX of the Articles of Confederation gave Congress the exclusive authority to establish courts for determining appeals in all cases of maritime captures. Unfortunately, during the months when Congress was debating with Pennsylvania over the case of the *Active* and was considering the establishment of an independent court of appeals, the Articles had not been ratified, and so, congressional power remained doubtful in theory and even more shaky in fact.

A committee of Congress reported in October 1779 that two courts of prize appeals should be established to sit in two different districts. The courts should have marshals and the power of fining and imprisoning for contempt and disobedience. State admiralty court judges and their officers were to be liable for contempt if they disobeyed the decrees of the court of appeals. Furthermore, the trial of all prize cases in state admiralty courts was to be according to ancient practice—that is, trial by the court and not by jury.

This pair of proposed courts of appeals would have been truly effective courts, capable of acting directly on recalcitrant litigants or court officials, had not Congress gradually pulled the courts' teeth in the process of debating this committee report: only one court of appeals would be established; no marshal would be appointed; the requirement of court, rather than jury, trials in the states was dropped; and, most significantly, the contempt power disappeared from the final compromise report. Instead of giving the court the power that would assure the effectiveness of its decrees, Congress meekly recommended that the states pass laws directing their admiralty courts to carry into full and speedy execution the final decrees of the newly created Court of Appeals in Cases of Capture. At least Congress had created an appellate court that, it fondly hoped, would have greater success in securing full respect for its authority. Congress appointed three legally trained judges to serve on this new court.

Congress had established the first federal court of the United States. Of course, the Committee on Appeals had acted as a court deciding some sixty appeals and on occasion had been called a court of appeals. For the first time, however, a judicial body with appellate jurisdiction over state courts existed outside of Congress, not as a committee made up of congressmen impeded by the rush of other pressing congressional business.

The Court of Appeals in Cases of Capture sat from 1780 until 1787, the year the new Constitution was drafted. Slightly more than fifty cases came before the new court. During most of its

brief existence, it sat with only two judges. Congress had made every effort—with some success—to assure that the most qualified, legally trained judges sat on the court. Though Congress had failed to give this court all the power many members of Congress thought appropriate, at least it had faced up to the problem of the constantly changing membership of the Committee on Appeals and the subtler problem of lack of judicial independence.

The Court of Appeals in Cases of Capture did not significantly change the procedures followed by the Committee on Appeals. Cases were carried forward for review either by appeal, granted by the trial court, or by petition to Congress when appeal had been denied or some technical obstacle, such as late filing, blocked an appeal. Both types of cases were handled under the same procedures once review had been granted. The party seeking review arranged to have the record of the trial court copied and sent forward, and sometimes original documents, not copies, came before the appellate court. The parties were permitted to expand the record by obtaining new depositions for consideration by the appellate court, so the review took on some of the characteristics of a trial de novo. Parties generally were represented by counsel.

The court seldom wrote opinions that gave the reasons for the court's determination. Except in five cases, the court merely issued a formalized decree affirming or reversing the trial court. This is the decree the prevailing party had to rely on when he retraced his steps and sought to have the state admiralty court execute the appellate court's judgment. Of course, when the trial court had been affirmed, no problems lay in the path of the successful party. But when the appellate court of Congress reversed a state trial court, as it did more frequently than it affirmed, the court's usual order to the state admiralty court to "issue all necessary process for carrying into Execution the Decree of this Court" was not always followed.

The case of the sloop *Active* was not the only case in which a decree of the appellate court of Congress was denied execution by the state court. There were cases in Connecticut, New Hampshire, and other states in which the admiralty court refused to execute the appellate court's decree. Three especially sensitive cases in Massachusetts involved Spanish property that had been condemned in the state court. The French minister complained to Congress of the unjust judgment of the Massachusetts court in these cases. The Spanish chargé d'affaires also sent a memorial to Congress objecting to the action of the state admiralty court.

Congress, of course, desperately needed the friendly support and financial aid of Spain and France. A special committee drafted a reply to the French minister assuring him that when the matter came before its appellate court in due course, Congress would make sure that the law of nations would be strictly observed. Congress promised that if it should turn out that the Spanish owners had suffered any injury from violations of neutral rights, reparations would be made to vindicate the honor of the Spanish flag. When these cases did come before the Court of Appeals in Cases of Capture, the court reversed the state's decrees in whole or in part. But there is serious doubt whether the appellate judgments were ever carried into execution by the Massachusetts admiralty court. It was much easier for Congress to write letters about vindicating neutral rights than it was actually to vindicate them. However, in most cases the decree of the congressional appellate prize court was given execution in the state admiralty court without objection.

CONCLUSION

Unsolved problems seldom disappear; they usually accumulate. The states had asserted their power to create a weak central government under the Articles of Confederation. It is hardly surprising that Congress under the Articles confronted far more problems than it could solve. In fact, the many significant accomplishments of the Continental Congress are quite amazing in light of its flimsy constitutional foundation. It successfully directed a war and entered into an advantageous peace treaty, it formed foreign alliances and somehow managed to finance the war, and it secured possession of vast western lands and wisely administered them.

The courts created by the Continental Congress likewise had deep, inherent weaknesses, yet they succeeded in resolving heated and divisive disputes just well enough to mitigate interstate or international rancor or hostilities. When compared with the strong federal judicial power under the Constitution, the judicial bodies created by Congress—the court to determine boundary disputes between the states and the appellate prize courts—are seen to have lacked the strong, sure-handed authority to determine finally all the disputes that came before them. The problems that these courts were established to address did not go away; they awaited the day a more effective court was established to address them.

Perhaps it is most helpful to consider the judicial bodies under the Articles of Confederation as a learning experience in which the participants—parties, counsel, and judges—gained a deeper insight into the utter necessity for a more effective federal judicial system. Many of the members of Congress and lawyers most closely associated with the judicial bodies set up under the Articles were also deeply involved in drafting the new Constitution in 1787 and supporting it through the process of ratification by the states. More than twenty of the fifty-five members of the constitutional convention of 1787 had some direct acquaintance with the workings of the judicial bodies created under the Articles. James Wilson and Oliver Ellsworth had both served as judges on the Committee on Appeals and had also served as counsel for parties before the committee. Wilson had represented the Olmsted claimants in the *Active* case, and Ellsworth had sat on the Committee on Appeals which decided that case and issued an injunction to the marshal in Pennsylvania. Wilson had also been one of the agents for Pennsylvania in its litigated boundary dispute with Connecticut. These same men, Wilson and Ellsworth, were clearly the most influential members of the constitutional convention in drafting Article III of the Constitution, which established the judicial power under the new government. The Judiciary Act of 1789, which set up the new federal judiciary, was largely the work of Ellsworth, who was then sitting in the United States Senate. Both Wilson and Ellsworth were appointed to seats on the Supreme Court. Many other lawyers and judges who had been involved with the courts under the Articles were appointed to serve on the Supreme Court or the various federal courts established under the Constitution.

The frustration for those associated with the courts under the Articles, and the ineffectual and wasteful manner in which these judicial bodies operated, educated many leaders in the need for an effective federal judicial system under a more perfect form of government. Though Congress, under the Articles, was unable to create fully effective courts, the marvel was that its judicial bodies worked as well as they did and made solid contributions to the first government of the United States.

BIBLIOGRAPHY

Bernard Bailyn, *The Ideological Origins of the American Revolution* (1967), drawing on the earlier work of Caroline Robbins, studies the English political writers who most influenced American revolutionary leaders. Henry J. Bourguignon, *The First Federal Court: The Federal Appellate Prize Court of the American Revolution, 1775–1787* (1977), is the most thorough study of the appellate prize courts established by the Continental Congress.

Edmund C. Burnett, *The Continental Congress* (1941; repr. 1964), is a lengthy survey of the work of Congress arranged as a day-to-day journal; and Burnett, ed., *Letters of Members of the Continental Congress*, 8 vols. (1921–1936), remains a valuable, well-edited collection of correspondence of members of Congress under the Articles. Joseph L. Davis, *Sectionalism in American Politics, 1774–1787* (1977), focuses on the implications of the sectional differences, rivalries, and conflicts in the work of the Continental Congress.

E. James Ferguson, *The Power of the Purse: A History of Public Finance, 1776–1790* (1961), presents the most thorough study of the public finances of the Continental Congress and of the role of Robert Morris. Worthington C. Ford, ed., *Journals of the Continental Congress, 1774–1789*, 34 vols. (1904–1937), a compilation of selected records of Congress, is the most complete published source available, but it suffers from inadequate and inconsistent editorial policy. Julius Goebel, Jr., *Antecedents and Beginnings to 1801*, vol. 1 of the Oliver Wendell Holmes Devise History of the Supreme Court of the United States (1971), is a comprehensive and difficult volume that studies in depth the background to the formation of the federal judicial system, including the judicial bodies set up by the Continental Congress. H. James Henderson, *Party Politics in the Continental Congress* (1974), analyzes the shifting factions and party alliances under the Articles.

Merrill Jensen, *The Articles of Confederation* (1940), is a pioneering study of the debates and divisions that led to the Articles of Confederation; and *The New Nation: A History of the United States During the Confederation, 1781–1789* (1950), studies the so-called critical years from a new point of view, stressing the positive accomplishments of Congress under the Articles. Forrest McDonald, *E Pluribus Unum: The Formation of the American Republic, 1776–1790* (1965), studies the crises and conflicts under the Articles that led to the adoption of the Constitution.

Jackson Turner Main, *The Antifederalists: Critics of the Constitution, 1781–1788* (1961), attempts to identify more precisely than Charles Beard had done the political, social, and economic status of the opponents of the federal Constitution; and *Political Parties Before the Constitution* (1973), expands the research of his earlier work to study the socioeconomic differences between those who opposed and those who supported the Constitution. Frederick W. Marks III, *Independence on Trial: Foreign Affairs and the Making of the Constitution* (1973), studies foreign affairs under the Articles, focusing on the military and commercial factors that created a sense of national insecurity. Peter S. Onuf, *The Origins of the Federal Republic: Jurisdictional Controversies in the United States, 1775–1787* (1983), studies with new depth and insight the boundary and other land disputes that threatened to create hostilities between the states.

Jack N. Rakove, *The Beginnings of National Politics* (1979), a controversial volume, unsuccessfully attempts a nationalist interpretation of political divisions in the Continental Congress. Paul H. Smith et al., eds., *Letters of Delegates to Congress, 1774–1789* (1976–), a superbly edited project, when complete, will be far more comprehensive than Burnett's eight volumes. Gordon S. Wood, *The Creation of the American Republic, 1776–1787* (1969), places the new state constitutions within the ideological and political context of the Confederation period.

[*See also* COLONIAL LAW AND JUSTICE; *and* FRAMING THE CONSTITUTION.]

FRAMING THE CONSTITUTION

S. Sidney Ulmer

THE fundamental charter of government in the United States is the federal Constitution, drafted by convention in 1787 and ratified by the required nine states in 1788. Subsequently, four additional states ratified the document, Rhode Island being the last and thirteenth on 29 May 1790. The sources of the Constitution are in a sense theoretical, since the document reflects certain theoretical perspectives regarding the government of men in a political system. These theories were known to most educated persons of the framers' era and their contributors ranged as far back as Aristotle. However, the theorists most influential in shaping the thinking that underlies the Constitution came from a much later age.

Writing in the sixteenth century, Niccolo Machiavelli incorporated in his *Discourses* a number of ideas about government and politics that eighteenth-century liberals found appealing. Some of these same ideas are basic to the Constitution and will be discussed at length later. Here we may simply note that the *Discourses* contain an explicit treatment of "checks and balances" and a noted emphasis on the values of liberty and republican government. Such ideas were common in the work of John Locke as well as in that of Montesquieu—both of whom were writers well known to the framers of the American Constitution.

The framers also had particular notions about man and government, which influenced the form and content of the document they drafted. In general, they tended to view man as fundamentally depraved—to accept the Calvinistic view that man was evil, damned, and in need of salvation. They did not quarrel with Thomas Hobbes's famous dictum that without government, life in a state of nature is "nasty, brutish,

and short." Like Hobbes, they did not think that life under government would somehow wash away those characteristics of man that, in a state of nature, made life a war of each against all. Hobbes and the framers did believe, however, that avarice, greed, ambition, jealousy, love of power—those qualities responsible for this war —could be curbed, checked, and balanced under government so that life would be not perfectly tranquil, but certainly less nasty, less brutish, and less short. Thus, while the framers understood human nature to be unchanging, it was that very quality that gave them confidence that man as citizen in a governmental system could be influenced and controlled with some degree of success.

The framers of the Constitution were, by and large, property holders or men who had a direct interest in the protection of property interests. This led the historian Charles Beard to conclude that the Constitution was essentially an economic document. Some framers undoubtedly shared Beard's notion that men act fundamentally out of economic considerations and that conflict is primarily economic in nature. However, others took a broader view—that conflict results from the unequal faculties of men, which in turn may produce economic disparities among them. A number of the framers believed in the concept of the enlightened statesmen who does not identify totally with either rich or poor. Many accepted the view that while such men may be biased, they remain capable of considering the interests of all the people and of avoiding decisions that simply reflect class interests. Thus, they thought, economics may influence politics but politics can also influence economics.

Experiential as well as theoretical considerations bore on the framers' constitutional decisions in the summer of 1787. In 1781 the thirteen states had established a common government under the Articles of Confederation. That government had certain distinctive characteristics: it featured a Congress in which each state had one vote; delegates were appointed by the states in a manner determined by each state; each state had no less than two and no more than seven delegates, and any delegate could speak; and the delegates were paid by each state and were subject to recall by each state for any reason whatsoever. These were not procedures designed to promote independence of decision-making in Congress. Indeed, the desire of the states to tightly control the decisions of Congress is reflected in other characteristics of the Confederation. There were no trial courts except those that Congress might set up for trying pirates and persons who committed felonies on the high seas. There was no executive beyond Congress or its agents; important powers could be exercised only by a two-thirds majority, and Congress lacked the means to enforce its own decrees—a matter of some significance when coupled with the fact that the government was funded by contributions from the states. Although Congress developed formuli for determining each state's proper quota, no way to ensure payment was available.

By the summer of 1787 the states and the leading statesmen of that period had accumulated six years of experience with government under the Articles of Confederation, and six years of concerns. Important needs were not being met by the confederated government. Common to most everyone's list of concerns were a uniform trade policy, a method of raising revenues directly, and increased central direction of foreign affairs.

There can be no doubt that the need for a coherent trade policy, both among the states and internationally, was a strong motivating force in the movement toward a new government. It was commonly thought that only a central government could exert uniform control over foreign and domestic trade, for only such a government could effectively lay and collect duties on goods and regulate interstate relations of a commercial nature. The confederated government, while ostensibly a central government, was not generally respected abroad and generated little esteem at home. By 1786 its credit was at a low ebb domestically and internationally. It was accumulating debts worldwide; commerce and agriculture were languishing; paper money was being issued in some states; and the ties of community, morality, and common interests so vital to the creation and existence of a new nation were beginning to show serious deterioration. Natural and commercially engendered animosities and conflicts among the states and their interests began to reappear. This state of affairs was of particular concern in Virginia, and its leaders moved to seek a remedy.

THE ANNAPOLIS CONVENTION

In 1786, Maryland and Virginia issued a call for a general trade convention to be held in Annapolis on the first Monday in September. In response to this call, nine states appointed delegates. For various reasons, delegates from only five states actually attended. After vainly waiting three weeks for additional state representatives to arrive, the delegates in attendance decided to take no action on the main question—trade and commerce—but to call for a later convention to consider this and other issues. The report of the Annapolis Convention suggested that there were important defects in the system of the federal government as it then existed and that questions of trade could not be adequately resolved without looking at and correcting some of these system defects. A new convention was needed to determine just what these defects were and to devise a plan for their remedy.

In spite of the vague language in the Annapolis report, the delegates in attendance there fully believed that they knew what the defects of the confederated government were, and most had fairly well developed ideas as to appropriate remedies. Good politics suggested the use of generalities at this stage. Thus, the Annapolis delegates limited themselves to a call for a convention to meet in Philadelphia on the second Monday in May 1787 for the purpose of revising the Articles of Confederation to meet the exigencies of the nation. Any such revisions were to be agreed upon by Congress and then submitted to the legislatures of the states for approval.

Since, under the Articles, only Congress could initiate amendments, the procedure that was suggested in the report of the Annapolis Convention might appear illegal, or at least extralegal. And although Congress approved the convention call in February 1787, six states had actually appointed delegates prior to that time. Subsequent to congressional approval, seven additional states quickly appointed delegates, and the 1787 Convention became a reality. Initially, Rhode Island declined to participate in the Convention. However, a group of merchants forwarded a letter to the Convention promising to use their good offices to get approval and adoption of the Convention's work by the state at the appropriate time. The understanding at large appears to have been that the Convention was for the purpose of amending the Articles of Confederation, as Congress had done before, and that the only difference lay in having the proposed amendments drafted by a convention prior to congressional consideration.

Given that Congress approved this procedure, one can view the Convention as a drafting committee of Congress, although the idea for such a committee did not originate in Congress, nor were the members of the committee appointed by Congress. That this "committee" did not represent Congress quickly became evident in the first days of the Convention when the intention to establish a new government became apparent. The prior intentions of a large number of delegates were indicated by the early presentation of proposals and plans not consistent with the continuation of the confederated government.

DELEGATES TO THE 1787 CONVENTION

One way to characterize the framers of the Constitution is by either national or state orientation. Those with a national orientation were sympathetic generally to weakening if not abolishing state governments and establishing a system of one central government of a nonmonarchial nature under certain restrictions and limitations. Those with a state orientation, on the other hand, were advocates of full protection of states' rights, fearful of a strong central or consolidated government, jealous of state sovereignty, and generally suspicious of all entrusted authority. In particular, they did not want a strong national government that might sub-

merge all states' rights and the privileges associated with state sovereignty. They believed that government need only maintain good order and the safety of the states.

These two perspectives were represented in varying degrees at the 1787 Convention, though at the individual level, positions were more complex than such generalizations imply. The perspectives of the delegates on the problems of the day were certainly broader than those encompassed by such labels as national and state parties.

Judging from their proposals, their debates, and their agility at finding appropriate compromises for their differences, the delegates to the 1787 Convention were probably as gifted a group as this nation has ever convened in pursuit of solutions to its political problems. This is not to say that they did not, individually, sometimes pursue narrow partisan advantage. But there was an unusually large number of what James Madison called "enlightened statesmen" who kept the larger good of the whole in mind and guided the Convention to its ultimate "bundle of compromises" that we know as the Constitution.

Although the states appointed a total of seventy-four delegates to the convention, only fifty-five from twelve states actually attended. These delegates by and large were young but experienced. The average age was only forty-two, yet nearly three-fourths had sat in the Continental Congress. A number of them had been members of their state legislatures and had helped write their states' constitutions. Eight had also been signers of the Declaration of Independence, seven had been state governors, and twenty-one had fought in the American Revolution. These were men whom life had tested. They also were men who had been chosen in particular states and thus reflected in their values, outlooks, and perspectives on the problems of the day the methods by which they were selected.

First of all, while the delegates were selected by state legislatures, these legislatures were chosen by severely restricted electorates with restrictions varying from state to state. Generally speaking, the legislators at the state level were put in office by considerably less than a majority of the adults in each state. Female suffrage did not exist, and male suffrage probably did not extend beyond the 20 percent level because of property restrictions placed on the entitlement to vote. As a consequence the voters tended to be a small minority of the public—those who were economically affluent or fairly well-to-do. Moreover, there were heavy property restrictions on holding a seat in a state legislature, and thus the members of such bodies also tended economically to be advantaged rather than disadvantaged. Given the circumstances in which the delegates were chosen to the 1787 Convention, it is not surprising to find that they were relatively well educated and generally well-off.

Members of the Convention included men with both national and state orientations. New York's ablest delegate was Alexander Hamilton, a small man but an intellectually superior one, thirty years of age, not popular in the Convention but respected for his ability and his originality. Very nationalist in his sentiments, Hamilton offered the "Hamilton Plan" to his colleagues, but it was far too nationalist for that time.

South Carolina sent several distinguished delegates. Two had the same surname—Pinckney. The older of the two was Charles Cotesworth Pinckney, a forty-one-year-old lawyer educated at Oxford under Blackstone. His father was chief justice of South Carolina. Pinckney was a brigadier general in the Revolution. In the Convention he stood for slavery and the rights of property. Like his cousin, Charles Pinckney was also oriented toward a national party. Only thirty years of age, he boldly offered the "Pinckney Plan" of government and later claimed to have authored large sections of the Constitution. A distinguished career preceded Pinckney's service in Philadelphia. At twenty, he had been a member of the Continental Congress and at thirty-one governor of his state. He appears to have been brilliant but vain, a quality that may have caused some delegates to pay less attention to his suggestions and to belittle Pinckney's contributions to the Constitution.

The state of Virginia sent numerous distinguished delegates to Philadelphia. First and foremost was James Madison, a thirty-six-year-old scholar of politics who in the Convention liked to quote Grotius, Malthus, Locke, and other thinkers of the age. Madison was small in stature, reticent, always dressed in black, and absolutely untiring in pursuit of what he saw as his responsibilities in the Convention. He had twice been a member of Congress and was commonly conceded to know more about the state of affairs in the United States than any other delegate. Most of what we know about the Convention proceedings is derived from detailed notes kept by Madison during the Convention debates.

A second important member of the Virginia delegation was Edmund Randolph, who refused to sign the Constitution but whose impact on the Convention via the "Randolph" or "Virginia Plan" was notable. In contrast to Madison, Randolph was six feet tall, a large, handsome man who was governor of Virginia at age thirty-four. In the Convention, Randolph favored a strong national government and opposed the slave trade, though he held over two hundred slaves at the time. Virginia also sent George Washington, George Mason, and George Wythe. Washington was the leader of the delegation and presided ably over the Convention. But he made only one speech, and his influence was felt primarily in the informal discussions that occurred between Convention sessions. Washington was at age fifty-five probably the richest man in America.

George Mason was the author of the Virginia Bill of Rights and attended the Convention at the advanced age of sixty-two. He owned three hundred slaves and possessed other great wealth, including over fifteen thousand acres of land. Yet he opposed slavery in the Convention and was largely responsible for the view that the central government should operate directly through the people rather than through the medium of the state. He also played a large role in the movement for a federal bill of rights, later added to the Constitution by amendments.

George Wythe, a year younger than Mason, was a lawyer who opposed slavery in deed and word. He freed his own slaves and supported them after doing so. He was a teacher of Thomas Jefferson, John Marshall, James Monroe, and other leading thinkers of the day. Wythe was also a signer of the Declaration of Independence and was chancellor of his state for ten years.

The small state of Connecticut was represented by Oliver Ellsworth and Roger Sherman, among others. Ellsworth was forty-two years of age, a justice in the state supreme court. He was an eloquent debater, respected for his general abilities and his integrity. An extremely rich lawyer, he was suspicious of a strong central government and did not sign the Constitution.

The mayor of New Haven, Roger Sherman,

was a self-made man, not rich, self-educated, said to be tall, ugly, awkward, and uncouth. Yet, he appears to have been a man of some wisdom and cunning. He had been a member of Congress and had signed the Declaration of Independence.

Finally, we may mention two distinguished delegates from Pennsylvania, James Wilson and Gouverneur Morris. Morris was thirty-five years old, the most frequent speaker in the Convention and according to some estimates the most brilliant. Morris was sharp-witted and eloquent, with an impressive command of the English language. He was a consistent aristocrat in the Convention and favored a strong national government. Later he opposed the War of 1812.

Another intense advocate of a strong central government, James Wilson, was a man many consider second in importance only to Madison in the 1787 Convention. Wilson was born in Scotland and came to America when he was twenty-three years of age. He was forty-five in 1787. Prior to the Convention, Wilson had served several times in Congress. He was a signer of the Declaration of Independence and was a member of the United States Supreme Court for the last ten years of his life.

THE INTENTIONS OF THE FRAMERS

On 25 May 1787, twenty-eight delegates representing nine states were present in Philadelphia. By 28 May, thirty-seven delegates representing eleven states were present in the city. On the following day, the delegates were finally able to begin their deliberations. What was their purpose? According to the call of the Annapolis Convention, the Philadelphia meeting was merely to revise the Articles of Confederation. Some delegates, however, had broader purposes in mind.

While it was commonly recognized that greater defenses against domestic and foreign dangers were essential and that increased regulation of commerce and the revenues derived therefrom were needed, a number of delegates believed that such ends could be accomplished by modifying the powers of the Congress. By contrast, the Virginia delegation favored a republican or nondemocratic form of government. A republican government, in their minds, featured the representative principle, with people acting on government through their representatives. Madison and Wilson added the view that such a government should act directly on the people. But no matter what the intentions of the framers might have been before they arrived in Philadelphia, their intentions once there became quite clear with the introduction of the Virginia Plan of government and reactions to it.

The Virginia Plan. The Virginia Plan was introduced on 29 May by Edmund Randolph. Recognizing that government under the Articles had both democratic and nondemocratic characteristics and that this same blend was present in the state governments, Randolph identified the major problem as the encroachment of the democratic parts of government on the nondemocratic parts. The solution proffered was to check democracy by establishing a republican form of government. Such a government would have at least one branch that was not purely democratic, with means to insure its independence from democratic pressures. The way to do this, said Randolph, was to establish a House elected by the people and a Senate chosen by the House from nominees proposed by the legislatures of the individual states. To insure the independence of the Senate, its members were to be given longer terms of office, though Randolph omitted a specific number of years from his initial resolution.

The House was to be subject to recall, the Senate not. Members of the House, moreover, were not to be allowed more than one term in office. No such restriction was to be imposed on the Senate. These arrangements, it was thought, would protect the Senate from undue influence by the people and provide protection against encroachment by the lower house. Individual senators chosen in the proposed manner would be in a better position to resist demands that unthinking, ignorant, or unreasonable constituents might place upon them. Indeed, the arrangements suggested would have made it difficult to even identify the constituency of the Senate, another measure by which the independence of the Senate from the people would be enhanced. Moreover, the fact that members of state legislatures at the time normally served terms of three years or less also had potential for increasing the independence of the Senate.

If the Senate was not to represent the people and the states except in a highly indirect fashion, who or what was to be represented? The answer, in part, was trade, commerce, and wealth. The constituency of a Senate composed in such a fashion would be the nation as a whole, but not all the people in that nation. The protection of those with wealth, property, and commercial interests appears, initially, to have been a driving force behind Randolph's idea of an appropriate Senate.

In addition to a two-house legislative body, the Virginia Plan favored a separation of the legislative, executive, and judicial branches of government. The legislature would have the legislative powers then residing in Congress plus all those other powers that the states were incompetent to exercise. In the event that one or more of the states should contravene the new Constitution, the national legislature would have a power to veto the state action. Moreover, if a state proved unamenable to acting consistently with the Constitution, the legislature would be empowered to employ force to ensure that the state did its duty. Voting in both houses of the national legislature would be proportioned using tax quotas or the number of inhabitants, or both.

The judicial branch of government would consist of a Supreme Court and such other courts as the legislature might think desirable. Judges would be chosen by the legislature and serve for good behavior. Federal jurisdiction would be limited to certain maritime questions, impeachment of national officers, and other questions pertaining to national peace and harmony.

The Virginia Plan suggested a single or plural executive chosen by the national legislature and limited to one term in office. In conjunction with a "convenient" number of federal judges, the executive was to form a council of revision with a veto on legislative acts, the veto being subject to overruling on a vote by both houses of the legislature. Thus, under the Virginia Plan ultimate power would reside in the national legislative body. This represented a dramatic departure from the status quo. State influence on Congress and control of its delegates would not be totally eliminated, but there is no question that state influence would be seriously attenuated. The extent of the attenuation soon became a troubling issue that plagued the framers throughout the Convention.

Randolph's plan also called for a republican form of government in each state, to be guaranteed by the federal government; the binding of state officers to support the federal Constitution; the amending of the new Constitution when needed, without the consent of the national legislature; and the admission of new states into the Union by less than a unanimous vote of the new Congress.

When one considers the contours of Randolph's suggestions in their entirety, the Virginia Plan appears starkly radical. To adopt such a plan of government would be to do much more than merely modify the Articles of Confederation, which was the official purpose of the Convention. The evidence indicates that Randolph was aware of the dramatic differences between a government structured consistently with the Virginia Plan and one operating under the Articles. Randolph's first resolution affirmed that the Articles of Confederation "ought to be . . . corrected and enlarged." But the Virginia Plan was such a gross departure from government under the Articles that, upon being questioned, Randolph quickly conceded that a confederated government could not do the job and proposed a "national government" consisting of supreme executive, legislative, and judicial branches. This was quickly adopted in the Committee of the Whole the following day. A committee of the Whole was the device that enabled the Convention to give detailed consideration to the Randolph Resolutions under less restrictive rules of procedure than those governing the Convention per se.

The importance of the Virginia Plan was twofold: it forced the delegates early in the Convention to decide whether their approach to their task was to be conservative or radical; and, as amended and enlarged, it became the Constitution of the United States. The changes that occurred in the plan as it made its way through Convention debates and committees can by no means be characterized as minor.

On the same day that Randolph presented the Virginia Plan, Charles Pinckney laid a second plan of government before the Convention. This plan was referred to the Committee of the Whole and did not constitute a focus for Convention debate at any time. However, there is evidence that the Pinckney Plan had some influence in shaping the recommendations of committees reporting to the Convention.

The New Jersey Plan. From 28 May to 13 June, the Committee of the Whole devoted its attention exclusively to the Virginia Plan. On 13 June, the committee brought in its report on the Randolph proposals as amended in the committee. The next day, as the Convention prepared to discuss the report, William Patterson of New Jersey asked that the discussion be postponed so that a new plan could be presented. The postponement was granted and Patterson offered the so-called New Jersey Plan on 15 June. The plan was the work of the New Jersey delegates, but the representatives of New York, Connecticut, and Delaware were also supporters of it.

Patterson offered the new plan as a substitute for the one approved by the Committee of the Whole. At this point a clearly defined conflict over the nature of the new government appeared. The discussions and votes in the Committee of the Whole had revealed a tendency for New Jersey, Connecticut, Delaware, New York, and Maryland to vote together. It was evident that these so-called small states had interests that set them apart from the large states. They represented a states-oriented party as against the national party represented in the large states. The conflict was also between states with claims to the western lands and those lacking such claims.

In the Committee of the Whole, the small states had resisted the suggestion that the Convention do anything other than amend the Articles of Confederation. Three of the small states had voted against proportional representation in the lower house; two opposed basing representation in the lower house on population and counting slaves as three-fifths; five voted in opposition to proportional representation in the Senate. Underlying these differences was a fear on the part of the small states that they would have less influence in the new government than in the old and that their interests would be swallowed up by the national party and the large states.

To alleviate their fears, the New Jersey Plan departed from the plan approved by the Committee of the Whole in substantial ways. The central feature of the plan was representation in the legislature. The plan proposed that each state retain equal voting power, irrespective of wealth, size, or population. The sovereignty of the states was to be retained. Revenue was to be raised primarily through import duties, stamp taxes, and postal charges. Additional revenue would be raised as in the old Congress—by requisitions upon the states. The New Jersey Plan also proposed a plural executive elected by the Congress, without right of veto, and a Supreme Court with limited jurisdiction. In essence, the Virginia Plan as approved by the Committee of the Whole would establish a national government while the New Jersey proposal would establish a confederated government.

The Hamilton Plan. The Hamilton Plan was the fourth plan offered to the Convention and apparently resulted from Hamilton's dissatisfaction with proceedings in the Convention up to 15 June. On 18 June, Hamilton made a wide-ranging speech expressing his disapproval of both the Virginia Plan and the New Jersey Plan—particularly the latter. He followed his remarks with a plan of government that radically departed from all previous suggestions. The central characteristic of Hamilton's plan was a strong central government, apparently modeled on that of Great Britain, which he greatly admired. Hamilton would have had a strong executive—chosen by electors who were elected by the people—who would serve for good behavior. He would have extensive powers, including an absolute veto. Hamilton also wanted the governors of the states selected by the central government and urged that they have a veto upon all legislation in their respective states. The Hamiltonian position thus represented the radical extreme of the national party, but it was too radical even for other nationalists in the Convention and did not provoke much discussion.

Two points of interest might be noted about the various plans presented to the Convention. The first is that by being given four plans incorporating various competing notions about the best government to construct, the delegates were able to compare and evaluate different options and to expressly reject those not to their liking. The debates on these various proposals, therefore, not only inform us as to preferences but also provide the reasoning behind the adoptions and rejections. The second point to note is the timing of the various presentations. Randolph and Pinckney presented plans on 28 May that had been prepared prior to the Convention, whereas the Hamilton and New Jersey Plans were developed as reactions to proceedings in the Convention. While the Pinckney Plan was not discussed in the Convention or the Committee of the Whole, the Virginia Plan was the exclusive focus of debate for the period 28 May through 13 June. During that period when no opposing plan was before the delegates, there occurred a shift in the thinking of some delegates as to the kind of government needed and the authority of the representatives of the eleven states in attendance to do more than merely amend the Articles of Confederation. Though it cannot be known with certainty whether the New Jersey Plan came closer to representing the initial thoughts of the delegates in Philadelphia than did the Virginia Plan, it seems likely that such was the case. However, by the time the New Jersey Plan was offered, it was too late, and the New Jersey Plan was rejected by a 7–3 vote with Maryland divided. This rejection occurred on 19 June, at which point the Convention returned to consideration of the amended Virginia Plan.

CONTROVERSIAL ISSUES

Although by 19 June the national party had won the day on most of the major points of contention, it was cognizant of substantial opposition to the provisions previously approved. No government could be formed with a mere majority of the states. The aim was for all the states to participate in the new political system and for all to ratify whatever scheme of government the Convention ultimately approved. Thus, a spirit of compromise was not totally lacking.

Representation in Congress. A major bone of contention was suffrage in the two legislative branches. Resolutions 7 and 8 of the report presented by the Committee of the Whole, after its consideration of the Virginia Plan, called for suffrage in the two houses of the legislature to be based on population, excluding Indians not paying taxes and counting slaves by the three-fifths formula. On 2 July, Oliver Ellsworth of Connecticut moved to amend Resolution 8 to allow each state one vote in the Senate. Although the motion was lost, the vote was evenly divided: 5–5. This caused Roger Sherman to observe that "we are now at full stop." This phrase was apt, and most of the delegates quickly recognized that the Convention might in fact break up over this issue. Thus a committee to seek some kind of compromise was suggested by Charles Pinckney. After a lengthy discussion in which Madison and Wilson strongly opposed this suggestion, the

Committee of Eleven was selected by ballot. That committee recommended on 5 July that each state have an equal vote in the Senate, but only if certain other provisions pertaining to the lower house were adopted simultaneously.

Given that the small states were already within a hair of getting equality in the Senate, the large states actually gave up little by granting equality in the committee report. The small states, on the other hand, made major concessions regarding the lower house—particularly in agreeing that "all bills for raising or appropriating money, and for fixing the salaries of officers of the Government of the United States shall originate in the first branch of the Legislature of the United States, and shall not be altered or amended in the second branch: and that no money shall be drawn from the public Treasury, but in pursuance of appropriations to be originated in the first branch." The small states were destined to have less power in the lower house, yet they gave the money power to that house.

On 5 July the Committee of Eleven also made certain recommendations pertaining to the basis of representation in the lower branch of the legislature. After discussion and amendments, it was finally agreed on 16 July that representation in the first legislature would be based upon an absolute number, that in future legislatures representation would depend on population, including slaves counted as three-fifths, and that direct taxation would be governed by that representation.

Selection of the President. The Articles of Confederation did not provide for a single unitary executive with powers independent of those possessed by Congress. It is not surprising, therefore, that the proposal to establish such an office led to considerable debate. Most of that debate centered on the method of choosing a president and the term of office to be allowed him. Terms of four, six, seven, eight, eleven, and fifteen years were proposed. At one point, a motion to have the president serve for good behavior got the votes of four states. The Virginia Plan, however, proposed that a single executive be established, that he be elected by the national legislature, that he serve for seven years, and that he be limited to a single term. This proposal was approved by the Committee of the Whole on 3 June.

On 18 June, Alexander Hamilton suggested

that the executive be known as "Governour", that he be elected by electors chosen by the people in electoral districts, and that he serve for good behavior. Hamilton's suggestions were not approved. On 19 June, the limitation of a single seven-year term was rejected by the Convention by votes of 8–2 and 5–3. But appointment by the legislature was approved five days later by a vote of 7–4, and on 26 July the Convention adopted the single executive serving for a single seven-year term. On that date the resolutions approved by the Convention were referred to a Committee of Detail whose function was to draft a Constitution. The provisions on the executive were retained by the Committee of Detail, but on 26 August a vigorous debate again ensued when the recommendations of the committee came up for discussion. The Convention easily agreed on a single executive to be known as President of the United States. The following motions then were offered in quick succession: to elect the president by the people rather than by the legislature, (failed); to give each state one vote in the legislature for the purpose of electing the president, (failed); to require a majority of the votes of the members of the legislature present to elect the president, (passed); to give the president of the Senate an additional vote in case of ties (failed); and to choose the president by electors chosen by the people (failed).

Yet the delegates were still not satisfied with what they had wrought concerning the executive, and on 31 August they referred a number of matters to a Committee of Eleven, including the provisions pertaining to the presidency. The committee reported four days later. The report included a dramatic modification of the provisions for choosing a president and changed the executive's term of office. The committee recommended that the president be chosen for a term of four years by electors selected in a manner to be determined by each state. A vice-president would be chosen at the same time. The number of electors would equal the number of senators and representatives assigned to each state. The electors' ballots were to be cast in each state and transmitted to the president of the Senate for counting. The person with the greatest number of votes would be elected president, with the first runner-up being designated vice-president. In case of ties, or in the event that no candidate received a majority of the votes, selection was to

be made by the Senate. These propositions are retained in the Constitution as adopted, with some exceptions—the major one being that selection of the president in case of ties or in the absence of a majority was shifted to the lower house, with each state receiving one vote. The same propositions govern the Constitution two centuries later, with one exception. In 1804, the Twelfth Amendment separated the election of president and vice-president, with the Senate choosing the vice-president in the event that no majority is obtained for that office.

The reason for the change is that the framers of the Constitution did not foresee the development of political parties. By 1796 the Federalist and Republican parties had formed, and both offered candidates for president and vice-president and conducted partisan campaigns. Due to a lack of party discipline, a Federalist president was elected (John Adams) to serve with a Republican vice-president (Thomas Jefferson). In 1800, however, the Republicans had most of the votes, and they were cast with discipline for Jefferson and Aaron Burr. The resulting tie vote required the House of Representatives to resolve the issue. Five days and thirty-six votes later, Jefferson was chosen president by a 10–4 vote with two states not voting. This episode led to the changes incorporated in the Twelfth Amendment.

The key issue that occasioned conflict over the executive in the 1787 Convention was this: Should the selection of the executive be by the people or done in some manner so as to insulate the selection process from the people? Those who feared election by the people thought the great mass of the electorate incapable of judging the qualifications of presidential candidates. They also feared such a system would give too much advantage to the large and populous states. On the other side, the nationalist party believed that election by the people would assure presidents of continental reputation, and they recognized, undoubtedly, that such a method would favor the populous states. The method finally chosen, then, may be viewed as a compromise between the competing strategies. Under the constitutional plan, the large states would have more electors. But the delegates from the small states apparently believed that elections would frequently produce no majority, thus throwing the choice of the president into the House of Representatives, where each state could have one vote. If this was their understanding, history has shown it to be a mistaken one, since the House has not selected a president since 1800.

The Supreme Court. Article III of the Constitution establishes federal judicial power. Although the drafting of this article gave considerably less trouble than the articles dealing with legislative and executive power, the Convention did have some difficulty in deciding how the Supreme Court was to be chosen and in determining its jurisdiction.

The initial suggestion was to have the national judiciary appointed by the national legislature. This was proposed in the Virginia Plan. However, in the Committee of the Whole, Madison and Wilson opposed the choosing of the national judiciary by any numerous body. Madison's objection was that legislators would be influenced in making their choices on grounds other than legitimate qualifications. He thought members of legislative bodies were likely to choose one of their own members. However, he asserted that the Senate was an exception to this generalization since it would be small in number, would have better motives than the lower house, and would have sufficient independence to make better judgments. Thus Madison's objection was not to legislative bodies per se but to those that might be subject to undue influence from the states and the people or those filled with men of inferior motives. Yet, having expressed himself on the question, he was willing to leave the matter open for the time being and merely moved to strike the offending clause, which was done. The 9–2 vote on the issue suggests little support in the Convention for Randolph's proposal on 5 June.

On 13 June, Charles Pinckney moved, in the Committee of the Whole, to have Supreme Court justices elected by the national legislature. Madison immediately restated his objections to involving the "whole legislature" in the selection process. He thought that many legislators were incompetent to make such choices, some were ignorant, and many could be expected to show an offensive partiality to other members of the legislature. He then proposed selection by the Senate, which was quickly agreed to without debate. When the Committee of the Whole made its report to the Convention on 13 June, it

recommended appointment by the second branch of the legislature.

When the Committee's recommendation came up for discussion in the Convention on 18 July, there were suggestions that appointment of Supreme Court justices ought to be made by the executive. Nathaniel Gorham of Massachusetts thought that the Senate was more responsible than the lower house would be, but he considered the executive an even better choice as the appointing agency. He argued for selection by the president with the advice and consent of the Senate. Madison did not object to the idea but thought the concurrence of at least one-third of the Senate would be better. Randolph noted that since the time when the Committee of the Whole had vested appointment of the justices in the Senate, each state had been given one vote in that body, and for this reason he preferred selection by the Senate. Wilson preferred selection by the president alone and moved to that effect. Subsequently, Wilson's motion was supported by only two states, the large and populous states of Massachusetts and Pennsylvania, thereby suggesting the persuasiveness of Randolph's political appeal to the smaller states.

The debate on the question was not yet completed. After the defeat of Wilson's motion for executive selection, Gorham moved for executive selection with the advice and consent of the Senate. As with Wilson's motion, Gorham's did not carry because it failed to get the support of the smaller states. Before the day was over, Madison moved to have Supreme Court justices appointed by the president with the concurrence of at least one-third of the Senate. This motion was postponed for consideration on 21 July. At that point Madison suggested that while the second branch was better suited than the whole legislature for choosing judges, the executive was better suited still. Should the executive make a mistake, the Senate could correct it by a two-thirds vote. He then underscored the political argument offered earlier by Randolph to support appointment by the Senate. But Madison's version differed. He thought it desirable that the states be represented in the process, and that this would be accomplished via Senate participation. The executive would represent the people. Though he had earlier favored selection by the Senate, he now thought that should the Senate alone select, a majority of the states but a minority of the people might choose the justices. He considered this unjustified since the Court was to act on the people rather than on the states. Thus, we see here the vestige of the Lockean notion of consent of the governed—if only by indirect means. After objections, Madison modified his motion to let a majority of the Senate reject a presidential choice. But again the small states defeated the motion, and selection by the Senate stood.

On 26 July, the Convention referred twenty-three resolutions that had been agreed upon to a Committee of Detail. Also referred at this time were the Pinckney and New Jersey Plans presented earlier. That committee reported on 6 August. Article 9 of the report retained the selection of Supreme Court justices by the Senate, but difficulty with the section remained and the matter was referred to a Committee of Eleven. That committee reported on 4 September, recommending that the justices of the Supreme Court be appointed by the president with the advice and consent of the Senate. This wording was adopted by the Convention on 7 September, reappeared in the report of the Committee of Style on 12 September, and appeared in the "engrossed" Constitution signed by the delegates on 17 September. Thus, Madison's amended motion of 21 July, defeated by a 6–3 vote on that date, reemerged on 4 September and became part of Article II, Section 2 in the Constitution.

The explanation for the change in the method of selecting Supreme Court justices accomplished by the Committee of Eleven can only be surmised. However, this Committee of Eleven formulated the first acceptable method of choosing the president, and with that difficult issue disposed of, the framers may have been more willing to give the executive the power to select Supreme Court justices—particularly those framers from the small states who had been resisting executive appointment.

CONSTITUTIONAL PRINCIPLES

Although there are a number of principles that might be abstracted from the 1787 Constitution, two stand out above all the rest—federalism and separation of powers.

Separation of Powers. The government of the United States is often referred to as a democratic government, its political system as a democratic system. Yet, the framers rejected what might be called a pure democracy in favor of republican government. Article IV, Section 4 of the Constitution even guarantees a republican form of government to every state in the Union. The republican form of government was designed to guard against what Madison called a "faction." Madison defined the term to mean "a number of citizens, whether amounting to a majority or minority of the whole, who are united and actuated by some common impulse or passion, or of interest, adverse to the rights of other citizens, or to the permanent and aggregate interests of the community." He thought that justice was the end purpose of all governments and that factions would surely threaten its realization.

He considered it better to try and control the effects of clashing interests. This was best done, he thought, in a "republic." In a pure democracy, as exemplified by a town meeting, the majority rules. As in a democracy, a republican government derives all its powers from the people, but it is administered by a select number of persons who hold their offices at the pleasure of the people, for a limited period of time or during good behavior. In such a system, theoretically, the views of the public are refined by passing them through representatives who seek the long-term interests of all citizens and are better able to resist temptations to partiality and short-term expediencies.

The framers appreciated Madison's argument, but they were not unfamiliar with corrupt legislators and other governmental officials. Thus with Madison they sought means of guarding against corruption in government and its consequences. They sought to do this by dividing power at two levels, the first being a division at the national level among legislative, executive, and judicial institutions, the second a division of power between state and federal governments. Coupled with this idea of separation of powers was the notion of checks and balances. Not only is our government divided into three branches, but the powers given one branch are first granted, then weakened by granting powers to the other two branches that may be used to influence or block action by the first.

This is done in three general ways. First, an

express power to control the operations of one branch may be vested in another. Thus it requires the approval of both houses of the legislature plus the president for a bill to become law. A second means is derived from the fact that the national government is a limited government and therefore may not legitimately exceed its assigned powers. Governmental acts that do so have no validity in the law and cannot be implemented. If implementation is attempted and challenged, the Supreme Court has the authority to block implementation. A third general method is also related to the concept of limited government. Each of the three branches has certain specific powers. One branch cannot exercise a power delegated to another. Thus, the Senate cannot originate a money bill, a power given to the House of Representatives. Nor can the House initiate a treaty, since the treaty power is lodged in the executive. And the Supreme Court is dependent upon Congress for its budget and upon the president to enforce its decrees.

Federalism. The second division of power adopted by the framers was between the national and state governments. This division had characterized government under the Articles of Confederation. But in the new Constitution, the idea was developed more fully, more explicitly, and with greater detail. In the process, the powers of the national government were drastically enlarged at the expense of the states. But the Tenth Amendment recognizes that all power begins with the people and the states and that the federal or national government has only those powers delegated to it under the Constitution. All powers not delegated are reserved to the states and the people.

In dividing power between state and federal governments, the important question was how much power and what kind of power to assign to the national government. The weaknesses in the confederated government that served as primary motivations for the 1787 Convention were noted previously. The framers had little difficulty agreeing that the new national government should be one of increased power vis-à-vis the states. The object of the Convention was to establish a government strong enough to ensure domestic peace and good order while avoiding a government that would stifle the liberties—particularly the economic or commercial rights—of

the people. The government adopted in the Constitution represents the framers' version of a compromise between these two extremes.

RATIFICATION

The Convention completed its work on 17 September 1787. Two days earlier, it had agreed to submit the Constitution to the states for ratification—with nine states being required to ratify in order to establish the new government. Before such submission, however, it was thought desirable that the framers sign the document. At this point, the states were unanimous in their approval of the document. But when it came time to sign, the framers were not unanimous. Randolph and Mason from Virginia and Elbridge Gerry from Massachusetts refused to sign.

Randolph reasoned that nine states would not ratify and confusion would then ensue. Gerry alluded to the democrats and antidemocrats in his state and expressed the view that the Constitution would put these two parties at each others' throats, thereby producing a civil war.

On 15 September, Randolph and Mason had expressed great concern over the "excessive" powers given Congress. They suggested that they could only support the plan for the new government if the states, in the process of ratifying, were allowed to offer amendments. Mason suggested that the Convention had labored without the knowledge of the people and that a second convention should be held. Thus he refused to sign the document. Mason, the author of the Virginia Bill of Rights, also wanted a bill of rights in the Constitution but had been rebuffed by his colleagues when he offered a motion to that effect. Eventually, thirty-nine of the fifty-five delegates who attended the Convention at one time or another signed the new Constitution.

In the state ratifying conventions, the so-called Federalists supported ratification. The Antifederalists opposed it. With some exceptions, the coastal areas supported the Constitution, the inland or back country opposed it. Similarly, the business community, large planters, and those possessed of great wealth favored ratification, while debtors, small farmers, and frontiersmen saw little reason to support the Constitution. Thus, extensive debates ensued in the state conventions. But with the ratification by New Hampshire on 21 June 1788, the requisite nine states had ratified the new Constitution, and by 29 May 1790, all thirteen states were in the fold.

THE BILL OF RIGHTS

The draft Constitution did not contain a bill of rights. In the state conventions that were called to ratify the Constitution, this omission was a highly controverted issue. In eight states the Constitution was ratified with the understanding that a bill of rights would be added later by amendment. Very shortly after commencing its first session, Congress received over one hundred resolutions for amending the Constitution. On 8 June 1789, Representative James Madison recommended to the House that it consider adding a bill of rights. His reason: many of the states expected Congress to initiate action leading to the adoption of a bill of rights. At that time, eleven of the thirteen states had already ratified the Constitution. Thus, the formation of the new government did not depend in any technical sense on the adoption of such a bill. But Madison knew that there was great dissatisfaction in the land over the matter and felt honor-bound to push the issue. That is why he said "I shall proceed to bring the Amendments before you as soon as possible, and advocate them until they shall be finally adopted or rejected by a constitutional majority of this House."

The position taken by Madison on the issue was, of course, good politics. Getting a new government was an accomplishment. Keeping it, as Benjamin Franklin had observed in the Convention, was another, and Madison well understood the distinction. The new government needed the support of those disaffected over the bill of rights issue and the two states not yet in the fold. This is not to suggest that Madison did not believe in the value of certain guarantees against federal authority. But it will be recalled that Madison was a strong advocate of a truly national government. He did not fear federal power or its abuse to the extent expressed by some of the framers. After reading the House debate on 8 June 1789, it is difficult to escape the conclusion that political considerations were important to those who voted for a bill of rights, irrespective of individual views regarding the need for such protection.

In August 1789, the House approved a number of provisions by a two-thirds vote. After some changes by the Senate, twelve amendments were sent to the states in September. The states subsequently ratified ten. These became known as the Bill of Rights, though some commentators have used that label to encompass only the first eight amendments.

BIBLIOGRAPHY

Charles A. Beard, *An Economic Interpretation of the Constitution of the United States* (1913). James M. Beck, *The Constitution of the United States* (1922). Morris L. Ernst, *The Ultimate Power* (1937). Max Farrand, *The Framing of the Constitution of the United States* (1913); and as ed., *The Records of the Federal Convention of 1787,* 4 vols. (1911–1937).

Charles S. Hyneman and George W. Carey, *A Second Federalist* (1967). Alfred H. Kelly, W. A. Harbinson, and Herman Belz, *The American Constitution: Its Origins and Development,* 6th ed. (1983). James Madison, *Notes of Debates in the Federal Convention of 1787 Reported by James Madison* (1966). Jackson T. Main, *The Anti-Federalists: Critics of the Constitution, 1781–1788* (1961).

[*See also* ARTICLES OF CONFEDERATION.]

THE MARSHALL COURT AND ERA

Robert K. Faulkner

T HE thirty-four years of the Marshall Court began with John Marshall's formal appointment as chief justice, on 31 January 1801, and concluded with his death in office, on 6 July 1835. While the Court contained several independent and gifted associate justices, especially William Johnson of South Carolina and Joseph Story of Massachusetts, Marshall's was the formative influence. He held office longer than has any other chief justice, Roger B. Taney being next with a term of twenty-eight years, and he dominated his associates more than has any other chief, with Charles Evans Hughes, William Howard Taft, and Earl Warren distant rivals. The Marshall Court was remarkably unified, dissents or concurring opinions appearing rather rarely. Its characteristic feature was the chief justice's famous expositions of the still new federal Constitution. Its era raised the Supreme Court from an erratic obscurity to the semipolitical eminence, as voice of a semisacred fundamental law, that it has since maintained. When, in 1833, Alexis de Tocqueville surveyed the new world of American democracy, he gave long and meditative accounts of the federal judiciary, especially the Supreme Court. "A more imposing court," he concluded, "was never constituted by any people."

The Marshall Court's achievement is the more remarkable because the times were the least promising and most dangerous ever to confront a new chief justice. Federal institutions had existed for but a dozen years, the Supreme Court was barely known and already rather discredited, and the political party of George Washington and the Constitution had just been driven from office by an overwhelming vote. The justices confronted the tumultuous triumph of Thomas Jefferson's popular republicanism, which was suspicious of Federalists, courts, and federal power. John Adams, lame duck and last of the Federalist presidents, nominated Marshall on 20 January 1801, and a lame-duck Senate, whose Federalist majority had been destroyed by the Republican landslide, confirmed him a week later. Marshall's term continued during the presidencies of James Madison and James Monroe, who also were Virginia Republicans inclined to strict construction of federal powers and to states' rights, and through the one ineffectual term of John Quincy Adams, a Whig who admired Marshall's work. It concluded amidst the pervasive triumph of Jacksonian democracy, which was suspicious of the Court's protection of federal powers, Indian rights, and vested property rights. These were times that tried the framers' project. Insofar as the United States remained one nation and a constitutional democracy, providing for individual rights, effective government, and economic enterprise as well as for popular control, the Court that bears Marshall's name deserves much of the credit.

During the course of its thirty-four years, the Marshall Court was engaged in five chief efforts. First, it established general judicial authority to construe the Constitution (and to restrict Congress, president, and states accordingly) in the face of Jefferson's plans and protests. Second, it held the executive branch to its statutory and constitutional duties. Third, it upheld federal legislative powers, especially extensive discretion to choose appropriate subordinate measures. Fourth, it secured creditors' rights and land titles in the face of virulent protests, several times verging on rebellion, from the states and the economically distressed. Last, it upheld international law that prescribed strict fidelity to treaties, regard for other governments as equally sovereign, and observance of the rights and duties necessary for free trade and mutual agreement.

TENTATIVE BEGINNINGS

Marshall took over a Court that, although respectable, had failed to establish firm authority before venturing into the dangerous struggle between Federalists and Republicans. Earlier, President George Washington had called the Supreme Court the "keystone of our political fabric," and he had worked to begin it well. Washington had presided over the Constitutional Convention, which had seldom discussed the judiciary but had relegated much to it. The "judicial power" was expressly extended to "all Cases, in Law and Equity, arising under this Constitution, the Laws of the United States, and Treaties . . . made under their Authority." The sweeping language implicitly gave sweeping responsibilities. In particular, the federal courts became the decisive barrier to the two domestic forces most feared by the framers, state governments and democratic legislatures. The convention rejected a legislative or executive veto of state laws (Virginia and Hamilton plans) and instead authorized judges to enforce upon the states "the supreme Law of the Land." Similarly, the Court was expected to hold the executive and legislature to the Constitution's mandates. If the *Federalist* is to be believed, the framers especially feared the more democratic House of Representatives and the humors of the people. Nor were direct judicial rebuffs to be the judges' only techniques. Firm judges, Hamilton suggested in no. 78, may mitigate by construction the impact of unfair and partial laws upon "the private rights of particular classes of citizens." Such checks to legislative inclinations will have an extensive, if quiet, influence upon the very "character of our governments."

President Washington took care to appoint to the Court prominent citizens from each section of the new nation, choosing especially those who had helped draft or defend the new Constitution. The justices made an immediate and favorable impression, and their decisions, together with charges to grand juries while on circuit, helped the new and distant government to win popular acceptance. In its first eleven years, the Court passed upon the constitutionality of an act of Congress, upheld federal treaties and laws against challenges from state legislatures and courts, and held unconstitutional a state law relieving debtors.

Nevertheless, the Court's authority was not yet firmly established. In the early years the judges' roles were in good part ceremonial; no cases reached the Court during the first few terms, and only about seventy were heard during its first eleven years. The impact of controversial decisions was cushioned by the public's ignorance of the potential conflict between the distant judiciary's powers and old familiar powers. A new Republican party fueled realization and resentment, when they arrived, and quickly inflamed the old antifederal animus of debtors, states, and legislatures. In *Chisholm* v. *Georgia* (1793) the Court disregarded express reassurances that the advocates of the Constitution had offered to states burdened with unpaid war debts, and held that a state might be sued for breach of contract by a citizen of another state. Retribution was swift. The Eleventh Amendment, a version of which was introduced into the House of Representatives on the next day, reversed the decision.

The Court's voice was often muffled. In most cases judges wrote individual opinions; there was no opinion for the Court, no reporter of decisions, and the vast majority of opinions were not even partially reprinted by newspapers. Also, the Court had three chief justices in eleven years. Chief Justice John Jay absented himself to negotiate with Britain, signed a highly controversial treaty, and then resigned in 1795 to become governor of New York. The federal judiciary appeared partisan, and this appearance was not mitigated by the Federalist Senate's rejection of John Rutledge as Jay's successor, for opposing Jay's Treaty, even after Rutledge had served a term in a recess appointment. Less than three years after Oliver Ellsworth succeeded Jay in March 1796, he was appointed to settle differences with France and so resigned as chief justice in December 1800 while still abroad.

Moreover, various federal judges directly challenged several favorite doctrines of the Republicans. They determined on circuit that France might be considered an enemy with whom the United States was engaged in partial war; that a citizen had no inherent right to expatriate himself (to fight for revolutionary France); that the Court (and government) had common-law jurisdiction to punish subversive acts; and, worst of all, that the Federalists' hated Alien and Sedition Acts were constitutional. The radical Republican paper *Aurora* urged that judges be impeached for political heresies; enmity toward the Court was one reason for the Republicans' electoral triumph of 1800. Meanwhile, the judges became more embroiled in partisanship. Justice Samuel Chase, irascible and rash, warned of Jeffersonian "mobocracy" and absented himself from the August 1800 term in order to electioneer for Federalist candidates in Maryland. The Federalists appointed Marshall as chief justice in January 1801 and pushed through their Judiciary Act on 13 February. Although the act relieved Supreme Court justices of the punishing task of riding circuit, it also opened up sixteen circuit judgeships that were promptly filled with good Federalists. These and other appointments of "midnight judges" were rushed through during the dying hours of Adams' presidency.

Jefferson was furious. Defeated at the polls, the Federalists "have retired into the judiciary as a stronghold . . . ," he commented in a letter to John Dickinson (19 December 1801), "and from that battery all the works of republicanism are to be beaten down and erased." Once in office, the Republicans took action. They repealed the Judiciary Act of 1801 and replaced it with their Republican Circuit Court Act of 1802, restoring Supreme Court justices to circuit duty. This act also postponed the meeting of the Supreme Court for fourteen months so that it could not declare unconstitutional either the cancellation of judicial offices or the joining to a supreme court of the duties of the circuit courts. Meanwhile, Jefferson and his chief congressional leaders awaited an opportunity (which Chase eventually provided) to transform the Court through a series of impeachments. The safety of the Court was further threatened by Jefferson's hatred for, and fear of, Marshall. The animosity was reciprocated by the new chief justice, who detested Jefferson and the Jeffersonian political creed.

There was an extraordinary unity of the sixteen disparate and often able judges who sat during the Marshall Court's thirty-four embattled years. At the beginning unity was easy; all six justices were Federalists who became secure against Jefferson's designs after the failure of the Chase impeachment in 1804. The Federalists were not secure against death, however. Beginning in 1804, with Jefferson's appointment of the spirited William Johnson of South Carolina to replace Alfred Moore, nine appointments lay with Republican and then Democratic presidents (and but one with the Whig John Quincy Adams). The majority tipped in 1810 when Madison appointed the great Joseph Story of Massachusetts to replace William Caleb Cushing. Yet, the Court's balance tipped only slightly. The old Federalists hung together. Justice Johnson followed Marshall's lead in essentials, Story became a protégé (but not a rubber stamp), and so on, until Marshall's final years. Then Marshall feared that the Court would fall to the states'-rights school, and he dissented in crucial cases affecting creditors' rights. On the other hand, Justice Henry Baldwin almost resigned in 1831, warning that Marshall's Court was extending its authority beyond "subjects clearly within the judicial power."

There were various causes for the unity that Marshall patiently cultivated and Jefferson repeatedly deplored. The Court was threatened from without. Justices such as Johnson, Thomas Todd, and Story were Republicans never fully devoted to Jefferson's creed. John McLean and James M. Wayne were appointed by Jackson but were far from being clones of "Old Hickory." Also, the justices lived and ate together (until 1845), a practice begun because of the District of Columbia's skimpy accommodations but encouraged by Marshall. Led by their genial chief and the witty Story, theirs was amiable, as well as efficient, fellowship. One reminiscer remarked that the best Madeira wine in Washington was called "The Supreme Court," imported by the justices and sipped as they deliberated after dinner. A letter from Story (24 February 1812) described his first term in 1812: "My brethren are very interesting men, with whom I live in the most frank and unaffected intimacy. Indeed we are all united as one, with a mutual esteem which makes even the labors of jurisprudence light. . . . My familiar conferences at our lodgings often come to a very quick, and I trust, a very accurate opinion, in a few hours." The justices' common deliberations were also aided by an extraordinary circle of lawyers, a Supreme Court bar chiefly composed of senators and representatives and led at different times by remarkable statesmen—counsel such as William Pinckney, William Wirt, and Daniel Webster.

Yet Marshall's superior prudence and force of reasoning were undoubtedly the unifying influences on his Court. During the early years of the Marshall era, Justice Johnson later reported to Jefferson, some of the old Federalists were tired and rather incompetent; but that does not explain Marshall's influence over such judges as Johnson and Story. Indeed, the six justices appointed by Jefferson, Madison, and Monroe entered not a dissent to the Court's key affirmations of federal power. Marshall was temperate— "No man is more temperate," said Wirt, who had been Jefferson's attorney general—and a master at avoiding needless quarrels while constructing necessary pronouncements. Of the more than 1,100 cases decided with opinions between 1801 and 1835, Marshall filed dissenting opinions in only six, fewer than any chief justice since. He wrote the opinion for the Court in 519 cases. Jay had written 3 opinions, and Ellsworth, 5. In his first five years Marshall wrote the opinion in every case in which he participated; in the next seven years he delivered 130 of the Court's 160 opinions. From the start he established the custom of one opinion for the Court; concurring opinions and dissents were discouraged. Jefferson hated and feared Marshall's "practice of making up opinions in secret and delivering them as the orders of the Court," opinions "huddled up in conclave, perhaps by a majority of one, delivered as if unanimous and with the silent acquiescence of lazy or timid associates, by a crafty chief judge, who sophisticates the law to his mind, by the turn of his own reasoning" (letter to Thomas Ritchie, 25 December 1820). Indeed, until his life's end Jefferson fought this "engine of consolidation" and tried to restore the old way that aired the Court's differences: a series of opinions by individual justices. Through a cascade of pungent letters, he sought allies in subordinating the Marshall Court to the nation's will. He advocated various schemes, including easier modes of impeachment and a six-year term for federal judges, with reappointment by the president after consent of both houses of Congress.

CONSTITUTIONAL REGULATOR OF GOVERNMENTS

The Marshall Court's first and crucial achievement was to establish the Supreme Court's authority, first as to the limits of the other federal branches and then as to the limits of the state governments. In this effort the Court was never free of dangerous challenges. It supervised the general government by all its decisions as to the relative constitutional powers of the Supreme Court, executive, and legislature. It maintained jurisdiction over state courts as to federal questions and then excluded particular state actions contrary to constitutional restrictions and the implications of the new federal powers. Three law cases resolutely ventilated these issues: *Marbury* v. *Madison* (1803), *Martin* v. *Hunter's Lessee* (1816), and *Cohens* v. *Virginia* (1821).

The Madison of *Marbury* v. *Madison* was the famous James Madison, at the time of this case Jefferson's secretary of state. William Marbury sued to obtain an office (justice of the peace in the District of Columbia) to which President Adams had appointed him under one of the Federalists' judiciary expansions of 1801. Madison, at incoming President Jefferson's behest, stopped the appointment by withholding delivery of the commission of office. The commission had been forgotten in the secretary of state's desk during the Adams administration's hectic last hours of premidnight judicial appointments on 3 March—forgotten by Marshall, who was serving as both the new chief justice and the old secretary of state. The filing of this suit and the Court's order in December 1801 that Madison show cause why he should not be commanded to deliver the commission made the Republicans postpone the Court's next term.

Marshall's opinion in *Marbury* is the classic judicial formulation of the American rule of law, a seminal little treatise that repays repeated readings. It managed to lay the foundation of Supreme Court predominance over the outlines of executive and legislative powers—and without much exacerbating the enmity of the party that controlled them. The Court decided first that Marbury had a right to his commission and that he might appeal from the executive to the courts for vindication of his right. But it finally denied him a remedy, holding that the law authorizing the writ for which he asked violated the Constitution. Marshall took the engaging position, as E. S. Corwin put it, of denying a certain judicial power while using the occasion to assert a transcendent judicial power, that of voiding legislation as unconstitutional. Jefferson grasped immediately the implications and fought all his life to discredit the decision. He failed. Marshall's establishment of judicial review was not seriously attacked by even the most zealously Republican newspapers.

Yet other parts of the opinion provoked immediate controversy. The Jeffersonians claimed that the findings as to Marbury's right to his office were unnecessary, since the Court disclaimed jurisdiction, and that they amounted to a hectoring lecture as to Jefferson's duties and the judiciary's authority. In fact, Marshall sought bigger game. He set forth a comprehensive ranking of federal powers and laws to govern all presidents, legislators, and judges. He required that a citizen's rights be determined by law and not by executive decree, when the executive is engaged in "ministerial" execution of law, as distinguished from the discretionary exercise of his "political" powers. Marshall insisted also that the citizen may appeal to the judiciary to make his legal right effective against the executive; else there would not be "civil liberty" or "a government of laws." Then he allowed an appeal from statute law to Constitution. A constitution is "deemed fundamental" and "designed to be permanent," and a law violating this fundamental law is void. This doctrine, the Court declared, is "essentially attached to a written constitution and is consequently to be considered, by this court, as one of the fundamental principles of our society." Finally Marshall insisted on the duty of judges to follow the Constitution in preference to an unconstitutional statute. Otherwise, the "very foundation of all written constitutions would be subverted" and the legislature, limited in words, would enjoy "a practical and real omnipotence."

In ways other than Marshall's emphatic arguments, the justices helped themselves to weather the political storms that assailed them. They resolved to return to circuit duty under the Republican Circuit Court Act of 1802, in light of precedent and despite their constitutional doubts, and affirmed the act's constitutionality in *Stuart* v. *Laird* (1803). Marshall himself was cautious, even timid, while testifying before the Senate during Justice Chase's impeachment trial. The impeachment failed, and impeachment, according to Jefferson, came to be "a mere scarecrow," a "bugbear" that the judges "fear not at all." Meanwhile, the Jeffersonian party began to weaken. John Randolph, the erratically brilliant leader of the House Republicans, was frantic after the Senate's acquittal of Chase. He introduced a bill for removal of judges by the president on joint address of both houses, and an ally introduced a constitutional amendment for recall of senators. These writhings further divided Randolph's radical Virginians from plainer northern democrats and moderates of both parties. While Jefferson had become immensely popular by the end of his first term, with his acquisition of Louisiana and the decline of the Federalists, Randolph was discredited and the Republicans in Congress nearly split. During his second term Jefferson's dominance dissolved; the Embargo of 1807, his pet weapon in foreign policy, had brought ruin and sedition at home and little but disdain abroad. The Marshall Court had managed to establish itself, flag unfurled, in the face of the newly democratized political branches and parties.

In *Martin* v. *Hunter's Lessee* and *Cohens* v. *Virginia,* the Court confronted challenges from the states to its protection of federal powers—a problem that had arisen early in Marshall's tenure. In 1803 a Pennsylvania law defied a federal district court decision and directed the governor "to protect the just rights of the State from any process issued out of any Federal Court." In 1809 the governor and legislature combined to forbid compliance with the Supreme Court decision, in *United States* v. *Judge Peters* (1809), that the district judge enforce his order. Only when armed conflict threatened between state troops and a United States marshal's posse of two thousand did the state back down. Recalcitrance on the part of the states continued. There was widespread disobedience to federal court orders enforcing the hated embargo in New England and South Carolina, enforcing the security of certain property rights and land claims in Pennsylvania, Georgia, Kentucky, and Virginia, and protecting the national bank in Kentucky, Ohio, and elsewhere. The worst crisis came in the last years. Georgia was near rebellion. It defied the Court's order, in *Worcester* v. *Georgia* (1832), to free missionaries whom the state had imprisoned for violating its rules governing valuable Cherokee territory. Georgia's seizure of the Cherokee lands violated the Constitution, the Court announced in an opinion by Marshall, because federal jurisdiction over the Cherokee, as a self-governing nation, was exclusive. Georgia's governor had threatened "the most determined resistance" to such a decision; the legislature denied the Supreme Court's jurisdiction in any proceedings interfering with a state court's criminal decision, and the state's highest court would not change its decision or free the missionaries. Finally, in January 1833, the governor pardoned the missionaries after they withdrew their suit. Georgia backed down only in the face of President Andrew Jackson's decisive proclamation against nullification of 10 December 1832 and the subsequent Force Bill to enforce federal laws. Both were directed against South Carolina's ordinance nullifying the tariff of 1832. The ordinance had specifically forbidden appeal to the Supreme Court of questions concerning the ordinance, state laws carrying it out, or the federal tariff law.

The Marshall Court's enforcement of federal supremacy provoked two Virginia challenges to its appellate authority. The twenty-fifth section of the original Judiciary Act of 1789 had authorized writs of error to the Supreme Court from judgments of state courts. The Court had taken jurisdiction in this manner sixteen times between 1789 and 1813 and had invalidated a state statute, all without serious opposition. In *Martin*, however, a state for the first time asserted the unconstitutionality of such jurisdiction. The case involved title to extensive and valuable lands and growing determination on the part of Virginia's Jeffersonian leaders, such as Judge Spencer Roane, to counter the Court's nationalism. Martin claimed by virtue of Lord Fairfax's title, as secured under the peace treaty with Britain (1783). Hunter's Lessee claimed by virtue of Virginia law, under which the lands were confiscated from the enemy during the Revolution and which denied that an alien might inherit land.

The Virginia Courts decided for Hunter's Lessee, and the Supreme Court, for Martin. The Virginia Court of Appeals then declared invalid the Supreme Court's decision. The Virginia judges unanimously held that Supreme Court review of state court decisions violated the constitutional division of independent state and federal powers. While controversies may arise between state and federal governments, wrote one of the Virginia judges, "the constitution has provided no umpire, has erected no tribunal, by which they shall be settled."

Justice Story wrote the Supreme Court's elaborate response. Marshall declined to participate, since he and certain relatives had made extensive purchases of other Fairfax lands. According to Article III of the Constitution, Story argued, it is the nature of the issue, and not the location of the court of first instance, that determines federal jurisdiction. That jurisdiction extends to all cases arising under the Constitution, laws, and treaties of the United States, whether the case arises in a state or federal court. This reach must be appellate unless a case is to be seized from state jurisdiction as soon as a federal issue is raised. The appellate authority is necessary if the Constitution and laws pursuant to it are to be the supreme law of the land, as Article VII requires. If there is a corresponding impairment of state courts and of state sovereignty in general, that is the inevitable and intended result of the Constitution's erection of an effectual and supreme national government. The Court's power, as Justice Johnson said while concurring in the judgment and dissenting from Story's opinion, is the government's "power of protecting itself in the exercise of its constitutional powers."

The Court's second important statement on the issue occurred in 1821. The Virginia believers in states' rights had been deeply alarmed by Marshall's authorization, in *McCulloch* v. *Maryland* (1819), of "ample means" for execution of the federal government's enumerated powers. The defense of implied powers, already linked to a controversy over the national bank, became entangled in the simmering debate as to Congress's power to limit slavery. The issue flared up when northerners tried to prevent Missouri's admission as another slave state. Despite the Missouri Compromise (1820), the incident was an ominous portent—an "alarm bell in the night," Jefferson called it. Southerners feared that the *McCulloch* decision had tacitly authorized further congressional conditions upon the admission of new states. Jefferson and Roane were now joined by the fiery publicist John Taylor of Caroline, who took specific aim at the Court's doctrine of implied powers and its supervision of state decisions. The Supreme Court may not construe fundamental law, Taylor argued, when "the Constitution operates upon collision between political departments," but only when it operates upon "collisions between individuals" (Taylor, 1822).

It was against this background that the Marshall Court decided *Cohens* v. *Virginia* in 1821. A Virginia court had convicted the Cohens brothers of selling a lottery ticket in Virginia, the sale being forbidden by state law and the lottery being authorized by the federal District of Columbia. When the Cohens sought to appeal, the state denied the Supreme Court's jurisdiction over a state court in a state criminal prosecution and denied also that Congress might authorize a lottery where state law forbade it. When the Supreme Court took jurisdiction, the Virginia legislature denied federal jurisdiction and resolved that counsel for the state were not to argue the merits of the case but only the question of jurisdiction.

Although Marshall eventually decided against the Cohens by construing the statute to authorize sales of lottery tickets only within the District, the famous *Cohens* opinion rebuts Virginia's attack on the Court. The people of the United States, Marshall declared, had made a "supreme government" to which "ample powers are confided." Virginia is subordinate to that government and to the judiciary that protects it, to the extent the Constitution requires. The Constitution expressly extends judicial jurisdiction to various cases involving a state as party. Moreover, the judicial power of any sound government should extend as far as its legislative power, and Virginia's construction is likely "to prostrate the government and its laws at the feet of every state in the Union." If courts of the Union cannot correct courts of the states in such cases, Marshall concluded, the government will be no better than the league that it replaced: "Each member will possess a veto on the will of the whole."

The *Cohens* opinion was widely circulated in the press, and it was followed within two weeks by the decision in *McClung* v. *Silliman* (1821), which denied the right of a state court to issue a writ commanding a federal official. The Court's opponents were furious. Jefferson redoubled his efforts, and a series of articles attacking the Court were written by Roane and reprinted in full in many southern and western papers. There

ensued years of congressional attacks upon the Court's powers and jurisdiction.

Meanwhile, Jefferson endeavored to move Justices Gabriel Duval, Todd, and Johnson to restore the old system of judicial opinions by individual justices in turn. Also, various other proposals percolated to give the Senate appellate jurisdiction whenever a state might be a party to a federal case, to provide for concurrence of five judges or even all seven judges when a state law was declared invalid, or to repeal Section 25 of the Judiciary Act. None of these attempts succeeded, but neither did attempts to relieve the judges of circuit duty and to provide an additional judge and circuit for the new states of the West and Southwest. These ten states, with a population equal to that of the whole Union in 1789, had only one judge on the Supreme Court. Although in 1807 a judge had been added to the original six, one who was responsible for a circuit encompassing Kentucky, Tennessee, and Ohio, subsequent bills all foundered on congressional distrust of the Court and partisan distrust of presidents from the other party.

As the doctrine of nullification took hold in the South and Georgia came close to rebellion in 1830, congressional animosity erupted again. South Carolina Senator Robert Hayne's famous defense of nullification in January 1830 justified veto of laws deemed unconstitutional by states even if validated by the United States Supreme Court. Marshall feared then that Section 25 of the Judiciary Act would either be repealed by Congress or nullified by an increasingly powerful segment of the Court.

The efforts of the Court's opponents reached their peak on 24 January 1831, when a majority of the House Judiciary Committee reported favorably on a repeal bill. The bill was rejected by the full House virtually without debate, and a subsequent motion to consider a constitutional amendment to limit the terms of federal judges also lost. The congressional attacks had failed, and Jackson's rebuff of South Carolina's venture into nullification served to secure the Marshall Court's last two years against state jealousies.

THE COURT AND THE PRESIDENTS

The Marshall Court's first sharp fights involved judicial limitation of executive actions.

Marbury portended this. The opinion divided executive authority into that directed by law (ministerial) and that involving executive discretion (political). An individual had a right to something denied him by the executive but due him by law, and the judiciary might vindicate such a right.

The Court applied this principle to hold an officer liable for civil suit for an action beyond statutory authorization, even if the action was prescribed by presidential instructions, in *Little v. Barreme* (1804). Adams' order could not "legalize an act which, without these instructions, would have been a plain trespass." The doctrine was soon turned against President Jefferson's pursuit of two favorite projects, punishment of Aaron Burr and the Embargo of 1807. Jefferson finally was convinced that his former vice-president and permanent enemy Burr was plotting an uprising in the West, to separate the Southwest from the Union. Burr and his followers were arrested, and transfered as prisoners from the West. Jefferson kept them under military arrest until they might be committed on a charge of treason, publicly declared their guilt, and sought from Congress authority to suspend the writ of habeas corpus for three months. In two trials Marshall stopped Jefferson's prosecutions. In *Ex parte Bollman and Swartwout* (1807) he held for the Supreme Court that a writ of habeas corpus might issue to free Burr's associates Bollman and Swartwout and that they could not be tried for treason; the evidence did not show levying of war and the crime, if any, could not be tried in the District of Columbia because it had not occurred there. The opinion was a humiliating rebuff to Jefferson, and it strengthened various legal barriers to partisan prosecutions for treason.

Jefferson's worst fears were realized when Marshall, serving on circuit in Richmond, defined treason so strictly that a jury reluctantly freed Burr. Marshall's ruling decided a sensational trial in which Jefferson was in effect prosecutor and yet, in a sense, defendant before the contemptuous rhetoric of Burr and his band of remarkable lawyers. To convict for treason, the Constitution requires either confession or testimony by two witnesses "to the same overt Act" of "levying War." No confession being forthcoming, Marshall would allow conviction only for an open act of levying war or, if for procuring the overt act charged, then only by testimony of

two witnesses to the procuring. While the prosecution had some witnesses to Burr's movements and forces, it lacked witnesses to prove either that Burr was present at the armed gathering specified, on the Ohio, or that he procured the gathering. After the verdict Marshall was hanged in effigy, charged with partisan bias, and furiously attacked by the Republican press. Nevertheless, he and his Court broadly provided what the framers of Article III, Section 3, seem to have intended: prevention of the abuse of treason prosecutions in political strife, by defining the crime strictly and requiring unequivocal evidence.

Jefferson intended the Embargo Acts of 1807 and 1808 to force a halt to French and British depredations on American trade, by cutting off American trade with France and Britain. Their purpose went beyond the particular circumstances, however. The embargo was Jefferson's crucial experiment in enlightened and humane foreign policy, conquering conquerors by peace. Jefferson persevered with a zeal and thoroughness that did not produce success but earned contempt for his country abroad, drove commercial New England toward ruin and to the brink of rebellion, deeply weakened the Republicans, almost prevented election of his heir Madison, and violated at every turn Jefferson's creed of strict construction of federal powers. He had to confront a variety of particular setbacks from Supreme Court judges on circuit, who limited some of his extensions of executive power, and yet he obtained a crucial affirmation of the embargo's general constitutionality.

The first and sharpest rebuff came from an unexpected source, Jefferson's appointee Justice William Johnson from Republican South Carolina. The president had ordered the customs-fees collectors in the ports to detain all vessels containing provisions, whereas the statute in question required collectors to detain all loaded vessels that, in the collectors' opinion, intended to evade the embargo. Johnson held the instruction void, as unwarranted by statute, and his opinion received more attention than any previous judicial decision except Marshall's decision as to Burr. Jefferson, furious, circulated a contrary opinion that he had obtained from Attorney General Caesar A. Rodney, which Federalists attacked as executive intimidation of the courts and executive construction of the law. Justice Johnson answered with a stinging defense of the primacy of law over executive order and of the primacy of judicial exposition of law. "You can scarcely elevate a man to a seat in a Court of Justice," wrote Rodney ruefully to Jefferson, "before he catches the leprosy of the Bench."

Despite the embargo, provisions seeped into Canada through Vermont, and Jefferson ordered out state troops and the regular army. Various acts of violence culminated in the murder of three state militiamen. When Rodney ordered the perpetrators tried for treason, thus to impress the citizenry, Justice Brockholst Livingston on circuit distinguished a general levying of war from willful opposition to a particular statute and would not sustain the indictment, in *United States* v. *Hoxie* (1808). Similarly, Marshall on circuit quashed criminal indictments for violations of an embargo act. Since the act mentioned no criminal penalties, the civil penalties provided must be supposed the exclusive remedies intended. In another case, Marshall refused to allow federal court processes to be governed by Virginia's stay laws, which postponed collection of legal judgments by execution, such as compulsory sale or garnishment of property, until six months after repeal of the embargo. Virginia had tried to ease the impact and unpopularity of Jefferson's measure, from which it suffered as much as any state, and Marshall's decision weakened Virginia's effort, since many creditors could obtain the aid of federal courts.

These small setbacks were countered by Jefferson's great judicial victory. In 1808, District Judge John Davis of Salem, Massachusetts, despite great pressure from the almost treasonous New England Federalist establishment, held the Embargo Acts constitutional in *United States* v. *Brigantine William*. Davis declared the embargo a valid regulation of commerce under the commerce power, a valid preparation for war under the war power, and a valid exercise of discretion for both purposes under the "necessary and proper" clause of the Constitution. The opinion rested on principles of implied powers broadly prefigured by the Marshall Court four years before in *United States* v. *Fisher* (1805). "Congress must possess the choice of means and must be empowered to use any means which are in fact conducive to the exercise of a power granted by the Constitution." The defeated counsel decided against an appeal. Years later, in deciding the

seminal commerce clause case of *Gibbons* v. *Ogden* (1824), Marshall noted "the universally acknowledged power of the Government to impose embargoes."

THE COURT AND NATIONAL POWERS

The most dramatic of the Marshall Court's cases were those elaborating and defending great national powers of war, taxation, and commerce. The judges were controversial not because they overturned legislation but because they justified national legislative powers that many states and many Republican leaders wished to restrict. The Marshall Court is famous as a nationalizing Court, and if that description slights the Court's deference to the states' residue of sovereign powers, it reflects the judges' priorities in a series of epic clashes with the states.

The classic is the great bank case, *McCulloch* v. *Maryland* (1819). Maryland had slapped a heavy tax on banks not chartered by the state, a tax designed to drive out branches of the Bank of the United States. The Baltimore branch refused to pay, and the state sued J. W. McCulloch, the cashier. Having lost in the Maryland courts, the bank appealed to the Supreme Court.

During the whole era of the Marshall Court the national bank was a chief target of those suspicious of national power. Jefferson's classic attack on implied powers of government was aroused in 1790 by Washington's first plan for a bank, and in 1811, opponents defeated recharter of the First Bank of the United States, which had been rather successful. Although a second bank was chartered in 1816, after desperate difficulties in financing the war and controlling the postwar boom, Jackson vetoed the rechartering of this "monster bank" in 1832. His veto message attacked implied powers, monopoly, governmental patronage of the rich and unproductive, and the authority of the Supreme Court as to constitutional questions.

The bank was a natural target. It was a federal power, but not constitutionally prescribed, and a central power that reached into daily life, encroached on local establishments, and made state banks and bankers pay off its loans and redeem their circulating paper. It regulated and promoted sound investments in a time of democratic laissez-faire and unbridled enterprise. National bankers seemed a distant financial elite that pressed the industrious and honest many. That the stockholders were often from the East Coast or Great Britain and usually antipathetic to Jeffersonian republicans and plain democrats did not help. While the Second Bank was outfitted with Republican stockholders, it was tainted with fraud and mismanagement during the crucial first years. The new directors complacently expanded credit with the boom and then contracted abruptly, reaping the blame, only partly deserved, for a whirlwind of bankruptcies and foreclosures. The combination of general animus and immediate grievances produced a small rebellion. By 1819, eight states had passed legislative or constitutional penalties to drive out the bank. The Baltimore branch had led all the branches in recklessly expanding credit, and cashier McCulloch proved to have been a ringleader in a sensational scheme of embezzlement.

Marshall's opinion for the Supreme Court ignores all such particulars; it elaborates Congress's ample power to charter a bank and the supremacy of Congress's power when exercised. The reasoning is spare, abstract, imperious, and unrelenting. Indeed, the Court's opinion was more shocking than its holding. Years of existence had warranted the bank to many who had once questioned its constitutionality, including Madison, and episodes of financial chaos moved some who had questioned its necessity. But these waverers were unprepared for Marshall's uncompromising exhibition of the constitutional extent of federal supremacy.

The United States is a government and not a league, Marshall unequivocally began, derived from the people and not dependent on the state governments. While limited in its enumerated powers, it is supreme within its sphere. It is true that no power to charter a corporation or incorporate a bank is enumerated. But the Constitution, unlike the Articles of Confederation, does not require that all its powers be expressly stated. And no government might have all its incidental powers enumerated, unless its constitution were to have have the "prolixity of a legal code." Only the "great outlines" can be marked; the subordinate powers must be implied. Here occurs the famous counsel to judges and others:

"We must never forget that it is a constitution we are expounding."

A government with the great powers to war, tax, and regulate commerce must be able to carry out its responsibilities. Marshall was far from saying that Congress's powers are boundless. Congress may not exercise a major power not enumerated; "under pretext of executing its powers pass laws for objects not entrusted to the government"; or exercise a subordinate power merely because it is secondary. But, Marshall insisted, a government responsible for great objects must be allowed to select the means. "The power being given, it is the interest of the nation to facilitate its execution." He pointed to the necessary-and-proper clause: Congress may "make all Laws which shall be necessary and proper for carrying into Execution" the powers explicitly granted. Maryland's counsel had tried to convert this confirmation of implied powers into a restriction, to insist that the Constitution condones only absolutely necessary means. Marshall concluded that "necessary" can mean, in common speech and public life, "convenient" or "useful" and was so used in the clause. Congress may select a "vast mass of incidental powers" and must have such discretion if the Constitution is not to be a "splendid bauble." It may appropriately select a national bank to execute the powers to war, tax, and regulate commerce. And what Congress may constitutionally do, no state may undo. Although states retain their sovereign power to tax, sovereign state powers are void when they contradict supreme federal powers. "It is of the very essence of supremacy to remove all obstacles to its action within its own sphere, and so to modify every power vested in subordinate governments as to exempt its own operation from their own influence." The Court declared void not only Maryland's tax aimed at destroying the national bank but any state tax on a federal function.

The *McCulloch* decision was met with ferocious indignation and then with defiance in the South and West. The *Richmond Inquirer* caught the states'-rights reaction: "If Congress can select any means which they consider 'convenient,' 'useful,' 'conducive to' the execution of the specified and granted powers; if the word 'necessary' is thus to be frittered away, then we may bid adieu to the sovereignty of the States; they sink into contemptible corporations; the gulf of consolidation yawns to receive them." Virginia's legislature solemnly protested and recommended the creation of a new tribunal to judge conflicts between states and the Union. Four states ratified a constitutional amendment to confine national banks to the District of Columbia. Ohio, which had suffered badly in 1818 from inflation and bank failures, refused to abide by the decision. Its newspapers were furious, and the Ohio legislature enacted a massive tax on every branch of the bank, which state officials proceeded to enforce by seizing bank funds. In 1821 the Ohio legislature declared the Bank of the United States completely deprived of the state's legal protection and passed resolves reaffirming its right to tax the bank, reaffirming the doctrines of the Kentucky and Virginia resolutions and protesting against judicial interference.

The Marshall Court passed on Ohio's claims in *Osborn* v. *Bank of the United States* (1824). Osborn, the state auditor, had appealed a circuit court's command that he return certain funds seized. Marshall's opinion for the Court reemphasized the *McCulloch* doctrine that Congress might select any necessary and proper means to carry out its great powers. It also emasculated the Eleventh Amendment while confirming the Court's jurisdiction. The amendment prohibits jurisdiction of federal courts over suits against a state by citizens of another state (or of a foreign state). Marshall held that the amendment applied only when a state was a party of record, and not to an agent of the state such as the auditor. This bit of reasoning follows a "pause" in his argument to reflect on "the relative situation of the Union with its members," should the objection to the court's jurisdiction prevail. A federal official fined or penalized by a state even through an agent could obtain no protection from the federal courts. Each state would be capable, "at its will, of attacking the nation, of arresting its progress at every step, . . . while the nation stands naked, stripped of its defensive armor, and incapable of shielding its agent or executing its laws." Nevertheless, the Court had to repudiate this doctrine four years later in *Governor of Georgia* v. *Madrazo* (1828).

The Court's development of the federal power to regulate commerce between the states had immediate and striking effects. Although the Marshall Court defended great powers of government, the presidents and the Congresses of the time were not disposed to exercise them. Lincoln, Cleveland, Wilson, and the Roosevelts were the presidents who exploited their constitutional inheritance. When the Court liberated commercial and entrepreneurial energy from state restrictions, however, thousands of individuals were panting for the opportunities it provided.

The Supreme Court's first and flagship commerce clause decision was *Gibbons* v. *Ogden* (1824), which declared void New York's authorization of a steamboat monopoly in New York waters. The grant of monopoly, under which Ogden's steamboat sailed, violated the "right to trade" of Gibbons' steamboat, which the Court derived from a United States coasting license.

Marshall's opinion in *Gibbons* begins by attacking those who would construe the Constitution strictly. It concludes by explaining the need to confront "refined and metaphysical" interpretations, which suppose that the powers of the nation are to be narrowed while "the original powers of the states are retained." The Court establishes in effect an extensive power of regulating the people's domestic economy in order to promote trade. First, Marshall defined commerce broadly as encompassing not merely buying and selling but also navigation and, indeed, all intercourse involved in trading. Then he held that the federal government might reach within the states to affect commerce among the states wherever it existed. He excepted "purely internal commerce" as not "among the states" if it did not "extend to or affect other states." Then he held that the commerce power was sovereign and not limited by the states' powers. It is "complete in itself, may be exercised to its utmost extent, and acknowledges no limitations, other than are prescribed in the constitution." Marshall's argument contrasted with opinions such as President Monroe's while vetoing the Cumberland Road Act in 1822: the federal power over commerce is merely that to impose duties and imposts as to foreign nations and prevent such taxes on trade among the states.

The Court was tempted to hold what Daniel Webster, as counsel for Gibbons, had urged upon it: that any state regulation of commerce among the states was void because the power of Congress was exclusive. But Marshall drew back and decided the case upon the conflict between Congress's particular law, giving a license for coastal navigation, and New York's grant of monopoly. He supposed that the laws of civilized man authorize a right to trade between man and man and that Congress's grant of a license implies grant of a power to exercise that "right to trade."

The Marshall Court later reinforced the priority of free trade among the states. *Brown* v. *Maryland* (1827) applied similar reasoning to trade with foreign nations. A Maryland tax on importers was held void as conflicting with a federal law. Ostensibly, the federal law merely levied duties on imports. But Marshall's opinion for the Court found that payment of the duty indicated a reciprocal and pervasive "right to sell" the goods imported. Any other construction would "break up commerce" with other nations.

Within a year after the *Gibbons* decision the number of steamboats working out of New York City increased from six to forty-three. The effects were not limited to New York; the monopoly had granted exclusive rights in four other states, and several states were providing for their own, often retaliatory, exclusive privileges. *Gibbons* halted this commercial warfare. It encouraged a massive expansion of steam transport and exploration on both coastal waters and inland rivers and lakes, notably in the distant West. Warren called *Gibbons* "the emancipation proclamation of American commerce." Others who were more politically minded called it a mighty strand in the cable by which Marshall sought to bind together the Union. *Gibbons* also undermined the power of economic and political privilege. For twenty-four years Robert Fulton, inventor of the steamboat, and the Livingston family, prominent Republican leaders, had held the New York monopoly. The Republican legislators and lawyers of New York had promoted it. The Court's elaboration of a simple coasting license into a "right to trade" free of state monopolies opened up transport and all exchange to free competition and lower rates.

Gibbons was the most popular of the Marshall Court's decisions. It was welcomed vociferously among all but the monopolists and the leading Republican strict constructionists—who feared consolidation and in particular a federal commerce power that could reach slavery within the states.

In 1823, Justice Johnson, on circuit in South Carolina, had hit the South's raw nerve. South Carolina and Virginia had statutes to discourage unrest among their slave populations. Among these were laws to prevent free blacks from entering and to provide for their detention in custody until their ships departed. Johnson held South Carolina's law unconstitutional, since the federal government's right to regulate commerce among the states and with foreign nations was "exclusive and paramount." State officials ignored the decision and ignored the implications of *Gibbons* when it was decided less than a year later.

Despite the priority the Court gave to national supremacy and to freedom of commerce, it also left some place for independent state action and for state regulation of health, police, and safety. The point of the commerce power was primarily to encourage commerce, to begin with. If embargoes on commerce were allowed, they were, per *Gibbons,* as retaliatory measures for the sake of future commerce or, at most, as instruments of the enumerated powers of war. In Marshall's opinion, as expressed in a letter, the Court would not under the commerce power authorize general patronage of such internal improvements as roads and canals but only internal improvements "for military purposes or for the transportation of the mail." Yet, as Jefferson complained, these purposes might justify many roads and canals. "Farther than this," Marshall said, "I know not why the government of the United States should wish" the power to extend.

The Court's tolerance of state police powers is visible in *Willson* v. *Blackbird Creek Marsh Company* (1829). The decision authorized a Delaware dam across a small navigable stream in tidewater, erected to promote health and the value of property, despite a contrary claim on behalf of a sloop holding the same coasting license that had freed Gibbons' steamboat. These were counterpoints, pianissimo but real, to the Marshall Court's principal melody: the primacy of few but sovereign political powers and of a pervasive national commerce.

In one important respect the Marshall Court retreated from the nationalism of its judicial predecessors. It decided against a common-law criminal jurisdiction for the federal courts. Offenses against the federal government might be prosecuted only under federal statutes and the Constitution, it decided, not under a national common law derived from Great Britain. The pre-Marshall Supreme Court had allowed indictments, as for perjury in federal court, despite the absence of a statute. The second chief justice, Ellsworth, explained to a circuit court grand jury in 1799 that they might indict for "acts manifestly subversive of the National Government, or of some of the powers specified in the Constitution," since "an offence consists in transgressing the sovereign will, whether that will be expressed, or obviously implied." The Republicans had been appalled. All the Federalists' political encroachments on the Constitution are as retail stuff, Jefferson complained to Charles Pinckney in 1800, besides "the wholesale doctrine, that there is a common law in force in the United States which and of all the cases within its provisions, their Courts have cognizance. It is complete consolidation." But in *United States* v. *Hudson and Goodwin* (1812), the Supreme Court concluded against a federal common-law jurisdiction as to crimes, throwing out an indictment of certain Federalist publicists for libeling Jefferson while he was president. Story and Marshall dissented, it seems. Story later complained that the national government was thus rendered defenseless against a variety of offenses that had been prosecuted as of course under the common law. But he failed to persuade the Court to reverse itself. He was instrumental in getting Congress in 1825 to pass the Crimes Act, which made certain of these offenses punishable.

COURTS AND THE SECURITY OF INDIVIDUAL RIGHTS

Apart from constitutional regulation of state governments and the political branches, the distinctive function of the federal courts remains the protection of individual rights. Marshall and his fellow justices developed this function also, although in a spirit that has been varied by recent Courts. The Marshall Court tried chiefly to assure personal security under law through judicial remedies and to protect rights to property obtained by contract. Its focus on individual rights to life and property may be compared with the post–New Deal Court's concern for freedom of expression, minimum human needs, and protection of disadvantaged minorities.

In providing for rights, the Marshall Court relied chiefly on statutes, treaties, and the Constitution, as well as on the "general principles" of civilized law that judges and legal writers had established and developed. For example, the Court protected Marbury's right to a commission according to statutory conditions of appointment, Burr's rights as a defendant in light of Article III's prescriptions for treason prosecutions, and creditors' rights in light of common "rules of property" and Article I's prohibition to any state of a "Law impairing the Obligation of Contract."

This judicial function was a mixture of obvious subordination and subtle direction. The Court had the task of a judicial branch of government, to apply the law to cases involving disputes as to individual rights. To that extent, courts "are the mere instruments of the law," as Chief Justice Marshall once put it, "and can will nothing." Yet the framers understood the Constitution and all government and law to provide for man's security and freedom, to be instruments of the rights to life, liberty, and property. The judiciary's special prerogative was to determine which rights existed, or "vested," by action of law. "The question whether a right has vested or not," as Marshall put it in *Marbury*, "is in its nature, judicial, and must be tried by the judicial authority." These views were derived from works on private and public law, such as the *Federalist* and Sir William Blackstone's *Commentaries on the Laws of England,* and less directly from teachings about the judicial function in John Locke's *Second Treatise of Civil Government* and Montesquieu's *Spirit of Laws.* Judges thus possessed an important responsibility for defining the sphere of individual liberty, sometimes in opposition to the other branches. Having decided that Marbury had a right to his commission, Marshall protected Marbury's appeal from the executive to a court: "The very essence of civil liberty certainly consists in the right of every individual to claim the protection of the laws, whenever he receives an injury."

Only a minor part of the Marshall Court's protection of rights involved the Bill of Rights, the first ten amendments that bulk large in modern constitutional litigation. It decided no cases under the First Amendment, whose provisions against establishing religion and for protecting free speech have come to seem of preeminent importance, nor under the next two amendments, which guarantee a right to bear arms and limit civilians' duty to board soldiers. The Court did have occasion to specify a few details of the next five amendments' regulation of criminal and civil proceedings. The search warrant required by the Fourth Amendment must state a good cause and be supported by oath if issued by a justice of the peace (*Ex parte Burford*, 1806). To bar prosecution under the prohibition of double jeopardy (Fifth Amendment), a former conviction must be pleaded (*United States* v. *Wilson*, 1833) or a prosecution for the identical offense (*United States* v. *Randenbush*, 1834); the bar to another trial applies when the defendant has been prosecuted in any civilized nation for robbery on the high seas, which is a crime against every such state (*United States* v. *Furlong*, 1820). While deprivation of life, liberty, or property may be only by due process of law, that does not bar the government from confiscating enemy property (*Brown* v. *United States*, 1814). Trial by jury in civil suits, for which the Sixth Amendment provides when more than $20 is at issue, is that which existed under English common law when the amendment was adopted (*Parsons* v. *Bedford*, 1830); jury trial may be waived by the parties (*Parsons* v. *Armor*, 1830). Despite the Eighth Amendment's prohibition of excessive fines, the Supreme Court lacks appellate jurisdiction to review the sentence of a lower court, even if the excessiveness is obvious (*Ex parte Watkins*, 1833).

The first amendments were of minor importance to the Marshall Court because they did not then apply to the states and because the vast bulk of legislation and of civil and criminal trials occurred in the states. In *Barron* v. *Baltimore* (1833), the Marshall Court confirmed what it said was obvious—that the Bill of Rights was intended to restrict federal powers alone. This changed only when twentieth-century courts incorporated such guarantees into the "due process of law" required of the states by the Fourteenth Amendment. Also, during the early national era the federal government passed rather few laws, federal courts allowed a large discretion to the political branches, and federal judges passed on comparatively few cases. Besides, the judges inclined to observe the civil and criminal procedures derived from the common law and to interpret the language of the amendments to require no more.

The Marshall Court is famous for the priority it gave to property rights, especially the rights of creditors. It characteristically overruled state attempts to take back land grants, to revise corporate charters, and to ease contractual obligations by bankruptcy, or stay, laws. Favoring investors, corporations, and creditors, while checking state legislatures, state courts, and the many debtors, the Court was plunged into bitter controversies. Its efforts have occasionally been portrayed as a reflection of sinister interests or as mindless reflections of a heartless capitalism. Whatever the defects of the Court's views, such explanations disregard its views and miss its motives. The justices thought they were doing what was right and also what was politic. They supposed an individual's right to the fruits of his labor and to dispose of his property. To protect this right was to encourage industry, commerce, and prosperity, and to discourage class conflict. The Marshall Court's protection of private enterprise and contractual agreements complemented its formulation of the government's commerce power to protect a right to trade. The Court was to some extent the nation's political economist, adjusting federal regulation and judicial regulation to protect private rights, industry, and a free national market.

In *Huidekoper's Lessees* v. *Douglass* (1807), Marshall strictly interpreted a Pennsylvania grant so as to favor a land company, although it had failed to fulfill certain specified conditions. A Pennsylvania court had given the opposite construction, and the Marshall Court would normally defer to a state court's interpretation of that state's statute. But the law was in its nature "a contract; and although a state is a party, it ought be construed according to those well-established principles" that secure rights that have been vested under contract.

Fletcher v. *Peck* (1810) occasioned the Marshall Court's classic limitation of state power to secure private rights: state grants were given the obligation of sacrosanct contracts. In 1795 the Georgia legislature granted huge tracts of land—the "Yazoo lands"—to several companies of speculators. The next Georgia legislature, elected in a burst of popular indignation at the fraud and bribery involved (every favorable vote but one had been repaid in land), revoked the grant. Those whose titles derived from the 1795 grant pressed claims for compensation. They pressed first Georgia, then Congress after Georgia ceded to the nation its claims to this land, and then the courts. The dispute was long and bitter, and partly caused the crucial split of the Republican party. John Randolph accused Jefferson and Jefferson's postmaster general, Gideon Granger, of toadying to the northern Yazoo speculators. Finally, in *Fletcher*, Marshall declared the Georgia revocation unconstitutional. The Court, Marshall said, might not meddle in the question of whether a law was invalid because of the legislators' motives. But it might decide that a law was invalid for meddling with a judicial function—that is, overturning vested property rights without following "those rules of property which are common to all the citizens of the United States" or "those principles of equity which are acknowledged in all our courts." Georgia's grant was a contract, Marshall argued, and Georgia's revocation was void because it violated either "general principles, which are common to our free institutions" or the Constitution's specific prohibition to the states of laws that impair the obligation of contracts.

The Marshall Court's most striking extension of the doctrine of contractual rights occurred in *Dartmouth College* v. *Woodward* (1819). An opinion by Marshall held that a state grant of a corporate charter was a contract not to be subsequently impaired. It protected corporate charters and thereby private institutions and interests, economic and otherwise. A New Hampshire legislature had rechartered Dartmouth College at the behest of a board of trustees that had overthrown the old board. The new charter enlarged the board, gave to the governor the additional appointments, and subordinated the trustees to a new board of overseers all appointed by the governor. Jefferson had written (21 July 1816) approvingly to the Republican governor, William Plumer,

> The idea that institutions established for the use of the nation cannot be touched nor modified, even to make them answer their end, because of rights gratuituously supposed in those employed to manage them in trust for the public, may perhaps be a salutary provision against the abuses of a monarch, but it is most absurd against the Nation itself.

Marshall reasoned otherwise. The charter is "a complete and legitimate contract" of a sort that the framers would have wished to protect. "Do donations for the purpose of education necessarily become public property," Marshall asked, "so far that the will of the legislature, not the will of the donor, becomes the law of the donation?" Neither the donor nor the professors nor the trustees necessarily become public figures. A corporation—"an artificial being, invisible, intangible, and existing only in contemplation of law"—is not necessarily a governmental body, nor is it made so because its purpose, education, is to be encouraged by government. Marshall replied to arguments from public policy: The framers had their own policy, to supply incentives for private giving. If the giver's wishes are respected, giving is encouraged. Charitable foundations as well as economic enterprises are served by withdrawing contracts from "the fluctuating policy and repeated interferences" of legislative bodies. Marshall refused to acquiesce in the Jeffersonian suggestion, made by the New Hampshire governor, that public reform was required for a charter that "emanated from royalty . . . [and] contained . . . principles . . . hostile to the spirit and genius of free government." One might rely, Marshall concluded dryly, on "learned and intelligent" trustees to benefit from the "light of science" and "liberal principles" and to choose other trustees who will alike participate in "the general improvement." The *Dartmouth College* case encouraged the American system of privately endowed foundations and educational institutions that are privately governed.

No doubt the sanctity thus provided to corporate charters meant additional security for economic corporations as well. Yet, the Marshall Court did not go very far in serving the economic corporation. It declined to infer from the mere grant of a charter an exemption from state taxation, even destructive taxation. The Court held that governments need taxing power, and for justice citizens must rely upon their elected representatives, in *Providence Bank* v. *Billings* (1830). Also, the Court seemed reluctant to establish the economic corporation as an independent person at law, in practice removed from its shareholders. It delayed federal protection of corporations by holding, in *Bank of the United States* v. *Deveaux* (1810), that shareholders of corporations suing in a circuit court (which held jurisdiction only by virtue of the parties' diverse citizenship) must be all citizens of a state different from that of the opposite party. Few corporations were parties before the Marshall Court. Later, however, the Court moved toward viewing the corporation as a legal person capable of acting and of enjoying the law's protection. In *Bank of the United States* v. *Dandridge* (1827), the Court decided over Marshall's dissent that a corporation's approval of its agents' acts may be shown by presumptive evidence without a written record and vote of the shareholders.

The Marshall Court's regulation of bankruptcy finally sympathized more with debtors (and less with security of commercial transactions) than the chief justice, at least, thought compatible with the Constitution. At first, in *Sturges* v. *Crowninshield* (1819), the Court had seemed to hold that a state bankruptcy or insolvency law, which discharges the debtor from a debt owed, unconstitutionally impairs the obligation of contracts. The framers, Chief Justice Marshall said for the Court, favored "the inviolability of contracts." Beset by laws delaying payment of debts and allowing payment in inflated currency, the framers had sought to "restore public confidence completely" among individuals. The *Sturges* decision shocked the states that had eased the plight of bankrupt debtors, and was restricted to the circumstances of that case. Eight years later the Court drew back. In *Ogden* v. *Saunders* (1827), a bare majority of four justices decided that bankruptcy laws were constitutional if they applied prospectively—that is, to contracts to follow—and construed *Sturges* to exclude only a retrospective application. Now in dissent, Marshall charged that a vital constitutional provision, "one on which the good and the wise reposed confidently for securing the prosperity and harmony of our citizens," was thus construed into an "inanimate, inoperative, unmeaning clause."

Perhaps the Marshall Court's most poignant decisions as to property and human rights concerned slaves and Indians. Although slavery violated a person's "natural right to the fruits of his own labor" (*The Antelope,* 1825) and the Indian tribes had been deprived of their original natural rights to their land, the Court held that the country's civil laws establishing slavery and subordinating Indian tribes had to take precedence over natural right. Justice Story had decided on circuit that the slave trade was contrary to the law of nations, because "a breach of all

moral duties." In *The Antelope,* the Supreme Court decided otherwise. It would adhere to international law as then formulated and not treat slave traders as pirates even if the trade was "unnatural." Similarly, the Court held that slavery was built into the country's laws. Courts, whose first duty was to apply the laws, whatever their sympathies with liberty, had to maintain the general policy of laws securing property.

Three great opinions as to Indian claims affirmed unequivocally that the laws and titles of a conqueror would control the conqueror's courts and then required that the conquered Indians be allowed their property and a certain independence until voluntarily ceded to the conqueror. In *Johnson* v. *Graham's Lessee* (1823), the Court confirmed a title derived from a Virginia grant in preference to a title derived from Indians who lived within the territory. Titles must turn on "the law of the nation in which they lie," Marshall argued, not merely on "abstract justice." Virginia and the United States inherited the European claim to title by discovery, and the Court had to respect the country's laws based on the European title. Similarly, the Court held that Indian tribes might not sue in federal courts as foreign nations; if "distinct political societies," they were nevertheless "domestic dependent nations" (*Cherokee Nation* v. *Georgia,* 1831).

Still, the Court indicated, even in these cases, that justification for further conquest had passed, insofar as danger from the Indians had passed. The conqueror should encourage "mingling" of the two peoples, or at least toleration of the Indians as "a distinct people." The Cherokee had an "unquestionable" right to their lands until their own "voluntary cession." In *Worcester* v. *Georgia* (1832), the Court declared void various Georgia laws that sought to abolish Cherokee independence and appropriate the tribe's territory. On the one hand, a federal treaty guaranteed the Cherokee territory. On the other, Georgia's cession of the land to the United States had been accompanied by a federal promise to extinguish the Indian claims. The Marshall Court favored the Indians' claim to exist as a self-governing nation; it supported the more humane national policy followed, if never successfully enforced, by every president from Washington to Andrew Jackson. The decision in *Worcester,* freeing two missionaries jailed for living among the Cherokee, flouted Jackson's encouragement of Georgia and provoked a crisis between the state and the Court.

THE COURT AND INTERNATIONAL LAW

We turn finally to the Marshall Court's enforcement of international law or, to use the Court's less optimistic name, the law of nations. The new federal government was confronted with threats from the world's great powers, Britain and France, and with opportunities from the decay of the Spanish empire. Furthermore, state courts and subordinate federal courts often reflected the feelings of a people sympathetic to the revolutions in Europe and South America and greedy for easy profits from privateering and armed adventuring. The Court's reaction was to self-consciously introduce to the country the "great system of public law" characteristic of enlightened nations. The United States was obliged, said Marshall in *Brown* v. *United States* (1814), to "receive the law of nations in its modern state of purity and refinement." This law was understood to be the common reason of civilized nations as devised by judges through a regular train of decisions and set forth in jurisprudential texts. In short, the Marshall Court followed the pre-Marshall justices in holding the law of nations part of the supreme law of the land, and it introduced various legal limits to the country's foreign policy. In particular, the Court was disposed to defer to the determinations of other nations' courts as decisions of equal sovereigns, to enforce stringently the obligations of treaties, and to be solicitous, where possible, of commercial rights, especially the rights of neutral traders during wartime.

During the Marshall Court's first dozen years the United States lived in the shadow of the Titans—of the epochal struggle between old Europe, led by Britain, and revolutionary France, exploited by Napoleon Bonaparte. That changed, however. There occurred the Louisiana Purchase from France in 1803, the United States' semivictory over Britain in the War of 1812, Britain's final defeat of Napoleon at Waterloo in 1815, the Rush-Bagot agreement of 1817 to limit British and American naval vessels on the Great Lakes, and the United States' acquisition of the Spanish Floridas in 1819. The rest-

less new nation was free to extend its trade and zeal into the Americas. During the first period, the Marshall Court chiefly upheld treaties with Great Britain and France and condemnations by their prize courts, even when these contradicted American advantage and violated the law of nations. It also insisted upon strict observance by American traders of their duties as neutrals. During the second period, the Court repeatedly enforced the treaties as to the Floridas and Louisiana and the duties of neutrals, so as to provide for Spanish land grants and to protect the Spanish and Portuguese from marauders and partisans of colonial independence.

In *Croudson* v. *Leonard* (1808), the Marshall Court upheld the condemnation of an American ship by a British prize court for trying to break Britain's blockade of Napoleon's continental empire. That the British orders-in-council far exceeded the traditional requirements for declaring a blockade, that decisions of British and French courts were manifestly self-serving and oppressed neutral ships trying to trade, and that the Republican administration was in a kind of war using its Embargo and Nonintercourse Acts, did not sway a majority of the Court from respecting the finality of the judgment of another sovereign's court. If Congress wished to vary this customary law by statute, it might; but it had not.

A more important case was *Schooner Exchange* v. *McFadden* (1812), which involved an American ship captured by the French, converted into a public ship of France, and seized while visiting this country. The Court rejected arguments based on the emperor's seizure of United States national ships and violation of the nation's neutral rights. Such questions were rather "of policy than law"; all public ships of friendly nations were exempt from the jurisdiction of United States courts.

Yet the Court would enforce its own government's sovereign authority. Merchants of New England, hating the War of 1812 against Britain, occasionally accepted British licenses to protect themselves from British warships. In *The Julia* (1814), Justice Story indignantly declared the practice illegal. Part of the people "may [not] claim to be at peace, while the residue are involved in the desolations of war"; the practice would foster "interests within the bosom of the country, against the measures of the government." In *The Rapid* (1814), one of many cases in which the Court enforced the Nonintercourse Acts against dissident New Englanders, Justice Johnson held illegal the importation during the war of goods purchased from England before the war and stored in Nova Scotia. "The whole nation are embarked in one common bottom, and must be reconciled to submit to one common fate. Every individual of the one nation must acknowledge every individual of the other nation as his own enemy—because the enemy of his country."

Where the Court found governmental actions equivocal, however, it inclined to suppose them limited by a concern for individual rights. *Brown* v. *United States* (1814) concerned the power of the United States to confiscate enemy property within its borders. Although the power over persons and property is plenary, Marshall declared, the president alone lacks such power without explicit congressional legislation. In *Murray* v. *Schooner The Charming Betsey* (1804), Marshall put the general point succinctly: "An Act of Congress ought never to be construed to violate the law of nations if any other possible construction remains, and consequently, can never be construed to violate neutral rights, or to affect neutral commerce, further than is warranted by the law of nations as understood in this country."

The Court's solicitude for neutral commerce went far. *The Nereide* (1815) decided that a Spanish neutral cargo was not good prize for an American privateer, even when carried aboard an armed British ship—this despite a declared war with Britain and the fact that Spanish law allowed confiscation. A neutral's right to ship in a belligerent's armed freighter was "part of the original law of nations"; retaliation was for the government and not for courts, which were to follow the law. However, American traders might not claim the mantle of neutrals while in fact aiding belligerents. A series of cases punished privateers that masked as freighters and preyed on the commerce of Spain and Portugal while their South American colonies were in revolt. These decisions opposed not only the greed of adventurers but also popular sympathy with rebels seeking self-government. In one set of cases, the Court held invalid prizes taken by ships fitted out in violation of the United States' neutrality. The leading case was *The Santissima Trinidad* (1822), a public ship of the "United

Provinces of Rio de la Plata." Justice Story held that the augmentation of the crew in United States ports, contrary to the requirements of neutrality, infected "the captures subsequently made, with the character of torts"—and restitution must be made. Many Portuguese and Spanish ships were restored, and relations with the two countries were pacified. A similar effect followed from various decisions as to piracy.

Mutineers and privateers often prowled under the flag of one patriotic movement or another, preying on neutral commerce. The lower courts, sympathetic or intimidated, inclined to acquit of piracy. In 1820 a series of decisions by the Supreme Court held that an American citizen sailing under the flag of a revolutionary government unrecognized by the United States might be convicted of piracy for attacking a Spanish vessel. The cases affirmed the convictions of some fifty men. The ensuing executions—two in each port city where convictions had been obtained—ended in the United States the fashion of piracy in South and Central America.

During 1832 and 1834 the Marshall Court reaffirmed the United States' duty to obey treaties despite treaty partners' frauds. The Court required scrupulous respect for Spanish grants of land protected by the Adams-Onís Treaty of 1819 and by the Louisiana Treaty of Cession of 1803. While the treaty of 1819 was pending, the Spanish authorities had added numerous doubtful new grants. Fraudulent titles abounded. Many claims had been assigned to financiers and speculators in New York and abroad, and the situation had aroused the indignation of President Jackson. Despite all this, Justice Henry Baldwin declared for the Court that a grant made by a public official purporting to act for his sovereign power was to be presumed an official act unless the United States proved lack of authority (*United States* v. *Arredondo*, 1832). Charles Warren concluded that the Court's decision significantly reduced America's public lands and unjustly enriched many private speculators whose claims lacked legal foundation. Nevertheless, an alternative determination would have shaken land titles in all older parts of the United States and thereby put into question the sanctity of treaties. Having obtained Louisiana and the Floridas, the Court seemed to say, it behooved the United States to observe religiously the terms on which these priceless bounties had been granted.

CASES

The Antelope, 10 Wheaton 66 (1825)

Bank of the United States v. Dandridge, 12 Wheaton 64 (1827)

Bank of the United States v. Deveaux, 5 Cranch 61 (1810)

Barron v. Baltimore, 7 Peters 243 (1833)

Ex parte Bollman and Swartwout, 4 Cranch 75 (1807)

Brown v. Maryland, 12 Wheaton 419 (1827)

Brown v. United States, 8 Cranch 110 (1814)

Ex parte Burford, 3 Cranch 448 (1806)

Cherokee Nation v. Georgia, 5 Peters 1 (1831)

Chisholm v. Georgia, 2 Dallas 419 (1793)

Cohens v. Virginia, 6 Wheaton 264 (1821)

Croudson v. Leonard, 4 Cranch 434 (1808)

Dartmouth College v. Woodward, 4 Wheaton 518 (1819)

Fairfax's Devisee v. Hunter's Lessee, 7 Cranch 602 (1813)

Fletcher v. Peck, 6 Cranch 87 (1810)

Gibbons v. Ogden, 9 Wheaton 1 (1824)

Governor of Georgia v. Madrazo, 1 Peters 110 (1828)

Huidekoper's Lessees v. Douglass, 3 Cranch 1 (1807)

Johnson v. Graham's Lessee, 8 Wheaton 543 (1823)

The Julia, 8 Cranch 181 (1814)

Little v. Barreme, 2 Cranch 170 (1804)

McClung v. Silliman, 6 Wheaton 598 (1821)

McCulloch v. Maryland, 4 Wheaton 316 (1819)

Marbury v. Madison, 1 Cranch 137 (1803)

Martin v. Hunter's Lessee, 1 Wheaton 304 (1816)

Murray v. Schooner The Charming Betsey, 2 Cranch 64 (1804)

The Nereide, 9 Cranch 388 (1815)

Ogden v. Saunders, 12 Wheaton 213 (1827)

Osborn v. Bank of the United States, 9 Wheaton 738 (1824)

Parsons v. Armor, 3 Peters 413 (1830)

Parsons v. Bedford, 3 Peters 433 (1830)

Providence Bank v. Billings, 4 Peters 514 (1830)

The Rapid, 8 Cranch 155 (1814)

The Santissima Trinidad, 7 Wheaton 283 (1822)

Schooner Exchange v. McFadden, 7 Cranch 116 (1812)

Stuart v. Laird, 1 Cranch 299 (1803)

Sturges v. Crowninshield, 4 Wheaton 122 (1819)

United States v. Arredondo, 6 Peters 691 (1832)

United States v. Burr, 4 Cranch 455 (1807)

United States v. Brigantine William, 28 F. Cas. 614 (1808) (No. 16,700)

United States v. Coolidge, 1 Wheaton 415 (1816)

United States v. Fisher, 2 Cranch 358 (1805)

United States v. Furlong, 5 Wheaton 184 (1820)

United States v. Hoxie, 1 Paine 265 (1808)

United States v. Hudson and Goodwin, 7 Cranch 32 (1812)

United States v. Judge Peters, 5 Cranch 115 (1809)

United States v. Randenbush, 8 Peters 288 (1834)

United States v. Wilson, 7 Peters 150 (1833)

Ex parte Watkins, 7 Peters 568 (1833)

Willson v. Blackbird Creek Marsh Company, 2 Peters 245 (1829)

Worcester v. Georgia, 6 Peters 515 (1832)

BIBLIOGRAPHY

Henry Adams, *History of the United States of America* (1891), is a penetrating but leisurely account of politics during the presidencies of Jefferson, Madison, and Monroe. Albert J. Beveridge, *The Life of John Marshall* (1919), details vividly the political circumstances and effects of the Marshall Court's constitutional decisions. Edward S. Corwin, *John Marshall and the Constitution* (1919), is a good brief account of the Court's life and times under Marshall. Robert K. Faulkner, *The Jurisprudence of John Marshall* (1968), clarifies Marshall's political and constitutional doctrines. Bray Hammond, *Banks and Politics in America* (1957), is first-rate political history, especially as regards the Bank of the United States.

James McClellan, *Joseph Story and the American Constitution* (1971), reviews informatively Story's views and judicial accomplishments. Donald G. Morgan, *William Johnson, The First Dissenter* (1954), is indispensable for understanding Johnson's contributions and frustrations. John Taylor, *Construction Construed and Constitution Vindicated* (1820) and *Tyranny Unmasked* (1822), provide a Jeffersonian indictment of the powerful government patronized by the Marshall Court. Charles Warren, *The Supreme Court in United States History* (1926), is spiced with comments by public figures and journalists; the first volume is the best study of the early Court from its beginning until Marshall's death.

[*See also* Articles of Confederation; Executive and Domestic Affairs; Federalism; Framing the Constitution; *and* Judicial Review.]

THE TANEY COURT AND ERA

Milton Cantor

HANNAH Arendt wrote of a world that shifts, changes, transforms itself "with ever-increasing rapidity from one shape into another." She might well have been describing the United States in the 1830s and 1840s. The pace and mode of transportation had markedly altered. Americans were spilling onto the Mohawk, Genesee, Catskill, and Baltimore turnpikes in a continuous stream of wagons and carts, lurching westward in a fluid crescent after the War of 1812. In the course of a lifetime, river channels were widened and deepened, and thousands of miles of canals were built in the Northeast and in the Old Northwest. The oxcart and stagecoach would give way to the clumsy flatboat and barge, then to the steamboat, and finally to the railroad operated by steam power.

By the mid-1840s, the entire Old Northwest was laced with waterways; and new projects had begun, financially supported and directed by such states as Ohio, Pennsylvania, and New York. Gradually, private entrepreneurial interests took over the states' financial role, with the private sector becoming the recipient of generous corporate charters and tax exemptions. The railroads would become the largest class of beneficiaries of municipal and state financial assistance, and the public sector would continue to play a very prominent, if less direct, role in determining the shape of transportation developments.

Clearly, Americans were not intent upon preserving Jefferson's agrarian republic. Every decade after 1800 spawned a legion of eagerly competitive entrepreneurs. With the rising need for capital, incorporation was on the ascendant, being an effective means of acquiring financial reserves needed for expansion. Banks were established by legislative acts. Insurance, manufacturing, railway, and canal companies also found the corporate form attractive, especially after *Dartmouth College* v. *Woodward* (1819) disclosed a judicial readiness to protect corporate charters from state legislative assault. Albert Gallatin noted in the 1800s that "the energy of this nation is not to be controlled; it is at present exclusively applied to the acquisition of wealth . . . and of course an immoderate expansion of credit receives favor." Thomas C. Cochran observed that "by 1860, business had assumed almost all the varied forms and functions with which we are familiar in the twentieth century."

Roger B. Taney was keenly aware of the dangers posed by the concentrated economic power that the corporate form promoted. As attorney general and a good Jacksonian, he expressed continual concern over the corporate threat to the rough egalitarianism of his age. The capitalist aspirations of Henry Clay and the Whig party —for protective tariffs and a national system of internal improvements—could never be endorsed by Democratic party leaders; though neither Jackson nor Taney, as a careful examination of their political and economic beliefs confirms, unequivocally opposed the entire Whig program.

Government aggressively assisted in economic growth; and so did the courts, by striking down state regulations adverse to business. The Marshall Court moved away from mercantilism while also acknowledging affirmative governmental acts that stimulated the economy. In effect, private enterprise was never wholly private; and "the line between private and public action is blurred, and always has been blurred" (Rostow). It has long been established that the holder of a liquor license had to use it in accord with the public good and not impair public morals, surely a restriction on what was considered the free exercise of private property. Chief Justice Lemuel Shaw of the Supreme Judicial Court of Massachusetts, in *Carey* v. *Daniels* (1844), neatly balanced "a use profitable" to the propertied with the "usages and wants of the community." So, we will see, did Taney and his associate justices.

It may be argued, then, that the legal system was recruited in the campaign to encourage and protect business enterprise. Massachusetts courts, for instance, sympathized with rising entrepreneurs and overturned many rules conferring exclusive property rights on initial resource users. The Pennsylvania Supreme Court frustrated riparian owners who claimed exclusive fishing rights in the large rivers of the state. Elsewhere, and again toward the end of promoting capitalist enterprise, legislative measures expressly conferred exclusive privileges on stagecoach franchises.

Such legal contention came at a time of rapid economic growth, the decline of an agrarian subsistence economy, the emergence of manufactories, and mounting market demands that would not be confined to a scattering of coastal towns. Gradually, as Morton Horowitz tells us, virtually all courts—first in Massachusetts and then elsewhere—abandoned prior appropriation precedents because, in the words of the New York Supreme Court, it meant that "the public, whose advantage is always to be regarded, would be deprived of the benefit which always attends competition and rivalry." Such thinking enabled the law to open the environment for private enterprise. State governments willingly conferred benefits upon "new" property anent the "old." In this antimonopoly spirit, Judge Shaw's celebrated holding in *Commonwealth* v. *Hunt* (1842) reflected his view that all competitors in the economy (including craftsmen) deserved an equal opportunity to engage in free and open competition (Levy).

The states, for instance, enjoyed virtually unlimited power to expropriate private property under the laws of eminent domain, a practice hardly consonant with laissez-faire. Such power was used positively by government and was enormously important to transportation develop-

ments. Equally inconsistent with laissez-faire, state legislators distributed public favors—in the form of franchises, tax exemptions, limited liability provisos and the like—to private beneficiaries, with corporations the most prominent of these. Finally, lawmakers shaped an entrepreneurial environment through the use of tax and police-power regulations. In effect, laissez-faire had at best a tainted sovereignty. The law, it was understood, would contribute to capital formation. It would be used to support and secure private initiatives and facilitate economic and social maturation.

Shifts in popular and legal perceptions of private property were accompanied by comparable changes in other areas. The old ethical principle that dominated moneylending in the colonial period—namely, that money should not be lent at a usurious rate of interest—gave way to the rule that individuals should make the rate for themselves. The contract clause was also being refashioned so as to promote economic growth rather than economic and social stability.

Finally, legal doctrine was never insulated from the stew of economic life. And litigation would bubble out of it. As business expanded and a small-scale capitalism burgeoned, legal change followed in attendance. First, as we have observed, the idea of competition was legitimated. Second, the evolving national economy prompted demands for federal participation in internal improvements, which raised complex questions about the states-nation relationship, the constitutional basis for federal assistance, and the legitimate reach of governmental power. Third, the meshing of law and business is strikingly evident: witness, for instance, Taney's innovative use of the government admiralty jurisdiction—rather than the commerce clause—in litigation involving the interior waterways, which carried a mounting volume of commercial traffic. Fourth, the very use of such waterways prompted soaring state and federal litigation that drew on the contract and commerce clauses as well as state police power. Taney was "keenly alive to the concentration of economic power which the corporate form promoted," as Frankfurter shrewdly concluded, and feared its impact on that equality of opportunity that his party promoted, even while encouraging such corporate growth. Fifth, these corporations—banks, railroads, manufactories—increasingly sought relief in federal courts and were permitted entry by the mid-1840s. Sixth, growing capital and credit formation required a series of legal adjustments and a positive judicial approach.

JUSTICES OF THE TANEY COURT

Roger B. Taney was born on 17 March 1777 of a long line of planter ancestors who worked slaves in tidewater southern Maryland. Shaped by the thinking of a planter aristocracy, he was educated at Dickinson College in Pennsylvania, trained for a career at the bar and in politics, was admitted to practice in 1798, became a staunch Federalist, and served in the Maryland legislature for a term. He practiced before the local and federal courts, including the Supreme Court in the 1820s, and energetically supported Andrew Jackson's candidacy in 1828. Appointed Maryland attorney general in 1827, he was predictably selected by Jackson to be United States attorney general after John C. Calhoun's supporters departed from the cabinet in 1831. Jackson made a good choice. Taney was a most competent, professional politician. He served the president loyally during the fight over the Second Bank of the United States and became a presidential favorite.

With the resignation of eighty-year-old Gabriel Duval of Maryland, who had presided over the fourth federal judicial circuit, consisting of Maryland and Delaware, a place on the High Court became vacant. Jackson sent Taney's name to the Senate in January 1835. The selection pleased Chief Justice John Marshall. In a confidential note to Senator Benjamin Leigh of Virginia, the chief justice wrote, "If you have not made up your mind on the nomination of Mr. Taney, I have received some information in his favor which I would wish to communicate" (Tyler). But not even Marshall could swerve the Bank and Whig forces from their covert war against the nomination, and they worked with untiring and careful tactics to defeat the president. Daniel Webster saw in Taney the symbol of all that was dangerous in Jacksonianism, and on his motion the Senate voted for indefinite postponement of the nomination. The nomination for associate judgeship had in effect died because the legislative session came to an end. But the effort to place Taney on the Court

hardly slackened. On 6 July 1835, John Marshall died. His passing produced an outpouring of grief across the country—and nowhere more so than in the parlors of the centralizers, the former Hamiltonians and the old-time Federalists. John Quincy Adams mourned the chief justice who had "cemented the Union, which the crafty and quixotic democracy of Jefferson had a perpetual tendency to dissolve." Joseph Story lamented, "Whoever succeeds him will have a most painful and discouraging duty. He will follow a man who cannot be equaled."

Predictably, Marshall's death prompted widespread speculation over his possible successor. The Whigs and nationalists advanced Story's name, evidently not believing that Jackson really meant his contemptuous dismissal of the "school of Story and Kent." Justice John McLean, a former Jackson appointee now drifting toward the Whigs, also sought the appointment. Taney headed the field of Democratic candidates; and the president, after a month's delay, submitted two names—Taney to succeed Marshall and Philip D. Barbour of Virginia to replace Duval as associate justice.

Again jeremiads poured from Whig and one-time Federalist presses. Story exclaimed, as Webster recounted, "The Supreme Court is gone and I think so too; and almost everything is gone or seems rapidly going." Intricate political maneuvering was renewed, with party lines sharply drawn and Webster and Clay leading the charge. This time Taney was confirmed, by a vote of 29–13, and then Barbour's nomination was also approved. The Whig reaction was just what had been expected. Charles Sumner, who had sought the chief-justiceship for his old friend Joseph Story grieved that Taney would now "hold the great scales which Marshall bore aloft" (Swisher).

The storm of protest was in vain. In January 1837, Taney began a judicial career that spanned more than twenty-eight years. In addition to the powerful, immensely strong-willed chief justice, his tribunal included Joseph Story of Massachusetts, who had been appointed in 1811 and was the outstanding leader of the old-court justices. He had most ardently admired his fallen chief, was Marshall's own choice as successor, and was the most reliable pro-Marshall judge—unlike Thompson, McLean, and Baldwin, who at times went their own way in constitutional interpretation. The politically minded Smith Thompson of the New York State Supreme Court had been appointed to the High Court in 1823. Then there were four Jackson appointees: John McLean of Ohio, who was closest to Story, a justice preoccupied for thirty years with becoming president and with extricating himself from financial difficulties; Henry Baldwin of Pennsylvania, a maverick known for his opposition to the emergence of equity in American law; the able, amiable, Savannah-born James M. Wayne, formerly a judge of the Georgia state court who became pro-Unionist and strongly opposed nullification; and, finally, Barbour, described by one local newspaper as holding "inflexible and uncompromising States-Rights principles," and a justice opposed to the Bank of the United States and to federally financed internal improvements.

John Catron of Tennessee, appointed in 1837, was yet another Unionist. A Jackson loyalist, he opposed the Bank and South Carolina's right to nullify federal law. Catron was also the architect of the new circuit-court bill that made its way through Congress in March 1837. It recast the Seventh Circuit and added the Eighth and Ninth Circuits. Jackson signed the bill and also submitted Catron's name for the Eighth Circuit and that of William Smith of Alabama for the Ninth, which was composed of Southern states. When Smith refused the appointment, President Martin Van Buren nominated John McKinley of Alabama, whom the Senate confirmed. McKinley had an undistinguished Court career, suffering from recurrent ill health before dying in 1852. Finally, among the early Taney Court justices, Peter V. Daniel is conspicuous. An ardent Jacksonian, he was confirmed in 1841. Daniel was a man of strong feelings and closed off from compromise toward those who held antislavery views. He feared the great corporations and New York's "mercantile community" like any good agrarian. Predictably, he opposed the Bank, rejoiced that his own Virginians were "yet an essential agricultural people" and, an ardent believer in states' rights, virtually embodied the 1798 Virginia and Kentucky Resolutions.

CONTRACTS

The Court's docket in its first year included fewer than sixty cases, but some had very important constitutional implications. These cases must be placed within the context of marked economic growth. The Court majority breathed the air of its times. State transportation measures would lead to constitutional challenge centering around the contract clause and to classic judicial dicta in favor of freedom for creative change, as against inflexible commitment to existing legal precedents. Like the state courts, the High Court recognized that exclusive property rights, in accord with precedent, would make economic development more difficult. Even the dissenters in the Massachusetts courts and the lower federal courts entertained positive views about economic progress, though they were more reluctant to overturn old property concepts. For dissenters like Justice Samuel Putnam on the Massachusetts bench and Story on the High Court, backward glances were in order, and they persisted in invoking the old rhetoric about liberty, sanctity of property, and social stability. But such rhetoric was growing less relevant in the new age. Landed wealth had become merely one of several commodities in the marketplace rather than the single keystone of a stable social order.

Taney surely was of similar mind. He had long displayed fixed views on monopolies and corporations, shaped by his agrarian background and Jacksonian ideology. His tenure on the bench, as Bruchey observed, "saw a phenomenal increase in incorporation, with nearly half of all corporations chartered between 1800 and 1860 appearing" in the 1850s. It is one of the ironies of legal history that Taney contributed to their growth. His penchant for laissez-faire—"corporate egalitarianism," as Bruchey aptly describes it—readily translated into the "ideal of publicly sponsored free competition in the interest of community welfare."

Taney, then, was very aware of the surging economic scene. In "a country like ours," he declared, "free, active and enterprising, continually advancing in numbers and wealth; new channels of communication are daily found necessary, both for travel and trade, and are essential to the comfort, convenience, and prosperity of the people." This perspective shines through in *Charles River Bridge Co.* v. *Warren Bridge Co.* (1837), a case which revealed as few others have the antimonopoly and antiprivilege sentiments that Taney brought to the Court. Indeed, no opinion of his more decisively affirmed state power over contractual sanctity and monopoly rights.

The story of the case goes back to 1650, when the Massachusetts legislature granted Harvard College permission to maintain a ferry between Charlestown and Boston. More than a century later, in 1785, the commonwealth's lawmakers passed a measure incorporating "the Proprietors of the Charles River Bridge" and authorizing them to replace the ferry with a bridge spanning the Charles River. Under the charter, limited to forty years, the company collected tolls and paid £200 annually to the college. When the grant expired, the bridge would become the commonwealth's property. In 1792 the legislature extended the franchise for seventy years. But in 1828, before the revised charter expired, the assembly incorporated the Warren Bridge Company. It was given the right to build and operate a toll bridge virtually alongside the Charles River Bridge, threatening the latter's income, especially given the provision that it would become a free roadway within a maximum of six years. Its competition would effectively destroy the value of the old bridge, as completely as if the lawmakers had directly repealed the charter. Thus, the legislators had in effect violated the Marshall Court prohibition on unilateral termination of corporate privilege. Story had powerfully endorsed this dictum in circuit, by ruling in *Allen* v. *McKeen* (1833) that even a reserved power to amend a franchise could not be used to abrogate vested rights.

The Charles River Bridge management's fears were realized in 1832, when the Warren Bridge earnings were such that conditions for free access had been fulfilled. Nothing in the old franchise promised exclusivity, and the Massachusetts Supreme Judicial Court rejected company contentions that its charter right was infringed upon. Appeal had been had to the High Court in 1831, with John Marshall presiding, but absences, subsequent vacancies, and a divided bench postponed reargument until January 1837.

Daniel Webster, counsel for Charles River Bridge, relied primarily on the contract clause. The first grant, he argued, was irrevocable and exclusive, existing titles must be scrupulously respected, and their rights liberally interpreted. His argument, Story wrote to Charles Sumner,

"was a glorious exhibition for old Massachusetts." The new chief justice, however, was not impressed. Speaking for the majority, he brushed aside Story's dissent, as well as immutable vested rights, and held that the state had not granted an exclusive franchise to the Charles River Bridge Company. The state, he concluded, "did not suppose that, by the terms it had used in the first law, it had deprived itself of the power of making such public improvements as might impair the profits of the Charles River Bridge." Hence, it followed that public grants conferring special rights of use in common resources were to be narrowly construed. Nothing may be implied. Otherwise, privilege might hamper economic opportunity or exigent community needs; otherwise, if narrow construction were not the rule, "you will soon find the old turnpike corporations awakening from their sleep, and calling upon this court."

Taney cited three Marshall Court decisions, *United States* v. *Arredondo* (1829), *Jackson* v. *Lampshire* (1830), and *Providence Bank* v. *Billings* (1830), in support of his finding that the Constitution would not be violated unless explicit contractual obligations were impaired. He also turned to the English rule of statutory construction, advanced in *Stourbridge Canal* v. *Wheely* (1831), which held that laws operate in favor of the public, not the grantee, if contractual terms are ambiguous.

Taney's opinion cannot be interpreted as a complete break with Marshall Court dicta, though it does single out a class of contractual relationships for special legal treatment. Certainly it does not indicate animosity toward the rights of private property. To the contrary, it suggests encouragement to new commercial and economic ventures. As such, the decision was as much in the interest of private investment as of community requirements. It reflected, as Frankfurter has observed, Taney's hostility to monopoly, readily transferred into denying corporate monopolies constitutional backing, by imposing a rule of strict construction. It also demonstrates his concern for economic expansion, for "the millions of property which have been invested in railroads and canals." The states, he insisted, must be allowed "to avail themselves of the lights of modern science, and to partake of the benefit of those improvements which are now adding to the wealth and prosperity and the convenience and comfort of every other part of the civilized world."

It could hardly be claimed that those involved in *Charles River Bridge* were hostile to private property. Surely not the chief justice or his great predecessor. But "the community also have [sic] rights," Taney exclaimed. Vested rights must be "sacredly guarded," but so must the "happiness and well-being of every citizen." At bottom, Taney's opinion was, as J. Williard Hurst has claimed, "the classic statement of policy in favor of freedom for creative change as against unyielding protection for existing commitments." Equally important, Taney adhered to an ethical conception of the social responsibility of private property; and when the rights of property collide with those of the community, the latter's rights are controlling. Lemuel Shaw may be numbered among many state judges who shared this view of a state's power to legislate for the common good, though it might "interfere with the liberty of action and even the right of property."

To further suggest that *Charles River Bridge* represented no drastic departure from the decisions of John Marshall's tribunal, Taney Court justices not only interpreted franchise charters strictly but would scrupulously enforce the rights expressly granted to private interests. Hence, if the decision watered down the doctrine of vested rights that Marshall so carefully erected, it nonetheless retained the old constitutional prohibition against impairment of explicit contractual obligations. Subsequent decisions demonstrated this underlying consistency. The justices carefully steered between the interests of private investors and the public good, applying the strict-construction rule in decisions between 1837 and 1865.

Strict construction in public contracts was frequently coupled with eminent domain, a legal proposition that had not arisen in the Marshall Court era but was now recognized. The issue of eminent domain first came to the Supreme Court in *West River Bridge Co.* v. *Dix* (1848). It arose after the Vermont legislature in 1795 granted a private bridge company the privilege of constructing a covered wooden toll bridge over the West River at Brattleboro, permitting it to maintain the bridge for a century. The tolls were fixed

for forty years, subject to revision thereafter if the company continued to make a minimum 12 percent profit. Long before the hundred years had expired, John Dix and thirty-four area residents protested the charter, believing it a "sore grievance" and asserting that a "wealthy town" like Brattleboro should maintain a free bridge. They petitioned the county court to take the bridge and make it part of a new free highway. Three court-appointed commissioners agreed with petitioners, and the court, under the right of eminent domain (as set fourth in an 1839 state statute), ordered the bridge made free on 1 June 1844. In effect, the state seized the entire property of a chartered bridge company. The company then appealed to the Vermont Supreme Court, claiming, among other things, that its charter was a contract and not to be abrogated. Rejecting this complaint, the court held that the contract clause was not violated by the state's power of eminent domain. Appeal was then made to the High Court. Webster, always the advocate of rigid construction of the contract clause, was (with Jacob Collamer) again counsel for a private bridge company, while Samuel S. Phelps of Vermont represented the state.

Webster's argument was his usual one: A corporate charter such as his client's was not "property" at all but rather a "franchise, a pure franchise," and could not be taken as if physical property. Hence, it was not subject to eminent domain. Further, state eminent domain power, if it reaches to a franchise at all, is nonetheless controlled by the contract clause; contracts, as Chancellor Kent asserted, were immune from the subsequent power of sovereignty; and, finally, compensation for the company should be an estimate of tolls to be received, less operating expenses—which would be more than the $4,000 awarded by the state (Frank). Webster then concluded with his inevitable prediction of the impending doom of the Republic and its financial interests if the Court ruled otherwise: "Our only security is to be found in this tribunal, to keep it [eminent domain] within some safe and well defined limits, or our State governments will be but unlimited despotisms over the private citizens." At issue was whether eminent domain or the contract clause governed. The former, he continued, was new to the American Constitution, a feature of arbitrary government, and the justices must carefully control this power. Vermont's effort to exercise it in this instance would lead to "the most levelling ultraisms of Antirentism or Agrarianism or Abolitionism."

State counsel brushed aside Webster's contentions and insisted that the just-compensation provision of the Fifth Amendment applied only to expropriation of property by the federal government and not by Vermont. Hence, the question of amount was not before the Court but only the one of whether the contract clause restricted the operation of the state's eminent domain power. Counsel insisted it did not.

Justice Daniel, with only Wayne in dissent (McLean concurred), rendered a sweeping opinion. It claimed that the power of eminent domain is "paramount to all private rights vested under the government, and these last . . . must yield in every instance to its proper exercise." In *Planters' Bank* v. *Sharp* (1848), Daniel dissented. Now he carried the Court with him. He found *Charles River Bridge* controlling and affirmed eminent domain to be an important function of sovereignty. Every contract, he found, is subject to "conditions inherent and paramount," and "such a condition is the right of eminent domain." Did the power of eminent domain, an implied power in the original contract, reach franchises? Daniel concluded that it did. A franchise was property, he stated, and with a few citations he waved away Webster's entire argument. Daniel, states' righter that he was, believed the state had the power to take, and the Court had nothing to decide regarding the adequacy of payment. Property rights, in sum, were not immutable, and state legislatures and courts were both indirectly invited to determine when older forms of property rights, such as contracts, had to be sacrificed in the quest for material progress or sacrificed in the course "of protecting and promoting the interests and welfare of the community," which was about as close to a police-power limitation on the contract clause as can be found at this early date.

The states, especially those in the West, would take up this judicial invitation to utilize the eminent domain power and to apply the contract clause strictly. They could do so because no clash with congressional power was present; no check on state authority to expropriate private property under eminent domain existed. And they could do so by corporate charter, which became the primary instrument of indirect subsidies— that is, not open state subsidies for internal improvements—to bridge companies, canal companies, and turnpike corporations. Without this privilege, as Scheiber (1982) observes, "private enterprise in transport was practically impossible." The states, moreover, would also transfer to private transport companies doctrines integral to eminent domain—for example, exemption from tort liabilities, such as trespass. Such privileges, an Indiana court ruled in *Rubottom* v. *McClure* (1838), were justified because the highest public good was involved: "The advancement of the wealth, prosperity, and character of the state." Taneyesque language and dicta became the norm in the West. For instance, in *Mills* v. *County of St. Clair* (1850), the Supreme Court ruled that an Illinois act of 1819 did not give an exclusive franchise. Illinois lawmakers had granted the charter to a family-owned ferry that crossed the Mississippi River and further provided that no competing ferry within a one-mile distance would be licensed. But the legislators also reserved the right to repeal the monopoly grant if it was "injurious to the public good"; and it did so in 1833. Six years later it took both the land and the franchise rights under eminent domain, authorized the county to operate a ferry, granted both a tract of land and a franchise to another operator, and offered no compensation to the first grantee. Daniel Webster, as counsel for the initial ferry owners, mostly repeated the *Charles River Bridge* argument, and with the exception of McLean, the justices were unmoved by his pleas. They acknowledged an obvious abuse of eminent domain but concluded it was the state's responsibility. It "rests with State Legislatures and State courts exclusively to protect their citizens from injustice and oppression of this description." Consequently, rejecting both pleas of exclusivity and compensation, they found no questions for review by the federal courts.

Still another case, *Richmond, Fredericksburg and Potomac Railroad* v. *Louisa Railroad* (1851), came up to the Court. At stake here was a franchise that had been given exclusively, insofar as it involved the right to carry passengers between Fredericksburg and Richmond. This grant did not prevent another railroad company, the Louisa Railroad, from being given the right to carry freight between the two cities, from crossing over the tracks of the first grantee, or from running tracks parallel to the initial user for part of the distance. But the Richmond railroad, as plaintiff, claimed that its grant prohibited the state from permitting a rival railroad to operate. The Court, Justice Robert C. Grier rendering the decision, concluded otherwise: The exclusive grant applied only to the transport of passengers, and hence, the state could indeed charter another carrier for a different purpose. The state's power of eminent domain was such that "when the public necessities require it," a grant of a franchise or a grant of land "may be taken for public purposes on making suitable compensation." As judicially defined, "suitable compensation" often involved disappointingly small payments to those who had to yield their rights. Judges seemed more concerned with approving the devolution of eminent domain powers upon those who built the canals, turnpikes, bridges, railways, and drainage projects—on the judicial grounds that those builders and their companies were vested with a "public purpose," as in New York's *Glover* v. *Powell* (1854). It was for the state to decide "when public necessity demands a surrender of private property," declared the New Jersey Supreme Court in *Sinnickson* v. *Johnsons* (1839), a case testing a law that authorized a private dam across a navigable river. This court, in determining "that the lands of individuals are holden subject to the requisitions of the public agencies," spoke for all the states. Theirs was the practical criterion that property rights must yield to public use.

In Taney's last term, another decision had obvious parallels to *Charles River Bridge*. In *Bridge Proprietors* v. *Hoboken Co.* (1864), the justices further honed the strict-construction guideline. In 1859, New Jersey authorized the Hoboken Company to construct a railroad bridge and viaducts within an area designated, by a 1799 statute, to be free of all bridges except one toll bridge that had been given a ninety-nine-year franchise. Seeking to build the railway bridge himself and thereby exact a toll from the railroad as well, the initial grantee sued, charging a violation of the contract clause. Speaking for the Court, Justice Samuel E. Miller conceded that the original charter was a valid contract but the passage of time and technological advances had to be considered. Sustaining the new franchise, he added that its bridge and viaducts could not carry the

kinds of traffic using the earlier toll bridge and, hence, the rights of the toll-bridge operators were not infringed upon by the subsequent grant.

State tribunals usually sustained grants when exclusivity was clearly and expressly given. But they recognized that such monopoly privileges often had an economically stunting impact. The use of the eminent domain doctrine offered an equitable resolution in that it provided some compensation for taken vested rights while permitting the community to develop economically. However, prior to the 1860s, eminent domain questions were seldom ruled upon by the Court, and such decisions as were made left franchise rights open to abrogation and, we have noted, gave a broad discretionary power to the states.

State courts followed the lead offered by the High Court. They upheld state grants of railroad rights-of-way through city streets and easements for stations and terminal facilities, as in New York's *Hudson & Delaware Canal* v. *Railroad* (1841) and Ohio's *Moorehead* v. *Little Miami Railroad* (1848). Such delegation of the eminent domain power rested on the public-use/public-purpose legal criterion, gave precedence to community needs over property rights, and simply required that fair and just compensation be given when private property was involuntarily surrendered. As the Massachusetts Supreme Judicial Court stated, it also meant that turnpike corporations were to be distinguished from ordinary "private" businesses. Hence, turnpikes and, later, railroads, bridges, and ferries were *publici juris*, to use Lord Chief Justice Matthew Hale's famous phrase, and eminent domain devolved upon them. Turnpikes were, as Chancellor Kent noted in an 1823 case, "the most public roads or highways that are known to exist . . . *are made entirely for public use,* and the community have a deep interest in their construction and preservation" (*Rogers* v. *Bradshaw*). In like manner, North Carolina's supreme court in 1837, when it upheld vesting the eminent domain power in a railroad company, declared in *Raleigh & Gaston Railroad* v. *Davis* (1837), "As to the corporation, it is a franchise, like a ferry or any other. As to the public, it is a highway, and in the strictest sense, *publici juris.*" Hence, land "taken" by the corporation under eminent domain was in effect "taken by the public for a public purpose." In the following year, South Carolina's supreme court upheld legislative delegation of the power to a railroad company by citing the company's special character, given the "general [public] right to use the road." The Ohio Supreme Court in 1854 offered the consensual validation that state tribunals gave to the taking of land "in the name [of] the state." Such a practice was legitimate so long as "the work for which it is taken is . . . as a matter of right and not merely of favor" (Scheiber, 1971).

The courts sometimes invoked a pragmatic consideration, one derived from the common law, which held that vested rights guaranteed by the contract clause must be measured against the collective interests of society in economic progress. Indeed, the "comfort, convenience and prosperity of the people" became justification enough for a legislative judgment that surrendered vested rights in property to eminent domain. Judges were very sensitive to the "public use or benefit" criterion, which "may depend somewhat on the situation and wants of the community for the time being" *(Scudder* v. *Trenton Delaware Falls Co.,* 1832). Thus, a New Hampshire court declared *(In re Mt. Washington Road Co.,* 1857), in sweeping aside the damage claims of those adversely affected by the charters granted to new corporations engaged in competitive businesses with their own,

> Every man, when he embarks in any business, or makes an investment of property, must do it at the risk of such changes as time and the progress of the age may introduce. There is no undertaking on the part of the government to protect him against new competitions, whether caused by individual enterprize or by improvements conducted under public authority.

This realistic criterion even applied to manufacturing corporations, for state lawmakers began to delegate the eminent domain power to them as well, when such corporations wished to build textile or other mills. These manufacturing establishments had always been deemed *privati juris* under the common law—unlike, say, gristmills, traditionally considered *publici juris.* But the pragmatic perspective of state judges persuaded them to validate such new measures. For example, Lemuel Shaw of the Massachusetts bench, a consistent pragmatist as to legislative definition of public purpose, concluded in *Hazen*

v. *Essex* (1851) that "manufacturing [had] come to be one of the greatest public pursuits of the commonwealth" and hence justified devolving powers traditionally given to gristmills on other types of manufacturing enterprises. Into the late 1840s at least, state courts usually assented to legislative discretion in determining "public purposes" and, it followed, to legislative delegation of eminent domain powers.

Another aspect of contract-clause application, that involving private persons rather than corporations, public or private, should be noted at this point. Litigation developed around state debtor-relief measures, something familiar to the national scene in the 1780s, when a number of state legislatures passed stay laws, measures literally staying the collection of debt. During the economic crisis of the late 1830s, more than ten states enacted comparable statutes. These laws, postponing the execution of contracts, were immediately challenged by creditors, though it was only in 1843 that a case involving such mortgage-moratorium measures reached the High Court.

Bronson v. *Kinzie* (1843) was the major case, one of four before the justices that involved staying the execution of contract, permitting payment on installment. It emerged out of a legal challenge to two Illinois measures enacted in February 1841, each spawned by the mounting bankruptcies in rural America. One state law enabled the debtor to repurchase property sold in foreclosure within a given time (one year) and at a given rate—namely, the purchase price plus interest set at 10 percent. The other, enacted at the same time, provided that no judicial sale of property should be made unless two-thirds of the appraisal value was bid for the foreclosed property. Both statutes were to apply retrospectively. Bronson, the mortgage holder, sought foreclosure of property under mortgage terms providing that if the debtor defaulted, on either principal or interest, he could legally sell the mortgaged premises at auction.

Taney, for the Court, held this attempt of Illinois lawmakers to change the contractual terms was an unconstitutional impairment of the obligations of contract. The state might alter such contracts, he agreed, "provided the alteration does not impair the obligation of the contract." But this statute sought to alter conditions of sale, in conflict with the contract, and it materially interfered with the right of the mortgagee. This opinion would have given pleasure to Marshall. It did delight Story. It demonstrated the judiciary's firm loyalty to the sanctity of private property. It aroused great resentment in the West, especially in Illinois, as was expected. Taney did not depart, as those deploring *Charles River Bridge* had feared, from Marshall's dicta on contracts, and Story should have been well pleased that the chief justice supported "sound constitutional doctrine" and "the rights of property and creditors." *McCracken* v. *Hayward* (1844) involved the second of the Illinois statutes, and it, too, was found invalid, the Court simply reaffirming *Bronson*. In *Rowan* v. *Runnels* (1847), a Court majority (only Daniels dissented) made it clear that state courts had no more right to void contracts—for the purchase of slaves, on this occasion—than did state legislatures.

Taney distrusted corporations, as we have observed, and wealth concentrated in the hands of banking and mercantile interests. However, he reluctantly accepted corporations as necessary to society and, highly pragmatic in his legal thought, believed there was a place for them. As a good Jacksonian, he tended to uphold state bank charter rights. But Taney also continually affirmed state powers vis-à-vis national jurisdiction and, consequently, when litigation turned on such questions, his reaction was hardly automatic and predictable. Nor were those of his colleagues, with opinions shifting from case to case. These shifts did not necessarily reflect technical distinctions but rather revealed a flaccid understanding of contract clause constitutionality.

In *Planters' Bank* v. *Sharp* (1848), Levi Woodbury, relying on the contract clause and speaking for seven justices, overturned an 1840 Mississippi law that denied the state's banks the authority given by their charters to transfer bills and notes. The measure had passed during the depression amid public resentment, when state banks were transferring the promissory notes of their debtors to other institutions in order to evade repayment in possibly depreciated paper; that is, these banks refused to receive their own depreciated paper in payment of debts due them. Mississippi's highest court upheld the legislation; some of the banks then took their appeal to the Supreme Court on the ground that the act unconstitutionally impaired contractual obligations—that is, their charters authorized discount

of bills and notes—and the justices agreed: the assignment and selling of notes was granted by the 1830 bank charter and was essential to banking operations. Thus, the state law, Woodbury held, violated the contract clause. Tending to place state actions in the most favorable light, he declared, "Those public bodies [state legislatures] must be presumed to act from public consideration, being in a high public trust; and when their measures relate to matters of general interest . . . the disposition in the Judiciary should be strong to uphold them."

More the anticorporate radical than Taney, Daniel dissented more vigorously. Alluding to the rascals who were fleecing Mississippi's citizens, he agreed with Webster, the counsel for Sharp, the debtor. The plaintiffs were corporations, he affirmed; their powers thus derived from the states that created them, their charter did not expressly confer the right to endorse promissory notes, and therefore, by strict construction of the charter, this power could not be implied. The Court majority, however, was not prepared to follow him or automatically sustain state banking measures.

Given the authority of stare decisis in Court history, such majority opinion occasions some surprise. But there is a plethora of instances in which continuity with *Providence Bank* and *Charles River Bridge* is also apparent. Of fourteen Court opinions involving contracts to which states were parties, six of which centered on tax-exemption grants, some were in the Marshall tradition and others were not. In one early case, *Armstrong* v. *Athens County* (1842), Justice Catron emphasized strict construction of the contract in question, one which made lands granted to Ohio University in 1804 tax-exempt "forever," but concluded that the benefits did not transfer to subsequent purchasers of the property. In effect, the Court majority had sub silentio departed from the Marshall Court opinion in *New Jersey* v. *Wilson* (1812).

Nearly a dozen years later, in another strict-construction decision, *Ohio Life Insurance and Trust* v. *Debolt* (1854), a fragmented Court upheld an 1851 state law taxing insurance companies at the same rate as other companies, notwithstanding a charter provision stipulating a tax rate no different from that of banks. Taney repeated the basic legal canon: strict construction of the corporate franchise. No attribute of sovereignty, such as the taxing power—"the community have . . . an interest in preserving this right undiminished"—would be considered as "relinquished, unless the intention to do so is clearly expressed." If a state made a mistake, the Court was not to function so as to rectify it or shield the state from its results: "The principle that they are the best judges of what is for their own interest, is the foundation of our political institutions." As in *Charles River Bridge,* Taney affirmed the right of lawmakers to act in behalf of the public interest with minimal judicial interference. Even contracts and charters "incautiously made" would be sustained, so long as the privileges were expressly granted and did not violate state constitutional requirements. Hence, the Ohio measure was upheld: a legislature may bind a successor by a grant of tax immunity only if the state constitution explicitly conferred this power upon it.

During the next decade, the *Debolt* ruling was applied in six more Ohio bank tax cases. In each, however, the Court, adhering to its own rule, did find explicit corporate privileges inhering in the charter and hence ruled that subsequent legislative acts impaired the obligations of contract. For example, in *Piqua Branch of the State Bank of Ohio* v. *Knoop* (1853), the Court majority supported the corporation exemption privilege as against state intent upon taxation. McLean's opinion, over the bitter opposition of the state and of four justices, held that such exemption in perpetuity was binding. Ohio had been one of a number of states whose lawmakers "had granted similar exemptions to state banks," and in this instance the original charter provided that the bank pay a fixed percent of the profits, exempting it from all other taxes. Consistent with Marshall Court dicta, the justices rejected the argument of state counsel—that the earlier charter arrangement signified only a method of taxation and was not a permanent charter. They fell back on the contract clause: the later legislative measure altering the tax provisions of the charter was an unconstitutional impairment. The dissenters, including Taney, relying on the implications of *Charles River Bridge,* denied that the state could ever surrender its sovereign right of taxation.

Under an 1845 measure, several Ohio banks were chartered with the proviso of a 6 percent tax on their profits—to be paid to the state in lieu of all other taxes. In response, Ohio's constitu-tional convention in 1851 responded by passing an amendment that repealed such tax exemptions and provided for uniform taxation. An act of 1852 was the capstone. It also taxed the banks in a way contrary to the 1845 charter provisions. The Court struck these measures down, in *Dodge* v. *Woolsey* (1855), as a violation of the contract clause. The three dissenters, deserted by Taney, stood on his earlier ground; no specific contractual exemption existed; the 1845 rate could be altered by the legislature; and even if an exemption had been specified, the people should be able to alter it by a change in their constitution.

Bank of Augusta v. *Earle* (1839) came up to the High Court with two other cases, *New Orleans and Carrollton Railroad* v. *Earle* and *United States* v. *Primrose,* known collectively as the *Alabama Bank Cases.* They derived from litigation centering on a provision in the Alabama Constitution that prohibited the legislature from establishing any bank except one in which the state held part of the stock and shared in the directorship. To protect these state banks, those in other states were prohibited by law from engaging in Alabama banking business. Bank agents of all three out-of-state corporations, in these three cases, had purchased bills of exchange in Alabama. Those who had issued and endorsed these bills (Earle and Primrose) refused to pay, on the grounds that, under Alabama law, state banks had a monopoly on banking and that foreign banking corporations were not permitted to operate in the state. When the Alabama debtors refused to honor their bills of exchange, the three plaintiffs went into circuit court.

Justice John McKinley, a Kentucky Democrat and Van Buren appointee who had become an avid states' righter, decided for the defendant in his circuit. He denied the right of a corporation of one state to so much as make a contract in another state, and surely not one that conflicted with the laws and policies of the foreign state. Alabama had rightfully prohibited foreign banking corporations from doing business within its borders, a decision that would have effectively deprived corporations from operating outside of the respective states in which they were incorporated. Reaction to his decision was immediate. Story, in a letter, declared that it "frightened half the lawyers and all the corporations of the country out of their properties." In an equally alarmed tone, he wrote to Justice McLean that the decision would "most seriously affect all banks, insurance companies and manufacturing companies doing an interstate business." Nor were New Englanders alone alarmed. The sale and shipment of Southern cotton was usually done by bills of exchange. Indeed, the interstate economic operations of the entire country were at stake. Small wonder, then, that the three banks, in three different suits, appealed to the Supreme Court.

Taney made a pragmatic accommodation to prevailing economic conditions. He was aware that "contracts to a very great amount have undoubtedly been made by different corporations out of the particular state by which they were created," but he did not wish to deprive states of all regulatory authority vis-à-vis foreign corporations. He rejected the most explosive aspect of Webster's brief—namely, that corporations, even if composed of citizens, were to be considered "persons" within the meaning of the privileges and immunities clause. They were not citizens because Taney feared "the enhancement of strength that such constitutional protection would give" (Frankfurter) rather than because of legal precedent or textual analysis. In any event, the privileges and immunities clause did not give out-of-state corporations the right to do business as they saw fit within a state's borders.

Proceeding then to the issue of comity, Taney recognized the resourceful possibilities of this doctrine. He closely followed the arguments of defense counsel (Webster and David Ogden), concluding that comity was relevant to the present litigation and that it legitimized the corporations' right to enter into contracts outside their own borders. Further, it permitted suit in federal court. In international law, he went on, foreign corporations, by the rule of comity, had the right to make contracts in other countries. "We think it is well settled," he declared, "that by the law of comity among nations, a corporation created by one sovereignty is permitted to make contracts in another, and to sue in its courts, and that the same law of comity prevails among the several sovereignties of this Union." Such rights, it follows, also existed in interstate relations. His decision circumscribed the constitutional rights of corporations and gave the states great potential power, in that by exclusion laws they could legislate against corporate entry—not that they wished to. It also meant that Taney, the enemy

of monopolies, gave corporations the security needed to operate nationally, that they were now free to do business in other states, exploit the national market, and enjoy the protection of the laws of the states (Cochran).

The second important constitutional decision in the 1837 term, after *Charles River Bridge,* was *Briscoe* v. *Bank of the Commonwealth of Kentucky.* Like cases already reviewed, it concerned a state bank, but the issue now turned on the definition of "bills of credit," which states were prohibited from issuing under Article I, Section 10, of the Constitution. Banking was a politically and economically sensitive issue. It had become a battleground in the 1830s, with rival state-national forces and agencies.

Kentucky's Commonwealth Bank was a model of the Jacksonian economic ideal. Though nominally a private corporation, its stock was owned exclusively by the state, its president and board of directors were selected by the legislature, and its notes circulated as money. Like the contract clause cases, the litigation surrounding the bank involved both constitutional matters of great moment and a broad spectrum of opinion as to the meaning of bills of credit. If these bank notes were so defined, their issuance by a state was explicitly prohibited. John Marshall's answer to the question of their legality had been given in *Craig* v. *Missouri* (1830), and he had then found that any paper medium circulated by the state for exchange purposes was under the constitutional ban. In 1834, when *Briscoe* was first argued, Marshall remained of the same opinion: the Kentucky bank notes could not be issued. No decision had been rendered, however, and the case was held over.

The litigation had its origins in 1820, when Kentucky chartered a state-owned and state-controlled bank. The legislature authorized it to perform the usual banking functions, including the issuance of state bank notes. Seeking to avoid repayment of a debt incurred in borrowing these notes, Briscoe challenged their legality. He claimed that they constituted state-issued bills of credit. The bank, after all, was intimately related to the state, even though its official acts were in its own name. The state, however, contended that there was a difference between notes issued by a state and those emitted by a chartered corporation. McLean's majority opinion relied heavily on the argument of Henry Clay, counsel for the bank. It sustained the state's position in an opinion that gave a strict reading of the constitutional clause involved: the notes were not bills of credit since they were issued by a bank, not by the state—even though the state owned the bank. He also accepted the state contention that if its bank notes were illegal, then so were the notes of all state-chartered banks, since the state could not do indirectly what it was prohibited from doing directly. Phrasing it more positively, he concluded that Kentucky, in establishing the bank, simply engaged in a constitutional exercise of state power and that the notes issued by the bank were not bills of credit within the meaning of the constitutional prohibition. Justice Baldwin observed that if the facts in *Craig* had been similar to those in *Briscoe*, Marshall would have been in the minority. Perhaps. But the later decision could have gone either way. Even Whigs like Clay, after all, recognized that the nation needed the currency provided by state banks, especially now that the Bank of the United States was no more than a mere state bank in Pennsylvania.

Story was unconvinced. For him and others, the case—like *Charles River Bridge* and *City of New York* v. *Miln,* both in the 1837 term—were determined by precedents established in Marshall's day. Remarking on McLean's failure to distinguish between state-owned banks and their notes, and those of privately owned, albeit state-chartered, banks (as all had to be), he bitterly arraigned the majority opinion:

> That a State may rightfully evade the prohibitions of the Constitution by acting through the instrumentality of agents . . . instead of acting in its own direct name, and thus escape from all its constitutional obligations, is a doctrine to which I can never subscribe, and which, for the honor of the country, for the good faith and integrity of the States . . . I hope may never be established.

Miln emerged out of an immigration controversy. At stake was the validity of a New York State measure that required captains of incoming vessels to provide local police with a passenger manifest and also give bond guaranteeing that their alien passengers would not become public charges. The larger issue turned on the powers of local police and on the commerce clause, with the latter taking on a crucial role in the nation-state debate; specifically, state efforts to exercise concurrently a good deal of power over transportation and the economy. In the background as well was the question of transportation of slaves across state lines and the volatile issue of congressional regulation of such interstate commerce. The Marshall Court had sketched the importance of the commerce clause in broad strokes and gave it a nationalist reading; the Taney Court would offer a more subtle approach, one which straddled the growing sectionalism—that is, find acceptance in the South while at the same time encouraging a national commerce. Inevitably, such an approach produced something less than clarity or consistency. Justice Barbour's opinion contributed to the ambiguity. His concept of commerce was vague and entirely uncertain as to when, if ever, congressional power took precedence over state authority.

The New York measure was "a regulation not of commerce but of police," with the police power defined diffusely as state authority to legislate for safety and general welfare. Barbour's opinion avoided any discussion of the extent of congressional power over commerce. *Gibbons* v. *Ogden* (1824), he claimed, was not applicable, since no federal law had been enacted that clashed with the state measure. Rather than being a regulation of commerce, the state act was a police regulation. Thus, as Kutler has observed, the decision not only assented to state laws touching commerce in the absence of congressional laws but also "seemed to take a step" toward the view that state police power might be held superior to the federal commerce power, that it might take precedence over federal supremacy. State police power, Barbour declared, was "complete, unqualified and exclusive," exceeding anything in the past.

Story composed a sharp dissent. The New York statute regulated commerce and clashed with congressional power, which, he claimed, was exclusive according to *Gibbons* and *Brown* v. *Maryland* (1827). Whether or not Congress enacted a law with which New York's might have clashed was irrelevant: congressional power was exclusive and Congress had preempted the field.

Contributing to the amorphous definition of the commerce clause and the extent of congressional power, the Taney Court accepted Story's nationalist reading of it in 1838, a year after *Miln*

70

—or at least it did so in this instance, for in *United States* v. *Coombs,* a case involving the 1825 Crimes Act, a measure that Story had drafted and his friend Webster had guided through Congress, Story carried the day. The statute provided for the punishment of various crimes against the United States and prohibited theft of goods from wrecked or stranded ships. The defendant had been indicted under this act for stealing merchandise from a wrecked vessel off the New York City coast. He had challenged the High Court's jurisdiction, with the Marshall Court's *Thomas Jefferson* (1825) precedent, which had ruled that the admiralty jurisdiction of the federal courts was limited to the sea and tidewaters, not to goods above the high-water mark, where the ship that the defendant had ransacked had been stranded. Congress, Story ruled, had full authority to punish the theft of goods under its commerce powers. The commerce power, he declared, did "not stop at the mere boundary line of State" and was not confined to acts committed upon the water. Rather, "any offense which thus interferes with, obstructs, or prevents such commerce, . . . though done on land, may be punished by Congress, under its general authority to make all laws necessary and proper to execute their delegated constitutional powers."

The issue of congressional exclusivity in regard to interstate commerce, which Barbour left open in *Miln,* continued to confront the Court in both the *License* and *Passenger Cases.* The Court remained divided, as the *License Cases* opinions indicate, with Justices McLean, Wayne, and Story the champions of total exclusivity, and Daniel and Taney in fierce opposition. These cases, like the *Passenger Cases,* raised the question of whether state welfare and reform statutes affecting interstate commerce were an unconstitutional encroachment on congressional authority in this field. The first of the *License Cases, Thurlow* v. *Massachusetts* (1847), immediately forced the justices to confront the issue of how the state might proceed in regulating commerce. *Thurlow* was first heard in 1845, with Webster and Rufus Choate, as counsel for Samuel Thurlow, attacking the validity of the state law under which their client had been convicted. The measure required licenses for retailers of spiritous liquors, even those selling in quantities of less than twenty-eight gallons—that is, selling in less than bulk quantity, which virtually prohibited all nonli-censed sales. Owing to vacancies, illnesses, and absences, the case was continued and reargued in 1847, in conjunction with similar appeals from Rhode Island and New Hampshire litigation, with Webster continuing to advocate congressional exclusivity anent commerce.

In seeking to answer the question of how far the state might go in regulating commerce, six justices wrote nine opinions. Taney was able to divide the three cases into two groups: in the Rhode Island and Massachusetts litigations, the liquor was already in the state, having been through its first stage of distribution; that is, the package had been "broken up" and the state liquor control law was applicable. Consequently, relying on Marshall in *Brown* v. *Maryland,* the chief justice found that these two state temperance laws did not involve a regulation of interstate commerce. But the New Hampshire statute at issue in *Pierce* v. *New Hampshire* (1847) put the really daunting question. This state measure required a license whether liquor was sold wholesale or retail, and no minimum in the amount sold had been stipulated. Moreover, in this case, the liquor was still in the original case in which the first importer received it. In effect, the process of intrastate distribution had not yet begun. Hence, the measure was a regulation of interstate commerce. John Holmes, counsel for plaintiff, argued that the state abused its police powers and interfered with interstate commerce, and he asked the Court to stand on precedent—namely, *Brown* v. *Maryland.* States' counsel relied on the police power as justification.

Taney's opinion explicitly rejected the exclusivist position and supported the states' right to legislate in the disputed field of interstate commerce: "The mere grant of power to the general government cannot, upon any just principles of construction, be construed to be an absolute prohibition to the exercise of any power over the same subject by the States." Taney did concede that in the event of a state-nation statutory conflict centering on the commerce power, the congressional statutes were controlling and supreme. Until then, however, the state might, "for the protection of the health of its citizens," regulate commerce. For him, the police-power doctrine was "nothing more or less than the powers of government inherent in every sovereignty to the extent of its dominions."

The *Passenger Cases—Smith* v. *Turner* (1849)

and *Norris* v. *City of Boston* (1842)—presented even greater difficulty than did the *License Cases,* with the laws of Massachusetts and New York producing two hundred pages of seriatim thinking that took eight judges seven hours to read. Consonant with the decision in *Miln,* these states had enacted measures that required bonds from ship masters carrying immigrants and a tax upon immigrant passengers arriving in their ports. Given the social and economic significance of immigration, then sharply increasing, the constitutional challenge attracted considerable interest. Justice Shaw concluded that the act's purpose was simply to help provide support for alien paupers; that is, it was designed to "secure the State and its citizens from unreasonable burdens, whilst providing for the exercise of a duty of humanity toward those, who in the ordinary course of life are placed within its borders." In upholding this measure, Shaw persuasively upheld the state's competency to legislate on the subject of paupers, affirmed that the means adopted by the state were appropriate, and rejected the contention that the act conflicted with congressional power over interstate commerce.

Webster, before the High Court, rejected this contention and, making a plea for exclusivity, found that the Massachusetts act "is a regulation of commerce of the strictest and most important class, and that Congress possesses the exclusive power of making such a regulation." A bare five-judge majority, reversing Shaw, found the state law unconstitutional, as it did the New York State statute. Justice Catron was the swing man, as the nonexclusivist majority that had upheld the state licensing laws two years earlier was depleted by one and the new majority invalidated these two state measures, and they did so by creating an artifical distinction between commerce and police, failing to realize, as did Taney and Woodbury in dissent, that the two categories often overlapped.

Taney was now one of four dissenters, along with Woodbury, Nelson, and Daniel. This quartet based their decision either on the ground that regulation of passengers was not regulation of commerce or that the tax did not conflict with any federal laws. Taney, for example, rejected the view "that the power to regulate commerce has abridged the taxing power of the States upon the vehicles or instruments of commerce." He was not, concluded Frankfurter, "willing to find in the commerce clause even an implied prohibition upon state taxation discriminating against foreign or interstate commerce." Frankfurter also observed that Taney's opinion "was not the dialectic of a states' rights doctrinaire like Calhoun." Rather his views seemed "to derive from his conception of the judicial function, from his unwillingness to open the door to judicial policy-making wider than the Constitution obviously required." But Frankfurter offers no evidence for such speculation, which sounds suspiciously self-serving, given his own predilections. He would possibly have been on firmer ground if *Luther* v. *Borden* (1849) or *Pennsylvania* v. *Wheeling and Belmont Bridge Co.* (1851) had been cited (though neither fell under the commerce power rubric of his study), for, in each case, judicial restraint carried the day. In *Luther,* an outgrowth of Dorr's Rebellion in 1842, the Court found that "political questions" were at stake and these belonged to the political branches: the conflicting claims of the rival state governments to legality were beyond the competence of the Court to decide. Again, when the majority sought to determine the competing claims of railroads and bridges in *Wheeling and Belmont,* Taney and Daniel dissented—to reaffirm the "narrow scope of judicial proceedings" and to reject a supralegislative role for the courts. Frankfurter would have been hard put to make a case for Taney's consistency, given *Dred Scott* v. *Sandford* (1857), where the Court majority recklessly abandoned the political realism of *Luther.*

The diversity of views in the *Passenger Cases* caused the court reporter to conclude that the tribunal left no opinion at all. Taney himself was troubled over the ebbing of "public confidence." Court-watchers did not know where the justices were going in regard to the commerce clause. At midcentury, then, the High Court seemed hopelessly fractured on the issue of nonexclusive congressional power, with a fragile majority believing the states could conditionally regulate.

On 4 September 1851 the enigmatic Levi Woodbury died, which was a misfortune for the minority bloc. Daniel anticipated the worst, because the Whigs, in the person of Millard Fillmore of New York, occupied the White House; and the president did solicit the advice of Webster, a consistent advocate of the cause of commerce-power exclusivity, on the vacancy. Upon receiving Webster's opinion, Fillmore, in September 1851, offered a recess appointment to Massachusetts-born Benjamin R. Curtis, a firm advocate of sanctity of contract and of property rights generally. Daniel's fears were now to be confirmed.

Curtis, who would be a very able associate justice, rendered the majority opinion in *Cooley* v. *Board of Wardens of the Port of Philadelphia* (1852), which established a formula for balancing the claims of state and national jurisdictions in interstate commerce; and we may assume that Webster, while not directly involved, took great satisfaction in his role in the selection process. By a 6–2 vote, the Court upheld a Pennsylvania statute regulating pilotage of vessels engaged in interstate and foreign trade. In so doing, the justices brought some predictable order to their views of the commerce power.

The provenance of this case lies in an 1803 pilotage law that the Pennsylvania legislature passed for the port of Philadelphia. It required vessels entering or leaving the harbor to take on pilots or pay half the pilotage fee into a fund for the relief of needy pilots. Pilotage is obviously related to navigation and thus to commerce, and consequently, the state law again raised the issue of state power to regulate commerce and the attendant question of exclusivity versus concurrency. Did the constitutional grant of authority delegated to Congress prohibit state regulation? Could the states regulate when such regulation was not in conflict with federal law? The Court had been divided on such basic questions for more than a dozen years—ever since *Miln* in 1837, if not since *Gibbons* in 1824.

Curtis rejected both exclusivist and concurrent formulas and, in a refreshingly brief ten-page opinion, held that the commerce power expressly delegated to Congress did not necessarily exclude the states and that the Pennsylvania statute was a legitimate regulation of a part of interstate commerce. In crisp, precise language, he found that state authority derived from the need to meet specific local conditions:

> Either absolutely to affirm, or deny, that the nature of this power requires exclusive legislation by Congress, is to lose sight of the nature of the subjects of this power, and to assert concerning all of them, what is really applicable but to a part. Whatever subjects of this power are in their nature national, or admit only of one uni-

form system, or plan of regulation, may justly be said to be of such a nature as to require exclusive legislation by Congress.

The subject of commerce was so broad and complex, he continued, that it did not lend itself to uniform federal measures, and the rule covering this "vast field" was simple: power depends on necessity. If the subject needed "a single uniform rule operating equally on the commerce of the United States in every port," then the power fell to Congress; if it, "like the subject now in question," demanded "that diversity, which alone can meet the local necessities of navigation," then it fell to the states.

In this instance, Curtis' Solomon-like compromise of partial concurrence belonged to the states. Daniel, while voting with the majority, listened to a distant drummer, reaffirming the doctrine of "original and inherent" state authority. McLean and Wayne, like Story and Webster before them, engaged in apocalyptic predictions. This retreat from the bastion of centralization, they lamented, would carry the nation back to the chaos of the Confederation. But, we might speculate, it simply indicated that the tribunal, in the absence of congressional action in the field of commerce, would articulate economic policy by means of constitutional construction.

Subsequent efforts to apply Curtis' formula indicate that *Cooley* failed to offer the final solution. Curtis himself, as noted, did not intimate what aspects of commerce required uniformity or permitted diversity. As Newmyer tells us, his "was less a doctrinal clarification than it was an agreement to stop looking for one." The majority simply abandoned the doctrinal imperatives, stare decisis, and the black-letter books of the law for economic and practical realities.

In *Veazie* v. *Moore* (1852), Justice Daniels, speaking for the majority, held that despite *Gibbons*, a Maine law granting exclusive navigational rights on the Penobscot to a single corporation was constitutional. The river being entirely within the state, the statute did not conflict with congressional commerce power. This restricted reading of the commerce clause was confirmed a decade later, when the High Court declared that a state might regulate a ferry that was obviously local in nature, even if its route of passage was interstate, in this instance a river boundary between two states. Similarly, the Court recognized the state's right to govern coastal fisheries against commerce clause claims, a right that extended even to seizing a vessel licensed by the United States when it violated state law (*Smith* v. *Maryland,* 1855).

In sum, significant powers were left with the states, especially when Congress took no positive statutory action. But the Court, in accordianlike fashion, could also lean toward the corporation and the national government in commerce as well as in contract cases and here, too, might offer emergent businesses very considerable protection against state legislative intrusion, as in *Searight* v. *Stockton* (1845).

In such fields as public lands and maritime law, the jurisdiction of the central government was given an expansive reading. Witness, for instance, *Propeller Genessee Chief* v. *Fitzhugh* (1851), a case arising in the context of the rapid growth in the tonnage and traffic on inland waterways, especially in the Midwest once the 1837 depression had run its course. Attendant upon such increases were expanding steamship capacity and, by 1850, substantial railroad construction, too. Congress recognized the lacunae in admiralty law, in particular those resulting from the long-standing doctrine that inland waterways, beyond the ocean's ebb and flow, were exempt from federal maritime jurisdiction, and a 1845 statute extended federal court authority to include most commercial navigation on inland waterways. The validity of this measure was soon tested in *Propeller Genessee.* Counsel for *Genessee Chief* contended that the collision between the two vessels involved, which left the *Cuba* sunk, had no basis in admiralty jurisdiction, because it did not occur on tidewater. Taney, as expected, found nothing attractive about an expansive reading of the commerce clause power giving greater authority to Congress at state expense. Indeed, he disavowed a commerce clause basis for the 1845 statute. But he sensed the need for an extension of admiralty jurisdiction. Acknowledging the "growing commerce on the lakes and navigable rivers of the Western states" weighed heavily in judicial deliberations, and Taney upheld the new measure and thus invalidated the majority opinion in *Thomas Jefferson,* which had limited navigable waters and, hence, federal authority to tidal ebb and flow, in accord with the old English rule.

The transportation revolution produced other centralizing decisions that suggest the currents were moving against the states. The second *Wheeling Bridge* case indicates as much. The tribunal's most important commerce case in the early 1850s, it further indicates that the Court did not always favor economic progress. At issue was jurisdiction over bridges spanning western rivers and the lively question of control of western trade. The immediate cause involved a span across the Ohio River at Wheeling, which Virginia and Ohio both wished to have erected and which authorized the Wheeling and Belmont Bridge Company to build. Pennsylvania opposed the span.

McLean rendered the majority opinion in February 1852, Taney and Daniel dissenting. Pennsylvania was not a party to the suit, he found, and no federal law was involved. Nonetheless, resort to equity could be had, and on the basis of the court-appointed referee's report, the bridge was considered an obstruction and the company could either raise the height or demolish it. Taney's terse and pointed dissent (like Daniel's more prolix one) was an appeal to judicial restraint: the federal courts could not, in the absence of congressional law on the subject, interfere in this matter. Such interference, he asserted, "appears to me much more appropriately to belong to the Legislature than to the Judiciary."

In 1856, after renewed argument and on complaint of Pennsylvania, the Court reversed itself. In the four-year interim, the original span had been destroyed by storm, the company had begun to build a new one, and Congress in August 1852 had passed a law placing the bridge in the public-road category, thereby making it a lawful structure. Hence, the Court majority, with three dissenters (McLean, Grier, and Wayne), now yielded to the congressional will and declared the statute a constitutional exercise of the commerce power.

Notwithstanding a majority of states' righters on the bench, the Taney Court took yet another step in 1842 to expand the field of federal power. *Swift* v. *Tyson* (1842) involved a Maine bill of exchange dated 1836 and some obscure litigants. The bill was drawn on George Tyson, a New York resident, by Nathaniel Norton and J. Keith. They endorsed the bill to John Swift, in part payment of a promissory note that they owed him. A number of complex and convoluted procedures were involved (Freyer, 1981). Suffice to find that the diversity of state citizenship of the litigants gave the Court jurisdiction, and the case was decided in January 1842. At issue was whether bills received in payment of debts qualified their holders as bona fide creditors. Even larger and more highly significant implications were involved for the negotiability of commercial instruments, and negotiable instruments were the most important circulating medium for long-distance exchanges of credit and capital in an age suffering from a chronic scarcity of specie and an absence of uniform currency. Also immediately at stake were procedural matters of equity, right of appeal, jury instructions, rules of decision—which really were caught up in more than the technical, because these practices, if uniformly ruled upon, would enable inferior federal courts to wield a unifying influence in commercial law. Settlement of such technical issues depended upon the uncertain meaning of section 34 of the 1789 Judiciary Act, which bound federal judges to follow local law in all cases where it applied—that is, whether federal courts had to apply the rules laid down by local law and by state court decisions.

By 1841, we have noted, there were signs that the High Court might offer a way out of the uncertainties inherent in the commercial laws of the states, that it might seek to remove the ambiguities surrounding section 34. In the *Alabama Bank Cases* (1839), the chief justice, invoking comity, upheld the rights of out-of-state corporations to make contracts in any state (unless said state enacted prohibitory measures). On circuit, in *Riley* v. *Anderson* (1841), with facts similar to those in *Swift*, McLean overruled an Ohio Supreme Court decision because it conflicted with the "general" commercial law.

Swift v. *Tyson*, we have noted above, turned on section 34 of the 1789 Judiciary Act, which provided "that the *laws* of the several States . . . shall be regarded as rules of decision in trials at common law [by federal courts] in cases where they apply" (italics added). Were local and state judicial decisions laws within the meaning of this statute? Or did the word *laws* refer only to state statutes and constitutions?

Considering Story's strong nationalist bias, his majority opinion was predictable. Story's great legal treatise *Commentaries on the Conflict of Laws* had sought codification of the laws of the

states in order to promote uniformity. The existing commercial instability had potentially grave consequences for a national market economy, and the judiciary, contemporaries reasoned, might be best able to eliminate commercial law Balkanization and bring order out of chaos. So it is no surprise that Story, for the Court, announced for the first time that the federal courts had authority to lay down rules of commercial law over state rules—without regard to state court decisions—even where no constitutional or federal issue was at stake, when this litigation came into federal court on diversity-of-citizenship grounds. Going even beyond Marshall's revered nationalism, Story asserted that state judicial decisions were not laws within the meaning of the 1789 Judiciary Act. The High Court, he declared, would give very "deliberate attention and respect" to such decisions, but it need not follow them; that is, it was not duty-bound to adhere to dicta laid down by New York's courts relative to the law of negotiable instruments, such as bills of exchange. "Questions of a more general nature, not at all dependent upon local statutes or local usages of a fixed and permanent operation" were at issue; and such questions require that the federal courts not be bound by state laws as laid down by state courts.

Further, Story added, the justices need not be bound by such law "if it differs from the principles established in the general commercial law." Rather, they would ascertain the law for themselves, a conclusion that introduced a novel doctrine into federal law—namely, that section 34 was relevant to local law and not intended to apply to more general matters; that there existed a general commercial law in the United States, one independent of state decisions; that the law applied in federal court governing commercial paper should be general commercial law as formulated by federal courts; and that "the law respecting negotiable instruments may be truly declared . . . to be in a great measure, not the law of a single country only but of the commercial world." In effect, Story here proclaimed the existence of a federal commercial law under the doctrine of a "general jurisprudence" in the field of commercial transactions. By this finding, the Court majority demonstrated a readiness to further interstate legal uniformity—by broadening the reach of equity, by restricting the applicability of the troublesome section 34, and by giving corporations standing in federal courts, as Freyer (1979) concludes.

Story's decision derived in part not only from a desire to give stability and commonalty to rules in multistate commercial transactions, as some commentators have observed, but also from an inclination to have banking activities and related commercial transactions involving fiscal exchanges placed under federal government supervision. His opinion in *Carpenter* v. *Providence Washington Insurance Co.* (1842) indicates as much. In this reassertion of *Tyson*, Story extended its holding from negotiable paper to an insurance policy. In interpreting such a policy, he declared,

> The questions under our consideration are questions of general commercial law, and depend upon the construction of a contract of insurance, which is by no means local in its character, or regulated by any local policy or customs. Whatever respect, therefore, the decisions of State tribunals may have on such a subject, and they certainly are entitled to great respect, they cannot conclude the judgment of this court.

In yet another case of the same term, *Martin* v. *Waddell's Lessee* (1842), the Court limited still further its obligation to follow state law under section 34 of the 1789 Judiciary Act. It centered on New Jersey's authority to grant exclusive oyster-bed rights in flats under its tidewaters. Long-standing state legal issues were involved, including royal charters and deeds of surrender as well as an 1818 state supreme court decision. Taney, though deciding in favor of the state, held that the state court ruling did not bind the federal court, though it was "unquestionably entitled to great weight." In *Dobbins* v. *Erie County* (1842), the Court reiterated its intention to protect federal governmental functions against state encroachment. In this instance, the income of a federal revenue officer was taxed under Pennsylvania state law. The measure was declared unconstitutional, an "interference with the constitutional means which have been legislated by the government of the United States to carry into effect its powers to lay and collect taxes, duties, imports, etc., and to regulate commerce."

Two years after *Swift*, the High Court extended that decision by greatly expanding the "general jurisprudence" dictum. Augmenting

Bank of Augusta of 1839, in which it was presumed—unless a state law to the contrary existed—that out-of-state corporations could carry on business within any state, *Louisville Railroad* v. *Letson* (1844) enlarged the force of this comity rule by virtually equating such corporations with citizens. The case was brought to the federal court on grounds of diversity of citizenship, and the corporation—no longer simply all of its members—was "deemed" by Justice Wayne to be a citizen of the state in which it was chartered.

Bank of Augusta, *Letson*, and *Swift* testified against the doubtful claim that Taney was an unqualified defender of agrarian ideology and state particularism. *Genessee Chief* expanded the maritime jurisdiction of the federal government; *Swift* developed a national common law for commerce; *Dobbins* denied state authority to tax the pay of federal officials; *Almy* v. *California* (1860) denied state power to tax goods leaving for out-of-state markets; *Bank of Commerce* v. *City of New York* (1863) restricted state interference with federal borrowing powers; *Holmes* v. *Jennison* (1840) affirmed exclusive federal power over extradition; *Vidal* v. *Girard's Executors* (1844) placed property under the protection of federal common law (that is, separating it from the state systems); *Rowan* v. *Runnels* (1847), yet another case involving property, property in slaves, found Taney's majority opinion affirming federal court primacy and power; *Ableman* v. *Booth* (1859) upheld federal government power to enforce national law without state interference. These last two cases bring us to the litigation surrounding slavery, the final area of Taney Court decision-making to be considered.

SLAVERY

Taney's first term on the bench included a series of cases that prefigured things to come. They centered on property rights in slaves, which of course was a dispute enfolded into the larger ethical issue of whether anyone could own property embodied in another man and in his labor. Nat Turner's revolt and the emergence of Garrisonian abolitionism, both in 1831, exacerbated legal and ethical issues. A slave case of six years later—the *United States* v. *The Ship Garonne* (1837)—sounded the tocsin, and cases would flood in, most on appeal from state courts. These cases often involved slaves disposed of in wills, deeds, and mortgage transferrals. The assumption was that slaves were property—to be disposed of in impersonal and formal terms, like all property, under the terms of the common law. At times, court cases, especially Southern court litigation, decided manumission-by-will disputes in favor of the would-be heirs; at other times, in favor of freedom for the slave. Southern judges, notably the Georgia state judiciary, held extreme proslavery sentiments and hence invariably held against manumission requests, as in *American Colonization Society* v. *Gartrell* (1857).

On occasion, litigation over slavery led to the adjudication of important constitutional questions. *Groves* v. *Slaughter* (1841) was one such instance. It was yet another commerce clause case after *Miln* (and before *Cooley* and the *Passenger Cases*), but one involving the slave trade. Robert Slaughter journeyed to Mississippi with some slaves, as he might to any state, and there sold them. He accepted notes as part of the payment and sought to collect on them when they came due. Suits were brought in Louisiana's circuit court in 1838 and 1839 for payment on these notes, and the court held for the plaintiff. But a complication had arisen in the interim, in May 1833. Mississippi lawmakers sought to end the drain of specie from the state and to stabilize slave auction prices within their borders and so passed an amendment to the state constitution prohibiting the importation or sale of slaves as merchandise. The Court had to decide whether this amendment unlawfully encroached on congressional power to regulate commerce. A fundamental and explosive issue was at stake: whether, if the amendment were valid, it was in conflict with congressional power over interstate commerce. But the majority, Smith Thompson writing the opinion, skirted the issue and settled on whether the state's constitution was self-executing. It was not. Since the state's legislators had not enacted the necessary statutes implementing their constitution, the ban upon slave importation was inoperative and the notes were valid.

Of the majority, McLean—understandably, given his national ambitions—was most intent on discussing the larger, more provocative issues —namely, the respective powers of states and federal governments in regard to the introduction of slaves into the states. Persons were commerce, he insisted, and as to navigation, "it is immaterial whether the cargo of the vessel consists of passengers or articles of commerce." Baldwin agreed. He obviously regretted McLean's insistence on discussing broader issues, "but since a different course has been taken by the judges who have preceded me, I am not willing to remain silent, less it be inferred that my opinion coincides" with theirs. The slaves, he concluded, were merchandise and thus articles of commerce; therefore, states could not prohibit their shipment in interstate commerce. Congressional power in this field was exclusive. Taney as well, against his preference, was forced to render an opinion on congressional power to regulate slave traffic between states. Not only did he believe that the state had a right to regulate interstate traffic in blacks, regardless of their condition, but also he believed that this right was exclusive. Congress could not control state actions by means of the commerce clause. Further, he speculated, the Court would never have to consider the question. So much for Taney's power of prophecy. *Groves* v. *Slaughter* had clearly touched a judicial nerve. Technically speaking, it simply concluded that from 1833 to 1838, Mississippi had not prohibited the introduction of slaves for sale as commodities. But the diversity of views and the depth of feeling evoked by commerce in slaves promised grave trouble for the tribunal.

United States v. *The Schooner Amistad* (1841) pushed the Court toward stage center on slavery matters. It concerned a cargo of forty-nine free blacks transported from Africa to Cuba. They had been captured in their homeland, in violation of treaties outlawing the slave trade and in violation of Spanish law. By the use of false documents certifying them as slaves, they were sold in Havana. They revolted in the course of being transshipped to another Cuban port, killed the captain and three crewmen, captured the two alleged owners, and ordered the latter to steer eastward for Africa. Instead, the owners tricked their passengers, steering the vessel toward American waters, where in 1839 it was captured as a prize off the Connecticut coast by a United States naval brig. The owners demanded that their alleged slaves be returned; the blacks sued for their freedom; and Attorney General Henry Gilpin, speaking for the Van Buren administration, sought to return schooner and human cargo to Spain, in accord with a treaty stipulating that stolen merchandise be surrendered. On the procedural issue, the district court ruled that it had the power to look into the documentation and determine whether the enslavement of the Africans had been legal. The circuit court, perhaps influenced by the region's antislavery sentiment, decided that the United States was not obligated to give over the prisoners to Spanish claimants, since they had enslaved the blacks in Havana contrary to the laws of Spain. The claimants then appealed to the High Court.

The seventy-four-year-old former president John Quincy Adams, counsel for the blacks, was an ardent antislavery man and naturally the object of national attention. His opening argument included the categorical claim that only "the law of nature and of Nature's God on which our fathers placed our own national existence" reached his clients. Story for the Court, with only Baldwin in dissent, upheld Adams' clients and claims. The treaties provided for extradition of legally held slaves, he admitted, but being kidnapped, they should be released and returned to Africa: "The eternal principles of justice and international law" demanded as much. The United States could not be a party to actions by which free Africans were deprived of their liberty.

Story did not propose to proceed "far beyond the record" and hence neglected a number of controversial matters raised by counsel. One would eventually lead to the great issue before Taney's Court—whether blacks, regardless of previous status, became free when entering a free state.

America's fugitive slaves had fewer rights than *Amistad*'s Africans, and fewer procedural rights than any white man accused of crime. After all, a state executive request for extradition was required for whites, but the 1793 Fugitive Slave Act made provision for the planter or his agent to recapture the alleged fugitive and remove him from the jurisdiction of a free state upon ex parte testimony of ownership in a federal or state courtroom. Even before this statute was supplemented by the 1850 Fugitive Slave Act, the fact of runaway slaves exacerbated sectional controversy.

Other developments also inflamed sectional opinion. The so-called underground railroad that helped fugitive slaves flee northward, often into Canada, deeply troubled Southerners. So did the personal-liberty laws of Northern states. Aware of the many instances of slave kidnappings and false claims of ownership, Northern state legislators approved measures providing that no blacks could be taken from their states without a certificate of a state magistrate and, in some states, without a jury trial affirming claimant's right to do so.

A year after *Groves* and *Amistad*, one of these state measures collided with the 1793 federal statute, and Story was presented with arguably the hardest decision of his entire judicial career (Dunne). It evolved out of an 1826 Pennsylvania measure that was unpopular with slaveholders because it repealed their previous statutory right of recapture without formal process and prohibited state judges from authorizing seizure solely on the slave-catcher's oath (Wiecek). The new law provided that a warrant would be issued only when the slaveholder, his agent or lawyer, produced the affidavit of ownership certified by claimant, in addition to the agent's own oath. Only then would the state magistrate, if satisfied that service was owed in another state, issue a certificate for removal of the fugitive from Pennsylvania. If a claimant exercised his right under federal law, evaded state procedures, and seized an alleged slave without warrant, he would be charged with kidnapping. And if he followed state legal guidelines, his oath was not admissible in evidence. Such procedural safeguards for the personal liberty of blacks frustrated Southern claimants, though it was not the law's intent.

In any event, Edward Prigg, the agent of a Maryland slaveholder, seized a fugitive slave woman, Margaret Morgan, together with her children, under a warrant issued by a justice of the peace of York County, Pennsylvania. When this same official refused to hold the hearing required by the 1793 statute and to issue a certificate without further proof of ownership mandated by state law, Prigg removed mother and offspring from Pennsylvania. The agent was then indicted by the state for kidnapping. The Maryland legislature, in reaction, adopted a report warning that the rights of all slaveholding states were in jeopardy.

Maryland, however, agreed to test the constitutionality of Pennsylvania's 1826 law, and Prigg voluntarily returned to the state and submitted to trial, thereby quieting the interstate friction. He was convicted under state law. His conviction was upheld on appeal in the higher state court, and his subsequent appeal to the High Court on writ of error provoked an extensive debate on the constitutionality of all such state measures and indirectly on that of the federal statute as well.

Story for the majority, in *Prigg* v. *Commonwealth of Pennsylvania* (1842), easily demonstrated the unconstitutionality of Pennsylvania law, since some of its provisions interfered with the enforcement of the 1793 measure. But he went further—down a road other colleagues refused to follow—and it prompted six of his brothers to write their own opinions, for a total of sixty-five pages. Story began with the dual premises that the 1793 measure was constitutional and that the Constitution's fugitive-slave clause guaranteed an unqualified right of recovery to the masters, which meant that any state law hindering that right, such as delay in apprehension, violated the Constitution. The clause was self-executing; that is, it mandated no legislation from federal or state governments: the master could apprehend the slave where he or she was found. Yet, he concluded, laws were needed to implement this right, since slaveholders usually required the assistance of public officials.

From this point onward, Story lost his concurring brethren, for in an obiter dictum, he insisted on national preemption, which would strike down all state laws, friendly or not, that touched on this field; that is, he affirmed congressional exclusivity in this field. Taney and Daniel had no use for Story's irrelevancies. They felt such dicta eroded the operation of federal law, since too few federal officials were available to implement, without state assistance, the 1793 measure. Taney affirmed the legal rights of the slave-owner, believing him to be entitled to state as well as federal assistance. Daniel's concurrence expressed fears about what would happen with "the removal of every incentive of interest in state officers" and with their entire neutralization.

On the question of whether states could legislate for the recovery of fugitives and whether state officials were obligated to assist, the justices were hopelessly divided, and it prompted bitter criticism nationally. The situation did lead many Northern states to administer measures discouraging their officials from assisting in the enforcement of the 1793 measure, thereby con-

tributing to its ineffectiveness and consequently further alienating the South. The subject of fugitive slaves was now opened to clamorous and abrasive debate—to be resolved only by the guns of war.

The impact of *Prigg* was felt directly in local cases, such as that of George Latimer, a black living in Boston. A Boston constable seized Latimer as a fugitive and brought him before Story, who detained him while counsel for Latimer's alleged master sent for further proof of his identity and status. Samuel Sewall, a convert to Garrisonian abolitionism, petitioned for a writ of personal replevin from Lemuel Shaw of the Massachusetts Supreme Judicial Court. He argued for the alleged fugitive's right to have his identity determined by a jury, a claim rejected by Shaw on the ground that even an initiation of such a process would constitute an infringement of exclusive federal power. Story had affirmed his obligation to the Constitution—the fugitive-slave clause in particular—and asserted that this clause, like the 1793 measure, must be given effect by the courts. Shaw, opposed to slavery like Story, admitted his helplessness: he could not interpose state authority between Latimer and slavery.

By this time, fugitive slaves were moving northward in growing number, with underground railroad networks stretching across the Midwest—the third and seventh judicial circuits —from New Jersey to the Mississippi River. One case that went to the circuit court in Cincinnati and eventually to the High Court suggests the complexity of the problem. In 1842 nine slaves owned by Wharton Jones of Kentucky escaped into Ohio and were picked up on a road north of Cincinnati by a wagon driven by John Van Zandt, who was charged with harboring and concealing fugitives in violation of the 1793 statute. Plaintiff sought civil damages against him. Counsel for the defense included William Seward of New York and Salmon P. Chase of Ohio, a friend of McLean. Chase sought reconsideration of *Prigg*. His plea in part centered on the principles of natural law and the Declaration of Independence, both of which he contended condemned slavery. Hence, the Constitution had to be interpreted narrowly to avoid conflict with natural right. McLean, in circuit, rejected the contentions of his friend. Considerations of conscience were invalid, so he instructed the jury, and he found the 1793 statute in accord with the *Prigg* precedent. However, McLean thought it best to have questions involving interpretation of this measure decided by the High Court.

In *Jones* v. *Van Zandt* (1847), Woodbury, for the Court, rejected Chase's contentions. The Constitution had struck a bargain with slavery—"one of its sacred compromises"—and the Court, he piously reminded the nation, had no recourse but to "stand by the Constitution and laws with fidelity . . . to go where the Constitution and laws lead, and not to break both, by travelling without or beyond them."

The Court was continually reminded—surely unnecessarily after *Amistad* and *Prigg*—that involvement on either side of the fugitive-slave issue would sharply undermine its popularity. The 1850 Fugitive Slave Act added fuel to the fires of sectional controversy—and being sufficiently different from the 1793 measure, provided grounds for reconsidering earlier decisions. At its core, the new statute provided for federal commissioners who would hear the apprehended fugitive and the slaveholder or agent, examine affidavits, and issue or deny certificates of removal.

The first legal test came in Boston—in the Thomas Sims case (*In re Sims*, 1851). In the same year that Justice Shaw refused a writ of habeas corpus to Shadrach, a detained fugitive slave, after which a black crowd dramatically rescued him, Sims, another fugitive, was captured and federal authorities prepared for a test of strength. Indeed, chains and ropes girded all entrances to Shaw's courthouse. Three antislavery lawyers sought a writ of habeas corpus on Sims's behalf and began a legal attack on the constitutionality of the 1850 measure. Robert Rantoul led the principal charge. The measure, he declared, vested judicial power in an officer who was not a judge within the meaning of Article III of the Constitution. Shaw was unmoved. He denied the writ and, turning to precedent, found no relevant differences between the 1793 and 1850 statutes, upholding the constitutionality of the latter. Sims, with military assistance, was returned to his owner.

Western abolitionists also hoped for legal success in their attack upon the 1850 measure. *Miller* v. *McQuerry* (1853) was the first important Ohio test of its constitutionality, and like Shaw, Justice McLean—the only Court justice who might be considered an abolitionist at this time—then sitting in circuit, found that precedent, specifically *Prigg*, was governing and the 1850 statute constitutional. Much like Story earlier and Shaw in his comparable confrontations, McLean confessed his inability to do anything but uphold the act. His decision helped persuade Southerners that free-state judges would do their duty in returning fugitives and surely frustrated abolitionist efforts to influence Northern courts.

The enactment of personal-liberty laws and the violence attendant upon efforts to release fugitives involved not only the issue of human bondage but also the nature of the federal polity. Both questions were central to the *Ableman* v. *Booth* case (1859), which occurred in an abolitionist area and prompted Taney's discourse on federal-state relations and the authority of the Supreme Court.

Joshua Glover, a slave belonging to a Missouri farmer, Benjamin Garland, escaped into Wisconsin in 1852. After maintaining his freedom for two years, he was captured in his Racine home by Garland and two federal marshals pursuant to a warrant of arrest. Injured in the scuffle and manacled, he was taken to a Milwaukee jail. A huge crowd assembled outside the courthouse, heard an emotional harangue by the abolitionist editor Sherman Booth, and thereupon battered in the jailhouse door, freed Glover, and sent him off to Canada. Booth and John Rycraft were arrested on a federal warrant and charged with violation of the 1850 statute by aiding Glover to escape. They sought discharge on a writ of habeas corpus from the Wisconsin Supreme Court on the ground of the unconstitutionality of the 1850 statute and were so discharged, in an opinion that affirmed a state's right to intervene. Judge Abram Smith, who rendered the opinion, upheld virtually all the arguments made against the 1850 statute and found it unconstitutional, the first time it was so held by a state supreme court. His grounds were that Article IV conferred on Congress no power to legislate with respect to fugitives and that the 1850 law denied a right of jury trial and thus denied due process to the fugitive. The full state bench, upon reconvening, affirmed this judgment.

Meanwhile, Booth was rearrested and his application for a writ of habeas corpus was now denied by the state, holding it should defer to the court that now had obtained jurisdiction (namely, the federal district court). When convicted, however, both Booth and Rycraft obtained the writ they sought from the state court, which found the prisoners unlawfully detained and which reaffirmed the unconstitutionality of the 1850 law. Thus did the state judiciary in effect nullify federal court procedures and invoke sub silentio the twin doctrines of interposition and nullification and the constitutional ghosts of the 1798 Virginia and Kentucky Resolutions.

In an arresting assertion of federal power, with an inner coherence in striking contrast to the strained, poorly crafted decision in *Dred Scott*, Taney emphasized the Constitution's transferral to the general government of many powers formerly in state hands, making it supreme within its sphere of authority, in order to frustrate local interests and prejudices. To maintain its supremacy, the general government was clothed with judicial power equal to the other branches, "for if left to the courts of justice in the several states, conflicting decisions would unavoidably take place, and the local tribunals could hardly be expected to be always free from the local influences of which we have spoken." The Constitution had provided for such a tribunal, "where all federal questions should be decided, whether arising in state or federal courts." A state court had the right to inquire by habeas corpus into the legality of the detention of any person held in the state, but it had no power to order the release when the person was held under federal authority.

Judicial encounters with race took many forms. Sometimes, as we have observed already, it involved runaways and Northern personal-liberty laws. At times, it centered on free blacks rather than slaves. In Massachusetts, Justice Shaw had to decide the merits of a black challenge to public school segregation, on the ground that Articles I and VI of the 1780 state constitution declared "all men are born equal and free" and prohibited grants of "particular and exclusive privileges." Charles Sumner argued that segregation conflicted with principles of natural law, but Shaw, in *Roberts* v. *City of Boston* (1849), rejected his claims, saying that the city school board had the power to segregate by race. For Shaw, the rights for which plaintiff argued were relatively meaningless. They could be granted or denied by state legislators and could be done on the basis of such arbitrary categories as race.

Some Northern states enacted "sojourner" statutes, which permitted retention of slaves for limited periods of residency. Pennsylvania, Missouri, and New York were among them. Pennsylvania's law was inconsistently interpreted. Massachusetts did not have such a measure, but its antislavery forces sought a common-law decision that would free all bondsmen coming into the state. In *Commonwealth* v. *Aves* (1836), Shaw found no law existed that permitted a visiting slaveholder to retain his slaves as slaves. The *lex domicilii* of the slave—Louisiana law in this instance—did not apply to a six-year-old black girl named Med who had been brought into the state by her mistress on a brief visit. Med could not be compelled to a slave jurisdiction. The maxim *Volenti non fit injuria* applied: those bringing slaves into Massachusetts must accept the legal consequences.

This dictum was precedent for *Commonwealth* v. *Taylor* (1841) and for later cases decided by courts in other Northern states. Moreover, as sectional conflict intensified, states that had earlier sought to accommodate sister states to the South began to refuse to recognize the enslaved status of anyone within their borders—whether passing through with their master or fleeing slavery in violation of federal law. Thus, the Illinois Supreme Court, which had affirmed the right of slaveowners accompanied by their slaves to travel through the state without change in the status of these bondsmen in *Willard* v. *People* (1843), held in *Rodney* v. *Illinois Central Railroad* (1857) that the state could not recognize any property right over a slave in Illinois. Suit had been brought against the railroad by a Missouri resident who claimed that the defendant had allowed the plaintiff's slave to escape by using railroad facilities. But the court affirmed:

> The law of Missouri, under which the negro owes service to the plaintiff, being repugnant to our law and the policy of our institutions, neither by the law of nations or the comity of States, can affect the condition of the fugitive slave in this State, or, within our jurisdiction, give the owner any property in or control over him.

This position was reversed in Southern courts, with freedom being denied to slaves who might otherwise have been emancipated. Thus, in Kentucky the state court of appeals abruptly reversed its 1848 decision that a former slave who had lived in Ohio for two years was free and no reversion occurred upon his return to Kentucky (*Davis* v. *Tingle*, 1848). But a year later, that same tribunal in *Collins* v. *America* (1849) refused to free a slave who had spent some time in a free state with her master's consent—on the ground that "the laws and Courts of Ohio may determine the condition of the slave while in that State [but] they cannot, by their own force or power, determine what shall be his condition when he has gone beyond their territorial jurisdiction." In *Mitchell* v. *Wells* (1859) a Mississippi court denied the validity of a manumission that occurred in Ohio.

The High Court took the least controversial judicial route whenever possible, as in *Strader* v. *Graham* (1851), a case that should be considered against the background of the then recently ended Mexican War and the spread of slavery westward as well as into the free states. Dr. Christopher Graham, a Kentucky slaveholder, permitted several of his slaves to be trained as professional musicians by a freedman and to be taken by the latter into other states, specifically Ohio and Indiana, to work temporarily as musical performers. Having lived on free soil, they were discontent with their existence as slaves in Kentucky and fled to Ohio. Under Kentucky law, an abettor of a fugitive is liable to the owner for the slave's value, and so Graham filed a suit against Jacob Strader, the owner of the steamboat *Pike*, on which the slaves made their escape. Strader argued that the blacks were freedmen, having been sent to free jurisdictions with their master's consent. The Kentucky Court of Appeals, standing by precedents, granted that a slave taken into a free state by its owner, becoming a permanent resident there, was free. But the slaves in this instance were sojourners, taken into free states for temporary purposes of wage work, and hence were not free; Strader was thus liable under state law and the owner was entitled to damages from those contributing to the slaves' escape. The case took six years in getting to the High Court. The justices had to determine whether slaves, having visited Ohio, had become free men by virtue of that state's laws, as well as the Northwest Ordinance, or whether, upon returning to Kentucky, they resumed their status as bondsmen. In a unanimous decision rendered by Taney, the Court refused to take jurisdiction on the ground that the status of slaves was determined by Kentucky law and exclusively by state courts. No federal question was at stake.

Taney, however, could not resist entertaining dangerous questions. Uneasy over mounting abolitionist attacks on slavery and anticipating his fateful opinion in *Dred Scott*, he left safe grounds for the jurisdictional thicket in an effort to offer some definitive, patently obiter dicta to forever put at rest abolitionist legal argument. The blacks' status, he conceded, was "not before us." It was determined by Kentucky law, not by Ohio or United States statutes. Every state, he affirmed, "has an undoubted right to determine the status, or domestic and social condition, of the persons domiciled within its territory"—except when the state's powers were restrained by the Constitution. Missourians, then, were assured that they were under no legal compulsion to enforce the laws of an antislavery jurisdiction. The Court had no jurisdiction over them. Thus, Taney gives expression to the doctrine of judicial restraint and places the federal stamp of approval on the doctrine of reversion: both were affirmed when Taney pledged noninterference by the federal courts with state court decisions on the subject.

Taney did not cease and desist at this point. He also found that the Northwest Ordinance of 1787 was superseded by the Constitution, the latter giving all states equality, which implied that Congress could not place conditions on a territory seeking statehood. Justice McLean in concurrence clearly had reservations about Taney's opinion. The Constitution's provisions, he admitted, might be substituted for those of the Northwest Ordinance, since the state of Ohio had adopted the ordinance's antislavery provisions in its own constitution, but McLean would go no further: "Anything that is said in the opinion of the court, in relation to the ordinance beyond this, is not in the case, and is, consequently, extrajudicial." Clearly a struggle was developing in the federal courts and particularly in the Supreme Court. It would further divide the country, politicize and nationalize the slavery issue, and contribute to the coming of the Civil War.

Dred Scott was the capstone case. It plunged the Court into the vortex of the slavery controversy. Once again, it involved the status of a slave who lived on free soil and returned to a slave state. And once again it could have been disposed of without comment upon the great controversial issues. But it was pushed by the political ambitions of Justice McLean and by the collective egotism of men who believed they could settle the vast issue finally and for all time, and so the *Dred Scott* Court made what was the greatest single miscalculation in American judicial history (Frank).

The story is familiar. At the height of the Kansas crisis, President Buchanan, in his inaugural address, predicted that popular sovereignty in the territories was "a judicial question" that was about "to be speedily and finally settled." The case itself was decided two days later—and along the lines he had sought. Dred Scott himself had been a slave of Dr. John Emerson, an army surgeon and a Missouri resident, and had been purchased from Peter Blow in 1833. Emerson took his slave on a tour of duty—to Fort Armstrong in the free state of Illinois and to Fort Snelling in the Wisconsin Territory, which was free under the 1819 Missouri Compromise. In 1838, Emerson returned with Scott, who now had a wife and daughter, to Missouri. He died in 1843, willing the Scott family to his widow. With the help of his original masters, specifically Taylor Blow—whose benevolence was inspired by personal affection, not antislavery views—Scott sued for his freedom in state court, his counsel arguing that residence in a free state and territory made him free. He won his suit in 1848 in the Missouri Supreme Court. A retrial took place after a series of bitter and intricate legal maneuvers and again Scott was declared a free man. Mrs. Emerson's counsel then appealed to the Missouri Supreme Court, which overturned the lower court judgment by a 2–1 vote. In so doing, the state's highest tribunal struck down a long line of precedents, in finding that neither the Missouri Compromise nor Illinois law had an extraterritorial effect upon Missouri (*Scott* v. *Emerson*, 1852). "The courts of one State," declared the majority, "do not take judicial notice of the laws of other States." Nor has territorial law any "force in the States of the Union, they are local, and relate to the municipal affairs of the territory." Hence, comity was held to be a matter of judicial discretion, and the status of Scott, upon returning to Missouri, was determined by the slave law of that state.

The case then went on appeal to the federal district court in 1853, on the issue of diversity of citizenship. Scott's lawyer argued his client was a citizen of Missouri suing John Sandford, a citizen of New York and the brother of Mrs. Emerson, to whom she had entrusted her husband's estate. Sandford pleaded to the jurisdiction of the Court—the celebrated plea of abatement—that since Scott was "a negro of African descent," he was not a citizen of the United States and thus incapable of suing in the federal courts. Counsel for Scott brought an action of trespass against Sandford and argued, conversely, that the fact of black blood and African descent did not deny citizenship. The circuit court agreed: This elderly black man was a citizen and thus able to bring suit in federal court. Its justices followed the *Strader* v. *Graham* precedent, however, in finding that the Scotts were slaves in Missouri, notwithstanding residence on free soil.

On appeal to the High Court, the case was first argued in February 1856, with the common impression that it would be decided against Scott on the authority of *Strader*. Scott's fate would be determined by Missouri law and would not touch on any other issue. In sum, the February conference decided that Nelson, who would simply uphold the circuit court decision, had prevailed, and he wrote a relatively innocuous short opinion of about five thousand words. It found Scott's status settled by Missouri law, as the highest state court had ruled in *Scott* v. *Emerson*. But, Grier recounted, the majority learned that two justices (surely he meant McLean and Curtis) intended to discuss the broader issues, opening up the whole Missouri Compromise question by declaring in favor of its validity. At this point, possibly owing to the impending McLean dissent or possibly for other reasons—since the background against which the justices deliberated tended to push them toward the broader constitutional questions—Wayne strongly urged that all the issues be dealt with, thereby disposing of the slavery controversy once and for all. The public, he said, had been led to expect it, and the Court would be derelict in its duty if it failed to take on the big questions. Thus, four days after deciding to stand on relatively noncontroversial grounds, the Court majority decided to enter the legal thicket. And, it should be emphasized, the Kansas-Nebraska Act (1854) had already explicitly repealed the Missouri Compromise, and so the decision could have been easily made—according to Missouri law.

The eighty-year-old chief justice, having originally assigned the opinion to Nelson, now, on Wayne's motion, took it on himself to render the majority opinion. Majority opinion it barely proved to be. Nine separate opinions—two in dissent—ran to 274 pages, with those justices who sought an emphatically pro-Southern decision prevailing. Seven colleagues concurred in the final result: Dred Scott was still a slave; six held the Missouri Compromise invalid; and only five accepted Taney's reasoning that it was actually unconstitutional. But these five did constitute a majority.

"The nature of citizenship, state and national, and whether it included free blacks," Fehrenbacher has concluded, "remained unsettled issues" at this time. Because at least "some free Negroes" were recognized as citizens in their own states and thus entitled to the privileges and immunities clause, it would be "reasonable to think" them citizens—with access to federal courts under the diversity-of-citizenship clauses. No federal or high state court had as yet expressly endorsed this view and Southern courts, of course, were always hostile to any connective between "Negro" and "citizen." Moreover, United States citizenship was generally considered as deriving from state citizenship.

The urgent question before Taney clearly involved Scott's citizenship, for if he were not a citizen, then the Court would lack jurisdiction. The first part of Taney's two-hour opinion, much like Daniel's, was a historical survey designed to prove that blacks were looked upon as inferior beings at the time that the Constitution was adopted. They were "regarded as beings of an inferior order; and altogether unfit to associate with the white race . . . and so far inferior, that they had no rights which the white man was bound to respect." They had not been included within the meaning of the Declaration of Independence. Nor did they have any standing under the Constitution, for they were not citizens of any state and hence not citizens of the United States. Because the Constitution was adopted at a time when no state had black citizens, the document intended to apply to whites only. In effect, Scott was not a citizen and could not bring suit, and here the case should have ended. But Taney decided upon an obiter dictum that denied Congress had constitutional authority to prohibit slavery in the territories, as it had attempted to

do in the Missouri Compromise, which, it followed, was unconstitutional. Slaves, Taney argued, were property, and Congress had no authority to deprive any person of his property, in whatever form, within the national domain. Hence, slaves, being property, could not be excluded from the territory. Further, the rights of property were protected against congressional intrusion by the due process clause of the Fifth Amendment. If Congress could not prohibit slavery in the territories, it followed that a territorial legislature, a creature of Congress, lacked the power to do so. In effect, the entire national domain was thrown open to slavery.

Taney maintained a mask of judicial propriety, but he had become over the years an angry critic of "Northern insult and Northern aggression." Now, in this polemical opinion, he defined the power to govern the territories in terms close to Southern hearts. Until a territory was admitted, Congress acted as the agent of the several states: "It was its duty to pass such laws and establish such a Government as would enable those by whose authority they acted to reap the advantages anticipated from its acquisition." This was a trustee concept, running back to 1798 and the Virginia and Kentucky Resolutions. Congress acted as trustee for the states. Its powers in the territory were those of a caretaker. The federal government, to be sure, had to preserve order and protect property. Taney insisted that it was obliged to do so in such a way as not to infringe on any property rights; and the holding of slaves was a state-protected property right.

Two justices rejected the majority conclusion that Scott was still a slave. McLean and Curtis upheld Scott's freedom as a citizen and his freedom under the Missouri Compromise. Having history on his side, Curtis ably refused Taney's contention that the Constitution was made for white men, and he noted that blacks were citizens at the time of its adoption and even had the right to vote. Both he and McLean argued that blacks had been citizens in 1787 and thereafter, denying Taney's holding that Congress had no right to prohibit slavery in the territory; that the Missouri Compromise had been constitutional until repealed in 1854; and that residence on free soil made Scott free.

The very diversity of opinions helped to cast disrepute on the decision and on the Court. It resulted in the downward plunge in Court prestige, perhaps the most lamentable result of the entire litigation.

Dred Scott and *Ableman* v. *Booth;* the galvanizing struggles in Kansas; successive political crises, concluding with the Democratic National Convention of 1860 in Charleston; the momentous presidential campaign; and Abraham Lincoln's election brought the nation to the brink of bloody civil war. With the conflict itself, the old struggle between the chaos of war and the rule of law began again, with innovative legal procedures, challenging constitutional issues, and a great debate. Congress and the chief executive were caught up in unique legal experiences. Both recognized that the Union was in danger and that its salvation demanded such measures as were taken. They were also uneasily aware that these measures often subverted the fundamental democratic propositions that held the government within the law at all times. Lincoln relied upon constitutional clauses anent the commander in chief, martial law, and the war powers; he proclaimed blockades of Southern ports, made unauthorized appropriations, called for volunteers to fill army ranks, mustered states' militias into federal service, and directed the army and the State Department to make "political arrests" of allegedly disloyal civilians under terms of executive proclamations suspending the writ of habeas corpus or instituting martial law in a region. Under the war power, he proclaimed martial law, placed persons under arrest without warrant and without a judicial showing of the cause of detention, seized the property of citizens, spent Treasury funds without congressional approval, called for conscription without waiting upon Congress, suppressed newspapers, and emancipated the slaves of those in arms against the Union. And understandably, all of these measures prompted widespread national reactions, pro and con.

The federal courts were depleted by hostilities, with judges leaving their posts owing to Southern loyalties. The High Court itself became enfeebled owing to frequent illness of Catron, Grier, Wayne, and Taney. Institutional continuity was disrupted by deaths, resignations, and the creation of a new judicial circuit, all of which added six new justices to the Court between 1857 and 1864. Lincoln made four appointments, all Unionists—Noah H. Swayne, David Davis, Samuel Miller, and Stephen J. Field

—to replace those who retired or died. Incumbents and recent appointees alike watched with concern executive wartime measures—naval blockades, militia calls, army increases, and so on —and heard the frequent appeal from law to necessity.

The conflict itself was of a dual character, which produced endless debate in and out of Congress and the courts: in theory, it was an insurrection, as the administration steadfastly proclaimed, but in conduct the Confederate forces were treated as those of a belligerent government. Witness, for instance, Lincoln's two proclamations of April 1861 establishing a blockade of Southern ports, which bears scrutiny because it introduced the High Court into the controversy over the nature of the conflict. In international law, blockade implicitly recognizes belligerent status. It is an act of war and potentially involved the use of naval force against neutral shipping; and yet the administration never admitted that the Southern ports were anything other than United States ports.

Cases emerging from the executive proclamations quickly came into federal courts. The Circuit Court for the District of Columbia held that the president had authority to determine whether the insurrection had culminated in a civil war. He had so determined, and finding no difference between a foreign and civil war, the circuit court upheld the administration. In a Philadelphia case (*The Parkhill,* 1861), the government won another decision, as it did in Baltimore and in New York. In February 1863, argument began in the Supreme Court on a number of prize cases, after the lower federal courts sustained the government and held that a blockade was a legitimate means for conducting both civil and foreign wars. At issue was the administration's right to institute this blockade of ports held by those in armed rebellion against the United States. By a 5–4 vote the Court agreed. On 10 March 1863 it found that the conflict was both a war and an insurrection; it thus let the administration, as Lincoln desired, have it both ways. The definition was left to the "political department" of government—that is, to Congress and the executive. They could determine what powers the nation employed, and their decision would be binding. Justice Grier for the majority declared that it was a civil war, even though one side called the conflict an insurrection: "The proclamation of blockade is, itself, official and conclusive evidence to the court that a state of war existed which demanded and authorized a recourse to such a measure, under the circumstances peculiar to the case."

The sympathies of many Marylanders for the Confederate cause made the Northern military position hazardous. Union troops en route from Philadelphia to the capital were in constant jeopardy. Acting with his usual circumspection, reluctance, and common sense, the president issued an order in April 1861 that did not suspend the writ of habeas corpus but left it to the discretion of the officer in charge to do so if necessity arose. The directive to General Winfield Scott stated that should action between Philadelphia and Washington occur that would "arm the people against the United States," he was to adopt "the most prompt and efficient means to counteract [it], even . . . to the extremest necessity, the suspension of the writ of habeas corpus."

By this directive, Lincoln opened up the question of whether the president or Congress had the right to take such action. The need to suspend the writ when public safety required it was one thing; but who was to judge of this need? Who was to judge of the existence of rebellion or invasion? The natural tendency was for the president to so decide. In Lincoln's view, the need was great, and moreover, the Constitution did not specify what branch of government was to exercise the suspending power. Many congressmen believed the legislature had exclusive power. And Taney, in *Ex parte Merryman* (1861), was the most vigorous exponent of this view.

Troops charged with the protection of railway track between Baltimore and Harrisburg entered the home of John Merryman, a prominent local politician, farmer, and officer in a secessionist drill company. They arrested him for participation in a destructive raid on railroad bridges and confined him in Fort McHenry, in the Maryland Department of the Army, commanded by General George Cadwallader. Merryman's counsel petitioned to the circuit court for a writ of habeas corpus; and Taney, sitting in circuit, signed the application. General Cadwallader replied that he was "duly authorized by the President of the United States . . . to suspend the writ . . . for the public safety. This is a high and delicate trust, and it has been enjoined upon him that it should be executed with judgment and discretion" and "errors, if any, should be on the side of safety to

the country." Taney refused to engage in a public debate with Cadwallader and simply rebuked him. Upon returning to the Supreme Court, he affirmed that "the President, under the Constitution and laws of the United States, cannot suspend the privilege of the writ of habeas corpus, nor authorize any military officer to do so." Suspension is associated with congressional action and must be within the power of Congress and Congress alone.

Taney tried to keep the Court on a collision course with the executive or the legislative departments, but his judicial brethren resisted these efforts. Consequently, the chief justice was limited to negative opinions on relatively minor administration actions, such as Treasury Department licensing of trade south of the Potomac, which he found destructive of federalism and the separation of powers. Only in *Ex parte Vallandigham* (1864) was the Court given an opportunity to render an opinion on the constitutionality of military rule in an area where civil courts were open, but it backed off on jurisdictional grounds. Other landmark Court decisions emerging out of the Civil War, such as the two test-oath cases, *Cummings* v. *Missouri* (1866) and *Ex parte Garland* (1866), and *Ex parte Milligan* (1866), occurred after Taney died.

Scholars have not been as kind to the Taney Court as to that of his great predecessor. Understandably so. Marshall's contributions will permanently overshadow Taney's. But Frankfurter justly places him second to the old chief justice in the nation's judicial history. In an era of swiftly expanding commercial capitalism, Taney's Court was sensitive to, and encouraged, growth. In an era of jealously guarded state sovereignty, the Court lessened its supervisory power over municipal law. It also strengthened the principle of judicial restraint, *Dred Scott* notwithstanding; laid down the basic distinctions between justiciable and nonjusticiable controversies; and displayed a greater faith in state legislative processes than did Marshall. Indeed, it satisfied all but extreme advocates of states' rights and sat secure in the scheme of government until *Dred Scott* and the Civil War.

The Taney Court stood for local responsibility as well as suspicion of power, whether from the national government or, befitting Jacksonian democracy, monopoly interests in alliance with government. It walked the narrow but distinct line between hostility to special privilege and encouragement to entrepreneurial interests. It offered a restricted interpretation of the doctrine of implied powers, thereby giving a large degree of autonomy to the states—to regulate the new economic forces in the public interest. Assuredly, it elevated the police power, via the "public welfare" criterion, to the status of a judicially enforceable restriction on the rights of individual property owners. Notwithstanding the twin doctrines of police power and eminent domain, however, vested rights remained secure, for by interpreting the police power, public welfare, eminent domain, and the tax power as it did, the Court intervened in the economy to fashion a legal environment favorable to the growth of enterprise. Its desire, Corwin (1936) shrewdly observed, was to clothe the states "so far as a faithful adherence to precedence would allow, with the sovereign and complete right to enact useful legislation for their respective populations."

The Taney Court also had a narrow view of the scope of the federal commerce power, especially when the chief justice's views and those of the Southern states coincided. To be sure, litigation surrounding the commerce clause failed to produce a solid majority bloc for any particular reading of the commerce clause but judicial dicta emerged, Corwin (1936) finds, that treated some of the reserved state powers "as exclusive in nature and hence as capable of setting an independent limitation to the delegated powers of the United States."

Nor can the chief justice be charged with completely reversing the Marshall Court's broad construction of the contract clause. Taney offset broad construction by strictly construing corporate charters, but there is no evidence that his tribunal "was reckless of property rights, as the Whigs had feared." The Taney Court was both conservative and forward-looking. It simply would not often expand the contract clause as to further limit state powers. In sum, while respectful of stare decisis and aware of its fiduciary obligations to the past, the Court gave new substantive life to its legal inheritance.

CASES

Ableman v. Booth, 21 Howard 506 (1859)

Allen v. McKeen, 1 Fed. 489 (1833)

Almy v. California, 24 Howard 169 (1860)

American Colonization Society v. Gartrell, 23 Georgia 448 (1857)

Armstrong v. Athens County, 16 Peters 281 (1842)

Bank of Augusta v. Earle, 13 Peters 519 (1839)

Bank of Commerce v. City of New York, 2 Black 620 (1863)

Bridge Proprietors v. Hoboken Co., 1 Wallace 116 (1864)

Briscoe v. Bank of the Commonwealth of Kentucky, 11 Peters 257 (1837)

Bronson v. Kinzie, 1 Howard 311 (1843)

Brown v. Maryland, 12 Wheaton 419 (1827)

Carey v. Daniels, 49 Mass. (8 Met.) 466 (1844)

Carpenter v. Providence Washington Insurance Co., 16 Peters 495 (1842)

Charles River Bridge Co. v. Warren Bridge Co., 11 Peters 547 (1837)

City of New York v. Miln, 11 Peters 102 (1837)

Collins v. America, 48 Ky. 565 (1849)

Commonwealth v. Aves, 18 Pick. 193 (1836)

Commonwealth v. Hunt, 4 Met. 111 (1842)

Commonwealth v. Taylor, 44 Mass. (3 Met.) 72 (1841)

Cooley v. Board of Wardens of the Port of Philadelphia, 12 Howard 299 (1852)

Craig v. Missouri, 4 Peters 410 (1830)

Cummings v. Missouri, 4 Wallace 277 (1866)

Davis v. Tingle, 47 Ky. 539 (1848)

Dartmouth College v. Woodward, 4 Wheaton 518 (1819)

Dobbins v. Erie County, 16 Peters 435 (1842)

Dodge v. Woolsey, 18 Howard 331 (1855)

Dred Scott v. Sandford, 19 Howard 393 (1857)

Ex parte Garland, 4 Wallace 333 (1866)

Gibbons v. Ogden, 9 Wheaton 1 (1824)

Glover v. Powell, 2 Stockton 211 N.Y. Chanc. (1854)

Groves v. Slaughter, 15 Peters 449 (1841)

Hazen v. Essex, 12 Cushing 475 Mass. (1851)

Holmes v. Jennison, 14 Peters 540 (1840)

Hudson & Delaware Canal v. Railroad, 9 Paige 323 N.Y. Chanc. (1841)

Jackson v. Lampshire, 3 Peters 280 (1830)

Jones v. Van Zandt, 5 Howard 215 (1847)

Louisville Railroad v. Letson, 2 Howard 497 (1844)

Luther v. Borden, 7 Howard 1 (1849)

McCracken v. Hayward, 2 Howard 608 (1844)

Martin v. Waddell's Lessee, 16 Peters 367 (1842)

Ex parte Merryman, 17 F. Cas. 144 (1861) (No. 9487)

Mills v. County of St. Clair, 8 Howard 569 (1850)

Miller v. McQuerry, 17 F. Cas. 335 (1853) (No. 9583)

Ex parte Milligan, 4 Wallace 2 (1866)

Mitchell v. Wells, 37 Miss. 235 (1859)

Moorehead v. Little Miami Railroad, 17 Ohio 340 (1848)

In re Mt. Washington Road Co., 35 N.H. 134 (1857)

New Jersey v. Wilson, 7 Cranch 164 (1812)

New Orleans and Carrollton Railroad v. Earle, 13 Peters 519 (1839)

Norris v. City of Boston, 4 Met. 282 (1842)

Ohio Life Insurance and Trust v. Debolt, 16 Howard 415 (1854)

The Parkhill, 18 F. Cas. 1187 (1861) (No. 10755a)

Pennsylvania v. Wheeling and Belmont Bridge Co., 9 Howard 647 (1851)

Pierce v. New Hampshire, 5 Howard 504 (1847)

Piqua Branch of the State Bank of Ohio v. Knoop, 16 Howard 369 (1853)

Planters' Bank v. Sharp, 6 Howard 344 (1848)

Prigg v. Commonwealth of Pennsylvania, 16 Peters 539 (1842)

Propeller Genessee Chief v. Fitzhugh, 12 Howard 443 (1851)

Providence Bank v. Billings, 4 Peters 514 (1830)

Raleigh and Gaston Railroad v. Davis, 2 Dev. & Batt. 451 N.C. (1837)

Richmond, Fredericksburg & Potomac Railroad v. Louisa Railroad, 13 Howard 71 (1851)

Riley v. Anderson, C.C.D. Ohio (1841)

Roberts v. City of Boston, 5 Cushing 59 Mass. 198 (1849)

Rodney v. Illinois Central Railroad, 19 Ill. 42 (1857)

Rogers v. Bradshaw, 20 Johns. R. 735 N.Y. Ct. Err. (1823)

Rowan v. Runnels, 5 Howard 134 (1847)

Rubottom v. McClure, 4 Blackford 505, 507 Ind. (1838)

Scott v. Emerson, 15 Mo. 577 (1852)

Scudder v. Trenton Delaware Falls Co., 1 N.J. Eq. 694 (1832)

Searight v. Stockton, 3 Howard 151 (1845)

In re Sims, 7 Cushing 285 (1851)

Sinnickson v. Johnsons, 2 Harr. 129 N.J. (1839)

Smith v. Maryland, 18 Howard 71 (1855)

Smith v. Turner, 7 Howard 283 (1849)

Stourbridge Canal v. Wheely, 2 Barn. Adol. 793 (1831)

Strader v. Graham, 10 Howard 82 (1851)

Swift v. Tyson, 16 Peters 1 (1842)

The Thomas Jefferson, 10 Wheaton 428 (1825)

Thurlow v. Massachusetts, 5 Howard 504 (1847)

United States v. Arredondo, 2 Peters 738 (1829)

United States v. Coombs, 12 Peters 72 (1838)

United States v. Primrose, 13 Peters 519 (1839)

United States v. The Schooner Amistad, 15 Peters 518 (1841)

United States v. The Ship Garonne, 11 Peters 73 (1837)

Ex parte Vallandigham, 1 Wallace 243 (1864)

Veazie v. Moore, 14 Howard 568 (1852)

Vidal v. Girard's Executors, 2 Howard 127 (1844)

West River Bridge Co. v. Dix, 6 Howard 507 (1848)

Willard v. People, 5 Ill. 4 Scamm. 461 (1843)

BIBLIOGRAPHY

John Quincy Adams, *Argument of John Quincy Adams Before the Supreme Court of the United States, in the Case of the U.S. v. Cinque and Others, Africans Captured in the Schooner Amistad* (1841), expresses his passionate belief that the Amistad blacks had been illegally enslaved and were freemen, and includes an attack on the administration, especially Van Buren and Secretary of State John Forsyth. Roy P. Basler, ed., *Collected Works of Abraham Lincoln,* vol. 4 (1953), cites Lincoln's views on the Vallandigham case.

Maurice Baxter, *Daniel Webster and the Supreme Court* (1966), meticulously describes Webster's arguments before the Taney Court, his advocacy of corporate rights and, especially illuminating, his arguments in various commerce clause cases. Stuart Bruchey, *The Roots of American Economic Growth, 1607–1861* (1965), offers a useful survey of American economic history down to the Civil War. Joseph Burke, "What Did the Prigg Decision Really Decide?" in *Pennsylvania Magazine of History and Biography,* 93 (1969), is an indispensable account of the Prigg case, and of the legal issues involved in the extradition of fugitive slaves.

Salmon P. Chase, *Reclamation of Fugitives from Service. An Argument for the Defendant, Submitted to the Supreme Court of the United States . . . in the Case of Jones v. Van Zandt* (1847), in a 108-page legal brief sets forth the Constitution argument with respect to the Abolitionist position. Thomas Cochran, *Business in American Life* (1972), surveys commercial conditions and commercial law at midcentury and the manner in which entrepreneurial interests were served. *Columbia Law Review* (1971), "American Slavery and the Conflict of Laws," contributes to slavery law, especially manumission and free-state residence legal dicta.

Moncure D. Conway, *Autobiography . . . of Moncure Daniel Conway with Two Portraits* (1904), discusses some important slavery cases and the impact of the Fugitive Slave Act. Edward S. Corwin, *The Commerce Power Versus States Rights* (1936), remains the classic account of the Court's interpretation of the commerce power in the Taney Court and Congress' discretionary power in this area, and "The Doctrine of Due Process Before the Civil War," in *Harvard Law Review,* 24 (1911), is especially useful for its study of the first use of substantive due process by the Supreme Court.

Robert Cover, *Justice Accused: Antislavery and the Judicial Process* (1974), describes the dilemma of antislavery judges and the conflict between law and morality, with Lemuel Shaw as paradigmatic. Gerald T. Dunne, *Justice Joseph Story and the Rise of the Supreme Court* (1970), is most helpful for some of the great Taney Court cases, Story's pervasive nationalism, his defense of the jurisdiction of the Court in interstate commerce litigation, and it offers an instructive corrective on the Taney-Story relationship.

Don Fehrenbacher, *The Dred Scott Case* (1978), is the definitive account of the Dred Scott decision and related judicial cases. John P. Frank, *Justice Daniel Dissenting: A Biography of Justice Peter V. Daniel, 1784–1860* (1964), offers important insights into Daniel's thinking on the regulation of business and slavery, and the nation-state relationship, especially in regard to bankruptcy and commerce law. Felix Frankfurter, *The Commerce Clause Under Marshall, Taney and Waite* (1937), is a thoughtful and succinct discussion of the Taney Court, its response to emergent economic forces and its view of the commerce power.

Tony A. Freyer, *Forums of Order: The Federal Courts and Business in American History* (1979), is a valuable account of the High Court's role in economic development across the nineteenth century, and *Harmony and Dissonance: The Swift and Erie Cases in American Federalism* (1981), is the definitive study of Swift, and includes a suggestive discussion of the larger question of the interaction of bench, bar, and business. J. A. C. Grant, "The 'Higher Law' Background of the Law of Eminent Domain," in *Wisconsin Law Review,* 6 (1930–1931), discusses the origins of the law of eminent domain.

Charles G. Haines and Foster H. Sherwood, *The Role of the Supreme Court in American Government and Politics, 1835–1864* (1944–1957), is an authoritative account of High Court opinions and judicial trends. Morton Horowitz, *The Transformation of American Law, 1780–1860* (1977), is a seminal study of the evolution of the common law, the transformation of concepts of property and property law, the relation of the bench to emergent commercial interests, and the judicial trend toward a utilitarian view of property usage.

James Williard Hurst, *Law and the Condition of Freedom in the Nineteenth-Century United States* (1956), is a pioneering work in antebellum legal history, with its "release of energy" theme —creative economic energy—an influential contribution to our understanding of the law in conjunction with new economic forces. Harold Hyman and William Wiecek, *Equal Justice Under Law* (1982), examine the nation's constitutional and legal history from 1835 to 1875, including judicial nationalism and constitutional problems under Lincoln. Stanley Kutler, *Privilege and Creative Destruction: The Charles River Bridge Case* (1971), is a reflective, admirably detailed monograph on the Charles River Bridge case and related cases, set against the economic and historical background.

"J. Catron [letter] to James M. Carlisle, Feb. 26, 1863," in *Legal Historian*, 1 (1958), has suggestive comments on the executive power and Lincoln's Blockade Proclamation. Leonard Levy, *The Law of the Commonwealth and Chief Justice Shaw* (1957), discusses Shaw's contribution to the police power, slavery and railroad law, interstate commerce, and contract case law in the Massachusetts Supreme Judicial Court. Leo Marx, *The Machine in the Garden: Technology and the Pastoral Ideal in America* (1964), offers an illuminating discussion of Webster, his views on the railroad and progress in the 1840s.

Robert G. McCloskey, *The American Supreme Court* (1960), (especially in chapter four on the Taney Court) comments on the due process clause. Thomas D. Morris, *Free Men All: The Personal Liberty Laws of the North, 1780–1861* (1974), is the basic text on the personal liberty laws of the five Northern states, the constitutional confrontation such statutes prompted, and how they contributed to the antislavery cause. A. E. Keir Nash, "Reason of Slavery: Understanding the Judicial Role in the Peculiar Institution," in *Vanderbilt Law Review*, 32 (1979), is a valuable account of slavery litigation and the judicial interpretation of slave law.

William Nelson, *Americanization of the Common Law* (1975), in a shrewd and illuminating analysis of the reception of English common law after 1780, discusses the evolution of public interest law, the legal conflict over competition versus monopoly, and law in the context of the changing social order. R. Kent Newmyer, "History Over Law: The Taney Court," in *Stanford Law Review*, 27 (1975), is a lucid account of certain aspects of the Taney Court; *The Supreme Court Under Marshall and Taney* (1968), offers important insights for the transitional years and the Taney Court case law; and *Supreme Court Justice Joseph Story* (1985) is a first-rate biography of the magisterial associate justice, one linking the man and the republic.

John G. Nicolay and John Hay, *Abraham Lincoln: A History*, vol. 4 (1890), describe Lincoln's reactions to the *Dred Scott* case. Lewis Orgel, *Valuation Under the Law of Eminent Domain* (1953), clarifies an important aspect of the state's legal right to expropriate property. Phillip Paludan, *A Covenant with Death: The Constitution, Law, and Equality in the Civil War Era* (1975), discusses the thought of five major legal thinkers, their legal-constitutional world, and how concern for social stability discouraged reforms in the slaves' status and the civil rights of freedmen. Eugene V. Rostow, *Planning for Freedom: The Public Law of American Capitalism* (1959), describes how economic activities shaped economic laws.

Harry Scheiber, "Federalism and the American Order," in *Law and Society*, 10 (1975), examines the evolution of the states' power of eminent domain in pre-Civil War America; *Ohio Canal Era: A Case Study of Government and the Economy, 1820–1861* (1969), traces the economic impact of the transportation revolution—new technology, the canal era, transportation investment—on antebellum America; "Property Law, Expropriation, and Resource Allocation by Government: The United States, 1789–1910," in *Journal of Economic History*, 33 (1973), examines the emerging theory and practice of property expropriation by state government; "The Road to *Munn*: Eminent Domain and the Concept of Public Purpose in the State Courts," in *Perspectives in American History*, 5 (1971), surveys eminent domain law, as well as riparian law and the growth of the state police power, including a thoughtful discussion of the reception of Hale's doctrine of *publici juris* in federal courts; and "The Transportation Revolution and American Law: Constitutionalism and Public Policy," in *Transportation and the Early Nation* (1982), discusses the qualitative changes in pre-Civil War transportation and the great legal issues attendant upon them: federalism, eminent domain, and federal jurisdiction.

William W. Story, ed., *Life and Letters of Joseph Story* (1851), describes the legal and personal values of Joseph Story. Carl B. Swisher, *The Taney Period, 1836–1864: History of the Supreme Court of the U.S.*, vol. 5 (1974), is the most detailed account of the cases and controversies of the Taney Court. Samuel Tyler, ed., *Memoir of Roger Brooke Taney* (1872), is the authorized biography of the chief justice, and while helpful, is obviously biased.

Charles Warren, *The Supreme Court in United States History* (1926), discusses the major Taney Court decisions, but is most useful for the exposition of public and private reactions to them and for the economic background materials. William Wiecek, *The Sources of Antislavery: Constitutionalism in America, 1760–1848* (1977), discusses the early legal-constitutional arguments of the Abolitionists in opposing slavery. Benjamin F. Wright, *The Contract Clause of the Constitution* (1938), examines the emergence and application of the contract clause and the major, as well as neglected, cases deriving from it in the Taney Court era.

[*See also* COMMERCE CLAUSE; FEDERALISM; MARSHALL COURT AND ERA; *and* RACIAL DISCRIMINATION AND EQUAL OPPORTUNITY.]

THE CHASE AND WAITE
COURTS AND ERAS

Jeffrey Brandon Morris

During the chief-justiceships of Salmon P. Chase and Morrison R. Waite, the United States Supreme Court repaired the damage to its prestige that had resulted from its *Dred Scott* decision of 1857, and continued a swift rise in influence and reputation vis-à-vis the other branches of the national government and the states. During Reconstruction the Court successfully sidestepped the dangers of tangling with Congress, while rendering civil liberties decisions of lasting importance. After 1871, an unusually able group of justices, confronted by the heaviest work load the Court had ever faced, functioned to general public satisfaction—a rare occurrence in the Court's history.

The most significant constitutional jurisprudence of the era resulted from encounters with the newly ratified Fourteenth Amendment. The Court, in general accord with its coequal branches and with public opinion, emasculated the protections accorded freed blacks by that amendment, choosing old principles of federalism and new nationalism over the ideals of Reconstruction. The Court did leave sufficient jurisprudence pointing in the other direction to enable the civil rights movement of the 1950s and 1960s to root its arguments in Waite Court decisions.

The Supreme Court lagged behind other American courts during the Chase and Waite eras in reading laissez-faire principles into the Constitution, giving to the due process clause substantive content and deriving a liberty of contract from the Constitution. The assertiveness of the Court during the Chase era (1864–1873) in wielding judicial review (except in 1868) would be widely emulated, where property rights were concerned, by state courts. During the period Waite was chief justice (1874–1888), the Supreme Court generally upheld laws made under the state police powers—the power to protect the health, safety, and welfare of the public. But it would be concessions to the rights of property, made in the reasoning in some of the very same opinions upholding regulation, that would be built upon after Waite's death to sharply constrict state and federal powers and to make the Supreme Court the virtual censor of laws regulating the economy.

THE CIVIL WAR

During the Civil War the Supreme Court had demonstrated little disposition to confront President Abraham Lincoln over issues bearing upon the constitutionality of how the war was being waged. The wartime Court did not interfere with newspaper censorship, the arrest and imprisonment of civilians, the draft, or the emancipation of the slaves. On the one major constitutional issue it did deal with—the legality of Lincoln's actions blockading southern ports—the president's actions were upheld by a narrow vote.

With the appointment of his former secretary of the treasury, Salmon P. Chase, to succeed Roger B. Taney on 6 December 1864, Lincoln had chosen half of the then ten-person Court and could anticipate support on challenges to the constitutionality of wartime actions. Although the war itself was almost over, such decisions would affect the constitutional environment of Reconstruction.

The first major decision involving the exercise of wartime powers to come before the Chase Court was *Ex parte Milligan* (1866), in which the Supreme Court effectively came to grips for the first time with Lincoln's policy of military trials of civilians outside war zones (that is, in regions where the civil courts were still in operation). Eighteen thousand civilians had suffered military arrests during the Civil War. The majority opinion in *Milligan* was at once an imperishable statement of the rule of law under the Constitution, an apparent threat to the basis of congressional Reconstruction, and an early manifestation of the activism that would characterize the Supreme Court and many other American courts in the late nineteenth century.

The case involved Lambdin P. Milligan, an officer of a pro-Confederate paramilitary secret society operating in Indiana, which, it was charged, had conspired to release forcibly Confederate prisoners and then to march into Kentucky and Missouri in conjunction with Confederate forces. Milligan was arrested in Indianapolis on 5 October 1864 and charged with conspiracy to overthrow the government, giving aid and comfort to the rebels, inciting insurrection, and violating the laws of war. Under the authority of Lincoln's suspension of habeas corpus and the 1863 Habeas Corpus Act, Milligan was tried by military commission and sentenced to be hanged. A petition for the writ of habeas corpus was filed in the United States circuit court in Indiana. There the two judges disagreed on the constitutional issue, and the case was certified to the Supreme Court.

The Supreme Court was unanimous in the *Milligan* case, insofar as it held that the president's establishment of military commissions was unconstitutional, as was the trial of civilians in zones remote from the war, where the civilian courts were open and their process unobstructed. Possibly because of the extreme claims of the government brief, the opinion for the Court written by Justice David Davis (who had been a close friend of Lincoln and his appointee to the Supreme Court) went beyond the narrow legal issue presented by the case. Davis stated that even if Congress had authorized the military commissions, those courts would have been unconstitutional, except where hostilities had effectively closed civilian courts. According to Davis, military power may govern by martial law only in the theater of actual military operations, only if there is foreign invasion or civil war, and only if the courts are actually closed and it is impossible to administer criminal justice according to law. Justice Davis gave expression to the ideals of

limited government under the Constitution, stating that "the Constitution of the United States is a law for rulers and people, equally in law and in peace, and covers with the shield of its protection all classes of men, at all times, and under all circumstances."

In *Texas* v. *White* (1869) the Supreme Court had to come to grips with the constitutional theories of secession and of Reconstruction. The case involved the Reconstruction government of Texas, which was suing to recover title to United States bonds. The sale of the bonds by the Confederate state government did not conform to certain restrictions upon alienation (transfer of title) imposed by an antebellum United States statute. To grant jurisdiction over the appeal, the Supreme Court had to clarify the status of Texas during and after the Civil War. Chief Justice Chase's opinion for the Court held that since the Union was indissoluble, secession had not destroyed the state of Texas or the obligations of Texans as United States citizens. The Confederate state government had been, in its relations with the United States, a mere illegal combination. But, because of the war, the rights of the state as a member of the Union and of its people as United States citizens had been suspended. The Court also held that laws made in the Confederate states which had not been made in furtherance of the rebellion—those related to the peace and good order of the community, such as ordinary business contracts—would be regarded as valid, while laws made in furtherance of the rebellion were invalid.

Regarding Reconstruction, the Court held that Congress had to assume the responsibility of reestablishing the states' relationship with the Union. Under Article IV of the United States Constitution, Congress was not to be limited to merely reviving the old order but could also take into account "the new conditions created by emancipation." However, the Court rejected the extreme "conquered province" theory of the Radicals. Echoing a theme that would sound throughout the jurisprudence of the Chase and Waite Courts, Chase posed a state-centered nationalism: "The preservation of the States and the maintenance of their governments, are as much within the design and care of the Constitution as the preservation of the Union and the maintenance of the National government."

The decisions in the *Legal Tender Cases* were a

less happy episode in the Supreme Court's history. The Legal Tender Acts of 1862 and 1863 created paper money that was declared by the government to be worth the same as hard currency (gold and silver dollars) even though it was not backed by gold but insured by the credit of the central government. These notes, known as greenbacks, were to be "lawful money and a legal tender in payment of all debts, public and private, within the United States." When greenbacks declined sharply in value because of wartime inflation, the groundwork for private litigation was laid. Questions were raised: Could a debt for a specified number of dollars be paid with an equal number of greenbacks? Could the creditor instead demand coin—or at least the amount in greenbacks equal to the gold value of the debt?

As secretary of the treasury, Chase had opposed the legal-tender bill at first, but with financial markets shaken, taxation inadequate, and loans unmarketable except at a discount, he gave in with reluctance. He viewed greenbacks as a temporary instrument for carrying on the war and expected that they would be redeemed in coin when the emergency was over. Chase had also proposed replacing the system of using state bank notes as the only currency in the country other than coin with a system of national banks whose notes would be serviced by reserves held in government bonds. Such a system had been authorized by an act of 25 February 1863. After Chase had left the Treasury, the federal government imposed a tax upon state bank notes in an attempt to eliminate this role for state banks. In *Veazie Bank* v. *Fenno* (1869), the Supreme Court, in an opinion by Chief Justice Chase, upheld that tax as a constitutional expression of Congress's power to provide a national currency. *Veazie Bank* would become the leading precedent for sustaining federal taxation as a means of regulating certain state and private activity.

The constitutionality of the Legal Tender Acts was a heavily litigated and politically divisive postwar issue. Depreciated greenbacks (one-third of the face value) became a matter of intense public interest inextricably entwined with every aspect of postwar finance—monetary policy, debt management, the tariff, interest rates, and price levels. *Hepburn* v. *Griswold* (1870) involved a note in which Susan and Henry Hepburn had promised to repay $11,250, a note

that came due before the enactment of the Legal Tender Acts. The Supreme Court, in conference, rejected Mrs. Hepburn's attempt to discharge the debt by payment of $11,250 in greenbacks, and voted to hold the laws unconstitutional as applied to debts contracted prior to passage of the act in 1862. Chase's opinion held that the Legal Tender Acts were violative of the obligations of contracts and of the "spirit of the Constitution" and that they deprived persons of property without due process of law. The Court held that to construe the acts as "an appropriate and plainly adapted means for carrying on war" would convert the federal government into a government of unlimited powers.

On the same day that the *Hepburn* decision was announced, President Ulysses S. Grant appointed William Strong and Joseph Bradley to the Court. When the second of the two justices to take his seat, Bradley, did so on 23 March 1870, Attorney General Ebenezer R. Hoar moved on 25 March that two cases pending for more than two years and dealing with the Legal Tender Acts be taken up. The Court agreed to do so by a vote of five to four, the *Hepburn* majority bitterly dissenting. The dispute between Chase, who contended that *Hepburn* was settled law, and the new majority, became bitter and public. At the end of the term, the Court ordered reargument in another case, *Knox* v. *Lee*.

On 1 May 1871 the Court decided *Knox* v. *Lee* and *Parker* v. *Davis*, sustaining the Legal Tender Acts as to both prior and subsequent debts. The opinions were not read until 15 January 1873. In *Knox* and *Parker* the Court, through Justice Strong, specifically overruled *Hepburn*, validating the acts, in the broadest possible manner, as a justifiable exercise of the national government's powers in time of emergency. The Court also suggested that even in the absence of an emergency, Congress had very wide discretion under the "necessary and proper" clause.

While the decisions in the *Legal Tender Cases* have been considered to be among the most serious wounds the Supreme Court has inflicted on itself, no lasting damage was done to the Court's rising prestige. In the short run, however, popular respect was shaken by the manner in which the Court handled the cases. The first decision had been made by a majority of the full court only by counting the vote of the enfeebled Justice Robert C. Grier, who may not have understood what he was voting on and who then left the Court. The decision was written by the same man (Chase) who had carried the burden of arguing for the propriety of the original law. Reopening the case was a serious error. Overruling the earlier decision with a new majority solely because of a change in the composition of the Court, with a division along party lines (except for Chase) accompanied by a public feud, compounded the damage.

Later, in *Juilliard* v. *Greenman* (1884), the Supreme Court ruled that Congress had the power to make treasury notes legal tender at any time, whether or not there was an emergency, under its constitutional power to borrow money on the credit of the United States, the "necessary and proper" clause, and the power to coin money. Justice Horace Gray would also rest his decision on broader grounds—the power "to make the notes of the tender of private debts [is] one of the powers belonging to sovereignty in other civilized nations."

POLITICAL ASPECTS OF RECONSTRUCTION

Three of the earliest surviving civil liberties decisions of the Supreme Court, handed down in the winter of 1866–1867, appeared to threaten the basis of congressional Reconstruction. In *Milligan*, Justice David Davis appeared to be reaching gratuitously beyond the principles necessary to decide the case by clearly implying that the army had no rightful role to play in the absence of war or insurrection. Milligan's conviction could simply have been invalidated by an opinion such as the one Chase had written, joined by three other justices, stating that establishment of martial law by the president without congressional action was unconstitutional, but indicating that Congress possessed constitutional powers to create military tribunals.

The result in *Milligan*, announced 3 April 1866, occasioned no great outcry. But by the time the opinions were released on 17 December 1866, a chasm had opened between President Andrew Johnson and the congressional Radicals. Johnson treated *Milligan* as an endorsement of his policies of prompt restoration of the Southern states to the Union on the basis of their acceptance of the abolition of slavery, and ordered

the dismissal of proceedings in military trials of civilians in the South. For their part, Radical orators, editors, and politicans savagely denounced the *Milligan* decision, as it appeared that, given the opportunity, the Court would strike down the military-trial provisions of both the Freedman's Bureau Act of 1865 and the Civil Rights Act of 1866 as well as like provisions in any future Reconstruction measures.

Immediately after *Milligan* had been argued in the Supreme Court in March 1866, the Court heard argument in two other cases that involved important aspects of Radical Reconstruction— laws disbarring and disfranchising ex-Confederates and their sympathizers. The results in these cases were announced in December 1866, and the opinions in *Ex parte Garland* and *Cummings* v. *Missouri* came down on 14 January 1867. The *Garland* case involved a rule of the United States Supreme Court itself (made pursuant to an act of Congress of 24 January 1865) that provided that no person should be allowed to practice in a federal court unless he had subscribed to an oath that he had never voluntarily borne arms against the United States or voluntarily given aid, counsel, or encouragement to persons in armed hostility. Augustus H. Garland, a member of the Confederate Congress who had been pardoned, moved for leave to practice in the Supreme Court, even though he was not able to take the oath.

In the *Cummings* case, Father John A. Cummings, a pro-Confederate Roman Catholic priest, had been indicted and convicted for violating a provision in the 1865 state constitution that required ministers, professors, attorneys, candidates for public office, and voters to swear that they had never engaged in rebellion against the United States, given aid to the rebels, or favored by act or word the Confederate cause.

By votes of 5–4, the Supreme Court, in opinions by Justice Stephen J. Field, held the oaths unconstitutional ex post facto laws and bills of attainder. Once again, the Court seemed to be challenging the Congress—this time, by asserting that even for those licensed after the laws in question had been passed, the laws might be unconstitutional. Justice Samuel F. Miller, writing for the four dissenting justices, maintained that the oaths were valid expressions of a government's right to protect itself by laying down certain qualifications for its officers and voters.

As the cleavage between Johnson and the Congress widened in 1867, the Court attempted to avoid being caught in the struggle. On 2 March 1867, Congress passed, over the president's veto, the first Reconstruction Act, which divided the South into five military districts subject to martial law. Restoration of states to the Union was made conditional upon new constitutional conventions, elected by universal male suffrage and obligated to establish state governments guaranteeing black suffrage and ratification of the Fourteenth Amendment. On 23 March, Congress passed a supplemental act that provided that upon failure to call constitutional conventions, military commanders would initiate constitutional conventions and the enrollment of voters.

On 12 April 1867, Mississippi invoked the original jurisdiction of the Supreme Court and sought an injunction restraining the president from enforcing the laws of 2 and 23 March. On 15 April the unanimous Court refused to grant the injunction. Writing for the Court, the chief justice drew a distinction between those ministerial acts performed by the president (acts under law in which he had no discretion) and those executive acts that involved political discretion. The Court held, in *Mississippi* v. *Johnson,* that it could not control the president in the performance of his political duties. While the attorney general had contended that the president was beyond legal process, the Court disclaimed decision on that ground.

When the state of Georgia, a few weeks later, invoked the original jurisdiction of the Court in an attempt to enjoin Secretary of War Edwin M. Stanton, General of the Army Grant, and a district commander from executing the two Reconstruction laws, the Court dismissed the suit. In an opinion by Justice Samuel Nelson, delivered on 10 February 1868, the Court held that the issue was a "political question" over which the Court had no jurisdiction; for the case to be appropriate for the exercise of judicial power, the rights in danger had to be rights of personal property, not political rights *(Georgia* v. *Stanton).*

When the Court received the case of William H. McCardle, it appeared ready to decide on the constitutionality of military Reconstruction. McCardle, the white racist editor of the *Vicksburg Times,* had written and published material strongly critical of Reconstruction. He was held for trial before a military commission, under au-

thority of the Reconstruction Acts, for disturbing the peace, inciting to insurrection, and libel. Contending that the military tribunal had no constitutional authority, McCardle sought habeas corpus in the circuit court. That court denied the writ and remanded him to military custody. McCardle then appealed to the Supreme Court under the jurisdiction of the Habeas Corpus Act of 1867. That law provided that all federal courts and judges could grant the writ of habeas corpus to any person restrained of liberty in violation of the Constitution or laws of the United States. The law provided for a specific appellate procedure: appeals were allowed from any inferior court to the circuit court and from the judgment of the circuit court to the Supreme Court. On 21 January 1868 the Supreme Court granted a motion to advance the *McCardle* case for a speedy hearing, and on 17 February the Court held that it had jurisdiction (*Ex parte McCardle* I).

Further developments in the potential crisis between Congress and the Court occurred during the constitutional crises between Congress and the president. On 24 February the House of Representatives voted to impeach President Johnson. The articles of impeachment were presented to the Senate on 4 March. The Supreme Court heard argument in the *McCardle* case on 2–4 March and, after a postponement when Chief Justice Chase was called to the impeachment proceedings, on 9 March. As legislation abrogating the relevant sections of the 1867 Habeas Corpus Act had passed both houses of the Congress on 12 March, the Court held back from announcing a decision of the *McCardle* case on the merits. On 27 March the bill, which repealed jurisdiction in the *McCardle* case, was enacted over the president's veto. On 30 March the president's trial actually began with opening statements, while in the Supreme Court, counsel asked for arguments in the *McCardle* case over the issue of Congress's power to take jurisdiction from the Court. As not all counsel were ready for argument, on 6 April the case was continued to the next term of the court, to begin in December.

On 12 April 1869, the unanimous Court, in an opinion written by Chase, held that the statute had deprived it of jurisdiction in the *McCardle* case (*Ex parte McCardle* II). The Court held that Congress had the power to make exceptions to the Court's appellate jurisdiction. The Court did not inquire into the motives of Congress.

Traditionally, the *McCardle* decision has been viewed as a confession of judicial impotence, as well as a precedent standing for Congress's power under Article III of the Constitution to prevent the Court from deciding certain cases or its power to punish or restrain the Court. Neither proposition may be true. In the last paragraph of the opinion in *McCardle* II, Chief Justice Chase broadly hinted that while the Court had been deprived of power under the 1867 Habeas Corpus Act, it might still retain appellate power in habeas corpus cases under earlier statutes.

Later that year, in *Ex parte Yerger*, in an appeal of the denial of habeas corpus by the circuit court to a man detained for trial by a military commission for killing an army officer, Chase, for a unanimous court, held that the Supreme Court had jurisdiction under the Judiciary Act of 1789 to hear an appeal in a habeas corpus case. *McCardle* apparently stood for the proposition that Congress could repeal the 1867 law, but the Court would not accept total denial of its power over habeas corpus, thus leaving citizens without remedy.

In *United States* v. *Klein* (1872), the Court dealt with a law depriving the Supreme Court of jurisdiction in those cases involving claims for land captured during the rebellion, where the Court of Claims had based its judgment in favor of the claimant, whose claim was dependent upon a presidential pardon. The Supreme Court held the statute unconstitutional, as an attempt to prescribe for the Court a rule for decision. Congress had therefore exceeded its power to regulate appellate jurisdiction and had passed the limit separating the legislative from the judicial branch. The *Klein* decision appears to stand for the principle that Congress must exercise its power to limit jurisdiction of the Supreme Court (or the other federal courts) in a manner consistent with the independence of the judiciary.

Recent scholarship has rejected the old view, taken by historians like Charles Warren, that the Court was at a low ebb during the Civil War and Reconstruction and, accordingly, that it was cowardly, political, and ineffectual. More recent historians, like Stanley Kutler and Harold Hyman, take a different view, arguing that the assault on the Court, which followed upon *Dred Scott*, largely ended in 1861, when the Republicans took over the White House and the presidency. Recent historians suggest that during the Civil War and Reconstruction, Congress respected judicial power and came to depend upon it for the protection and enforcement of particular legislation and for the fulfillment of other nationalistic impulses. The only real blow at the Court was the statute withdrawing jurisdiction in *McCardle*, and while the Court gave way there, it recouped in *Ex parte Yerger*.

Nonetheless, it is fair to say that a Court that included antebellum Democrats (James M. Wayne, Samuel Nelson, Nathan Clifford, and Robert C. Grier) and Lincoln appointees unsympathetic to important aspects of Reconstruction (Stephen J. Field, David Davis, and Salmon P. Chase), with a penchant for judicial activism in other areas, did run a risk during the Civil War and Reconstruction. That it escaped long-term harm is a tribute to its general prudence.

The resolution of controversies arising out of the war and the political aspects of Reconstruction from 1864 to 1871 was acceptable to almost all Americans. In addition, the members of the Court, in their roles as judges of the circuit courts, made separate contributions to sectional reconciliation and to stability in the South. Led by Chase, they refused to ride circuit in the South until all possibility of claims that judicial power was subordinate to military power was removed by actions of the political authorities. Even so, district judges were encouraged to convene the circuit courts. Those courts, whether manned by district judges, Supreme Court justices, or both, made a major contribution to stability by accepting as valid, years before the decision in *Texas* v. *White*, the nonwar business transactions (insurance policy coverages, indebtedness, estate conveyances) that had been carried out under the Confederate flag. By signaling the stability of constitutional forms and institutions during a time of great instability, the Court became popular in the South and reconciled that region to its defeat. In addition, Chase found technical reasons to delay (and then to make impossible) the treason trial of Jefferson Davis, a prosecution finally dropped in 1869, and assisted the growing desire of the nation to put the war behind it.

THE RIGHTS OF THE FREEDMAN

In its handling of cases involving the rights of the freedman, the Supreme Court mirrored the majority views in the nation. The Chase Court demonstrated solicitous concern, certainly until 1871. The Waite Court, however, withdrew support and, when Reconstruction was ended in 1877, came close to legitimizing the abandonment of the black American.

The Chase Court. Soon after passage of the 1866 Civil Rights Act, which bestowed citizenship on blacks and granted them the same civil rights as all those born in the United States (other than American Indians), lower federal court decisions by Chief Justice Chase and Justice Noah H. Swayne upheld its constitutionality. Chase, for example, released through habeas corpus a black child held as an apprentice under a Maryland law that treated black apprentices more harshly than whites (*In re Turner,* 1867).

The justices on circuit had interpreted the 1866 Civil Rights Act and the Thirteenth Amendment sympathetically. But the first pronouncement by the full Supreme Court interpreting the Fourteenth Amendment, which had been declared ratified on 28 July 1868, sharply constricted it as far as the freedman was concerned. The case, on the surface, had little to do with the freed black. Businessmen were seeking relief from legislation that, they contended, was passed as the result of corruption. At issue in the *Slaughterhouse Cases* (1873) was a monopoly established by the Republican legislature of Louisiana in 1869. In the guise of a health regulation to reform the unsanitary meat-slaughtering industry, the Crescent City Live-Stock Landing and Slaughter-House Company, owned largely by former Unionist Whigs, was incorporated and given total control of the landing and butchering of livestock in New Orleans. The law had been procured by bribery. Seeking to enjoin the operation of the law, the Butchers' Benevolent Association, consisting of four hundred butchers, invoked the Fourteenth Amendment.

The Supreme Court divided 5–4. The views of the dissenters will be discussed later, as they constitute an important part of the chronicle of the evolution of the Fourteenth Amendment as a protection of property rights. Here an understanding of Justice Samuel F. Miller's majority opinion, restrictively interpreting the amendment, is vital to understanding the manner in which the Court would interpret the Fourteenth Amendment where the rights of blacks were involved.

The first clause of the Fourteenth Amendment states, "No State shall make or enforce any law which shall abridge the privileges or immunities of citizens of the United States; nor shall any State deprive any person of life, liberty, or property, without due process of law; nor deny to any person within its jurisdiction the equal protection of the laws." Miller began by stating that the pervading purpose of the Reconstruction amendments had been to bring peace and security to the black freedmen—to free the slaves, to secure their freedom, and to protect them from white oppression. But then Miller interpreted away the privileges and immunities clause by holding that it protected only the rights of federal citizenship and that these rights were few in number. Such rights included only the right to come to the seat of the government to assert claims upon the government, the right to the protection of the federal government on the high seas or within the jurisdiction of foreign nations, and perhaps a few more. As a result, most civil rights remained under the protection of the states. All the clause had done, Miller asserted, was to codify the previous relationship between the national government and the states. Miller then dismissed with a few words contentions that the livestock monopoly violated the due process and equal protection clauses.

Miller's opinion flew in the face of the congressional debates over the amendment. It permanently devitalized the privileges and immunities clause and certainly failed to carry out the nationalist revolution in the constitutional system that at least the Radical framers of the amendment had intended. In the states, the *Slaughterhouse Cases* would be used as a precedent to uphold laws establishing segregated schools, limiting the practice of law to whites, and making it a crime for blacks and whites to intermarry.

The Waite Court. In cases involving the application of Reconstruction laws and the Reconstruction amendments, the Supreme Court would treat the relationship between the states and the central government much as it had before the Civil War, without slavery but with the other rights of the states intact. The Fourteenth Amendment was interpreted narrowly so as to avoid any substantial shift in the power relations within the federal system. These decisions presented monumental obstacles to the enforcement of black rights. Not all of this was the Court's doing, for many of the constitutional amendments, federal laws, and criminal indictments that it had to interpret would have profited from better draftsmanship. Still, the Court need not have exalted technicalities over the spirit of the Reconstruction amendments.

The first important decisions of the Waite Court involving the Reconstruction laws were handed down in 1876. *United States* v. *Cruikshank* arose out of the Colfax, Louisiana, massacre, a clash between armed whites and black militia during which seventy blacks had been killed in cold blood after they had surrendered. A hundred whites had been indicted under the Civil Rights Enforcement Act of 1870 for conspiracy to deprive blacks of their rights as citizens. Only nine were found, brought to trial, and convicted. In an opinion for all the justices but Clifford, Chief Justice Waite dismissed the indictments in a way that suggested the Court would not make enforcement of the Reconstruction laws come easily. According to the chief justice, federal rights had to be involved for the Fourteenth Amendment protections to apply, and under the *Slaughterhouse Cases*, there were not many of these. In *Cruikshank*, neither the right to peacefully assemble nor the right to bear arms was protected by the privileges and immunities clause. The Fourteenth Amendment had not itself added rights but only guaranteed existing rights against their denial by the states. Congress could, under the Thirteenth and Fifteenth Amendments, punish private discrimination, but racial discrimination had to be expressly averred in the indictments. Furthermore, racial motivation had to be proven as connected to the deprivation, and that would be difficult to accomplish.

United States v. *Reese* involved an indictment of a Kentucky election official under the 1870 Enforcement Act, which had made interference with voting rights a federal offense punishable in the federal courts. The defendant had refused to count a black man's vote. The Court struck down two sections of the law because they had not been expressly restricted to racially motivated offenses, and emphasized that the Fifteenth Amendment had not conferred the right to vote upon anyone but merely prohibited the federal and state governments from denying persons the franchise because of race. Justice Ward Hunt was alone in dissent.

The practical outcome of *Reese* and *Cruikshank* was to make federal law almost wholly ineffective to protect blacks. Already blacks were barred by violence from many ballot boxes in the South. Many of their votes went uncounted. Before 1876, convictions had occurred in only 20 percent of the cases attempting to enforce the voting rights of blacks. But at least in 1875 there had been two hundred prosecutions. By 1878 there were only twenty-five.

The Court was in step with the national mood. Within a year of *Reese* and *Cruikshank*, the settlement of the disputed election of 1876 led to the withdrawal of federal troops in the South, signaling the end of active federal intervention in civil rights. The "Compromise of 1877" would restore stability in the South and open the South to capitalism. *Cruikshank* and *Reese* arranged for one of the essential conditions of North-South reconciliation: the ending of meaningful political participation by blacks.

There were, however, Supreme Court decisions demonstrating sympathy with protection of black suffrage and hostility to systematic exclusion of blacks from juries. In *Ex parte Siebold* (1880) the Court upheld the constitutionality of the 1871 law requiring state election officials to enforce both state and federal laws when supervising elections at which both state and federal officers were chosen. In *Ex parte Yarbrough* (1884) the Court sustained the convictions of nine men for beating a black who voted in a congressional election. In effect, this meant that the Court had recognized voting in national elections as a federal right, which Congress might protect against both public and private abuse. In *Strauder* v. *West Virginia* (1880) the Court held that a state law excluding nonwhites from serving as jurors violated the equal protection clause. These cases would be resurrected during the civil rights movement of the 1950s and 1960s. In the short run, they were undercut by *Virginia* v. *Rives* (1880). In that case, a county judge had been indicted under the 1875 Civil Rights Act for deliberately excluding qualified blacks from juries because of their race. The Court held that the absence of blacks from a jury could not be taken to imply unlawful racial discrimination per se in the absence of a state law prohibiting blacks from serving on juries. Thus, by cautious use of discretionary authority, local officials could, as a practical matter, exclude blacks from juries.

Equally characteristic of the drift of the Court was its use of the commerce clause in 1878 to strike down a Louisiana law requiring public carriers operating in the state to provide all passengers regardless of race with equal facilities. This was, Chief Justice Waite wrote, an unconstitutional burden on commerce (*Hall* v. *De Cuir*, 1878). Soon the lower federal courts would be upholding laws mandating racial segregation in transportation. The Court would not hold antimiscegenation laws as violative of equal protection, even though they punished interracial sexual relations (married or unmarried) more harshly than sexual relations between partners of the same sex (*Pace* v. *Alabama*, 1883). The treatment of the Alabama law in *Pace* would foreshadow the decision in *Plessy* v. *Ferguson*, which would sanction American apartheid thirteen years later.

But the most important of all the Waite Court decisions affecting the freedman were those in the *Civil Rights Cases* (1883), involving the constitutionality of the public-accommodations provisions of the Civil Rights Act of 1875. That law had guaranteed equal rights in public places such as inns, restaurants, public conveyances, theaters, and other places of amusement, without distinction of color. From the moment of its passage, there had been widespread resistance to that law and, at best, desultory enforcement. Still, during the 1870s and early 1880s, integrated public facilities in both North and South had been increasing.

The decisions in the *Civil Rights Cases* sealed the triumph of American federalism over the freedman. Writing for eight members of the Court, Justice Joseph P. Bradley held that the Fourteenth Amendment was directed only against action by states, their political subdivisions, and their officers, agents, and instrumentalities. Congress had to wait to take corrective action until there was discriminatory state action. Furthermore, while the Thirteenth Amendment was not limited to state action, the "badges and incidents of slavery" and "involuntary servitude" were limited to such matters as compulsory work; restraint upon movements; and the right to hold property, to make contracts, to have standing in the courts, and to testify as a witness against a white person. Eighty years later, the *Civil Rights Cases* remained such an obstacle to passage of a public-accommodations law by the federal government under the Fourteenth Amendment that Title II of the Civil Rights Law

of 1964 was passed by the Congress under its commerce clause powers. In the *Civil Rights Cases,* Justice John Marshall Harlan would be alone in dissent, as he would be again in *Plessy* v. *Ferguson*.

If the Waite Court began the march away from Reconstruction, it should nonetheless not be judged in the same light as the Fuller Court, which handed down *Plessy* v. *Ferguson*. When Americans sought finally to fulfill promises of racial equality in the mid-twentieth century, they were not entirely limited to Harlan's great dissents but were able to find in the jurisprudence of the Waite era something to build upon. Not only had that Court taken a view that prevented later adoption of the position that nothing had been changed by the Reconstruction amendments other than the abolition of slavery, but also it had, in cases such as *Strauder* and *Ex parte Yarbrough*, sown moderately nationalist seeds. Nonetheless, it would be grimly ironic that the Supreme Court, which gave such a cramped reading of the amendment where the freedman was concerned, came to read it with amplitude where the rights of property were involved.

GOVERNMENT REGULATION OF THE ECONOMY

During the period under consideration, the United States Supreme Court and other American courts began to evolve a series of doctrines that would be employed to protect business from regulation by the state and federal governments and which asserted that the judiciary was the ultimate arbiter of the constitutionality of economic regulation. While few such cases would be decided by the Chase Court, that Court would strongly oppose municipal repudiation of bond obligations; launch in its dissenting opinions in the *Slaughterhouse Cases* substantive due process; and, by its assertiveness in the exercise of judicial review, set an example for later state and federal courts. On the whole, the Waite Court was sympathetic to the exercise of state police power and was restrained in its exercise of judicial power. It would, however, leave enough in its dicta so that within a few years the Supreme Court would be employing the due process clause without appearing to disrupt doctrinal continuity.

The Supreme Court during Waite's chief-justiceship held that corporations were "persons" and thus protected by the Fourteenth Amendment; sustained the new invention of the railroad receivership, which would be employed by lower federal court judges to protect railroads from strikes and regulation by the states; and left room in its dicta for the development by later courts of the doctrines of freedom of contract and economic liberty. On the other hand, it generally sustained, under the commerce clause, federal and state laws. State courts during these years would be far more sympathetic to the property rights contentions of business than the Supreme Court.

Legal developments during this period reflected the prevailing national preoccupation with rapid development that followed the Civil War and the growing acceptance of the philosophy of laissez-faire. Between 1870 and 1890 the population of the nation increased by two-thirds, and its character became more urban and industrial. The economy was transformed from agrarian to industrial, from handicraft to machine technology, from specialized to integrated industry, from small, local to large, national enterprises. Simple business organizations gave way to the modern corporation; individual ownership was replaced by wage-earning status.

Leading members of the bar accepted the philosophy of social Darwinism—that every man should have freedom to do all he wills, provided he does not infringe upon the equal freedom of any other man, and that the role of government was to administer this principle and to keep its hands off the economic system. The jurisprudential doctrines they advanced were, at first in the 1870s, strange and ill-supported by precedent. Cases were skillfully manipulated, and doctrines were spread through university law schools and newly created bar associations. While judges were at first reluctant to make radical departures, they kept their options open through their dicta. Ultimately, the doctrines were repeated often enough to become familiar and then immemorial. By often referring to the concurring and dissenting opinions of Field and Bradley, the state courts forged a climate to which the majority of the United States Supreme Court would capitulate soon after Waite's tenure ended.

The Chase Court. Perhaps the most lasting heritage of the Chase Court was the example it set through its vigorous assertions of judicial power.

From 1864 to 1873, the Supreme Court held unconstitutional ten federal and forty-six state laws, sometimes doing so even when it could not clearly cite the particular clause of the Constitution that was being violated. For example, in the *Hepburn* case, Chief Justice Chase relied upon the obligation of contracts clause to help void the federal law, even though that was but a prohibition upon the states; a federal law that violated the obligation of contracts would, said Chase, be inconsistent with the "letter and spirit of the Constitution."

Prior to the Civil War, the restraints upon the power of state governments to promote, regulate, prohibit, or otherwise control economic activity under their taxation, eminent domain, and police powers were contained in Article I, Section 10 of the Constitution (the contract clause) and in the restrictions upon the kind of taxes that could be levied. Because of the doctrine of strict construction of public grants and because of the general adoption of clauses in state constitutions and laws reserving to states the right to alter, amend, or modify charters, the contract clause had been of declining usefulness to the protection of property.

During the era of the Chase Court, the great treatise writers Thomas M. Cooley and John F. Dillon (the former a Michigan Supreme Court justice and dean of Michigan Law School, the latter the chief justice of Iowa and later a judge for the Eighth Circuit) supplied the bar with numerous constitutional principles on which to restrict the powers of legislative bodies and popularized within the profession those principles which encompassed laissez-faire policies desired by much of the emerging business class. Cooley, in particular (in his *Treatise on . . . Constitutional Limitations*), gave widespread currency to the New York Court of Appeals decision in *Wynehamer* v. *People* (1856) and thus rescued what would become the powerful doctrine of substantive due process from the constitutional cul-de-sac of *Dred Scott,* by identifying it with the older doctrine of vested rights, making this small constitutional phrase comprehend most of the other implied limitations upon interference with property rights.

During the Chase era, neither the United States Supreme Court nor the state judiciaries were particularly concerned with property rights when cast against state regulatory powers. Even extraordinary exercises of state police power were being upheld. In 1866 the New York Court of Appeals, for example, upheld the creation of a unified, nonpartisan Metropolitan Board of Health in New York City, with mixed executive, legislative, and judicial functions delegated by the state, which had the capacity to condemn property, issue summonses, fix penalties, compel testimony, and require cooperation from municipal workers *(Coe* v. *Schulz).* The struggle in state courts between proponents of legislative sovereignty and supporters of laissez-faire had barely begun, and not until the middle 1880s would there be decisive victories registered in favor of business.

One of the first doctrines employed after the Civil War to limit state power was that of "taxation for a public purpose." Within a very few years it would become a settled proposition that aid to private business enterprises (other than railroads) was not a public purpose for which the state legislatures could exercise their taxing and spending powers. Cooley's treatise and the opinions of both Cooley and Dillon were influential. In *People* v. *Salem* (1870) the Michigan Supreme Court struck down a state law that authorized townships to pledge their credit in aid of railroads. The limits upon the power of taxation, wrote Cooley, were inherent in the subject itself and "inflexible and absolute." As Iowa's chief justice in 1869, Dillon had written the opinion in *Hansom* v. *Vernon,* where he suggested that a tax for private purposes would deprive of property the persons taxed without due process of law. In *Loan Association* v. *Topeka* (1875) the Supreme Court affirmed a decision of Circuit Judge Dillon that a municipal bond issue authorized by the Kansas legislature to aid in the establishment of a privately owned bridge factory was unconstitutional.

Although the Supreme Court under Chase made no major change in its approach to interpreting the commerce clause, it did, for the first time, declare an act of Congress unconstitutional as violative of that clause, as well as ten state laws. In *United States* v. *De Witt* (1870) Congress had inserted into a revenue bill a provision making naptha adulteration of kerosene a federal misdemeanor. Writing for a unanimous Court, Chase said that Congress could not limit state police powers by labeling its laws revenue measures. The regulatory clause was too remote and

too uncertain to warrant Court sanction of the prohibition as an appropriate and plainly adopted means for carrying into execution the power of laying and collecting taxes. In *Crandall* v. *Nevada* (1868) the Court struck down a Nevada tax on each person leaving the state by railroad, coach, or vehicle for hire, as against the national rights of citizens.

But the Supreme Court would often uphold state laws under the commerce clause during Chase's chief-justiceship. In probably the most significant case, *Paul* v. *Virginia* (1869), the Court upheld a state law requiring out-of-state insurance companies doing business in Virginia to obtain a license. It held that contracts of insurance are not articles of commerce "in any proper meaning of the word," that they are not commodities to be shipped or forwarded from one state to another and then put up for sale.

While some state courts prior to the Civil War had seen in the phrase "due process of law" potential for the protection of natural rights, it is fair to say that at the time of the ratification of the Fourteenth Amendment in 1868, the word *liberty* signified personal liberty and freedom from restraint; the word *property* referred to a static right of possession and use, suggesting something material and tangible. Through judicial interpretation, "due process" would evolve toward a substantive guarantee against "arbitrary" legislation, while "liberty" (or "property") would begin to encompass the right to follow any lawful calling. The "right to property" would also come to embrace such intangibles as exchange value and expected earning power. Substantive due process would become the concept that government may not enact a particular law if that law is inherently unfair and unjust and therefore can never meet the requirement of due process of law. Central to this evolution were the dissenting opinions in the *Slaughterhouse Cases.*

The majority in the *Slaughterhouse Cases* dismissed the contentions that the creation of the monopoly violated Fourteenth Amendment rights. Paying major attention to the contention that the law violated the privileges and immunities clause, the majority accepted without debate the procedural interpretation of due process. Former Justice John Archibald Campbell, who argued the case for the Butchers' Association, contended that the Fourteenth Amendment applied not merely to the emancipated slave but to every class and every condition of the population. Campbell gave the amendment a laissez-faire interpretation. According to Campbell, the amendment "was designed to secure individual liberty, individual property, and individual security and honor from arbitrary, partial, proscriptive and unjust legislation of state governments" (Twiss).

Field, Bradley, Chase, and Swayne all dissented. Field saw the question largely in terms of the doctrine of vested rights and the privileges and immunities clause, which, he stated, referred to inalienable rights derived from the Creator, belonging to the citizens of all free governments; among these were the right to pursue a lawful employment in a lawful manner. Justice Bradley based part of his dissent on the substantive interpretation of due process. The New Orleans butchers, Bradley stated, had been deprived of their lawful calling in an arbitrary and capricious manner and without due process of law.

The Waite Court. The Supreme Court during Waite's chief-justiceship struck down little or nothing of substance that might be called social legislation. From 1872 (just before Waite became chief justice) to 1886 (just before his tenure ended), forty of forty-six cases involving Fourteenth Amendment claims were decided on behalf of the state. The Court sustained quarantine regulations; wharfage fees on public docks; prohibitions on the sale and manufacture of liquor; and condemnation of businesses as public nuisances. State railroad regulations were upheld, as were laws setting rates charged by water companies and laws prohibiting businesses that engaged in the liquor trade or operated lotteries. Under Waite, the Court greatly modified the doctrine of *Dartmouth College* v. *Woodward* (1819) that corporate charters constitute contracts, the impairment of the obligations of which are prohibited by the contract clause. In *Stone* v. *Mississippi* (1880) the Court, through Waite, laid down the principle that a state may repudiate charter rights deemed harmful to the public welfare; that is, a state may not contract away the exercise of its police power.

However, between 1877 and 1882, five men whose conservatism had been largely cast in terms of traditional principles of federalism left the Supreme Court either because of death or resignation, and were replaced by justices who were committed to the rights of property. During the 1880s this was reflected not so much in the Court's holdings but in explanatory language scattered throughout an opinion but not essential to it—so-called dicta. These dicta were built upon from 1890 to 1937 by the Supreme Court in such a way as to couple vested rights with the due process clause, so that the clause became a substantive limitation upon the powers of the state to regulate private property in the interests of the public welfare. Thus, Field, who, untroubled by doubt, saw issues in absolute terms and wrote with force, casting constitutional issues in prophetic, moralistic tones, would emerge the victor in his great duel over these principles with Waite, but not until after Waite's death.

The most important cases involving regulation of the economy during the Waite era were the *Granger Cases,* known largely for the case that was the leading decision, *Munn* v. *Illinois* (1877). The *Granger Cases* dealt with state laws establishing strong railroad commissions that could set maximum rates, eliminate rate discrimination, and initiate court action. *Munn* itself dealt with an Illinois law that outlawed warehousemen's fraudulent practices and created the Railroad and Warehouse Commission, which was empowered to investigate costs, receipts, earnings, and indebtedness of railroads. To prevent abuse of the monopoly of grain elevators, rates were fixed for the storage of grain in Chicago.

In *Munn* v. *Illinois* the Supreme Court held that businesses affected by the public interest must submit to public control, including rate regulation. Waite's opinion was reminiscent of Chief Justice Roger B. Taney in its recognition that property rights were not absolute, its broad view of the state police powers, and its conscious deference to legislative policy judgments. Heavily influenced by Justice Bradley, Waite harkened back to an ancient British doctrine and to decisions of the Massachusetts Supreme Judicial Court in the first half of the nineteenth century. He held that when private property is devoted to a public use, it is subject to public regulation, and that when property is devoted to a use in which the public has an interest, the owner in effect grants to the public an interest in that use and must submit it to be controlled by the public for the common good. For Waite, the reasonableness of public regulation was a political question for the legislature to decide, not a legal one for the courts.

Field, joined by Strong, dissented with passion, predicting that the reasoning of the majority implied an almost unlimited scope for regulatory power. But Waite had left room for inroads into his opinion. He suggested that under some circumstances a regulatory statute might be so arbitrary as to be unconstitutional under the due process clause. It could be inferred as well from *Munn* that if there were businesses "affected by the public interest," there were also some businesses "not affected with a public interest," and those could not be regulated.

During the Waite era, the Court would continue to sustain state regulation of railroads as within the police power and not a deprivation of property, even though considerable costs were imposed upon the railroads. In the *Sinking Fund Cases* (1879) the Court, through Waite, would sustain a federal statute requiring certain railroads to set aside a portion of their profits as insurance against the accumulation of debts so that they would be able to repay loans to the United States. But the Court did add that the United States, like the states, was prohibited from depriving persons or corporations of property without due process of law. The positions advanced by corporate counsel made headway in the mid-1880s. During oral arguments in the case of *Santa Clara County* v. *Southern Pacific Railroad* (1886), Chief Justice Waite announced from the bench that all of the justices agreed that the guarantees of the Fourteenth Amendment encompassed corporations.

In *Stone* v. *Farmers Loan & Trust Co.* (1886; *Railroad Commission Cases*), the Court upheld a Mississippi law establishing a railroad commission with full regulatory powers. The power to regulate was not to be viewed as confiscation. But for the first time the Court acknowledged that the power of regulation might not itself be without limit, that "under pretence of regulating fares and freights, the State cannot require a railroad corporation to carry persons or property without reward; neither can it do that which in law amounts to a taking of private property for public use without just compensation, or without due process of law." The ground was thus laid for the Supreme Court to hold a rail-rate regulation unconstitutional, which it would do in *Chicago, Milwaukee & St. Paul Railway* v. *Minnesota* (1890). Then eight years later, in *Smyth* v. *Ames*, the Court held unconstitutional a Nebraska law

setting intrastate freight rates so low as to be unreasonable and amounting to a deprivation of property without due process of law.

In moving toward a doctrine that would exalt freedom of contract over state regulation, the United States Supreme Court lagged behind state courts. The most influential state court decision was that written by Judge Robert Earl of the New York Court of Appeals in 1885 in *In re Jacobs*. At issue in *Jacobs* was a state law restricting the manufacture of cigars in tenement housing on any floor used as living quarters. Synthesizing a number of laissez-faire ideas—economic liberty, substantive due process, prohibitions against class legislation, and pretended exercises of police power—the court held that it was for the courts to decide whether a statute was a real or pretended exercise of the police power. The New York statute was held invalid.

That the Supreme Court had not really come this far afield is clear from a comparison of two cases from Waite's last terms. In *Mugler* v. *Kansas* (1887) the Court, through Justice Harlan, upheld a Kansas prohibition law, indicating that there were differences between legitimate and pretended exercises of the police power and that not every statute enacted ostensibly to promote public health, safety, or welfare would be accepted as legitimate. The courts, said Harlan, would not be bound by mere forms but were duty-bound to look at the substance of things. But the next year, in *Powell* v. *Pennsylvania*, the High Court refused to go beyond the face of a Pennsylvania law prohibiting the manufacture and sale of oleomargarine, accepting the legislative judgment that margarine was an impure food.

Solicitude for the rights of business, coupled with growing judicial activism, can be seen in the development of the railroad receivership in the 1870s, which evolved from the capacity of district judges as chancellors in equity.

Railroad receiverships constituted an enormous increase in the work of the federal courts as well as the assumption of new duties. Receivership was used by the federal courts to protect the existing railroad system from the threats of heavy indebtedness and labor unrest. Receivers were almost always chosen from existing management, and the railroads were taken from the control of state commissions and state officials.

Out of this environment emerged an increasingly antilabor attitude among federal judges, protecting "their roads" from strikes and boycotts. Judges like Thomas Drummond of the Seventh Circuit (Wisconsin-Illinois-Indiana), who administered the affairs and conducted the operations of many railways, laid down the doctrine that men may work or not as they saw fit, but that they may not lawfully prevent others from working (*Secor* v. *Railway,* 1877). The first injunctions against labor were employed against unions on strike against railroads in receivership, rulings that essentially commanded a group of workers to avoid any hint of a disturbance. In the wake of widespread strikes in 1877, judges like Drummond declared the action of the workers to be in contempt of court and issued special warrants empowering federal marshals to intercede in these labor disputes. After the railroad strikes of 1885–1886, federal judges issued writs of assistance and bench warrants, and held contempt proceedings on the basis of their receivership jurisdiction. By the years 1886–1888, the labor injunction had emerged in its modern form.

During the Waite period, because of the development of railroad and telegraph systems, the commerce clause began to assume great importance. Until 1870, the Court had dealt with only 30 cases involving the commerce clause; that number rose to 77 by 1880 and to 148 by 1890. The Court under Waite upheld national authority over commerce in practically every case of importance before it. The most important of these was *Pensacola Telegraph Co.* v. *Western Union Telegraph Co.* (1877), where the Supreme Court upheld federal power under the commerce and postal clauses over telegraphic communication and denied the states the power to interfere with the expansion of this means of communication. In doing so, the Court held that congressional power is not confined to the instrumentalities of commerce in evidence when the Constitution was adopted but keeps pace with the progress of the country.

While in the *Granger Cases* the Court had held that in the absence of congressional legislation, the states could regulate railroads even when their operations were interstate in character, it retreated in *Wabash, St. Louis & Pacific Railway* v. *Illinois* (1886). There, Illinois' attempt to end ruinous rate discrimination by prohibiting long-short haul clauses in transportation was held to be an infringement upon Congress's exclusive control over interstate commerce. This made national legislation imperative, and Congress responded by creating the Interstate Commerce Commission in 1887.

INSTITUTIONAL DEVELOPMENTS

The Supreme Court. During the era of Chase and Waite, the Supreme Court's membership finally stabilized at nine by the Act of 10 April 1869, which reduced the circuit-riding duties of the justices to once every two years. The business of the Court greatly expanded. During Chase's first term, the Court heard 60 cases. During Waite's last term, it terminated 422. The Court's backlog grew from 636 in 1870 to 1,563 in Waite's last term, in spite of enormous efforts by the justices.

The quality of the justices during this period was extremely high. A 1970 poll of professors of constitutional law, history, and politics rated five members of the Court "great" or "near great": Samuel F. Miller, sympathetic to national power, skeptical about the new capitalism, and committed to a role of balanced restraint for the judiciary; Stephen J. Field, whose powerful but not subtle mind saw the truth as a series of broad, incontestable generalities; Joseph Bradley, a man of great learning and a craftsman; John Marshall Harlan, result-oriented and stubborn, but also independent, prophetic, and right by modern-day standards; and Morrison Waite, virtually unknown at the time he became chief justice but an excellent manager and harmonizing leader, well equipped to preside over the Court that one scholar described as "the ablest all-around Court that ever sat" (Frank). Waite's 872 opinions rank him second only to Oliver Wendell Holmes, and his average output of 62.29 majority opinions per year is by far the greatest of any justice—an extraordinary achievement, even though many of the cases would have been dealt with by the contemporary Court simply by denial of the writ of certiorari.

Although Salmon P. Chase has not been regarded as highly as others who have held the chief-justiceship, Chase was singularly well equipped for the questions of constitutional law, international law, and the prize cases that came before his Court. While his ambition for the presidency evoked criticism and distracted from his overall effectiveness as chief justice, Chase's contribution as a circuit justice to national reconciliation, his insistence that the impeachment trial of Andrew Johnson (over which he presided) be conducted in a judicial atmosphere, and his performance in preventing the Court from entering into destructive combat with the Reconstruction Congresses suggest that as a chief justice, he was a statesman of a high order. One more of Chase's achievements is entitled to mention: his role in fostering the admission of the first black member of the bar of the Supreme Court, John S. Rock, whose admission was moved by Charles Sumner on 1 February 1865.

Lower Courts. During the years 1864–1888, the case load of courts throughout the United States increased greatly. Judges were rushed and dockets crowded. Procedure was elaborate and often stultifying. Judges were poorly paid and lacked staff. There was no one in charge in either state or federal courts to monitor the flow of litigation, to shift or to coordinate judges to meet that flow, or to call upon the legislatures to reform the court system. Such reforms in judicial administration would not occur until the early decades of the twentieth century.

The instrumentalist conception of judging, which had dominated American courts in the first half of the nineteenth century, gave way to the philosophy of legal formalism. In the earlier period, men like James Kent, Lemuel Shaw, and John B. Gibson molded the common law and adapted it to American needs, and Marshall and Taney and their brethren made the Supreme Court the supreme arbiter of the Constitution. But after the Civil War, conscious legal creation was driven underground and replaced with the view that law was a system of rules that could be found and ought to be strictly applied; that is, judges did not make the law but merely declared law, which, in some Platonic sense, already existed. Law in this period appeared as a science, operated by abstract first principles, dictating concrete results.

Law, of course, continued to be "made," but judges refused to admit to it, even to themselves. By changing and expanding the common law, courts assisted in the adaptation of the nation to the new conditions of an urban-industrial society. New areas of law emerged or expanded greatly—among them municipal corporations, torts, contracts, agency, and insurance. The touchstone in all branches of the law, Spencerian laissez-faire, particularly dominated contracts, property, and other private law subjects. Judges wielded judicial review but also controlled lower courts and juries with an iron hand.

CASES

Chicago, Milwaukee & St. Paul Railway v. Minnesota, 134 U.S. 418 (1890)
Civil Rights Cases, 109 U.S. 3 (1883)
Coe v. Schulz, 47 Barbour 65 (1866)
Crandall v. Nevada, 6 Wallace 35 (1868)
Cummings v. Missouri, 4 Wallace 277 (1867)
Dartmouth College v. Woodward, 4 Wheaton 518 (1819).
Dred Scott v. Sandford, 19 Howard 393 (1857)
Ex parte Garland, 4 Wallace 333 (1867)
Georgia v. Stanton, 6 Wallace 50 (1868)
Hall v. De Cuir, 95 U.S. 485 (1878)
Hansom v. Vernon, 27 Iowa 28 (1869)
Hepburn v. Griswold, 8 Wallace 603 (1870)
In re Jacobs, 98 N.Y. 98 (1885)
Juilliard v. Greenman, 110 U.S. 421 (1884)
Knox v. Lee, 12 Wallace 457 (1871)
Loan Association v. Topeka, 20 Wallace 655 (1875)
Ex parte McCardle, 6 Wallace 318 (1868) [McCardle I], 7 Wallace 506 (1869) [McCardle II]
Ex parte Milligan, 4 Wallace 2 (1866)
Mississippi v. Johnson, 4 Wallace 475 (1867)
Mugler v. Kansas, 123 U.S. 623 (1887)
Munn v. Illinois, 94 U.S. 113 (1877)
Pace v. Alabama, 106 U.S. 583 (1883)
Parker v. Davis, 12 Wallace 457 (1871)
Paul v. Virginia, 8 Wallace 168 (1869)
Pensacola Telegraph Co. v. Western Union Telegraph Co., 96 U.S. 1 (1877)
People v. Salem, 20 Mich. 452 (1870)
Plessy v. Ferguson, 163 U.S. 537 (1896)
Powell v. Pennsylvania, 127 U.S. 678 (1888)
Santa Clara County v. Southern Pacific Railroad, 118 U.S. 394 (1886)
Secor v. Railway, 7 Bissell's Reports 513 (7th Cir. 1877)
Ex parte Siebold, 100 U.S. 371 (1880)
Sinking Fund Cases, 99 U.S. 700 (1879)
Slaughterhouse Cases, 16 Wallace 36 (1873)
Smyth v. Ames, 169 U.S. 466 (1898)
Stone v. Farmers Loan & Trust Co. (Railroad Commission Cases), 116 U.S. 307 (1886)
Stone v. Mississippi, 101 U.S. 814 (1880)
Strauder v. West Virginia, 100 U.S. 303 (1880)
Texas v. White, 7 Wallace 700 (1869)
In re Turner, 24 F.Cas. 787 (C.D.Md.1867) (No. 14,247)
United States v. Cruikshank, 92 U.S. 542 (1876)
United States v. De Witt, 9 Wallace 41 (1870)
United States v. Klein, 13 Wallace 128 (1872)
United States v. Reese, 92 U.S. 214 (1876)
Veazie Bank v. Fenno, 8 Wallace 533 (1869)
Virginia v. Rives, 100 U.S. 313 (1880)

Wabash, St. Louis & Pacific Railway v. Illinois, 118 U.S. 557 (1886)
Wynehamer v. People, 13 N.Y. 378 (1856)
Ex parte Yarbrough, 110 U.S. 651 (1884)
Ex parte Yerger, 8 Wallace 85 (1869)

BIBLIOGRAPHY

Loren Beth, *The Development of the American Constitution* (1971), is the leading constitutional history of the period. Albert Blaustein and Roy M. Mersky, "Rating Supreme Court Justices," in *American Bar Association Journal,* 58 (1972), gives the results of a poll of scholars. Thomas Cooley, *A Treatise on the Constitutional Limitations Which Rest upon the Legislative Power of the States of the American Union* (1868), is the most influential jurisprudential work of the Chase and Waite eras. John F. Dillon, *Treatise on the Law of Municipal Corporations* (1872), is the leading treatise emphasizing national judicial constraints upon municipal bond repudiation when cities are not controlled by the states.

Charles Fairman, *Mr. Justice Miller and the Supreme Court, 1862–1890* (1939), is one of the finest of all judicial biographies; and *Reconstruction and Reunion, 1864–88, Part One,* vol. 6 of the Oliver Wendell Holmes Devise History of the Supreme Court of the United States (1971), is the major resource for the history of the Chase Court. Sidney Fine, *Laissez Faire and the General-Welfare State* (1956), in chapter 12, provides an account of the triumph of laissez-faire in the courts. John Frank, *Marble Palace* (1958), describes the workings and history of the Court. Lawrence M. Friedman, *A History of American Law* (1973; rev. 1986), is the standard text in American legal history. Howard Jay Graham, *Everyman's Constitution* (1968), is a series of essays about the origin and interpretation of the Fourteenth Amendment by a leading scholar.

Harold M. Hyman and William M. Wiecek, *Equal Justice Under Law* (1982), is a leading constitutional history of the period 1835–1875. Clyde E. Jacobs, *Law Writers and the Courts* (1954), studies the influence of three great treatise writers, Cooley, Dillon, and Tiedeman, on constitutional law. Morton

Keller, *Affairs of State* (1977), is a history of American public life in the late nineteenth century, with a chapter on "The Province of the Law." Alfred H. Kelly, Winfred A. Harbison, and Herman Belz, *The American Constitution* (6th ed., 1983), is the standard American constitutional history text. Stanley I. Kutler, *Judicial Power and Reconstruction Politics* (1968), a short but important book, asserts that Congress during Reconstruction was not dominated by hostile attitudes toward the federal judiciary but in fact contributed significantly to increasing its powers, and that the Court exhibited tenacity and toughness.

Robert G. McCloskey, *American Conservatism in the Age of Enterprise* (1951), is a study of the evolution of conservative political thought, focusing on Sumner, Carnegie, and Field; and *The American Supreme Court* (1960), the standard one-volume history of the Court, takes the position that the Court under Chase and Waite was activist and pro–property rights. C. Peter Magrath, *Morrison R. Waite* (1963), is an excellent biography of a figure who should be better known. Phillip S. Paludan, *A Covenant with Death* (1975), studies representative legal thought of the Civil War era, discerning the threads that would influence postwar treatment of the freedman.

James G. Randall, *Constitutional Problems Under Lincoln* (1926), is a classic study of such issues as treason, suspension of habeus corpus, confiscation, and emancipation. James G. Randall and David Donald, *The Civil War and Reconstruction* (2nd ed., 1961), is an excellent one-volume history and basic reference tool. Bernard Schwartz, *The Law in America* (1974), is an illustrated history of American law, with text by an able scholar. Benjamin R. Twiss, *Lawyers and the Constitution* (1942), is a classic describing the influence of lawyers on the acceptance of laissez-faire principles by the courts. Charles Warren, *The Supreme Court in United States History,* 2 vols. (rev. ed., 1926), is the classic work, covering the Chase and Waite Courts in volume 2. G. Edward White, *The American Judicial Tradition* (1976), collects relatively brief essays on American judges, including Miller, Field, Bradley, Harlan, Cooley, and Doe.

[See also COMMERCE CLAUSE; DUE PROCESS OF LAW; EQUAL PROTECTION CLAUSE; EXECUTIVE AND DOMESTIC AFFAIRS; MILITARY LAW; RACIAL DISCRIMINATION AND EQUAL OPPORTUNITY; *and* TANEY COURT AND ERA.]

THE FULLER COURT AND ERA

Loren P. Beth

DURING the Fuller era the Supreme Court reached man's estate. For the first time it realized the potentialities of judicial review as a means of checking and directing the states and the other branches of the federal government in their use of policymaking powers under the Constitution. Melville W. Fuller—a genial and capable man if not a great chief justice—had little to do with this development, since it had begun before his appointment in 1888 and would no doubt have proceeded with anyone else at the head of the Supreme Court. There seems to be something ineluctable about the process by which the Court "responds to a changing society."

The changes to which the Court, and indeed the entire American judiciary, were responding were primarily economic in nature. As a result the law was pulled in two directions. First, it was necessary, in Hurst's felicitous phrase, to "release the energy" for the industrial revolution by using the law to free America's resources for rapid exploitation. This meant, among other things, the accommodation of the law to the gathering and use of huge amounts of capital by ever-larger business corporations. Although historians, particularly those of the "progressive" tradition, think that much of this development was evil or at least unfortunate, it can be thought of as distinctly creative in meeting the felt needs of the time.

Nevertheless, such freedom for development led to great problems: the spoliation of natural resources and the development of a new wage-dependent work force, to name two. So while lawmakers—legislators no less than judges—were making policy to "free" free enterprise, they were also under great pressure to limit this freedom through government regulation. This second need was never as clearly articulated as the first, mostly because the problems took time to identify and because there was no agreement as to what they were or how to deal with them. Nevertheless, there was a great volume of regulatory legislation, both state and federal, enacted or seriously considered during the Fuller era; and courts participated by often upholding legislation and by sometimes developing their own approaches. Thus, contrary to the theories of many later legal writers—Karl Llewellyn and Grant Gilmore come to mind—the Fuller era was one of great legal and judicial innovation. After all, whatever one thinks of their wisdom, the doctrines of freedom of contract and substantive due process were astonishing acts of creativity to come from judges who were presumably bound to the strict rule of precedent.

The theme of this essay, then, is that the law was used instrumentally during the Fuller era—conservatively, to create the conditions necessary for a free-enterprise industrial society, and progressively, to create the regulations necessary to ameliorate the hardships engendered by such a society. How successful law was in these two respects is another question. Answering this question will necessitate an examination of the law's uses in areas such as civil rights.

THE ROLE OF LAWYERS IN THE FULLER ERA

The fact that lawyers constitute a major portion of the political elite in the United States is well known. It has apparently been a characteristic of American politics since colonial times, and it certainly held true during the Fuller era. Legislatures were packed with lawyers, and members of the bar were frequently elected to the presidency- and state governorships. Consequently, the legal profession played a predominant role in the enactment of statutes. The American penchant for solving problems by passing laws may in large part be due to the lawyer's natural faith in the utility of law, which was probably at its height during what Gilmore calls the Age of Faith, a period encompassing the Fuller years.

But the indirect effect of lawyers on law is less obvious, though still tremendously important, and more interesting. It came about, as implied above, because American courts were makers of private and public policy through their decisions as both common-law and constitutional interpreters. Theories of law, passed from the academics through their students to the courts, were thus exceptionally influential in determining not only the decisions themselves but also the techniques by which the decisions were reached and justified. And if, as one may assume, the predominant legal theories were a response to the felt needs (as Oliver Wendell Holmes might have said) of the times, one might also expect that these theories would be picked up and used by judges. Whether the theory was cause or effect is somewhat more ambiguous.

Legal theory, in the broad sense, was dominated during the latter part of the nineteenth century by the ideas of John Austin and Christopher Columbus Langdell. Austin, the English follower of utilitarianism, had a great influence on both British and American developments, such as the rigid use of precedent as the basis for decisions. He emphasized law as a closed system in which, from existing principles, answers could be derived by deductive logic without so much as a glance at conditions in the real world. His attempt was to systematize the common law into a restricted body of rules, thus reducing decision-making to a purely formal process of matching the rule to the case. Austin viewed law as a science consisting of rationally derived concepts, in which the original concept (rule, principle) served as the decision guide.

Austin's conceptualism, fortuitously, was a neat fit with Langdell's theories of legal education. As dean of the Harvard Law School from 1870 to 1895, Langdell made Harvard America's preeminent law school. He instituted the case method of teaching, which fast became the dominant method of teaching law. Like Austinianism, the case method depended on rules derived from previous judicial decisions on a subject. The law student learned the rules by studying the precedents. Langdell's approach presupposed that law was a science consisting of ascertainable principles or doctrines that could be found in printed books. These principles were at least national in scope, so that the law of individual states became subordinate to commonly held principles. Appellate decisions would be analyzed by the professor in terms of doctrinal logic, and a new decision could be judged by whether it conformed with the precedents. Gilmore points out that Langdell and his followers tried "with considerable success, to formulate theories which would cover broad areas of the common law and reduce an unruly diversity to a manageable unity." Law could thus be learned in libraries; the chief "trick" was to choose the proper overmastering rule. Theoretically, one could start to write a treatise or casebook by sorting out from the mass of case decisions those few that have been decided correctly and then merely follow them. Langdell believed that since the common law stemmed from England, English cases would in most cases provide the rule, which should then be followed by American courts. In a real sense, however, the law writer—Langdell, for instance, in his casebook on contracts—became the lawmaker, since it was he who was responsible for "finding" the rule in some preceding decision.

This law of concepts typified the American lawyer's approach to his profession in the latter part of the nineteenth century. Lawyers used it in arguing before the courts, and appellate judges attempted to use it in their decisions. The most successful law writers, as it happened, were conservatives, so it was natural that conceptualism became in practice a tool for conservatives. In the American context, the rule was often based on a precedent that aided free enterprise in one way or another. In private law the courts developed, and the law writers fostered, principles like the "fellow-servant rule," under which employers were never to be held liable for injuries to their employees caused by other employees. In public law the basic concept was that freedom was the rule and state intervention the exception: the "police power" doctrine thus limited the areas in which states could regulate private businesses. In addition, common-law judges looked askance at legislation, preferring to keep legal change in their own hands. Politically they might have to accept a statute, but they could at least limit its applicability.

It was thus an age of the legal treatise, and some law writers (especially Thomas M. Cooley, John F. Dillon, and Christopher G. Tiedeman) enjoyed tremendous influence. Cooley's *Treatise on Constitutional Limitations,* for instance, was largely responsible for developing the ideas of liberty of contract and substantive due process in public law, which were taken up by lawyers arguing before state and federal appellate courts and eventually were adopted by the Supreme Court in cases such as *Allgeyer* v. *Louisiana* (1897) and *Lochner* v. *New York* (1905).

But Americans were by nature too pragmatic to go to extremes in the use of conceptualism, and judges grew too fond of power to let rules govern their use of it. The rule of precedent in the hands of American judges allowed them to do pretty much as they pleased. This was because there was often doubt as to which of two different lines of precedent governed, because many cases had no precedents, and because statutes were often used to abrogate precedents. Thus, the fellow-servant rule was never applied rigidly: both legislatures and courts set to work creating exceptions to it. And if the police power limited state regulation of business, it did so only in ways approved by judges. What happened—intentionally or not—was that the power of the courts was maximized because of the flexibility that the system allowed in practice to judges. And the actual course of decisions was more liberal than might be expected.

DOMINANT LEGAL TRENDS

The ambivalence described above was not due to liberal thought as such but to the distrust of extremes and to the diversity of economic and political forces. If railroads wanted freedom to charge their customers whatever they wished, the shippers—who were also businessmen—were happy to obtain government help in regulating such charges. Thus, one must be very careful in speaking about dominant trends: in fact, they were seldom truly dominant. It is customary, for instance, for legal historians to aver that

individualism was the dominant trend, but upon investigation one finds that the individualism of which Bernard Schwartz writes is confined largely to the economic sphere. At the turn of the century, in fact, individualism as a legal doctrine was largely confined to white males who held or manipulated corporate property. Regulation by the states of noneconomic matters was seldom thought of as improper. States were thus left free —the Supreme Court said so—to regulate the relations between races, through the enactment of Jim Crow laws; to interfere with the liberty to refuse to be vaccinated; to protect women by prohibiting them from working as barmaids; and to enact "blue laws," restricting the activities of citizens on Sunday. They were not, on the other hand, free to ban child labor, to make basic changes in the liability of employers for industrial accidents to their workers, or to regulate wages for white males in industries where the work was safe.

Paradoxically, even in areas usually thought of as economic (where free enterprise might be assumed to be the ruling canon), this "dominant" legal canon was not after all dominant. Prices could not be regulated—except for businesses "affected with a public interest," which included all public utilities. Wages and hours could not be restricted—except for women in "dangerous" occupations. Similarly, the law might not regulate employer-employee relations—except that state safety and health regulations were upheld. In fact, it is difficult to find a single area in which the "dominant legal trend" was unambiguously dominant. It is, however, safe to say that by 1910 there were strong tendencies for law to be denied power to interfere with the conduct of private businesses that were truly private. In the large area of trusts and combinations, the power of law was greater, but to an uncertain extent, especially if the business involved was not a public-interest business. And the power of government was still greater (even the federal government got into the act) where public-interest businesses were concerned. But the power of government was greatest in purely private noneconomic matters.

One might approach the matter of legal trends somewhat differently by looking not at the type of business or person involved, but instead at the motivation for a particular regulation. Thus, the police power was normally held to extend to questions of health (quarantine and vaccination laws), safety (safe place and safe equipment laws), and morals (prohibition or Sunday laws). But it was not upheld for less traditional subjects of legislation, such as the regulation of labor relations or price fixing in purely private businesses.

One final tendency might be noted. When looking at court decisions of this period, especially those in which a court has found laws unconstitutional, the impression is of a mighty battle between courts and legislatures. Legal historians seem often to have believed that legislatures were "good" because they represented the public interest and that courts were "bad" because their decisions protected "big business." Aside from the difficult question of what is really the public interest, this view tends to ignore the obvious venality and corruption of the legislatures, and their responsiveness to "interests," which was fully as great as the courts', although perhaps to different interests. Also, this view tends to rely strongly on a few "great" cases and to play down or ignore the many decisions in which both state and federal courts upheld legislation even when it restricted business enterprise.

This essay takes a closer look at the courts, including the Fuller Court, in an attempt to balance two extreme views: the "progressive" view that the era was one of almost unmitigated disaster, especially where the courts were concerned, and the conservative view that all was right in the best of all possible worlds.

The degree to which judges did or did not use their powers to protect minorities and to assert the values of the Bill of Rights will also be looked at. Courts built perhaps a sorrier record regarding minorities than in those areas discussed above.

DEVELOPMENTS AND TRENDS IN STATE COURTS

Most American law is made and enforced by state agencies: legislatures, administrative agencies, local governments, and state courts. This was even more true during the Fuller era than it is now. Under the Constitution state courts were left with the responsibility for most lawmaking. This means that most criminal law; the law governing birth, marriage, divorce, death, and family relationships generally; the law regulating business incorporation, commercial transactions, and the holding and use of property; and the law concerning relations between the races were all primarily left to the state courts unless there was a federal constitutional issue presented (a rather rare circumstance in the 1890s) or federal courts assumed jurisdiction under the diversity-of-citizenship clause (less and less common after 1891).

We should add that the state courts were preeminently common-law courts. This meant that they could make decisions even in areas in which there were no statutes, that they assumed that previous decisions made by other common-law courts were normally to govern their own decisions, and that statutes were often construed narrowly so as not to disturb the existing common-law rules. Also, in the English tradition, common-law courts have a creative function: despite the separation of powers, common-law courts have always made law in the course of deciding cases.

As noted above, the courts during the Fuller era were at least partly under the influence of a dry formalism along with a tendency to favor freedom of enterprise generally. If the initial premise of legal formalism (that there is a rule of law by which every case can be decided) governed absolutely, the courts would have been much more conservative than they in fact were. The premise, however, was not valid. Consequently, courts indulged in a great deal of innovation, even if the judges did not admit or realize that they were doing so.

The Supreme Court, we have said, was ambivalent in its attitudes toward the developing business corporations; the state courts were no less so. Even allowing for differences from state to state, no court was wholeheartedly laissez-faire in its decisions. Thus, some state judges struck down laws setting maximum hours for working women, prohibiting payment of workers in scrip, requiring payment by the week, prohibiting payment in goods, or banning the payment of miners by measuring the weight of coal produced after screening out unusable materials. Such decisions were usually based on the idea of a sacrosanct freedom to contract, but there was a large admixture of pure sentiment involved, as the following statement (fairly typical) indicates:

"[Government is not authorized] to do for its people what they can do for themselves. . . . It is an attempt to degrade the intelligence, virtue and manhood of the American laborer, . . . it assumes that the employer is a knave, and the laborer an imbecile" (*State* v. *Goodwill*, 1889).

Such decisions are not surprising, nor is the sentiment accompanying them. But there was no unanimity. Other state courts upheld scrip laws and weekly payment laws; and some judges dissented, as did Judge Oliver Wendell Holmes of the Supreme Judicial Court of Massachusetts when his court invalidated a law preventing employers from withholding wages for imperfect work and upheld one outlawing picketing. The balance of decisions was against workers.

In cases that saw one set of businessmen pitted against another set, of course, courts were more likely to uphold state regulation; this was also true when obvious public interests were involved, as in health matters or when "noxious" articles such as liquor were banned or controlled. In addition, the public-private distinction noted above was much used by state courts.

Such considerations provide some explanation of the fact that state courts accepted railroad regulation so readily, even though they were not generally in favor of government interference. Shippers were powerful politically, and most of the time their interests were opposed to those of the railroads. The burgeoning "big" businesses —Andrew Carnegie's steel industry, for instance —had no wish to leave themselves at the mercy of the railroad magnates, even though their size gave them certain advantages as compared with small enterprises. Then, too, railroads during the Fuller era and earlier had dismayingly high accident rates, especially in so-called minor accidents involving nothing more than the life or limb of an employee: courts were not likely to oppose requirements for safety devices intended to curb accidents. And finally, the influence of rail transportation on the American economy was so pervasive (modern industrialism would never have developed without it) that even conservative courts could hardly hold that railroads were strictly private businesses or that they could not be regulated by government.

For similar reasons state courts erected few barriers to the regulation of public utilities. The right to regulate—as a principle—was invariably upheld. The innovative use of state regulatory commissions was also accepted. Specific regulations, especially of rates, were not as readily accepted; but as early as the 1890s, state acts regulating smoke emission, spark damage, and even the requirement of "on time" notices in passenger railroad stations were upheld. As the Wisconsin Supreme Court said, "the business of operating railroads [or gas or electric services] differs from other business in its nature and is subject to special regulation to meet the conditions peculiar to it" (*Kiley* v. *Chicago, Milwaukee & St. Paul Railway*, 1909). Since the courts were making these decisions, the question of whether the public nature of the business actually justified state regulation was up to them: they were left broad discretion, and consequently the decisions varied a good deal from one state to another and from one time to another.

Another tendency was for state courts to use federal decisions or statutes as pretexts for limiting state action. This could mean merely that state regulations could not be stricter than those of the federal government. But often the mere existence of a federal rule was held to bar state action completely, and still more often, state courts held that acts of their legislatures violated the federal commerce clause, even if there was no applicable federal law or decision. It is hard to tell in such decisions whether the state judges were only trying to "apply" the constitutional principle or whether they were opposed to the regulations themselves. It is probable that much of the time they themselves did not know.

Health and safety regulations were generally upheld as being within the proper police powers of the states. Thus, states were allowed the power to destroy diseased fruit or animals summarily, to regulate the medical and dental professions and enact quarantine and inoculation laws, to enact inspection and certification statutes, to require the provision of safety devices in mines and factories, and to require that animals be fenced in or otherwise prevented from roaming at large. Here the public interest seemed clear: the needs of densely populated urban centers and the dangers posed by the widespread use of hazardous machinery were so clear that even conservative judges could accept such limitations on otherwise "free" enterprise.

Courts were, however, hesitant to accept legislation based solely on aesthetic considerations. Early zoning and building-permit laws were often struck down. For instance, an Illinois statute regulating the distance of billboards from parks and boulevards was declared invalid as an attempt "to limit the proper use of private property for aesthetic reasons." Holmes himself led the Massachusetts court in condemning an attempt to protect the view of the state capitol building by restricting the height of buildings near it. Holmes based the decision on technical grounds but went on to say that while one object of the law was to "save the dignity and beauty of the city at its culminating point," nevertheless this is a purpose "of luxury rather than necessity," so that to sustain the law "under the police power would be a startling advance upon anything heretofore done" (*Parker* v. *Commonwealth*, 1901).

The regulation of businesses or products regarded as harmful was acceptable to the courts, but they reserved to themselves the right to make independent judgments of what was or was not harmful. Liquor and saloons being putatively bad, states could prohibit women from entering them or from serving as barmaids. But some courts struck down laws prohibiting the use of trading stamps even though something equally innocuous in itself, such as the sale of yellow oleomargarine, could be prohibited. (Of course oleo was not universally considered innocuous, and the incident illustrates the strength of the butter lobby as opposed to the oleo interests.) Almost all of the many and varied regulations of the liquor trade were upheld, although they were often of doubtful effectiveness. Judges no doubt felt a glow of righteousness when they aided the legislators in the battle against Demon Rum.

Laws that created classifications considered invidious were struck down; but again, the pattern varied from court to court. One court might hold that a tax on oil trucks was invalid because it did not apply to all trucks; another, that a license fee for peddlers of stoves, ranges, and wagons was invalid because these were harmless items, and peddlers of other, equally harmless ones were not required to pay. Other courts, however, might uphold similar laws. The catalog of such cases is endless.

This confusion in the state courts was, of course, a reflection of a similar confusion in the legislatures, which were experimenting—sometimes wildly—with new types of regulations intended to meet the problems of the spreading industrial and communications revolutions. Perhaps, given the nature of judicial review and the inherent conservatism of the legal profession, one ought to be surprised at how much of the legislative product was found constitutional. Certainly the courts did not meet the regulatory age with a solid phalanx of opposition. Nor is there much evidence that court decisions unduly restrained the states from meeting the problems of the day as they wished.

In the area of human rights and liberties, the record of the state courts was not commendable. They did not distinguish themselves by their attachment to the spirit of their bills of rights. There were, naturally, major differences between states. Massachusetts started on its long career of strict (even silly) application of the obscenity laws; southern states were less willing—even less willing, one ought to say—than others to accord rights to blacks. And states differed in their interpretations of the demands of separation of church and state. The courts were, in most of these areas, merely acceding to legislative acts that probably reflected popular majority opinions. In addition to the above, popular majorities often showed little tolerance for the huge numbers of immigrants then arriving in the United States, and little active concern for working people in general. The agrarian and middle-class perspectives that dominated politics in most states were reflected faithfully by the courts.

In church-state relations there were two major concerns: Sunday laws and the status of religion in the burgeoning public schools. In general, Sunday laws were upheld, even though in view of the strong church-state separation clauses in most state constitutions, secular reasons for the observance of a religious holiday had to be articulated. This was done generally by saying that under the police powers, the state had a right to provide for a day of rest as a health or general-welfare measure.

In the schools, many experiments with religion were tried. Most of them involved some form of Bible-reading and the recitation of the Lord's Prayer. State courts varied widely in their reactions to these (although, since no two laws were exactly the same, it is difficult to compare one state with another). Some accepted these practices on the assumption that the Bible is not a sectarian book if read without comment. The

Nebraska court, for instance, said, "Certainly the Iliad may be read in the schools without inculcating a belief in the Olympic deities, and the Koran may be read without preaching the Moslem faith. Why may not the Bible also be read without indoctrinating children?" (*Nebraska* v. *Scheve*, 1903).

But other courts struck down such laws. The Wisconsin court condemned religious instruction even when objectors were excused. The practice, said the court, results in a loss of caste and a subjection to "reproach and insult," as well as tending "to destroy the equality of the pupils which the constitution seeks to establish and protect" (*Wisconsin* v. *Weiss*, 1890). Even Louisiana, deep in the Bible Belt, held that the Bible is a religious book, not suitable for use as a textbook (*Herold* v. *Parish Board*, 1915). Washington outlawed the granting of credit for religion classes (*State ex rel. Dearle* v. *Frazier*, 1918), and various state courts banned the use of state funds for the aid of sectarian schools (*Otken* v. *Lamkin*, 1879). Most states held that the wearing of religious garb by teachers in public schools was a violation of religious liberty (*O'Connor* v. *Hendrick*, 1910).

The Jim Crow laws that grew up in the South and, to some extent, in the North were not hindered by the state courts. While the judges had to obey the Supreme Court's dictum that blacks must be allowed on juries, they did so only grudgingly. Miscegenation laws, for instance, were generally considered to be constitutionally proper (for instance, *Green* v. *State*, 1877) even in the North, and the Texas court upheld a prohibition of interracial sexual intercourse (*Strauss* v. *State*, 1915).

The distressing record of the courts extended into other areas as well: Maryland was permitted to bar blacks from becoming lawyers, and segregation in theaters, schools, railroads and their stations, soda fountains, skating rinks, places of residence, saloons, cemeteries, and many other areas of social and economic life was accepted (*In re Taylor*, 1877; *Younger* v. *Judah*, 1892; *State* v. *Gray*, 1883; *Central Railroad* v. *Green*, 1878; *Cecil* v. *Green*, 1896; *Bowlin* v. *Lyon*, 1885; *Harris* v. *Louisville*, 1915; *State ex rel. Tax Collector* v. *Falkenheimer*, 1909; *People* v. *Forest Home Cemetery*, 1913; *Sparks* v. *State*, 1912).

Northern courts were sometimes more sensitive to the race issue. Pennsylvania's court found school segregation unconstitutional; so did California's—at least the segregation of Chinese children. Several state courts ruled that local-option segregation in schools was impermissible unless authorized by state law. And there were scattered decisions upholding black rights in other areas (*Kaine* v. *Commonwealth*, 1882; *Tape* v. *Hurley*, 1885; *People* v. *Quincy*, 1882).

Despite such decisions, the position of blacks was nowhere even approximately equal legally to that of whites, and perhaps that involves the most serious accusation that can be made against jurists (and legislators) in the period. It goes without saying, nevertheless, that on the whole the white public supported such laws and decisions, and one notices the ordinary consonance between what the public seemed to want and what the judges did.

Before the 1930s states were free to develop their own rules regarding police and court practices in dealing with those accused of crimes. In an era in which public sentiment was "hard" on criminals, the state courts reflected this fact. It would be an error to regard this situation as an unmixed evil. After all, the states had to deal with the vast majority of all criminal cases. This meant a tremendous and ever-increasing case load and a consequent need to experiment with methods of coping with it. Not all such experiments would produce injustice; nor, probably, did the framers of the federal Bill of Rights hold all wisdom on the subject of criminal justice.

Thus, the use of the criminal information—a document by which a prosecutor can bring cases to court without a grand jury indictment—became common in the states near the turn of the century. Even though it was a break with tradition, it made such good sense in terms of the saving of time and manpower that the courts generally upheld the practice, as did the Supreme Court, much later (*In re McNaught*, 1909; *Palko* v. *Connecticut*, 1937). Similarly, the new and spreading use of indeterminate-sentence laws was accepted (*Woods* v. *State*, 1914). On the whole, police methods of interrogation were not closely supervised or checked by the courts, and this was probably the worst single feature of criminal justice around 1900.

While all state constitutions guaranteed freedom of expression, there were, then as now, many temptations for state and local governments to limit speech in one way or another.

State courts often concurred in these limitations. Thus, a Kansas law prohibiting the publication of papers "devoted largely to the publication of scandals, intrigues, and immoral conduct" was upheld, even though the law could obviously be used, and perhaps was intended, to prevent political criticism (*In re Banks*, 1895). Libel law was extended by some states without interference from the courts: Idaho banned the publication of "deliberate falsehoods" (*McDougall* v. *Sheridan*, 1913), and Montana prohibited even good-faith accounts of "infamous" acts if they were untrue (*Kelly* v. *Independent Publishing Co.*, 1912). By contrast, courts held that a law compelling publications to disclose their sources of facts about candidates was unconstitutional (*Ex parte Harrison*, 1908); that laws preventing criticism of the courts were invalid (*State* v. *District Court*, 1916); and that the previous news stories of a publication may not be used to prevent its future issuance (*Ulster Square Dealer* v. *Fowler*, 1908). Anthony Comstock provided the impetus for the passage of numerous state laws prohibiting obscene publications. And while even Massachusetts courts would sometimes use technicalities to avoid enforcing these laws—the Bay State's high court held in 1895 that Boccaccio's *Decameron* could not be held obscene because the indictment did not specify exactly which passages offended the law (*Commonwealth* v. *McCance*, 1895)—that state in general gained a bad reputation among devotees of literary freedom, especially when the judges upheld a conviction in the case of Elinor Glyn's novel *Three Weeks*. This puerile (to present-day eyes) effort was castigated as appealing to the animal and the impure thoughts of its readers (*Commonwealth* v. *Buckley*, 1909). In the Victorian age, one might expect nothing else.

Most affairs, of course, were left to private control, and the courts were usually reluctant to interfere. Judges always had the power to void contracts that were against public policy, but they seldom did so, usually restricting this power to those situations in which men had done social harm willfully. Such obvious values as public health or the conservation of natural resources could not, however, be served well by private endeavor, and the courts, by allowing legislatures to grant public lands without substantial controls, made conservation rather difficult later on.

Law, as we have seen, also operated to encourage the growth and concentration of capital, without which industrial America could not have developed. But by the time Fuller acceded to the bench, it was becoming clear that this growth presented problems. While both state legislatures and courts attempted to cope with the era of corporate consolidation, their efforts were inadequate, and federal action became necessary.

THE FULLER COURT: PERSONALITIES AND PRACTICE

Despite its active use of judicial review and the consequent "strength" of its decisions, the Fuller Court was not for most of its existence a distinguished body. The appointments by a succession of presidents—Benjamin Harrison, Grover Cleveland, William McKinley, Theodore Roosevelt, and William Howard Taft—were, with the exception of Holmes (almost accidentally) and Charles Evans Hughes (at the very end of the period) at most adequate, usually mediocre, and sometimes unfortunate. Nevertheless, Fuller inherited a very strong Court, although a fractionated one. Several of the judges sitting in 1888 are among the most prominent in judicial history: Samuel F. Miller, Stephen J. Field, Joseph P. Bradley, and John Marshall Harlan. Samuel Blatchford was a workhorse, valuable because he wrote numerous of the more routine opinions, and Horace Gray was more than adequate. This left only Stanley Matthews and Lucius Q. C. Lamar in the mediocre category. Both served only short terms and might have proved more valuable had they survived longer.

Fuller symbolized the deterioration that would affect his court. He presided over the Court for twenty-two years—longer than any chief justice except John Marshall and Roger B. Taney—without stamping his personality on it. Born in Maine and educated at Bowdoin and Harvard Law, he moved to Chicago and established what was eventually to be one of the city's largest law practices. He was a lifelong Democrat who campaigned for Stephen Douglas in the exciting campaign of 1860, but never was elected himself to any office and was largely unknown, except in his own state and to lawyers, at the time of his appointment in 1888 by President Cleveland.

As chief justice, Fuller excelled in the administration of the Court's business, his sense of fitness in the assignment of opinions was remarkable, and his ability to maintain close friendships with his colleagues was notable. Miller and Holmes both thought him the best chief justice under whom they served—which may not be saying much, since there was no really strong chief justice between Taney and Taft's appointees. He was certainly the one most loved by his colleagues. He was an indefatigable worker who normally wrote more opinions than anyone else on the Court, but most of the important cases he assigned to others. His talents and interests were largely in the kinds of private law cases that constituted the bulk of the Court's practice early in his tenure. He was less at home with the burning public issues that came to the Court increasingly often later in his tenure. Ideologically, Fuller tended toward conservatism: in his later years he frequently voted with David J. Brewer and Rufus W. Peckham either in majority or dissent. He thus found himself out of sympathy with much that the Court's majority was doing, and dissented more frequently than he had in the early 1890s.

Justices Miller, Bradley, and Field all died within ten years of Fuller's accession, and Field was practically useless for several years before his death. In general, it must be said that their replacements were less able, and certainly less strong-minded. Other judges, some of whom had only brief tenures, came and went during the twenty-two year period. Of them all, Harlan and Holmes stand out as being in the tradition of strong judges who left their marks on the Court's history. Brewer and Horace Gray were more than adequate, and Edward Douglass White was certainly adequate as well, although much of his present-day reputation stems from his years as chief justice (1910–1921). The rest are almost forgotten.

When Fuller became chief justice, the Supreme Court labored under onerous burdens. The sheer amount of litigation in the United States had increased exponentially after the Civil War; much of it was related to population expansion and the industrialization of the nation. The High Court found that most of its cases involved private law, with public law and constitutional litigation accounting for only a small part of the work. The Court, under the appeal rules, took hundreds of appeals from the district and circuit courts, and many of these came into federal jurisdiction only because of the diversity of citizenship of the litigants (often fictional or artificial). Patent, copyright, and trademark cases were frequent, as were admiralty matters.

To add to the problem, the federal court system had not been reorganized for many years. Circuit courts were still made up of one local district court judge plus the Supreme Court justice who was assigned to that circuit. This practice added significantly to the burdens of each individual Supreme Court justice.

These particular problems were alleviated a good deal by the passage of the Circuit Court Act in 1891. Enacted under some pressure from the judges themselves, and certainly with their advice, it relieved the judges of their circuit duties, creating a new set of circuit courts of appeals. By routing most nonconstitutional diversity cases and patent appeals to these new courts, Congress succeeded, for twenty years or so, in restoring manageability to the Supreme Court's docket; this was so even though the same act actually increased the Court's load of criminal cases. The Court took 623 new cases in 1890; in 1892 it handled 290. The Supreme Court became at one stroke much more of a constitutional court and, in a broader sense, a public law court than it had ever been.

CONSTITUTIONAL LAW: THE OLD CONSTITUTION

Except in the area of substantive due process, most of the Fuller Court's significant constitutional decisions involved the "Old Constitution" —that is, the Constitution as it was before the adoption of the Civil War Amendments (XIII–XV). The extent of the power of the national government was the crux of these decisions legally, although from a policy perspective the issue often was how far the Court would allow private business to be regulated by Congress. Although there were many contract clause cases, they were of diminishing importance and will not be reviewed here.

The most important, both numerically and otherwise, were the commerce clause cases. The Fuller Court explored, for the first time, the idea that congressional power was limited even when interstate commerce was clearly involved in a case. Does the word *regulate* include the power to prohibit? Since many things ought to be prohibited, the judges were reluctant to say that the power did not exist; on the other hand, they apparently did not want Congress to be able to prohibit indiscriminately. So the well-known "noxious articles doctrine" was born, which held that even in interstate commerce Congress could not prohibit trade in items or in ways that were considered beneficial or unobjectionable. The Fuller Court got around to identifying only a few noxious items, such as lottery tickets and diseased cattle. But the doctrine was industriously used later by the White Court. Liquor was putatively harmful, so Congress was allowed to regulate trade in alcohol.

Perhaps more important were the cases in which the Court had to decide whether or not interstate commerce existed at all. Here the Court developed the idea that manufacturing and other forms of production are not in themselves commerce and thus are not interstate activities. Sometimes this concept merely meant that states could regulate, as in prohibition of the production of liquor for interstate trade, but it could also be used to bar regulation by Congress. When the Court held that the sugar trust was only involved in the production of sugar, that meant that the Sherman Antitrust Act could not be applied to it. There was, indeed, a possible exception: If the actions of the trust had a direct effect on interstate commerce, Congress might have the power to regulate even production; Chief Justice Fuller held that any effects of the sugar trust on interstate commerce were too indirect to endow Congress with this power, but a few years later Justice Holmes led the Court in holding that a monopoly of the stockyards in Chicago was part of a "stream of commerce" and thus that the effects of the monopoly on interstate commerce were direct (*United States* v. *E.C. Knight Co.*, 1895; *Swift and Co.* v. *United States*, 1905). Again, the Fuller Court held that railroad workers who were not themselves in interstate commerce could not be protected by Congress, even if the railroad for which they worked did cross state lines (*First Employers' Liability Cases*, 1908); but in 1914 the White Court contrarily held that the interstate and intrastate railroad rates of a particular firm were essentially inseparable, so that the Interstate Commerce Commis-

sion (ICC) could regulate even intrastate rates if those rates had a direct impact on the interstate freight business (*Shreveport Rate Case*, 1914).

These opposing approaches could be—and were—manipulated by the Court to reach the results it wished. Thus, Congress could not outlaw the use by employers of "yellow-dog contracts," which made union membership impermissible (*Adair* v. *United States*, 1908), but federal rules for the use of safety equipment on railroads were upheld, even for equipment not used in interstate commerce (*Southern Railway* v. *United States*, 1911). The Court used doctrines that enabled it to negate at will the regulatory power of Congress under the commerce clause, but in fact it used these doctrines selectively, if not realistically, and one could hardly say that the Court was wholeheartedly against regulation by national authorities.

Other powers granted to Congress in Article I were also sometimes construed so as to limit the power of Congress to regulate firms. Most of these clauses were not as easily used in accord with free enterprise dogma, since they could not readily be used by Congress for regulatory purposes; but there were possible other limitations. For instance, the doctrine of intergovernmental tax immunity inherited from the Chase Court (by which neither the state nor the federal government can tax the other) could have been used to limit the reach of Congress' tax power: it was not, however, used this way by the Fuller Court except in the *Income Tax Cases* (1895). The Court also allowed Congress to spend its revenue money practically any way it saw fit. Similarly, the use of the tax power to regulate the packaging of tobacco and margarine, and taxes on the sale and transfer of drugs, were upheld (*Felsenheld* v. *United States*, 1902; *In re Kollock*, 1897; *United States* v. *Doremus*, 1919). Whether Congress can use a tax to prohibit an activity rather than merely to regulate it or to collect revenue was a question of some importance during this period. When Congress imposed a prohibitory tax on margarine, the Court chose to regard the tax as being, on its face, a revenue measure—which could, of course, be said of any tax (*McCray* v. *United States*, 1904).

By all odds the most significant and notorious tax case, and possibly the most criticized of all the Fuller Court's decisions, was the *Income Tax* decision. Congress, faced with a pressing need for more federal revenue as the size and complexity of the nation and the government increased, enacted the first peacetime income tax in 1894. It was targeted at the wealthy, a very low tax of a flat 2 percent on all annual incomes above $4,000. The Court unanimously held that the tax, since it was imposed on income from state and municipal bonds, violated the principle of intergovernmental tax immunity. Only two dissenters, White and Harlan, were willing to uphold the tax on income from land; the majority felt that this was a direct tax and thus unconstitutional unless apportioned by the populations of the states. But the Court split evenly on two other issues (Howell E. Jackson being ill): the tax on income from real estate and the tax on income from personal property. The issues being so important, the Court held them over for reargument, and Jackson struggled to Washington so as to make up a full Court. Chief Justice Fuller's opinion decided that all taxes on incomes from land and personal property were direct taxes and therefore unconstitutional, and he gained four supporters, despite the knowledge that the same type of tax, when imposed during the Civil War, had been upheld by the Court. Thus having mutilated the law, the majority held that the rest of it could not stand either. Some, if not all, of the majority seemed more concerned with politics than with constitutionality, and Justice Brown (in dissent) accused the majority of taking "the first step toward the submergence of the liberties of the people in a sordid despotism of wealth." The result was adoption of the Sixteenth Amendment, which specifically empowers Congress to levy taxes regardless of the source of the income.

The Pullman strike of 1894 gave the Court a chance to demonstrate its distrust of organized labor. Eugene V. Debs, the strike leader, was convicted of violating a court injunction forbidding his union to act in such a way as to interfere with the mail or with interstate commerce. On appeal Justice Brewer held for the Court that the injunction was an appropriate use of the national government's power (*In re Debs*, 1895). He used a broad interpretation of national sovereignty somewhat at odds with the narrow reading the Court almost concurrently used in the *Sugar Trust Case*. Again, the Court was willing to use a broad interpretation of the antitrust laws so as to include organized labor under the epithet "combi-

nation in restraint of trade" (*Loewe* v. *Lawler*, 1908).

Another set of cases involving federal power —but this time not bringing in questions of economic regulation—were the *Insular Cases* (1901–1905). When the United States absorbed some of the former Spanish colonies after the Spanish-American War (mainly Puerto Rico and the Philippines), a question arose as to the extent constitutional provisions were applicable to these new territories. By narrow majorities the Court held that unless the conquered territory had been "incorporated" by Congress, the Constitution did not apply, but the judges had great difficulty in deciding what the criteria for incorporation were, so that decisions had to be reached separately for each territory.

CONSTITUTIONAL LAW: STATE REGULATION OF BUSINESS

While the Court through the use of the commerce clause doctrine opened up the possibility that federal regulation of business might on occasion be found unconstitutional, it was not willing to give its unambiguous blessing to state regulation either. The result was that, as generations of commentators have pointed out, the judges constructed a "twilight zone" in which federal action could be banned if it did not involve interstate commerce, while similar state regulations could be struck down as violations of due process. Since this use of the due process concept was new and since its application in this way is not apparent upon reading the clause, it needs some elaboration.

The states had always been assumed to possess a broad and undefined set of powers that Chief Justice Marshall had dubbed "the power of police." In a sense these powers consisted of all governmental power not given by the Constitution to the national government. Over the years the term *police power* came to be regarded as definable and thus limited. It was eventually to be defined as the power of the states to legislate for the protection of the public health, safety, and morals, as Justice Harlan wrote in 1887 (*Mugler* v. *Kansas*).

This doctrine gave, by itself, no license for Supreme Court invalidation of state laws, even if such laws exceeded health, safety, or moral limits, since there appeared to be no constitutional provision bearing on the subject. It was the task of lawyers to find such a provision; and after some preliminary skirmishing with the privileges or immunities clause of the Fourteenth Amendment, they settled on the use of the due process clause instead. The argument they used was not obviously logical, and it took them some time to convince the Supreme Court that *due process* could mean such a thing. The argument was essentially that the protection of life, liberty, and property (especially the last two) envisaged by the clause was not limited to process at all but included the substance of the law, too. In effect, they were asking the judges to read the words *due process* as though they read *proper substance*. It would then be up to the courts, advised the lawyers, to decide which state laws were proper. Thus was a provision initially intended only to ensure proper procedures—"the process and proceedings of the common law," as Justice Story had written—and enacted mainly to protect the freed slaves (although obviously the use of the word *person* made the same protections available to everyone, including business corporations) converted into a broad and undefined limit on state legislation. This new doctrine, now known as substantive due process, was accepted and available for use by the Supreme Court (and equivalently for lower courts) by 1890. It was not, however, actually used to invalidate a law until 1897 in *Allgeyer* v. *Louisiana,* in which the Court held that a law prohibiting Louisianians from buying marine insurance from out-of-state companies was unconstitutional.

Substantive due process was not used frequently—at least by the Fuller Court. Mainly, it put the states on notice that there was an undefined area in which their legislation was constitutionally suspect. It has often been regarded as a natural-law doctrine because its use depends on the judges' own conceptions of wise or good public policy. It also gave the judges two alternatives to use at their own discretion: the old idea that laws are presumptively valid or the new notion that they may even be presumptively invalid. Nevertheless, out of the hundreds of due process cases presented to the Fuller Court, only sixteen laws at most (some decisions were ambiguous as to what constitutional provision was being used) were actually struck down. Thus, while the Court's adoption of the doctrine is sometimes

viewed as pernicious, the judges' use of it was restrained, and few decisions were unanimous.

The two cases usually cited as typifying the Court's use of substantive due process—but that actually show it at its extreme—are a railroad rate case, *Smyth* v. *Ames* (1898), and the bakers' hours case, *Lochner* v. *New York* (1905). Justice Harlan, who wrote the opinion in the railroad case, held that Nebraska's rate structure denied the railroads due process because it would not allow a "fair return on a fair valuation of the investment" and thus was unreasonable. To do so he had to plunge into the thickets of transportation economics—in which he, like the other judges, was far from expert. But some questions were not even economic: What is a fair return? Any figure (6 percent was commonly chosen in such cases) was purely arbitrary. Economically, how does one figure the valuation? Harlan listed the original cost of construction, cost of permanent improvements, value of stocks and bonds, present cost of construction, earning capacity (this had to be figured as a probability under the proposed rates), and operating expenses as factors to be considered, and then he added that there may "be other matters to be regarded."

Perhaps the most difficult of these questions was what the earnings were likely to be under a rate scheme that had not yet even gone into effect. The simple way to figure this was to take the company's business in the last year or two and project it into the future at the new rates; but this left out the possibility that new rates might affect the amount of business or that general business activity might affect the return regardless of rates (in the event of a depression, for instance). Since its central concern is fairness, *Smyth* stands for the proposition that courts can and should be willing to substitute their judgment as to what is fair for that of a legislature or commission. The concern for fairness is laudable, the lack of expertise deplorable, and the view of the judicial function questionable.

In the nonrate area, doubtless the most extreme use of substantive due process by the Fuller Court was the invalidation of the New York bakers' hours law in *Lochner.* This is so at least in part because of the uncompromising language used by Justice Peckham in his opinion for the Court. New York argued that the law—which prohibited bakery employees from working more than ten hours a day or sixty a week—was a legitimate protection of the bakers' health. Peckham was perfectly willing to substitute the Court's judgment on this matter for that of the legislature. He pointed out that most people did not regard baking as particularly unhealthy; he cited statistics to prove that it was no more so than other industries; and he concluded that since hours could not be limited (his own conclusion, it must be said) in other industries, they could not be limited in bakeries either. He refused to accept the argument that workers were in an unequal bargaining position. Unless the work was dangerous, he said, the limitation of hours constituted "mere meddlesome interferences with the rights of the individual"—in this case, the freedom of workers and employers to contract for hours of work.

Harlan's dissent is significant, for it investigated with some thoroughness the health conditions for workers in bakeries and concluded that there was sufficient evidence of hazards to health to render the legislature's judgment reasonable. The opinion was, in a way, an anticipation of Louis D. Brandeis' development of the same argumentative technique (the "Brandeis brief"). Holmes also dissented in a short, trenchant opinion in which, refusing, with his usual vast Olympian detachment, to discuss the health conditions of the workers, he attacked the whole concept of liberty of contract. Arguing that legislation should be upheld unless it could not be accepted by a rational and fair man, he further accused the majority of applying its economic predilections rather than the Constitution. "The Fourteenth Amendment," he drily remarked, "does not enact Mr. Herbert Spencer's *Social Statics.*" But he really failed to meet the majority on its own ground: Peckham was sure that the law was unreasonable and that the state's power did not extend beyond the protection of health, safety, and welfare; having "proved" that this was not a health measure, he could only view the regulation as in favor of labor and hostile to employers.

If the Fuller Court did not overuse substantive due process, it was nevertheless responsible for precedents that could, and would, be used in the 1920s. Fuller's bench, however, was marked by hesitance, ambiguity, indecisiveness, and inconsistency—and in fact most of its decisions favored the states' regulatory powers.

CONSTITUTIONAL LAW: CIVIL RIGHTS AND LIBERTIES

Although the Fourteenth Amendment's primary purpose was the protection of the freedmen, no real protection was offered them by the Supreme Court under either Waite or Fuller—or, indeed, for quite awhile thereafter. The Court inverted the amendment so that it protected business corporations to a greater degree than blacks, defendants claiming that their trial rights had been violated, or anyone presenting claims under the First Amendment.

The Fuller Court, against Harlan's vehement objections, continued its predecessor's course of providing little or no protection to blacks. The most significant cases were *Plessy* v. *Ferguson* (1896) and *Berea College* v. *Kentucky* (1908).

Plessy involved Louisiana's Jim Crow laws, which were similar to those imposed in other southern states. Plessy, who was a black only legally—under Louisiana law even one-sixteenth black blood made a person legally black—was refused seating in a car reserved for whites under a state law requiring segregation in transportation. He sued the state under the equal protection clause, claiming that forced segregation is by its very nature discriminatory action by the state. In an opinion notable for its casuistry, Justice Brown for the eight-man majority wrote a short sociological dissertation, claiming that since the law on its face did not speak of an inferior race but merely of separation, harm resulted only because the blacks chose to interpret the law as implying inferiority. He went on to say that the police power of a state was broad enough to prevent "a comingling of the two races upon terms unsatisfactory to either." In an interesting anticipation of William Graham Sumner's dictum that "law ways cannot change folkways," he concluded (in words that live in constitutional history largely because of their inaccuracy) that "legislation is powerless to eradicate racial instincts or to abolish distinctions based upon physical differences, . . . [and] if one race be inferior to the other socially, the Constitution . . . cannot put them upon the same plane." Since Jim Crow laws were in reality quite new, he was in effect claiming that law could not change conditions brought into being by earlier enactments.

Harlan contributed perhaps his greatest dissent. He started from the proposition that the Constitution does not permit any authority "to know the race of those entitled to be protected in the enjoyment" of the rights it grants. Segregation, he pointed out, is in itself discriminatory: It implies black inferiority and in fact would not be used on any other assumption. Even though whites may privately desire segregation, the law may not obey their wishes, since the Constitution commands that "the common government of all shall not permit the seeds of race hate to be planted under the sanction of law."

Neither Brown nor Harlan felt it necessary to discuss whether the separate facilities provided for Plessy were in fact equal to those provided for whites. Segregation, said Brown, is not discrimination per se; but apparently Plessy's lawyers had not come to court prepared to argue the equality issue, so Brown merely assumed that the facilities were equal. Harlan, on the other hand, was claiming that segregation in itself creates inequality, so he did not have to raise the question either. Much constitutional law was, however, to be based on the separate-but-equal notion.

Berea concerned a Kentucky statute prohibiting integration in private incorporated educational institutions. The Supreme Court performed a neat tactical exercise in evasion by interpreting the issue as involving only technical questions concerning the power of a state to change the terms of a corporate charter, thus entirely avoiding the real racial issue. It was a 7–2 decision, with Day joining Harlan in dissent. In his last great dissent in a race case, Harlan pointed to the obvious fact that Kentucky's law was not merely a corporate regulation but an official act of discrimination entirely beyond the state's power. "Have we become so inoculated," he asked, "with prejudice of race that an American government . . . can make distinctions between . . . citizens in the matter of their voluntary meeting for innocent purposes, simply because of their respective races?" The Court's decision was mute evidence of its answer. Perhaps corporations could not be regulated where their profits were concerned, but could where mere people were involved.

The race question carried over into the area of trial rights. While early cases established that

black defendants had the right to juries that did not exclude blacks, their affirmative right to serve on juries was not supported. Further, the absence of blacks from any individual jury was not an invalidating factor, and long, expensive litigation was required before rulings could be obtained on whether there was systematic exclusion of blacks. The essential conservatism of these holdings was emphasized by an 1898 decision upholding a Mississippi law restricting jury service to qualified voters. Since every possible device had been used to disqualify blacks from voting, the law had the effect of excluding them from jury service, too. The Supreme Court held that since the voting law was constitutional, the jury provision must be also. The Court looked only at the surface fairness of the voting law (*Williams* v. *Mississippi,* 1898).

The Court was unwilling to accord the Fourteenth Amendment any meaning as far as other trial rights were concerned. The majority took the view that the due process clause imposed no new requirements upon the states in this area except those needed to protect blacks, showing a distinct lack of interest in the protection of other citizens; putative criminals were given short shrift by a Court more concerned with the preservation of the liberty of contract of corporations. Again, Justice Harlan was a signal—and usually lonely—exception. Before Fuller became chief justice, Harlan had argued that the Fourteenth Amendment, primarily through its privileges or immunities clause, protected all defendants against violations of the fair trial provisions of the Bill of Rights (*Hurtado* v. *California,* 1884). He continued this course in an 1892 case in which the Court refused to hold that cumulative punishment for a number of violations related to the same offense violated the cruel-and-unusual-punishment clause of the Eighth Amendment (*O'Neal* v. *Vermont,* 1892). Then, in *Maxwell* v. *Dow* (1900), which raised the question of indictment without a grand jury, Harlan argued against the majority that either privileges or immunities, or due process, applied correctly against the states, would prevent states from using such a procedure. He accused the majority of being more interested in property rights than in individual rights.

Harlan's last pronouncement on this issue came in *Twining* v. *New Jersey* (1908). The majority (with Justice William H. Moody as spokesman) upheld a state law permitting judges to comment on the defendant's failure to testify. Moody seemed to feel that there might be some substance to Harlan's arguments, but he was unwilling to break a solid line of precedents, merely saying that "the question is no longer open in this court." After arguing that the right of freedom from self-incrimination was not historically viewed as fundamental, Moody (while claiming a vast potential power for the Court) stressed that "nothing is more fundamental than the full power of the state to order its own affairs." Harlan wrote another long dissent, and finally ended by saying that "as I read the opinion of the Court, it will follow from the general principles underlying it . . . that the Fourteenth Amendment would be no obstacle whatever in the way of a state law" allowing the rack or thumbscrew, censorship, unreasonable search, or double jeopardy.

The Court did not apply the First Amendment rights of freedom of religion and speech through the Fourteenth Amendment to the states during Fuller's tenure. Such cases as were decided are distinctly unsatisfactory, with even Justice Holmes acting as though free speech were at the mercy of the states. In one case, for instance, Holmes wrote that "for the legislature absolutely or conditionally to forbid public speaking in a highway or public park is no more an infringement of the rights of a member of the public than for the owner of a private house to forbid it in the house" (*Davis* v. *Massachusetts,* 1897). And when a newspaper editor was punished for contempt in Colorado for publishing remarks critical of judges, the Court could find no constitutional issue at all, suggesting that the judges did not take the First Amendment seriously where the states were concerned (*Patterson* v. *Colorado,* 1907).

The Court saw few First Amendment issues with federal dimensions. Lower federal courts upheld the Comstock laws prohibiting the use of the mail for obscene materials, and the Supreme Court, although not deciding this issue specifically, made approving comments in cases involving other matters. In one religion case the Court followed up its 1879 decision upholding Congress' prohibition of polygamy in the federal territories by observing that a "crime is not less odious, because sanctioned by what any particu-

lar sect may designate as religious" (*Davis* v. *Beason,* 1890). Here again, the Court was not wrong except in dealing with the issue as if the answers were clear-cut. The Court also approved a federal grant for a hospital to be run by a Roman Catholic order, regarding hospitals as secular no matter who operates them (*Bradfield* v. *Roberts,* 1899). It also upheld a federal contract for the support of Indian Catholic schools, apparently on the assumption that this was a matter for the Indians to decide rather than Congress (*Quick Bear* v. *Leupp,* 1908).

On the whole, then, the contributions of the Supreme Court to Bill of Rights jurisprudence were minimal if not always negative—a slight improvement on its performance in the racial discrimination cases. Nevertheless, there was nothing in the decisions that foreclosed the possibility of later courts applying these rights more vigorously.

CONCLUSION

The Fuller Court's niche in constitutional history is ambiguous. Most of its major decisions advanced principles or reached conclusions that later courts reversed. Thus, although substantive due process remains, it is not used to strike down state economic regulations. The separate-but-equal doctrine has been rejected; the Court's limitations on the commerce power of Congress have given way to an increasing awareness that the American economic system is a seamless web; the Sixteenth Amendment was a stinging rebuke to the Court's declaration that an income tax was unconstitutional; the First Amendment has by now taken its place as one of the Court's primary concerns, and it has been used effectively both in the church-state area and in cases involving freedom of speech; and finally, the Court's reluctance to impose national standards for the rights of defendants in criminal cases has been replaced by an eagerness (on the part of the Warren Court, at least) to create such standards.

The fact that the Fuller Court was ambivalent in its attitudes toward economic regulation has normally been seen as less important than the doctrines it developed for use in such issues. It must be said, then, that at least in the area of constitutional law, the Fuller era may have been the least effective in American history. Attempting to emulate Canute by harnessing the wave of the future, the Court failed utterly.

CASES

Adair v. United States, 208 U.S. 161 (1908)
Allgeyer v. Louisiana, 165 U.S. 578 (1897)
In re Banks, 42 Pac. 693 (1895, Kans.)
Berea College v. Kentucky, 211 U.S. 45 (1908)
Bowlin v. Lyon, 25 N.W. 766 (1885, Iowa)
Bradfield v. Roberts, 175 U.S. 291 (1899)
Cecil v. Green, 4 N.E. 1105 (1896, Ill.)
Central Railroad v. Green, 86 Pa. St. 421 (1878)
Commonwealth v. Buckley, 200 Mass. 346 (1909)
Commonwealth v. McCance, 164 Mass. 162 (1895)
Davis v. Beason, 133 U.S. 333 (1890)
Davis v. Massachusetts, 167 U.S. 43 (1897)
In re Debs, 158 U.S. 564 (1895)
Felsenheld v. United States, 186 U.S. 526 (1902)
First Employers' Liability Cases, 207 U.S. 463 (1908)
Green v. State, 29 Am. Rep. 739 (1877, Ala.)
Harris v. Louisville, 177 S.W. 472 (1915, Ky.)
Ex parte Harrison, 110 S.W. 709 (1908, Mo.)
Herold v. Parish Board, 68 Sou. 116 (1915, La.)
Hurtado v. California, 110 U.S. 516 (1884)
Income Tax Cases (1895). *See* Pollock v. Farmers' Loan and Trust Co.
Insular Cases (1901–1905):
    De Lima v. Bidwell, 182 U.S. 1 (1901)
    Dooley v. United States, 182 U.S. 222 (1901)
    Dorr v. United States, 195 U.S. 138 (1904)
    Downes v. Bidwell, 182 U.S. 244 (1901)
Kaine v. Commonwealth, 101 Pa. St. 490 (1882)
Kelly v. Independent Publishing Co., 122 Pac. 735 (1912, Mont.)
Kiley v. Chicago, Milwaukee & St. Paul Railway, 119 N.W. 309 (1909, Wis.)
In re Kollock, 165 U.S. 526 (1897)
Lochner v. New York, 198 U.S. 45 (1905)
Loewe v. Lawler, 208 U.S. 274 (1908)
Maxwell v. Dow, 176 U.S. 581 (1900)
McCray v. United States, 195 U.S. 27 (1904)
McDougall v. Sheridan, 128 Pac. 954 (1913, Idaho)
In re McNaught, 99 Pac. 241 (1909, Okla.)
Mugler v. Kansas, 123 U.S. 661 (1887)
Nebraska v. Scheve, 93 N.W. 169 (1903, Nebr.)
O'Connor v. Hendrick, 184 N.Y. 421 (1910)
O'Neal v. Vermont, 144 U.S. 323 (1892)
Otken v. Lamkin, 56 Miss. 758 (1879)
Palko v. Connecticut, 302 U.S. 319 (1937)

Parker v. Commonwealth, 178 Mass. 199 (1901)
Patterson v. Colorado, 205 U.S. 454 (1907)
People v. Forest Home Cemetery, 101 N.W. 219 (1913, Ill.)
People v. Quincy, 40 Am. Rep. 196 (1882, Ill.)
Plessy v. Ferguson, 163 U.S. 537 (1896)
Pollock v. Farmers' Loan and Trust Co., 158 U.S. 601 (1895)
Quick Bear v. Leupp, 210 U.S. 50 (1908)
Shreveport Rate Case, 234 U.S. 342 (1914)
Smyth v. Ames, 169 U.S. 466 (1898)
Southern Railway v. United States, 222 U.S. 20 (1911)
Sparks v. State, 142 S.W. 1183 (1912, Tex.)
State ex rel. Dearle v. Frazier, 102 Wash. 369 (1918)
State v. District Court, 155 Pac. 278 (1916, Mont.)
State v. Goodwill, 33 W. Va. 179 (1889)
State v. Gray, 93 Ind. 303 (1883)
State ex rel. Tax Collector v. Falkenheimer, 49 Sou. 214 (1909, La.)
Strauss v. State, 173 S.W. 663 (1915, Tex.)
Sugar Trust Case. See United States v. E. C. Knight.
Swift and Co. v. United States, 196 U.S. 375 (1905)
Tape v. Hurley, 6 Pac. 129 (1885, Calif.)
In re Taylor, 30 Am. Rep. 451 (1877, Md.)
Twining v. New Jersey, 211 U.S. 78 (1908)
Ulster Square Dealer v. Fowler, 111 N.Y.S. 16 (1908)
United States v. Doremus, 249 U.S. 86 (1919)
United States v. E.C. Knight Co., 156 U.S. 1 (1895)
Williams v. Mississippi, 179 U.S. 213 (1898)
Wisconsin v. Weiss, 44 N.W. 967 (1890, Wis.)
Woods v. State, 169 S.W. 558 (1914, Tenn.)
Younger v. Judah, 19 S.W. 1109 (1892, Mo.)

BIBLIOGRAPHY

Loren P. Beth, *The Development of the American Constitution, 1877–1917* (1971). Lawrence M. Friedman, *A History of American Law* (1973). Grant Gilmore, *The Ages of American Law* (1977). James Willard Hurst, *Law and the Conditions of Freedom in the Nineteenth-Century United States* (1956). Willard L. King, *Melville Weston Fuller: Chief Justice of the United States, 1888–1910* (1950).

Karl N. Llewellyn, *The Common Law Tradition: Deciding Appeals* (1960). Jonathan Lurie, *Law and the Nation, 1865–1912* (1983). John E. Semonche, *Charting the Future: The Supreme Court Responds to a Changing Society, 1880–1920* (1978). Benjamin R. Twiss, *Lawyers and the Constitution: How Laissez-Faire Came to the Supreme Court* (1942). G. Edward White, *The American Judicial Tradition: Profiles of Leading American Judges* (1976). [*See also* COMMERCE CLAUSE; CORPORATIONS AND THE LAW; COURTS AND CONSTITUTIONALISM; JUDICIAL REVIEW; LEGAL EDUCATION; *and* LEGAL PROFESSION AND LEGAL ETHICS.]

THE WHITE AND TAFT COURTS AND ERAS

Paul L. Murphy

WITH the death of Chief Justice Melville W. Fuller on 4 July 1910, President William Howard Taft got the opportunity to appoint a new chief justice, Edward D. White. In his single term, Taft enjoyed the unique privilege of appointing six justices, the other five being Horace Lurton, Charles Evans Hughes, Willis Van Devanter, Joseph Lamar, and Mahlon Pitney. Taft appointed more justices than any president since George Washington. Taft's objectives in selecting these men were several. One was to reactivate the Court, the condition of which he called "pitiable," especially because of superannuation. He wanted younger, more vigorous justices with judicial experience, men who would "preserve the fundamental structure of our government as our fathers gave it to us." What this meant was no liberals but, rather, men who would work through the Court "to protect the essential features of the existing social order" and to strengthen the bench as a bulwark against progressive reconstruction of society. Taft had been deeply shaken by the emotional intensities that surrounded the reform of the time, which was anathema to him as a man who revered the stability of the law and legal institutions. By elevating White, a sitting justice with a sixteen-year record on the Court, he hoped for an administrative leader who would use the authority of his position to restore detached and dispassionate jurisprudence, regain unanimity, and lessen dissent.

Taft's desire for an active but conservative tribunal was a response to numerous developing tendencies in the law and in public policy generally that he felt should be slowed down. The years of his predecessor, Theodore Roosevelt, had seen a mild legal revolution in the country at virtually all levels of government. The presidency had become the focus of public interest and constitutional power, at least in outline and potential. Administrative government was also well under way. Congress had become more effective and more powerful than it had ever been. And there was in progress a general ascension of the locus of political power from local to state government and from state to national government. Taft was anxious to contain, if not reverse, these tendencies and looked to White and his other appointees to carry through this responsibility.

The legal and constitutional basis for these developments had evolved in the early years of the twentieth century. Government had ceased to be viewed as a limited public caretaker that responded to events rather than actively planning and supervising public policy. To condone such positive government, at a variety of levels, entailed turning away from narrow, restrictive commerce, taxing, and due process formulas in public policy. This did not necessarily mean rejecting such formulas, for the courts had a certain freedom to choose. And since courts inevitably respond to popular pressures and demands in the area of public law, judicial leaders had found legal ways to accept certain reform tendencies; more specifically, different aspects of the Constitution were now emphasized, with older formulas held in reserve. The test was frequently in the enforcement. Congress, far more active in passing new social legislation, came to depend upon the development of new administrative techniques and institutions by which laws could be enforced. The scope of authority of new agencies required clarification, as did the relationship of the federal government to the states.

With new federal authority had come new state authority, and, consequently, a structure of intergovernmental relationships wherein the new power of city, state, and federal government had to be rationalized. For a conservative such as Taft, this meant reemphasizing that the enumerated powers of the national government were limited by the existence of the states' reserve powers and that both sets of powers were fixed so that they could only be changed by amendment.

Taft's successor, Woodrow Wilson, was prepared to move in quite another direction. More sanguine regarding the general use of governmental power, he encouraged the states and the federal government to push progressivism even further. Vehicles included informal cooperation, wherein state and federal laws complemented one another, and formal supportive agreements or contracts between the two units of government were implemented in such areas as highway construction, agricultural extension services, and vocational education. Another means of sharing within the federal system entailed joint or cooperative use of personnel. This evolved from interdependent law and administration, wherein federal laws were dependent upon state enforcement or state laws were dependent upon federal enforcement. Finally, there was financial aid flowing from one level of government to another, with such grant programs requiring cooperation, but with a careful delineation of authority.

Legal theory of the day tended more to support the Wilsonian view. Sociological jurisprudence, a new school of legal thought that evolved after the turn of the century but drew upon earlier theorizing, especially by Oliver Wendell Holmes, Jr., shifted law away from the closed system of the nineteenth century, which emphasized that the answers to new legal questions could be derived from deductive logic. Law, the new generation contended, should respond to the underlying needs and desires of society; it could, and should, be used deliberately to shape that society. Such a view had been conducive to the development of vast new bodies of state and federal police power. Further, public hostility to the voiding of socially progressive legislation had produced strong attacks on the "obstructive force of scholastic legalism." Felix Frankfurter wrote in 1912, "More and more government is conceived as the biggest organized social effort for dealing with social problems. . . . Growing

democratic sympathies, justified by the social message of modern scientists, demand to be translated into legislation for economic betterment, based upon the conviction that laws can make men better by affecting the conditions of living" (quoted in Bickel and Schmidt, 200).

At the legislative level, this view resulted, in the White Court years, in a great body of positive federal, state, and local action. Between 1910 and 1921, Congress passed the Webb-Kenyon Act (1913) over Taft's veto, using a broad interpretation of the commerce clause to prohibit the interstate shipment of liquor into states where its sale was forbidden; enacted the Owen-Glass (Federal Reserve) Act (1913), overhauling and regulating the nation's money system; set up the Federal Trade Commission (FTC; 1914) to deal with unfair business practices; amended the Sherman Act of 1890 through the Clayton Antitrust Act (1914), defining more clearly what constituted proscribable business practices and extending greater freedom to labor under the antitrust structure; struck at the narcotic industry with the Harrison Antinarcotic Act (1914); passed the Federal Farm Loan Act (1916); enacted the Adamson Act later the same year, providing for the eight-hour day on the railroads; and passed a body of wartime legislation that included the 1917 Selective Service Act and Espionage Act and the 1918 Sedition Act.

Congress also imposed a minimum-wage law on the District of Columbia (1918); provided for national prohibition enforcement through the Volstead Act (1919); returned the railroads to private ownership through the Esch-Cummins Act (1920), which also strengthened the power of the Interstate Commerce Commission (ICC); and set up the Federal Power Commission with the Federal Water Power Act (1920). Along with such statutory action, Congress sent four constitutional amendments to the states for successful ratification: the Sixteenth (income tax), 1913; the Seventeenth (direct election of senators), 1913; the Eighteenth (Prohibition), 1919; and the Nineteenth (woman suffrage), 1920.

Simultaneously, the states were assuming new legal functions. These entailed increased control of banking and insurance, expansion of public school systems and higher education, the beginning of state park development, and utility and franchise regulation. Along with this kind of centralization came social legislation: workmen's compensation; employer-liability laws; maximum-hour and minimum-wage laws; police-power measures addressing the health, safety, and welfare of citizens; and laws restricting the civil rights of minorities and the free speech of dissidents. Laws also guaranteed citizens the initiative and referendum so that further popular legislation could be more easily placed upon the statute books.

At the local level, municipal reform was in the air and was widely pursued. So was enhanced regulation. Cities paved, cleaned, and lighted streets; administered parks, playgrounds, and recreational and educational facilities; developed dependable water and sewage systems; attacked problems of public health; regulated franchises; monitored utility rates; drafted building and electrical codes; zoned neighborhoods; condoned restrictive covenants; regulated industries, from plumbers to laundries; and worked with the state to control the rights to marry and divorce. They thus shared with the other branches of government the responsibility and rule-making power at the heart of an expanded regulatory structure.

While the law was responding to the needs of popular majorities and to their economic and political power, many Americans remained outside this system. There was little participation by blacks, women, and the poor, and even less by recent immigrants. Pressure groups spoke for a number of these constituencies, particularly on the state and local levels. Thus, the National Association for the Advancement of Colored People (NAACP), the National Consumer's League, the National Child Labor Committee, and woman-suffrage and "dry" groups became instruments for seeking greater access to legal rights and protection and such concrete reforms as voting rights, better representation, apportionment, and the dismantling of racially discriminatory legislation and policies.

It was to this changing society that the newly reconstituted Supreme Court was called upon to react. The results were mixed but important. The justices saw their primary task as defining the proper constitutional role of government regulation of the economy. A great deal of judicial creativity went into the development of doctrines that could either justify or limit that role. The commerce clause was central in this process. Judicial action was thus a patchwork of often conflicting decisions, reflecting differing views about what could, or should, be done to solve the novel and difficult problems of the day. The White Court, while conservative, largely rejected extreme laissez-faire and accommodated moderate proposals for reform, especially if social improvement did not involve interference with vested rights. Its handicap was its vacillation, resulting from divisions on issues by members who were, apart from Holmes, unprepared philosophically for the new age. On the other hand, it was, if not hospitable, at least tolerant toward measures designed to produce industrial and financial change.

In the constitutional area, the Court reviewed very little truly important litigation during Taft's administration. A half dozen cases do stand out. The two major ones involved the antitrust laws and the giant Standard Oil and American Tobacco corporations. Ever since Theodore Roosevelt had drawn the distinction between good trusts and bad trusts, the Court had been cautious in enforcing antitrust regulations, avoiding the determination of what was an unreasonable restraint of trade. The Justice Department lacked adequate funds for the enforcement of the Sherman Antitrust Act, but public pressure was mounting. A Roosevelt-inspired prosecution of the oil trust had been begun by the government in 1906. After lengthy testimony, the district court had held the Standard Oil combination to be in violation of the Sherman Act and had ordered the company's dissolution into its component parts. The trust had appealed.

In his decision in *Standard Oil Co.* v. *United States* (1911), Chief Justice White denied the appeal and read into the Sherman Antitrust Act the "rule of reason," the interpretation that only unreasonable restraints were prohibited by law. Such reasonableness, White contended, was to be determined by the courts. Taft was pleased. The Court, he maintained, had merely adopted common-law terminology: "A reasonable restraint of trade at common law is well understood and clearly defined." Nevertheless, the language of the opinion created the impression that the Court was arrogating power to itself by enlarging its own discretion in the interpretation of an important statute, a view expressed in dissent by Justice John Marshall Harlan, who considered the rule of reason nothing more than judicial usurpation.

The implications of White's opinion were revealed two weeks later in *United States* v. *American Tobacco Co.* (1911). There the Court passed on the government's suit against the tobacco trust. Although it ordered the company to reorganize, the Court refused to impose absolute dissolution on the grounds that the combination was not altogether an unreasonable one. This put the full seal of approval upon the rule of reason, but not without bitter protest from Harlan, whose dissent further reflected his hostility to judicial rule-making.

The net result was that after 1911 it proved virtually impossible to prosecute any great trusts successfully. Almost any monopoly could put up a plausible argument for its social respectability and thus claim to be a reasonable combination. This was seen clearly in the shoe-machinery trust case, *United States* v. *Winslow* (1913), and in *United States* v. *United States Steel Corp.* (1920). It encouraged the merger movement of the 1920s, an unprecedented era of combination and monopoly, which, even with the availability of the Clayton Antitrust Act and the FTC, limited the Court's capacity to curtail business' increasing power. Woodrow Wilson also opposed the rule, which he hoped could be given more statutory precision by the terms of the Clayton Act and the FTC Act of 1914.

The Court's generally antilabor attitude had also been a factor in both of these measures. In 1911, in *Gompers* v. *Bucks Stove & Range Co.*, the White majority responded to the pressure of the American Anti-Boycott Association to outlaw labor boycotts by bringing them within the purview of the Sherman Act. It handed down a ruling making any such boycott a conspiracy in restraint of trade. The personal involvement of Samuel Gompers, the president of the American Federation of Labor (AFL), in this Bucks Stove case brought home to organized labor the necessity of congressional repeal of such "judicial legislation." The Clayton Act, with enforcement support from the new FTC, specifically exempted labor unions and farm organizations from the terms of the antitrust laws. This was hailed as the "Magna Carta of labor," since it limited "government by injunction" and legalized strikes, peaceful picketing, and boycotts.

When it came to more modest social regulation, the Court was considerably more solicitous. In March 1911 it sustained the Pure Food and Drug Act of 1906, which authorized seizure of adulterated goods in interstate commerce *(Hipolite Egg Co.* v. *United States).* Justice Joseph McKenna reminded the appellants that there were very few limits to the federal commerce power. The power, he argued, was complete in itself and subject to no limitations except those found in the Constitution. There was no dissent. Two years later, in *Hoke* v. *United States* (1913), the Court ruled favorably on the constitutionality of the Mann Act, which proscribed the interstate transportation of women for immoral purposes. Answering the contention that the statute invaded the police powers of the states in violation of the Ninth and Tenth Amendments, McKenna declared explicitly that the commerce clause could be used to promote the general welfare. Since most social legislation was geared to this end, the ruling seemed to lend conscious sanction to the concept that the federal government could interpret its authority so as to adjust itself to new social conditions.

Meanwhile, the Court, in the *Second Employers' Liability Cases* (1912), had sustained the constitutionality of a revised law that fixed liability for employee injury on interstate carriers without reference to contributory negligence. The opinion by Justice Van Devanter was a persuasive brief for the right of Congress to regulate virtually every phase of carrier-employee relationships. The ruling, as Alfred H. Kelly has written, "reflected the spirit of liberal nationalism on the Court at the height of the Progressive era."

Other important aspects of governmental regulatory powers were clarified by the White Court in its early years. In *United States* v. *Grimaud* (1911), the Court took on the ticklish issue of the constitutional status of federal commission rulings, thus addressing the new administrative structure. The case involved delegation of authority of the secretary of agriculture to make rules and regulations for the administration of public lands. A 1905 act of Congress had made violations of the secretary's rules subject to fine and imprisonment. Using this authority, the Department of Agriculture had issued regulations to limit grazing on such lands. In its ruling, the Court extended the doctrine of administrative discretion to recognize that administrative rulings had the force of law and that violations of them might be punished as infractions of a criminal statute if Congress should so provide. The decision seemed to remove doubts as to the constitutionality of administrative rulings and, in the process, to condone growing commission government.

When Woodrow Wilson entered the White House in March 1913, the Court was considering an important commerce clause case involving railroad rates that had been fixed by a Minnesota state commission. The railroads had contended that the measure did not permit a fair return on their investment and was thus a violation of the due process clause of the Fourteenth Amendment. The Court, speaking through Justice Charles Evans Hughes, rejected this contention and sustained the rate, holding that the exclusive authority of Congress over interstate commerce did not inhibit state action in nonconflicting areas. Further, it confirmed that if rates did affect interstate, as well as intrastate, rates, the federal government could regulate the latter (*Minnesota Rate Cases*, 1913). The following year, in the landmark *Shreveport Rate Cases*, the Court held that the Interstate Commerce Act and the commerce clause of the Constitution gave the United States plenary power in rate-making. By ruling that local activity affecting interstate commerce came within the scope of federal power, the justices created an "affect" doctrine, which became a key constitutional device for extending national authority over widely divergent areas of local activity.

As American entry into World War I loomed, Congress, to prevent a nationwide rail strike, passed the Adamson Act, establishing the eight-hour day on interstate railroads. In *Wilson* v. *New* (1917), a bare majority of the Court upheld the establishment of temporary wages and hours as an emergency measure. Chief Justice White went further and took the occasion to declare that authority for congressional control of such subjects was latent in the Constitution.

The upholding of federal authority and federal reform legislation was complemented in these years by the Court's generally permissive attitude toward state regulatory and police-power statutes. This seems to have stemmed from general acquiescence in the positive social use of law and from a revulsion against the efforts of the bar to trivialize the Fourteenth Amendment guarantees of liberty and equality by seeking to convert political defeats into constitutional grievances. The pattern was generally positive, with some important exceptions. The Court, in *Bunting* v. *Oregon* (1917), extended to all employees in all industries an Oregon statute relating to maximum hours, first upheld with reference to women in *Muller* v. *Oregon* (1908). The statute also affected minimum wages of women and minors, and this aspect of the law was implicitly upheld as well. The ruling was complemented by one in *Stettler* v. *O'Hara* (1917), in which the Court sustained a state court ruling upholding an Oregon minimum-wage law for women. Also in 1917, the Court upheld the constitutionality of a New York workmen's compensation act (*New York Central Railroad* v. *White*) and a more stringent measure in the state of Washington (*Mountain Timber* v. *Washington*). The latter provided for a system of enforced compensation by the employer to a state compensation fund, where the New York law had merely required the employer to carry compensation insurance or show ability to pay probable claims. At the local level, the justices sustained a Los Angeles ordinance that required certain businesses which constituted a health hazard to be operated outside the city limits (*Hadacheck* v. *Los Angeles*, 1915). "There must be progress. And if in its march private interests are in the way, they must yield to the good of the community," McKenna stated resolutely.

On the other hand, in *Coppage* v. *Kansas* (1915) the justices held unconstitutional a state statute forbidding "yellow-dog" contracts. Pitney maintained that the right of an employer to buy labor on his own terms, and the right of a laborer to sell on his own terms were a part of the freedom of contract protected by the Fourteenth Amendment. In *Truax* v. *Raich* (1915), Hughes, for the Court, invalidated a state law that sought to limit the number of foreign nationals who could be employed by local employers. And in *Adams* v. *Tanner* (1917), McReynolds, speaking for a badly split Court, invalidated a Washington law forbidding employment agencies to collect fees from those whom they placed, as a deprivation of a property right, without due process of law. In a lengthy dissent, which Holmes and Clarke joined, Justice Louis D. Brandeis, who had ascended the bench just a year earlier, presented a mass of detailed sociological data to show the "vast evils" associated with the employment agency business as justification for the state's right to prohibit it entirely. The case brought into sharp focus the reality that the Court's acceptance or rejection of a police statute under the Fourteenth Amendment was to a great degree a function of the justices' social philosophy.

These years cannot be fully understood without an awareness of the effect of the European war on American public policy. Experts on this period note that after 1915 a general hardening of lines occurred regarding the approbation of further expansive reform. Indeed, the ruling in *Hammer* v. *Dagenhart* (1918) seemed almost to mark the end of an era, and the rejection of much of previous doctrine on the broad use of the commerce clause for social reform. *Hammer* involved a federal statute, the Owen-Keating Child Labor Act of 1916, which undertook to inhibit the flow of goods produced by child labor in interstate commerce. The Court, in a split decision, declared the act unconstitutional as an invalid use of the commerce power to prohibit shipment of goods not inherently harmful. Herman Belz has written, "This part of the opinion, an unconvincing exercise in judicial ingenuity, revived a distinction apparently long since discredited." Justice William R. Day also stressed that regulation of child labor was a local issue and contended that the Tenth Amendment precluded an invasion of the state police power by federal authority. This use of the Tenth Amendment subsequently increased as a device for limiting federal authority. Less than nine months after the decision, Congress passed a second child labor act, this one based on the taxing power, a hopeful constitutional substitute, given the Court's own ruling in *United States* v. *Doremus* (1919) at almost the same time, sustaining the Harrison Antinarcotic Act as a reasonable use of the taxing power as a police measure to outlaw a practice contrary to the general welfare.

While this action came in a wartime context, more direct evaluation of concrete wartime legislation was also occurring. As early as 1916, an army appropriations act had authorized the president "in time of war . . . to take possession and assume control of any system of transportation." After the president's seizure of the railroads in December 1917, Congress passed the Railway Administration Act (1918), providing for government operation of the roads and compensation for their owners. The Court upheld executive seizure in *Northern Pacific Railway* v. *North Dakota* (1919). The Lever Act (1917) was a dramatic enactment to authorize federal control of the domestic economy, a sphere normally reserved for the states. Only one feature of this law, certain of its price-fixing provisions, was declared unconstitutional, in *United States* v. *L. Cohen Grocery Co.* (1921). The Selective Service Act of 1917 asserted the federal authority to register and classify for military service all American men from twenty-one to thirty years of age. Challenged as "involuntary servitude" within the meaning of the Thirteenth Amendment and as an assault upon the states, the measure was unanimously sustained in the *Selective Draft Law Cases* (1918). A flag-waving opinion by Chief Justice White contended that the power of the federal government, both as an inherent element of sovereignty and as a direct consequence of the Constitution's provision to raise and support armies, provided an adequate constitutional base for the law.

The war period also saw the first major federal assault upon free speech and free press since the Alien and Sedition Acts of 1798. The 1917 Espionage Act and the 1918 Sedition Act sought to punish criticism of the armed forces; "disloyal, profane, scurrilous, or abusive language about the form of government" of the United States; and general opposition to the war. Postal censorship was established through the former measure, which banned treasonable or seditious material from the mails. In *Schenck* v. *United States* (1919) the Supreme Court sustained both, but not until Oliver Wendell Holmes enunciated the "clear and present danger" rule, as a defense against overzealous enforcement. Holmes argued in *Abrams* v. *United States* (1919) for each case to be weighed on a new scale, contending it served the public dialogue and should be limited only when it became an overt threat to public security. These rulings marked the beginnings of a modern jurisprudence of civil liberties, which was supported by the new American Civil Liberties Union (ACLU), and became an important dimension of public law and public controversy in subsequent years.

The same period also saw the beginnings of two other interesting trends. One trend entailed judicial action giving unprecedented scope to all three "Civil War amendments," the Thirteenth, Fourteenth, and Fifteenth. The other reflected the first glimmering of concern for the probity of criminal processes. This new softening of judicial racial attitudes reflected, according to Benno Schmidt, the White Court's spirit of trying to introduce national cohesion at a time of race riots and war. Schmidt also sees it as a by-product of laissez-faire constitutionalism from the 1900–1910 period and as rooted in the institutional revival of the Court in that period. In any event, minor breakthroughs were important. In one of the first cases to reach the White Court, *Bailey* v. *Alabama* (1911), Hughes, for the Court, invalidated an Alabama statute requiring individuals to "work out" their debts by service on the land of the creditor—a variation of peonage—because it was in conflict with the Thirteenth Amendment. Three years later in *United States* v. *Reynolds,* the Court struck down the Alabama criminal-surety system once again as a form of proscribed involuntary servitude. The criminal-surety system had made it possible, under state law in Alabama and Georgia, for a black arrested for a minor crime to be contracted over to a white employer who paid his fine. Such employment, or surety contracts, were put in writing and approved in open court by the judge before whom the defendant had been sentenced. The aforementioned rulings lay at the junction of race and economic arrangements that fixed the distinctive character of the South during the Progressive Era. They were the most lasting of the White Court's contributions to justice for blacks and were among its greatest achievements.

As to the Fourteenth Amendment, the Court in *McCabe* v. *Atchison, Topeka & Santa Fe Railway* (1914) began the first assault on the "separate but equal" doctrine of *Plessy* v. *Ferguson* (1896). In 1914 an Oklahoma law that required separation of the races but allowed railroads not to provide sleeping and dining cars for blacks if there was little demand for them was castigated as a violation of the equal part of "separate but equal." This ruling was to be built upon in the 1940s until that doctrine was retired in *Brown* v. *Board of Education* (1954). In *Buchanan* v. *Warley* (1917) the Court for the first time found in the Fourteenth Amendment limits on the spread of laws requiring racial separation and struck down a Louisville ordinance which provided that in any block in which the majority of houses was occupied by whites, property could not be sold to blacks. The decision, in effect, made segregation by zoning impossible. This led to segregation through private restrictive covenants, a practice that later produced further constitutional ques-

tions. Less important, but symbolically significant, was the Court's overturning of Oklahoma's and Maryland's grandfather clauses. A grandfather clause was a state provision whereby males who had voted before 1867 or had served in the military in the Civil War or in certain earlier wars or who were descended from such persons would vote automatically without need to meet property, literacy, or other voter qualifications. Since very few blacks voted before 1867, and none at all in the South, this effectively protected poor whites and excluded black voters altogether. The Court overturned these clauses by applying the Fifteenth Amendment and what was left of the federal civil rights statutes at that time, in *Guinn* v. *United States* (1915) and *Myers* v. *Anderson* (1915). With this set of rulings the White Court breathed life into Reconstruction principles that had been left for dead by the Waite and Fuller Courts for three decades.

As to criminal procedure, the Court's landmark ruling in *Weeks* v. *United States* (1914) saw the Court, for the first time, holding that in prosecutions in federal courts the Fourth Amendment barred the use of evidence seized through illegal search and seizure. While the ruling did not apply to the states, it sent a message as to federal standards which were eventually extended in later decades. In *Frank* v. *Mangum* (1914, 1915) an infamous case involving southern justice, the body took jurisdiction and explored the meaning of due process in state courts. It eventually ruled, over dissents by Holmes and Hughes, that the Fourteenth Amendment did not impose upon the states any particular form or mode of procedure but merely required that essential rights not be interfered with; but a few years later, in *Moore* v. *Dempsey* (1923), the Taft Court went much further. There, partially as a result of the NAACP's litigation activities, a locally sanctioned judicial lynching was ruled a denial of due process, indicating that the Court would in the future look beyond the mere forms of proceedings and inquire whether state criminal defendants had, in fact, been afforded a fair trial. The Court, wrote Holmes, had a clear duty to "secure the petitioners their constitutional rights." Thus began to emerge the "fair trial" rule, under the due process clause, a rule that required the states for the first time to afford criminal defendants a fair trial, not the mere form of a trial.

The state courts in this period clearly had

greater overall influence than the federal. Possessing the power to review the constitutionality of state and federal acts and to interpret state and local statutes, they also possessed the power and status of the English common-law courts. Most law was made and enforced at the state level. As Loren Beth has written, the holy trinity of the American civil lawyer—property, contract, tort—was almost solely the province of the states. Generally the state courts did little to protect the rights of individuals and less to retard the development of social legislation. Their attitude toward business and its regulation by government reflected a modified laissez-faire. The New York Court of Appeals, for example, first invalidated and then upheld a workman's compensation statute (*Ives* v. *South Buffalo Railway,* 1911; *Jensen* v. *Southern Pacific Co.,* 1915). Other states tended to follow suit.

Antilabor activities in the state courts reflected those in the federal, with state courts often abusing their equity powers to restrict strikes, picketing, and boycotts, often by ex parte injunction. State courts generally embraced the doctrine of liberty of contract, although differing patterns are observable. Washington upheld the limiting of the hours of work for women (*State* v. *Somerville,* 1912); North Carolina outlawed the employment of children under twelve (*Starnes* v. *Albion Manufacturing Co.,* 1908); Illinois struck down a law prohibiting the assignment of wages (*Massie* v. *Cessna,* 1909); Massachusetts banned the limiting of working hours in "steam railroad stations" (*Commonwealth* v. *Boston & Maine Railroad,* 1915); Missouri struck down the limiting of baker's hours (*State* v. *Miksicek,* 1910); and several states struck down statutes prohibiting employers from firing or threatening workers involved in union activities. On the other hand, state courts put up few bars against legislation regulating public utilities and generally sustained health and safety regulations. In the struggle between "growth" and protection of the environment, however, growth generally won.

In the area of human rights, there seemed little enthusiasm by state courts for extending Bill of Rights guarantees. The *Twining* decision of 1908 had made clear that the states were under no constitutional obligation even to observe the minimal rules contained in the Bill of Rights, since these limited only the federal authorities. This seemed an invitation to the state courts to handle a variety of individual-rights cases as best they could, a practical approach, given their limited personnel. State courts worried little about local restrictions on free speech and press. Censorship was widely imposed. The state courts were not inclined to interfere with attempts to reform the political process or, in the South, with attempts to keep blacks from the polls. They did go along with burgeoning government, changing and expanding the common law to aid in the adoption of the political system to the new conditions of an urban and industrial society. Further, the common law was helpful in the large freedom it gave for private associations in an age when pressure groups became major influencers of governmental action. It did allow pressure groups to exist and further enhanced social action in dealing with public problems. Thus, at the state level there occurred a shift from legislative to powerful executive and administrative agencies and an increasing power of judicial review, along with the growth and influence of interest groups.

When Warren G. Harding became president in March 1921, the nation entered a decade of conservatism, a trend reinforced by the Supreme Court. The death of Chief Justice White in May 1921 finally opened that position to the eager William Howard Taft. Harding, in his two and a half years in office, made three other appointments, all comfortably conservative and approved by the new chief justice. The legal climate had changed since 1910. The Taft of 1921 viewed conservative Republican principles as being at once happily ascendant in the White House and dangerously menaced within the Court. He was particularly suspicious of Brandeis and Holmes but was reassured with the appointments of Pierce Butler, George Sutherland, and Edward Sanford that a conservative Court could now play a vital role in erecting new safeguards for private property and undermining its most dangerous enemies—Socialists, Communists, Progressives, and militant champions of labor and labor unions. For Taft it was time to move away from Progressive expansionism and restore the country to its traditional constitutional bases, through the re-creation of a predictable and minimal legal system that rested upon judicial defense of a static Constitution and an immutable natural law. In specific terms, this meant restrictive, although selectively restrictive, interpretations of the taxing and commerce powers; an emphasis on the Tenth Amendment for precluding federal intrusion into the reserve powers of the states; and a limitation on the states themselves, through an interpretation of the Fourteenth Amendment, which emphasized substantive due process and liberty of contract, constitutional constructs that could be invoked to protect property against restrictive state laws while leaving the states free to use their police power to inhibit legislatively the activities of those whose private actions might threaten property.

But Taft also wanted to strengthen the Supreme Court. He thus lobbied through Congress a new judiciary act in 1925, granting the Court almost unlimited discretion to decide for itself what cases it would hear. He was anxious to remove the bulk of ordinary private litigation from the Court's agenda and make it the final authority in adjusting the relationship of the individual to the several states and to the United States, of the states to one another, and of the states to the United States. It could thus better mediate between the individual and the government and mark the boundaries between state and national action. This would, he hoped, upgrade the importance of the cases that the Court did hear and ensure a commensurate enhancement of the Court's own power and prestige. In practice, such a looming constitutional presence dampened the enthusiasm of activist legislatures, state and national, for pushing social reform legislation and made those members of regulatory commissions who sought to make their agencies aggressive forces cautious in the utilization of their frequently limited authority.

Legal theory of the day tended to split sharply over this development. Conservatives cheered and began a decade of Constitution worship, which encouraged scholastic legalism and a return to legal formalism. Liberal reaction tended to rally around a series of eloquent dissents by Brandeis, Holmes, and, after his appointment in 1925, Harlan Fiske Stone. It found form in the legal realist movement. The realists, heavily concentrated in the law schools, sought to go beyond the sociological jurisprudence of the prewar period and focus legal adjudication on the consideration of societal reality. Their overall effect was to call attention to social needs and policy implications and to prepare the ground for the introduction of new kinds of information on social relationships into the process of making legal decisions. Influenced by pragmatism, behaviorist psychology, psychoanalysis, and statistical sociology, the realists deplored the decade's emphasis on rigid formulas and the application of the rules of law, rather placing emphasis on the role of the judge and his own psychological composition as a prime factor in decision-making. Law to them was what judges did, rather than what they said, and central was a consideration of the impact of what they did as a practical remedy for immediate legal problems. By the years of the Great Depression, their star had risen and influenced a new generation impressed by their prescience.

At the legislative level, the decade was strikingly empty. Harding had begun his presidency with an ambitious legislative docket. This included a Wilson-vetoed national budget and accounting act, a new farm-credit law, the creation of a system of national highways, laws regulating aviation and radio, and even an antilynching law. A surprised Congress, conditioned to think of "normalcy" as inaction, passed little legislation, and, indeed, the major federal statutes of the decade included the Packers and Stockyards Act of 1921, the Railway Labor Act of 1926, and stopgap depression legislation, principally the Agricultural Marketing Act of 1929.

Other than these, the primary statutory activity in the decade included modest measures appropriating money for disabled veterans' rehabilitation (the Fess-Kenyon Act of 1920) and state infant and maternity welfare activities (the Sheppard-Towner Maternity Act of 1921). Congress did approve a proposed child labor amendment in June 1924, but its ratification was stymied by opposition from manufacturers' associations and certain religious groups. The Johnson-Reed Immigration Act of 1924 imposed stringent quotas on entry to the United States and was consonant with the strong tendency of the courts in the period to define the rights of aliens narrowly. But again, to the extent that significant legislation was passed, most was at the state level, but by the end of the decade the courts had voided much of that. In fact, judicial action generally demonstrated once again that the Court had returned to its old role as a "brake on the social mechanism." Between 1921 and 1930, it ruled unconstitutional 11 acts of Congress, 131 state laws that had placed governmental restraints on one or another form of business activity, and 12 city ordinances. Conversely, its majority had no trouble sustaining federal measures that aided business and sanctioning numerous state laws and city ordinances that abridged the civil liberties of labor, radicals, too-outspoken pacificists, and other critics of the capitalist system.

At the federal level, the courts swerved between permissiveness and expansion in noneconomic cases, on the one hand, and contraction of power in areas that might adversely affect business, on the other. In *Missouri* v. *Holland* (1920), Justice Holmes interpreted the treaty-making power broadly, ruling that a treaty once ratified could be implemented by legislation that would have been invalid in the absence of the treaty. If the subject matter was sufficiently related to the general welfare and it was in a national interest that could be protected "only by national action in concert with another power," the treaty-making power could be used to expand the regulatory power of Congress. Congress' power was also expanded in connection with investigations to obtain information necessary for legislation. The Court, in *McGrain* v. *Daugherty* (1927), ruled that Congress might exercise the judicial power of subpoenaing witnesses and punish them for contempt if they failed to appeal. In 1929, in *Barry* v. *United States ex rel. Cunningham,* this was expanded to authorize punishing a witness for contempt if he refused to answer questions. Regarding the presidency, the Court in *Myers* v. *United States* (1926) invalidated a congressional statute to deny the president the power to remove certain federal officials without congressional consent, as an improper restraint on the executive powers.

At the regulatory level, the Court sustained full federal control over interstate as well as intrastate commerce, and went well beyond the *Shreveport* ruling in giving new sweep to the commerce clause in *Railroad Commission of Wisconsin* v. *Chicago, Burlington and Quincy* (1922). In *Stafford* v. *Wallace* (1922), it gave new emphasis to the stream-of-commerce doctrine as a source of federal regulatory power, insisting that the federal government could remove burdens to the free flow of commerce. The federal taxing power received a similar sanction when in *Massachusetts* v. *Mellon* (1923) the Court implied that revenue raised by national taxation could be used for economic and social purposes that were usually within the domain of the states. The effect of the ruling was to leave to congressional discretion federal grants-in-aid.

The 1920s were a business decade. Jerold Auerbach has written, "Corporate lawyers enjoyed unchallenged professional hegemony and unsurpassed opportunity to articulate their wishes as professional values. They spoke for the profession, asserted their clients' interests as professional and national interests and served as role models for those who aspired to the most rewarding professional careers." Calvin Coolidge respected this reality in his oft-quoted contention that "the business of America is business." The era saw renewal of the old system of business agreements, which now took the form of price and policy arrangements by trade associations.

Originally hostile, the Court soon followed the lead of Secretary of Commerce Herbert Hoover, who was persuading businessmen to standardize their products and adopt codes of fair practice. In *Maple Flooring Association* v. *United States* (1925), six of the justices agreed that such activities, rather than violating the restraints of the antitrust laws, "stabilized trade and industry . . . and avoided the waste which inevitably attends the unintelligent conduct of economic enterprise." The Court curtailed the FTC's right to define unfair trade practices in *Federal Trade Commission* v. *Gratz* (1920), and severely restricted its fact-finding authority in *Federal Trade Commission* v. *Curtis Publishing Co.* (1923). The justices not only restricted federal regulatory power over business but also utilized federal legislation to protect employers and curtail labor-union practices. In 1921 the anti-injunction provisions of the Clayton Act were virtually emasculated, and the way was paved for the renewed use of the antitrust laws against unions (*Duplex Printing Press Co.* v. *Deering,* 1921). This process was extended even into local labor disputes in *Bedford Cut Stone Co.* v. *Journeymen Stone Cutters Association* (1927).

Confronting the renewed use of federal police power during the decade, the Court was cautiously ambivalent. While upholding the 1921 Packers and Stockyards Act (*Stafford* v. *Wallace,* 1922) and the 1919 National Motor Vehicle Theft Act (*Brooks* v. *United States,* 1925), which forbade the movement of stolen automobiles in interstate commerce, it once again ruled the fed-

131

eral Child Labor Act, this time based on the taxing power, unconstitutional as a violation of the Tenth Amendment (*Bailey* v. *Drexel Furniture Co.*, 1922).

State police power fared poorly as well. As in the Progressive Era, the justices constantly scrutinized laws with the idea of determining their social objectives, but only if those social objectives seemed sufficiently compelling were the laws sustained. Normally this meant that if the laws unduly restricted private property or the owner's use of private property, they were ruled in violation of the due process clause of the Fourteenth Amendment. Sutherland set the tone for the decade by overruling, in *Bailey* v. *Drexel Furniture Co.*, a minimum-wage law for women in the District of Columbia. Despite the fact that similar state laws had previously received judicial sanction, Sutherland returned to the concept of freedom of contract enunciated in *Lochner* v. *New York* (1905) and condemned wage legislation as economically and socially unsound and a violation of due process of law. Following this precedent, the Court overruled a wide range of state regulatory laws, from anti-injunction laws to statutes placing conditions on business that the conservative majority deplored. Holmes and Brandeis deplored the conservative majority, frequently dissenting on the grounds that state legal experiments in the regulatory field properly reflected "contemporary conditions, social, industrial, and political, of the community." A Virginia statute permitting sterilization of inmates in institutions for the feebleminded, however, was sustained in *Buck* v. *Bell* (1927), as were a variety of other restrictions on individual freedom and individual rights.

Civil liberties and civil rights cases thus did come up during the 1920s, and the Court gradually evolved new legal concepts for dealing with them, which, nonetheless, reflected the temper of the times. Early in the decade, the Court still remained convinced that only if local laws directly affected property rights were they a threat to people's liberty. In *Meyer* v. *Nebraska* (1923) the Court threw out a state law prohibiting the teaching of, or teaching in, any language other than English to children in the first eight grades. Parents who paid for this type of education, argued Justice McReynolds, had a right to have their children educated on their terms without state interference. Since the children were essen-

tially their property, this was interfering with they way they wanted that property treated. In *Pierce* v. *Society of Sisters* (1925), McReynolds held an Oregon statute unconstitutional as attempting to force parents to send children to public schools. The statute, he argued, was destroying the property rights in private schools as well as the freedom of parents to utilize educational facilities of their own choice for which they were willing to pay.

But breakthroughs occurred in the civil liberties field. Brandeis had argued in a free-speech case in 1920 (*Gilbert* v. *Minnesota*) that it was time to reject the view that the liberty guaranteed by the Fourteenth Amendment included only liberty to acquire and enjoy property. For him, and others, the guarantees of the federal Bill of Rights should also apply to the states, and in a crucial case, *Gitlow* v. *New York* (1925), Justice Sanford stated for the Court, "We may and do assume that freedom of speech and of the press —which are protected by the First Amendment from abridgement by Congress—are among the fundamental personal rights and 'liberties' protected by the due process clause of the Fourteenth Amendment from impairment by the states." The statement opened the door to a new era in the constitutional law of civil liberties. Other cases soon followed, confirming the new association between due process and the guarantees of the Fourteenth Amendment; and by the depression year of 1931, both freedom of speech and of the press had been firmly incorporated against state interference.

As to the civil rights of minorities, the decade was a highly conservative period. The momentum that had carried woman suffrage to a successful amendment continued. In 1922, Congress passed the Cable Act, providing that a married alien woman would retain and determine her own citizenship and make her own application for naturalization after lawful admission for permanent residence, which the act reduced to three years. The same period saw all native-born Indians granted full citizenship through the Curtis Act of 1924. The measure did not automatically entitle Indians to vote, and some states still disfranchised Indians as "persons under guardianship." The National Woman's Party got the equal rights amendment (ERA) introduced into Congress in 1923, even though it was opposed by most of the large women's organizations because it was seen as a threat to protective labor legislation. Thus, the measure floundered, not to be revived until World War II.

As for black Americans, returning black veterans looked to the NAACP to push for rights. They quickly learned that World War I had not been fought for racial democracy in America, and race riots erupted in a dozen cities in the years following the war. This led to the introduction into Congress of antilynching bills, although none was successful in these explosive years. Judicial conservatives offered little encouragement to rising black expectations. The Court in 1926 unanimously upheld a restrictive racial covenant that provided that property should never be leased or sold to a black, maintaining that since no state action was involved, no violation of due process was present (*Corrigan* v. *Buckley*). On voting rights, Holmes speaking for a unanimous Court made clear that Texas could not, by statute, exclude blacks from the Democratic primary without thereby violating the equal protection clause of the Fourteenth Amendment (*Nixon* v. *Herndon*, 1927). This ruling had little impact, since party leaders promptly found ways to make the essential primary decisions prior to that election.

The 1920s was also an anti-alien decade, with economic hostility fueling racial bias toward Chinese, Japanese, Filipinos, and Hindus, striking particularly at their rights of naturalization. The Court considered the rights of those aliens who were ineligible for citizenship and curtailed such rights as holding land or even owning stock in a corporation that held land for agricultural purposes (*Terrace* v. *Thompson*, 1923). Deportation was also condoned for "undesirable" aliens, a subjective definition that did not have reference to any criminal behavior.

Regarding the procedural rights of the Fourth through Eighth Amendments, the majority of justices took few steps decisive enough to create permanent precedents. Generally the Court left standards to the states and only injected federal authority where flagrant flouting of procedural rights brought national demands for minimal decency. The Fourth Amendment's guarantee against unreasonable searches and seizures did present new challenges, especially during the Prohibition years. Holmes had set the tone in this regard in *Silverthorne Lumber Co.* v. *United States* (1920), which arose from the fact that the Department of Justice and a United States marshal had, "without a shadow of authority," seized books and papers in the office of two suspects who were being detained at the time. His opinion insisted that "the knowledge gained by the government's own wrong cannot be used by it in the way proposed." On the other hand, the Court in 1925, in *Carroll* v. *United States*, permitted search and seizure, without warrant, of automobiles used for illegal transport of liquor. The only qualification was Taft's assertion "that where the securing of a warrant is reasonably practicable it must be used."

The technology of the 1920s also produced judicial response. Wiretapping was a new method by which evidence could be secured, and questions early arose as to whether this technique violated the Fourth Amendment. In *Olmstead* v. *United States* (1928), Taft, for a badly split Court, maintained that it did not, since nothing was searched and nothing was seized. Brandeis, on the other hand, responded bitterly that when "the government becomes a law-breaker, it breeds contempt for law." Holmes joined in, saying that it was "less evil that some criminals should escape than that the government should play an ignoble part."

State courts in this decade tended to follow national trends, with local variations. Judicial review at the state level continued to grow and become even more extensive, with the number of cases coming before the courts testing the constitutionality of laws, ordinances, proceedings, and administrative measures increasing out of all proportion to those of former decades. In some states, such as Virginia, this was the result of new, progressive constitutions that included limitations on the power of the legislature, rigid supervision and control of corporations, and a more detailed concern with economic matters. But it also stemmed from a more extensive use of the police power at the state level and from the desire, particularly of corporate bodies, to use the courts to cut down on public interference with their freedom.

Interesting anomalies occurred, however. In certain states, new constitutional provisions curtailed the power of the legislature to enact local, special, or private laws. This revealed both a distrust of the legislative body and a desire to keep local issues out of state-level litigation. In some respects, this paralleled Taft's new role for the Supreme Court in the Judiciary Act of 1925. It also represented the apparent willingness of the citizenry to trust the courts to concentrate on "straightening out" the legislature rather than on local issues. Thus, the court's role in statutory construction, as in judicial review, was enhanced in seeing to it that legislation generally tended to serve the state's interests. Variations occurred, emphasizing the ongoing tension between uniformity and diversity, centralism and localism. Issues of power and control were at the root of such tensions. This was particularly true in the South, where such an issue as centralization of public education was clearly opposed, with the state courts frequently leaving discretion in such matters to the local citizenry.

In New York, the expansion of judicial review was also a notable development, again emphasizing the importance of the courts over elected bodies, particularly ones wherein corruption and extravagance and the pernicious influence of lobbyists and economically powerful people had led to venality and wastefulness. Because people wanted a check on legislative action, the courts were encouraged to test questionable legislation against higher standards. During the 1920s the courts tended to sustain legislatures, but not until critical assessment had been carried out. Again, in the industrial states, there was a marked tendency for the courts to view positive labor legislation with a particularly hostile eye, reflecting the business orientation of the era.

In sum, the hopes of those who pushed for greater state-level judicial review were not fulfilled. Such action neither cured legislative misbehavior nor acted as an insuperable obstacle to essential laws. Rather, in an era that distrusted the democratic process, it left large bodies of policymaking discretion to judges and lawyers—an elite that generally empathized with, and found itself comfortable serving, the business elite of the age.

CASES

Abrams v. United States, 250 U.S. 616 (1919)
Adams v. Tanner, 244 U.S. 590 (1917)
Bailey v. Alabama, 219 U.S. 219 (1911)
Bailey v. Drexel Furniture Co., 259 U.S. 20 (1922)

Barry v. United States ex rel. Cunningham, 279 U.S. 597 (1929)
Bedford Cut Stone Co. v. Journeymen Stone Cutters Association, 274 U.S. 37 (1927)
Brooks v. United States, 267 U.S. 432 (1925)
Brown v. Board of Education, 347 U.S. 483 (1954)
Buchanan v. Warley, 245 U.S. 60 (1917)
Buck v. Bell, 274 U.S. 200 (1927)
Bunting v. Oregon, 243 U.S. 426 (1917)
Carroll v. United States, 267 U.S. 132 (1925)
Commonwealth v. Boston & Maine Railroad, 222 Mass. 206, 110 N.E. 264 (1915)
Coppage v. Kansas, 236 U.S. 1 (1915)
Corrigan v. Buckley, 271 U.S. 323 (1926)
Duplex Printing Press Co. v. Deering, 254 U.S. 443 (1921)
Federal Trade Commission v. Curtis Publishing Co., 260 U.S. 568 (1923)
Federal Trade Commission v. Gratz, 253 U.S. 421 (1920)
Frank v. Mangum, 235 U.S. 694 (1914); 237 U.S. 309 (1915)
Gilbert v. Minnesota, 245 U.S. 325 (1920)
Gitlow v. New York, 268 U.S. 652 (1925)
Gompers v. Bucks Stove & Range Co., 211 U.S. 418 (1911)
Guinn v. United States, 238 U.S. 347 (1915)
Hadacheck v. Los Angeles, 239 U.S. 394 (1915)
Hammer v. Dagenhart, 247 U.S. 251 (1918)
Hipolite Egg Co. v. United States, 220 U.S. 45 (1911)
Hoke v. United States, 227 U.S. 308 (1913)
Ives v. South Buffalo Railway, 201 N.Y. 271, 94 N.E. 431 (1911)
Jensen v. Southern Pacific Co., 215 N.Y. 514, 109 N.E. 600 (1915)
Lochner v. New York, 198 U.S. 45 (1905)
McCabe v. Atchison, Topeka & Santa Fe Railway, 235 U.S. 151 (1914)
McGrain v. Daugherty, 273 U.S. 135 (1927)
Maple Flooring Association v. United States, 268 U.S. 563 (1925)
Massachusetts v. Mellon, 262 U.S. 447 (1923)
Massie v. Cessna, 239 Ill. 352, 88 N.E. 152 (1909)
Meyer v. Nebraska, 262 U.S. 390 (1923)
Minnesota Rate Cases, 230 U.S. 352 (1913)
Missouri v. Holland, 252 U.S. 416 (1920)
Moore v. Dempsey, 261 U.S. 86 (1923)
Mountain Timber v. Washington, 243 U.S. 219 (1917)
Muller v. Oregon, 208 U.S. 412 (1908)
Myers v. Anderson, 238 U.S. 363 (1915)
Myers v. United States, 272 U.S. 52 (1926)
New York Central Railroad v. White, 243 U.S. 188 (1917)
Nixon v. Herndon, 273 U.S. 536 (1927)
Northern Pacific Railway v. North Dakota, 236 U.S. 585 (1919)
Olmstead v. United States, 277 U.S. 438 (1928)
Pierce v. Society of Sisters, 268 U.S. 510 (1925)
Plessy v. Ferguson, 163 U.S. 537 (1896)
Railroad Commission of Wisconsin v. Chicago, Burlington and Quincy, 257 U.S. 563 (1922)
Schenck v. United States, 249 U.S. 47 (1919)
Second Employers' Liability Cases, 223 U.S. 1 (1912)
Selective Draft Law Cases, 245 U.S. 366 (1918)
Shreveport Rate Cases, 234 U.S. 342 (1914)
Silverthorne Lumber Co. v. United States, 251 U.S. 385 (1920)

Stafford v. Wallace, 258 U.S. 495 (1922)
Standard Oil Co. v. United States, 221 U.S. 1 (1911)
Starnes v. Albion Manufacturing Co., 147 N.C. 5, 61 S.E. 525 (1908)
State v. Miksicek, 225 Mo. 561, 125 S.W. 507 (1910)
State v. Somerville, 67 Wash. 638, 122 P. 324 (1912)
Stettler v. O'Hara, 243 U.S. 629 (1917)
Terrace v. Thompson, 263 U.S. 197 (1923)
Truax v. Raich, 239 U.S. 33 (1915)
Twining v. New Jersey, 211 U.S. 78 (1908)
United States v. American Tobacco Co., 221 U.S. 106 (1911)
United States v. Doremus, 249 U.S. 86 (1919)
United States v. Grimaud, 220 U.S. 506 (1911)
United States v. L. Cohen Grocery Co., 255 U.S. 81 (1921)
United States v. Reynolds, 235 U.S. 133 (1914)
United States v. United States Steel Corp., 251 U.S. 417 (1920)
United States v. Winslow, 227 U.S. 202 (1913)
Weeks v. United States, 232 U.S. 383 (1914)
Wilson v. New, 243 U.S. 332 (1917)

BIBLIOGRAPHY

The most detailed study of the White Court is Alexander M. Bickel and Benno C. Schmidt, Jr., *The Judiciary and Responsible Government: 1910–1921* (1984), vol. 9 of the Oliver Wendell Holmes Devise History of the Supreme Court of the United States. The early segments, completed by Bickel before his death in 1974, deal in detail with the Court's personnel, and its rulings, especially in the area of antitrust law and the rule of reason, and social legislation, both federal and state. In the last three chapters, Schmidt deals almost exclusively with the civil rights of black Americans, exploring peonage, discrimination, and the denial of voting rights. The same Supreme Court focus is present in William F. Swindler, *Court and Constitution in the Twentieth Century: The Old Legality, 1889–1932* (1969), and in Alfred H. Kelly, Winfred A. Harbison, and Herman Belz, *The American Constitution: Its Origin and Development,* 6th ed. (1983). This edition departs sharply in emphasis from the previous five, moving from a liberal orientation to a neoconservative one with Belz's revision. Loren P. Beth, *The Development of the American Constitution, 1877–1917* (1971), includes valuable material on the White Court, the era, and especially on state-court behavior in this period. The emphasis is more constitutional than legal and covers a broad range of topics. John E. Semonche, *Charting the Future: The Supreme Court Responds to a Changing Society, 1890–1920*

(1978), spends five of twelve chapters on the White period, again with Supreme Court emphasis and with a revisionist thrust. Paul L. Murphy, *World War I and the Origin of Civil Liberties in the United States* (1979), treats civil liberties issues in wartime and a portion of the White era, and traces the emergence of the American Civil Liberties Union. The standard biography of White is Marie Carolyn Klinkhamer, *Edward Douglass White: Chief Justice of the United States* (1943). Its uncritical focus is partially compensated for by Robert Highsaw, *Edward Douglass White: Defender of the Conservative Faith* (1981). Good personal and bibliographical data regarding the careers of both the White and Taft justices is contained in Leon Friedman and Fred L. Israel, eds., *Justices of the United States Supreme Court, 1789–1969* (1969), vol. 3. A particularly useful study of one of the central figures in this period is Philippa Strum, *Louis D. Brandeis: Justice for the People* (1984).

The Taft Court and era is discussed in the early chapters of Paul L. Murphy, *The Constitution in Crisis Times, 1918–1969* (1971); in Swindler; and in Kelly, Harbison, and Belz. Alpheus T. Mason, *William Howard Taft: Chief Justice* (1965), treats Taft's behavior as chief justice and the climate he created for law in the 1920s. The study is valuably augmented by Walter F. Murphy, "In His Own Image: Mr. Chief Justice Taft and Supreme Court Appointments," in *1961 Supreme Court Review* (1961). Richard C. Cortner, *The Supreme Court and the Second Bill of Rights* (1981), is the best treatment of the incorporation of the Bill of Rights against the states.

State courts themselves still cry for modern reassessment. Two early works do include material on this period: Margaret V. Nelson, *A Study of Judicial Review in Virginia, 1789–1928* (1947), and Franklin A. Smith, *Judicial Review of Legislation in New York, 1906–1938* (1952).

G. Edward White, *Patterns of American Legal Thought* (1978), includes a valuable essay on the move from sociological jurisprudence to legal realism. The standard work on the latter movement is Wilfred E. Rumble, Jr., *American Legal Realism* (1968). A broader study of the context of legal development in this period is John W. Johnson, *American Legal Culture, 1908–1940* (1981).

General treatments of law in these years are inadequate. Lawrence M. Friedman, *A History of American Law* (1973), includes a brief chapter on the twentieth century, setting forth major trends. Jerold Auerbach, *Unequal Justice: Lawyers and Social Change in Modern America* (1976) presents a highly critical assessment of the legal profession generally, with pithy chapters on the White and Taft eras.

[*See also* AMERICAN JURISPRUDENCE; CIVIL LIBERTIES TO 1937; DUE PROCESS OF LAW; FEDERALISM; FREE SPEECH AND EXPRESSION; *and* FULLER COURT AND ERA.]

THE HUGHES COURT AND ERA

David J. Danelski

O N the day the New York stock market crashed —Black Thursday, 29 October 1929—Chief Justice William Howard Taft was desperately ill. A dying man, he was obsessed with preserving the conservative makeup of the Court. He viewed Oliver Wendell Holmes, Louis D. Brandeis, and Harlan Fiske Stone, his liberal colleagues, as hopeless in preserving his notion of the Constitution. But there were five justices other than himself, he thought, who could hang on for many years and keep the Court steady—Willis Van Devanter, James C. McReynolds, George Sutherland, Pierce Butler, and Edward T. Sanford. By January 1930, Taft knew that he could no longer hang on, but he would try to pass on his office to Charles Evans Hughes. With Taft's resignation imminent, both conservatives and liberals on the Court sought to influence the choice of his successor. Taft by this time was too ill to do more than make his support of Hughes known. His conservative colleagues, Van Devanter and Butler, could do more, for they had access to Attorney General William D. Mitchell, a friend of Van Devanter and a former law partner of Butler. Harlan Fiske Stone was also in a favored position to influence the appointment, for he too had access to Mitchell and, more important, to President Herbert Hoover, a close friend.

Stone discussed the chief-justiceship with both Hoover and Mitchell. Stone told Hoover that he thought a man of liberal tendencies should be chosen and gave the president a short list of names headed by Chief Judge Benjamin N. Cardozo of the New York Court of Appeals. When Hoover raised Hughes's name, Stone responded negatively on three grounds— Hughes's age (which was sixty-seven), his resignation from the Supreme Court to run for the

presidency in 1916, and his representation of corporate clients after leaving the Court. Stone's conversations with Mitchell also indicated that Hoover was likely to appoint Hughes. Stone concluded that Hoover was inclined to choose Hughes because he did not want a liberal.

At the time he talked to Stone, Mitchell had already decided to recommend Hughes to Hoover. Aware of Van Devanter's and Butler's strong support of Hughes, he dispatched the two conservative justices to New York to persuade Hughes to accept the chief-justiceship if Hoover were to offer it. Hughes's comments over dinner with Van Devanter and Butler convinced them that he would probably accept. Soon after Mitchell received that report, Hoover invited Hughes to the White House, where the president offered him the chief-justiceship. But Hughes demurred. He said he was too old and had no desire to accept the responsibility. Hoover urged him to accept. Finally, Hughes said he would accept if Hoover would assure him there would be no confirmation fight. Hoover gave the assurance. The next day Taft resigned, and two days later Hoover sent Hughes's name to the Senate.

Hoover's assurance notwithstanding, Senate opposition to Hughes's nomination was predictable. Progressive senators had mounted campaigns against Warren G. Harding's nomination of Butler in 1923 and Calvin Coolidge's nomination of Stone in 1925, on the grounds that the nominees' representation of corporate interests would bias their interpretation of the Constitution. Although the progressives had been able to muster only a few votes against the confirmations of Butler and Stone, they had fought their battles in the boom times of the 1920s. The early days of the Great Depression were another matter. The Senate reacted predictably. Senators argued that Hughes had regularly represented corporations of "untold wealth" after resigning from the Court. "The man who has never felt the pinch of hunger," George W. Norris told his colleagues in the Senate, "and who has never known what it was to be cold, who has never been associated with those who have earned their bread by the sweat of their faces, but who lived in luxury, who has never wanted for anything that money could buy, is not fit to sit judgment in a contest between organized wealth and those who toil." This was a powerful argument in 1930. Ultimately the Senate confirmed Hughes's nomination, but the vote was 53–26.

Considering Hughes's public stature and his impeccable character, the fact that twenty-six senators voted against him is remarkable. A lesser man probably would have been defeated. Two months later, Justice Sanford, one of the five justices Taft had counted on to continue the conservative character of the Court, died at the age of sixty-five, and Hoover nominated John J. Parker of North Carolina, a federal circuit judge. The American Federation of Labor objected to him because of his labor decisions, and the National Association for the Advancement of Colored People objected to him because reputedly he had opposed suffrage for black people. To the progressives, Parker had to be blocked for the same reasons that Hughes had been opposed. The Senate rejected Parker's nomination by a vote of 41–39. Hoover then nominated Owen J. Roberts, a Republican lawyer from Philadelphia who had been chief prosecutor in the Teapot Dome case. After a perfunctory examination of Roberts' background, the Senate speedily confirmed his nomination.

Early in 1932, Justice Holmes retired at the age of ninety. Stone immediately pressed Hoover to appoint Cardozo, and this time Hoover yielded. With Cardozo's appointment, the Hughes Court personnel settled in for a five-year period.

Cardozo joined the Court in the bleakest year of the Great Depression. Banks were closed, and business was stagnant. More than 13 million people were unemployed. Many had neither homes nor food. More than 2 million men, women, and children wandered across the country in a fruitless quest for work. The homeless wanderers built makeshift shacks of packing boxes and scrap metal in empty lots and outskirts of towns, creating "Hoovervilles" throughout the nation. In this period of national despair, Franklin Delano Roosevelt conducted a successful campaign for the presidency. After repeating his oath of office before Chief Justice Hughes on 4 March 1933, Roosevelt told the nation that the only thing it had "to fear is fear itself—nameless, unreasoning, unjustified terror which paralyzes needed efforts to convert retreat into advance." Concluding, he said, "This Nation asks for action, and action now."

It did indeed seem to be a time for action, not legal hairsplitting about the Constitution. But the prevailing interpretation of the Constitution in 1933 stood in the way of necessary action. In the half-century that preceded the New Deal, the Supreme Court had limited governmental activity. It held that the federal government's delegated powers were limited by the states' police powers and that broad construction of the Constitution's general-welfare and commerce clauses was insufficient to support federal legislation regulating the economy. As for state regulation, the Court held that the exercise of state police powers was rigorously limited by the due process clause of the Fourteenth Amendment. The result was a no-man's-land in which laissez-faire reigned and the use of property was generally immune from government regulation.

In drafting legislation enacted by Congress during the "Hundred Days" of the Roosevelt administration, New Deal lawyers knew that the constitutional doctrine on which they relied had the adherence of only a minority of the Court. The legislation they wrote created a host of new federal agencies, including the Civilian Conservation Corps, the Federal Emergency Relief Administration, the Federal Deposit Insurance Corporation, the Home Owners' Loan Corporation, the Public Works Administration, and the Tennessee Valley Authority. The newly enacted National Industrial Recovery Act, the Agricultural Adjustment Act, and a joint resolution of Congress empowering the president to devalue the dollar by reducing its gold content raised especially difficult constitutional problems.

In 1933 there was considerable speculation about the Supreme Court upholding New Deal legislation. The conservatives (Van Devanter,

McReynolds, Sutherland, and Butler) seemed certain to declare it unconstitutional, while the liberals (Brandeis, Stone, and Cardozo) seemed likely to uphold it. That left the deciding votes with Hughes and Roberts.

Cases challenging New Deal legislation did not reach the Supreme Court until 1934. Early that year the Court decided two important state cases involving economic regulation, *Home Building & Loan Assn.* v. *Blaisdell,* which upheld the Minnesota Moritorium Act, and *Nebbia* v. *New York,* which upheld the New York Milk Control Law. Both were 5–4 decisions, and the split in the cases appeared to be ideological. Van Devanter, McReynolds, Sutherland, and Butler were on one side, and Brandeis, Stone, and Cardozo were on the other. The three liberals prevailed only because Hughes and Roberts joined them.

Although the language of the majority opinions in *Blaisdell* and *Nebbia* reassured New Deal advocates, the closeness of the vote did not. Those cases did not prove to be harbingers of judicial approval of New Deal legislation. They were among a few liberal decisions in an oscillating ideological pattern of decision-making. During the same term in which the Court decided *Blaisdell* and *Nebbia,* it also decided *Booth* v. *United States* and *Lynch* v. *United States,* cases that unanimously struck down provisions enacted during the Hundred Days. The laws in *Booth* and *Lynch,* however, were economy measures that did not go to the heart of the New Deal program. Far more important was *Panama Refining Co.* v. *Ryan Co.* (1935), which the government had chosen to test the constitutionality of the National Industrial Recovery Act. By a vote of 8–1 (Cardozo dissenting), the Court ruled against the government on the ground that the act unconstitutionally delegated power to the president because it did not set adequate standards for executive guidance.

Less than two months after *Panama Refining Co.,* the Court again swung to the left in the *Gold Clause Cases,* in which it had to decide whether Congress had the power to nullify the gold clause in private and public contracts. The clause required payment of principal and interest in United States gold coin. In one of the cases, *Perry* v. *United States* (1935), Hughes took the position that the congressional resolution repudiating the gold clause in government bonds was unconstitutional, but despite the resolution's unconstitutionality, bondholders could not recover because they had not shown more than nominal damages. In the other cases, *Norman* v. *Baltimore & Ohio Railroad* (1935) and *Nortz* v. *United States* (1935), Hughes upheld the validity of the gold clause resolution. Brandeis, Cardozo, and Roberts concurred in Hughes's opinion, and Stone concurred in the result. Thus, the government, though chastised in *Perry,* prevailed in all the cases. In delivering a dissenting opinion for himself, Van Devanter, Sutherland, and Butler, McReynolds exclaimed angrily from the bench, "This is Nero at his worst. The Constitution is gone!" Had the decision gone the other way, Roosevelt was prepared to deliver a defiant radio address to say that he would not enforce the Court's decisions. Roosevelt rejoiced "that the Supreme Court has at last definitely put human values ahead of the 'pound of flesh' called for by a contract." He added, "In spite of our rejoicing, I shudder at the closeness of five-to-four decisions in these important matters."

Three months after the Court decided the *Gold Clause Cases,* it swung to the right again, this time striking down the Railroad Retirement Pension Act in *Retirement Board* v. *Alton Railroad Co.,* with Hughes, Brandeis, Stone, and Cardozo dissenting. Then, in a series of unanimous decisions, the Court struck down provisions of the Frazier-Lemke Act in *Louisville Bank* v. *Radford,* the Federal Home Owner's Loan Act of 1933 in *Hopkins Federal Savings & Loan Assn.* v. *Cleary,* and the National Industrial Recovery Act in *Schechter Poultry Corp.* v. *United States.* On the same day that *Radford* and *Schechter* were announced, 27 May 1935, the Court also unanimously decided *Humphrey's Executor* v. *United States,* which held that the president could not remove members of regulatory commissions unless Congress gave him authority to to do so. Roosevelt was stunned by these decisions, particularly *Humphrey's Executor,* which vexed him more than the other decisions because he thought the Court had acted personally against him in denying what it would have upheld if someone else had been in the White House.

Schechter was the most important of these decisions because it had rejected the government's broad interpretation of the commerce clause and thus killed the National Recovery Administration (NRA), which more than any other agency symbolized the New Deal. Reacting to the decision,

Roosevelt told reporters that its implications were "more important than any decision since the *Dred Scott Case.*" He added that the nation had been relegated to a "horse-and-buggy" definition of interstate commerce. The response of the press to Roosevelt's remark was chilly. It supported the Court rather than the president. Even some New Dealers welcomed the demise of the NRA, which they regarded as either a failure or an agency that fostered monopoly.

The conservative trend of decisions continued in *United States* v. *Butler* (1936). In that case, the Court, with Brandeis, Stone, and Cardozo dissenting, invalidated the Agricultural Adjustment Act, saying in an opinion by Roberts that the power of Congress to tax and spend for the general welfare was inadequate to uphold the act. Stone, writing in dissent, made an outraged plea for judicial self-restraint. Calling the majority's construction of the Constitution "tortured," he wrote,

> Courts are not the only agency of government that must be assumed to have capacity to govern. Congress and the courts both unhappily may falter or be mistaken in the performance of their constitutional duty. But interpretation of our great charter of government which proceeds on any assumption that the responsibility for the preservation of our institutions is the exclusive concern of any one of the three branches of government, or that it alone can save them from destruction, is far more likely, in the long run, "to obliterate the constituent members" of "an indestructible union of indestructible states" than the frank recognition that language, even of a constitution, may mean what it says: that the power to tax includes the power to relieve a nation-wide economic maladjustment by conditional gifts of money.

Stone's words may have affected the votes of some of his colleagues in later cases, for in *Ashwander* v. *Tennessee Valley Authority* (1936) all the justices except McReynolds voted to uphold the validity of a contract between the Tennessee Valley Authority and the Alabama Power Company to sell surplus power. But soon thereafter the Court struck down the Bituminous Coal Conservation Act of 1935 in *Carter* v. *Carter Coal Co.* and the Municipal Bankruptcy Act in *Ashton* v. *Cameron County Water Improvement District*. In *Carter*, the Court split as it had in *Butler* (6–3), but

Hughes wrote a separate opinion in which he dissented in part. In *Ashton*, the Court split 5–4, with Hughes, Brandeis, Stone, and Cardozo in dissent. This same division in the Court occurred in *Morehead* v. *New York ex rel. Tipaldo* (1936), which struck down New York's minimum-wage law for women. Overwhelmingly the press and the public thought that the majority had gone too far in *Tipaldo*. Even the Republican National Convention in 1936 repudiated the decision.

Why the Supreme Court oscillated between the left and right in the mid-1930s is one of the most fascinating questions in its history. A large part of the answer is ideology. Both the conservative bloc and the liberal bloc remained intact in all but two of the decisions mentioned above. But there was a difference between the conservatives and liberals: conservative justices supported only one liberal outcome, whereas the liberal justices supported seven conservative outcomes. Given the 4–3 division of votes in the two ideological blocs, the votes of Hughes and Roberts were obviously crucial in determining decisions when the Court split into blocs.

Although Hughes had been the candidate of the conservatives for the chief-justiceship, he was personally disposed to agree with the liberals. On the minimum-wage issue, he had taken a liberal position before his appointment as chief justice, and in the 1930s he acknowledged privately that he sympathized with most New Deal legislation. His votes were generally in accord with his liberal disposition; in all but two decisions mentioned above, he voted with at least two of the liberal justices. In one of the cases in which he parted company with the liberals, *Carter*, he wrote a separate opinion partly agreeing with them. In the other case, *Butler*, he thought Brandeis might vote with him, for Brandeis had voted "pass" in the conference.

The importance of Hughes's liberal inclinations in the New Deal cases cannot be underestimated, but other aspects of his behavior on the bench are also important. First, there was his leadership ability, which he used to increase the size of majorities on the premise that unity contributes to the legitimacy of decisions. Nine of the decisions mentioned above were decided unanimously or by 8–1 votes. He also used his leadership ability to keep the Court from suffering "self-inflicted wounds," an expression he had earlier coined. He had been successful in

Blaisdell, Nebbia, and the *Gold Clause Cases,* but he failed in *Tipaldo.* Second, there was Hughes's profound concern for the Court's reputation, which he sought to protect by reinterpreting precedents rather than overruling them. Third, there was his use of his power to assign opinions to enhance the legitimacy of decisions. He assigned to liberal justices the Court's opinion in three of the cases that struck down New Deal legislation—two to Brandeis and one to Cardozo —presumably on the premise that liberals would find the decisions less objectionable if liberal justices wrote in support of them. Of the remaining cases mentioned above in which he had the power of assignment, he wrote in seven himself, including the *Gold Clause Cases, Panama Refining,* and *Schechter,* thus adding the prestige of the chief-justiceship to those decisions.

Ideology accounts less for Roberts' voting behavior than it does for any other justice in the New Deal period. Although his colleagues viewed him as a conservative, Roberts' votes in the mid-1930s lacked a clear ideological pattern. In the ten closely divided decisions mentioned above—those with 5–4 and 6–3 votes—Roberts voted with the liberals five times and the conservatives five times. His votes explain in large part the Court's oscillation in the mid-1930s. Roberts' commitment to legal formalism, together with his conservatism, is the best explanation of his behavior. Soon after he was appointed to the Court in 1930, he expressed his approach to judicial decision-making in a letter to Felix Frankfurter:

> It seems to me that in every case, when the facts and circumstances are clearly understood and properly weighed, there is a position that must be eternally right. It only beclouds the issue to call the result either a conservative or a radical victory. My hope is that I may be able to view situations with calmness and without predisposition, and at least in a fair percentage of cases put my finger on that which is eternally right, as a result of analysis and deliberation.
>
> (quoted in Chambers, 68)

In *Butler,* Roberts wrote,

> When an act of Congress is appropriately challenged in the courts as not conforming to the constitutional mandate the judicial branch of the Government has only one duty—to lay the

article of the Constitution which is invoked beside the statute which is challenged and to decide whether the latter squares with the former.

Because Roberts was a legal formalist, Hughes was able to persuade him to join the liberals in some important decisions, for Hughes was formidable in legal argument. But Van Devanter, Sutherland, and Butler could hold their own in legal argument, and most of the time they had precedent on their side; so it is not surprising that Roberts frequently went along with them.

Roberts' formalism played a crucial role in the decision of *Tipaldo.* In a memoir he later wrote and gave to Justice Felix Frankfurter, he explained his vote as follows:

> Both in the petition for certiorari, in the brief on the merits, and in oral argument, counsel for the State of New York took the position that it was unnecessary to overrule the *Adkins* case [which held unconstitutional a minimum-wage law passed by Congress for in order to sustain the position of the state of New York]. It was urged [by some of the justices in conference] that further data and experience and additional facts distinguished the case at bar from the *Adkins* case. The argument seemed to me to be disingenuous and born of timidity. I could find nothing in the record to substantiate the alleged distinction. At conference I so stated, and stated further that I was for taking the State of New York at its word. The State had not asked that the *Adkins* case be overruled but that it be distinguished. I said I was unwilling to put a decision on any such ground.
>
> (quoted in Frankfurter, 314)

Roberts then went on to say that he was willing to reexamine *Adkins* when a case came to the Court requiring it to do so.

Two and a half months after the Court decided *Tipaldo,* a case came before it that raised the same issue, this time in regard to Washington's minimum-wage law. The case was *West Coast Hotel Co.* v. *Parrish* (1937). Between 5 and 10 October 1936, the Court, by a vote of 5–4, noted probable jurisdiction in *Parrish.* (Four votes are required to note probable jurisdiction or grant a petition for certiorari, which are means of granting appellate review.) The fact that the fifth vote was Roberts' was significant.

Roberts later said he voted for review in *Parrish* because counsel in that case, unlike counsel in *Tipaldo,* had asked the Court to overrule *Adkins.*

On 14 October, Stone became seriously ill. On 16 and 17 December, while Stone was lying comatose at home, the Court heard oral arguments in *Parrish.* Sometime before the conference on 19 December, at which the Court decided the case, Hughes and Roberts met privately to discuss *Parrish.* In that discussion, Roberts said he was willing to vote to sustain the Washington law. Hughes told his biographer Merlo J. Pusey that the disclosure made him so happy that he almost hugged Roberts. Roberts maintained that he had not in fact changed his position, for he had not faced the issue of overruling *Adkins* until the fall of 1936. Historians have criticized Roberts' explanation, and some of them have pointed out that a critical event, the presidential election of 1936, occurred between the Court's decision in *Tipaldo* and Hughes's conversation with Roberts in December 1936, suggesting that Roosevelt's overwhelming victory in the election affected Roberts' vote in *Parrish.* The influence of Hughes must also be considered. He had been unsuccessful in his attempt to persuade Roberts in *Tipaldo,* but he had not given up. Roberts knew that Hughes wanted his vote in *Parrish.* In view of Roberts' respect and affection for Hughes, whom he regarded like a father or an older brother, it is likely that Hughes at least partly influenced Roberts' vote in *Parrish.*

The conference vote in *Parrish* on 19 December 1936 was 4–4 because Stone was still ill and absent from the Court. That tie vote upheld the constitutionality of the Washington minimum-wage law and marked the beginning of judicial restraint in cases challenging state economic regulation under the due process clause of the Fourteenth Amendment. But because Stone was certain to contribute the fifth vote for that position, the justices agreed not to announce the Court's decision until Stone returned to the Court.

Meanwhile, Roosevelt, unaware that a crucial shift had occurred in the Supreme Court, was planning to do battle with it. Following his overwhelming electoral victory in 1936, Roosevelt returned to Washington elated, overconfident, and angry at the Supreme Court, which he was determined to vanquish. He had considered moving against the Court earlier, but after the chilly response of the press to his "horse-and-buggy" criticism of *Schechter,* he decided to bide his time. The only decision he commented on was *Tipaldo,* and that comment was restrained. But months before the *Tipaldo* decision, Roosevelt had been studying plans to curb the Court.

One approach was to amend the Constitution. Felix Frankfurter, then a professor at Harvard and one of Roosevelt's advisers, favored that approach. "If we're to have amending," he wrote to a friend in 1935, "we need (1) *expansion,* through declaratory defining Amendment, of the Commerce Clause, (2) *contraction,* through declaratory defining Amendment, of the Due Process Clause" (quoted in Irons, 274). The Court's unannounced decision in December 1936 had already accomplished contraction, and expansion now seemed likely. But Roosevelt and his advisers knew none of this, and furthermore Frankfurter was not privy to the Court-curbing plans developed after the 1936 election.

The key figure in devising those plans was Attorney General Homer Cummings, who was an astute politician but not a scholarly lawyer. Six days after the election, Roosevelt summoned Cummings for a progress report. It was clear to Cummings that the president was ready to act, but how he would act was unclear. Edward S. Corwin, a Princeton political scientist who had been advising Cummings, suggested in December 1936 "that the President be authorized, whenever a majority of the Justices, or half of the Justices, are seventy or more years old, to nominate enough new Justices of less than that age to make a majority. This . . . would require only an act of Congress" (quoted in Leuchtenburg, 1966, 389). Corwin's suggestion appealed to Cummings, but Cummings was not sure that a constitutional amendment was unnecessary until he came across a recommendation Justice McReynolds had made in 1913 when he was Woodrow Wilson's attorney general. McReynolds had recommended that federal lower-court judges be permitted to retire at full pay at the age of seventy after ten years of service and that if any judge over the age of seventy failed to retire, the president, with advice and consent of the Senate, be empowered to appoint another judge. This procedure, according to McReynolds, would ensure the presence of a judge sufficiently active to discharge promptly and adequately the duties of the courts. Cummings liked the recommendation for two reasons: first, it showed no constitutional amendment was necessary; second, it had been made by McReynolds, who could now be neutralized by a procedure he had himself devised.

Cummings, consulting only with Solicitor General Stanley Reed and a few others, drafted the Court-reorganization plan that Roosevelt announced publicly on 5 February 1937. The proposed legislation, which the press immediately called the "Court-packing plan," empowered the president to appoint an additional justice for each justice over the age of seventy up to a total of six. At the time there were six justices, including Brandeis, who were more than seventy years old. The typical reaction of contemporaries and later historians was that the proposal was simply too clever. To many, Roosevelt's justification was worse than the proposal itself because it was disingenuous. Roosevelt said the proposed bill was necessary because the aged justices had fallen behind in their work—which was patently false—instead of stating his true purpose, which was to transform the Court by naming justices who would be sympathetic to the New Deal.

From Roosevelt's perspective in 1937, however, his Court plan was almost certain to be a splendid success. First, as the 1936 election had shown, the people overwhelmingly supported him. Second, Senate leaders, particularly southerners such as James F. Byrnes of South Carolina, Pat Harrison of Mississippi, and the powerful majority leader, Joseph T. Robinson of Arkansas, also supported him. Third, Roosevelt did not have to rely on Cummings for executive-legislative liaison; Tom Corcoran and Ben Cohen, gifted lawyer-politicians, would assume that task. Fourth, the justices were apparently in no position to defend themselves. With such advantages, vigorous debate in the Senate, strong vocal opposition in the nation, and even the outrage of the news media did not worry Roosevelt. He was supremely confident of victory, but he had miscalculated.

Roosevelt underestimated the political skills of Brandeis and Hughes, the resentment of many nonsouthern senators to the disingenuous plan, and the Court's popular support. Roosevelt tried to soften the proposal's blow for Brandeis by having Corcoran inform him of it before it was announced, but the gesture was ineffective. Brandeis saw Roosevelt's plan as an affront to the Supreme Court that had to be countered.

Hughes's reaction was similar. He thought it was an assault upon the Court's independence, and he especially resented the assertion that the Court was behind in its work. When three senators, Burton K. Wheeler of Montana, William H. King of Utah, and Warren Austin of Vermont, called on Hughes to ask him to appear before the Senate Judiciary Committee, which was holding hearings on the Court plan, Hughes not only agreed to see them but also said he was willing to appear if at least one other Court member would accompany him, preferably Brandeis because of his standing as a Democrat and liberal. Brandeis, however, did not want Hughes or any other justice to appear before the committee. Wheeler then met with Brandeis and asked for a letter from the Court stating the facts as to its work, and Brandeis told him to call Hughes. After discussing the matter with Wheeler, Hughes wrote the letter the next day (21 March 1937) and took the letter to Brandeis and Van Devanter, who approved it.

Hughes's letter, which Wheeler read at the Senate hearings the next day, was a devastating attack on Roosevelt's proposal. It not only demonstrated the falsity of the president's assertion that the Court was behind in its work, but it also raised questions about the feasibility and constitutionality of the plan. Hughes's letter concluded with a statement that because of shortness of time he had not been able to consult with all the members of the Court on the letter. But he added that he was confident that it was in accord with the views of his colleagues. This statement gave the impression that all nine justices agreed with it, even though six of them had not seen it. Soon after Wheeler read Hughes's letter to the Judiciary Committee, several members of the Roosevelt administration acknowledged that the tide of public opinion in the Supreme Court battle had turned against the president.

Exactly a week later, on 29 March 1937, Hughes delivered the Court's opinion in *Parrish*. Stone had returned to the Court about 1 February and, as expected, agreed to uphold the constitutionality of the Washington law. Two weeks after *Parrish*, Hughes delivered the Court's opinion in *National Labor Relations Board* v. *Jones & Laughlin Steel Corp.*, which held constitutional the National Labor Relations Act. The vote was the same as in *Parrish*, 5–4, with Roberts voting with

Hughes, Brandeis, Stone, and Cardozo. The majority rested its decision on a broad interpretation of the commerce clause, thus providing the expansion that Frankfurter earlier thought would require a constitutional amendment. "Admirably done," Brandeis wrote on the back of Hughes's opinion in *Jones & Laughlin* when it had been circulated. "Yes sir," wrote Cardozo, "a magnificent opinion."

Parrish and *Jones & Laughlin*, taken together, constituted a constitutional revolution. There was no longer a no-man's-land in governmental regulation of the economy. Stone's dissenting view in *Butler* was now the law of the land. Roosevelt was jubilant.

On 1 March 1937, Roosevelt had signed legislation assuring Supreme Court justices that when they left the Court, their retirement pay would not be reduced, as it had been for Justice Holmes in 1933, and on 19 May 1937, Van Devanter exercised his right of retirement with full pay. Van Devanter's retirement had been timed at the request of Senators Wheeler and William E. Borah to contribute most to defeating Roosevelt's Court plan. The retirement, together with the death of Senator Joseph T. Robinson, who had led the fight for the president's proposal in the Senate, effectively ended any chance of the bill's passage. Roosevelt nominated Senator Hugo L. Black of Alabama, a New Deal stalwart, to Van Devanter's place, and within three years, four other Roosevelt appointees joined the Supreme Court.

One of Roosevelt's biographers wrote,

> All in all, the court fight was a stunning defeat for the President. Whether or not it was a fatal or irretrievable one, however, depended on the events to follow. Two years later, with his eye on a string of pro–New Deal Court decisions, the President exulted that he had lost the battle but won the war. As matters turned out in Congress and party, it could better be said that he lost the battle, won the campaign, but lost the war.
>
> (Burns, 315)

Roosevelt's losses in the Court struggle were enormous. The struggle blunted the most important reform drive in the nation's history. It divided the Democrats and reformers, unified the Republicans, undermined bipartisan support for the New Deal, led to the rebirth of the conservative coalition, and undercut the overwhelming support of the middle class that Roosevelt had mobilized in 1936. Tangentially, it even created distrust for Roosevelt's foreign policy, for some senators thought it revealed a deviousness and an overreaching for executive power.

Hughes believed that the Court struggle could have been averted if Congress had not reduced Holmes's retirement allowance in 1933, for that action was notice to the justices that they could not rely on the congressional promise of retirement compensation after resignation. Unlike lower federal judges, they did not have the right of retirement, which would have permitted them to retain their offices and given them constitutional protection of their salaries, for there may be no diminution of judges' compensation while in office. According to Hughes, the result of Congress's action in regard to Holmes was that Van Devanter and Sutherland, who otherwise would have retired, remained on the bench. Stone agreed that Congress' tinkering with Holmes's retirement allowance was a serious drawback to retirements in the Court.

In 1935, Representative Hatton W. Sumners, chairman of the House Judiciary Committee, introduced a bill to permit Supreme Court justices to retire like other federal judges, rather than to resign, thereby according them constitutional protection of their compensation; however, the House rejected the bill. Two months later Sumners reintroduced it. As early as May 1935, James M. Landis and Donald R. Richberg, leading New Deal lawyers, were aware of the purpose of the Sumners bill and also that the justices were considerably disturbed by the reduction of Holmes's retirement allowance. Why the Roosevelt administration did not support the Sumners bill prior to 1937 is puzzling. Robert H. Jackson's explanation is that Roosevelt was probably unaware of the bill.

Roosevelt was also apparently unaware that prior to the disclosure of his Court plan, Van Devanter had decided to retire. Corcoran recalled in his memoir that when he informed Brandeis of Roosevelt's Court plan on the morning of 5 February 1937, the justice responded, "Tell your President he has made a great mistake. All he had to do is wait a little while." Corcoran regretted not pressing Brandeis for an explanation of the remark, for he believed that if he had done so, Brandeis would have told him what every member of the Court already knew—that Hughes in effect had Van Devanter's retirement letter in his pocket. Corcoran thought that if he had been able to convey that information to Roosevelt, the doomed campaign against the Court could have been called off the day after it had been announced, and the president would have thereby averted one of his worst political defeats.

The Supreme Court emerged from its struggle with Roosevelt stronger than it had been since 1930. The final years of Hughes's chief-justiceship witnessed important doctrinal changes that justified a new role for the Court in American government. The most important of these changes were the "selective incorporation theory," which Cardozo set forth in *Palko* v. *Connecticut* (1937), and the "double standard," which Stone set forth in *United States* v. *Carolene Products Co.* (1938).

The selective incorporation theory, which holds that certain guaranties in the Bill of Rights apply to the states through the due process clause of the Fourteenth Amendment, was a striking development in constitutional jurisprudence. As late as 1922, a majority of the Supreme Court, which included Holmes and Brandeis, agreed in *Prudential Insurance Co.* v. *Cheek* that the First Amendment's guaranty of free speech was not within the protection of the Fourteenth Amendment. Three years later, the Court took a diametrically opposed position in *Gitlow* v. *New York.* "For present purposes," wrote Justice Sanford, "we may and do assume that freedom of speech and of the press—which are protected by the First Amendment from abridgment by Congress—are among the fundamental personal rights and 'liberties' protected by the due process clause of the Fourteenth Amendment from impairment by the States." The Court upheld the New York statute challenged in *Gitlow,* with Holmes and Brandeis dissenting, but those justices accepted the majority's dictum that the Fourteenth Amendment's due process clause incorporated the First Amendment's guaranty of free speech.

The Hughes Court extended the *Gitlow* dictum in 1931 in *Stromberg* v. *California* and *Near* v. *Minnesota,* decisions that protected freedom of speech and press from state actions. Among the Bill of Rights guaranties that Hughes and his colleagues applied to the states were the right to counsel in capital cases (*Powell* v. *Alabama,* 1932),

free exercise of religion (*Hamilton* v. *University of California,* 1934), the right not to be coerced into giving evidence against oneself in a criminal proceeding (*Brown* v. *Mississippi,* 1936), and the right to assemble peaceably (*De Jonge* v. *Oregon,* 1937).

The Hughes Court acknowledged, however, that certain other guaranties in the Bill of Rights, such as indictment by grand jury and trial by jury, were not incorporated. In *Palko,* Cardozo explained why some guaranties applied to the states and others did not:

> The line of division may seem to be wavering and broken if there is a hasty catalogue of the cases on the one side and the other. Reflection and analysis will induce a different view. There emerges the perception of a rationalizing principle which gives to discrete instances a proper order and coherence. The right to trial by jury and the immunity from prosecution except as the result of an indictment may have value and importance. Even so, they are not of the very essence of a scheme of ordered liberty. To abolish them is not to violate a "principle of justice so rooted in the traditions and conscience of our people as to be ranked as fundamental."

Less than a year after Cardozo's opinion in *Palko,* Stone set forth the doctrine of the double standard in *Carolene Products Co.* He stated in a single sentence the standard for review in economic cases: "Regulatory legislation affecting ordinary commercial transactions is not to be pronounced unconstitutional unless in the light of the facts made known or generally assumed it is of such a character as to preclude the assumption that it rests upon some rational basis within the knowledge and experience of the legislators." In short, the Court should exercise self-restraint in economic cases and accord legislation a presumption of constitutionality that will not be overcome unless the justices find there is no rational basis for such legislation.

But this was not the Court's standard in reviewing cases involving fundamental personal rights. At the end of the sentence quoted above was the famous footnote 4, which stated that there may be a narrower scope for the presumption of constitutionality when legislation appears to prohibit fundamental rights guaranteed specifically by the Constitution, to restrict the operation of political processes, or to discriminate against religious, national, or racial minorities. Legislation falling into any of these categories has been held subject to searching judicial inquiry. Stone's statement of the double standard is the basis of the Supreme Court's modern role as an active protector of fundamental personal rights, particularly those necessary for operation of the democratic process, and of its abandonment of its former role as active protector of property rights.

By the time Hughes left the Court in 1941, the institution had changed greatly. In 1940 there were five Roosevelt appointees on the Court—Black, Reed, William O. Douglas, Frankfurter, and Frank Murphy. Hughes retired a year later, and Roosevelt promoted Stone to the chief-justiceship. During the Hughes era, the Court succeeded in protecting its institutional prerogatives in a fierce struggle with a popular president, and at the same time, it managed to transform its principal role from protector of property rights to protector of personal rights and to lay the foundation for the nationalization of the Bill of Rights. This was a watershed for constitutional decision-making for at least the next half-century. Few periods in the Court's history were as important as the eleven years of Hughes's chief-justiceship.

CASES

Ashton v. Cameron County Water Improvement District, 298 U.S. 513 (1936)

Ashwander v. Tennessee Valley Authority, 297 U.S. 288 (1936)

Booth v. United States, 291 U.S. 339 (1934)

Brown v. Mississippi, 297 U.S. 278 (1936)

Carter v. Carter Coal Co., 298 U.S. 238 (1936)

De Jonge v. Oregon, 299 U.S. 353 (1937)

Gitlow v. New York, 268 U.S. 652 (1925)

Hamilton v. University of California, 293 U.S. 245 (1934)

Home Building & Loan Assn. v. Blaisdell, 290 U.S. 398 (1934)

Hopkins Federal Savings & Loan Assn. v. Cleary, 296 U.S. 315 (1935)

Humphrey's Executor v. United States, 295 U.S. 602 (1935)

Louisville Bank v. Radford, 295 U.S. 555 (1935)

Lynch v. United States, 292 U.S. 571 (1934)

Morehead v. New York ex rel. Tipaldo, 298 U.S. 587 (1936)

National Labor Relations Board v. Jones & Laughlin Steel Corp., 301 U.S. 1 (1937)

Near v. Minnesota, 283 U.S. 697 (1931)

Nebbia v. New York, 291 U.S. 502 (1934)

Norman v. Baltimore & Ohio Railroad, 294 U.S. 240 (1935)

Nortz v. United States, 294 U.S. 317 (1935)

Palko v. Connecticut, 302 U.S. 319 (1937)

Panama Refining Co. v. Ryan Co., 293 U.S. 388 (1935)

Perry v. United States, 294 U.S. 330 (1935)

Powell v. Alabama, 287 U.S. 45 (1932)

Prudential Insurance Co. v. Cheek, 252 U.S. 567 (1922)

Retirement Board v. Alton Railroad Co., 295 U.S. 330 (1935)

Schechter Poultry Corp. v. United States 295 U.S. 495 (1935)

Stromberg v. California, 283 U.S. 359 (1931)

United States v. Butler, 297 U.S. 1 (1936)

United States v. Carolene Products Co., 304 U.S. 144 (1938)

West Coast Hotel Co. v. Parrish, 300 U.S. 379 (1937)

BIBLIOGRAPHY

Henry J. Abraham, *Freedom and the Court* (1982), explains selective incorporation and the double standard. Joseph Alsop and Turner Catledge, *The 168 Days* (1938), is an account of the Court-packing fight. Leonard Baker, *Back to Back: The Duel Between FDR and the Supreme Court* (1967), is a book-length study of the Court-packing struggle. James MacGregor Burns, *Roosevelt: The Lion and the Fox* (1956), covers the president's encounters with the Hughes Court.

John W. Chambers, "The Big Switch: Justice Roberts and the Minimum-Wage Cases," in *Labor History*, 10 (1969), is a critical analysis of Roberts' change of position from *Tipaldo* to *Parrish*. Richard C. Cortiner, *The Supreme Court and the Second Bill of Rights: The Fourteenth Amendment and the Nationalization of Civil Liberties* (1981), is a valuable history of the process of selective incorporation. Felix Frankfurter, "Mr. Justice Roberts," in *University of Pennsylvania Law Review*, 104 (1955), includes Roberts' memoir explaining his votes in *Tipaldo* and *Parrish*. Max Freedman, ed., *Roosevelt and Frankfurter: Their Correspondence, 1928–1945* (1967), also reprints Roberts' *Tipaldo-Parrish* memoir.

Charles Evans Hughes, *The Autobiographical Notes of Charles Evans Hughes*, edited by David J. Danelski and Joseph S. Tulchin (1973), expresses the view that the Court controversy could have been averted. Peter Irons, *The New Deal Lawyers* (1982), is an excellent study of litigation before the Supreme Court during the New Deal. Alfred H. Kelly, Winfred A. Harbison, and Herman Belz, *The American Constitution: Its Origins and Development* (1983), covers the cases of the Hughes era. William E. Leuchtenburg, *Franklin D. Roosevelt and the New Deal* (1963); "The Origins of Franklin D. Roosevelt's 'Court Packing' Plan," in *Supreme Court Review* (1966); and "Franklin D. Roosevelt's Supreme Court 'Packing' Plan," in Harold M. Hollingsworth, ed., *Essays on the New Deal* (1969), include some of the most insightful work on the Court-packing plan.

Robert S. McElvaine, *The Great Depression: America, 1929–1941* (1984), provides historical background. Alpheus Thomas Mason, *Harlan Fiske Stone: Pillar of the Law* (1956), is the best study of the Supreme Court under Hughes. Paul L. Murphy, *The Constitution in Crisis Times, 1918–1969* (1972), includes cases of the Hughes era. Merlo J. Pusey, *Charles Evans Hughes*, 2 vols. (1952), gives Hughes's perspective on the period. Arthur M. Schlesinger, Jr., *The Age of Roosevelt*, 3 vols. (1956–1960), is a classic portrait of the era.

[See also EXECUTIVE AND DOMESTIC AFFAIRS; JUDICIAL REVIEW; JUDICIAL SELECTION; and WHITE AND TAFT COURTS AND ERAS.]

THE STONE AND VINSON
COURTS AND ERAS

James Bolner, Sr.

Harlan Fiske Stone assumed the chief-justiceship of the United States on 3 July 1941 and served until his death on 22 April 1946; he was succeeded by Fred Moore Vinson, who assumed the office on 24 June 1946. The United States had declared war on Japan and Germany in early December 1941. The global conflict lasted until 1945; in May 1945, Germany surrendered, but the war with Japan did not end until the dramatic surrender aboard the USS *Missouri* on 2 September. Some 292,000 Americans were killed in battle, while another 670,000 were wounded; more than 139,000 serviceperson were taken prisoner or missing in action; over 6,000 American civilians died in war-related activities. The war witnessed the total mobilization of the nation's resources, and at peak strength over 16.1 million Americans were in military service. Clearly, the war left its mark on American institutions and on the values, culture, and outlook of the American people.

World War II saw the introduction of nuclear weapons. The first atomic bomb was dropped on Hiroshima, Japan, by order of President Harry S. Truman on 6 August 1945, and the second on Nagasaki three days later. The extended period of continued military preparedness that followed the war—the "cold war"—served to put the United States into a permanent state of quasi-military emergency. The war created the condition for the assertion of broad claims of presidential power both domestically and abroad. These claims survived the war, as did congressional claims to the power to deal with the aftermath of the war. Measures were taken against individuals both at home and abroad in the name of national security. The liberties of those who held quaint and unorthodox religious views were threatened. It was also the age of McCarthyism and political hysteria about domestic subversion.

The times generated genuine challenges to free institutions.

The war and its aftermath also had a pervasive sociological impact. Blacks gained new political power through their service in the armed forces. In July 1948, President Truman issued an executive order banning racial discrimination in the armed services. Of equal significance was the mass migration of blacks to urban centers outside the South. The presence of sizable black voting blocs in these politically competitive states gave blacks considerable political power, especially in the context of the selection of the president by the electoral college. In practical political terms, black voters were in a position to exert great influence on, if not determine, the outcome of the electoral vote in presidential elections.

World War II was also seen as a turning point in the evolution of American values. Social scientists in the postwar period claimed that the traditional American dedication to the principles of "rugged individualism" were giving way to a new conformity. Massive government regulations that were alleged to be hostile to the accumulation of large fortunes created an environment conducive to the development of an ethic of group and corporate conformity. With the mass migration of urban workers to the comfortable environment of the suburbs, the automobile became a virtual necessity for every family. At the end of the period under consideration, television was coming upon the scene—a medium oriented to the creation of consumer desires and to the transformation of these desires into "needs." Psychology became a major field of study for the business community, for not only was it important to know "what makes people tick" in order to get ahead in the close quarters of the corporate environment, but it was also essential to know how consumers

146

thought and what they liked and disliked. The methods of political pollsters and market-research specialists became indistinguishable. The "selling" of products and candidates became the focus of much of national life.

A variety of forces appeared to be at work, all aiming at the creation of a consumer society in the context of an economy that required rapid growth as a prerequisite of economic health. In a real sense, the industrial productivity of the war years was reoriented to production for the consumer market. The population increase (over 19 million between 1940 and 1950) meant the presence of both more consumers and new producers. Producers were increasingly of the "white collar," as opposed to the "blue collar," class; indeed, by 1956, those in service occupations would outnumber those engaged in production. By the late 1940s it had become increasingly acceptable for families to live out their lives in a totally consumption-oriented milieu. "Consumer credit" became a mainstay of the economy, especially after credit cards were introduced in 1950. Suburbanites were typically "buying" their homes and living from month to month by taking advantage of the "revolving charge" method of the growing chain of general-service department stores.

The publication in 1948 of *Sexual Behavior in the Human Male*, by Alfred C. Kinsey, signaled a reassessment of sexual mores. A new frankness about sex appeared in magazines, books, and films. The new openness was not limited to the exploitation of nudity and heterosexual relationships: artistic and commercial media began to devote increasing attention to miscegenation, homosexuality, and drug addiction—subjects considered taboo in the preceding decades.

POLITICAL DEVELOPMENTS

In 1940, President Franklin Delano Roosevelt was reelected for a third term over Republican Wendell Willkie. With the advent of World War II, the nation united behind the President, but as the conflict wore on, the administration's domestic policies were to provoke more and more criticism. In 1941 the Senate established the Special Committee to Investigate the National Defense Program, to monitor executive decision-making in connection with military procurement and defense policies. Chaired by Senator Harry S. Truman, Democrat of Missouri, the committee soon established its role as a "friendly watchdog" and did nothing to embarrass the administration. In the 1944 presidential election, Roosevelt defeated Thomas E. Dewey and won a fourth term, even though Roosevelt had provoked a major clash with his own party in February: disregarding the counsel of his Democratic colleagues, he vetoed an important revenue measure; Senator Alben Barkley of Kentucky, the Democratic majority leader, resigned his post in protest but was immediately reelected by Senate Democrats. The Roosevelt proposals for social reform made after the election were ignored by Congress, and the president secured the confirmation of his choice for secretary of commerce only after making major compromises.

When Roosevelt died on 12 April 1945, Truman assumed the presidency amid high expectations that as a former senator, he would enjoy improved relations with Congress. It soon became clear that while Truman was capable of adroit handling of foreign affairs, he was to have little success in dealing with the intractable coalition of conservative Democrats and partisan Republicans in the Congress. In the 1946 congressional elections the Republicans made major gains in both the House and Senate. A major piece of legislation enacted by the Republican-dominated Eightieth Congress was the Taft-Hartley Act, a measure designed to create categories of "unfair labor practices" for which labor unions could be held accountable. The law was enacted over Truman's veto, a fact that was to play a large role in his refusal to adhere to its provisions for an eighty-day injunction in dealing with strikes when he was faced with the prospect of a steelworkers' strike in 1952.

Subversion was a major preoccupation of the era. In 1940, Congress enacted the Alien Registration Act (Smith Act); in 1950 the Internal Security Act (McCarran Act) established the Subversive Activities Control Board, a body that soon declared the Communist party to be a subversive organization; and in 1954 the Communist Control Act outlawed the Communist party.

CHANGING AMERICAN VALUES

The quality of life in the period following the war was symbolized in two of the major public figures of the day: General of the Army Douglas

A. MacArthur and Senator Joseph McCarthy of Wisconsin. The public attention that each of these men received gave the era a distinctive coloration. Both of their careers were shaped by the war and its continuing impact and appeared to provide the public with a pageant of national affairs that rivaled the war itself in its emotionalism and intensity.

MacArthur, who had had a distinguished military career as a commanding general in the Pacific theater during World War II, was given the command of United Nations forces in the Korean War by President Truman in September 1950. The active intervention by the Chinese Communists in the Korean conflict in support of the North Koreans so alarmed MacArthur that he wanted to employ nuclear weapons against them. When he failed to remain silent about his military views, which were at odds with those of President Truman, the president removed MacArthur from his command in April 1951. It was a highly charged moment for the country. MacArthur, the conquering hero, was accorded a boisterous patriotic welcome home topped by an emotional and moving, if somewhat self-dramatizing, address to a joint session of both houses of Congress.

This vindication by President Truman of the principle of civilian supremacy was so important that it deserves the status of a constitutional event. The removal of MacArthur at a time when his popularity was at its highest and Truman's was at its lowest has done much to nourish the growth of the "Truman cult" of recent years. Moreover, the importance of Truman's action against a background of atomic warfare appeared to announce to the public that the awesome powers of destruction represented by the new weaponry would be released only within the limitations of responsible representative institutions and not on the basis of military judgments.

Truman's removal of MacArthur set the stage for McCarthy's more outlandish claims. The successful prosecution of Alger Hiss for perjury during his trial as a Soviet spy was sparked by the investigations conducted by Congressman Richard M. Nixon as a member of the House Committee on Un-American Activities. McCarthy claimed that there were large numbers of persons more or less like Hiss still within government and that the authorities were doing nothing to prosecute them. His favorite accusation

was that the activities of the "Communist sympathizers" and "fellow travelers" had debilitated the ability of the United States to respond to Soviet aggression. As the chairperson of the Senate Subcommittee on Investigations beginning in January 1953, McCarthy launched an attack on the work of the United States Information Services Libraries (the Voice of America), which are responsible for dissemination abroad of information about the United States. In October 1953, McCarthy overextended himself by launching an attack against the Department of the Army. It was at this point that President Eisenhower indicated opposition to McCarthy, and the Senate proceeded to pass a resolution condemning his conduct in December 1954.

THE SUPREME COURT AND THE WAR

During World War II the justices of the Supreme Court reflected a certain self-conscious attempt to strike a delicate balance between support for the war effort and solicitude for the rights of the "enemy" and "sympathizers" in ways that would hold the United States up as a model of constitutional democracy and government under law. In the *Japanese Exclusion Cases*—*Hirabayashi* v. *United States* (1943) and *Korematsu* v. *United States* (1944)—the Court approved severe racially based restrictions on the freedoms of persons of Japanese ancestry. Taken together, these cases project a doctrinal lesson that in the name of military exigency the authorities may subject persons to a curfew (*Hirabayashi*) and may incarcerate others (*Korematsu*), and do this without proof of the disloyalty of the individuals in question. Once loyalty to the United States has been established, however, an incarcerated individual must be released (*Ex parte Endo,* 1944).

The Court's handling of the disloyalty cases stemming from the war shows a disposition to uphold harsher treatment of Americans of Japanese descent than that of German saboteurs. Convictions of German saboteurs who landed on the east coast and of those assisting them were upheld in *Ex parte Quirin* (1942) and *Haupt* v. *United States* (1947), respectively. In *Cramer* v. *United States* (1945) the Court ignored Cramer's testimony in open court and reversed his treason conviction on the ground that the government had not brought forward the two witnesses required by the Constitution. A Nazi sympathizer had his conviction for treason reversed in *Hartzel* v. *United States* (1944); and in *Keegan* v. *United States* (1945), the conspiracy convictions of the leaders of the German-American Bund for anti-draft activities were reversed on the ground that the government had failed to provide adequate evidence. But in 1946 the Court reversed the convictions of civilians in Hawaii who had committed offenses during the war and who had been convicted by a military court, asserting that the civilian courts were capable of functioning at the time the military proceedings were held and that the Organic Act establishing the territory of Hawaii did not sanction the suspension of civilian liberties.

On the related subject of denaturalization, the Court's decision-making showed a concern for careful analysis of the facts of each case. The Court blocked the government's attempt to denaturalize a Communist party member and a Nazi sympathizer on the ground that the government had failed to provide sufficient proof, in *Schneiderman* v. *United States* (1943) and *Baumgartner* v. *United States* (1944), respectively.

ECONOMIC POWERS

The period 1941–1954 was characterized by continued judicial self-restraint (verging on judicial abdication) in the area of economic regulation, a growing solicitude for individual and minority rights, and a cautious attitude toward broad claims of presidential power. The pattern for judicial self-restraint in the economic regulation area had been set in the years 1937–1940, when the Court had undergone a virtual judicial revolution. By the time Stone assumed the chief-justiceship, there remained little to add to the constitutional proposition that Congress and the states had free rein to regulate business and the economy. Indeed, Stone himself, just months before he became chief justice, authored the opinion for the Court in *United States* v. *Darby Lumber Co.* (1941), which upheld the constitutionality of the 1938 Fair Labor Standards Act and sustained Congress' power to close the channels of interstate commerce to goods manufactured by workers paid below a federally established minimum wage and its power to regulate the hours and

wages of workers producing goods "for interstate commerce." Three years earlier the Court had upheld the 1938 Agricultural Adjustment Act, drawing a fine distinction between the production and the marketing of agricultural goods (*Mulford* v. *Smith,* 1939). In *Wickard* v. *Filburn* (1942) the Court handed down what was perhaps its most dramatic judicial approval of federal economic legislation, in a case brought by an individual farmer seeking to escape a federal penalty for growing wheat (for use on his own farm) in excess of his allotment under a federal agricultural marketing program. Speaking for a unanimous Court, Justice Robert H. Jackson found that "Congress may properly have considered that wheat consumed on the farm where grown, if wholly outside the scheme of regulation, would have a substantial effect in defeating and obstructing its purpose to stimulate trade therein at increased prices."

The justices were disposed to uphold the application of the Fair Labor Standards Act to circumstances only tangentially related to interstate commerce, yet it would be inaccurate to describe the Court as a rubber stamp. On the same day in 1945, the Court ruled that the operators of an elevator in a building occupied by an interstate company were covered by the law but that workers servicing the building, one-fourth of whose tenants were engaged in interstate activities, were exempt (*Borden Co.* v. *Borella,* 1945; *10 East 40th St. Building* v. *Callus,* 1945).

The Court was inclined to favor broad national power where economic issues related to questions of federalism. In 1944 the Court held that state regulation of the insurance business encroached on Congress' constitutional prerogatives, in *United States* v. *Southeastern Underwriters Assn.* (1944). Responding to pressures from the insurance industry, Congress shortly overturned the decision and, in essence, divested insurance of its interstate character so as to permit state regulation. The justices also found that Congress' power exercised in the National Labor Relations Act extended to mining company employees. In a decision that reflected a readiness to uphold Congress' power even when Congress had not exercised it, the Court ruled that a state could not burden and disrupt interstate commerce by limiting the length of trains traveling through the state (*Southern Pacific Co.* v. *Arizona,* 1945). This broad acknowledgment of federal power in the commerce field served the Vinson Court well, as it used the commerce clause as a vehicle for protecting the rights of blacks: *Henderson* v. *United States* (1950) ruled that racially segregated dining facilities on interstate trains violated the Interstate Commerce Act section protecting parties from being placed at an "undue disadvantage"; and *Morgan* v. *Virginia* (1946) invalidated a state law, applied to interstate commerce, that required racial segregation on public motor carriers, on the ground that the policy burdened interstate commerce.

The post–World War II Supreme Court's position supportive of federal government economic regulation was thoroughgoing. Not only were federal economic regulations consistently upheld, but when the Court was rebuffing one branch of the central government in *Youngstown Sheet and Tube Co.* v. *Sawyer* (1952), it was giving a generous endorsement to federal regulatory power. The judicial disposition to uphold federal regulation is well illustrated in the rulings supporting broad regulatory claims stemming from the war powers, even when hostilities were long over. The upholding of comprehensive wartime economic regulations came in *Yakus* v. *United States* (1944), wherein the Court upheld the Emergency Price Control Act and the Inflation Control Act (both of 1942). Soon after this, the Court sustained the powers of the Office of Price Administration, established to implement the legislation (*Steuart and Bros.* v. *Bowles,* 1944). Of a different order was the decision in *Woods* v. *Miller* (1948), upholding Congress' power, under the war powers, to enact peacetime rent-control legislation. In an opinion by Justice William O. Douglas, a unanimous Court found that Congress' war powers authorized it to deal with war-related problems even after the cessation of actual hostilities.

These rulings in support of federal regulatory powers often featured judicial rhetoric underscoring national power and calls for judicial self-restraint. Perhaps emboldened by this rhetoric, President Truman, claiming that steel was needed for the Korean War effort, ordered executive seizure of the nation's major steel mills in April 1952, to forestall a nationwide strike by the steelworkers' unions. The Court's decision against the president constitutes one of the most dramatic cases decided during any period. Seven of the Court's nine members wrote opinions in

Youngstown. Justice Hugo Black, as senior justice in the majority of six, wrote an opinion for the Court, but Justices Douglas, Felix Frankfurter, Harold H. Burton, Tom C. Clark, and Robert H. Jackson each wrote separate concurring opinions. Chief Justice Vinson, joined by Justices Stanley F. Reed and Sherman Minton, filed a dissenting opinion. The opinions of the majority reflected variations on the theme of the need to keep the modern presidency restrained by law. With the passage of time, it is Justice Jackson's concurring opinion that has come to be regarded as most valuable because of its analysis of the constitutional limits on presidential power. The Court should be vigilant, argued Jackson, when a president tries to assert authority over domestic matters on the grounds that foreign-policy interests and involvements are at stake; this is especially true when these involvements, like the commitment of American forces in the Korean War, were largely of the president's own making. When the president acts within the constitutionally prescribed powers and is supported in this by Congress, wrote Jackson, the president's power is at its height. Next in constitutional soundness is a presidential action that, while not specifically sanctioned by the Constitution's language, is fully supported by Congress. When the president, however, acts without constitutional and/or congressional support, then there must be extraordinary justifications brought forward to support the actions. In the steel seizure case, reasoned Jackson, there were no such extraordinary circumstances.

CONSTITUTIONAL RIGHTS

A second major facet of the work of the Stone and Vinson Courts—the first being a continued validation of federal regulatory power—was the development of the constitutional law protective of individual rights, especially in the areas of freedom of conscience and the rights of racial minorities. Beginnings had been made in both areas in the 1920s and 1930s: previous Courts had invalidated a number of laws and regulations limiting the constitutional rights of Jehovah's Witnesses to conduct their ministries. But the stream of Jehovah's Witness cases reaching the Court during the 1940s gave the Court an opportunity to delineate in detail the contours of the First Amendment's "free exercise" religious guarantee. In 1941 the Court had upheld a state law (challenged by Witnesses) requiring a special permit to parade or process on city streets; this, the Court said, was a reasonable police power measure (*Cox* v. *New Hampshire*). Similarly, the next year the Court upheld the conviction of a Jehovah's Witness under a state law forbidding the use of offensive or derisive public name-calling (*Chaplinsky* v. *New Hampshire*). These were virtually the only setbacks for the Witnesses in the Supreme Court, for the Court ruled in case after case in their favor. The Court voided a state law requiring a permit from a state official before conducting religious solicitations; in the same case, the Court reversed a breach-of-the-peace conviction of the same Witnesses, who had played anti-Catholic phonograph records to residents of Catholic neighborhoods (*Cantwell* v. *Connecticut*, 1940).

In a series of decisions in the 1940s and 1950s, the Supreme Court reflected a decided preference for religiously based public expression—all of the decisions involving Jehovah's Witnesses. Outstanding examples involve the use of public loudspeakers and door-to-door solicitation. In 1948 the Vinson Court found unconstitutional, as a prior restraint on free speech, an ordinance requiring those using a sound amplification device to secure a permit (*Saia* v. *New York*), but the very next year, it upheld a similar ordinance in a case involving the Witnesses (*Kovacs* v. *Cooper*). In 1951 the Court upheld a city ordinance banning door-to-door solicitation (*Breard* v. *Alexandria*) but did so in such a way as to leave standing its 1943 ruling striking down a similar ordinance challenged by the Witnesses (*Martin* v. *Struthers*).

On two dramatic occasions the Witnesses lost their cases, only to have the Court reverse itself in their favor. Both of these occasions reflected the volatile nature of the Court's decision-making and the readiness of the justices to respond to their colleagues' arguments. In 1940 the Court, with only Justice Stone in dissent, reversed lower federal courts by upholding a state law requiring public school children to salute the United States flag and recite the pledge of allegiance (*Minersville School District* v. *Gobitis*). Two years later a majority of the Court sustained the constitutionality of a state licensing requirement for peddlers as applied to Witnesses (*Jones* v.

Opelika). Justices Black, Douglas, and Frank Murphy dissented and took the occasion to announce that they had changed their minds on the issue of the flag salute and the pledge of allegiance. (The restrictive *Jones* decision was overruled in 1943 in *Murdock* v. *Pennsylvania*.) Within the next two years Justice James F. Byrnes was replaced by Justice Wiley B. Rutledge and Justice Jackson joined the Court. In 1943, Stone, Black, Douglas, Murphy, Rutledge, and Jackson decided *West Virginia State Board of Education* v. *Barnette*. Justice Jackson's opinion in this case constitutes one of the finest models of judicial writing of any era. Wrote Jackson:

> We can have intellectual individualism and the rich cultural diversities that we owe to exceptional minds only at the price of occasional eccentricity and abnormal attitudes. When they are so harmless to others or to the State as those we deal with here, the price is not too great. But freedom to differ is not limited to things that do not matter much. That would be a mere shadow of freedom. The test of its substance is the right to differ as to things that touch the heart of the existing order.

During the Vinson era the Court was faced with challenging questions pertaining to the relationship between church and state. The first of these cases, *Everson* v. *Board of Education* (1947), involving local government rebates to parents who incurred public transportation expenses to send their children to religiously affiliated schools, set the tone of political-religious accommodation that persists in contemporary American constitutional law. Writing for a 5–4 majority, Justice Black declared:

> The "establishment of religion" clause of the First Amendment means at least this: Neither a state nor the Federal Government can set up a church. Neither can pass laws which aid one religion, aid all religions, or prefer one religion over another. . . . No tax in any amount, large or small, can be levied to support any religious activities or institutions, whatever they may be called, or whatever form they may adopt to teach or practice religion.

Having said this, however, Black went on to uphold the rebates in question, not as aids to religion but as exercises of the state's police power

—analogous to providing "police and fire protection, connections for sewage disposal, public highways and sidewalks." The dissenters criticized Black's opinion for ignoring constitutional history and for failing to recognize that the subsidies aided religious schools while ostensibly aiding the children attending them.

Subsequent rulings in the church-state area demonstrated that it was not possible to force the Court's decision-making into a neat pattern. The Court struck down on "establishment of religion" grounds a scheme whereby teachers of religion entered public schools to teach pupils technically released from public school attendance (*McCollum* v. *Board of Education*, 1948). But in 1952 the Court, without overruling *McCollum*, held that it was constitutionally permissible for pupils to be dismissed from public schools to receive religious instruction off of school premises (*Zorach* v. *Clauson*).

Another important development in the field of individual rights—one that was to receive considerable attention after 1952—concerned heightened judicial scrutiny where encroachments on fundamental human rights were in question. In *Skinner* v. *Oklahoma* (1942), the Court struck down a state law providing for sterilization of persons convicted three times of crimes involving "moral turpitude." The defendant in the case had been convicted first of stealing chickens and then twice of armed robbery. Speaking for the Court, Justice Douglas found that the distinctions between crimes made in the state law did not satisfy constitutional standards. While pointing out that states had broad powers to classify in legislating, Douglas found that "strict scrutiny of the classification which a State makes in a sterilization law is essential, lest unwittingly or otherwise, invidious discriminations are made against groups or types of individuals in violation of the constitutional guaranty of just and equal laws."

POLITICAL SPEECH AND ASSOCIATION

Even before the post–World War II era became the era of the cold war, with the Soviet Union and the United States assuming an increasingly hostile stance toward each other, the Court was faced with a number of questions in-volving political loyalty and subversion of persons unconnected with the war itself, persons who were neither alleged saboteurs nor alleged traitors. In 1945 the Court sustained Illinois' refusal to admit an applicant to the practice of law on the ground that he had claimed conscientious objection to military service (*In re Summers*). In 1952 the Court also upheld a New York law disqualifying from public school employment all those who held membership in any organization judged to advocate violent overthrow of the government (*Adler* v. *Board of Education*). In the same year, however, the Court struck down, on grounds that it was too broad, a state law denying state employment to anyone who had belonged to allegedly subversive organizations; the law failed, said the Court, to distinguish between knowing and innocent (or unknowing) association (*Wieman* v. *Updegraff*).

Although the pattern is difficult to characterize, the Court gave a quite narrow interpretation to free expression guaranties where economic, as opposed to political, interests were being pursued. In *Thornhill* v. *Alabama* (1940), the Court interpreted peaceful picketing as constitutionally protected expression, and in *Thomas* v. *Collins* (1945), it ruled that labor organizing activity could not be subjected to a state permit system. Of course, the Court easily held that picketing which was not peaceful could be enjoined (*Milk Wagon Drivers Union* v. *Meadowmoor Dairies*, 1941), but the liberal rulings were balanced against a number of cases in which the Court sanctioned injunctions against picketing where the justification for limiting such activity was not so apparent, as in *Carpenters and Joiners Union* v. *Ritter's Cafe* (1942), involving picketing at a site not immediately related to the labor dispute; *Giboney* v. *Empire Storage and Ice Co.* (1949), concerning picketing in violation of state antitrust laws; and *International Brotherhood of Teamsters* v. *Hanke* (1950), challenging a state court decision that had found the union's goals objectionable.

In the related area of "street advocacy," the Vinson Court handed down a number of important decisions. The best known of these is perhaps *Beauharnais* v. *Illinois* (1952), upholding an Illinois law that made it an offense to publish anything casting aspersions on a race or religion. The Court viewed the law as a species of group libel and therefore not to be evaluated by regular standards. In *Terminiello* v. *Chicago* (1949), however, the Court showed it was prepared to play an activist role as it extended itself to overturn Terminiello's breach-of-the-peace conviction, even though his remarks had been highly provocative of the violence that had occurred; the trial judge, reasoned the majority, had given the jury an overbroad standard in instructing that it could find the defendant guilty if it found his speech to be "speech which stirs the public to anger, invites dispute, brings about a condition of unrest, or creates a disturbance."

Perhaps the most important decision of the Stone and Vinson eras in the First Amendment field was *Dennis* v. *United States* (1951), upholding the conspiracy convictions under the Smith Act of eleven leaders of the United States Communist party. Writing for the Court, with only Justices Black and Douglas dissenting, Chief Justice Vinson adopted Court of Appeals Chief Judge Learned Hand's adaptation of the "clear and present danger" test (183 F. 2d at 212), formulated over thirty years before by Justice Oliver Wendell Holmes, Jr. In judging subversion cases, Hand (and Vinson) declared, "the gravity of the 'evil' [must be] discounted by its improbability." A corollary to this, in plainer words, is that the graver the evil, the less probable does its occurrence need to be before government can act. Thus, the government did not have to wait for subversives to take specific action before curbing the Communist leaders. Justices Black and Douglas wrote strong dissents, and once the cold war had subsided, the Court undermined the *Dennis* ruling by drawing a distinction (indicated by Douglas in his dissenting opinion) between advocacy of overthrow as an abstract doctrine and incitement to overthrow as a concrete action.

RACIAL DISCRIMINATION

In decisions handed down in the 1940s and early 1950s, the Stone and Vinson Courts laid the foundation for *Brown* v. *Board of Education* (1954). Indeed, so weak were the theoretical bases of racial segregation that the Hughes Court's ruling in *Missouri ex rel. Gaines* v. *Canada* (1938) had left the doctrine in shambles. *Gaines* ruled that, while racially separate facilities were constitutionally permissible, they must have some degree of genuine equality. Acting on this

premise, the Court in 1948 ordered the admission of a black applicant to the University of Oklahoma Law School on the grounds that there was no equal separate facility for blacks (*Sipuel* v. *Board of Regents*). Also in 1948 the Court ruled that state and federal courts could no longer enforce agreements to discriminate on the ground of race in the sale of real estate (*Shelley* v. *Kraemer; Hurd* v. *Hodge*). Four years earlier the Stone Court, in a dramatic reversal of a position it had taken only nine years before, declared the "white primary" unconstitutional and thereby ended the practice of excluding blacks from voting in Democratic primaries—often the only meaningful elections—in the Deep South states (*Smith* v. *Allwright;* the earlier ruling was *Grovey* v. *Townsend*).

In 1950 the Court delivered two near-fatal blows to all educational segregation by race. First, it ruled that states could not deny blacks the educational advantages to be gained by free association among all students within an institution. Thus, Oklahoma could not segregate blacks admitted to its graduate school by relegating them to separate desks, study areas, cafeteria tables, and the like (*McLaurin* v. *Oklahoma State Regents*). Second, in *Sweatt* v. *Painter,* the Court declared that Texas' attempt to provide a "separate but equal" legal education for blacks by hurriedly establishing a separate law school failed to satisfy the equal-protection standard. Counsel for the blacks in the 1950 cases had asked the Court to outlaw segregation in all levels of public education. The Court carefully limited its ruling to the facts of the cases before it, and its ruling, therefore, affected only graduate and legal education.

RIGHTS OF CRIMINAL DEFENDANTS

The Stone and Vinson eras were veritable battlegrounds in the area of defendants' rights, largely because of the provocative debate that raged among the justices over the relationship between the Bill of Rights and the Fourteenth Amendment. The question with which the justices wrestled was this: In limiting the states by prohibiting them from denying persons "life, liberty, or property without due process of law," does the Fourteenth Amendment thereby prohibit the states from adopting practices forbidden by the Bill of Rights (Amendments IV–VIII)? In other words, does the Fourteenth Amendment "incorporate" the constitutional limitations and make them applicable against the states?

The position defended by Justice Black, and supported from time to time by other justices, was that the adoption of the Fourteenth Amendment had made the entire Bill of Rights applicable to the states. Justice Frankfurter headed up the group espousing the opposite view: that the Fourteenth Amendment's due process clause did not incorporate the Bill of Rights, and that the Court was obligated to interpret the clause independently of the specific limitations on federal authority in the Bill of Rights. The Frankfurter contingent was successful in getting the Court to stand by the doctrine of selective (as opposed to wholesale) incorporation; but it appears that as the Court came to discern more and more of the federal limitations in the contours of the Fourteenth Amendment's due process clause, Black's position was in fact triumphant. Typifying the Court's difficulties in dealing with the question of incorporation is the case of *Wolf* v. *Colorado* (1949), which asked the Court to decide whether or not illegally seized evidence (inadmissible in federal court) was admissible in state court. The Court ruled that while the states were free to admit such evidence, they were subject to the constitutional requirements of the "essence" of the Fourth Amendment. The Court's ruling was essentially conservative, but it laid the foundation for a later Court to find that the exclusion of illegally seized evidence is constitutionally required.

Amid florid rhetorical skirmishes—often led by Black and Frankfurter—the Stone and Vinson Courts incorporated only the right to a public trial into the Fourteenth Amendment, as in *In re Oliver* (1948). Many of the decisions of the period exhibit judicial reluctance to encroach upon the constitutional powers of the states. In the major case of *Betts* v. *Brady* (1942), a divided Court ruled that the due process clause of the Fourteenth Amendment did not require state courts to appoint counsel for indigent defendants facing noncapital sentences such as fines and imprisonment. Black's spirited dissent was vindicated many years later when the Court reversed *Betts* in *Gideon* v. *Wainwright* (1963).

Another important confrontation between the forces of incorporation and those championing "fundamental fairness" was *Adamson* v. *California* (1947), in which the Court held that the Fourteenth Amendment's due process clause did not incorporate the Fifth Amendment's privilege against self-incrimination and, therefore, did not bar a state prosecutor from commenting unfavorably on a defendant's refusal to take the stand. (Such a comment was not permissible under federal criminal procedure.) It was in *Adamson* that Black set forth his "historical" doctrine of "total incorporation." Black persistently inveighed against the use of an open-ended judicially defined version of fundamental fairness. In *Rochin* v. *California* (1952), the Court reversed the conviction of a defendant whose stomach had been pumped by the police as part of a drug search. Speaking for the Court, Frankfurter found that the conduct of the police "shocked the conscience" and therefore violated due process. Black sharply attacked Frankfurter's standard, arguing that it left any judge free to invalidate a law simply because he did not like it.

One of the period's more dramatic rulings involving defendants' rights was *Louisiana ex rel. Francis* v. *Resweber* (1947). Francis was a convict who had survived the state's first attempt to execute him when the electric chair malfunctioned. The Court found nothing constitutionally offensive in the state making a second attempt, refusing to find that the Fourteenth Amendment embodied a "cruel and unusual punishments" prohibition similar to that found in the Eighth Amendment.

Although the Court was unprepared to embrace Black's theory of total incorporation, a large number of decisions show considerable sensitivity to improper applications of the doctrine of fundamental fairness. The Court regularly reversed state court judgments secured on the basis of coerced confessions and coercive investigations, as in *Chambers* v. *Florida* (1940), *Ward* v. *Texas* (1942), and *Ashcraft* v. *Tennessee* (1944). This concern was eloquently expressed in *Malinski* v. *New York* (1945), in which the Court reversed a conviction even in the face of evidence sufficient to obtain a conviction. The Court upheld New York's rule requiring the trial judge to exclude confessions that were patently involuntary and to allow the jury to determine the voluntariness and truthfulness of confessions in questionable cases.

The Court was sensitive to the fact that coercion takes many forms. In *Watts* v. *Indiana* (1949), the defendant had been arrested for an assault but was a suspect in a murder. The police worked in relays to question him for six nights before he confessed. The Court stressed that the defendant had been isolated from counsel and friends and was unable to invoke any of his constitutional rights.

The Court on occasion also held investigating officers to strict requirements of probable cause (the basis of an officer's belief that an offense has been or is being committed and that the suspect or arrestee is the guilty party), as in *Brinegar* v. *United States* (1949). The Court's rulings in the search-and-seizure area, however, often rested on unstable and shifting majorities and are best characterized as contradictory and confusing. In *Johnson* v. *United States* (1948), the Court held that the detection of opium smoke by experienced narcotics officers did not constitute adequate probable cause for a warrantless search. Without any apparent doctrinal justification, two years later the Court upheld a thorough search of a desk, safe, and file cabinets in a one-room office on the theory that the officers were executing a valid arrest warrant (*United States* v. *Rabinowitz*, 1950). In *Goldman* v. *United States* (1942), a sharply divided Court held that evidence acquired by using a detectaphone (a device that, when attached to a wall, permits one to overhear conversations on the other side) was admissible. The federal statute barring interception of phone conversations (which were overheard) was not violated, reasoned the Court, since the listener had merely eavesdropped; the Fourth Amendment had not been violated because there had been no trespass. In a similar vein, the Court upheld the admission of a voice recording made by a police informant of questionable reliability and used at trial to corroborate his testimony concerning the defendant (*On Lee* v. *United States*, 1952).

While much of the constitutional adjudication in the area of defendants' rights involved state authority, the federal government did not escape the Court's supervisory scrutiny. In *McNabb* v. *United States* (1943), the Court ruled inadmissible a confession secured during a delay in presenting the defendant before a committing officer in keeping with the Rules of Federal Procedure. The same approach was taken in *Upshaw* v. *United States* (1948), in which the Court reversed a conviction even though no improper pressure had been used in securing a confession during an impermissible delay.

JUDICIAL PERSONNEL AND POLITICS

Despite changes, the Court remained relatively stable in its membership throughout the period 1941–1952. Consider that five of the justices (Black, Frankfurter, Douglas, Reed, and Jackson) served for virtually the entire period and that Burton served with these five from 1945 on. To understand the work of the Court during the era, it is helpful to examine the political views of the justices and the patterns of voting alignments that characterized the Court. The Hughes Court had been characterized by relatively stable and predictable voting blocs. During the Stone and Vinson eras the judicial blocs persisted with the added dimension of personal hostilities among some justices.

Roosevelt's first choice for a successor to retiring Chief Justice Charles Evans Hughes was his attorney general, Robert H. Jackson. Jackson was well regarded for his legal acumen; of equal importance was the fact that his political views were in close accord with the president's. Roosevelt was equally well aware that the legal community expected him to elevate Associate Justice Harlan Fiske Stone, whose preparation for the chief-justiceship clearly outshone Jackson's. Stone's biographer Alpheus T. Mason narrates how Roosevelt sought counsel from another Roosevelt appointee, Felix Frankfurter, and how Frankfurter advised the appointment of Stone on the ground that the appointment of a Republican would unify the country as it prepared for war. Stone was named chief justice, and Jackson was appointed associate justice to replace Stone. In addition to Stone and Jackson, the Court consisted of Owen Roberts, a moderate justice appointed by President Hoover in 1930, and appointees of President Roosevelt: Hugo L. Black, former senator from Alabama, who had been appointed by Roosevelt in 1937 and who, during his long tenure on the Court, articulated a theory of constitutional interpretation calling for strict fidelity to the text of the document, especially where constitutional limitations were involved;

Stanley Reed, another moderate-to-conservative justice, who had served as Roosevelt's solicitor general; Felix Frankfurter, a former Harvard law professor and a prominent member of Roosevelt's "brain trust"; William O. Douglas, another former law professor (Yale), who, at the time of his appointment in 1939, was serving as chairman of the Securities and Exchange Commission; Frank Murphy, Roosevelt's former attorney general, who had served as governor of Michigan before being named to the Court in 1940; and James F. Byrnes, another former senator (from South Carolina), who served only one term before being appointed to serve as "assistant president" to Roosevelt. Byrnes was replaced by Wiley Rutledge, a former lower court federal judge who was decidedly liberal in his views.

Truman's appointments to the Court were markedly less colorful than Roosevelt's. All of them turned out to be comparatively conservative. Roberts' retirement in 1945 made it possible for Truman to name Harold H. Burton, a Republican Senator from Ohio, an associate justice, giving the Court a semblance of bipartisan balance. Stone's death in 1946 presented Truman with a difficult decision. He had recently appointed Jackson as chief prosecutor of the German war trials at Nuremberg, and Jackson was evidently keenly interested in the chief-justiceship. Feuding among the justices prompted Truman to go outside the Court for a nominee, and he selected his personal friend, Fred Moore Vinson of Kentucky, who was serving as his secretary of the Treasury. The untimely deaths of both Murphy and Rutledge in the summer of 1949 made it possible for Truman to name to the Court his attorney general, Tom C. Clark, and another personal friend and political associate, Sherman Minton of Indiana.

As chief justices, Stone and Vinson had no success in preserving unity on the Court. Throughout their tenure on the Stone and Vinson Courts, Black and Douglas formed a consistently liberal voting pair, although the strength of their agreement (measured by the agreement rate) was often weaker than that prevailing within other blocs. In the 1941 term Black, Douglas, and Murphy had an agreement rate of 82 percent; in 1942 these three, along with Rutledge, faced a conservative bloc formed by the remainder of the Court (Roberts, Reed, Frankfurter, Stone, Byrnes, and Jackson). Throughout

the remainder of the Stone era (the 1943–1945 terms), Black and Douglas formed one discrete voting bloc; Murphy and Rutledge formed a second; and Stone, Roberts, Reed, Frankfurter, Jackson, and Burton constituted a conservative bloc. In the 1946–1948 period, two conservative blocs emerged, with Vinson, Reed, and Burton in one and Frankfurter and Jackson in the other. In the 1949–1952 period, Minton and Clark joined the Vinson-Reed-Burton bloc, while the Frankfurter-Jackson and Black-Douglas blocs remained intact.

These blocs rested on definite policy differences. The four liberals voted well above the Court average in favor of economic liberalism and civil liberties. The divisiveness among the justices is mirrored in the important decision of *Colegrove* v. *Green* (1946). Only seven justices participated, since Jackson was still in Nuremberg, and the chief-justiceship was vacant. The issue was the thorny one of judicial involvement in legislative redistricting and reapportionment. A malapportioned state legislature (caused by rural overrepresentation) had created congressional districts in which rural inhabitants were grossly overrepresented. The arrangement was challenged as violative, among other things, of the federal guaranty of a "republican form of government." Black, Douglas, and Murphy thought the Court should take the case and grant relief. Frankfurter, Reed, and Burton suggested that the Supreme Court lacked jurisdiction and considered the matter a "political question" in a "political thicket." That left Rutledge, who appeared to straddle the fence: he sided with the three champions of judicial restraint, but on the narrow ground that he thought this an injudicious occasion for the exercise of federal equity jurisdiction; yet he agreed with the three dissenters that the Supreme Court indeed had jurisdiction. Thus, the Court ruled against Colegrove, but only three justices considered the Court without power to act. The *Colegrove* ruling, with its sharply clashing views, may well be taken as the Stone and Vinson Courts in miniature.

THE COURT'S WORK LOAD

During the Stone and Vinson periods the number of cases reaching the Court increased dramatically. The number of cases on the regular appellate docket remained stable (ranging from 1,302 in 1941 to 1,678 in 1946), but in 1945 the Court began maintaining a "miscellaneous docket," on which were entered cases filed by litigants, mainly prisoners, unable to pay the customary filing fees and unable to prepare their pleadings in keeping with the technical rules of the Court. In 1945 there were 131 cases on this special docket, but by 1952 it had grown to over 600. Viewed in another light, during the Vinson period these paupers' cases made up about a third of the Court's entire docket.

There were also dramatic changes in the types of cases with which the Court was concerned. The focus of Supreme Court litigation reflected the Court's posture of judicial self-restraint: there was a decrease in the number of cases involving federal regulatory statutes based on the commerce clause and a drop in federal taxation cases; constitutional questions appeared more prominently in the Court's work, especially questions dealing with the rights of criminal defendants and racial minorities. These figures reflect the Court's growing preoccupation with the rights of individuals and a concomitant decline in its concern with questions involving economic and property rights.

While the volume of cases reaching the Court increased, the number of cases disposed of on the basis of a full-scale review (oral argument and signed opinion) remained small (at about 150 cases per term). During the 1960s and 1970s this fact played a major role in prompting proposals for judicial reform aimed at lightening the burden on the Supreme Court by creating some form of intermediate appellate court to screen cases so as to assure that only the truly important questions reached the Court and to permit the appellate system as a whole to discharge its duties more efficiently and effectively. For a variety of reasons, most of them having to do with opposition from the members of the Court, no major reforms were adopted.

ASSESSMENT

The Stone and Vinson eras were paradoxically years of seminal philosophical debate among the justices and a time that evidenced the Court's vulnerability to the pressures of the political process. Much of the work of the Supreme Court during the period shows the justices (some more than others, of course) to have been sensitive to popular hysteria, especially that associated with Senator Joseph McCarthy.

Neither Stone nor Vinson demonstrated outstanding administrative qualities as chief justice, although certainly Stone made major contributions to the development of American law. Dissension among the justices, especially the bitter feud between Jackson and Black, cast a cloud over the work of the Stone Court. While life among the justices was more cordial under Vinson, it would not be accurate to say that under Vinson's leadership the Court became a place of harmony.

The legal-philosophical giants of the period were Frankfurter and Black, each of whom attempted to articulate the bases of his respective position. Frankfurter, the scholarly professor, attempted to find in the Constitution definite constraints on judicial power, claiming that legislatures, not courts, were better qualified to make judgments about such matters as school administration, legislative redistricting and reapportionment, and even threats posed by subversives. The Frankfurter-Black clash represented a major debate about the meaning of the New Deal. Frankfurter's view was favorable to the claims of states' rights and reflected the view that the growth of the judicial power of the central government posed a threat to the delicate equilibrium of the federal system. Applied to concrete cases, Frankfurter's principles appeared biased in favor of conservative outcomes—preserving the established doctrines and deferring to legislative judgments.

Frankfurter's approach was rooted in the rich learning of the law schools and steeped in reverence for skepticism about judicial power advocated by great judges of the past, such as Learned Hand and Oliver Wendell Holmes, Jr. Like Frankfurter, Black doubted the judicial capacity to make wise policy, but, in contrast to Frankfurter, he was inclined to hold that the Constitution's text itself precluded certain judicial choices. In addition, Black retained the New Dealer's Populist streak, distrusting abstract doctrines that served the interests of the wealthy and of large corporations. Black consistently argued for a literal interpretation of the Constitution's prohibitions, an approach that forced Black to espouse doctrines apparently at odds with historical facts. (Black argued, as indicated above, that the text of the Fourteenth Amendment's first section was "intended" by its authors to "incorporate" the limitations of the Bill of Rights against the states—a position that accorded well with Black's literal approach but one that reputable historians have effectively shown to be at odds with the truth.) By the time Vinson's chief-justiceship ended, Black had worked out a kind of interpretational "system," at least in the area of freedom of expression: the language of the First Amendment ("Congress shall make no law . . ."), he argued, places an "absolute" prohibition on Congress in these areas; the Fourteenth Amendment applies the identical limitations to the states. Thus, when legislatures seek to limit expression, association, or religion, it is the Constitution, not the courts, that checks them. The judges have no competence in evaluating policies of governments outside the areas referred to by the Constitution. Courts should not strike down, or even seriously review, laws that regulate the economy, for instance, because the economy is none of the judiciary's business.

Black's position corresponded roughly to a doctrine articulated by Stone in *United States* v. *Carolene Products Co.* (1938), in which Stone had declared that judicial scrutiny of legislation which did not threaten the processes whereby laws were made or amended should be at a minimum, while judicial scrutiny of laws that affected freedoms of expression and association should be at a maximum. This position is the immediate intellectual ancestor of the contemporary champions of "strict judicial scrutiny" to protect "insular minorities" and "fundamental freedoms." The approach fit well with the goals of the progressives behind the New Deal: take the courts out of regulatory review, but invite courts to play an active role in protecting minorities and civil liberties generally. Frankfurter and his disciples were quick to point out that such a simplistic approach to constitutional interpretation was a kind of special pleading to cover up policy goals, which offered little guidance in resolving real questions; the meaning of "due process" or "reasonable searches and seizures" or "speech" still called for judicial interpretation, they argued. Moreover, it failed to explain why certain guaranties should be more sacred than others.

The clash between Frankfurter and Black represented, of course, a perennial struggle with basic questions of legal-political philosophy. The major contribution of the Stone and Vinson eras may well be the presentation of these perennial questions in such stark relief.

CASES

Adamson v. California, 332 U.S. 46 (1947)
Adler v. Board of Education, 342 U.S. 485 (1952)
Ashcraft v. Tennessee, 322 U.S. 143 (1944)
Baumgartner v. United States, 322 U.S. 665 (1944)
Beauharnais v. Illinois, 343 U.S. 250 (1952)
Betts v. Brady, 316 U.S. 455 (1942)
Borden Co. v. Borella, 325 U.S. 679 (1945)
Breard v. Alexandria, 341 U.S. 622 (1951)
Brinegar v. United States, 338 U.S. 160 (1949)
Brown v. Board of Education, 347 U.S. 483 (1954)
Cantwell v. Connecticut, 310 U.S. 296 (1940)
Carpenters and Joiners Union v. Ritter's Cafe, 315 U.S. 722 (1942)
Chambers v. Florida, 309 U.S. 227 (1940)
Chaplinsky v. New Hampshire, 315 U.S. 568 (1942)
Colegrove v. Green, 328 U.S. 549 (1946)
Cox v. New Hampshire, 312 U.S. 569 (1941)
Cramer v. United States, 325 U.S. 1 (1945)
Dennis v. United States, 341 U.S. 494 (1951)
Ex parte Endo, 323 U.S. 283 (1944)
Everson v. Board of Education, 330 U.S. 1 (1947)
Giboney v. Empire Storage and Ice Co., 336 U.S. 490 (1949)
Gideon v. Wainwright, 372 U.S. 335 (1963)
Goldman v. United States, 316 U.S. 129 (1942)
Grovey v. Townsend, 295 U.S. 45 (1935)
Hartzel v. United States, 322 U.S. 680 (1944)
Haupt v. United States, 330 U.S. 631 (1947)
Henderson v. United States, 339 U.S. 816 (1950)
Hirabayashi v. United States, 320 U.S. 81 (1943)
Hurd v. Hodge, 334 U.S. 24 (1948)
International Brotherhood of Teamsters v. Hanke, 339 U.S. 470 (1950)
Japanese Exclusion Cases. *See* Hirabayashi v. United States *and* Korematsu v. United States.
Johnson v. United States, 333 U.S. 10 (1948)
Jones v. Opelika, 316 U.S. 584 (1942)
Keegan v. United States, 325 U.S. 478 (1945)
Korematsu v. United States, 323 U.S. 214 (1944)
Kovacs v. Cooper, 336 U.S. 77 (1949)
Louisiana ex rel. Francis v. Resweber, 329 U.S. 459 (1947)
McCollum v. Board of Education, 333 U.S. 203 (1948)
McLaurin v. Oklahoma State Regents, 339 U.S. 637 (1950)
McNabb v. United States, 318 U.S. 332 (1943)
Malinski v. New York, 324 U.S. 401 (1945)
Martin v. Struthers, 319 U.S. 141 (1943)
Milk Wagon Drivers Union v. Meadowmoor Dairies, 312 U.S. 287 (1941)
Minersville School District v. Gobitis, 310 U.S. 586 (1940)
Missouri ex rel. Gaines v. Canada, 305 U.S. 337 (1938)
Morgan v. Virginia, 328 U.S. 373 (1946)
Mulford v. Smith, 307 U.S. 38 (1939)

Murdock v. Pennsylvania, 319 U.S. 105 (1943)
In re Oliver, 333 U.S. 257 (1948)
On Lee v. United States, 343 U.S. 747 (1952)
Ex parte Quirin, 317 U.S. 1 (1942)
Rochin v. California, 342 U.S. 165 (1952)
Saia v. New York, 334 U.S. 558 (1948)
Schneiderman v. United States, 320 U.S. 118 (1943)
Shelley v. Kraemer, 334 U.S. 1 (1948)
Sipuel v. Board of Regents, 332 U.S. 631 (1948)
Skinner v. Oklahoma, 316 U.S. 535 (1942)
Smith v. Allwright, 321 U.S. 349 (1944)
Southern Pacific Co. v. Arizona, 325 U.S. 761 (1945)
Steuart and Bros. v. Bowles, 322 U.S. 398 (1944)
In re Summers, 325 U.S. 561 (1945)
Sweatt v. Painter, 339 U.S. 629 (1950)
10 East 40th St. Building v. Callus, 325 U.S. 578 (1945)
Terminiello v. Chicago, 337 U.S. 1 (1949)
Thomas v. Collins, 323 U.S. 516 (1945)
Thornhill v. Alabama, 310 U.S. 88 (1940)
United States v. Carolene Products Co., 304 U.S. 144 (1938)
United States v. Darby Lumber Co., 312 U.S. 100 (1941)
United States v. Rabinowitz, 339 U.S. 56 (1950)
United States v. Southeastern Underwriters Assn., 322 U.S. 533 (1944)
Upshaw v. United States, 335 U.S. 410 (1948)
Ward v. Texas, 316 U.S. 547 (1942)
Watts v. Indiana, 338 U.S. 49 (1949)
West Virginia State Board of Education v. Barnette, 319 U.S. 624 (1943)
Wickard v. Filburn, 317 U.S. 111 (1942)
Wieman v. Updegraff, 344 U.S. 183 (1952)
Wolf v. Colorado, 338 U.S. 25 (1949)
Woods v. Miller, 333 U.S. 138 (1948)
Yakus v. United States, 321 U.S. 414 (1944)
Youngstown Sheet and Tube Co. v. Sawyer, 343 U.S. 579 (1952)
Zorach v. Clauson, 343 U.S. 306 (1952)

BIBLIOGRAPHY

Henry J. Abraham, *Freedom and the Court: Civil Rights and Liberties in the United States* (1977), is a survey of the Supreme Court's interpretation of constitutional limitations; and *Justices and Presidents: A Political History of Appointments to the Supreme Court* (1974), is a study of the appointment process through history; it contains valuable biographical information about the members of the Supreme Court. Administrative Office of the United States Courts, *Annual Report, 1948* (1949), presents detailed statistical information on the work of the Supreme Court of the period from 1937 to 1947. Liva Baker, *Felix Frankfurter* (1969), is recognized as an outstanding biography of a leading member of the Court during the Stone and Vinson eras.

Congressional Quarterly, *Guide to the U.S. Supreme Court* (1979), is a one-volume encyclopedia on the Supreme Court and its role in the American system of government. Leon Friedman and Fred L. Israel, eds., *The Justices of the United States Supreme Court, 1789–1969: Their Lives and Major Opinions*, 4 vols. (1969), is a collection of scholarly essays on the justices accompanied by excerpts from one or two of their major opinions. Roger A. Geimer, "The Demise of the Puritan Ethic in America," in *Great Events From History*, Worldwide Twentieth Century Series, 1 (1980), examines the changes in American values brought about by World War II and its aftermath. Sheldon Goldman, *Constitutional Law and Supreme Court Decision-Making* (1982), is a casebook arranged chronologically and contains excellent introductory articles on each of the major periods of American constitutional development. J. Woodford Howard, "On the Fluidity of Judicial Choice," in *American Political Science Review*, 62 (1968), is an interesting study of the complex ways whereby members of the Supreme Court arrive at their decisions.

Alfred H. Kelly, Winfred Harbison, and Herman Belz, *The American Constitution: Its Origins and Development* (1983), is a thorough and readable account of American constitutional development in a historical perspective. Alpheus T. Mason, *Harlan Fiske Stone: Pillar of the Law* (1956), is a classic study of the life and contributions of Chief Justice Stone. C. Herman Pritchett, *Constitutional Law of the Federal System* (1984), is a critical survey of Supreme Court interpretations of the separation of powers, federalism, and the powers of the central government; *Constitutional Civil Liberties* (1984), a companion volume to the preceding item, is a highly readable analysis of judicial interpretation of constitutional limitations; and *The Roosevelt Court* (1969), is a classic study of the work and contributions of the Supreme Court during the Franklin D. Roosevelt era.

John R. Schmidhauser, *Judges and Justices: The Federal Appellate Judiciary* (1979), is a critical survey of the politics of appellate courts, including the Supreme Court's relationship to other appellate tribunals. Mark Silverstein, *Constitutional Faiths: Felix Frankfurter, Hugo Black, and the Process of Judicial Decision-Making* (1984), is a study of the legal-philosophical views of the two justices. "The Supreme Court, 1952 Term," in *Harvard Law Review*, 67 (1953), contains valuable statistical information on the work of the Supreme Court for the 1948–1952 period and complements the information in the 1948 *Annual Report* cited above. U.S. Congressional Research Service, *The Constitution of the United States: Analysis and Interpretation* (1973) and *1980 Supplement* (1982), present a detailed, provision-by-provision discussion of the meaning of the Constitution.

[See also CIVIL LIBERTIES AFTER 1937; CONGRESS; DUE PROCESS OF LAW; EXECUTIVE AND FOREIGN AFFAIRS; and FREE SPEECH AND EXPRESSION.]

THE WARREN COURT AND ERA

Bernard Schwartz

THERE have been two great creative periods in American public law. The first was the formative era, when the Marshall Court laid down the foundations of American constitutional law, giving specific content to the broad general terms in which the federal Constitution is written. The judicial task at that time was to work out from the constitutional text a body of legal doctrines adapted to the needs of the new nation and the new era into which it was entering. The second great creative period was the Warren Court era. The judicial task then was to keep step with the twentieth century's frenetic pace of societal change. To do this, the Warren Court had to perform a transforming role, usually thought of as more appropriate to the legislator than the judge. In the process it rewrote much of the corpus of American constitutional law. Indeed, in terms of creative impact on the law, the Warren Court's tenure can be compared only with that of the Marshall Court.

WARREN AND HIS COURT

Earl Warren, the fourteenth chief justice of the United States, was appointed on 2 October 1953 and served until 23 June 1969, when he administered the oath of office to his successor, Warren E. Burger. Warren was born (1891) and raised in California; he grew up in Bakersfield, then a small town that was a microcosm of the burgeoning West itself. The last vestiges of the American frontier, the town and state quickly came to be the paradigm of twentieth-century America. While Warren lived there, growth was the prime element of California life. In his later years the chief justice would recall proudly that during his years as California's governor, his state had been able to absorb 5 million new arrivals "without any confusion or discord whatsoever."

The man, like the state, displayed a capacity for growth throughout his career. The popular conception of Warren's judicial career has been one of a virtual metamorphosis, with the political grub suddenly transformed into the judicial lepidopteron. Certainly, Warren as chief justice appeared to be an entirely different person than he had been before his elevation to the Court. As his state's leading law enforcement officer, Warren had been perhaps the foremost advocate of what a *Harper's* article was to term "our worst wartime mistake"—the forced evacuation and internment of persons of Japanese ancestry from the West Coast after the Japanese attack on Pearl Harbor in December 1941. As chief justice, Warren was the foremost proponent of racial equality. From his crucial role in the *Brown* school segregation case to the end of his Court tenure, he did more than any other judge in American history to ensure that the law, in W. H. Auden's phrase, "found the notion of equality."

As governor, Warren strongly opposed reapportionment of the California legislature, even though, as he later conceded, "My own state was one of the most malapportioned in the nation." As chief justice, Warren led the movement to bring the apportionment process within the "equal protection" guaranty—a movement that culminated in his opinion in *Reynolds* v. *Sims* (1964).

Like John Marshall, Earl Warren had a political background. In 1920, soon after he had obtained his law degree from the University of California, Warren began his legal career in the office of the district attorney of Alameda County, across the bay from San Francisco. He was elected district attorney five years later and served in that position until 1938. A 1931 survey

160

of American district attorneys declared without hesitation that Warren was "the best district attorney in the United States."

In 1938, Warren was elected attorney general of California, and in 1942, governor. He was a most effective chief executive; he reorganized the state government and secured major reforming legislation—notably, measures for modernizing the state's hospital system, improving its prisons and its correctional system, creating an extensive highway program, and increasing old-age and unemployment benefits. Warren proved an able administrator and was the only governor of his state to be elected to three terms. He was appointed by President Dwight D. Eisenhower to head the Supreme Court before he could serve out his third term and resigned as governor so that he could take up his new duties as chief justice.

The designation of a Supreme Court by the name of its chief justice was, during Warren's tenure, more than a mere custom, for the Supreme Court took on his image as unmistakably as the earlier Courts of John Marshall and Roger B. Taney had reflected the unique leadership of those two men. Many students of the Supreme Court dispute this, claiming that while Warren may have been the nominal head of the Court that bears his name, the actual leadership was furnished by other justices. Thus, Gerald Dunne's biography of Hugo Black is based upon the proposition that the justice was really responsible for the "judicial revolution" that occurred during the Warren years. Others have asserted that Justice William J. Brennan dominated the high bench while Warren sat in its center chair. Justice Black himself always believed that he had indeed led the judicial revolution that took place while Warren was chief justice and resented the acclaim that the chief justice received for leading what everyone looked upon as the Warren Court. As Black saw it, the Court under Warren had only written into law the constitutional principles that he had been advocating for many years. When Warren retired as chief justice, the justices prepared the traditional letter of farewell. The draft letter read, "For us it is a source of pride that we have had the opportunity to be members of the Warren Court." Black changed this to "the Court over which you have presided."

The other justices who served with Warren all recognized his leadership role. Justice Douglas'

autobiography ranks Warren with Marshall and Charles Evans Hughes "as our three greatest Chief Justices." The justices who sat with him have personally stressed that Chief Justice Warren may not have been an intellectual, but then, as Justice Potter Stewart put it, "he never pretended to be one." More important, says Stewart, he possessed "instinctive qualities of leadership." When Stewart was asked about claims that Justice Black was the intellectual leader of the Court, he replied, "If Black was the intellectual leader, Warren was the *leader* leader."

Warren himself brought more authority to the chief-justiceship than had been the case for years. The most important work of the Supreme Court occurs behind the scenes, particularly at the private conferences where the justices discuss and vote on cases. The chief justice controls the conference discussion; his is the prerogative to call and discuss cases before the other justices speak. All those who served with him lay stress on Chief Justice Warren's ability to lead the conference. "It is incredible," said Justice Brennan just after Warren's death, "how efficiently the Chief would conduct the conferences, leading the discussion of every case on the agenda, with a knowledge of each case at his fingertips."

The conference notes of justices on the Warren Court quickly confirm that after an inevitable period of feeling his way, the chief justice was as effective a leader as the Court has ever had. In almost all the important cases, the chief justice himself led the discussion toward the decision he favored. During his tenure, the High Court was emphatically the Warren Court, and without arrogance, he, as well as the country, knew it. A consideration of the work of the Warren Court reveals a constitutional corpus that was directly a product of the chief justice's leadership.

Even the most inspiring general must have troops who are willing and able to follow his lead, and so the designation of the Court by the name of its chief justice should not be allowed to obscure the role of its other members. The Warren Court contained some of the most noted justices in Supreme Court history, who played important roles in supporting or opposing the chief justice's lead. Among Warren's supporters on the Court, the most important were Justices Black, Douglas, and Brennan. When Warren was appointed, Hugo L. Black was the senior associate justice and the leader of the Court's liberal wing. Like Warren, Black had a political background, having served as senator from Alabama before his Court appointment in 1937. Before Warren became chief justice, Black had been the leader in the effort to have the justices actively interpret the Constitution in favor of individual rights. In particular, he urged an absolutist interpretation of the First Amendment—that is, one that permitted no restrictions at all upon freedom of speech—as well as the view that all the guaranties in the federal Bill of Rights were binding upon the states. The latter approach would have meant a substantial broadening of the Supreme Court's review power, because it meant full scrutiny of state as well as federal action for conformity to the Bill of Rights.

Black's chief supporter in the pre-Warren Court was Justice William O. Douglas. Before Warren's appointment, the heading "Mr. Justice Black and Mr. Justice Douglas, dissenting," was as common as a similar heading for Justices Holmes and Brandeis a generation earlier. Douglas had been a law professor and chairman of the Securities and Exchange Commission when he was named to the Court in 1939 at the age of forty, the youngest justice in over a century. On the bench, he followed Black's activist approach and wrote some of the strongest dissents in support of their position in the pre-Warren years. In declining to write an article about Douglas, Black averred, "Our views are so nearly the same that it would be almost like self praise for me to write what I feel about his judicial career."

Though Black and Douglas were regarded by the public as Warren's leading supporters, the chief justice always considered his most effective ally on the Court to be Justice William J. Brennan. Appointed in 1956 after having served as a New Jersey judge for seven years, Brennan had more judicial experience than any member of the Warren Court and was the only one to have served as a state judge. Soon after his appointment, Brennan became Warren's closest colleague. The chief justice would usually turn to Brennan when he wanted to discuss a case or some other matter on which he wanted an extra-conference exchange of views.

Unlike Black and Douglas, who tended to be uncompromising in their views, Brennan was always willing to mold his language to meet the objections of some of his colleagues, a talent that would become his hallmark on the Court and

one on which Warren would rely frequently. It was Brennan to whom the chief justice was to assign the opinion in some of the most important cases decided by the Warren Court.

The activist position increasingly assumed by the Warren Court was opposed by what was usually called the Court's conservative wing. Its leader until his retirement in 1962, and the chief justice's principal opponent until then, was Justice Felix Frankfurter. He had been a noted Harvard law professor, a proponent of libertarian causes, and a principal unofficial adviser to President Franklin Roosevelt, who chose him for the Court in 1939. Frankfurter was a consistent opponent of the Black-Douglas position, to which the chief justice increasingly adhered. Frankfurter rejected the view that elevated freedom of expression and other personal rights above economic rights, because he believed that it created an unwarranted hierarchy of rights not provided for in the Constitution. Frankfurter also rejected the view that the entire Bill of Rights was binding upon the states. That position, Frankfurter contended, distorted the proper working of federalism. It would make the Supreme Court the hierarchical head of both state and federal judicial systems, merging them into one common mass subject equally to the overriding supervisory authority of the one Court in Washington. The difference between the Frankfurter approach and that of Warren and his supporters ultimately resulted in a fundamental disagreement on the proper role of the Supreme Court. Frankfurter urged a restrained role opposed to the increasingly activist approach taken by the Warren bloc.

While Frankfurter remained on the Court, the justices remained split between the two views. The trend was, however, clearly toward the Warren position and, after Frankfurter's retirement, the chief justice had a solid majority. It was then that Justice John Marshall Harlan succeeded to the Frankfurter mantle of opposition to the Warren approach. Harlan had been a member of a leading Wall Street law firm and a federal appellate judge before he was elevated to the Supreme Court in 1955. He was the best legal technician on the Warren Court and became a sound justice who could be relied on for learned opinions that thoroughly covered the subjects dealt with. Harlan's voice calling for judicial restraint was, however, what one reporter termed a voice increasingly "heard in a symbolic wilderness," as the chief justice and his supporters increasingly dominated the Court's decisions.

ACTIVISM VERSUS JUDICIAL RESTRAINT

In his widely read *Inside U.S.A.*, John Gunther asserted that Warren, then governor of California, was a pragmatic politician who had "little coherent philosophy." As soon as he took his place on the bench, the chief justice was faced with a choice between the two antagonistic judicial philosophies that have contended in American courts throughout the twentieth century. In simplified terms, the division was between judicial activism and judicial self-restraint. The rule of restraint had been the handiwork of that seminal figure of modern American law, Justice Oliver Wendell Holmes.

In the years before Warren's appointment, the Supreme Court had moved from judicial activism in cases involving economic regulation to the judicial restraint that Holmes had advocated so vigorously in dissent. Before 1937, the justices construed the Constitution as authorizing them to pass on the wisdom of legislative policies in exercising review power. As the Court conceded in *Ferguson* v. *Skrupa* (1963), "There was a time when the Due Process Clause was used by this Court to strike down laws which were thought unreasonable, that is, unwise or incompatible with some particular economic or social philosophy."

Critics contended that the justices were arrogating to themselves a veto power never contemplated by the Constitution—what Theodore Roosevelt once termed "the political function which American courts alone among the courts of the world possess." The frequency with which the Court interposed the power to negate social legislation led to the famous charge by Justice Brandeis that it was exercising "the powers of a super-legislature" (*Burns Baking Co.* v. *Bryan*, 1924).

All this began to change in 1937 with the reversal in the Court's jurisprudence that Edward S. Corwin characterized as "Constitutional Revolution, Ltd." Now the Holmes approach of judicial self-restraint could virtually take over the field. By the time Warren came to the Supreme Court, the Holmes approach had become established doctrine and had furnished the jurisprudential foundation for the transition from laissez-faire to the welfare state. By midcentury, the welfare state had become an accepted fact—constitutionally as well as politically.

With the adoption of the Holmes restraint doctrine, the justices have come to recognize governmental restrictions on property rights to an extent never before permitted in American law. At the same time, they have seen that unless the rights of the person are correlatively expanded, the individual will virtually be shorn of constitutional protection—hence, the recent shift in American public law to emphasis on the protection of personal rights. The justices are disturbed by the growth of governmental authority and are seeking to preserve a sphere for individuality even in a society in which the individual stands dwarfed by the power concentrations that confront him.

In such a society the issues confronting the courts have also begun to change. Judges like Chief Justice Warren came to believe that even the Holmes canon could not suffice as the bedrock of judicial review. Warren was willing to follow the rule of restraint in the economic area. It was, in truth, the 1963 *Ferguson* decision of the Warren Court that sounded the death knell for judicial activism in that area. Notwithstanding this judicial deference in the economic realm, however, Warren believed that restraint was not the proper posture in the cases involving claimed infringements on personal rights that increasingly came before the Supreme Court. In such cases, he advocated active intervention by the Court to ensure enforcement of the guarantees for individual rights as they existed in the Bill of Rights. In the Warren view, the tenet of judicial self-restraint should not bind judges in cases involving restraints on life and liberty. In those cases, challenged legislation must be scrutinized with greater care.

During the first years of the Warren Court, this activist approach was opposed most strongly by Justice Frankfurter. The Warren-Frankfurter difference ultimately came down to a fundamental disagreement on the proper role of the judge in the constitutional system. Frankfurter remained true to the Holmes approach, insisting that self-restraint was the proper posture for a nonrepresentative judiciary, regardless of the nature of the asserted interests in particular cases. Warren was willing to follow the canon of judicial restraint in the economic area, but he felt that the Bill of Rights provisions protecting personal liberties imposed on the judges more active enforcement obligations. When a law was alleged to infringe upon the personal rights guaranteed by the Bill of Rights, Warren refused to defer to the legislative judgment that the law was necessary.

Warren rejected the Frankfurter philosophy of judicial restraint because he had come to believe that it thwarted effective performance of the Court's constitutional role. Judicial abnegation, in the chief justice's view, meant all too often judicial abdication of the duty to enforce constitutional guaranties. "I believe," Warren declared in an interview on his retirement, "that this Court or any court should exercise the functions of the office to the limit of its responsibilities." Judicial restraint meant that "for a long, long time we have been sweeping under the rug a great many problems basic to American life. We have failed to face up to them, and they have piled up on us, and now they are causing a great deal of dissension and controversy of all kinds." To Warren, it was the Court's job "to remedy those things eventually," regardless of the controversy involved.

THE COURT AND CIVIL RIGHTS

In any qualitative list of the important decisions of the Warren Court, the first place would have to be given to the 1954 decision in *Brown* v. *Board of Education,* which at last gave real meaning to the constitutional right of equality. That right had been elevated to the organic plane with the ratification of the Fourteenth Amendment in 1868, but it was not until the latter half of the twentieth century—or, more precisely, after the appointment of Warren as chief justice—that the right began to be vigorously enforced by the Supreme Court. According to Justice Reed, who participated in the *Brown* decision, "If it was not the most important decision in the history of the Court, it was very close."

Before the *Brown* case, the Fourteenth Amendment had not succeeded in securing equality for blacks. This was true in large part because of Supreme Court decisions, particu-

larly that in *Plessy* v. *Ferguson* (1896). Plessy, who was one-eighth black, had been arrested on a train out of New Orleans for refusing to move from a "white" railway car to a "colored" coach. The conductor had acted under a Louisiana law that required railroads "to provide equal but separate accommodations for the white and colored races," and the Supreme Court had not only rejected the contention that this law violated the Fourteenth Amendment's guaranty of equal protection of the laws but even held that racial segregation was not in itself unconstitutional. Upon the "separate but equal" doctrine approved by the *Plessy* Court was built a whole subsequent structure of racial discrimination. Jim Crow replaced equal protection, and legally enforced segregation became the dominant feature in much of the United States.

The *Brown* decision changed all that. At issue in *Brown* was the constitutionality of segregated schools, with separate schools for white and black pupils, of the type that was then required by law in much of the country, particularly in southern states and even the nation's capital. When the justices first discussed the case in 1952 under Warren's predecessor, Chief Justice Fred M. Vinson, they were sharply split. According to a letter by Justice Frankfurter to Justice Stanley Reed, a decision at that time would have produced only a 5–4 vote against segregation. The closeness of the division led the justices to postpone decision until the following year. By then Warren had succeeded to the Court's central chair. That the Court ultimately seized the constitutional issue and unanimously outlawed school segregation was due, in the main, to the new chief justice's efforts. "It looks like a unanimous decision—a major accomplishment for his [Warren's] leadership," Justice Harold Burton wrote in his diary a week before the *Brown* decision was announced.

The importance of judicial unanimity cannot be overemphasized. It was no mean feat for the Court's neophyte (as he then was), vested only with the moral prestige of the chief-justiceship, to induce eight individualists, accustomed to arriving at decisions in their own ways and never hesitant at articulating their separate views, to join in the unanimous decision, without even a single concurring voice to detract from the majesty and forthrightness of his opinion. Warren's

Brown decision is typical of his straightforward, almost nonlegal style. The opinion opens by stressing that the Court could not "turn the clock back to 1868 when the [Fourteenth] Amendment was adopted, or even to 1896 when *Plessy* v. *Ferguson* was written. We must consider public education in the light of its full development and its present place in American life throughout the Nation." In today's conditions, segregation in schools on the basis of race must be held to "deprive the children of the minority group of equal educational opportunities." Segregated schools, by their nature, said the chief justice, could not provide equal educational opportunities: "To separate them [black children] from others of similar age and qualifications solely because of their race generates a feeling of inferiority as to their status in the community that may affect their hearts and minds in a way unlikely ever to be undone."

The *Plessy* decision had said that the assumption that segregation supposed colored inferiority was fallacious, but Warren declared that segregation did signify the inferiority of blacks: "Whatever may have been the extent of psychological knowledge at the time of *Plessy* v. *Ferguson*, this finding is amply supported by modern authority. Any language in *Plessy* v. *Ferguson* contrary to this finding is rejected." This statement was supported by a footnote that listed seven works by social scientists. The chief justice then stated the Court's far-reaching conclusion: "We conclude that in the field of public education the doctrine of 'separate but equal' has no place." The *Brown* opinion ended with the holding that plaintiffs "and others similarly situated" had been deprived of equal protection by the segregation complained of.

Almost never before, wrote the columnist Arthur Krock the next day in the *New York Times,* had "the high tribunal disposed so simply and briefly of an issue of such magnitude." The *Brown* opinion was strikingly short for an opinion of such consequence: only ten pages in the *United States Reports.* Critics of the *Brown* decision have been disturbed by what they claim is its inadequacy in explaining its vindication of the new right. They allege a lack of legal craftsmanship in the Warren opinion that has tended to deprive it of the respect to which it would otherwise be entitled. They point to the opinion's laconic nature, its failure to rely upon legal precedent, and its literary weakness, as compared with those produced by past American masters of the judicial art.

It may be unfortunate that the *Brown* opinion was not written by a Holmes or a Cardozo. However, it is doubtful whether those virtuosos could possibly have secured a unanimous decision, which was Warren's forte. Taken as written, *Brown* certainly ranks as one of the great opinions of judicial history—plainly in the tradition of Chief Justice Marshall's seminal dictum in *McCulloch* v. *Maryland* (1819) that the Court must never forget that it is a constitution that it is expounding. Perhaps the *Brown* opinion did not demonstrate as well as it might have that the mere fact of segregation denies educational equality. But *Brown* is so clearly right in its conclusion in this respect that whether more was really necessary becomes questionable.

It has since become apparent that the contemporary criticisms of the Court's performance have lost their relevance. What is plain is that *Brown* has taken its place in the very forefront of the pantheon of historic decisions. In the light of what Justice Arthur J. Goldberg once termed the American commitment to equality and its part in helping to fulfill the commitment, *Brown* will occupy a paramount position long after the contemporary criticisms will have ceased to have any more continuing significance than those voiced against the great decisions of the Marshall Court at the very outset of the nation's constitutional development.

After the *Brown* decision, the Warren Court moved to outlaw racial segregation in all public institutions. In 1955 the Court prohibited segregation in public beaches in Baltimore and a municipal golf course in Atlanta. The next year it invalidated the segregated bus system in Montgomery, Alabama. In the following year the Court ruled segregation invalid in all public buildings, housing, transportation, and recreational and eating facilities. By 1963, in *Johnson* v. *Virginia,* the Court could declare categorically, "It is no longer open to question that a State may not constitutionally require segregation of public facilities."

In its 1954 *Brown* decision, the Court had held that school segregation was unconstitutional, and a year later, in its second *Brown* decision, the

Court ordered the district courts to take such action as was necessary and proper to ensure the nondiscriminatory admission of plaintiffs to schools "with all deliberate speed." The enforcement of *Brown* was left to the lower courts, which met massive resistance in many southern school districts. The Warren Court intervened in several cases to force desegregation, particularly in *Griffin* v. *County Board of Prince Edward County* (1964), in which a Virginia county had closed down its school system rather than have blacks attend schools with whites. Then, in *Green* v. *County Board of New Kent County* (1968), the Court invalidated "freedom of choice" plans, under which most southern school districts then operated. The Court held that a school board had a duty to come forward with a desegregation plan that "promises realistically to work *now*." This holding led the way to the ruling in *Alexander* v. *Holmes County Board of Education* (1969) under Chief Justice Burger, that the delay countenanced by the "all deliberate speed" formula was no longer constitutionally permissible.

The Warren Court decisions furthering racial equality were an important catalyst to the civil rights protests of the 1960s and congressional action to protect civil rights. Both developments received support from decisions of the Warren Court. Convictions of civil rights demonstrators in public places and at sit-in demonstrations at restaurants, lunch counters, and libraries were reversed in a number of cases, thereby establishing the right to use the streets and other public places as "public forums" for the dissemination of even unpopular views.

Soon after the Court decided the last of the important sit-in cases, the Civil Rights Act of 1964 became law—the first time since Reconstruction that Congress had passed an important statute to protect civil rights. The 1964 law prohibited racial discrimination in hotels, restaurants, and other public accommodations. The decision in the *Civil Rights Cases* of 1883 had invalidated a similar law (the Civil Rights Act of 1875) on the ground that the Fourteenth Amendment's guaranty of equal protection was limited to "state action" and did not reach the discrimination of private hotel and restaurant owners, but the Warren Court upheld the 1964 act. The Court ruled in *Heart of Atlanta Motel* v. *United States* (1964) that Congress could pass the law under its commerce power and a law under

that power was not subject to the "state action" limitation. In *South Carolina* v. *Katzenbach* (1966) the Court also upheld the Voting Rights Act of 1965, which contained far-reaching provisions protecting the right of blacks to vote. Though the act provides for the supplanting of state election machinery by federal law and federal officials, the opinion of Chief Justice Warren found it a valid congressional measure to enforce the Fifteenth Amendment.

LEGISLATIVE INVESTIGATIONS AND SUBVERSION

Though the Warren Court gave wide scope to the congressional power to protect civil rights, it did not hesitate to intervene when it determined that Congress had acted in violation of those rights. The first part of Warren's tenure coincided with the excesses associated with Senator Joseph R. McCarthy. When Warren was appointed, McCarthy was at the apex of his power. He had won the approval of seven of every ten Americans in a January 1954 Gallup poll and his permanent Senate Investigating Subcommittee had been voted a large appropriation. The investigations conducted by McCarthy and the House Un-American Activities Committee (HUAC), as well as similar state committees, had cast a pall on expression throughout the country.

During Warren's early years, his Court acted to curb abusive conduct during legislative investigations. In 1955 the Court reversed contempt-of-Congress convictions because of violations of the privilege against self-incrimination by HUAC (*Quinn* v. *United States; Emspak* v. *United States*). The following year a similar decision was rendered in *Slochower* v. *Board of Education of the City of New York*, in which a city employee was dismissed for refusing, on grounds of self-incrimination, to answer a Senate committee's questions. Then, in 1957, the Court handed down two decisions significantly restricting legislative investigatory power. *Sweezy* v. *New Hampshire* limited legislative power to inquire into a professor's academic activities. *Watkins* v. *United States* went further. In reversing a conviction for refusing to answer questions before HUAC, the opinion of the chief justice laid down broad limitations upon congressional investigatory power. It contained a lecture against abuses by congressional investigators and ruled that they were subject to constitutional restrictions. In particular, they were limited to inquiries for valid legislative purposes: "There is no congressional power to expose for the sake of exposure."

In addition, during the first part of Warren's Court tenure, the Court acted to curb other aspects of the governmental program against subversive activities. In *Pennsylvania* v. *Nelson* (1956), the Court struck down state antisubversion laws, holding that they were preempted by federal action on the subject. The next year *Yates* v. *United States* drastically limited the Smith (Alien Registration) Act, the law passed by Congress in 1940 to deal with subversion. The Court reversed the Smith Act convictions of fourteen leaders of the Communist party on the ground that more than advocacy of forcible overthrow of government as an abstract principle was required for a Smith Act conviction. Under *Yates* and later Warren Court decisions, it became all but impossible for successful Smith Act prosecutions to be brought.

Other Warren Court decisions greatly restricted the operation of the extensive loyalty programs that had been set up by the federal government and many states. In a number of cases the Court invalidated dismissals under the loyalty programs, holding the government strictly to the procedures specified in the relevant regulations. The decision in *Greene* v. *McElroy* (1959) was of broader significance. The Warren opinion there relied upon the denial of the right of cross-examination—a basic right in all adjudicatory proceedings. The Court also invalidated a statute that barred members of Communist-action organizations from defense facilities (*United States* v. *Robel*, 1968) and struck down loyalty oaths insofar as they applied to passive members of organizations—that is, those who had no intent to further their illegal aims (*Elfbrandt* v. *Russell*, 1966).

Few decisions of the Warren Court encountered such strong opposition as those limiting governmental power to suppress subversive activities. Critics referred to the day on which the *Yates*, *Sweezy*, and *Watkins* decisions were handed down as "Red Monday." Senator McCarthy declared that "Warren has become a hero to the *Daily Worker*." The newly organized John Birch Society began an unsuccessful campaign to impeach the chief justice. The landscape soon blossomed with "Impeach Earl Warren" billboards,

and congressmen were deluged with letters urging impeachment.

REAPPORTIONMENT

The *Brown* decision signaled the expansive attitude of the Warren Court toward the constitutional guaranty of equality. From the field of racial equality involved in *Brown*, the Court spread the equal-protection mantle over an increasingly broad area, notably in the field of political rights. The key decision here was *Baker* v. *Carr* (1962), in which the federal courts were ruled competent to entertain an action challenging certain legislative apportionments as contrary to the doctrine of equal protection. The problem arose from the fact that though American legislative districts had originally been apportioned on an equal population basis, over the years population shifts had made for extreme malapportionment. Thus, the seats in the Tennessee legislature, where *Baker* arose, had last been apportioned in 1901. By the time the case was brought, a vote from the most populous county had only a fraction of the weight of one from the least populous: the population ratio of the most and least populous districts was then over nineteen to one.

Before *Baker*, the Supreme Court had held that the federal courts had no jurisdiction in such cases. The question of legislative apportionment was ruled a "political question" and therefore beyond judicial competence. The leading pre-*Baker* apportionment decision, *Colegrove* v. *Green* (1946), had declared, "Courts ought not to enter this political thicket." In *Baker*, Warren and his colleagues overruled the earlier cases and held that attacks on legislative apportionments on equal-protection grounds could be heard and decided by the federal courts.

Then, in *Reynolds* v. *Sims* (1964), the chief justice's own opinion ruled that the United States Constitution lays down an "equal population" principle for legislative apportionment. Under this principle, substantially equal representation is demanded for all citizens. According to the most noted passage in Warren's opinion, "Legislators represent people, not trees or acres. Legislators are elected by voters, not farms or cities or economic interests." It follows, Warren said, that "the Equal Protection Clause requires that the seats in both houses of a bicameral state legislature must be apportioned on a population basis." Legislative districts must represent substantially equal populations, which means that the "one person, one vote" principle is now enshrined in the United States Constitution: equal numbers of people are entitled to equal representation in their government.

Warren himself characterized the reapportionment cases as the most important cases decided by the Court during his tenure. In those cases, the Warren Court worked an electoral reform comparable to that achieved by Parliament in translating the program of the English Reform Movement into the statute book. The result has been a virtual transformation of the political landscape, with voting power shifted from rural areas to the urban and suburban areas in which most Americans have come to live.

The chief justice never had doubts about the correctness of the reapportionment decisions. He maintained that if the "one person, one vote" principle had been laid down years earlier, many of the nation's legal sores would never have festered. According to Warren, "Many of our problems would have been solved a long time ago if everyone had the right to vote, and his vote counted the same as everybody else's. Most of these problems could have been solved through the political process rather than through the courts. But as it was, the Court had to decide" (Pollack, 209).

EQUALITY AND CRIMINAL JUSTICE

If one great theme recurred in the jurisprudence of the Warren Court, it was that of equality before the law—equality of races, of citizens, of rich and poor, of prosecutor and defendant. The result was what Justice Abe Fortas once termed "the most profound and pervasive revolution ever achieved by substantially peaceful means." More than that, it was the rarest of all political animals: a judicially inspired and led revolution. Without the Warren Court decisions giving ever-wider effect to the right to equality before the law, most of the movements for equality that have permeated American society would have encountered even greater difficulties.

In addition to racial and political equality, the Warren Court moved to ensure equality in criminal justice. The landmark case was *Griffin* v. *Illinois* (1956). Griffin had been convicted of armed robbery in a state court. He filed a motion for a free transcript of the trial record, alleging that he was indigent and could not get adequate appellate review without the transcript. The motion was denied. In the Supreme Court's conference on the case, Warren pointed out that the state had provided for full appellate review in such a case. A defendant who could pay for a transcript should not be given an advantage over one who could not. "We cannot," declared the chief justice, "have one rule for the rich and one for the poor." Hence, he would require the state to furnish the transcript. The Court followed the chief justice's lead and held that it violates the Constitution for a state to deny to defendants alleging poverty free transcripts of trial proceedings, which would enable them adequately to prosecute appeals from criminal convictions. As Justice Arthur Goldberg later explained,

> The state law at issue in *Griffin* conditioning appeal on the purchase of a transcript applied on its face to rich and poor alike. Its effect, however, was to deny an appeal to potential appellants lacking sufficient funds to purchase a transcript. The Court, laying to rest the notion that equal protection requires only equal laws and that the state is never obliged to equalize economic disparities, held the law unconstitutional. Justice Black's opinion stated that: "There can be no equal justice where the kind of trial a man gets depends on the amount of money he has. Destitute defendants must be afforded as adequate appellate review as defendants who have money enough to buy transcripts."

As it turned out, *Griffin* was a watershed in the Warren Court's jurisprudence. In it the Court made its first broad pronouncement of economic equality in the criminal process. After *Griffin* the Warren Court appeared to agree with Bernard Shaw that "the worst of crimes is poverty," as it tried to equalize criminal law between those possessed of means and the less affluent. It was the *Griffin* approach that was the foundation of the landmark decision in *Gideon* v. *Wainwright* (1963), which required counsel to be appointed for indigent defendants.

The *Gideon* case was one of the most famous decided by the Warren Court. Indeed, Clarence Gideon and his case have become part of American folklore. In *Gideon* the Court overruled an earlier case that had refused to hold that the right to counsel was so fundamental as to be included in the due process guaranty. Again following Warren's lead, the Court reversed Gideon's conviction, because his request to the trial judge to have a court-appointed lawyer to assist him was denied. "Reason and reflection," declares the *Gideon* opinion, "require us to recognize that in our adversary system of criminal justice, any person haled into court, who is too poor to hire a lawyer, cannot be assured a fair trial unless counsel is provided for him. This seems to us to be an obvious truth."

CRIMINAL PROCEDURE

Gideon made plain that the Constitution requires public provision of counsel for criminal defendants who cannot afford to hire their own attorneys. The need for the assistance of counsel is not, however, limited to the courtroom. *Gideon* was based on the express constitutional guaranty of the right to counsel in "all criminal prosecutions." But, the case only raised another critical question: When does the right to counsel begin?

The Warren Court answered this question in *Miranda* v. *Arizona* (1966). Miranda had been convicted in a state court of kidnapping and rape. He had been arrested and taken to an interrogation room, where he was questioned without being advised that he had a right to have an attorney present. After two hours, the police secured a confession, which was admitted into evidence over Miranda's objection. The state's highest court affirmed the conviction, but the Warren Court reversed. The majority agreed with Chief Justice Warren that for the police to be able to use any confession, they must show that they gave full effect to the defendant's right to remain silent and to the presence of an attorney, either retained or appointed. Warren had no doubt that the right to counsel began as soon as there was what his opinion termed "custodial interrogation"—that is, interrogation while an individual is in police custody. To the chief justice, the constitutional right came into play when Miranda was arrested. "I didn't know," he commented during the argument before the Court, "that we could arrest people in this country for investigation. Wouldn't you say it was accusatory when a man was locked in jail?"

The *Miranda* decision worked a drastic change in American criminal law and its application by policemen, prosecutors, and judges. The Warren Court in effect laid down the rule that an accused who wants a counsel should have one at any time after he is taken into custody. Under Warren's decision, the police must give so-called *Miranda* warnings: that the person arrested has a right to remain silent, that anything he says may be used against him, that he can have a lawyer present, and that he can have counsel appointed if he cannot afford one.

Protection of the rights of criminal defendants had become a primary concern of the Warren Court. The *Miranda* decision, as much as anything, exemplified Warren's own concern in such cases. Every so often in criminal cases, when counsel defending convictions would cite legal precedents, Warren would bend over the bench to ask, "Yes, yes—but were you fair?" The fairness to which the chief justice referred was no jurisprudential abstraction. It related to such things as methods of arrest, questioning of suspects, police conduct, and the like—matters that Warren understood intimately because he had been involved with them as a prosecutor in Alameda County, California. The *Miranda* decision was the ultimate embodiment of the Warren fairness approach.

It was also illustrated by *Mapp* v. *Ohio* (1961), wherein the Warren Court adopted the "exclusionary rule," which bars the admission of illegally seized evidence in state criminal cases. The Supreme Court had refused to follow that rule before *Mapp*, holding that the exclusionary rule was not required by the Constitution in state criminal cases. Now, under Chief Justice Warren, the *Mapp* state conviction was reversed because illegally seized evidence had been admitted at the trial. Such a holding, the Warren Court affirmed, closes "the only courtroom door remaining open to evidence secured by official lawlessness" in violation of the Constitution's guaranty against unreasonable searches and seizures.

FROM PROPERTY TO PERSONAL RIGHTS

The dominant trend in the Supreme Court during Warren's tenure as chief justice was a shift in emphasis from property rights to personal rights. "When the generation of 1980 receives from us the Bill of Rights," Warren declared in a 1955 article, "the document will not have exactly the same meaning it had when we received it from our fathers." The Bill of Rights as interpreted by the Warren Court had a meaning much different from that handed down by its predecessors.

In the early 1950s, legal observers expected the adoption of the judicial self-restraint approach to signal a decline in the Supreme Court's position. The subdued role played by the Court under the Holmes doctrine led many to expect the Court to wither away, much as the state was supposed to do in Marxist theory. Yet, one thing is clear: neither the Soviet state nor America's high tribunal has withered away in the second half of the twentieth century. Still, the work of the Warren Court differed from that of prior Supreme Courts. In enforcing the liberties guaranteed by the Bill of Rights, the Warren Court forged a new and vital place for itself in the constitutional structure. More and more, the Court came to display its solicitude for individual rights. Freedom of speech, press, religion, the rights of minorities and those accused of crime, those of individuals subjected to legislative and administrative inquisitions—all came under the Warren Court's fostering guardianship.

There were three principal developments in the Warren Court regarding the protection of personal rights: (1) acceptance of the "preferred-position theory," (2) extension of the trend toward holding Bill of Rights guaranties binding on the states, and (3) broadening of the substantive content of the rights themselves:

The preferred-position theory was first stated in the decision in *United States* v. *Carolene Products Co.* (1938), though only tentatively in a footnote. Under Chief Justice Warren it became accepted doctrine. The theory is based on the view that the Constitution gives a preferred status to personal, as opposed to property, rights. The result is a double standard in the exercise by the Supreme Court of its review function. The tenet of judicial self-restraint does not rigidly bind the judge in cases involving civil liberties and other personal rights. The presumption of validity for laws gives way far more readily in cases where life and liberty are restrained. In those cases, the legislative judgment must be scrutinized with much greater care.

Critics say that the preferred-position ap-

proach, with its elevation of personal rights, creates a hierarchy of rights not provided for in the Constitution. It should, however, be recognized that each generation must necessarily have its own scale of values. In nineteenth-century America, concerned as it was with the economic conquest of a continent, property rights occupied the dominant place. A century later, in a world in which individuality was dwarfed by concentrations of power, concern with the maintenance of personal rights had become more important. With the focus of concern on the need to preserve an area for the development of individuality, judges were naturally more ready to find legislative invasion when personal rights were involved than in the sphere of economics.

A century and a half ago, the Supreme Court had ruled the federal Bill of Rights binding only on the federal government, not on the states. It has been urged that the Fourteenth Amendment changed that result, incorporating the entire Bill of Rights in the Fourteenth Amendment's due process clause. The Court has never accepted this view, adopting instead a selective approach, under which only those rights deemed "fundamental" are included in due process. Yet if advocates of full incorporation seemingly lost the incorporation battle, after midcentury they came close to winning the due process war, for the Warren Court, without formally abandoning its selective incorporation approach, held many of the Bill of Rights guaranties to be fundamental and hence absorbed by due process.

The key decisions were *Mapp* and *Gideon*, which reversed earlier refusals to hold the right against the use of illegally secured evidence and the right to counsel to be so fundamental as to be included in due process. Both *Mapp* and *Gideon* spoke in broad terms of the need to protect individual rights; they signaled a trend to include ever more of the Bill of Rights guaranties in the Fourteenth Amendment. In the following decade the Warren Court held these rights fundamental and hence binding upon the states: rights against double jeopardy and self-incrimination and rights to jury trial in criminal cases, to a speedy trial, and to confrontation. Add to these rights those that had been held binding on the states before midcentury, and they include all the rights guaranteed by the federal Bill of Rights except the rights to a grand jury indictment and to a jury in civil cases involving more than $20. The two exclusions hardly alter the overriding tendency to make the due process clause ever more inclusive.

The Warren Court did more than merely apply the Bill of Rights to the states: it also broadened the substantive content of the rights guaranteed, giving virtually all personal rights a wider meaning than they had theretofore had in American law. This was particularly true in two crucial areas: criminal justice and freedom of expression. The former has already been discussed, but it remains to say a word about the latter.

As has already been seen, two members of the Warren Court, Justices Black and Douglas, consistently urged an absolutist view of the freedom of speech guaranty. Their view was based upon the unqualified language of the First Amendment, which says that "Congress shall make no law . . . abridging the freedom of speech." In the Black-Douglas view, when the amendment says that no laws abridging speech shall be made, it means flatly that *no* laws of that type shall, under any circumstances, be made. Under the Black-Douglas approach, no speech may ever be restricted by government action, even speech which is libelous, obscene, or subversive.

The Warren Court did not adopt the Black-Douglas absolutist view, but it did place increasing emphasis on freedom of expression as a preferred right. The primacy of the First Amendment was firmly established. The right to use the streets and other public places as public forums was extended to those using them for civil rights protests and demonstrations. Most criticisms of conduct by public officials and public figures were exempted from the law of libel. Freedom of the press was broadened, censorship laws were struck down, and the power to restrain publication on grounds of obscenity were drastically limited.

In addition, the Warren Court began to recognize new personal rights not specifically guaranteed in the federal Bill of Rights. Foremost among these was a constitutional right of privacy. Justice Douglas urged the existence of such a right in a 1961 dissent: "This notion of privacy is not drawn from the blue. It emanates from the totality of the constitutional scheme under which we live" (*Poe* v. *Ullman*). The Douglas notion of a right to privacy as part of the area of personal right protected by the Constitution was accepted by the Warren Court only four years later.

In *Griswold* v. *Connecticut* (1965) defendants

had been convicted of violating a state law prohibiting the use of contraceptive devices and the giving of medical advice in their use. In reversing the conviction the Supreme Court held that the law violated the right of privacy. The opinion expressly recognized the existence of a constitutionally protected right of privacy—a right said to be within the protected scope of specific Bill of Rights guaranties.

During Chief Justice Warren's tenure, protection of personal rights and liberties became the very focus of the Court's enforcement of the contemporary Constitution. With property rights constitutionally curtailed, compensatory scope had to be given to personal rights if the ultimate social interest—the individual life—was not to be lost sight of. Furthermore, the need to broaden the constitutional protection of personal rights received added emphasis from the growth and misuse of governmental power in the twentieth century. Totalitarian systems showed dramatically what it meant for the individual to live in a society in which Leviathan had become a reality. The "Blessings of Liberty," which the Constitution's framers had taken such pains to safeguard, were placed in even sharper relief in a world that had seen so clearly the consequences of their denial.

CONCLUSION

In 1966, Vice-President Hubert Humphrey declared that if President Eisenhower "had done nothing else other than appoint Warren Chief Justice, he would have earned a very important place in the history of the United States." By then, it was widely recognized that Earl Warren had earned a place in the front rank of the American judicial pantheon. To be sure, Warren was never a legal scholar. "I wish that I could speak to you in the words of a scholar," the chief justice once told an audience, "but it has not fallen to my lot to be a scholar in life." As one of Warren's colleagues put it, Warren "never pretended" to be an intellectual in the sense that Frankfurter was. Warren's forte was not so much scholarship as leadership. During his tenure Warren was to lead the Supreme Court as masterfully as Marshall had.

As a judge, Warren was never content to deem himself a mere vicar of the common-law tradition. Instead, he was the paradigm of the "result-oriented" judge, who used his power to the full to secure the result he deemed right in the cases that came before his Court. Employing the authority of the ermine to the utmost, he never hesitated to do whatever he thought necessary to translate his own conceptions of fairness and justice into the law of the land. His Court's principal decisions have taken their place in the forefront of historic judicial decisions. Their impact on a whole society's way of life can be compared only with that caused by political revolution or military conflict.

"It is a delicious irony," reads a famous passage by Anthony Lewis, "that a President who raised inactivity to a principle of government should have appointed a Chief Justice for whom action was all" (quoted in Friedman and Israel, 2726). President Eisenhower said that one of the reasons he chose Warren was because he felt that Warren did not "hold extreme legal or philosophical views." Yet this criterion of moderation in legal and philosophical views is not necessarily valid as a measure by which to judge greatness on the bench. When people object to extremism in legal and philosophical views, they are really objecting to judicial activism. The judge who holds strong views is bound to take a more expansive view of the judicial function.

Perhaps the period of judicial activism that took place under the Warren Court was unprecedented in legal history. But almost all the outstanding judges in American law have been characterized by a more affirmative approach to the judicial role than that taken by their lesser colleagues. The great American judges have been jurists who used the power of the bench to the full. This was particularly true of Chief Justice Warren. The Marshall Court and the Warren Court have now become major parts of American legal history. The two men who sat at the center of those Courts were strong leaders who acquired their influence by the force of their character and their integrity.

We need not, in Justice Frankfurter's phrase, subscribe to the "hero theory of history" to recognize that great judges make a profound difference in the law. It did make a vast difference that Earl Warren and his colleagues rather than some other judges sat when they did. If Warren could not have made his judicial reputation without the opportunity that his position afforded him, it is also true that he forced the opportunity to make the creative contributions that escaped lesser chief justices. This, after all, has been the common characteristic of the greatest judges. Not all of them were masters of the common law or consummate craftsmen of judicial techniques. But all seized the occasion to make the creative contributions that eluded their lesser brethren.

CASES

Alexander v. Holmes County Board of Education, 396 U.S. 19 (1969)
Baker v. Carr, 369 U.S. 186 (1962)
Brown v. Board of Education, 347 U.S. 483 (1954); 349 U.S. 294 (1955)
Burns Baking Co. v. Bryan, 264 U.S. 504 (1924)
Civil Rights Cases, 109 U.S. 3 (1883)
Colegrove v. Green, 328 U.S. 549 (1946)
Elfbrandt v. Russell, 384 U.S. 11 (1966)
Emspak v. United States, 349 U.S. 190 (1955)
Ferguson v. Skrupa, 372 U.S. 726 (1963)
Gideon v. Wainwright, 372 U.S. 335 (1963)
Green v. County Board of New Kent County, 391 U.S. 430 (1968)
Greene v. McElroy, 360 U.S. 474 (1959)
Griffin v. County Board of Prince Edward County, 377 U.S. 218 (1964)
Griffin v. Illinois, 351 U.S. 12 (1956)
Griswold v. Connecticut, 381 U.S. 479 (1965)
Heart of Atlanta Motel v. United States, 379 U.S. 241 (1964)
Johnson v. Virginia, 373 U.S. 61 (1963)
McCulloch v. Maryland, 4 Wheaton 316 (1819)
Mapp v. Ohio, 367 U.S. 643 (1961)
Miranda v. Arizona, 384 U.S. 436 (1966)
Pennsylvania v. Nelson, 350 U.S. 497 (1956)
Plessy v. Ferguson, 163 U.S. 537 (1896)
Poe v. Ullman, 367 U.S. 497 (1961)
Quinn v. United States, 349 U.S. 155 (1955)
Reynolds v. Sims, 377 U.S. 533 (1964)
Slochower v. Board of Education of the City of New York, 350 U.S. 551 (1956)
South Carolina v. Katzenbach, 383 U.S. 301 (1966)
Sweezy v. New Hampshire, 354 U.S. 234 (1957)
United States v. Carolene Products Co., 304 U.S. 144 (1938)
United States v. Robel, 389 U.S. 258 (1968)
Watkins v. United States, 354 U.S. 178 (1957)
Yates v. United States, 354 U.S. 298 (1957)

BIBLIOGRAPHY

James M. Clayton, *The Making of Justice: The Supreme Court in Action* (1964), is a reporter's account of the Warren Court during the 1962 Court term. William O. Douglas, *The Court Years, 1939–1975: The Autobiography of William O. Douglas*

(1980), is by a leading justice on the Warren Court. Gerald Dunne, *Hugo Black and the Judicial Revolution* (1977), is a biography of one of Warren's principal supporters. Leon Friedman and Fred L. Israel, eds., *Justices of the United States Supreme Court, 1789–1969*, 4 vols. (1969), discusses and reprints notable opinions by the justices. Arthur Goldberg, "Equality and Governmental Action," in *New York University Law Review*, 39 (1964), is by a former justice of the Supreme Court. Luther Huston, *Pathway to Judgment: A Study of Earl Warren* (1966), is a journalist's study of the chief justice in action.

Leo Katcher, *Earl Warren: A Political Biography* (1967), emphasizes Warren's pre-Court career. Richard Kluger, *Simple Justice: The History of Brown v. Board of Education and Black America's Struggle for Equality* (1975), is a massive account of the school segregation case. Leonard W. Levy, ed., *The Supreme Court Under Earl Warren* (1972), is a series of essays on the Warren Court. Anthony Lewis, *Gideon's Trumpet* (1964), concerns a leading Warren Court decision. Jack Harrison Pollack, *Earl Warren: The Judge Who Changed America* (1979), is an account of Warren's life by a journalist.

Bernard Schwartz, *Super Chief: Earl Warren and His Supreme Court—A Judicial Biography* (1983), is a biography of Warren as chief justice, with emphasis on the decision process in the cases decided by the Warren Court; and, with Stephan Lesher, *Inside the Warren Court* (1983), is an account of how the Warren Court operated. James Simon, *Independent Journey: The Life of William O. Douglas* (1980), is a biography of an important justice on the Warren Court. Earl Warren, *The Public Papers of Chief Justice Earl Warren*, edited by H. Christman (1959), is an essential source; and *The Memoirs of Earl Warren* (1977), is the chief justice's posthumously published memoirs. John D. Weaver, *Warren: The Man, the Court, the Era* (1967), devotes itself in large part to Warren's political career. G. Edmund White, *Earl Warren: A Public Life* (1982), stresses Warren's judicial philosophy.

[*See also* Burger Court and Era; Civil Liberties After 1937; Criminal Procedure; Franchise; Judicial Review; Marshall Court and Era; *and* Racial Discrimination and Equal Opportunity.]

THE BURGER COURT AND ERA

Richard Funston

THE retirement of Chief Justice Earl Warren at the conclusion of the 1968 term of the Supreme Court marked, symbolically at least, the termination of an extraordinary decade and a half of constitutional creativity. Not since the era of the great chief justice John Marshall had the Supreme Court rendered decisions of such scope with such consequences for public policy in so many areas of American life. With courage and compassion, the Warren Court had led a transformation of the law, while other agencies of government seemed to tarry.

Such decisional style, of course, did not endear the Warren Court to all Americans. Significant elements of society, disagreeing with the results reached, vehemently charged that the Court was usurping the role of the legislatures and illegitimately amending the Constitution by judicial fiat. Even many legal scholars, who were generally sympathetic to the results produced, pointed out that while the Warren Court might be courageous and compassionate, many of its decisions could find no support in either reason or history. Rather, the opinions that the Court advanced to explain and legitimate its policy choices often proceeded from factually inadequate or erroneous premises through the most inarticulate reasoning and cavalier handling of precedent to conclusions that were empirically and logically questionable. Decisions, often the product of bare 5–4 majorities, supported by such opinions, the scholarly critics warned, would prove to be peculiarly vulnerable if personnel changes on the Court occurred in the near future.

At the very moment Chief Justice Warren announced his intention to retire, Richard Milhous Nixon was campaigning for the presidency on a platform that not too subtly held the Warren Court responsible for many of the ills besetting America. Nixon promised that if elected, he would "remake" the Court by appointing "strict constructionists," who would return the judiciary to its appropriate role and strike the legal balance in favor of the "peace forces" and against the "criminal forces." Once in office and aided not only by the retirement of Chief Justice Warren and the virtually forced resignation of Justice Abe Fortas but also by the untimely deaths of two of the intellectual giants in Supreme Court history, Justice Hugo Black and Justice John Harlan, President Nixon set out to redeem his campaign promise.

Such presidential efforts to restructure the Court were not illegitimate, and in nominating those who agreed with his policies, Nixon was behaving as other presidents had before him. But, perhaps more than any of his predecessors, Nixon's choices seemed to disregard considerations of ability, competence, and character, in favor of ideology. Before he ignominiously departed the Oval Office, Richard Nixon had secured the appointment of four new members of the Supreme Court, including a chief justice, and the news media had proclaimed his success in redirecting judicial policymaking.

The Court under Chief Justice Warren Earl Burger was, or so the journalists claimed, significantly different from the Warren Court. Chief Justice Burger and the other Nixon appointees (Justices Harry Blackmun, Lewis Powell, and William Rehnquist), often joined by Justice Byron White and somewhat less often by Justice Potter Stewart, were seen as reversing many policies established during the Warren era, committing the Court to a new conservatism, and generally dismantling the Warren legacy. Not only did the American public apparently accept this media-created image but also, if contemporary opinion polls are to be believed, it approved of it.

But to what extent did the image conform with the reality of Burger Court decision-making? Was the Burger Court a Nixon Court? To answer these questions, one must turn to the *United States Reports*, not the *New York Times*.

THE UNFINISHED BUSINESS OF THE WARREN COURT

In an interview granted shortly after his retirement, Chief Justice Warren stated that he thought the three most important decisions rendered by the Court during his tenure were *Brown* v. *Board of Education* (1954), *Baker* v. *Carr* (1962), and *Gideon* v. *Wainwright* (1963) (*New York Times*, 27 June 1969). *Brown* had held that "separate but equal" educational facilities were inherently unequal and had started the country down the long road to eradicating legally required segregation of the races. *Baker*, overturning a generation of precedent to the contrary, had ruled that cases involving legislative apportionment presented justiciable questions and had opened the way for the subsequent "one man, one vote" decisions, requiring that legislative districts be reapportioned on the basis of equality of population. *Gideon* had decided that in all serious criminal cases the accused must have the assistance of counsel at trial and that, were the defendant too poor to afford an attorney, counsel must be appointed at state expense. As such, *Gideon* had represented a major step in the process of "incorporation" by which the Bill of Rights guaranties were made applicable against the states through the Fourteenth Amendment, but it had also been the precursor of decisions such as *Miranda* v. *Arizona* (1966), which extended the right to counsel from the courtroom into the station house. These, then, were the areas of Warren Court decision-making that, according to the assessment of the late chief justice himself, were the most significant: race relations, reapportionment, and the rights of the criminally accused. How did Warren Court precedent in these areas fare at the hands of the Burger Court?

Race Relations and Equal Educational Opportunity. In *Brown* the Warren Court outlawed segregated public schooling. Subsequently, by process of logical extension, it struck down state-compelled separation of the races in all other aspects of social intercourse. Never, however, did it abandon the theory that it was the involvement of public officials that was necessary to bring the Fourteenth Amendment into play; purely private discrimination was beyond the reach of the Constitution. And, in the case of desegregation of education, the Warren Court commanded only that the transition from segregation to desegregation should take place "with all deliberate speed."

The result was that for a decade America witnessed a great deal of deliberation but very little speed in the matter of integration. It was not until a large federal bureaucracy was created by Congress through the passage of various civil rights acts—each of which the Warren Court quickly and cheerfully sustained—to enforce the mandate of *Brown* that significant advances began to be made to improve the condition of black Americans. For its own part, however, although some of its later decisions stretched the concept of "state action" almost beyond recognition and indicated growing displeasure with the formula of "all deliberate speed," the Warren Court continued to adhere to both doctrines.

Ironically, the very first decision of the Supreme Court under the chief-justiceship of Warren Burger, an extremely brief memorandum decision entitled *Alexander* v. *Holmes* (1969), struck the death knell for "all deliberate speed." The time for immediate school desegregation had come. Further procrastination would be constitutionally impermissible; every school district was to desegregate immediately.

Having decided when desegregation must occur, the Burger Court then moved to consider the means that might be employed to achieve desegregation. In *Swann* v. *Charlotte-Mecklenburg Board of Education* (1971), it approved the use of racial quotas (at least as flexible starting points); the rezoning of school attendance districts; and, despite the public opposition of President Nixon, busing of children in order to attain meaningful school integration.

In *Milliken* v. *Bradley* (1974), however, the Burger Court balked at recognizing a power in federal district judges to compel the amalgamation of school districts to obtain a desirable black-white mixture in the schools. In *Milliken* the lower-court judge had ordered interdistrict busing of children, because without such busing significant desegregation was impossible. Since the population of the Detroit school district was almost entirely black, the desegregation of the Detroit schools would still result in racially identifiable, nearly all-black schools. The Supreme Court, however, ruled that the extent of the judicial remedy could extend only to the extent of the violation; and, since the school districts surrounding the Detroit area had not themselves been found to be segregated in violation of *Brown,* interdistrict remedies were inappropriate.

But, if one area of a school district were found to be segregated as the result of official policy or action, as was the case in *Keyes* v. *Denver School District No. 1* (1973), then the entire district was subject to judicially mandated remedies, including busing. On the other hand, the majority in the Denver case refused to surrender the idea that it was only de jure segregation, separation of the races as required by law, that was constitutionally objectionable. Justice William O. Douglas, the Court's most liberal member, and Justice Powell, the Court's only southern member and a Nixon appointee, urged that the mandate of *Brown* was violated whenever the state, through its compulsory attendance laws, forced a child to attend an identifiably one-race school; for Justices Douglas and Powell the cause of the segregation was irrelevant. But the majority in *Keyes* continued to insist, as had the Warren Court, that de facto segregation, segregation of schools as a matter of fact arising from racially separate residential patterns, while perhaps undesirable, was constitutionally permissible. The decisions in *Keyes* and *Milliken,* nevertheless, represented a recognition by the Burger Court, a recognition never indulged by the Warren Court, that what was once considered to be a southern problem was in fact a national problem.

The *Keyes* approach was continued and, in a seemingly unrelated case, extended to alleged employment discrimination in *Washington* v. *Davis* (1976). *Washington* involved a suit by two unsuccessful black candidates for positions on the Washington, D.C., police force. They argued that the written verbal-ability test administered to them as part of the police department's hiring practices unconstitutionally discriminated against black applicants to the force, in that

blacks failed at a rate roughly four times as great as whites. The Burger Court majority held that government action having a racially disproportionate impact was not a denial of equal protection unless racially motivated, a showing that the black plaintiffs in *Washington* had not even attempted to make.

By making official motive or intent the factor to distinguish unconstitutional discrimination from coincidental disadvantage, the holdings in *Keyes* and *Washington* appear to contradict the Burger Court's own precedent of *Palmer* v. *Thompson* (1971). In *Palmer,* the Court held that the decision of the city of Jackson, Mississippi, to close its municipal swimming pools in the face of a court order to integrate did not violate the equal protection clause. The majority refused to consider the argument that the city's closing had been racially motivated. Whether government is motivated by "good" or "bad" reasons, the Court noted, is irrelevant to the question of whether it is constitutionally prohibited from doing what it has set out to do. Several members of the majority, moreover, were apparently strongly influenced by the fact that Jackson had been losing money for a period of years on its operation of public pools, and they were concerned that a decision against the city would lock southern cities into the continued operation of fiscally unjustified services simply because of a coincidence of the historical fact of segregation in those areas.

Palmer to the contrary notwithstanding, *Dayton Board of Education* v. *Brinkman* (1977), expressly following *Washington* v. *Davis,* made clear what may only have been implicit in *Keyes:* de facto segregation is not a violation of the Constitution; only intentional actions by school authorities to produce racial imbalance violate the equal protection clause. Subsequently, though, in *Columbus Board of Education* v. *Penick* (1979) and the second *Dayton Board of Education* v. *Brinkman* (1979), the Burger Court relaxed the burden upon plaintiffs of demonstrating racial motivation in school board decision-making and thus broadened the scope of northern school districts' affirmative duty to desegregate their schools.

Theoretically, the states remained free to deal with de facto segregation under their own state laws. But, in the seemingly inconsistent decisions of *Washington* v. *Seattle School District* (1982) and *Crawford* v. *Los Angeles Board of Education* (1982), the Burger Court threw the question of the availability of relief for such segregation into confusion.

In the *Seattle School District* case the Court, divided 5–4, invalidated a state initiative that barred school boards from assigning students to schools for purposes of racial balance, on the ground that the initiative created a particularly burdensome process for integration advocates. On the same day, however, in *Crawford,* an eight-justice majority affirmed the validity of a California constitutional amendment (passed by voter initiative) that limited court-ordered busing by state courts for desegregation purposes to those cases in which a federal court would order busing to remedy an equal-protection violation. The *Crawford* majority essentially ignored the *Seattle* decision. Only Justice Blackmun, concurring, attempted to reconcile the two decisions. Dissenting in *Crawford,* Justice Thurgood Marshall found the cases indistinguishable.

For purposes of comparing Burger Court and Warren Court decision-making in this area, however, perhaps the Burger Court's most significant precedent was *San Antonio Independent School District* v. *Rodriguez* (1973). In *Rodriguez* the Burger majority declined to extend *Brown*'s logic and concern for equal educational opportunity to purportedly wealth-based classifications; thus, *Rodriguez* upheld local property taxation as a scheme for financing public education.

While local property taxation unquestionably results in differential educational expenditures between districts, the *Rodriguez* Court could not conclude that this was the kind of inequity proscribed by the Constitution. There was no evidence that local property taxation worked a discrimination against identifiable ethnic groups or even that it operated to disadvantage the poor. Indeed, the poor—at least in Texas—tended to live in school districts with relatively large tax bases due to the presence of concentrations of industrial and commercial property with high assessed valuations. Since education is not a right specifically protected by the Constitution, the majority in *Rodriguez* felt that restraint and discretion were, if not the better part of valor, the appropriate judicial virtues to be exercised in this case. Undoubtedly, the justices were influenced by the fact that the central assumption of the appellees in *Rodriguez*—that there is a correlation between educational expenditure and educational quality—had not yet been proved and was, in fact, the subject of vigorous dispute in the social sciences.

The Burger Court was also less likely to find state involvement in racial discrimination where it arguably existed than the Warren Court might have been. In *Moose Lodge No. 107* v. *Irvis* (1972), for example, the Court rejected a claim under a nineteenth-century civil rights statute, passed under Congress' power to enforce the Fourteenth Amendment, on the ground that while the refusal of service involved had been racially motivated, there had not been sufficient official involvement to constitute state action. The Moose Lodge, to be sure, was the recipient of a liquor license from the state of Pennsylvania and, as such, was subject to extensive state regulation. But the state had played no part in the adoption of the club's racially discriminatory policies; it did not encourage them; it had not enforced them; it had not granted the Moose Lodge a monopoly on the retail sale of liquor within Pennsylvania; and its involvement with the club did not approach the intimacy of a partnership arrangement.

On the basis of precedent, however, there were grounds to find that the Moose Lodge's actions were sufficiently clothed with a public character to elevate them to the status of constitutional significance. That the *Moose Lodge* majority did not take advantage of these precedents in order to rule for Irvis could be seen as an indication that the Burger Court was eroding the rights of blacks established by the Warren Court. But it might as logically have been interpreted as signifying that the Burger Court was more sensitive to claims of privacy and individual associational freedom than the Warren Court had been.

In short, the Burger Court, while it showed no enthusiasm for extending the logic of *Brown* beyond racial classifications or for expanding the concept of state action, manifested no intention to undermine the Court's previously contracted commitment to achieve a racially neutral legal order. It was unwilling to abandon the distinction between de jure and de facto segregation, a distinction itself recognized and perpetuated by the Warren Court, but the Burger Court did abandon the "all deliberate speed" formula; pushed the application of *Brown* north of the Mason-Dixon line; and, where it found de jure segregation, as in *Swann, Keyes,* and *Penick,* approved the use of sweeping remedial measures. There was even an ironic continuity of approach, if not of result, in *Rodriguez,* in which the Burger Court, as had the Warren Court in *Brown,* took judicial notice of, and was influenced by, contemporary scholarship in the social sciences, although in *Rodriguez* that scholarship counseled judicial restraint.

Legislative Apportionment. As in its school desegregation decisions, the Warren Court's approach to the constitutional questions of legislative apportionment was characterized by strong rhetoric and simple arithmetic. Contrary to American philosophical and historical tradition, the Warren Court mandated the apportionment of both houses of a bicameral state legislature on the basis of population equality (*Reynolds* v. *Sims,* 1964). Only the unicameral legislature of the state of Nebraska and the Senate of the United States, which was constitutionally immune, escaped this egalitarian onslaught. The Court did experience some difficulty in its efforts to define "population" and a "substantial equality" thereof, but its general intention and direction were clear. Indeed, apart from school integration, the Warren Court's reputation rested most upon its one-man, one-vote rulings. (Interestingly enough and for all too obvious reasons, over the years the Court, without comment, modified the slogan, first enunciated by Justice Douglas in 1963 in *Gray* v. *Sanders,* to read "one person, one vote.")

It was during Burger's chief-justiceship, however, that the Court went to the logical extreme of applying the dogma of one-person, one-vote to the tens of thousands of special district governments within the United States, those governmental units, such as school districts or local housing authorities, that are organized to provide only a few particularized services. And in *White* v. *Weiser* (1973), the Burger Court outdid even the Warren Court in its insistence upon precise arithmetic equality across congressional districts.

But the new Court did relax the standard as applied to local and state governments, on the ground that at these levels the preservation of the integrity of local political subdivisions, insofar as reasonably feasible, was a legitimate state concern. Thus, the Burger Court approved apportionments deviating from exact mathematical

equality by margins greater than those approved by the Warren Court. Indeed, the Burger Court went so far as to hold that deviations of less than 10 percent between the largest and smallest districts within a jurisdiction were constitutionally *de minimis,* too small to trigger judicial concern. Beyond this, one-person, one-vote remained the rule, and population disparities of more than 10 percent had to be justified by some countervailing state interest that a majority of the justices would find compelling, though none ever did.

In *Whitcomb* v. *Chavis* (1971) the Burger Court was faced with one of those distressing collisions of constitutional rights. In *Whitcomb,* it was alleged that multimember districting—the apportionment of legislative districts in which a single district elects more than one representative, the candidates running at large within the jurisdiction—deprived an identifiable ethnic minority, blacks, of the legislative representation to which their numbers within the district would seem to have entitled them. The Court, however, noted that in multimember districting schemes, equal numbers of people voted for equal numbers of representatives and, finding that simple arithmetic was satisfied, upheld such apportionments.

While the result in *Whitcomb* might be interpreted as evidence of the Burger Court's hostility to the claims of blacks, it is also true that it was perfectly consistent with the Warren Court's disparagement of the consideration of any factors other than population in the apportionment of legislative seats. Concern for group interests is, by definition, foreign to a rule of law that reduces people to faceless ciphers and focuses only upon numbers. But, if an electoral scheme operates systematically to deny effective representation to a distinct group of voters, voting itself becomes a futile, meaningless exercise. While multimember districts might fulfill the arithmetic requirements of *Reynolds,* they can operate to leave minority voters with only the right to vote and lose.

Troubled by this, the Burger Court, in *White* v. *Regester* (1973), overturned a multimember districting scheme because the plan invidiously discriminated against black and Chicano voters. Although multimember districts and at-large voting systems were not per se unconstitutional, the Court indicated, they could be invalidated if adopted or maintained for the purpose of diluting the voting strength of identifiable ethnic minority groups. Thus, even a mathematically precise districting plan that operated to effect a racial discrimination could be nullified on equal-protection grounds.

Subsequently, relying upon *Washington* v. *Davis,* the Court held that a violation of the equal protection clause could be established in a vote-dilution case only upon a showing of discriminatory intent. But *Rogers* v. *Lodge* (1982) also indicated that discriminatory intent need not be proved by direct evidence but, instead, could be inferred from a totality of relevant factors. Among those factors, the Court held, was an electoral system's political history, despite the fact that Chief Justice Warren had, in *Reynolds*, expressly rejected history as a factor relevant to consider in drafting an apportionment plan.

Voters in electoral districts gerrymandered to serve partisan purposes may also complain that they have been denied a chance to have an effective voice in the political process. But, in *Gaffney* v. *Cummings* (1973) the Burger Court spurned the claim that an apportionment plan was unconstitutional because it was based upon improper political motives. It was conceded in *Gaffney* that the plan adopted had been intended to perpetuate the relative strengths of the Republican and Democratic parties as reflected in recent elections, but the mere fact that partisan (as opposed to racial) considerations had played a role in the formulation of the districting was insufficient for the Court to label it unconstitutional.

Six justices in *Davis* v. *Bandemer* (1986) did reject the idea that partisan gerrymandering claims present nonjusticiable "political questions," although three members of the Court, including Chief Justice Burger, would have held such claims to be never amenable to judicial resolution. But, of the six justices in the majority, four then voted to reverse the lower court's ruling that Indiana's legislative apportionment was an unconstitutional political gerrymander. Despite substantial evidence to support the district court's finding, the four-justice plurality held that the mere fact that an apportionment scheme made winning elections more difficult for a particular political party did not make the plan unconstitutional; proportional representation is not required by the equal protection clause.

It is apparent, then, that the Burger Court was no more anxious than the Warren Court had been to attack the problem of gerrymandering. Indeed, the Court's continued insistence that population equality across districts was the primary, if not the only, consideration, regardless of traditional geographic, political, cultural, or ethnic boundaries, made gerrymandering much more difficult to recognize and prove legally, even if the rationale of the reapportionment decisions might make it unconstitutional. The result was that one-person, one-vote continued to be the rule, although whatever philosophic foundation it might have had took a severe beating. The Supreme Court therefore remained lost in the "political thicket" that Justice Felix Frankfurter had warned it against entering in *Colegrove* v. *Green* (1946). In its struggle to penetrate this virtually impenetrable jungle, however, the Burger Court continued to rely upon the torch first lighted by the Warren Court.

Criminal Defendants' Rights. So vastly accelerated was the process of applying the Bill of Rights protections to the states during the Warren era that by the time of Chief Justice Warren's retirement virtually all of the protections of the first eight amendments—and certainly all of the really significant ones—were required of the states. The Warren Court did not stop there, however, but in its interpretation of the substantive content of those requirements sought to fashion the Bill of Rights into a code of police conduct. In *Miranda* v. *Arizona* (1966) it held that prior to conducting a process of custodial interrogation designed to elicit incriminating statements, the police must advise the suspect that he has a right to remain silent, that anything he says may be used against him at trial, that he has a right to consult with counsel, and that if he cannot afford counsel an attorney will be appointed to represent him. If the suspect indicates a desire to exercise either his right to silence or to counsel, the police must honor that request; and if the interrogation continues and a statement is taken, the prosecution must bear a heavy burden to prove that the defendant knowingly and intelligently waived his rights.

In *United States* v. *Wade* (1967) the Court ruled that a suspect exhibited in a lineup had the right to have defense counsel present. Many of the rights available to adult defendants were accorded to juveniles in *In re Gault* (1967). In *Chimel* v. *California* (1969) the Warren Court radically restricted the permissible scope of a police search incident to a valid arrest, and in *Mapp* v. *Ohio* (1961) it held that the fruits of any search violative of the Fourth Amendment must be excluded at trial.

Many of these controversial decisions directed at the constitutionalization of criminal procedure were achieved only by the barest of majorities and were all too frequently supported by opinions that merely pronounced rather than persuaded. Such results were exceptionally susceptible to reversal; and, in truth, no area of Burger Court decision-making suggested a greater disjunction with its predecessor than this. *Wade*'s recognition of a right to counsel was limited to postindictment lineups. The warrantless use of "bugged" informers was upheld. The emerging doctrines of the right to confrontation were stunted. Full-scale arrest searches of persons stopped for mere traffic violations were approved. The end of the road in extending the procedural safeguards of criminal trials to juvenile proceedings was apparently reached. Statements obtained in violation of *Miranda* were admitted for purposes of impeaching the credibility of the defendant who had testified in his own behalf. Even acknowledged violations of constitutional rights were dismissed as harmless errors, having no significance upon the outcome of the trial and thus not worthy of appellate notice.

In particular, the Burger majority was hostile to the exclusionary rule of the Fourth Amendment, which provides that evidence obtained by virtue of an unreasonable search and seizure must be excluded at trial. First recognized in a 1914 federal case and extended to state police activities in *Mapp*, the exclusionary rule has been justified as a deterrent of unconstitutional searches. Empirical studies, however, have raised doubts about its deterrent effect, especially with regard to searches directed at so-called possessory crimes, such as narcotics offenses, in which the police may be at least as interested in confiscating the contraband as in securing convictions. Moreover, even if the rule does function to deter the police, many judges, including some as respected as Benjamin Cardozo, have expressed doubts as to whether its benefits exceed its costs.

Sympathetic to these doubts, the Burger Court increasingly limited the scope of the exclu-

sionary rule, though never actually abandoning it, by broadening the constitutional definition of a "reasonable" search. In *New York* v. *Belton* (1981), for example, focusing on police efficiency concerns rather than upon privacy expectations, the Court held that no warrant was required to search the interior of a car and its contents if the search were incident to a lawful, custodial arrest of recent occupants of the vehicle; and in *United States* v. *Ross* (1982) the Court continued this trend, ruling that closed containers and packages found during a legitimate warrantless search of an automobile might themselves be opened and searched without a warrant.

Even more significantly, in *United States* v. *Leon* (1984) and its companion case, *Massachusetts* v. *Sheppard* (1984), the Court modified the exclusionary rule by adopting a "good faith" exception, allowing illegally obtained evidence to be admitted where the police conducting the search had reasonably relied upon a technically defective search warrant. So long as *Leon* and *Sheppard* were confined to instances in which law enforcement officers had relied upon invalid warrants, those decisions created a relatively narrow exception to the exclusionary rule; neutral, detached, and independent magistrates would, after all, continue to review the evidence supporting each search. But, were the good-faith exception to be extended to warrantless searches, its impact would be enormous.

While limiting the scope of the exclusionary rule, the Burger Court also limited the class of criminal defendants who might invoke it. Whereas the Warren Court, in *Katz* v. *United States* (1967), had held that the Fourth Amendment's protection was predicated on the claimant's legitimate expectations of privacy, the Burger Court, in *Rakas* v. *Illinois* (1978), refused to equate a legitimate presence in the searched premises with a legitimate expectation of privacy while there. This came close to reviving the pre-*Katz* rule that to invoke the protection of the Fourth Amendment, one need have either a property or a possessory interest in the premises searched or the property seized.

Thus, at the hands of the Burger Court, the Fourth Amendment's exclusionary rule was, rightly or wrongly, significantly circumscribed. Though obviously displeased with the rule, however, the Court neither abandoned it nor *Mapp*'s application of the rule to state, as well as federal, police activities.

Miranda v. *Arizona,* perhaps the Warren Court's most famous (or infamous) criminal defendants' rights ruling, was accorded similar treatment. *Michigan* v. *Tucker* (1974), for example, declined to apply the doctrine of "the fruit of the poisonous tree" to exclude the testimony of a witness to whom the prosecution had been led only as the result of an interrogation at which the suspect had not been fully advised of his rights as required by *Miranda.* Then, in *Oregon* v. *Elstad* (1985), relying upon *Tucker,* the Court still more sharply qualified *Miranda* by holding that a suspect's voluntary confession, though obtained in violation of *Miranda,* did not presumptively taint a later confession secured after proper warnings had been given. Some commentators thought that such decisions evinced both practical and theoretical doubts about the continuing vitality of *Miranda.*

But the Burger Court's blunting of *Miranda* was by no means consistent. It found that a defendant's *Miranda* rights had been violated by the introduction, for impeachment purposes, of the fact that the defendant had remained silent after receiving the *Miranda* warnings. It held that even though a suspect had initially spoken with the police after receiving the *Miranda* admonitions, he had not waived his rights, and therefore, when he subsequently invoked his right to counsel under *Miranda,* the officers were precluded from initiating any further interrogation of the suspect before his attorney arrived. Also, completely disregarding its own language in *Michigan* v. *Tucker,* the Court ruled that the introduction, at the penalty phase of a capital murder trial, of psychiatric testimony based upon interviews conducted without *Miranda* warnings was a violation of the defendant's Fifth Amendment rights.

Reports of *Miranda*'s demise, therefore, were greatly exaggerated. (Ernesto Miranda himself was subsequently stabbed to death in a barroom brawl.) The Burger Court's approach to *Miranda* was very much that expressed by the chief justice, concurring in *Rhode Island* v. *Innis* (1980): "I would neither overrule *Miranda,* disparage it, nor extend it at this late date."

Moreover, to achieve a balanced picture of Burger Court decision-making in the area of criminal defendants' rights, the catalog of cases limiting the extension of Warren Court decisions must be viewed in contrast with the Burger Court's own decisions expanding the rights of the criminally accused. *Argersinger* v. *Hamlin* (1972), for example, extended the indigent defendant's right to an appointed attorney, established in *Gideon,* to those charged not only with serious offenses but also with misdemeanors. Whereas *Gideon* had held only that the state must provide counsel in serious criminal matters, *Argersinger* ruled that representation by counsel was mandatory in any prosecution that might result in the defendant's imprisonment.

In *Mayer* v. *Chicago* (1971) the Burger Court went even further than it had gone in *Argersinger. Mayer* expanded the Warren Court's ruling in *Griffin* v. *Illinois* (1956), which had required the provision of free transcripts to indigents seeking to appeal serious convictions. But, in requiring free transcripts even in misdemeanor cases, the Burger Court's ruling covered appeals in cases in which the maximum punishment was only a fine and not imprisonment.

Ake v. *Oklahoma* (1985) was yet more expansive. In *Ake* the Court held that an indigent criminal defendant was entitled to the assistance of a psychiatrist at state expense if the defendant's sanity would be a significant factor at trial or if, in a capital sentencing proceeding, the prosecution intended to introduce expert testimony regarding the defendant's potential future danger to the community. The Court's due process analysis, however, was so broadly phrased as to be applicable to a wider range of circumstances, including the right of indigent defendants to the assistance of expert witnesses at state expense. *Ake* thus demonstrated the Burger Court's willingness to consider seriously the evolving requirements of modern criminal practice.

A corollary of this flexible realism was that the Burger Court began to chart directions of its own in the field of criminal procedure. It delivered a serious blow to those who would argue that plea bargaining is unconstitutional, even upholding, in *Corbitt* v. *New Jersey* (1978), a statutory scheme designed to encourage guilty pleas to lesser offenses. On the other hand, the Court also established that as a constitutional matter the prosecution was required to keep its bargain with the defendant. This recognition of plea bargaining as the necessary, if regrettable, means by which the criminal justice system keeps its head above the ever-rising waters of criminal prosecutions introduced a refreshing air of reality into Supreme Court decision-making in this area and apparently was dictated in no small part by Chief Justice Burger's concern for the reform of judicial administration.

This interest in the efficient administration of justice also began to manifest itself in the Court's anxious, albeit inconsistent, efforts to address the Sixth Amendment's mandate of a "speedy trial." Chief Justice Burger's expression, in extrajudicial remarks, of his conviction that reform was more needed in the area of sentencing than in the area of procedure similarly found its way into the decision-making of the Court under his stewardship. Although the central issues of criminal sentencing have not yet come to the Supreme Court, the Burger Court did decide questions of no small importance, perhaps most significantly making a valiant, if contradictory and ultimately unsatisfactory, effort to restrain capital punishment.

Indeed, the Burger Court's Eighth Amendment jurisprudence reflected a doctrinal odyssey as thrilling, as unpredictable, and ultimately as incoherent as Ulysses'. In the landmark case of *Furman* v. *Georgia* (1972) the Court struck down the death penalty as then applied, on the ground that standardless capital sentencing schemes violated the Eighth Amendment's prohibition against cruel and unusual punishment because such schemes created a substantial risk that the death penalty would be inflicted in an arbitrary and capricious manner. Four years later, the Court attempted to clarify the conditions under which a statute imposing the death penalty for the crime of murder would be found constitutional. The Court held that mandatory sentences of death for particular crimes were unconstitutional, but it also ruled that capital punishment could be inflicted without violating the Eighth Amendment's prohibition where the statutory sentencing scheme both preserved and guided the sentencer's discretion.

Thus, the Burger Court's capital punishment decisions embodied an inherent tension between two goals: promoting consistency in inflicting the sanction and requiring individualized sentencing determinations. Later cases, such as

Lockett v. *Ohio* (1978), reversing a death sentence, and *Pulley* v. *Harris* (1984) and *Spaziano* v. *Florida* (1984), both affirming death sentences, failed to resolve or relieve this tension. If anything, it appeared that a decade after *Furman* the Court was in danger of losing sight of the origins of that holding.

It could, then, be argued that the strongest evidence of a Burger Court reversal of Warren Court policy was manifested in the field of criminal procedure. But a more honest assessment would have to conclude that the picture was confused and the precedents in disarray. Philip Kurland's early analyses of the Court's performance are still applicable: while there were changes, they were "neither basic nor widespread" (1971, 298); the Burger Court was "neither so hard-nosed nor so soft-headed about this part of its business as its critics would have it" (1972, 307). The Nixon appointees did not create a rebuttable presumption that the prosecution was always right. But it was also correct to note that they did not adopt the Warren majority's tendency to indulge the opposite presumption.

More specifically, *Gideon,* which Earl Warren had regarded as one of the milestones of his tenure, survived undiminished. Indeed, the new regime was even willing to inflate it. But the Warren precedents on its periphery were sentenced to early desuetude.

First Amendment Freedoms. Significantly, assessing the major advances of the Court during his career, Chief Justice Warren mentioned no First Amendment decisions. His silence was appropriate. Except for saving a few hapless souls from the worst excesses of McCarthyism and rousing a storm of protest from those who thought a public schoolroom the appropriate place from which to address the Lord, the Warren Court's First Amendment cases afforded few decisions seminal in the development of the law. While it contributed little to the creation of First Amendment doctrine, the Warren Court did render opinions of more than passing interest to both lawyer and layperson. Thus, it is worthwhile to examine the relation between Warren and Burger Court decision-making in these areas also, even though they are, by Chief Justice Warren's own testimony, areas of "lesser" importance.

Under Chief Justice Warren, the Court tended to be favorably disposed toward peaceful protest, demonstrations, and other forms of symbolic expression as means for exercising First Amendment freedoms. The Warren Court was the first in history to address the constitutional problems presented by efforts to censor obscenity. Its efforts to fashion a constitutional law of pornography control, however, were less than successful, and upon his retirement the chief justice pronounced obscenity to be the Court's "most difficult area" (*New York Times,* 27 June 1969).

The Warren Court's decision in *New York Times Co.* v. *Sullivan* (1964) also added constitutional dimensions to the law of libel. *Sullivan* and its progeny held that the press was immune from libel judgments unless the complainant could demonstrate actual malice or a reckless disregard of the truth on the part of the press. While *New York Times* attempted to confine this constitutional protection to libels of public officials, subsequent cases relaxed the requirement to cover the libel of "public figures." The Court did not, however, adopt Justice Black's absolutist position that all defamation laws are unconstitutional, although it may have come close to it. Nor did Warren Court decision-making consistently favor press claims. Its attempts to protect the criminally accused from prejudicial pretrial publicity raised a howl of angry protest from the news media.

The Burger Court, though perhaps less sympathetic to protesters, continued to affirm the First Amendment rights of those who choose novel, annoying, or objectionable methods to express their beliefs, reaffirming such Warren Court precedents as *Shelton* v. *Tucker* (1960), *Cox* v. *Louisiana* (1965), and *Freedman* v. *Maryland* (1965). In wrestling with the problem of how to reconcile freedom of the press with the right of a criminal defendant to a fair trial, the Burger Court relied upon Warren Court decisions in the area, reaffirming the various protective devices available to trial judges first canvassed in *Sheppard* v. *Maxwell* (1966). *Nebraska Press Assn.* v. *Stuart* (1976), however, held that attempts by trial judges to protect the criminally accused by controlling the content of news stories were a form of prior restraint, presumptively invalid under the First Amendment. *Nebraska Press* specifically declined to address the question of whether the trial court might close its proceedings to the media, but subsequently *Richmond*

Newspapers, Inc. v. *Virginia* (1980) ruled that the First Amendment guarantees a right of public access to criminal trials.

As for the constitutional law of defamation, the Burger Court continued to adhere to the *New York Times* rule. One problem presented by the Warren Court's extension of that rule from public officials to public figures, however, related to the question of how one became a public figure. Since it could be argued that anyone worthy of press comment is, by definition, a public figure, the rule could potentially become a tautology, virtually immunizing the media from all defamation judgments; and in fact, the Burger Court initially adopted such a position.

But, in *Gertz* v. *Robert Welch, Inc.* (1974) the Court reversed itself in favor of a more subjective standard: a public figure was one who had engaged in publicity-seeking activities or had assumed a role of special prominence in the affairs of society. *Gertz* and *Time, Inc.* v. *Firestone* (1976) indicated that the Burger Court intended to employ this standard with rigor, to limit the scope of the public-figure rule, and *Herbert* v. *Lando* (1979) further held that the First Amendment did not bar a public-figure defamation plaintiff from inquiring, during the discovery phase of the litigation, into editorial communications and reporters' states of mind.

Gertz, however, was more of a victory than a defeat for press interests, for it overturned the traditional common-law rule of strict liability in defamation actions. After *Gertz,* even private individuals would need to prove negligence in order to recover in defamation suits, and public figures and public officials would still have to prove knowing falsity or reckless disregard of the truth. Moreover, *Dunn & Bradstreet, Inc.* v. *Greenmoss Builders, Inc.* (1985) rejected the idea that the *New York Times* rule was limited to publications by the news media. *Gertz* and *New York Times,* the Court held, were designed to protect not merely the institutional press but all speakers, including private credit-reporting agencies.

Such developments led some legal scholars to conclude that if the law of defamation were to be eroded as a protection for injury to reputation, it would be desirable to provide alleged defamation victims with a statutory right to reply. A few commentators went even further and argued that such access was affirmatively mandated by the First Amendment. But the Burger Court refused to compel public access to the news media, and in *Miami Herald Publishing Co.* v. *Tornillo* (1974) it unanimously held that a Florida statute requiring newspapers that assailed the character of a political candidate to afford free space to the candidate for reply was unconstitutional as a violation of the First Amendment guaranty of a free press.

Contrasted with this record, however, must be *Branzburg* v. *Hayes* (1972), which occasioned a chorus of dismay from the news media. *Branzburg* held that news reporters did not have a constitutional privilege to refuse to reveal the sources of their information to a properly constituted judicial tribunal. Despite the media's cries of anguish, it should be borne in mind that until quite recently the privilege claimed in *Branzburg* had never been thought to exist and that even though *Branzburg* was resolved against the reporter's claim, it was the first Supreme Court opinion ever to recognize news gathering as a constitutionally protected activity, a doctrinal development that paved the way for the outcome in *Richmond Newspapers.*

Whatever these decisions may say about the relationship between the Burger Court and the press, they do not support a claim that the Burger and Warren Courts differed significantly on questions of press freedom. There is little, if any, solid evidence to suggest that any of these cases would have been resolved otherwise by the Warren Court.

In the area of obscenity, on the other hand, there is every reason to believe that the results produced by the Burger Court would have been different if the cases had been decided just a few years earlier. The Warren Court's last major obscenity decision, *Stanley* v. *Georgia* (1969), had recognized a First Amendment right to the private possession and use of obscene materials. Logically, this seemed to suggest a concomitant right of access to such materials for the private perusal of consenting adults. The Burger Court, however, refused to extend *Stanley*'s logic and expressly held that there was no such constitutional right of access.

Similarly, the Burger Court revised the test for obscenity established in *Roth* v. *United States* (1957). Rejecting *Roth*'s emphasis that to be censorable, the allegedly obscene material must be utterly without redeeming social value, the Burger Court held that before such material

could be constitutionally protected, it must possess some serious literary or scientific value. Moreover, unlike the Warren Court, the Burger Court permitted the use of local standards of sexual candor rather than national mores to be used as the yardstick to measure the obscenity of a challenged work.

It must be remembered, however, that the Warren Court itself revised *Roth* several times, and it never held that obscene expression was protected by the First Amendment. Rather, the Warren Court consistently took the position that obscenity was beyond the protection of the Constitution and then busied itself with trying to define the obscene. The Burger Court's position was consistent with this definitional approach. The new justices appeared to believe that the Warren Court's position had been correct; it just had not been sufficiently rigorous in its definition of the key term. As a result the Burger Court, like the Warren Court, remained mired in semantics, its obscenity opinions no more—but certainly no less—unclear or unpersuasive than those of the Warren Court.

Perhaps the Burger Court's most celebrated First Amendment decision will turn out to be one of its least significant. *New York Times Co.* v. *United States* (1971), otherwise known as the *Pentagon Papers Case,* is unlikely to prove important in the development of constitutional jurisprudence. This is so because of the novelty of the factual situation involved, the extraordinary speed with which these issues were brought to the Court for consideration, and the confusing welter of opinions that the Court produced. Each justice filed a separate and individual statement of his position, no two of which adopted the same reasoning. Most interestingly, while the vote was 6–3 against the government (Burger, Blackmun, and Harlan dissenting), the chief justice later told an interviewer that on the substantive issue, the justices actually had been unanimous (*New York Times,* 6 July 1971). Finding that the government had not established that serious and adverse consequences would flow from the publication of the *Pentagon Papers,* the majority simply reiterated the position first taken forty years before in *Near* v. *Minnesota* (1931) that absent a clear and present danger of the realization of some grave social injury, the publication of the news may not be subjected to prior restraint.

Indeed, the holding in the *Pentagon Papers Case*

was even narrower than that in *Near*, for in *Near* the challenged injunction had applied to all future editorials, the content of which was unknown, while in the *Pentagon Papers Case* the substance of the publications complained of was well known. That fact alone argues against the significance of the *Pentagon Papers* decision. It is difficult to foresee that in future cases the publication of "secret documents" will be announced in advance, thus affording the government the opportunity to resort to the courts in order to attempt to suppress them.

As for the First Amendment law of church and state, the Warren Court did arouse the wrath of many by banning prayer and Bible reading from the public schools. But it also approved indirect public aid to parochial education through textbook loan programs and refused to strike down mandatory Sunday-closing laws in the face of strong establishment and free-exercise challenges.

For its part, the Burger Court approved construction grants and other forms of aid to sectarian institutions of higher education but was far less solicitous of state efforts to assist parochial secondary and elementary schools. The Court created and repeatedly reaffirmed a three-part test to assess the constitutionality of state aid to religious schools. But this test proved to be self-contradictory, condemning virtually all forms of purchase of services programs, whereby the state contracted with parochial schools and paid them for their provision of secular instruction. On the one hand, the Court told the schools that to be eligible for state aid, their secular and religious teaching must be completely separated, but, on the other hand, the Court invariably found that public enforcement of such separation required excessive government entanglement with religion, thus violating the First Amendment. The result was a series of extraordinarily ad hoc decisions, occasionally approving public programs aiding parochial education, as in the provision of testing and counseling services, but more often invalidating such programs, as in the case of "shared time" or "dual enrollment" arrangements.

The Burger Court was no less suspicious of religion in the public schools, overturning so-called moment-of-silence statutes, which provided that elementary pupils should begin each class day with a period of quiet for meditation or voluntary prayer, and striking down a law that required the posting of a copy of the Ten Commandments on public classroom walls. Outside of the classroom, however, the Court took a more lenient view toward accommodation between government and religion. In *Marsh* v. *Chambers* (1983) it upheld, against an establishment clause challenge, the Nebraska state legislature's practice of opening each day's session with an invocational prayer by an official, state-compensated chaplain. More controversially, *Lynch* v. *Donnelly* (1984) allowed the inclusion of a nativity scene, or crèche, in a municipal Christmas display, on the theory that the crèche was not primarily a religious symbol but merely depicted the historical origins of a national holiday.

The Court also sustained state tax exemptions for church properties against claims that such exemptions violated the religion clauses of the First Amendment, although why this decision, in view of the practice's firm roots in centuries of constitutional tradition, was even necessary is not easy to explain. Certainly, the Burger Court's predecessors, including the Warren Court, had steadfastly refused to consider it.

On the free-exercise front, the Burger Court was not only less creative but also markedly less active, perhaps reflecting America's increasing secularization. It did, however, rule that the states could not use their compulsory school-attendance laws to require the Amish to violate the tenets of that sect's religious beliefs.

The Burger Court's First Amendment cases, then, were uneven. But so, too, were the Warren Court's. Only in the area of obscenity were the results produced by the two Courts markedly different, and even there the doctrinal approach was extremely constant. Generally speaking, there was no indication by the Burger Court of a retreat from the First Amendment frontiers established by the Warren Court.

NEW DIMENSIONS IN CONSTITUTIONAL FREEDOMS

While many of the areas of Warren Court concern would continue to confront the Supreme Court for some time to come, it was equally clear that the business of the Court under Chief Justice Burger would have attributes of its own. Among the foremost of these was the issue of the constitutionalization of the welfare state. As regards wealth-based classifications, the Burger Court took a less ambitious view of the scope of the equal protection clause than had the Warren Court. But, on the other hand, the Burger Court expanded the procedural rights of the poor and other government beneficiaries.

It was also predictable that ecology problems would eventually find their way to the Supreme Court. The Burger Court's response, however, was to avoid the issue, if at all possible. Where it could not, it energetically deferred to Congress. Thus, it refused to interfere with the Amchitka nuclear explosion, and it invalidated a municipal ordinance controlling the times of jet takeoffs, basing its decision on the federal Noise Control Act of 1972. But it also gave preponderant weight to the environmentalist policy expressed in the Federal-Aid Highway Act of 1970, construing the secretary of transportation's authority to approve the use of public parkland for highway projects much more narrowly than the secretary himself would have desired, and it declined to impede the enforcement of the Florida Oil-Spill Prevention and Pollution Control Act, where there was no evidence to show that this statute infringed upon Congress' constitutional power to regulate interstate commerce. Natural scientists tell us that there will be no quick solutions to environmental problems, and the Burger Court appeared disinclined to indulge the hopes of a few that what science could not provide the judiciary could.

Gender Discrimination. The body of law that was most eminently of Burger Court creation was the constitutional law of sex-based discrimination. But, lacking much, if any, assistance from precedent, the Burger Court's approach to the subject was confused. Apparently, a sizable plurality, perhaps even a majority, of the Court would have preferred to await ratification of the equal rights amendment (ERA) rather than achieve sexual parity through judicial construction and was therefore unwilling, although not unable, to expand traditional equal-protection doctrine to cover sexual discrimination.

The Court, however, was not hostile to the claims of females. In *Reed* v. *Reed* (1971) the Court struck down a mandatory preference for males contained in the Idaho probate code. *Frontiero* v. *Richardson* (1973) overturned federal statutes that provided that a female member of the armed forces could receive dependent's benefits for her husband only if she could prove that she was the source of more than half of her husband's living expenses, whereas a male in the service was accorded these benefits regardless of his contributions to his wife's living expenses. Similarly, *Weinberger* v. *Wiesenfeld* (1975) held the practice of providing social security survivors' benefits to the widow and minor children of a deceased husband-father but only to the minor children, not to the widower, of a deceased wife-mother to be an unconstitutional discrimination against women workers. In *Stanton* v. *Stanton* (1975) an eight-justice majority invalidated a statute mandating different ages of majority for males and females; and in *Taylor* v. *Louisiana* (1975) the same majority struck down a blanket exemption from jury service for women, thereby reversing in result, if not in reasoning, the Warren Court's holding in *Hoyt* v. *Florida* (1961).

The outcome of these decisions was the development of a new equal-protection standard. Traditionally, equal-protection challenges had been analyzed under a so-called mere-rationality test: to be valid, a legislative classification need only be rationally related to a legitimate state interest. During the Warren years, however, the Court had created a new standard, labeled "strict scrutiny" by some: to be valid a legislative classification employing a suspect category or touching a fundamental interest had to advance a compelling state interest. The difficulties of defining "suspect" categories and "fundamental" interests—other than by recourse to the judge's own personal preferences, prejudices, and predilections—and the problems inherent in determining whether the governmental interest in the legislation was "compelling" led many scholars to criticize the strict-scrutiny standard as "substantive equal protection," recalling the days when a conservative Court had employed the due process clauses of the Fifth and Fourteenth Amendments in a substantive manner so as to deny government the power to enact economic regulatory measures and legislate to improve the conditions of labor.

Perhaps influenced by such criticism, the Burger Court, while never abandoning strict scrutiny, moved to confine its application, as in *San Antonio Independent School District* v. *Rodriguez.* Thus, gender was never accorded the status of a suspect classification. However, while the Burger

186

Court's initial sex-discrimination cases employed the language of traditional equal-protection analysis, they produced results associated with strict scrutiny. Many commentators concluded that an intermediate standard of equal-protection review had emerged, a development acknowledged by the Burger Court itself in *Craig v. Boren* (1976): "Classifications by gender must serve important governmental objectives and must be substantially related to achievement of those objectives." In short, the new standard was more demanding than the traditional rule, which almost always sustained legislation, but less rigid than substantive equal protection, which invariably overturned legislation. Academic Court-watchers hailed this development, encouraged its extension to classifications other than gender, and argued that eventually the Court must recognize that there is only one equal protection clause—not two or three.

The Burger Court, however, proved to be extremely cautious about extending its new, intermediate standard to other than sex-based discriminations. It did apply the standard in cases involving discrimination against illegitimate children, but in at least one case, *Matthews v. Lucas* (1976), it was used to sustain the discrimination. In contrast, *Plyler v. Doe* (1982) utilized the new standard to address for the first time the rights of "illegal" aliens under the equal protection clause. *Plyler* voided an attempt by the state of Texas to deny state-provided education to illegal-alien children. (Interestingly, all of these few cases extending intermediate equal-protection analysis involved, in one way or another, children, although the legislative classifications themselves were not age-based. *Plyler* also suggested that issues arising out of the massive and continued flow of undocumented immigrants into the United States might come to constitute a significant portion of the Court's docket.)

The new standard of intermediate equal-protection review developed in gender-discrimination cases did little to avail male appellants, however, even though they, too, alleged discrimination based on sex. In *Kahn v. Shevin* (1974), the Court upheld a Florida law granting widows a property tax exemption that was denied to widowers. *Rostker v. Goldberg* (1981) sustained male-only draft registration—a decision that may, however, be limited to the context of

military affairs, an area in which the judiciary has traditionally deferred to congressional judgment. In *Michael M.* v. *Sonoma County Superior Court* (1981) the Court approved a statute that penalized males, but not females, for having sexual intercourse with a nonspousal partner under eighteen years of age. In fact, the Court argued that such gender-based statutory-rape laws promoted sexual equality, because underage females are naturally deterred from engaging in intercourse by the possibly serious consequences of pregnancy, whereas males are not. Singling out males for criminal sanctions, therefore, tended to equalize the deterrents as between the sexes.

Reproductive Rights. Related to the Burger Court's advances on behalf of women's rights was its position in the abortion cases. *Roe* v. *Wade* (1973) and *Doe* v. *Bolton* (1973), which, respectively, left women free to choose to terminate pregnancy at any time during the first trimester of gestation and significantly limited state power to regulate abortion operations during the second trimester, paralleled, if they did not entirely coincide with, the demands of many feminist groups. Rejecting the claim that life begins at conception, the Court did, however, accept the argument that the state's interest in the preservation of potential life would justify the prohibition of abortions (except those necessary, in appropriate medical judgment, to preserve the life or health of the mother) after viability—that is, the point at which the fetus could survive with artificial aid outside the uterus. But, by placing viability at the stage at which a fetus can survive with artificial aid, the Court implicitly conditioned the right to choose to terminate pregnancy upon the state of medical technology; as that technology progresses and the stage of viability is pushed further back into the pregnancy (perhaps even to conception), the due process right recognized in *Roe* is concomitantly restricted.

The Court also held that the legitimate state interest in preserving potential life might be used by the state to determine how to allocate public funds. Thus, the potential reach of *Roe* was limited by ruling that state and local governments had no affirmative constitutional duty to provide public funding for nontherapeutic (elective) abortions, and the exclusion of even therapeutic abortions from federal Medicaid coverage was also upheld.

The Court's approval of restrictions on abortion funding, however, did not signal a retreat from its treatment of government restrictions of abortion itself. In *City of Akron* v. *Akron Center for Reproductive Health* (1983) the Court reaffirmed its commitment to *Roe* v. *Wade*, overturning various provisions of Akron's sweeping abortion ordinance, including requirements that all abortions after the first trimester be performed in hospitals, that the attending physician recite a detailed list of "facts" about fetal development and the risks of abortion, that women wait twenty-four hours after signing a consent form before the abortion could be performed, and that no abortion be performed upon an unmarried minor under the age of fifteen without the written consent of one of her parents unless the minor obtained a court order that the abortion be carried out. Given public agitation over the question of abortion, however, it was apparent, even as the *Akron* decision was announced, that it would not be the Burger Court's last word on the subject.

Affirmative Action. Almost as intractable as the question of abortion was the issue of "affirmative action"—or "reverse discrimination" or "preferential treatment" or whatever one chose to call it. The Warren Court's emphasis upon equality of opportunity had produced some resounding rhetoric but little in the way of statistically demonstrable racial integration of American life. In the 1970s, therefore, some began to argue not for equality of opportunity but for equality of result, for affirmative action to promote measurable integration. Such arguments, however, seemed to collide head-on with the principle advanced by the Warren Court that race was never a constitutionally valid classification.

In addressing the constitutionality of affirmative-action programs, the Burger Court was once again encountering an issue of first impression. In its first brush with the question, *De Funis* v. *Odegaard* (1974), it managed to avoid decision by invoking the doctrine of mootness, a procedural response that allowed the Court to remain silent on the validity of such programs.

But in *Regents of the University of California* v. *Bakke* (1978) the Court could not evade the question. Its response, however, was, to put it most charitably, opaque. A highly fragmented Court produced six separate opinions, no more than four justices concurring on any point. Five jus-

tices agreed that the racial minority set-aside admissions program practiced at the medical school of the University of California at Davis was unconstitutional. A different group of five, however, agreed that professional schools (and presumably undergraduate institutions of higher education) could constitutionally consider race in their admissions procedures. The critical vote in the case was cast by Justice Powell, who, while maintaining that race might be considered as a factor in university admissions decisions, at least in a flexible, individualized process, was troubled by the rigid racial-quota system employed by the university. Justice Powell also was unable to accept the use of race-conscious "remedial" programs where there had been no official finding of past discrimination. *Bakke* thus left many issues unresolved, and its overall impact upon affirmative-action programs remains to be seen.

The Burger Court, however, was not inhospitable to minority-preference programs. In *United Steelworkers of America* v. *Weber* (1979), for example, decided in the Court term immediately following *Bakke*, five justices held that the prohibition on employment discrimination contained in Title VII of the 1964 Civil Rights Act did not apply to an affirmative-action plan voluntarily adopted by private parties to eliminate traditional patterns of racial discrimination; and *Local 28 of the Sheet Metal Workers' International Assn.* v. *Equal Employment Opportunities Commission* (1986) sustained the power of federal judges to order preferential hiring programs in order to remedy violations of Title VII, even though the individuals hired were not themselves the actual victims of past discrimination.

The *Sheet Metal Workers'* decision built upon *Fullilove* v. *Klutznick* (1980). Although the 6–3 decision yielded no majority opinion, *Fullilove* recognized a congressional power to sanction race-conscious action predicated upon past discrimination. By upholding the congressionally enacted 10 percent set-aside for minority business enterprises under any federally funded public work, *Fullilove* explicitly approved the use of racial quotas. In doing so, however, the *Fullilove* Court appeared to contradict *Bolling* v. *Sharpe* (1954). In *Bolling*, eliminating racial segregation in the public schools of the District of Columbia, the Warren Court had held that Congress was as constitutionally prohibited from classifying on the basis of race as were the states. But in *Ful-*

lilove all six members of the majority seemed to suggest that there were really two principles underlying the Fourteenth Amendment: a general antidiscrimination principle of racial neutrality and a more specific remedial purpose. The remedial purpose is addressed to Congress only. *Fullilove* took the position that when the two principles conflict, as with remedial preferential treatment, the remedial purpose controls. This seemed to suggest, although it was never expressly indicated, that Congress did have power to take certain actions with respect to race that state legislatures and other government agencies lacked.

In its approval of "benign" discriminations, the Burger Court was even willing to reject the logic, if not the language, of the reapportionment cases. *United Jewish Organizations* v. *Carey* (1977) upheld a race-conscious apportionment plan adopted for the purpose of creating "safe" voting districts for blacks and thus producing state legislative representation roughly proportional to the racial composition of the state. While the legislative districts were essentially equal in population, the use of racial criteria to define communities of interest for purposes of allocating representation was foreign to the earlier reapportionment decisions' monomaniacal concern for numbers alone.

The attraction of preferential-treatment programs, however, could not be contained. Soon groups other than blacks were agitating to be included in such programs on the rationale that past societal discrimination against their particular group required a contemporary "remedy." Often these were other ethnic groups—Chicanos, Native Americans, Asian-Americans—but there were also groups defined by characteristics other than ethnicity, most particularly women. Ironically, the Burger Court's reluctance to label sex a suspect classification made it, as a constitutional matter, easier to justify reverse discrimination on the basis of gender. Thus, *Schlesinger* v. *Ballard* (1975) found no constitutional defect in military discharge provisions allowing longer terms of service for female naval officers than for their male counterparts, because the different classifications were allegedly designed to correct for the women officers' more-limited promotion opportunities.

Commercial Speech, Campaign Contributions, and the First Amendment. In addressing the contours of the First Amendment, the Burger Court's principal contribution was to abandon the aged doctrine that "commercial" speech was not entitled to First Amendment protection. First enunciated in *Valentine* v. *Chrestensen* (1942), the commercial-speech doctrine maintained that a merchant's advertising of his wares was utterly different from political expression and thus unprotected by the Constitution. But this theory was undercut, first, by the fact that the print media—admittedly protected by the First Amendment—were themselves in business to make a profit and, second, by the increasing importance of advertising in American culture as a consequence of the spread of television.

In 1976 the Burger Court overruled *Chrestensen,* holding that an advertisement that did no more than propose a commercial transaction was entitled to some First Amendment protection, though perhaps less than that accorded to political expression. While government remains able to control false and deceptive advertising, *Virginia State Board of Pharmacy* v. *Virginia Citizens Consumer Council, Inc.* emphasized the important role that commercial information plays in the efficient allocation of resources in an essentially free-enterprise economic system.

Interestingly enough, the *Virginia State Board* decision set the Burger Court on a collision course with the justices' professional brethren, the organized bar. Traditionally, the legal profession had banned attorney advertising as unethical and sanctioned, through suspension from practice or even disbarment, those who engaged in it. The Burger Court, however, neither shrank from the logic of its position nor showed special favor to the bar but, rather, invalidated such blanket bans on professional advertising.

Related to its extension of the parameters of constitutional protection to encompass commercial speech was the Burger Court's recognition that the use of political resources other than traditional expressive forms merited First Amendment defense. The foremost precedent in this area, *Buckley* v. *Valeo* (1976), declared most of the regulations on federal campaign spending enacted by Congress in its overreaction to Watergate to be unconstitutional. While *Buckley* upheld ceilings on campaign contributions and approved in principle federal financing of presidential campaigns, it struck down limitations on direct expenditures in support of federal candidates, invalidated restrictions on total spending by a candidate, and declared limits on the amount a candidate might spend from his or her own funds to violate the First Amendment. In *First National Bank of Boston* v. *Bellotti* (1978), the Court held that states could not prohibit corporations from contributing or expending funds in ballot-measure campaigns, because there is no risk of corruption that could outweigh First Amendment interests where the voters decide an issue directly; and in *Citizens Against Rent Control* v. *Berkeley* (1982) the Court extended the logic of *Buckley* and *Bellotti* to prohibit the imposition of any contribution limits in ballot-measure elections. The *Berkeley* decision may have brought to a halt the well-intentioned but constitutionally defective populist efforts to equalize political power by restraining the rights of a disfavored few.

CONCLUSION

The volume and significance of the cases brought before the Supreme Court did not diminish with the appointment of Nixon, Ford, and Reagan nominees. Law generally, and constitutional law in particular, is a reflection of time, place, and circumstance. As society changes, its constitutional problems and their resolution change. As long as Americans continue to indulge their traditional confidence that the Constitution must mean what they want it to and as long as the Supreme Court continues to be that document's final arbiter, the Court will bear a heavy burden in the application of the Constitution to new and difficult problems of American society.

During the Burger era, therefore, the Supreme Court was presented with new and difficult issues. The Burger Court probed the resolution of those issues cautiously, but not unsympathetically. The results were mixed; the doctrinal advances modest, but not insignificant. The Court under Chief Justice Burger showed a heightened sensitivity to sex as a basis for legislative classification but never declared gender to be a constitutionally suspect criterion. The Court created for women a right to private choice in matters of procreation but did so on a theory that could permit the constriction of that right in the future. The Court approved of affir-

mative action in theory but, in the most publicized case involving that issue, found the specific program to be constitutionally defective. The Court broadened the sweep of the First Amendment to include commercial speech but was unwilling to accord that speech full First Amendment protection. It was a judicial style that one commentator has aptly characterized as "an activism of ambivalence" (Nichol, 315).

Undoubtedly there were differences between the decision-making of the Warren and Burger Courts. The outcomes produced by the two Courts, however, tended to vary in degree rather than in kind. Differences did exist, but they were not as simple or as great as the media generally advertised them to be. The real and significant differences involved more profound questions of philosophical approach.

Scholarly students of the Court have generally agreed that the two most important tendencies manifest across the broad spectrum of Warren Court decision-making were nationalism and egalitarianism. The Warren Court preferred uniform, national solutions to America's political problems and, in order to secure such solutions, was willing to countenance substantial growth in the power of the federal government. Often these accretions of power were recognized to promote equality, as defined by the Court, although more often than not the definition came by way of a slogan rather than a carefully thought-out statement of the relationship between the competing interests and principles involved.

The Burger Court, on the other hand, proved to be far more tolerant of diversity and local decision-making control. With the seating of the Nixon appointees there was a shift of attitude on the Supreme Court regarding the appropriate distribution of power in the federal system. In several decisions, the Burger Court exhibited a desire, conscious or unconscious, to redress the pronationalist balance struck by the Warren Court and to allow greater state and local control, even if that might sustain decisions with which the justices themselves were not necessarily in agreement. Local property taxation, for example, was upheld as a permissible means for financing public education, even though the majority opinion expressed criticism of that system and a hope that it would be reformed. State legislative apportionments substantially deviating from precise mathematical equality were sustained on the ground that the preservation of the territorial integrity of local political subdivisions was a constitutionally legitimate concern. The use of subnational standards was approved for obscenity prosecutions, and the power of federal courts to intervene in ongoing state criminal proceedings was narrowly circumscribed.

The principle of federalism was not merely tolerated but actively encouraged by the Burger Court. For example, although the Court had held the First Amendment afforded no right of public access to private property for expressive purposes, *PruneYard Shopping Center* v. *Robins* (1980) held that state courts could construe state law to authorize individuals to speak and petition in a privately owned shopping mall, regardless of the owner's wishes. This state expansion of expressive rights, the Court found, neither deprived the owner of property without due process of law nor "took" the property for public use without just compensation. At the very least, the outcome in *PruneYard* belied the argument of some critics that the recrudescence of property rights had been the foremost principle of civil liberties during the first decade of the Burger Court.

True, *Garcia* v. *San Antonio Metropolitan Transit Authority* (1985) did abandon the Burger Court's misguided effort to resurrect the Tenth Amendment as a substantive bar to congressional power. But, in sundry opinions, the Court emphasized the value of "community" as a valid, even constitutionally compelling, interest. Church-property tax exemptions, for example, were sustained in large part because of the churches' contributions to the stabilization of community life. *Village of Belle Terre* v. *Boraas* (1974) allowed a town to exclude nontraditional family units in order to preserve its distinctive ambience. The Court upheld the use of zoning ordinances to regulate theaters showing sexually explicit, but not obscene (and, thus, constitutionally protected), "adult" films because of the city's interest in protecting the community environment and the quality of life in its neighborhoods. *Warth* v. *Seldin* (1975) even restricted the ability of litigants to challenge local zoning ordinances in the first place.

On the equality front, the Burger Court withdrew from the more advanced positions established by its predecessor. The Warren Court increasingly tended to interpret the equal protection clause in a substantive manner, denying to legislatures the power to make certain decisions, even though not explicitly prohibited by the Constitution and even though the legislative means chosen were rationally related to the ends sought, if the decision would involve the sacrifice of some value that the Warren Court defined as fundamental, albeit unenumerated in the Constitution. The Burger Court, however, tended to adopt the position that if the choice in question had not been specifically forbidden to the legislature, the only appropriate judicial question was whether the means chosen were rational. But the Court, while invoking a means-oriented test, did not always retreat to the traditional mere-rationality test but created a more intensive means-scrutiny, dubbed by the *Harvard Law Review* as "strict rationality." This new technique was not consistently employed and surfaced primarily, though not exclusively, in the sex-discrimination cases. But, when viewed within the history of American constitutional development, it was a development of considerable significance.

The development of an intermediate equal-protection test, however, was linked to another of the trends of Burger Court decision-making that set it apart from that of the Warren Court, a greater deference to legislative judgment. In truth, much of the rhetoric and many of the decisions of the Warren Court betrayed a distrust of legislatures. But the Burger Court displayed a desire to shift the burden for solving society's problems from the judiciary to society's elected representatives.

This preference for legislative rather than judicial resolution of social controversy was perhaps most marked when the issue was one of equality. *Washington* v. *Davis*, for example, holding that official action having a racially disproportionate impact was not a denial of equal protection unless discriminatorily motivated, drew a sharp contrast between the constitutional standard and that of Title VII of the Civil Rights Act of 1964, outlawing discrimination in employment. But in *Griggs* v. *Duke Power Co.* (1971), speaking through Chief Justice Burger himself, the Court had already issued an extremely strong opinion joined by all of the justices nullifying employment tests that were not job-related and that operated to exclude a disproportionate number of minority applicants, even though there was no evidence that the employer in question had operated in bad faith or that the test was not racially neutral on its face. So, too, in *Fullilove* the Court gave controlling weight to congressional choice in order to sustain a patently race-conscious quota system. Similarly, in the area of gender discrimination, the Burger Court was inclined to give Title VII a broader interpretation than it would have given the equal protection clause.

In its deference to legislative judgment, the Burger Court was not willing to countenance congressional violation of the constitutional principle of separation of powers. In *Immigration and Naturalization Service* v. *Chadha* (1983), the Court rejected that political invention of the modern Congress, the "legislative veto." This device enabled Congress, most often by simple resolution of either house, to reject a federal agency's regulation or an executive official's decision. Relying upon a strict construction of the bicameralism provisions of the Constitution, the Burger Court majority declared the legislative veto unconstitutional; any exercise of "legislative power," the Court ruled, must be approved by both houses of Congress and presented to the president for signature or veto before becoming legally effective.

Chadha's very own strict construction, however, taken together with the ambiguity of the concept of legislative power, made it a likely candidate for limitation by distinction. While some analysts predicted extreme consequences would flow from *Chadha,* it seemed that Congress' position vis-à-vis the federal bureaucracy would, in the future, turn more on Congress' attitude than that of the Court.

The Burger Court was therefore more committed to the principle of federalism, less egalitarian, and more deferential to legislative judgment than was the Warren Court. Such differences of emphasis and perspective between the two Courts, while they produced no striking discontinuities, had their consequences. The heritage of the Warren Court extended not only to a set of decisions in the *United States Reports* but also to a climate of opinion generated in prospective appellants. Although the volume of judicial business continued to increase under Chief Justice Burger, a new and perceptible caution about appealing began to surface in some

legal circles. Reformers, fearing reversals, eschewed resort to the Supreme Court, sometimes turning to state judiciaries instead. Any normative evaluation of this phenomenon necessarily turned upon an individual's understanding of, or feelings about, democracy, majority rule, legislatures, and the institution of judicial review.

But, in arriving at one's judgment, it was important to remember that in terms of those areas singled out by Chief Justice Warren as the most significant of his tenure, the relationship between the Warren and Burger Courts was marked by less change than was generally and originally believed. Upon close, scholarly, and dispassionate examination, the continuities were more impressive than the discontinuities. The Burger Court was not as conservative as was generally believed; but neither had the Warren Court been as liberal as was generally believed. The Burger Court extended First Amendment freedoms, struck down antiabortion laws, and attempted to confine the death penalty. The Warren Court, on the other hand, approved restrictions of press freedom where necessary to protect an accused's right to a fair trial, held that technological searches were not per se violations of the Fourth Amendment, and approved police "stop and frisk" tactics.

Courts, like individual justices, may be "liberal" in some areas and "conservative" in others. It is popularly fashionable to stereotype them as one or the other, but in truth the handful of issues that actually make their way to the Supreme Court for final resolution seldom permit of such blatant oversimplification.

The most important cleavage between the Burger majority and the Warren majority resulted not from differences over results but was rooted in fundamental differences concerning the nature of the judicial task. What dissimilarities there were between the Warren majority and the Burger majority largely were the reflection not of divergent ideologies but of divergent conceptions of the appropriate role of the Supreme Court in American politics. That is still the most significant debate in American constitutional history.

Had the Burger Court followed any other than the Warren Court, it would have been regarded and be remembered as a liberal Court. It not only consolidated Warren precedent in the areas of race relations, legislative apportionment, freedom of expression, and, to a lesser extent, criminal procedure but also rendered several pathbreaking decisions—particularly regarding women's rights, reverse discrimination, and the establishment of religion—that were anything but reflective of a reactionary spirit. Of course, had the Burger Court not followed the Warren Court, the liberal precedent upon which it built would not have been in place.

In the final analysis, the Burger Court was a moderate, centrist Court. Its decision-making was pragmatic rather than ideological. At times this decisional style produced ambiguous, even apparently contradictory results. It also produced mixed reviews from the commentators. Some scholarly critics carped that the Court was "unpredictable," "leaderless," or "fragmented." But, relying upon the same evidence, one might as easily—and more justifiably—conclude that the Burger Court was independent, uncommitted, and open-minded.

Rather than approach its cases with a preconceived notion of the just society and then force its decisions to meet its preconceptions, the Burger Court resolved legal controversies on a case-by-case basis and left it to the commentators to identify (or create), if they could, its themes or patterns of values. The Court itself, guided, but not shackled, by the doctrine of *stare decisis,* decided individual cases on their own merits. That, after all, is the difference between judging and legislating.

On 24 June 1986 President Ronald Reagan went on national television to announce the resignation of Warren Earl Burger, who stood at the president's side, as the fifteenth chief justice of the United States. The chief justice's wholly unanticipated decision to resign was, in a way, characteristic of the "unpredictable" Burger Court. So, too, was Burger's reason for resigning: he chose to devote his energies to his role as chairman of the Commission on the Bicentennial of the United States Constitution, a celebration that Burger viewed as presenting the opportunity for a year-long dialogue to educate the public to the principles of American constitutionalism. It would be a fitting end to the public service of a man who had led a Supreme Court that, in contrast with its predecessor, had shown a greater skepticism of the capacity of an activist judiciary to guarantee the maintenance of republican institutions and, thus, had been less inclined to equate the rule of the Constitution with rule by the Court.

CASES

Ake v. Oklahoma, 105 S. Ct. 1087 (1985)
Alexander v. Holmes, 369 U.S. 19 (1969)
Argersinger v. Hamlin, 407 U.S. 25 (1972)
Baker v. Carr, 369 U.S. 186 (1962)
Bolling v. Sharpe, 347 U.S. 497 (1954)
Branzburg v. Hayes, 408 U.S. 665 (1972)
Brown v. Board of Education, 347 U.S. 483 (1954)
Buckley v. Valeo, 424 U.S. 1 (1976)
Chimel v. California, 395 U.S. 752 (1969)
Citizens Against Rent Control v. Berkeley, 454 U.S. 290 (1982)
City of Akron v. Akron Center for Reproductive Health, 462 U.S. 416 (1983)
Colegrove v. Green, 328 U.S. 549 (1946)
Columbus Board of Education v. Penick, 443 U.S. 449 (1979)
Corbitt v. New Jersey, 439 U.S. 212 (1978)
Cox v. Louisiana, 379 U.S. 536 (1965)
Craig v. Boren, 429 U.S. 190 (1976)
Crawford v. Los Angeles Board of Education, 458 U.S. 527 (1982)
Davis v. Bandemer, 106 S. Ct. 2797 (1986)
Dayton Board of Education v. Brinkman, 433 U.S. 406 (1977); 443 U.S. 526 (1979)
De Funis v. Odegaard, 416 U.S. 312 (1974)
Doe v. Bolton, 410 U.S. 179 (1973)
Dunn & Bradstreet, Inc. v. Greenmoss Builders, Inc., 105 S. Ct. 2939 (1985)
First National Bank of Boston v. Bellotti, 435 U.S. 765 (1978)
Freedman v. Maryland, 380 U.S. 51 (1965)
Frontiero v. Richardson, 411 U.S. 677 (1973)
Fullilove v. Klutznick, 448 U.S. 448 (1980)
Furman v. Georgia, 408 U.S. 238 (1972)
Gaffney v. Cummings, 412 U.S. 735 (1973)
Garcia v. San Antonio Metropolitan Transit Authority, 105 S. Ct. 1005 (1985)
In re Gault, 387 U.S. 1 (1967)
Gertz v. Robert Welch, Inc., 418 U.S. 323 (1974)
Gideon v. Wainwright, 372 U.S. 335 (1963)
Gray v. Sanders, 372 U.S. 368 (1963)
Griffin v. Illinois, 351 U.S. 12 (1956)
Griggs v. Duke Power Co., 401 U.S. 424 (1971)
Herbert v. Lando, 441 U.S. 153 (1979)
Hoyt v. Florida, 368 U.S. 57 (1961)
Immigration and Naturalization Service v. Chadha, 462 U.S. 919 (1983)
Kahn v. Shevin, 416 U.S. 351 (1974)
Katz v. United States, 389 U.S. 347 (1967)
Keyes v. Denver School District No. 1, 413 U.S. 189 (1973)
Local 28 of the Sheet Metal Workers' International Assn. v. Equal Employment Opportunities Commission, 106 S. Ct. 3019 (1986)

BIBLIOGRAPHY

Albert W. Alschuler, " 'Close Enough for Government Work': The Exclusionary Rule After Leon," in *Supreme Court Review* (1984), provides, as of this writing, the latest scholarly analysis of an area in almost constant flux. Vincent Blasi, ed., *The Burger Court: The Counter-Revolution That Wasn't* (1983), a collection of essays by major commentators analyzing the Court's performance in a number of substantive fields, is presently the definitive work in this area. Archibald Cox, *Freedom of Expression* (1981), discusses various First Amendment issues in the Burger Court. E. Donald Elliott, "INS v. Chadha: The Administrative Constitution, the Constitution, and the Legislative Veto," in *Supreme Court Review* (1983), reviews the Burger Court's separation-of-powers doctrine.

Richard A. Epstein, "Substantive Due Process by Any Other Name: The Abortion Cases," in *Supreme Court Review* (1973), and Laurence H. Tribe, "The Abortion Funding Conundrum: Inalienable Rights, Affirmative Duties, and the Dilemma of Dependence," in *Harvard Law Review*, 99 (1985), present differing perspectives on a difficult contemporary legal issue. Leon Friedman and Fred L. Israel, eds., *The Justices of the United States Supreme Court, 1789–1978* (1980), contains biographies and excerpts from the major opinions of those who served on the Burger Court, except Justice O'Connor; information on Justice O'Connor can be found in Robert E. Riggs, "Justice O'Connor: A First Term Appraisal," in *Brigham Young University Law Review* (1983), and Comment, "Justice Sandra Day O'Connor: Token or Triumph from a Feminist Perspective," in *Golden Gate University Law Review*, 15 (1985). Richard Funston, "The Double Standard of Constitutional Protection in the Era of the Welfare State," in *Political Science Quarterly*, 90 (1975), examines the consequences of the Burger Court equal protection doctrine for the reappraisal of property as a constitutional value; and *Constitutional Counterrevolution?* (1977), gives a general account of the subject, emphasizing continuity in the constitutional jurisprudence of the 1970s.

Julius G. Getman, "The Emerging Constitutional Principle of Sexual Equality," in *Supreme Court Review* (1972), and Ruth Bader Ginsburg, "Gender in the Supreme Court: The 1973 and 1974 Terms," in *Supreme Court Review* (1975), track the development of the Burger Court doctrine of gender discrimination. Gerald Gunther, "In Search of Evolving Doctrine on a Changing Court: A Model for a Newer Equal Protection," in *Harvard Law Review*, 86 (1972), examines the broader doctrinal significance of Burger Court equal protection decisions and is a classic. Richard Harris, *Decision* (1971), provides another journalistic—and mean-spirited—account of the Haynsworth-Carswell fiasco.

Philip B. Kurland, "Enter the Burger Court," in *Supreme Court Review* (1970); "1970 Term: Notes on the Emergence of the Burger Court," in *Supreme Court Review* (1971); and "1971 Term: The Year of the Stewart-White Court," in *Su-*

preme Court Review (1972), are lengthy, albeit sometimes witty, analyses of the years of transition from the Warren Court to the Burger Court. Alpheus T. Mason, "The Burger Court in Historical Perspective," in *Political Science Quarterly,* 89 (1974), is a valuable broad portrait of the Court from an eminent constitutional historian. Gene R. Nichol, Jr., "An Activism of Ambivalence," in *Harvard Law Review,* 98 (1984), gives an excellent review of Blasi, cited above. Richard Schiro, "Commercial Speech: The Demise of a Chimera," in *Supreme Court Review* (1976), reviews the Burger Court's most original contribution to First Amendment theory. Symposium, "United States v. Nixon," in *University of California, Los Angeles Law Review,* 22 (1974), presents a thoughtful exchange of views by leading scholars on the case that saw the end of a presidency.

William Van Alstyne, "The Recrudescence of Property Rights as the Foremost Principle of Civil Liberties," in *Law and Contemporary Problems,* 43 (1980), argues that the protection of property interests was an increasingly central theme of Burger Court jurisprudence. J. Harvie Wilkinson III, *From Brown to Bakke: The Supreme Court and School Integration, 1954–1978* (1979), provides a detailed treatment of the desegregation issue from a former law clerk to Justice Powell. Bob Woodward and Scott Armstrong, *The Brethren* (1978), is interesting less for what it has to say about the Burger Court—much of which is trite, inaccurate, or both—than as an example of uninformed journalistic bias against the Court. [*See also* CIVIL LIBERTIES AFTER 1937; CRIMINAL PROCEDURE; DUE PROCESS OF LAW; EQUAL PROTECTION CLAUSE; FEDERALISM; FRANCHISE; FREE SPEECH AND EXPRESSION; LAW AND THE MEDIA; RACIAL DISCRIMINATION AND EQUAL OPPORTUNITY; RELIGIOUS LIBERTY; SEX EQUALITY UNDER THE CONSTITUTION; SEXUALITY AND THE LAW; STATE CONSTITUTIONAL LAW; *and* WARREN COURT AND ERA.]

CIVIL LIBERTIES TO 1937

Gary L. McDowell

IT was not until near the end of the Constitutional Convention of 1787 that the idea of a national bill of rights was introduced. But the summer had been long and grueling; despite the concerns of George Mason of Virginia, the delegates were simply not willing to plunge into so fundamental and politically divisive a debate. After a series of hard-fought compromises, they had reached a consensus that would allow them to offer a new federal constitution for the approval of the states. Better, they thought, to leave the issue of a bill of rights to a later day. Besides, all the states had bills of rights, and the soon-to-be-debated Constitution was, as Alexander Hamilton would argue in *The Federalist,* a bill of rights itself, insofar as it created a limited government of well-defined and checked powers. There were those who remained unpersuaded, however, and when the proposed Constitution wound its way along the ratification route, the demand for a bill of rights became the primary issue.

To the Antifederalists, who opposed the document proposed by the convention, the Constitution had departed too far from the tried and true principles of confederalism and state sovereignty that characterized the Articles of Confederation. In the Antifederalist view, the new Constitution created a national government of nearly unbridled power. The result in time would be, they argued, that the states would be "devoured" by the national authority. In particular, there was nothing in the proposed charter to protect fundamental individual rights and liberties from the national power. The state constitutions secured more rights against state abuse by state bills of rights; the national constitution should offer similar protections.

During the ratification debates the Antifederalists were able to extract concessions from the friends of the new Constitution, the Federalists. They agreed that the first order of business of the First Congress would be the proposal of a bill of rights to be added by the new amendment process to the Constitution. Though the final Bill of Rights fell far short of what most Antifederalists demanded, the First Congress, under the leadership of James Madison, delivered on the Federalist promise to offer a bill of rights for ratification by the states. Thus were the first ten amendments added to the Constitution as a means of restricting the powers of the national government.

From the outset it was clearly understood that the Bill of Rights secured the liberties of the people only against national abuse; the Bill of Rights did not restrict state power. In time, this view came to be challenged. It seemed to some that the states should surely be held as accountable as the national government when it came to civil liberties; and in 1833 the traditional understanding of the applicability of the Bill of Rights to the states was challenged before the Supreme Court of the United States.

In the case of *Barron* v. *Baltimore,* John Barron, the owner and operator of a wharf, brought suit against the city of Baltimore. The city's plan for paving its streets demanded that certain streams be diverted from their natural courses; as a result, Barron's wharf was rendered useless. Barron claimed that the actions of the city of Baltimore violated the clause of the Fifth Amendment that expressly prohibits the taking of private property "for public use without just compensation." Though Barron won a damage award of $4,500 in the lower court, he lost on an appeal by Baltimore, and the case found itself before the Supreme Court.

196

In response to Barron's claim that the provisions of the Fifth Amendment were a restraint on both state and national governments, the Court disagreed. "The Constitution," Chief Justice John Marshall argued, "was ordained and established by the people of the United States for themselves . . . and not for the Government of the individual states. . . . These amendments [the Bill of Rights] contain no expression indicating an intention to apply them to the state governments. This Court cannot so apply them." Thus, with characteristic precision Chief Justice Marshall reaffirmed the original understanding of the role of the Bill of Rights in securing civil liberties. But even as he wrote, storm clouds were gathering over the issue of slavery, and in time the storm would break out in the Civil War. Thereafter, public thinking about the proper constitutional relationship of nation to states would never be the same.

In the wake of the Civil War, Congress undertook the arduous task of reconstructing the Union. But there were doubts as to how far the national authority would be able to reach into the domestic affairs of the states, even the former rebel states. Reconstruction acts and civil rights acts meant to provide the freedmen with their rightful liberties seemed doomed to failure when challenged before a Supreme Court still rather friendly to state sovereignty. To prevent this from happening, the Fourteenth Amendment was proposed and ratified (1868). The original federal balance of the Constitution was thus formally altered.

The question of the applicability of the Bill of Rights to the states would arise again. Did the Fourteenth Amendment in effect overrule Justice Marshall's opinion in *Barron?* In the *Slaughterhouse Cases* (1873), the logic of *Barron* was reconfirmed: the Bill of Rights was not applicable to the states by virtue of the Fourteenth Amendment. Again in *Hurtado* v. *California* (1884) the limited scope of the Bill of Rights was affirmed. Still later, in *Brown* v. *New Jersey* (1899), the Court insisted that "the first ten amendments to the Federal Constitution contain no restrictions on the powers of the states, but were intended to operate solely on the Federal government." But, however insistent the Court had been, the breezes of constitutional change were beginning to blow.

Beginning with a vigorous dissent in *Hurtado,*

Justice John Marshall Harlan pushed for recognition by the Court that the Fourteenth Amendment did indeed "incorporate" the Bill of Rights through its due process clause. To Harlan's way of thinking, the entire Bill of Rights should apply to the states because the rights were so fundamental as to inhere in the very meaning of "due process of law." Harlan argued in *Hurtado* that "there are principles of liberty and justice, lying at the foundation of our civil and political institutions, which no State can violate consistently with that due process of law required by the Fourteenth Amendment in proceedings involving life, liberty or property." Despite his zeal and his scholarly determination, Justice Harlan had a steep jurisprudential path to take in convincing his brethren of the virtues of incorporation. But he never gave up.

In 1900, Harlan was again pitted against a solid majority of the Court in *Maxwell* v. *Dow.* Again, over his dissent, the Court totally rejected the notion of incorporation. They were unpersuaded by Harlan's insistence that all federal rights were comprehended by the Fourteenth Amendment's privileges and immunities clause. Eight years later in *Twining* v. *New Jersey* (1908), Justice Harlan was argued down; but this time there was a glimmer of hope. In his opinion for the 8–1 majority, Justice William Moody, though rejecting the contention that the Bill of Rights was incorporated in toto, did admit that there was at least the "possibility" that due process of law meant that "some of the personal rights . . . may also be safeguarded against state action." Though Justice Harlan never lived to see it, his arguments in behalf of the doctrine of incorporation would eventually become the standard judicial position on the role of the Bill of Rights.

The first official statement came in *Gitlow* v. *New York* (1925) when the Court asserted without elaborate argument that "freedom of speech and of the press—which are protected by the First Amendment from abridgment by Congress —are among the fundamental personal rights and 'liberties' protected by the due process clause of the Fourteenth Amendment from impairment by the States." It was not until 1937 that the doctrine of incorporation received its most famous theoretical defense. In *Palko* v. *Connecticut* (1937), Justice Benjamin Cardozo suggested that certain provisions—but not all—

of the Bill of Rights did apply to the states through the Fourteenth Amendment. The key was that only those rights which are "of the essence of a scheme of ordered liberty" were to be considered incorporated. Only those rights were to be applied that, if abolished, would constitute a violation of a principle of justice "so rooted in the traditions and conscience of our people as to be ranked as fundamental."

Though not so sweeping an endorsement of incorporation as Justice Harlan would have had, Cardozo's argument in behalf of an "honor roll of superior rights" in *Palko* clearly set the stage for constitutional politics after 1937, when cases involving the Bill of Rights would become the dominant strand of constitutional litigation, and the number of provisions of the Bill of Rights applied to the states would increase. A scanning of political history up to 1937 reveals a relative paucity of civil liberties cases. But the consequences of those few cases were often more far-reaching than those of later cases. The history of pre-1937 civil liberties litigation breaks down into three rather neat periods: the founding period, 1789–1857; the Civil War period, 1857–1898; and the substantive due process period, 1898–1937.

THE FOUNDING PERIOD, 1789–1857

After the new government came into being through the adoption of the Constitution, the great controversies that captured public attention had not much to do with civil liberties. The focus of attention largely continued to be the relationship between national and state authority; the major issues were issues of federalism. Indeed, nearly all efforts were directed at drawing an acceptable line between national power and state sovereignty.

The first several decades of the republic were characterized by the Federalists—first under the leadership of Alexander Hamilton and then under John Marshall—pushing to secure in practice their theories of an extensive commercial republic against the resistance of the political heirs of antifederalism, the Jeffersonian Republicans. Under the long tenure of Chief Justice Marshall, the Supreme Court made great headway in freeing the national government from the shackles of confederalism; sectionalism was pushed

back by the jurisprudential likes of Marshall and Justice Joseph Story as they fleshed out the meaning of the national commerce power and the contract clause.

After the Court passed in 1836 from the hands of Marshall to his successor as chief justice, Roger Taney, the debates over federalism continued. Jacksonian democracy nudged Hamiltonian nationalism a bit out of the way. It was clear that the old doctrine of state sovereignty, or states' rights, had not been snuffed out by the Federalist ascendance, but during the 1830s, 1840s, and 1850s, precisely what lay at the heart of the debate became more evident. The older antifederalist constitutional arguments for state sovereignty and small republics had come to be tainted by the increasingly controversial presence of America's "peculiar institution," slavery. The arguments for state power and state autonomy were becoming more pointedly arguments for the perpetuation of that morally troubling institution. The analysis of the federal problem that Madison had offered in the Constitutional Convention was clearly accurate. The lines of division, Madison had told his fellow delegates, were not between large states and small states; the demarcation was between slave states and free states. As the public mood darkened and political rhetoric grew more rancorous, the still young and growing nation of states stumbled toward the bloody debate over the question of state sovereignty, the Civil War.

During this period when the political wrinkles of the Constitution were being ironed out, the issue of civil liberties came to the fore on at least two occasions that would prove to have lasting historical significance. In the Supreme Court decision of *Calder* v. *Bull* (1798) and in the political debates over the Alien and Sedition Acts (1798), concerns about the nature and scope of civil liberties were expressed that would inform later judicial traditions.

As a result of the theory of "natural rights," which had so informed the Enlightenment and influenced early American constitutional and political thought and practice (exemplified by the Declaration of Independence), there rushed beneath the calm institutional surface of the Constitution a current of thought that embraced the notion of "vested rights." The doctrine of vested rights held that there were certain individual rights so fundamental as to lie beyond the legitimate reach of any government. Those which had been included in the various bills of rights did not exhaust the catalog of natural rights. The vested rights theory had at its core, in addition to the rights of conscience and political speech, the belief in rights that derived from the scarcity of private property. Any law by any government that violated these basic rights was deemed unconstitutional—even though it might not clearly violate any specific provision of the Constitution. The judiciary, it was argued, was the institution best suited to protect such vested rights against any heavy-handed legislative encroachments. Thus, the argument ran, it was appropriate for the courts to protect these principles of abstract justice in the name of constitutional liberty.

The first effort by the federal judiciary came at the circuit court level in 1795 when Justice William Paterson declared unconstitutional a Pennsylvania statute that sought to transfer ownership in a disputed piece of land. Not only did such a state action impair the obligation of a contract as prohibited by Article I, Section 10, of the Constitution, but it also violated natural rights. Paterson wrote in *Vanhorne's Lessee* v. *Dorrance* (1795),

> The right of acquiring and possessing property and having it protected is one of the natural inherent and unalienable rights of man. . . . The legislature, therefore, had no authority to make an act divesting one citizen of his freehold, and vesting it in another, without a just compensation. It is inconsistent with the principles of reason, justice, and moral rectitude; it is incompatible with the comfort, peace, and happiness of mankind; it is contrary to the principles of social alliance in every free government.

In 1798 the Supreme Court engaged in a debate over the doctrine of vested rights in *Calder* v. *Bull.* The issue was whether the constitutional prohibition against ex post facto laws extended to state laws interfering with property and contractual rights. Against the claim that it did, the Court decided that "ex post facto laws extend to criminal, and not to civil cases." Justice James Iredell, rejecting the claims of vested property rights, argued that "some of the most necessary and important acts of legislation are . . . founded upon the principle that private rights must yield to public exigencies."

Justice Samuel Chase was not so sure. To his way of thinking, there are

certain vital principles in our free Republican governments which will determine and overrule an apparent and flagrant abuse of legislative powers; as to authorize manifest injustice by positive law; or to take away that security for personal liberty, or private property, for the protection whereof the government was established. An act of the legislature . . . contrary to the great first principles of the social compact, cannot be considered a rightful exercise of legislative authority.

Though this doctrine of vested rights would find its way, to an extent, into Chief Justice Marshall's later decisions on the contract clause and would be given passing notice by Chief Justice Taney in *Dred Scott* v. *Sandford* (1857), it would generally lie dormant until the late nineteenth and early twentieth centuries, when it would be revived and fused to the due process clause. This union would produce the doctrine of substantive due process, which would create and protect property rights. Later still, it would come to inform yet newer variants of substantive due process and substantive equal protection in the area of personal rights in such cases as *Griswold* v. *Connecticut* (1965), where the Supreme Court would create a constitutional "right to privacy," and in the controversial abortion decision *Roe* v. *Wade* (1973), which was rooted in *Griswold*'s right to privacy. The arguments over vested rights during the last decade of the eighteenth century in fact foreshadowed the dominant judicial view of civil liberties during the entire nineteenth century: civil liberties had as much, if not more, to do with property rights as with personal rights.

This is not to say that during the founding period there were no controversies over the status of personal rights under the Constitution. The debate between the Federalists and the Republicans reached perhaps its most intense pitch on precisely this issue; the ostensible subject of debate was the Alien and Sedition Acts. In response to the Quasi War, the undeclared war with France that broke out in 1798, the Federalists undertook to pass legislation that would suppress the Republican opposition to the war. The Federalist-dominated Congress passed four laws: the Naturalization Act, a relatively uncontroversial act demanding fourteen years' residence for citizenship; the Alien Friends Act, which authorized the president to deport aliens deemed dangerous to the United States; the

Alien Enemies Act, which empowered the president to deport during wartime those aliens who were from an enemy country; and the Sedition Act, the most controversial of the acts, which in effect sought to bring back as a federal statute the old English common-law crime of seditious libel.

The Sedition Act was vigorously enforced by the Adams administration (fifteen indictments, ten convictions), to the constitutional horror of the Jeffersonians. The act not only made it a crime to conspire to oppose or impede the operation of any law, but also made illegal "any false scandalous and malicious writing . . . against the government of the United States, or either house of the Congress, . . . or the President, . . . or to bring them, either of them, into contempt or disrepute; or to excite against them, or either or any of them, the hatred of the good people of the United States." To the Jeffersonians this was intolerable. To their way of thinking, the First Amendment, aimed as it was at securing a free and robust public debate over important issues, rendered such laws beyond the constitutional pale. To make political criticism a punishable criminal offense struck at the very heart of free, popular government; such a law ran counter to the basic principles of the American experiment in republican government.

Though the laws were never successfully challenged in the Court (not for a lack of Jeffersonian efforts, but the Federalist-dominated judiciary simply played partisan politics and refused to entertain such suits), the Alien and Sedition Acts, especially the Sedition Act, served as the efficient cause for the laying of the jurisprudential foundation on which future theories of First Amendment rights would be built. The Jeffersonians staked out what they thought to be the proper liberal position. The First Amendment by its text, they argued, simply prohibited Congress from passing any such law; seditious libel had no place under the Constitution. Further, the "necessary and proper" clause of the Constitution was not a wild card for Congress to use in such instances; rather, laws deemed politically necessary must also be constitutionally proper. The Alien and Sedition Acts, by virtue of the First Amendment, were certainly not constitutionally proper.

Though the Alien and Sedition Acts were too extreme, the Federalist argument that Congress had the constitutional power to pass such laws was not crushed by the Jeffersonian assault. Indeed, it has since become an accepted article of faith that Congress does possess such a power. The later constitutional controversies over such statutes as the Sedition Act of 1918 and the Smith Act of 1940 demonstrated that while seditious libel might go too far to be legitimate, laws against conspiracy to overthrow the government do pass muster. The dilemma is where to draw the juridical line. Judicially created doctrines such as "clear and present danger" and the "balancing test" have been the responses to this vexing constitutional and political question of civil liberties.

As the nation moved from the Federalists to the Jeffersonians, to the Jacksonians, the moral shadows of the crisis of the house divided began to darken the political and constitutional landscape. As the principle of confederalism was transformed into the doctrine of states' rights, which issued in calls for nullification of disagreeable federal laws by the states, any and all attention to civil liberties came to focus on the question of slavery. How, the opponents of slavery queried, could a nation dedicated to the principles of equality and liberty expressed in the Declaration of Independence tolerate human bondage in its midst? But how, responded the defenders of slavery, could a nation dedicated to the sanctity of private property condone the abolition of rights to property, whether that property was an acre of land or a slave? The differences proved politically irreconcilable. They proved judicially irreconcilable, as well, for in the *Dred Scott* case the Supreme Court ushered in a new era of political thinking over precisely what civil liberties under the Constitution were all about.

THE CIVIL WAR PERIOD, 1857–1898

The political and moral arguments over slavery came to a constitutional head when Dred Scott's effort to sue his owner, John F. A. Sandford, for his freedom finally worked its way to the Supreme Court of the United States. Though the issues to be decided upon were rather technical —Scott's right to sue Sandford in a federal court as a citizen of Missouri as against Sandford's claim that Scott, as a slave, had no such right to sue—the broader import of the case was distinctly political. The issue was national power versus state sovereignty: Did a slave's presence in a free state or territory make him a freeman under the federal Constitution?

In an effort to end the increasingly bitter public debate over slavery, the Supreme Court offered nine separate opinions—seven concurrences for Sandford and two dissents for Scott. The most famous of these opinions was that of Chief Justice Taney. There were two basic reasons, Taney explained, why Dred Scott could not sue in a federal court. First, he was a black, and since 1787, blacks were not comprehended under the term *citizen* in the Constitution. There were, Taney argued, two levels of citizenship in the United States: state citizenship, which could be conferred by the states, and federal citizenship, which could be conferred only by Congress. State citizenship was not sufficient to make an individual "a citizen of the United States within the meaning of the Constitution." This doctrine of dual citizenship precluded a slave's presence in a free state from being enough to free him from his legal and physical shackles.

The second reason Dred Scott could not sue for his freedom in a federal court was that he was a slave, and a slave was property. Thus, Congress could not prohibit slavery in the territories, because such a prohibition would violate the property rights a slaveholder had in his slave. Taney argued that any act of Congress (such as the Missouri Compromise Act, which prohibited slavery in certain new territories) "which deprives a citizen of the United States of his liberty or property merely because he came himself or brought his property into a particular Territory of the United States, and who had committed no offense against the laws, could hardly be dignified with the name of due process of law." Reaching back to the philosophic debates of the Revolution, Taney revived the dormant theory of vested rights, fused it to the due process clause of the Fifth Amendment, and prohibited Congress from tampering with the spread of slavery. This decision, which would come to be described as the Court's "self-inflicted wound," further frayed the already unraveling fabric of the Union.

To a good many, the *Dred Scott* decision was intolerable. To one man in particular, it was a devastating attempt to sever the Constitution from the source of its fundamental principles, the Declaration of Independence, and was a denial of the maxims of natural rights and human equality upon which the entire American structure rested. In Abraham Lincoln's view it was this departure from the animating principles of the Union that rendered *Dred Scott* constitutionally unacceptable.

Though Lincoln's efforts against the *Dred Scott* decision constituted the heart of his 1858 campaign for the Senate against Stephen A. Douglas, his political efforts failed. But he was able in a series of debates to reduce Douglas to a position of attempting to reconcile the contradictions of his Democratic party in order to keep Northern and Southern Democrats from pulling apart over the question of slavery. Though he lost in 1858, Lincoln laid the foundation for his successful quest for the presidency in 1860 against Douglas. Lincoln's articulation of the moral problem presented by the presence of slavery in a nation dedicated to the proposition that all men are created equal and are endowed by their Creator with certain inalienable rights became the focus of the national debate. But as Lincoln stepped into the presidency, the Southern states began to step out of the Union. The theory of states' rights became the practice of secession. If the Union was to be preserved, it would have to be by means of a bloody and seemingly endless civil war.

During the course of the war the issue of civil liberties created a strong undercurrent beneath the already stormy surface of national politics, for in waging the war, President Lincoln assumed prerogative powers that clashed with what many saw as the most basic guaranties of due process of law and limited constitutional government. In Lincoln's view, the Constitution was not a mere compact of sovereign states that the states could leave at will; the states had never seceded from the Union but were merely in a state of illegal and unconstitutional rebellion. Lincoln took seriously his oath of office: he was going to protect and defend the Constitution at all costs. Harsh and swift punishment for treason, confiscation of the enemies' private property, compulsory military service, and the emancipation of the slaves by presidential proclamation all raised fundamental constitutional questions. What underlay them was an even more fundamental question: How far could the government go in impairing basic civil rights in wartime?

The question was brought into sharp focus by the Lincoln administration's use of military police activities and its suspension of the writ of habeas corpus. The conflict between civil and military authorities deepened when President Lincoln—the head of both—officially proclaimed that any person interfering with military recruitment or "guilty of any disloyal practice affording aid and comfort to the rebels . . . shall be subject to martial law, and liable to trial and punishment by courts-martial or military commissions." The suspension of the writ of habeas corpus by presidential order was especially troubling. Though the Constitution does in fact provide that the habeas corpus privilege may indeed be suspended "when in Cases of Rebellion or Invasion the public Safety may require it," the suspension provision is part of Article I of the Constitution, the legislative article, not Article II, the executive article. The constitutional question was not whether the privilege could be suspended but only whether the president had, like Congress, the legitimate authority to do so. To allow that the president did would go far toward embracing the arbitrary administration of national power. It was inevitable that the federal judiciary would become involved.

In *Ex parte Merryman* (1861) the courts entered the fray. John Merryman had been arrested and imprisoned for his military activities in Maryland against the Union. Merryman then petitioned for a writ of habeas corpus from Chief Justice Taney, in Taney's capacity as a circuit judge. Taney granted the writ, but the military refused to comply; it was, after all, their commander in chief who had suspended the privilege of the writ. In a vigorous assault on the policies of the Lincoln administration, Justice Taney argued that the suspension of habeas corpus was exclusively a congressional power. The presidential substitution of military authority for civilian authority violated the clear language and meaning of the Constitution. Under such an arrangement, Taney believed, "the people of the United States are no longer living under a Government of laws, but every citizen holds life, liberty and property at the will and pleasure of the army officer in whose military district he may happen to be found." Lincoln was unpersuaded. He refused to

back down. In 1863, Congress confirmed Lincoln's stand by passing the Habeas Corpus Act, which authorized presidential suspension of the writ in certain, now legally defined circumstances.

Related to the suspension of the writ of habeas corpus was the use of martial law and military tribunals for the trial of civilians in those states not in rebellion. This situation was especially controversial in those states that were far from the battlefields and in which the ordinary civil courts were still operating. Zealous Democrats (dubbed Copperheads) who were opposed to the president and his conduct of the war were being arrested by military officials and charged with "disloyal practices affording aid and comfort to the rebels." Those arrested and charged then found themselves being tried and sentenced by military commissions.

In one instance, a former congressman from Ohio, Clement L. Vallandigham, was arrested for denouncing the Lincoln administration in a speech. He was tried by military commission and found guilty; he was sentenced to confinement for the duration of the war. Vallandigham challenged the assertion that the jurisdiction of such military commissions extended to civilians. He appealed to the Supreme Court, claiming that the Court had the authority to review the work of these commissions. But in *Ex parte Vallandigham* (1864), the Supreme Court disagreed, saying it had no jurisdiction over military commissions.

Then came *Ex parte Milligan* (1866). Unlike Vallandigham, who had only spoken against Lincoln's war efforts, L. P. Milligan had actually engaged in treasonable activities for which he had been arrested by the military commander in the district of Indiana, tried by a military commission, found guilty, and sentenced to death. President Andrew Johnson commuted the death penalty to life imprisonment. Milligan petitioned for a writ of habeas corpus from the federal circuit court. The division of the judges led the circuit court to certify the question to the Supreme Court for resolution. The Court held unanimously in favor of Milligan.

Rejecting the decision in *Vallandigham*, the Court now held that it did have the power to review the proceedings of a military commission, for in this case the military commission was unlawful. Going further, Justice David Davis and four other justices argued that neither Congress nor the president could order civilians tried before military commissions in areas where the civilian courts were still working. Such commissions were a violation of the civil liberties secured by the Constitution and the Bill of Rights. Military expediency was no excuse for violating basic rights of individuals. "The Constitution," Justice Davis concluded, "is a law for rulers and people, equally in war and in peace."

After the war, there remained the awesome task of putting the nation back together again. Lest there were any doubt that the war was meant to end the presence of slavery, in 1865 the Thirteenth Amendment was adopted, banishing slavery and involuntary servitude forever. But to end slavery constitutionally and secure the rights of the freedmen politically were two very different matters. As Congress undertook to pass various Reconstruction acts and civil rights acts, it became clear that such acts might fall if challenged before a Supreme Court still clinging to the notion that when it came to a state's domestic policy, federal power largely stopped at the state's borders. The key, then, was to affirm constitutionally the power of Congress to reach into the states and secure certain fundamental rights for the former slaves. That effort led to the Fourteenth Amendment, adopted in 1868.

The purpose of the Fourteenth Amendment was to secure for all persons within a state the "privileges or immunities of the citizens of the United States," "due process of law," and the "equal protection of the laws." In other words, it empowered Congress to assure the freedmen the various civil rights that *Dred Scott* had denied them, such as the rights to sue, to marry, to enter into contracts, and to hold property. As the Thirteenth Amendment sought to overrule *Dred Scott* by abolishing slavery, the Fourteenth sought to bestow citizenship on those freed. In 1870 came the Fifteenth Amendment, designed to enfranchise blacks.

With this trilogy of "Civil War Amendments," the federal theory of the Constitution was altered. But giving the new constitutional provisions their intended effect would be easier said than done. In part because of a lingering attachment of many citizens to the old constitutional order, President Andrew Johnson found his position on such matters besieged by the Radical Republicans in Congress. To complicate matters, the Supreme Court gave every indication of being willing to all but gut the Reconstruction efforts. Since many of the Reconstruction measures contained provisions for military trials like that struck down in *Milligan,* it seemed a safe assumption that most Reconstruction policies would not easily survive the scrutiny of the Court.

In *Cummings* v. *Missouri* (1867) the Court struck down a test-oath provision of the Missouri constitution as an unconstitutional bill of attainder and ex post facto law. In *Ex parte Garland* (1867) the Court invalidated a similar oath at the national level. In *United States* v. *Reese* (1876) the Court began its assault on Reconstruction in earnest: the Enforcement Act of 1870, passed pursuant to the Fifteenth Amendment, was declared unconstitutional. The Third Enforcement Act (1871; also called the Ku Klux Klan Act) was invalidated in *United States* v. *Harris* (1883) insofar as the Court found that it sought to enforce the provisions of the Fourteenth Amendment against persons—especially members of the Klan—rather than against the states as states. In the Civil Rights Act of 1875, Congress sought to prohibit racial segregation in all places open to the general public, such as inns, theaters, and restaurants. This, too, was declared an unconstitutional effort to extend the reach of the Fourteenth Amendment. The *Civil Rights Cases* (1883) confirmed the doctrine that the provisions of the Fourteenth Amendment reached only to "state action."

The judicial doctrine of state action thwarted congressional efforts to give full federal protection to the liberties of blacks under the Civil War Amendments. In *United States* v. *Cruikshank* (1876) the Court had ruled that the Fourteenth Amendment added "nothing to the rights of one citizen against another. It simply furnishes an additional guaranty as against any encroachment by the States upon the fundamental rights which belong to every citizen as a member of society." Confirming this in the *Civil Rights Cases,* the Court stated emphatically that "individual invasion of individual rights is not the subject matter of the amendment."

In one of the most famous cases, *Plessy* v. *Ferguson* (1896), the Court argued that separate facilities for blacks and whites did not deny equal protection of the laws as long as the separate facilities were equal facilities. In *Cumming* v. *Rich-*

mond County Board of Education (1899) this "separate but equal" doctrine was accepted as a constitutionally legitimate basis for states having separate schools for blacks and whites. The separate-but-equal logic would persist until 1954, when it was officially abandoned by the Court in *Brown* v. *Board of Education.*

In other areas, too, the Court consistently restricted the scope of congressional power under the Civil War Amendments. By limiting the power of Congress to confer legal rights and by denying the right of individuals to claim violations of constitutional rights against anything but clear state action, the Supreme Court so limited the Civil War Amendments as to render them all but useless for the protection of civil liberties. But while the original intention of all three amendments was dwindling in constitutional significance, there were those who began to see new possibilities for applying the provisions of the Fourteenth. In particular, that amendment seemed a means for the full resuscitation of the doctrine of vested rights in an age increasingly industrial and economically complex.

The first case wherein such notions were raised was also the first time the Court was called upon to rule on the meaning of the Fourteenth Amendment. The *Slaughterhouse Cases* (1873) involved an 1869 Louisiana statute that all but created a monopoly in the slaughterhouse business in New Orleans. Some of the slaughterhouses banned as a result of the legislation brought suit that the law violated the privileges-and-immunities clause of the Fourteenth Amendment; to their way of thinking, the whole body of traditional civil liberties, including the right to acquire and possess property, was, by the Fourteenth Amendment, placed in the hands of the federal government for protection. The Court was not convinced.

In an opinion that effectively annihilated the original purpose of the amendment, the Court held that the protection of those traditional liberties still remained with the states. The privileges-and-immunities clause did nothing to restrict state regulation of private property. Against the plaintiff's further claim that the legislation was a deprivation of property without due process of law, the Court sought to establish clearly that the phrase *due process of law* had a precise, technical meaning. But against the majority there were ringing dissents, most notably one by Justice Stephen Field. In Field's view, the due process clause was not merely a procedural guarantee; it was connected to that abstract notion of vested rights. For the moment however, over Field's vehement objections, the Court was willing to leave protections for civil liberties—property rights as well as personal rights—to state discretion.

The Court returned to this notion of substantive due process in *Munn* v. *Illinois* (1877), but, again over Field's dissent, the Court refused to legitimate the doctrine. The states, the majority opinion held, had every right to regulate private property—in this instance, fixing the rates for the storage of grain—in the public interest. The *Slaughterhouse* meaning of due process was affirmed.

But other currents were beginning to move in ways that would erode the strict procedural notion of due process. Between *Slaughterhouse* and *Munn,* the Court, in *Loan Association* v. *Topeka* (1875), struck down a Kansas statute because it allowed taxation for a private purpose, an end the Court believed was a violation of "the essential nature of all free governments." By 1878, the notion of vested rights was increasingly seen as connected to the due process clause in some way. In *Davidson* v. *New Orleans* (1878), while affirming the *Slaughterhouse* doctrine of due process, the Court at least conceded that certain "extreme" state regulations of private property may indeed violate the due process of law. Between 1877 and 1890 seven new justices were added to the Court, replacing those who had constituted the majority in *Munn.* Their conservative presence would in a short time push the *Slaughterhouse* and *Munn* readings of due process out of the constitutional light for good. By 1890, in *Chicago, Milwaukee, and St. Paul Railway* v. *Minnesota,* the Court was willing to invalidate a Minnesota rail rate as a violation of the Fourteenth Amendment, if only on procedural grounds. By the time of *Smyth* v. *Ames* (1898), in which a Nebraska rail rate was held invalid as a deprivation of property without due process of law, the doctrine of substantive due process was firmly established. For the next forty years substantive due process, with its principle of "liberty of contract," would all but reduce judicial concern for civil liberties to a single-minded attention to the vested rights of property.

THE SUBSTANTIVE DUE PROCESS PERIOD, 1898–1937

America, as it edged toward a new century, was hardly the same country it had been a century earlier. The power of commerce had been unleashed; while it brought unprecedented opportunities for wealth and a general rise in the standard of living, it also brought unforeseen problems. Industries had no incentive to serve the public interest when public interest came into conflict with profits. Corporations grew and flourished; large endeavors began to gobble up all competition monopolistically. Gone were the days of a largely self-sufficient agrarian society. The population shifted from rural to urban areas, farms were replaced by factories, and nearly everyone was considered a candidate for a largely underpaid and overworked labor force.

These social changes inspired a growing movement to pass legislation at both the state and federal levels to render this new industrial world more humane. Efforts were made to establish decent and safe working conditions, with minimum-age and maximum-hour requirements; to allow workers to bargain collectively with employers; and to set standards for quality of goods produced. Many viewed every piece of progressive social and economic legislation as a direct assault on the institution of private property. In particular, those who viewed property as a vested right took to the courts and there found a great deal of judicial comfort.

At bottom, the debate concerned the constitutional question of the extent of a state's police power to regulate the health and welfare of its citizens. In their efforts to deal with the problems born of increasing industrialization, the states found themselves blocked by the Supreme Court's insistence that the Fourteenth Amendment barred any solutions that tampered with the liberty of contract and free, private enterprise. The classic statement came in *Lochner* v. *New York* (1905), a case involving a New York statute that limited the hours of labor in bakeries. The Court's majority, under Justice Rufus W. Peckham, was not pusillanimous: "There is

no reasonable ground for interfering with the liberty of person or the right of free contract, by determining the hours of labor, in the occupation of a baker." Such regulation was unconstitutional. Justice Oliver Wendell Holmes offered a scathing dissent, arguing especially against the tendency of the Court to confuse what was constitutionally permissible with what the justices thought was "reasonable":

> A constitution is not intended to embody a particular economic theory, whether of paternalism . . . or of laissez faire. It is made for people of fundamentally differing views, and the accident of our finding certain opinions natural and familiar or novel and even shocking ought not to conclude our judgment upon the question whether statutes embodying them conflict with the Constitution of the United States.

But the Court generally did so conclude for the next several decades.

Statutes seeking to allow collective bargaining were struck down at the national level through the due process clause of the Fifth Amendment in *Adair* v. *United States* (1908) and at the state level through the Fourteenth Amendment in *Coppage* v. *Kansas* (1915). Though political efforts at the state and federal levels persisted, the Court generally held firm. The Court effectively created a free zone for enterprise, a zone protected from interference by either state or federal legislation. Though it did not consistently forbid all legislative efforts, the Court did regularly embrace the "rule of reason" as the basis of its determinations; thus, while some social and economic regulatory acts passed muster, they did so only because they seemed "reasonable" to a majority of the justices when viewed through the judicial lens of substantive due process. It was a murky constitutional time.

The era of substantive due process was not to die completely until well into Franklin D. Roosevelt's New Deal when, in *West Coast Hotel Co.* v. *Parrish* (1937), the Court allowed a Washington minimum-wage law to stand. Until that time, a good many pieces of legislation that sought to regulate everything from child labor (*Hammer* v. *Dagenhart*, 1918; *Bailey* v. *Drexel Furniture Co.*, 1922) to the sale of diseased chickens (*Schechter Poultry Corp.* v. *United States*, 1935) were deemed constitutionally unacceptable. But although during this time civil liberty was largely confined by the Court to considerations of liberty of contract, other civil liberties cases were beginning to carve out definite constitutional theories that would, when substantive due process and judicial protection of property rights subsided in 1937, be in place to serve as new standards for judicial decision-making.

Once again it was a war that brought personal-rights issues of civil liberty to the attention of the Court; World War I, like the Civil War, made it necessary for the Court to attempt to draw the line where governmental necessity ended and individual liberty began. In response to the war, Congress had passed two pieces of legislation aimed at two of the most troubling activities wars spawn, espionage and sedition. The Espionage Act of 1917 and the Sedition Act of 1918 provided the context for the great judicial debates over civil liberties.

The Espionage Act was first ruled upon by the Court in *Schenck* v. *United States* (1919). The plaintiff contended that his conviction for distributing pamphlets against the draft to members of the military under the military censorship provisions of the act violated his First Amendment rights. Justice Holmes took a balanced view. The right to free speech had never been, and could never be, considered absolute. "Free speech," as he famously put it, "would not protect a man in falsely shouting fire in a theatre, and causing a panic." The exercise of one's liberties, Holmes argued, depended to a degree upon circumstance. When a nation is at war, especially, "many things that might be said in time of peace are such a hindrance to its [war] effort that their utterance will not be endured so long as men fight." No court, he concluded, could regard such utterances as protected by the Constitution. But that is not to say any and all speech was fair game for governmental interference. "The question in every case," Holmes explained, "is whether the words used are used in such circumstances and are of such a nature as to create a clear and present danger that they will bring about the substantive evils that Congress has a right to prevent. It is a question of proximity and degree."

In *Abrams* v. *United States* (1919), the Court turned its critical eye toward the Sedition Act, under which Abrams and others had been con-victed for publishing pamphlets criticizing America's intervention in Russia. The Court, under the opinion of Justice John H. Clarke, upheld the convictions, arguing that the purpose of the publication had been to "excite, at the supreme crisis of the war, disaffection, sedition, riots, and . . . revolution." Such incendiary efforts fell outside the bounds of the First Amendment.

Justice Holmes dissented vigorously. Joined by Justice Louis Brandeis, he again argued in behalf of what he understood to be the only legitimate constitutional standard for governmental interference with First Amendment freedoms: the clear-and-present-danger test. The pamphlet in question, he insisted, posed no such threat. "The surreptitious publishing of a silly leaflet by an unknown man" was so far from posing a clear and present danger to the legitimate war effort as to be ludicrous. To convict Abrams could encourage the government to suppress all criticism of its efforts, as it had under the despised Sedition Act of 1798. This would not do; free speech under the Constitution meant more. "The best test of truth," Holmes asserted, "is the power of the thought to get itself accepted in the competition of the market. . . . That, at any rate, is the theory of our Constitution." Thus, legitimate grounds for the curtailment of free speech or press existed only when such expression presented a danger at once clear and present. Any other criticism was protected by the Constitution.

Holmes and Brandeis again found themselves united in an effort to prevent the Court from moving away from their standard of clear and present danger in *Pierce* v. *United States* (1920). They again found the majority of the justices unwilling to grant so great an expansion to free speech as their test afforded. Rather, the Court, speaking through Justice Mahlon Pitney, found that a Socialist pamphlet critical of the draft and the war could indeed be grounds for conviction under the Espionage Act. The fact that there was no evidence that the publication had any effect at all on the war effort was not the point. It sufficed that such a publication might indeed have "a tendency to cause insubordination, disloyalty, and refusal of [military] duty." Pitney further averred, despite the *Schenck* decision, that there need be no demonstrable clear and present danger. The "bad tendency" of a publication was sufficient to allow governmental punishment, if not suppression. After *Abrams* and *Pierce* the clear-and-present-danger test of *Schenck* lay dormant. It would not be until after 1937 that the libertarian logic of Holmes and Brandeis would ascend from the constitutional cellar of dissenting opinions and become the dominant jurisprudential view of First Amendment liberties.

As Court and country headed into the Roaring Twenties the dominance of property rights continued unabated, but judicial efforts to establish a firmer foundation for personal rights continued to gain strength. In *Meyer* v. *Nebraska* (1923) the Court, in an opinion by the curmudgeonly Justice James McReynolds, struck down a statute that was designed to prohibit the teaching of German. Such a statute violated the liberty of conscience of parents to bring up their children as they see fit, a liberty secured against state abridgment by the Fourteenth Amendment. Though rooted in the same logic of individualism as the property rights cases, *Meyer* at least opened up substantive due process to liberties that went beyond liberty of contract. In a similar case, *Pierce* v. *Society of Sisters* (1925), the Court, again under McReynolds, declared unconstitutional an Oregon law that required children from ages eight to sixteen to attend public schools. Not only did such a law violate the property rights associated with private schools, but it also infringed the parents' rights of educating their children.

The high-water mark of civil liberties litigation in the 1920s came in *Gitlow* v. *New York* (1925). Rejecting the logic of *Barron* and *Hurtado,* the Court announced that the Bill of Rights —or at least portions of it—were assumed to apply to the states through the due process clause of the Fourteenth Amendment. The issue in *Gitlow* was again subversive activity. A New York statute had made the advocacy of any "doctrine that organized government should be overthrown by force and violence" illegal as criminal anarchy. Benjamin Gitlow's "The Left Wing Manifesto" and "The Revolutionary Age" had been found to violate the New York law. The Supreme Court, while allowing that the Bill of Rights touched such state legislative efforts, also upheld the law and Gitlow's conviction. Applying the bad-tendency test rather than the clear-and-present-danger test, Justice Edward T. Sanford argued for the majority that because "a

single revolutionary spark may kindle a fire that, smoldering for a time, may burst into a sweeping and destructive conflagration . . . [a state] may, in the exercise of its judgment, suppress the threatened danger in its incipiency."

Against this logic, Holmes rose to the challenge. Holmes fumed,

> It is said that this manifesto was more than a theory, that it was an incitement. Every idea is an incitement. . . . The only difference between the expression of an opinion and an incitement in the narrower sense is the speaker's enthusiasm for the result. Eloquence may set fire to reason. . . . If in the long run the beliefs expressed in proletarian dictatorship are destined to be accepted by the dominant forces of the community, the only meaning of free speech is that they should be given their chance and have their way.

But to the majority this free-market approach to ideology was naive. There was no sound reason to assume that civil liberty meant that a liberal regime was obligated to allow the doctrines of illiberalism to sweep away the very foundation of that liberty.

In *Whitney* v. *California* (1927) the Court had before it another Red-scare case. Again under Justice Sanford, the Court employed the bad-tendency test and upheld Whitney's conviction under the California criminal syndicalism statute. Though now joining the majority (there was considerable evidence), Justices Holmes and Brandeis joined also in a concurrence to extol the constitutional virtues of the clear-and-present-danger test over the now firmly rooted bad-tendency test. In *Stromberg* v. *California* (1931) the Court was unwilling to accept as constitutional a California statute that made illegal the display of a red flag as a symbol of anarchism. Such a prohibition, Chief Justice Charles Evans Hughes argued, was too broad. Unless precise, such prohibition violated the right of free speech embraced by the due process clause of the Fourteenth Amendment. Though still not dominant, the clear-and-present-danger standard was clearly thriving.

Connected to the free-speech and -press issues of the Red-scare period were statutes aimed at excluding certain nationalities from citizenship. In *Ozawa* v. *United States* (1922) the Court upheld the exclusion of resident Japanese; in

United States v. *Bhagat Singh Thind* (1923) the ban was stretched to cover Hindus; and in *Toyota* v. *United States* (1925) those Japanese who had served the United States in World War I were also not eligible for citizenship. The deportation of "undesirable aliens" was upheld in *United States ex rel. Bilokomsky* v. *Tod* (1923) and in *Mahler* v. *Eby* (1924). All told, the fear of Communism and subversion generally rendered the Court unsolicitous of civil liberties for individuals.

In the war against subversion the Court went far in removing constitutional shackles from the arms of the law by deciding in *Olmstead* v. *United States* (1928) that wiretapping did not qualify as "search and seizure" within the meaning of the Fourth Amendment's prohibition of "unreasonable" searches and seizures. Despite several vigorous dissents (the case was decided 5–4) and Holmes's acerbic snipe that wiretapping was "a dirty business," *Olmstead* would stand as ruling law until the more judicially liberal 1960s.

Having established the applicability to the states of the free-speech provision of the First Amendment in *Gitlow* and bolstered it in *Stromberg*, the Court had the opportunity to do the same for freedom of the press. In *Near* v. *Minnesota* (1931) the issue was censorship of the press; the Minnesota Gag Law allowed prior restraint of the press in certain defined circumstances by permitting the suppression of malicious or defamatory newspaper articles. To allow such a law, Chief Justice Hughes declared, was to allow an unconstitutional "infringement of the liberty of the press guaranteed by the Fourteenth Amendment." Such a statute outstripped anything remotely considered to be appropriate to libel law. Though the issue of punishment for publication in other circumstances was left to be hashed out in the future, there was no doubt that prior restraint of publication was censorship and beyond the constitutionally legitimate powers of the states.

Adding to the growing enthusiasm for personal liberties that was beginning to characterize the 1930s was *Powell* v. *Alabama* (1932), one of the famous Scottsboro Boys cases. The issue was whether the Sixth Amendment's provision for a right to counsel for the accused in criminal trials reached the states through the Fourteenth Amendment. Reviewing the conviction of several black men convicted of the rape of two white women, the Court found that indeed the accused had been denied opportunity for adequate legal counsel; such a failure to allow defendants "reasonable time and opportunity to secure counsel was a clear denial of due process" as secured by the Fourteenth Amendment. Though cautious not to give carte blanche, the Court established the applicability to the states of yet another provision of the Bill of Rights and for the first time a provision outside the First Amendment.

Of course, the entire First Amendment had yet to be construed as applying to the states, and in 1934, the Court returned to the amendment for a consideration of its religion clauses. In *Hamilton* v. *Regents of the University of California* (1934), Albert Hamilton claimed that the California requirement that all students at the University of California take military drill, on threat of expulsion, violated his freedom of religion. Arguing that his religious convictions forbade his bearing of arms, Hamilton insisted that the California requirement violated his rights under both the First and Fourteenth Amendments. Conceding that indeed Hamilton's religious freedoms were safeguarded against the state through the incorporation of the First Amendment into the Fourteenth Amendment, the Court was unwilling to find that the California requirement was such a violation. After all, Hamilton chose to attend the University of California; he was not required to attend. Thus, he was not entitled to an exemption from an otherwise legitimate requirement. As in so many of the early civil liberties cases, a fundamental principle was articulated but then held not to apply to the plaintiff.

By 1937, when the Court decided *Palko* v. *Connecticut*, the applicability of the Bill of Rights to the states by the Fourteenth Amendment was already relatively well established. A few months before the *Palko* decision, *De Jonge* v. *Oregon* (1937), another criminal syndicalism case, incorporated the First Amendment protections for the right "peaceably to assemble, and to petition the Government for a redress of grievances." Chief Justice Hughes argued there that "peaceable assembly for lawful discussion cannot be made a crime." What remained was the need for a theoretical context in which to place the doctrine of the incorporation of the Bill of Rights. That is precisely what Justice Cardozo sought to provide in *Palko*. In considering whether the Fourteenth Amendment incorporated the Fifth Amendment's guarantee against being "twice put in jeopardy of life or limb," Justice Cardozo concluded that it did not. The Court ruled against Palko on every point.

As noted earlier, only those rights deemed so fundamental as to be "of the very essence of a scheme of ordered liberty" were included in the Fourteenth Amendment. Procedural rights generally and the guaranty against double jeopardy in particular were not so fundamental. (Double jeopardy would not be incorporated until 1969, in *Benton* v. *Maryland.*) Those rights deemed properly fundamental were the more substantive guaranties such as the freedoms of thought and speech in the First Amendment. Such substantive rights, Cardozo argued, lie on "a different plane of social and moral values" than mere procedural rights. In looking especially at that freedom of conscience at the heart of the First Amendment, Cardozo suggested, "one may say that it is the matrix, the indispensable condition of nearly every other form of freedom." Thus, those substantive First Amendment guaranties had to be considered "absorbed" by the Fourteenth Amendment, for "neither liberty nor justice would exist if they were sacrificed."

After 1937, Cardozo's limited view of incorporation would gradually erode as new justices on the Court had occasion to ponder new claims of civil liberties under the Constitution. But the theoretical justification for an incorporation, or "absorption," had been firmly laid. As the 1940s faded into the 1950s, civil liberties would gradually become one of the primary issues before the Supreme Court, and by the 1960s and the heyday of the Supreme Court under Chief Justice Earl Warren, they would be, by and large, the main focus of the justices. The seeds of the more judicially liberal attitudes toward individual liberty that had been planted before 1937 would be brought to full constitutional fruition.

CASES

Abrams v. United States, 250 U.S. 616 (1919)
Adair v. United States, 208 U.S. 161 (1908)
Bailey v. Drexel Furniture Co., 259 U.S. 20 (1922)
Barron v. Baltimore, 7 Peters 243 (1833)
Benton v. Maryland, 395 U.S. 784 (1969)
Brown v. Board of Education, 347 U.S. 483 (1954)
Brown v. New Jersey, 175 U.S. 172 (1899)
Calder v. Bull, 3 Dallas 386 (1798)
Chicago, Milwaukee, and St. Paul Railway v. Minnesota, 134 U.S. 418 (1890)
Civil Rights Cases, 109 U.S. 3 (1883)
Coppage v. Kansas, 236 U.S. 1 (1915)
Cumming v. Richmond County Board of Education, 175 U.S. 528 (1899)
Cummings v. Missouri, 4 Wallace 277 (1867)
Davidson v. New Orleans, 96 U.S. 97 (1878)
De Jonge v. Oregon, 299 U.S. 353 (1937)
Dred Scott v. Sandford, 19 Howard 393 (1857)
Ex parte Garland, 4 Wallace 333 (1867)
Gitlow v. New York, 268 U.S. 652 (1925)
Griswold v. Connecticut, 381 U.S. 479 (1965)
Hamilton v. Regents of the University of California, 293 U.S. 245 (1934)
Hammer v. Dagenhart, 247 U.S. 251 (1918)
Hurtado v. California, 110 U.S. 516 (1884)
Loan Association v. Topeka, 20 Wallace 655 (1875)
Lochner v. New York, 198 U.S. 45 (1905)
Mahler v. Eby, 264 U.S. 32 (1924)
Maxwell v. Dow, 176 U.S. 581 (1900)
Ex parte Merryman, Fed. Cases No. 9487 (1861)
Meyer v. Nebraska, 262 U.S. 390 (1923)
Ex parte Milligan, 4 Wallace 2 (1866)
Munn v. Illinois, 94 U.S. 113 (1877)
Near v. Minnesota, 283 U.S. 697 (1931)
Olmstead v. United States, 277 U.S. 438 (1928)
Ozawa v. United States, 260 U.S. 178 (1922)
Palko v. Connecticut, 302 U.S. 319 (1937)
Pierce v. Society of Sisters, 268 U.S. 510 (1925)
Pierce v. United States, 252 U.S. 239 (1920)
Plessy v. Ferguson, 163 U.S. 537 (1896)
Powell v. Alabama, 287 U.S. 45 (1932)
Roe v. Wade, 410 U.S. 113 (1973)
Schechter Poultry Corp. v. United States, 295 U.S. 495 (1935)
Schenck v. United States, 249 U.S. 47 (1919)
Slaughterhouse Cases, 16 Wallace 36 (1873)
Smyth v. Ames, 169 U.S. 466 (1898)
Stromberg v. California, 283 U.S. 359 (1931)
Toyota v. United States, 268 U.S. 402 (1925)
Twining v. New Jersey, 211 U.S. 78 (1908)
United States v. Bhagat Singh Thind, 261 U.S. 204 (1923)
United States ex rel. Bilokomsky v. Tod 263 U.S. 149 (1923)
United States v. Cruikshank, 92 U.S. 542 (1876)
United States v. Harris, 106 U.S. 629 (1883)
United States v. Reese, 92 U.S. 214 (1876)
Ex parte Vallandigham, 1 Wallace 243 (1864)
Vanhorne's Lessee v. Dorrance, 2 Dallas 304 (1795)
West Coast Hotel Co. v. Parrish, 300 U.S. 379 (1937)
Whitney v. California, 274 U.S. 357 (1927)

BIBLIOGRAPHY

Henry J. Abraham, *Freedom and the Court,* 4th ed. (1982), is a classic survey of the history of civil liberties under the Constitution. It includes perhaps the most thorough treatment of the doctrine of incorporation. Raoul Berger, *Govern-*

ment by Judiciary (1977), is probably the most controversial work on constitutional law in the past fifty years. It presents a critical account of the "transformation" of the Fourteenth Amendment. Walter Berns, *The First Amendment and the Future of American Democracy,* 2nd ed. (1985), is a valuable guide to the intentions of those who framed and ratified the First Amendment as well as subsequent judicial interpretations of it.

John Hart Ely, *Democracy and Distrust* (1980), is one of the more controversial contributions to the theory of civil liberties and judicial review. Robert Faulkner, *The Jurisprudence of John Marshall* (1968), is the standard work on the legal and constitutional theory of the man generally recognized as the greatest chief justice ever to sit on the Supreme Court. Alfred H. Kelly, Winfred A. Harbison, and Herman Belz, *The Ameri-can Constitution,* 6th ed. (1983), is the single best history of the development of the American Constitution from pre-Revolutionary times to the present.

James McClellan, *Joseph Story and the American Constitution* (1971), is the best survey of the jurisprudence of one of the great justices of the Supreme Court. Richard E. Morgan, *Disabling America* (1984), is a critical assessment of how civil rights litigation has come to dominate and, in the author's view, transform American politics. Robert A. Rutland, *Birth of the Bill of Rights, 1776–1791* (1983), is the standard history of the creation of the Bill of Rights during the battle over ratification of the Constitution and through the First Congress.

[*See also* CIVIL LIBERTIES AFTER 1937; HUGHES COURT AND ERA; *and* WHITE AND TAFT COURTS AND ERAS.]

CIVIL LIBERTIES AFTER 1937

John Brigham

The Constitution has become identified with the Supreme Court, and decisions of the Court have been the source for civil liberties policy since 1937, when the Court shifted its attention to political rights in the Constitution. This became a basis for the way we understand individual rights in America, because it is primarily in this court that modern civil liberties are shaped. Lower courts, federal and state, are most significant as the arena for civil liberties. Because of the range and magnitude of their activity, they will be discussed as we focus on doctrines associated with the Bill of Rights, recognizing that lower courts and state constitutions largely but not entirely reflect national doctrines.

INCORPORATION

Although originally governing the relationship between individuals and the federal government, by midway through the twentieth century, federal constitutional rights had been effectively applied to the relationship between citizens and government at every level. By then, the protections in the Bill of Rights joined protection for equality and property, which had been applied to the states through the Fourteenth Amendment in a process known as incorporation. The decision by Justice Benjamin Cardozo in *Palko* v. *Connecticut* (1937) dealt with "double jeopardy," the protection against being tried twice. After this benchmark decision, there was little doubt about the supremacy of federal constitutional rights, and all that remained was to determine whether incorporation was relevant in specific contexts. The standard announced in *Palko* was that rights would be applicable to the states if they were the very essence of a "scheme of ordered liberty."

Gradual expansion of the protections in the Bill of Rights to the states continued until the 1960s, which witnessed a nearly wholesale application of criminal procedure protections to cases tried in state courts. The change has been so dramatic that double-jeopardy protection, which was not incorporated under the standard announced in *Palko,* has now joined the entire Bill of Rights as essential to a "scheme of ordered liberty."

The tables may, however, be turning. In the future, we may look to the states for new developments and definitions of civil liberties. This movement is under way. Massachusetts distinguished itself from the federal system with a capital punishment decision in 1980. California allowed textbooks to be loaned to private schools in 1981. And, in 1980, West Virginia provided for press access to the courtroom. The high court in each of these states based its decision on the state constitution. In most cases the strategy of going to the state courts was a response to decisions from the federal courts. Consequently, the ideas on which the decisions are based reflect the discussion of civil liberties fostered by federal judges. Signs of resistance to federal court decisions in the states were increasing in the 1980s.

THE DOUBLE STANDARD

Incorporation exemplified the post-1937 shift of the Supreme Court from constitutional protection of property to protection of political freedoms. The shift was acknowledged in *United States* v. *Carolene Products Co.* (1938). Justice Harlan Fiske Stone inserted a footnote proposing a turn away from judicial intervention in public regulation of business and toward judicial supervision of the more narrowly defined political and legal process. The footnote is the interpretive source for what has come to be known in constitutional discourse as "the double standard," an institutional practice that distinguishes the economy from politics for the purpose of attention by the Supreme Court.

By this distinction, the justices have given "certain fundamental freedoms" closer scrutiny than others. According to Henry Abraham, "what the post-1937 judiciary did was to assume as constitutional all legislation in the proprietarian sector . . . but to view with a suspicious eye legislative and executive experimentation with other basic human freedoms" (p. 13). The standard is triggered when the Court reviews a statute passed by Congress or a state legislature in the area demarcated roughly as the economy. According to the practice, the justices have merely asked that there be a reasonable basis for regulatory legislation. This deference to the legislative process has meant less attention to economic regulation as a civil liberties question. But property was never entirely absent from constitutional adjudication.

A corollary to explicit judicial concern for political rights is that civil liberties have become identified with protection for the powerless. Although this protection came from the federal level until the 1980s, it may well come from the states in the future. Both a focus on political rights and regard for the powerless are strongly associated with the 1937 shift in judicial politics.

SUBSTANTIVE DUE PROCESS

Procedural due process holds that citizens may not be put in prison and thus deprived of their liberty unless they have first been convicted by jury trial. The belief that citizens have a right to go where they please unless convicted is associated with due process in a broad sense. Since 1937 these general constitutional rights have been referred to as substantive due process, a not altogether attractive characterization associated with judicial conservatism from the nineteenth century to the Great Depression. The battles during the Depression over judicial capacity to limit legislative regulation in the economic and social sphere depicted judicial decisions as "substantive" rather than "procedural" due process. Rights associated with the due process

clauses of the Fifth and Fourteenth Amendments that are not expressed in so many words in the Constitution as ratified in 1789 or in the amendments, such as the right to privacy or the right to travel, are sometimes viewed as judicial inventions. Yet, civil liberties rely heavily on judicial interpretation in all areas, and the measure of a right's existence cannot simply be a passage in the text of the Constitution. There must, in the case of every right, be a tradition of interpretation in the legal community amounting to a belief that the right exists. These traditions rather than words in a text are the sources of meaning.

"Libertarian" values associated with individual freedom and privacy have consistently been found to lack doctrinal foundation. Yet, these liberties have developed according to the political orientations on the Court for most of the period since 1937. The result is current interest in general due process guaranties associated with privacy and autonomy. A right to privacy, created from a panoply of related protections, has had real impact. Applications of this right to birth control and abortion, particularly in cases subsequent to *Roe* v. *Wade* (1973), have been among the most dramatic in recent constitutional history. They reveal interpretive standards and recognition of the right even where it is not applied in a particular case.

The Renaissance humanism of the Founding Fathers and their commercial inclinations, together with modern expectations, have also led to protection for a sphere of autonomous action. This is reflected in a right to travel, a right to minimally restrictive treatment for mental illness, and protection against nonrebuttable statutory presumptions such as those having to do with sex and age. Homosexuality, as a civil liberties issue, has generally been avoided by the Supreme Court, so that decisions such as *Gaylord* v. *Tacoma School District No. 10* (1977), which held that "immorality" as a ground for discharging a teacher was too vague, have set the legal framework.

Because substantive due process came to describe excessively creative interpretation of the Constitution, decisions associated with this tradition carry an implication of arbitrariness. Yet, an aspect of due process in the broadest sense is the elimination of arbitrariness. For instance, the "void for vagueness" doctrine "requires that a penal statute define the criminal offense with sufficient definiteness that ordinary people can understand what conduct is prohibited and in a manner that does not encourage arbitrary and discriminatory enforcement" (*Kolender* v. *Lawson*, 1983). Justice Sandra Day O'Connor's words in this case set a substantive requirement about the sort of laws that are permitted. It came in response to a California statute that made loitering a misdemeanor. The justice linked her opinion to maximizing individual freedom "within a framework of ordered liberty."

DOCTRINAL CONCEPTS

Civil liberties will be outlined here through four conceptual categories: freedom, property, due process, and equality. The first freedoms of expression and religion are characterized by tolerance, a value reflecting social diversity in the United States and serving as a safety valve for the expression of dissent. The twin functions of maintaining respect for the individual and providing an open forum for gaining access to the truth are associated with due process. The doctrines of due process apply to the criminal and the civil context whenever people are in jeopardy. Property is the concept associated with legal protection of settled or legitimate expectations in land, personal effects, and entitlements that come from government. Equality has a limited doctrinal foundation, but it has developed dramatically as the state has taken on increasing responsibility for the maintenance of public welfare. These constitute the central doctrines of civil liberties.

FREEDOM

The First Amendment is a multifaceted guaranty with a number of specific rights. It reads,

> Congress shall make no law respecting an establishment of religion, or prohibiting the free exercise thereof; or abridging the freedom of speech, or of the press; or the right of the people peaceably to assemble, and to petition the Government for a redress of grievances.

Although the roots of the First Amendment lie in struggles over religion, modern First Amendment developments, particularly since the 1920s, have most often concerned secular, political ex-

pression. Expression needing protection inevitably threatens something, and the standard of protection extended to the point when the expression presented a "clear and present danger." The standard, in place before 1937, came to depend on the metaphorical guide concerning shouting "Fire!" in a theater and causing a panic. Protection for expression has taken different forms within the general clear-and-present-danger framework. In each instance, the boundary of protection juxtaposes legitimate governmental interests, such as domestic peace, against the constitutional right to free and unfettered expression.

A variant of the more pragmatic tradition is an "absolutist" or literal interpretation. Although it has seldom commanded a majority of the Court, it reflects the concern for purity. Grounded in the work of Alexander Meiklejohn, who was a major contributor to ideas about free speech between the world wars, its influence on the Court came from Justices Hugo L. Black and William O. Douglas. Meiklejohn argued that we cannot help but be startled by the absoluteness of the First Amendment because it "holds good in war as in peace, in danger as in security." The American Civil Liberties Union (ACLU) has accepted this interpretation, and its reading has characterized doctrine in this area. Called "pure tolerance," the absolutist interpretation derives its strength from a refusal to make distinctions over the value of speech. This was evident in the ACLU's position that Nazis marching in Skokie, Illinois, a predominately Jewish community, should be protected so that other groups, such as Communists, could march where they might be prohibited from marching. This kind of tolerance is associated with pluralism, reflecting the reality of a very diverse society and rooted in "interest aggregation," guaranteeing something for everyone (Wolff).

Free Speech and Subversion. Liberal societies value open discussion and public discourse as safety valves for inevitable disagreements. Yet, during the development of modern free-speech doctrine, danger to some legitimate national interests became a constitutional basis for prosecution of speech. Under Chief Justice Charles Evans Hughes, the most important case may well have been *De Jonge* v. *Oregon* (1937). The speaker in *De Jonge* was convicted under an Oregon law for presiding at a meeting of the Communist party, because the party was viewed as advocating political violence and revolution. The Court was willing to overturn De Jonge's conviction because the meeting at which he appeared was peaceful. According to Hughes, laws must deal with particular abuses because of "the need to preserve inviolate the constitutional rights of free speech."

The first peacetime sedition law since the Alien and Sedition Acts of 1798 was the Alien Registration Act of 1940, known as the Smith Act. Section 2 of the act, dealing with advocacy, conspiracy, and membership, made it illegal for any person to advocate the overthrow of the government by force, hold membership in any group dedicated to such purposes, or print or disseminate written matter advocating such overthrow. The act did not get a hearing in the Supreme Court until 1951. In this case, *Dennis* v. *United States,* the conviction was upheld in the midst of the cold-war hysteria over Communism. In *Dennis,* fear bridged the gap between the clear-and-present-danger standard and the fact that no demonstrable danger had been posed.

Few of the celebrated draft evasion cases of the 1960s reached the Supreme Court, but its doctrinal stance was evident in the lower courts. Wartime dissent is sometimes thought to involve external rather than internal security. It reached a particularly high level over Vietnam, and the "danger" it posed was a matter of contention at the time. In *United States* v. *Spock* (1969), five leading opponents of the Vietnam War, including the pediatrician Benjamin Spock, were indicted for conspiracy to "counsel, aid and abet . . . Selective Service registrants to evade the draft." The convictions of these antiwar activists were dismissed by the Court of Appeals for insufficient evidence of intent to participate in an illegal conspiracy. The government did not appeal to the Supreme Court, fearing, perhaps, the embarrassment of an adverse ruling.

Freedom of Assembly. The American Nazi party and other groups outside the conventional political sphere continue to make some of the most dramatic claims upon the right to assemble, along with their civil liberties advocates and the judiciary. In 1978 and 1979, American Nazis planned to march through Skokie, Illinois, a predominately Jewish Chicago suburb, seven thousand residents of which had been confined in Nazi concentration camps during World War II. The march involved not only an affront to the

residents but also the threat of violent retaliation. The situation became a rallying point for the ACLU and is characteristic of the kind of case that the ACLU has used to develop its view of the First Amendment. Although the local courts in the *Skokie* case issued an order to stop the Nazi march, the appellate court responded with a "stay," upheld by the Supreme Court. This opinion shows a commitment to "pure tolerance" that is outside conventional practice.

Owing much to the "general" freedom of expression, freedom of assembly raises the possibility of dangers or threats to public order. This freedom has come to include the right to gather and the right to associate for political purposes. Modern encounters with the freedom to assemble can be traced to *Hague* v. *Committee on Industrial Organization* (1939). In that case, Jersey City had prohibited assemblies in streets, parks, or public buildings without a permit. When the mayor denied the CIO permission for a rally because he considered it a Communist organization, the labor union successfully challenged the decision. Justice Owen J. Roberts ruled that streets and parks have been "held in trust for the use of the public" and that their use may be regulated but not abridged or denied under the guise of regulation. A procedure for acquiring a permit cannot delegate so much power to public officials that they are able to base their decision on the content of the expression or the purpose of the assembly. In *Watt* v. *Community for Creative Non-Violence,* which was appealed to the Supreme Court in 1983, the Circuit Court of the District of Columbia ruled that demonstrators had a right to sleep in tents in a park across the street from the White House as a way of dramatizing the plight of Washington's homeless. Federal regulations against camping in downtown Washington had been interpreted by the National Park Service as prohibiting the demonstration, but the appeals court ruled against the government because sleeping outside was part of the message that the demonstrators had a First Amendment right to communicate.

Purely private property is not open to public demonstrations, but some of the most difficult assembly issues involve quasi-public property such as shopping centers. In *Amalgamated Food Employees* v. *Logan Valley Plaza* (1968), the Court upheld the right of a labor union to picket a store in a shopping center, because there did not seem to be any other way to convey the facts of a labor dispute to the public. In *PruneYard Shopping Center v. Robins* (1980), the justices had an opportunity to rule on whether the California Constitution violated that of the United States. The case was unusual because of this confrontation of constitutional values. The shopping center owner had appealed a judgment of the California Supreme Court holding that California's constitution protects speech and petitioning exercised in a reasonable way in privately owned shopping centers. The decision by Justice William H. Rehnquist held that the ruling did not deny owners' rights under the Fifth Amendment or the free-speech rights associated with the ownership of property. Thus, the decision on the California Constitution was sustained.

Free Speech and Institutions. In institutional settings, free speech has traditionally been balanced against authority. In schools, the application of the right of free speech involves issues such as the authority of administration over teaching personnel (as in the issue of loyalty oaths) and the authority of administration over students. In 1969, students had been suspended from school in Iowa for wearing black armbands as a protest against the Vietnam War after school officials had forbidden the gesture. The controversy focused on the extent to which official authority had been compromised by the violation of the administrative ban on armbands. The justices ruled that the authorities in Des Moines had expected too much and reminded them that "state-operated schools may not be enclaves of totalitarianism" (*Tinker* v. *Des Moines Independent Community School District*, 1969). Preventing disturbances was not a strong enough foundation to justify suspension. The justices laced the opinion with exhortations to the following effect: "It can hardly be argued that either students or teachers shed their constitutional rights to freedom of speech or expression at the schoolhouse gate."

While *Tinker* involved issues of expression versus order in the institution, another body of litigation deals with institutional authority over the curriculum. As with the maintenance of order, institutional decisions about what is to be part of the education process do not usually entail clashes over constitutional rights. But expectations about curriculum content (for instance, such topics as evolution, sex education, and the literature available in the school library) may give rise to such clashes. Following five years of cases in the lower courts, the Supreme Court took up *Island Trees Board of Education* v. *Pico* (1982) and gave a reading of how the First Amendment applied in this context. In a plurality opinion, Justice William J. Brennan commented on the limits a school board faced regarding library books. He would have precluded removal where the board simply disapproved of the political ideas or philosophies expressed in the books.

It may well be that a freedom based on uncertainty and relativism about values is at odds with democracy and social cohesion. In the school library censorship cases, when books are challenged by outraged parents because they are "un-Christian, anti-Semitic, or racist," as in *Pico*, the response has become a defense of a neutral or "pure" freedom to read rather than a substantive defense of the materials. The refusal to take sides seems to neutralize opposition and to take the edge off critical discourse to the point where a great deal can be said but without much effect.

Unprotected Expression. The prevailing interpretation of the First Amendment views some speech as unprotected because its contents are offensive. In *Chaplinsky* v. *New Hampshire* (1942), the majority opinion by Justice Frank Murphy found that "certain well defined and narrowly limited classes of speech" had never raised constitutional problems. They included "the lewd and obscene, the profane, the libelous and the insulting or 'fighting words.'" Murphy reasoned that these utterances are neither essential to any "exposition of ideas" nor a "step to truth." Any benefit they might have was outweighed by society's interest in preventing evil. From this proclamation, a distinction has developed that is clear in its outlines but ambiguous in its details.

The kind of unprotected speech that sparked the controversy in *Chaplinsky*, "fighting words," is the least litigated. Libel has received more attention. Its common-law roots exemplify how crosscutting areas of law create conflicts that define civil liberties. Here, standards for protecting public reputation have been developed to take account of press freedoms. Commercial speech is an area of expression capable of regulation. Early in the women's movement, newspapers were prohibited from making sex designations in their help-wanted columns, but in the 1980s pharmacists and lawyers were given the right to advertise under the First Amendment, where professional and trade associations had previously restricted that free expression.

Obscenity has been the most fully litigated of the unprotected areas. Americans have known limits to expression from colonial times, yet early governments faced few constitutional challenges to their moral authority. As the country became more diverse and challenges to regulation of conventional morality arose, the issue came to the forefront of civil liberties. In 1957 a standard was established in *Roth* v. *United States.* Justice Brennan depicted a history of limited freedom evident in laws against blasphemy and profanity in nearly all of the original states. Like the early moral wrongs, obscenity would not be considered "within the area of constitutionally protected speech." Brennan defined the obscene as that which involved lascivious longings associated with a perverse (rather than healthy) interest in sex, and he suggested a new test that would safeguard legitimate expression by looking to the average person rather than the most susceptible and by taking the material as a whole. Juries would be the obscenity filter, in lieu of an explicit definition of material not protected by the First Amendment.

The standard "utterly without redeeming social importance" survived until a change in personnel on the Supreme Court resulted in *Miller* v. *California* and *Paris Adult Theatre I* v. *Slaton* in 1973. *Miller* involved a mass mailing of sexually explicit advertising material to unwilling recipients. This led the Court, under the pen of Chief Justice Warren E. Burger, to announce a new test for obscenity. To ease the prosecutorial burden of proving material obscene, pornography would be specifically defined by state law as appealing to the prurient interest, patently offensive, and lacking in serious literary, artistic, political, or scientific value. The Court returned authority to the state and local level and emphasized community-based offensiveness, with a focus on hard-core pornography. This meant "ultimate sexual acts, masturbation, excretory functions, and lewd exhibition." Exposure has been the "core" in pornography. Unlike subsequent concerns expressed by feminists, violence is not discussed. Whether the old standard of morality can be transformed to one more clearly associated with defamation has made this a challenging issue.

Freedom of the Press. The "press" mentioned in the First Amendment has come to mean professional journalists and the media they work for. Whether that was initially the case is a subject of some debate. Press protection intersects with private law and the criminal process, but its structure is determined by the First Amendment. Just prior to the beginning of the period covered by this essay, the Supreme Court reiterated its traditional commitment to protection from prior restraint on publication in *Near* v. *Minnesota* (1931). During most of the subsequent period it has been assumed that this is one of the basic tenets of First Amendment protection, and much of the litigation has been elsewhere; but one of the most dramatic cases of the period involved this issue.

In the "Pentagon Papers" case (*New York Times* v. *United States,* 1971), restraint took place when the Nixon administration stopped the *New York Times* and the *Washington Post* from publishing Defense Department documents that examined, sometimes critically, the escalation of the Vietnam War. The Supreme Court expedited the proceedings and in a matter of weeks held that the government had not sufficiently justified its restraint of the press. The old standard, which had been treated as an absolute, was beginning to be treated more conditionally. An injunction was issued against the magazine *The Progressive* in 1979 for an article on defense secrets that told how to make a hydrogen bomb. The restraint was lifted when it became clear that the information was already available to the public.

Two traditional problem areas for the press are trials, with the related court-governed proceedings, and traditional common-law protections associated with contractual relations and libel. In a case where a former Central Intelligence Agency (CIA) agent broke an agreement not to publish articles about the agency without prior review, the courts treated the issue as a matter of contractual obligation and determined that the former agent was bound by his agreements (*Snepp* v. *United States,* 1980). Interpretation of the intersection between libel and press freedom is traceable to *New York Times Co.* v. *Sullivan,* a 1964 case in which libel of a public official was limited to occasions when the media reported something they knew to be untrue that damaged the official's reputation. The decision widened the sphere of public discourse and established a continuum allowing greater discussion, the more public the subject.

There has been a running battle between the press and the trial judges over the often conflicting norms of fair trial and free press. Press liability for subpoena of news sources stems from the presumption that the government has an obligation to provide defendants with a fair trial. One of the most dramatic controversies came when the reporter Bill Farr was jailed in the 1970s because he refused to reveal sources that a trial judge believed had a bearing on the guilt or innocence of a defendant. Judicial control of publicity at trials has run from the reversal of convictions because of undue publicity, in the case of the Texas "high-roller" Billy Sol Estes in 1965, to holdings that there is no constitutional right to ban television from court when it is permitted by state law (*Chandler* v. *Florida,* 1981). As with other First Amendment questions, the clash of issues and the way they are resolved determines the nature of the civil liberties.

Freedom of Religion. The tolerance that has recently become so evident in First Amendment protection for expression operates less conspicuously in matters of religion, because of the longstanding tradition of constitutional protection against excessive government involvement. Provisions for religious toleration, particularly those which stipulate that there be no official involvement with religion, have produced, in some contemporary interpretations, a view that religious establishments suffer a kind of discrimination. Thus, there is a tension in constitutional protection for religion between guaranties of freedom to practice and the "wall" between church and state.

Since the 1940s, religion has been an effective shield from some of the explicit demands and conditions imposed by the state. The initial cases, like many that have come later, involved the Jehovah's Witnesses and their refusal to "pay homage to false gods," such as the American flag. After initially declining to protect this form of religious expression, the Court ruled that the Constitution required withholding from the state "any authority to compel belief or the expression of it where that expression violates religious convictions" (*West Virginia State Board of Education* v. *Barnette,* 1943). In current practice, toleration is seen as a far better cement for the polity than the more primitive, yet certainly evocative, instruments of patriotism.

Free exercise has developed as one of the classic "negative" liberties. Perhaps the best examples of the immunity it provides are the right to claim exemption from military service and the opportunity to become a conscientious objector. The tradition has been that immunity from the draft was a guarantee grounded in religious toleration. In cases arising from the Vietnam War, however, the definition of religious conviction was expanded to include "a sincere and meaningful belief" occupying a place "parallel to a belief in God" (*United States* v. *Seeger,* 1965). This rule extended the mantle of religion to "a belief that is equally paramount in the lives of their possessors" as belief in God is in the more traditional definition of religion. The tradition has been upheld with less reliance on organized belief and more reliance on personal conviction.

Government in the United States is prevented by the Constitution from making laws "respecting an establishment of religion." Under the growth of the welfare state and pressure for public assistance, the establishment clause has been a source of tension. In the middle of the twentieth century, higher standards of toleration led to increased separation of church and state. In *Everson* v. *Board of Education* (1947), the issue was provision by New Jersey of bus fares for all schoolchildren, including those going to parochial schools. In this case, the Supreme Court upheld the principle of a wall between church and state, but found bus fares outside the wall. The idea that support for buses was without a religious purpose became one of the tests in determining when the state had become involved with religion in an unconstitutional fashion. Another Supreme Court decision on this issue came in *Mueller* v. *Allen* (1983), where a 5–4 ruling endorsed tuition aid to parochial schools for the first time. The aid came in the form of a Minnesota tax credit amounting to $700.

The establishment issue that has epitomized liberal tolerance since it first emerged involves prayer in the public schools. The controversy began in the 1960s over a nondenominational daily prayer designated by the New York State Board of Regents for use in the public schools of that state. The prayer, which went, "Almighty God, we acknowledge our dependence upon Thee, and we beg Thy blessings upon us, our parents, our teachers, and our country," was recommended for reading at the beginning of each school day. It was invalidated by the Supreme Court in 1962 as inconsistent with the establishment clause. Similar decisions upholding the basic principle have continued to be handed down while the controversy rages in Congress. In January 1983, for instance, the Court decided not to take an appeal by a school district in Texas from a lower-court ruling that had struck down the district's policy of permitting student religious groups to meet on school property before and after regular school hours.

In the end, expression is always subject to the interests of society and the state. This practice in American constitutional politics has coexisted with real distaste for limits on speech. There have always been limits; the issue is which ones are acceptable. Recognizing the political and social reality of freedom of expression will do more to give expression back its cutting edge than will an uncertain and relativistic tolerance.

PROPERTY

The meaning of property is in flux. Public regulation of economic interests, always more significant than generally understood, has expanded with the growth of government, planning, and environmental concerns, while governmental obligations to holders of statutory entitlements have been recognized as a property right. Thus, the rights associated with "real" property are less comprehensive than they appear to the public, and protection of entitlements is more substantial than is conventionally understood. Property rights protected by the Constitution will be the focus here, and they will be discussed with reference to the concept of legitimate expectations. We begin by discussing the shift away from protection of "economic" rights that set the context for the modern concept of property.

Once central to liberal theory, the property right has been missing since at least 1937 from treatment as a civil liberty protected by the Constitution. That is, the property right has not been considered alongside the right to speak freely or the guaranty of equal protection in the Constitution. Property in the traditional sense of an individual right is absent from many of the civil liberties treatises. Of course, protection of property has not disappeared, but its status as a civil liberty, a constitutionally protected right of every citizen, has received little attention. Since the early part of the twentieth century, reform move-

ments have attacked the protection of property as actually the protection of the power of the few over the many rather than as the protection of individual autonomy. As a consequence, this right slipped from the debate on constitutional principles after 1937. While legal scholarship occasionally noted the peculiarities of a double standard, property remained on the periphery of civil liberties. This was true in spite of the economic implications for recognized liberties such as right to counsel for indigent defendants and protection against discrimination in employment. Although the Supreme Court officially avoided constitutional property for more than forty years, the growth in civil liberties protection has brought the Court back. Now, "real" property draws on the support for civil liberties, the result of two generations of activism over fundamental rights in the federal courts and around the nation.

The term *property* in the Constitution is used only in the Fifth Amendment: "nor shall private property be taken for public use without just compensation." The early Supreme Court protected personal interests as well as real property by reference to various constitutional provisions. As far back as 1803, in *Marbury* v. *Madison,* the Supreme Court recognized that actions by government create expectations. In *Fletcher* v. *Peck* (1810) and subsequent cases, Chief Justice John Marshall relied on the contract clause to prevent governmental whim from denying legitimate expectations. Before the Civil War, slavery and franchises to do business constituted important forms of property. After the Civil War, property was viewed in terms of its value in the market, linking the right to an expanding industrial order. By the time judicial attention had turned from regulation of the economy to political rights in 1937, a conception of constitutional property had already been laid down.

In his treatise on constitutional law, Laurence Tribe considered a model of "settled expectations" to be a distinctive form of constitutional adjudication composed of "restraints on government power" that vest rights in property on the grounds "that certain settled expectations . . . should be secure against governmental disruption, at least without appropriate compensation" (p. 456). Property in the Constitution is a matter of expectations rather than of possession of tangible things, and protection comes from those expectations having been "settled" or deemed legitimate.

Settled expectations can be found in *Penn Central Transportation Co.* v. *New York,* a 1978 case in which the Supreme Court subordinated state power over historic preservation to a reasonable expectation of profit. The case involved questions of how the city of New York could restrict development of historic landmarks and whether the restrictions that it applied to Grand Central Terminal constituted a "taking." Writing for the majority, Justice Brennan admitted an inability to develop any set formula for determining when "economic injuries caused by public action must be compensated." He indicated that although takings are more readily found where there is a "physical invasion" by government, a broader understanding exists. To require compensation, a taking may simply interfere with interests "sufficiently bound up with the reasonable expectation of the claimant to constitute 'property' for Fifth Amendment purposes." The Court held that Penn Central had insufficient loss to constitute a violation of legitimate expectations.

The compensation question had become a matter of balancing rights to determine when property could be taken from private hands. One of the traditional requirements was that property could be taken only "for public use." This issue has never arisen more dramatically than in the 1984 case of *Hawaii Housing Authority* v. *Midkiff,* in which the state had instituted a land condemnation program to transfer property to those who had been leasing from the island's large landowners. According to Justice O'Connor, regulating oligopoly and the evils associated with it is a classic exercise of a state's police powers. This decision points up an old maxim concerning the unexceptional fact of limits on property ownership delivered by Justice Jackson: "Rights, property or otherwise, which are absolute against all the world are certainly rare" (*United States* v. *Willow River Power Co.,* 1945).

Grounded in the relationship between individuals and the state, decisions on compensation involve weighing expectations. The relationship is the structural dimension in the Constitution that triggers the "just compensation" provision when private control and use of property is diminished. By the era at which this essay begins, the Supreme Court had acknowledged that "property . . . may be construed to include obligations, rights, and other intangibles as well as personal things" (*Fidelity and Deposit Co. of Maryland* v. *Arenz,* 1933). A balance between social interests and principled standards has characterized the evaluation of expectations ever since.

New Forms of Property. A distinction between the individual rights surrounding what is called real property and the privileges associated with public services and employment can be traced to *McAuliffe* v. *City of New Bedford* (1892), a Massachusetts case in which Oliver Wendell Holmes, Jr., before going to the Supreme Court, distinguished between "a constitutional right to talk politics" and a job as a policeman, to which no constitutional right applied. At the Supreme Court, the justices had distinguished between traditional property and entitlements to licenses, goods, or services provided by government. Under the doctrine that this government largesse was a privilege, the justices placed minimal constraints on revocation of entitlements. The distinction between property rights and privilege began to break down by the mid-twentieth century.

Beyond Privilege. The initial application of constitutional protection for property to public programs involved social security. The program had been held constitutional in 1937. Twenty-three years later, in *Flemming* v. *Nestor* (1960), the justices addressed the legal status of benefits. Although they listened to the due process claim, the Court allowed benefits to be denied to a family following their deportation. But in 1961 the Court established the principle that when benefits were withdrawn, there would have to be an unusually important government need to outweigh the right to a prior hearing *(Cafeteria and Restaurant Workers Union* v. *McElroy).* In an influential article published in 1964, Charles Reich, a law professor, argued that the welfare state had altered the status of individuals. He felt that benefits such as unemployment compensation, public assistance, and old-age insurance urgently "need the concept of right," and he made the case so forcefully that this academic treatment became the referent for modern constitutional property.

The case that recognized statutory entitlements as property, *Goldberg* v. *Kelly,* was decided in 1970. It pitted New York City and state welfare authorities against a beneficiary who had been cut off without a hearing because he refused to accept counseling for a drug addiction that he denied having. Justice Brennan noted that since much of the wealth in the country, such as tax exemptions, employment security, and unemployment compensation, "takes the form of rights that do not fall within traditional common-law concepts of property . . . it may be realistic today to regard welfare entitlements as more like 'property' than a 'gratuity.'" This position was amplified by Justice Potter Stewart, who held that "a person's interest in a benefit is a 'property' interest for due process purposes if there are such rules or mutually explicit understandings that support his claim of entitlement to the benefits" (*Board of Regents of State Colleges* v. *Roth,* 1972).

The new understanding replaced the minimal protection that had existed by which benefits were revoked with a presumption favoring continuation of the benefit. Thus, in *Goss* v. *Lopez* (1975), the Court found this form of property where high school students were suspended from their classes without a hearing following protests over the bombing of Cambodia at the end of the Vietnam War. The deprivation was held to be substantial enough to overcome concern about the educational process, and the property interest determined the extent of the due process required.

The Modern Practice. During the mid-1970s, the conservative swing on the Supreme Court affected case outcomes, but even the conservatives acknowledged property in entitlements. The justices allowed termination of federal disability benefits without a prior hearing while granting that benefits provided by the government are a "statutorily created property interest protected by the Fifth Amendment" (*Mathews* v. *Eldridge,* 1976). Other failed litigation recognizing the property right to entitlements involved a foster family desiring to remain intact, a state prisoner being transferred, and a medical student who claimed to have been unjustly dismissed from school. Not all appeals in this period were unsuccessful, however. In *Memphis Light, Gas and Water Division* v. *Craft* (1978), the utility company claimed an absolute right to discontinue service when bills had not been paid. The Supreme Court saw an exception when the bill was the subject of a "bona fide dispute." The company would be liable for damages if the dispute turned out to be legitimate. Here, state protection against termination, except for cause, amounted to a property interest that the Court was willing to recognize. This combined the civil libertarian concern for the powerless with an economic issue.

The rise of protection for statutory entitlements came at a time of diminished concern for more marketable forms of property, but these gains would ultimately enhance protection of traditional property. Gerald Gunther, in his treatise on constitutional law, denied that there was a workable distinction between property and political rights. He sought support in Justice Stewart's observation that "property does not have rights, people have rights" (*Lynch* v. *Household Finance Corp.,* 1972), which had been an effort to enhance constitutional protections for homes and savings accounts by associating them with "established" rights to travel and to the continuation of welfare benefits.

After Justice Stewart had been replaced by Justice O'Connor, the Court continued to draw on civil rights to protect economic interests. The opinion in *Logan* v. *Zimmerman Brush Co.* (1982), by Justice Harry A. Blackmun, boldly restated the definition of property as "an individual entitlement grounded in state law" and ruled in favor of a shipping clerk with a short leg who claimed that he "had been unlawfully terminated because of his physical handicap." The protected property was a traditional common-law entitlement, a "cause of action" provided by the Fair Employment Practices Act. The opinion reveals an enthusiasm for protection of the powerless very different from that expressed by the Supreme Court 150 years earlier when it viewed the poor as a "moral pestilence." Similarly, in *Loretto* v. *Teleprompter Manhattan CATV Corp.* (1982), a "taking" claim arose over a New York statute that provided that a landlord must permit a cable television company to install its equipment in her building. The concern here was for a very old right in the face of state support for an expanding form of entertainment. This sensitivity to property is a consequence of the concern for civil liberties as much as it is traditional protection for economic interests.

DUE PROCESS

Perhaps the most eloquent argument for constitutional due process came in a concurrence by

Justice Felix Frankfurter in *Joint Anti-Fascist Refugee Committee* v. *McGrath* in 1951. The committee, one of the cold war's casualties, had been designated "Communist" without notice, justification, or the chance to confront the evidence, without, as Frankfurter argued, the fairness of procedure that is "due process in the primary sense." This kind of fairness on the part of the government was important, he said, for two reasons: "No better instrument has been devised for arriving at truth than to give a person in jeopardy of serious loss notice of the case against him and opportunity to meet it. Nor has a better way been found for generating the feeling, so important to a popular government, that justice has been done." The sections that follow examine the elements of due process that are considered fundamental constitutional liberties.

Criminal Procedure. The criminal process is built on the rights in the Constitution. This "deep structure" is found in the Fourth, Fifth, Sixth, and Eighth Amendments to the Constitution. These provisions outline a process begun by the police, carried out by the prosecutor and the judiciary, and concluded by prison guards and probation officers. It has three main stages: the period prior to trial when the investigation, arrest, and initial appearance before a magistrate take place; the period of the trial, including the selection of a jury and the evidentiary matters that constitute the business of the trial; and the posttrial period, which focuses on sentencing, punishment, and the appellate process.

Investigation in the pretrial period is governed by "search and seizure," where the basic rule is that a warrant issued by a disinterested magistrate and showing "probable cause" must be obtained. The warrant provision requires prior justification when the government undertakes a search to collect evidence against an individual, but it does not operate in every instance. There are six major exceptions: (1) consent, where an individual has agreed to let the police search; (2) searches provided for by statute, such as those at borders to minimize the spread of insects and disease; (3) nontestimonial personal evidence, such as lineups and fingerprints; (4) volatile situations in which police officers in the field are suspicious and thus have the right to at least "stop and frisk"; (5) searches of automobiles, where probable cause exists in a volatile situation; and (6) a search subsequent to a valid arrest.

A 1982 case, *United States* v. *Albert Ross, Jr.*, involved a narcotics dealer known as Bandit and linked the automobile exception with the exception to the warrant requirement when a search accompanies an arrest. In this case District of Columbia police had followed a tip that identified Bandit as selling narcotics out of the trunk of his "purplish maroon Chevrolet Malibu." The police arrested the individual, and searching the car without a warrant, they found heroin in a "lunch-type brown paper bag" in the trunk and cash in a red leather pouch. The decision was that when police had legitimately stopped a car and had probable cause to believe that it contained "contraband," they could conduct a search as thorough as a magistrate could authorize by warrant. The limitation was that "the search is limited by its object." Thus, as Justice John Paul Stevens pointed out, if a van is being searched for illegal aliens, the police could not examine the contents of the glove compartment. This is an area of considerable interest, and *Ross* itself has been rejected on state grounds by Washington in *State* v. *Ringer* (1983).

Technological intrusion is a special threat to human dignity, and statutory wiretaps are a problematic exception to the warrant requirement. Modern concern in this area stems from a dissent by Justices Holmes and Louis D. Brandeis in the 1928 case of *Olmstead* v. *United States*, where they argued that protection from warrantless telephone wiretaps was part of the Fourth Amendment. The protection for the individual in the Fifth Amendment led to broader due process protection from wiretapping in 1967 in *Katz* v. *United States*. The justices threw out the old requirements that for constitutional protection to obtain, there had to be a trespass and some physical object had to have been seized. This extended the safeguards to bugging devices, wiretaps, and other forms of electronic eavesdropping.

Another phase of the pretrial investigation takes place while the defendant is in custody. The right to remain silent during interrogation by state law enforcement officers has been upheld since 1964, when rough treatment of Danny Escobedo by the police in Illinois led the Supreme Court to require counsel during questioning. The implications were spelled out in *Miranda* v. *Arizona* in 1966, when the Court announced a series of rules now known as Miranda warnings. These require the police to notify arrested suspects that they have the right to remain silent, that what they say may be used against them in court, that they have a right to counsel, that counsel will be provided for them without charge if they cannot afford to pay an attorney, and that any information that they give must be given voluntarily. These warnings came to represent the "due process revolution" of the 1960s, in which state governments, which do most of the criminal law enforcement, were subjected to constitutional review of their actions. The Supreme Court restated the authority of the warning requirement in *Edwards* v. *Arizona* (1981), although its decisions since then have allowed some flexibility in application.

The "exclusionary rule" links the pretrial period and the trial. This rule stems from the principle that if the police or prosecution have failed to obey the laws governing the criminal process, any evidence gathered illegally by them cannot be used for a conviction. Having been applied in federal courts since 1914, the rule was made applicable to the states in *Mapp* v. *Ohio* in 1961, a case in which the police broke into the home of Mrs. Dollree Mapp—allegedly in pursuit of a fugitive—and used obscene literature that they found in Mapp's home to convict her. To some, the principle has represented the sanctity of the due process system; to others, it has represented a systemic propensity to "coddle criminals." The rule has undergone intense scrutiny since the early 1970s, when President Nixon made his appointments to the Supreme Court. One of the most puzzling in the Constitution from an ordinary observer's point of view, the exclusionary rule has appeared destined to be excluded itself. While there has been much attention to this issue, its place in the ideology of constitutional due process is marginal. The rule is a gloss on the Constitution given widespread application in the 1960s as a mechanism for disciplining the police. The reasonableness of letting the accused go free because the police have blundered is easily missed.

Knowledge of the accusation, protection against undue delay, an impartial jury, and a right to counsel distinguish the American process from the horrors depicted by Franz Kafka in his novel *The Trial*. The right to a public trial has been guaranteed since the 1940s and subject to relatively little controversy. The right to a speedy trial is of more recent vintage. The Constitution's provision was applied to the states in *Klopfer* v. *North Carolina,* a 1967 case arising out of civil rights struggles in which the defendant, Peter Klopfer, a professor at Duke University, was tried for participating in a sit-in at a segregated restaurant. Klopfer was brought to trial for trespass. The trial was suspended, and Klopfer faced the threat of renewed prosecution at North Carolina's discretion. This was considered a denial of a speedy trial. The courts were initially reluctant to specify the length of time allowed by the constitutional provision. Willie Mae Barker's case, however, stimulated such a quantification of the permissible delay. Initially scheduled in 1958, Barker's trial was postponed eleven times while the prosecution sought a conviction of his partner. Barker objected to the twelfth continuance, which would have postponed his trial to at least five years after he was arrested. Although the Supreme Court let it pass in *Barker* v. *Wingo* (1972), the Speedy Trial Act of 1974 was a partial response to this case, and in general, it has been through statutory authority rather than judicial decision that the parameters of access to timely justice have been delineated.

The right to an impartial jury also protects the defendant. In *Williams* v. *Florida* (1970), Justice Byron R. White argued that the jury must place itself "between the accused and his accuser" and that the jury had to be large enough "to promote group deliberation . . . and to provide a fair possibility for obtaining a representative cross-section of the community." The common-law jury had been twelve persons; it is against this standard that the smaller and allegedly more efficient juries of today are measured. Six has been the lower limit since *Williams*.

Another aspect of the jury, the requirement of unanimous agreement, has come under pressure since the early 1970s. Although part of the common-law tradition, unanimity has been treated by some members of the Supreme Court as a historical accident. The number of votes required for conviction began to be viewed functionally as necessary for determining "reasonable doubt," and fewer persons, nine or ten, have been needed for conviction. The justices drew the line in *Burch* v. *Louisiana* in 1979 when they held that a nonunanimous six-person jury for a petty criminal offense was unconstitutional. Justice Rehnquist, while not passionate in his commitment to the common-law jury, was not willing to yield the constitutional provision for a jury to the state's interest in saving money and time. Here, too, states set the appropriate requirements for juries, while the Supreme Court simply monitors the constitutional minimum.

Provision of counsel began in capital cases and was broadened to include felonies in the federal courts in 1938. When the Supreme Court expanded this protection to the states in *Betts* v. *Brady* in 1942, it was "special circumstances" such as the complexity of the trial that required counsel to be provided. This led to a series of ad hoc decisions in which the justices of the High Court determined the circumstances requiring the provision of counsel. Tiring of these ad hoc decisions, the justices brought up *Gideon* v. *Wainwright* in 1963. Clarence Earl Gideon was a hapless petty offender with a strong sense of his rights. Indigent and charged with felony breaking and entering in Florida, he requested a lawyer but was turned down at his trial and on appeal in the state appellate courts. The ruling, a high point in the Warren Court's protection for civil liberties, established a provision for court-appointed counsel in serious criminal trials. Later, the Burger Court made counsel a requirement where imprisonment was possible. Related to procedural fairness, adequacy of counsel has been assessed in terms of "reasonable competence" (*Tollett* v. *Henderson*, 1973), although Justice Thurgood Marshall has suggested a higher standard of "competence in law." In California, the state supreme court held in 1982 that the right to counsel included a defendant's qualified right to decide who could best decide the case (*Maxwell* v. *Superior Court*).

The conclusion of a trial presents an opportunity for appellate review and results in the imposition of punishment consistent with the Eighth Amendment, which protects against excessive bail and penalties that are cruel and unusual. The posttrial stage also includes procedural protection against having to defend oneself more than once for the same crime and appellate review of a conviction. Here, state courts have contributed a great deal to setting procedural standards, especially where the issue is prosecution by the state and the federal government. While the federal Constitution has been understood to allow dual prosecution, some states have prohibited subsequent prosecution in state courts after a federal conviction (*People* v. *Cooper*, 1976).

A tragic case, *Louisiana ex rel. Francis* v. *Resweber*, involving both double jeopardy and cruel and unusual punishment, came to the Supreme Court in 1947 after the state of Louisiana had attempted to execute Willie Francis and failed because of technical difficulties. Lawyers for Francis argued that a second attempt would place him in jeopardy twice, as well as being cruel and unusual. Both claims were rejected, and the state succeeded on its second attempt.

Generally, the Eighth Amendment relies on a conventional standard of reasonableness when evaluating punishment. There are, for instance, equity considerations that prevent the government from turning a fine into a prison term for those unable to pay and that require punishment to be proportionate to the offense. In 1983 a life sentence without the possibility of parole for a series of nonviolent petty offenses was ruled cruel and unusual in *Solem* v. *Helm*. Courts in Washington and West Virginia have made similar decisions about excessive punishment. Similarly, capital punishment for rape was held to be unconstitutional in 1977 because the seriousness of the punishment exceeded the seriousness of the crime.

Capital punishment, however it is executed, draws the most attention to the Eighth Amendment and has been a subject hotly contested in the states. In 1972, by a 5–4 vote, the Supreme Court held that the death penalty violated constitutional due process. The opinion was that its capriciousness, rather than the penalty itself, made execution cruel and unusual. Many states responded with new statutes addressing how the penalty was applied. In *Gregg* v. *Georgia* (1976) the Court was asked whether a reconstituted Georgia statute was constitutional. Gregg had been convicted of having killed two men who had given him a ride while he was hitchhiking. Death was a possible penalty when a case involved "aggravating circumstances" such as aircraft hijacking, treason, prior conviction of a capital felony, commission in the act of another capital felony, or when the murder was "horribly vile." Gregg's case included some of these circumstances, and the justices found the Georgia statute constitutional.

By the 1980s, the death sentence was on the rise. While the federal government sought the penalty for treason, espionage, and presidential assassination, thirty-five states enacted new statutes to meet constitutional requirements. In 1981 there were 780 people on death row in the United States. Opponents of the death penalty claim that the same arbitrariness and racial discrimination that led to its temporary abolition in 1972 still exist. Supporters such as Justice Rehnquist criticize the procedural protection that allows imposition of the sentence to be delayed. In 1983 the Court upheld the use of expedited procedures to review habeas corpus petitions from death row inmates in a 5–4 decision (*Barefoot* v. *Estelle*) reflecting the continuing division over capital punishment. The death penalty has special procedural significance, since the penalty cannot be revoked. The search for truth is more significant, and pressure to eliminate the penalty as the ultimate indignity is likely to remain strong.

Civil Procedure. With expansion of the roles and services provided by the government, substantial issues arise outside the criminal sphere to which due process may be applied. Whatever the object of struggle, be it an education or a welfare benefit, procedural guarantees set standards for how people are to be treated when government action threatens them with a loss. Civil due process is a growing area in civil liberties. Beginning with public employment, due process challenged the old distinction between a right and a privilege. The higher federal standard of procedural guarantees fueled early developments in criminal rights, but after a decade of incorporation in that area, there followed the application of procedural safeguards to other institutional settings. In prisons, schools, the civil service, and welfare offices, the institutional setting began to look different as it was influenced by new standards for protection of liberty and property rights, as in the *Goldberg* case.

In *Goss* v. *Lopez* (1975), due process rights were provided to students who had been temporarily suspended from their high schools without a hearing. Having found that the state of Ohio promised the students an education, Justice White held that this benefit could not be taken away without due process. The process "due" was a function of the right in jeopardy. In this case, due process would apply because the guaranteed education was threatened. White emphasized the practical nature of the procedural requirement. The minimal standard was "the opportunity to be heard." In this decision, the Court considered the burdens that due process required in relation to the interests of school authorities in carrying out their institutional functions. The requirement for suspensions of students for ten days or less was "an informal give-and-take" between the school authorities and the student. Although confrontation in a high school corridor has few of the trappings of formal hearings, it does reflect the twin functions of due process identified by Justice Frankfurter in the *Joint Anti-Fascist Refugee Committee* case. In addition, if the student denied the charges, he or she deserved an explanation and an opportunity to present his or her side of the story.

Due process in institutional settings links the procedure to the weight of the deprivation. This approach was evident in *Board of Curators of the University of Missouri* v. *Horowitz* (1978), where the fact situation produced an important distinction between disciplinary and academic judgments. In the *Horowitz* case, a medical student had been dismissed on the basis of "erratic attendance at clinical sessions, poor performance around patients, and poor personal hygiene." She claimed that she had been unconstitutionally deprived of liberty and property. According to Rehnquist, Horowitz was entitled to invoke a liberty interest in the opportunity to continue her medical education and gain employment as a doctor. The justice deferred to faculty and administrative prerogatives where educational evaluations were at stake, and because there had been "deliberation," the Court found that the medical school met the minimal requirements due when the issue is "purely academic."

Distinctions like the one in *Horowitz* have broad consequences. By recognizing the liberty interest but requiring little because of the academic setting, the Court diluted the value of due process. It would, of course, be odd to ask a jury whether a student would make a good doctor or deserved an A in a civil liberties class. Discrimination on the basis of sex and religion, however, such as Horowitz claimed, can taint the evaluation process. A charge of bias is the sort of thing for which neutral adjudication and procedural safeguards were developed. To dismiss them as "substantive" is to ignore the functions of procedural fairness. It is a hedge against arbitrary state action; it honors the individual; and perhaps it even gets at the truth. Due process becomes operative when claims are made concerning subjects, such as sexual harassment, about which society is particularly sensitive.

EQUALITY

The Constitution requires that no state "deny to any person . . . the equal protection of the laws." Battles over how to interpret this provision have been as heated as any in constitutional law. Interracial marriage, busing for school desegregation, and male-only draft registration are some of the more contentious issues that have arisen in this area of civil liberties. The pitched battles that have developed over these and other issues take on a distinctive character as a result of the fact that "constitutional equality" is not the same as "equality" in its conventional sense. What the justices and lawyers have extrapolated from the constitutional text has its own strengths and limitations. According to the constitutional view, distinctions between the races and similar classifications are "suspect," whereas gross inequalities of condition in America seem beyond scrutiny.

The promise of equality was not a dominant principle of the American Revolution, as it was of the French Revolution only a few years later. Although equality was mentioned prominently in the Declaration of Independence, the decision not to include equal protection as a founding principle was partly due to the status of the black population, unresolved until the Civil War. Thus, equality in the Constitution dates from that war. Emancipation was followed by a series of constitutional amendments: the Thirteenth, Fourteenth, and Fifteenth, which attempted to protect the new status of the former slaves. The Thirteenth Amendment abolished slavery; the Fifteenth Amendment guaranteed voting rights; and the Fourteenth Amendment, the cornerstone of constitutional equality and nationalization of the Constitution, provided that no state shall "deny to any person within its jurisdiction the equal protection of the laws."

For all its obvious callousness, the Supreme Court opinion in *Plessy* v. *Ferguson* (1896) represents a shift in the basis for evaluating the segregated institutions being erected in the South. The old standard had been the commerce clause. The new standard would be the constitutional guaranty of equal protection. Building on the ambiguity in the Fourteenth Amendment, the justices cleverly accommodated constitutional equality in *Plessy* with the conventional perception of what it meant to be equal. The racist Jim Crow system was legitimated by a doctrinal construction designed to separate material conditions and political equality from social equality.

To understand the doctrine of separate but equal, it is useful to understand this distinction between a political, a social, and a material basis for comparison. Material equality applies to such things as shelter, transportation, and food. The segregated rail cars in *Plessy* would be materially equal in at least one sense if they got to their destination at the same time as the cars reserved for whites. Social equality refers to how people are treated and is evident in the value they place on such treatment. Some cultures have made social distinctions between the front and back seats of a bus, although there may be little material difference between them. Political equality refers to equality in the area of citizenship, such as the right to vote or hold public office. This equality is "distant" from basic needs, but it cannot exist independently of material and social considerations.

The *Plessy* opinion acknowledged the need to protect political equality, but it distinguished between the rights of citizenship and separation of the races in schools, theaters, and other public places. The majority saw nothing fundamentally "unequal" about material separation and proposed that the attitudes that made separation offensive were social and beyond the reach of the law. The concession to those being segregated was a guarantee of material or physical equality. The law separated the races in railroad cars, but because the Constitution required that the cars be "equal," the separation was not considered discriminatory. Equal, in this sense, would have to mean the same conditions of transportation.

Modern Equality. The legal politics of equal protection at the constitutional level began to ferment thirty years after the *Plessy* decision. The focus was on a new reading of equality to wipe out the doctrine of separate but equal. Led by the NAACP Legal Defense Fund, the litigation strategy employed the promise of material equality to make it so costly to maintain segregation that the South would give it up. The plan was known as the Margold strategy, after its proponent, Nathan Margold, a lawyer for the

NAACP. The first success attributable to this claim came in *Missouri ex rel. Gaines* v. *Canada* (1938), where Missouri was ordered to admit a black law student to its law school or to create a new one. It was not enough, according to the Court, to simply pay Lloyd Gaines's tuition at another state's law school, since this would not provide him with an equal education in Missouri. This initial success was based on the failure of institutions in the South to live up to the promise of equality in *Plessy,* rather than on the evil of separation per se.

The authoritative source of modern constitutional equality, *Brown* v. *Board of Education,* eliminated "separation" from constitutional protection in 1954. After the decision, attention shifted from the refusal to see separation as a violation, to a view of separation as the primary violation of constitutional equality. The consequence was a view of equal protection that no longer included material equality.

Since *Brown,* constitutional equal protection has been expanded beyond race to sex and some other classifications. Where it has been employed, the doctrine checks certain statutory classifications when important interests are affected. The result is a level of "scrutiny" or prejudice against such distinctions. Economic hardship, indigence, and the ability to pay have been peripheral under this rubric. Although American society would not function the way it does without distinctions based on wealth, these distinctions bring back the issue of material deprivation.

Political Equality. Under the Constitution a person cannot be absolutely deprived of political rights. These rights, generally associated with citizenship, are grouped around participation, including the right to vote and to run for office, and criminal procedure. In the case of political participation, for instance, the fact that people were being deprived of the right to vote on the basis of ability to pay led to the abolition of the poll tax, first by the Twenty-fourth Amendment at the national level and then in the states (*Harper* v. *Virginia State Board,* 1966). Similarly, in *Bullock* v. *Carter* (1972), the Supreme Court held a Texas practice of supporting primary elections through candidate filing fees to be unconstitutional. This area is fairly well settled, and relatively few equal-protection cases arise.

A more extensively litigated aspect of political equality involves the criminal process. The first holdings came soon after *Brown* and were followed throughout the due process revolution by instances in which people were deprived of criminal due process rights because of some form of discrimination. Since the 1930s, the necessity of avoiding capital punishment has been of sufficient interest to call for provision of counsel. But it was not until *Gideon,* in 1963, that the states were required to provide a lawyer when the possible punishment was less severe. Although the *Gideon* decision was based on the Sixth Amendment, it reflected the idea of fairness in the Fourteenth.

The appeal, although more costly than the trial, is considered discretionary. Consequently, the courts have not been clear about equal protection here. At the very least, appellants have the right to be provided with a transcript from their trial (*Griffin* v. *Illinois,* 1956). After that, what is available depends on how compelling a claim can be made.

Punishment has been problematic at least since such economically sensitive sanctions as fines have been employed. But there is a more generic bias to modern punishment, since middle-class and higher-status convicts may have the humiliation of punishment deducted from their sentences. In 1982, Danny Bearden took the state of Georgia to the Supreme Court when he was sent to prison after he had failed to pay a fine. Justice O'Connor made it clear that a defendant cannot be sent to jail for lack of funds. She wrote that when the trial court automatically revoked Bearden's probation, it did not exercise adequate care and violated his constitutional rights (*Bearden* v. *Georgia*).

Equality has also been a factor in civil proceedings. Until 1971, Connecticut required a fee to file for divorce. People without funds contested this infringement in the Supreme Court and the state was forced to stop this practice (*Boddie* v. *Connecticut*). Counsel has been provided by the Maryland Court of Appeals where an indigent defendant was subject to incarceration in a civil contempt proceeding. Courts have sometimes ordered payment of witness fees in civil cases, but provision of counsel as a matter of right has been rare. Concern about sex discrimination has had an impact here, especially in the states. Maryland prohibited such discrimination in child-support cases (*Rand* v. *Rand,* 1976) under its equal rights amendment, and New Hampshire extended the protection of its ERA to alimony in 1980 *(Buckner* v. *Buckner)*. Given the failure of the national ERA, it is not a surprise that there has been a lot of state action in that area.

Social Equality. The modern period of constitutional equality began with a turn toward the issue of discrimination in social life, and equal rights for racial minorities and for women continue to concern American courts, particularly in the states. Although less forcefully than in the political sphere, economic conditions have played a role here, particularly in terms of commitments to social programs such as those for education and medical care.

In *San Antonio Independent School District* v. *Rodriguez* (1973), the issue was whether children were being deprived because the public school system was funded by a tax on property that reflected the wealth of the community. Although the state of Texas, like most states, tried to "equalize" the disparities between districts by spreading part of its support according to need, the claimants in San Antonio, Texas, argued that the barrio in which they lived was unable to provide the same level of education as the wealthier, largely Anglo suburbs. Because distinctions based on wealth had been mitigated by the state and no one was absolutely deprived of an education, the property-tax basis for financing survived the challenge in 1973. A decade after *Rodriguez,* a decision struck down a Texas statute denying funding to schools that enrolled undocumented alien children *(Plyler* v. *Doe,* 1982).

Health insurance and public services have raised some compelling equal protection challenges. In *Maher* v. *Roe* (1977) the Court held that a state's decision not to pay for abortions, even though it paid for childbirth, did not violate the Constitution. The district court had ruled that the presence of a fundamental right to an abortion required strict scrutiny of the distinction between abortion and childbirth. The constitutional protection for abortion brought the case to the Court's attention. Justice Lewis F. Powell, writing for the majority, held that the lower court had "misconceived the nature and scope of the fundamental right recognized in *Roe*" and that past decisions do not indicate "that financial need alone identifies a suspect class for purposes of equal protection analysis."

He found no "restriction on access to abortions that was not already there." The holding was extended in *Harris* v. *McRae* (1980), a similar public-assistance case where the justices reasoned that the liberty in *Roe* includes the freedom of a woman to decide whether to terminate a pregnancy but not a public obligation to make the choice a reality.

An important development linked to social equality is the controversy over comparable pay for men and women who do comparable work. The issue has been described as one of wage discrimination or "comparable worth." As a matter of equal protection, this issue is associated with sex discrimination. Although it involves "wealth," the courts' concern is governed by sex discrimination. In 1983 the Supreme Court encouraged advocates of comparable worth when it ruled that claims of sex-based discrimination in wages not covered by the Equal Pay Act of 1963, with its formula of "equal pay for equal work," could be brought under Title VII of the Civil Rights Act of 1964 *(County of Washington* v. *Gunther,* 1981).

Material Equality. Few cases in the appellate courts are in this category, but *Warth* v. *Seldin* (1975) comes close. Warth claimed that Penn-field, a suburb of Rochester, New York, had adopted a zoning ordinance that made it "economically impossible" to construct "sufficient numbers of low and moderate income" houses. Although racial exclusion was also alleged, the issue primarily concerned discrimination against low-income people. In what Tribe called a "harsh and bizarre" result, Warth lost his case. Other litigation concerning material deprivation has involved utilities threatening to terminate service *(Memphis Light, Gas and Water Division* v. *Craft,* 1978) and repossession of goods for nonpayment of a loan *(Flagg Brothers, Inc.* v. *Brooks,* 1978). These cases are linked to doctrines of due process and protection for entitlements that have existed since *Goldberg,* but constitutional protection stemming directly from material deprivation has been unusual.

In the area of constitutional equality, as in other civil liberties, judges and justices have been generally sympathetic since 1937, and on occasion they have been significant advocates. For most of the period the federal courts have taken the lead in expanding civil liberties protection, although the state courts began to come to

227

the fore in the 1980s. Perhaps the most important conclusion to be drawn from the history of these rights is that while each new right creates interests on either side, the existence of fundamental rights and liberties in the Constitution gives a decided advantage to those who would preserve or even extend them.

CASES

Amalgamated Food Employees v. Logan Valley Plaza, 391 U.S. 308 (1968)

Barefoot v. Estelle, 463 U.S. 880 (1983)

Barker v. Wingo, 407 U.S. 514 (1972)

Bearden v. Georgia, 461 U.S. 660 (1983)

Betts v. Brady, 316 U.S. 455 (1942)

Board of Curators of the University of Missouri v. Horowitz, 435 U.S. 78 (1978)

Board of Education, Island Trees Union School District No. 26 v. Pico, 457 U.S. 853 (1982)

Board of Regents of State Colleges v. Roth, 408 U.S. 564 (1972)

Boddie v. Connecticut, 401 U.S. 371 (1971)

Brown v. Board of Education, 347 U.S. 483 (1954)

Buckner v. Buckner, 120 N.H. 402, 415 A.2d 871 (1980)

Bullock v. Carter, 405 U.S. 134 (1972)

Burch v. Louisiana, 441 U.S. 130 (1979)

Cafeteria and Restaurant Workers Union v. McElroy, 367 U.S. 886 (1961)

Chandler v. Florida, 449 U.S. 560 (1981)

Chaplinsky v. New Hampshire, 315 U.S. 568 (1942)

County of Washington v. Gunther, 452 U.S. 161 (1981)

De Jonge v. Oregon, 299 U.S. 353 (1937)

Dennis v. United States, 341 U.S. 494 (1951)

Edwards v. Arizona, 314 U.S. 160 (1981)

Everson v. Board of Education, 330 U.S. 1 (1947)

Fidelity and Deposit Co. of Maryland v. Arenz, 290 U.S. 66 (1933)

Flagg Brothers, Inc. v. Brooks, 436 U.S. 149 (1978)

Flemming v. Nestor, 363 U.S. 603 (1960)

Fletcher v. Peck, 6 Cranch 87 (1810)

Gaylord v. Tacoma School District No. 10, 88 Wash. 2d 286, 559 P.2d 1340 (1977)

Gideon v. Wainwright, 372 U.S. 335 (1963)

Goldberg v. Kelly, 397 U.S. 335 (1970)

Goss v. Lopez, 419 U.S. 565 (1975)

Gregg v. Georgia, 428 U.S. 153 (1976)

Griffin v. Illinois, 351 U.S. 12 (1956)

Hague v. Committee on Industrial Organization, 307 U.S. 496 (1939)

Harper v. Virginia State Board, 383 U.S. 663 (1966)

Harris v. McRae, 448 U.S. 297 (1980)

Hawaii Housing Authority v. Midkiff, 467 U.S. 229 (1984)

Joint Anti-Fascist Refugee Committee v. McGrath, 341 U.S. 123 (1951)

Katz v. United States, 389 U.S. 347 (1967)

Klopfer v. North Carolina, 386 U.S. 213 (1967)

Kolender v. Lawson, 461 U.S. 352 (1983)

Logan v. Zimmerman Brush Co., 455 U.S. 422 (1982)

Loretto v. Teleprompter Manhattan CATV Corp., 458 U.S. 419 (1982)

Louisiana ex rel. Francis v. Resweber, 329 U.S. 459 (1947)

Lynch v. Household Finance Corp., 405 U.S. 538 (1972)

McAuliffe v. City of New Bedford, 155 Mass. 216 29 N.E. 517 (1892)

Maher v. Roe, 432 U.S. 464 (1977)

Mapp v. Ohio, 367 U.S. 643 (1961)

Marbury v. Madison, 1 Cranch 137 (1803)

Mathews v. Eldridge, 424 U.S. 319 (1976)

Maxwell v. Superior Court, 30 Cal. 3d. 705, 639 P.2d 248, 180 Cal. Rptr. 177 (1982)

Memphis Light, Gas and Water Division v. Craft, 436 U.S. 1 (1978)

Miller v. California, 413 U.S. 15 (1973)

Miranda v. Arizona, 384 U.S. 436 (1966)

Missouri ex rel. Gaines v. Canada, 305 U.S. 337 (1938)

Mueller v. Allen, 463 U.S. 388 (1983)

Near v. Minnesota, 283 U.S. 697 (1931)

New York Times v. United States, 403 U.S. 713 (1971)

New York Times Co. v. Sullivan, 376 U.S. 254 (1964)

Olmstead v. United States, 277 U.S. 438 (1928)

Palko v. Connecticut, 302 U.S. 319 (1937)

Paris Adult Theatre I v. Slaton, 413 U.S. 49 (1973)

Penn Central Transportation Co. v. New York, 438 U.S. 104 (1978)

People v. Cooper, 398 Mich. 450, 247 N.W.2d 866 (1976)

Plessy v. Ferguson, 163 U.S. 537 (1896)

Plyler v. Doe, 457 U.S. 202 (1982)

Powell v. Alabama, 287 U.S. 45 (1932)

PruneYard Shopping Center v. Robins, 447 U.S. 74 (1980)

Rand v. Rand, 33 Md. App. 527, 365 A.2d 586 (1976)

Roe v. Wade, 410 U.S. 113 (1973)

Roth v. United States, 354 U.S. 476 (1957)

San Antonio Independent School District v. Rodriguez, 411 U.S. 1 (1973)

Snepp v. United States, 444 U.S. 507 (1980)

Solem v. Helm, 436 U.S. 277 (1983)

State v. Ringer, 52 100 Wash. 2d 686, 674 P.2d 1240 (1983)

Tinker v. Des Moines Independent Community School District, 393 U.S. 503 (1969)

Tollett v. Henderson, 411 U.S. 258 (1973)

United States v. Carolene Products Co., 304 U.S. 144 (1938)

United States v. Ross, 456 U.S. 798 (1982)

United States v. Seeger, 380 U.S. 163 (1965)

United States v. Spock, 416 F.2d 165 (1st.Cir. 1969)

United States v. Willow River Power Co., 324 U.S. 499 (1945)

Warth v. Seldin, 422 U.S. 490 (1975)

Watt v. Community for Creative Non-Violence, 703 F.2d 586 (D.C.Cir 1983), cert. granted, 464 U.S. 812, rev'd sub nom. Clark v. Community for Creative Non-Violence, 104 S. Ct. 3065 (1984)

West Virginia State Board of Education v. Barnette, 319 U.S. 624 (1943)

Williams v. Florida, 399 U.S. 78 (1970)

BIBLIOGRAPHY

Henry J. Abraham, *Freedom and the Court: Civil Rights and Liberties in the United States* (1982), is one of the standard references since the late 1950s. Bruce A. Ackerman, *Private Property and the Constitution* (1977), presents with great sophistication a modern treatise on constitutional protection for property. John Brigham, *Civil Liberties and American Democracy* (1984), examines this body of constitutional law by pushing beyond the dominant political view to a treatment of law as ideology.

Henry Steele Commager, "Keynote Statement," in Stephen C. Halpern, ed., *The Future of Our Liberties* (1982), discusses the place of equality in the constitutional tradition. John R. Commons, *The Legal Foundations of Capitalism* (1924), approaches the law from the perspective of institutional economics. Norman Dorsen, ed., *Our Endangered Rights* (1984), reports on the American Civil Liberties Union.

Sheldon Goldman, *Constitutional Law and Supreme Court Decision Making* (1982), combines history, behavioral science, and doctrinal analysis in a very valuable collection of information on the Constitution. Gerald Gunther, *Cases and Materials on Constitutional Law* (1980), is a lawyer's casebook. Gerald L. Houseman, *The Right of Mobility* (1979), treats emerging rights through a focus on issues associated with a right to travel.

Peter Irons, *Justice at War* (1983), examines Japanese-Americans as a challenge to constitutional principles in World War II. Richard Kluger, *Simple Justice* (1976), gives a monumental account of the various litigation struggles to overturn segregation as waged by the NAACP and its legal arm. Anthony Lewis, *Gideon's Trumpet* (1964), epitomizes the hope and spirit of the due process revolution that took place in the 1960s with a metaphoric portrayal of access to the Supreme Court.

Catharine A. MacKinnon, *Sexual Harassment of Working Women* (1979), presents an influential argument for treating sexual harassment as an aspect of sex discrimination. Alexander Meiklejohn, *Free Speech and Its Relation to Self-Government* (1948), philosophizes on free expression. Paul Murphy, *World War I and the Origin of Civil Liberties in the United States* (1979), is the best historical discussion of how constitutional ideas come into vogue.

C. Herman Pritchett, *The Roosevelt Court* (1948), is the first and probably still the best study of the relationship between political orientation and doctrinal developments on the Supreme Court. Charles A. Reich, "The New Property," in *Yale Law Journal*, 73 (1964), articulates a framework for constitutional property rights, with an impact few law review articles have had.

Mark Silverstein, *Constitutional Faiths: Felix Frankfurter, Hugo Black, and the Process of Judicial Decision Making* (1984), is one of the good biographies linking civil liberties to the lives of the justices through their commitment to an institutional role. Laurence H. Tribe, *American Constitutional Law* (1978), presents an illuminating interpretation of the Constitution employing different models to investigate its structure. Robert Paul Wolff, *A Critique of Pure Tolerance* (1968), offers a philosophical investigation of tolerance by Wolff, Herbert Marcuse, and Barrington Moore that explains the modern idea of free expression.

[*See also* BURGER COURT AND ERA; CIVIL LIBERTIES TO 1937; CONSTITUTIONAL INTERPRETATION; COURTS AND CONSTITUTIONALISM; CRIMINAL PROCEDURE; DUE PROCESS OF LAW; EQUAL PROTECTION CLAUSE; RACIAL DISCRIMINATION AND EQUAL OPPORTUNITY; SEX EQUALITY UNDER THE CONSTITUTION; STATE CONSTITUTIONAL LAW; SUPREME COURT OF THE UNITED STATES; *and* WARREN COURT AND ERA.]

Part II
SUBSTANTIVE
LAW

ADMINISTRATIVE LAW

Michael J. Glennon

ADMINISTRATIVE law is the body of law governing the activities of administrative agencies. It thus encompasses virtually every entity of government other than legislatures and courts. This essay deals with federal administrative law, although similar principles apply in most states.

Fundamental to nearly every aspect of administrative law is the rationale underlying the creation of administrative agencies. One reason they exist lies in a changed conception of the role of government. Citizens have come to expect governmental protection from unscrupulous business practices, unrestrained competition, environmental degradation, and unsafe working conditions. Administrative agencies are thought to perform such functions more effectively than either legislatures or courts. They are capable of achieving greater expertise than are legislatures, and are thus more adept at addressing certain kinds of complex issues. They are capable of greater flexibility in resolving disputes than are courts, and are thus able to save litigants time and money.

As a consequence administrative agencies typically engage in two kinds of activities: rule making and adjudication. To distinguish these activities from those performed by the legislative and judicial branches, agency rule making is considered a "quasi-legislative" function and agency adjudication is considered a "quasi-judicial" function. In reality, the substance of an agency's activities may differ very little from that of the legislative and judicial branches.

It is not necessarily true that a particular agency or particular agency action will serve the objective of efficiency. Congress surely has the expertise to have enacted as laws some rules promulgated by administrative agencies; the temptation is ever present to authorize agencies to promulgate rules that will resolve controversial issues that legislators feel it politically wise to avoid. Conversely, where the scope of an agency's authority is unclear, agency officials may seek to aggrandize the agency's power by regulating matters not clearly within its statutory authority. And while the procedure that governs agency dispute resolution may be less formal than that governing the courts, because the procedural safeguards are less rigorous, the result may be less fair. Administrative agencies may therefore offer theoretical advantages that do not always accrue in actual practice or that are offset by other problems that would not arise through strict adherence to legislative or judicial processes.

ADMINISTRATIVE OFFICIALS

Can Congress appoint administrative officials? The Constitution provides, in Article II, Section 2, that the president "shall nominate, and by and with the advice and consent of the Senate, shall appoint . . . all other Officers of the United States . . . but the Congress may by law vest the appointment of such other inferior Officers, as they think proper, in the President alone, in the Courts of Law, or in the Heads of Departments." In *Buckley* v. *Valeo* (1976), the Supreme Court considered the application of this provision to congressional appointments. Congress had provided by law that of the eight members of the Federal Election Commission, two were to be appointed by the president pro tempore of the Senate, and two by the Speaker of the House; two additional congressional officials, the secretary of the Senate and the clerk of the House of Representatives, were to be made ex officio members of the commission; and the remaining two were to be named by the executive. Because the commission exercised administrative and enforcement powers, the Supreme Court held this appointment scheme impermissible. Congress, the Court said, cannot have it both ways: if administrative officials are to exercise such powers, they must be appointed by the president; if they are appointed by Congress, administrative and enforcement functions may not constitutionally be conferred upon them.

Although the Constitution contains no provision expressly governing the process of removing administrative officials, the Court has viewed it as an incident of the appointment power and has accordingly construed broadly the scope of the chief executive's authority to remove administrative officials. In *Myers* v. *United States* (1926), the Court struck down a statute requiring congressional approval as a condition for the removal of a postmaster. The availability of removal as a "disciplinary influence," the Court said, was vital to the proper performance of the president's responsibility to take care that the laws be faithfully executed.

Nine years later, however, the Court read *Myers* narrowly in *Humphrey's Executor* v. *United States* (1935) and held invalid the president's removal of a member of the Federal Trade Commission (FTC). The postmaster in *Myers,* the Court said, was a purely executive official, whereas the FTC member exercised quasi-legislative and quasi-judicial functions. In *Humphrey's Executor,* removal was prohibited by statute in the absence of "inefficiency, neglect of duty, or malfeasance," but the Court appeared to conclude in *Wiener* v. *United States* (1958) that even without such language, presidential removal would be invalid if the official in question exercised quasi-legislative or quasi-judicial functions.

gated by Congress to another entity. The doctrine seeks to ensure that important decisions on matters of public policy are made by Congress. Early statements of the doctrine suggested that no delegation of legislative power was permissible. As the role of government in society expanded, however, it became apparent that such strict proscription of delegation was impractical, and the Court in the early New Deal era moved to a more moderate version of the doctrine. Yet even under the less rigorous version the Court invalidated two key pieces of legislation in 1935. It did so, it said, because one statute failed to indicate with sufficient specificity precisely what power was delegated to administrative officials *(Schechter Poultry Corp.* v. *United States)* and because another failed to specify the circumstances under which the exercise of statutorily conferred power was permissible *(Panama Refining Co.* v. *A. D. Ryan).* In subsequent cases the Court paid lipservice to the doctrine, but it declined to apply even this more moderate version, causing some commentators to conclude that the doctrine is a legal dinosaur. It has admittedly been more than fifty years since the doctrine was employed to invalidate a statute. Recently, however, the Court construed narrowly the statutory authority conferred upon administrative officials, citing the earlier delegation cases as its authority. It should thus not come as a complete surprise if the delegation doctrine is one day resurrected; resuscitation has been recommended by both liberal and conservative jurists and commentators. The vexing question is whether in light of the vast number of federal statutes arguably vulnerable to a delegation challenge, any version of the delegation doctrine could be applied in a principled fashion without regard to the substance of the legislative authority delegated.

THE DELEGATION DOCTRINE: LEGISLATIVE POWER

The "delegation doctrine," or, as it is sometimes called, the "nondelegation doctrine," is in reality a corollary of the doctrine of separation of powers, which requires that legislative functions be performed by Congress, judicial functions by the courts, and executive functions by the president. The delegation doctrine is addressed to situations in which legislative power (the power to affect private rights and obligations) is dele-

LEGISLATIVE VETO

During the administration of Herbert Hoover, Congress, working with the executive, devised a unique mechanism for governmental reorganization. The device allowed the president to propose changes in the structure of government subject to the possibility of legislative disapproval. As the mechanism evolved, it developed two principal variables: whether Congress would act by approval or disapproval, and whether one or both Houses would so act. Because the president did not participate in the process after his initial proposal—that is, because he did not have the opportunity either to sign or veto the subsequent action of Congress—the device became known as the "legislative veto."

By 1983, some 270 provisions of federal law contained legislative vetoes, including some of the most important federal statutes, such as the War Powers Resolution of 1973, the Congressional Budget and Impoundment Control Act of 1974, and the Trade Act of 1974. The legislative veto represented one of the central methods used by Congress to control administrative agencies. Nonetheless, every president since Hoover had objected to the constitutionality of the legislative veto on the grounds that it violated the "presentment clause" of the Constitution, which was argued to require presentment of a measure to the president for his veto or signature before it has the force of law. Members of Congress argued that the legislative veto was constitutional because the legislation containing the device had been presented to the president.

The argument was not persuasive to the Supreme Court, which in 1983 struck down the device in *Immigration and Naturalization Service* v. *Chadha*. In that case, the Court by implication invalidated more provisions of federal law than had been struck down during the entire history of the Republic. Yet the ramifications of the decision remain unclear. Some commentators have suggested that it will compel Congress simply to write more detailed legislation. To do so, however, could in many instances require overriding a presidential veto, quite possibly by a president far more capable of sustaining the veto than were his predecessors. In addition to more detailed legislation, a number of more technical devices are available if Congress is genuinely interested in restoring the balance of legislative-executive power to the pre-*Chadha* state. Whether Congress will muster the political will to do so is another question.

DELEGATION OF JUDICIAL POWER

As noted earlier, the delegation doctrine, strictly speaking, applies only to the delegation of legislative power to administrative agencies. Similar questions arise with respect to the exercise of judicial power by administrative agencies: for example, could Congress, by statute, take

cases traditionally decided by the courts and assign them to administrative agencies to decide? This question is complicated by the Seventh Amendment guaranty of a right to jury trial in all suits at common law. In *Crowell* v. *Benson* (1932), the Court answered the question in the affirmative, holding that workmen's compensation disputes could be statutorily assigned to an administrative agency for adjudication. The Court did not, however, found its decision on the inapplicability of the Seventh Amendment; rather than holding, as it might have, that workmen's compensation awards were new, statutorily created entitlements not available in suits at common law, the Court arrived at its conclusion after an examination of the principles of separation of powers. In 1977, the Court complicated matters in *Atlas Roofing Co.* v. *Occupational Safety and Health Review Commission* by holding that Congress may create a new statutory cause of action in favor of the government and enforceable in an administrative agency without violating the Seventh Amendment right to a jury trial. The statute in question, the Court reasoned, created a public right, as distinguished from private rights such as tort, contract, and property actions. Although this distinction seems inconsistent with the broader holding of *Crowell* that even questions concerning private rights may be adjudicated by administrative agencies, it is difficult to believe that the Court intended to overturn all statutorily created procedures for the adjudication of private rights by administrative agencies.

The Sixth Amendment guaranty of a jury trial in criminal cases is similarly relevant. Minor offenses such as traffic violations can constitutionally be assigned to administrative agencies for disposition, provided the defendant is not subject to the imposition of a sentence of incarceration in excess of six months. (It is at that point, the Supreme Court has held, that the Sixth Amendment's jury trial guaranty applies.) It is thus clear that an administrative agency could not try a criminal case in which the penalty was greater than six months' imprisonment.

INSPECTIONS AND INFORMATION

Administrative action, whether by rule or adjudication, can be no more reliable than the information upon which it is based. The objective of efficiency is thus undercut to the extent that needed information is denied. Yet efficiency cannot be sought at the expense of discarding another important, countervailing value: procedural fairness. With respect to administrative investigations, the concept of fairness is reflected largely in the rights guaranteed by the Fourth and Fifth Amendments.

The Fifth Amendment privilege against self-incrimination comes into play when a person is asked to turn over records that may serve as evidence against him or her for the imposition of a criminal penalty. Given the pervasiveness of record-keeping requirements in federal law and consistent opinions of the Supreme Court upholding the power of federal agencies to require record keeping and reports, the question arises whether such records are protected by the privilege against self-incrimination. In *Shapiro* v. *United States* (1948), the Supreme Court reiterated the so-called public records exception to the Fifth Amendment: "The privilege which exists as to private papers cannot be maintained in relation to 'records required by law to be kept in order that there may be suitable information of transactions which are the appropriate subjects of governmental regulation and the enforcement of restrictions validly established.' " There must, the Court said, simply be a sufficient relation between the activity sought to be regulated and the public concern. Twenty years later, however, in *Marchetti* v. *United States* (1968), the public records exception was narrowed. The Court there suggested that the exception would not apply unless the defendant is obliged to keep and preserve the records in question, unless there are "public aspects" to the records, and unless the requirements are imposed in "an essentially non-criminal and regulatory area of inquiry."

With respect to Fourth Amendment defenses, it is clear that the prohibition against warrantless searches and seizures applies to those conducted by administrative agencies. To require that the traditional probable-cause standard be fulfilled, however, would obviously preclude spot-check inspections of regulated industries not reasonably suspected of violating the law. The Court's solution has been twofold. First, a lesser level of probable cause is required in administrative inspection cases; generally, a showing that the business selected for inspection was selected on the basis of a general enforcement plan is all that is necessary to meet probable-cause require-

ments. Second, pursuant to the Court's traditional doctrine that the Fourth Amendment does not apply where there exists no reasonable expectation of privacy, the Court has held that no warrant requirement attaches where the business has been the subject of long-standing regulation or where it is under the jurisdiction of an administrative agency with pervasive regulatory authority (including licensing power) over it. The firearms, liquor, and mining industries are classic examples.

Although the Fourth Amendment has not been held applicable with respect to subpoenas issued by administrative agencies, requirements of specificity similar to those prescribed by the Fourth Amendment for search warrants were earlier held applicable to administrative subpoenas. In *Federal Trade Commission* v. *American Tobacco Co.* (1924) the Court declined to order enforcement of a subpoena for all business records, because its breadth made compliance unduly burdensome. Later, however, in *Endicott Johnson Corp.* v. *Perkins* (1943), the Court declined to allow lack of jurisdiction to be set up as a defense in an agency enforcement proceeding. The subpoena in question was alleged by the defendant to seek documents relative to activities beyond the scope of the agency's regulatory power. The Court, however, sustained the subpoena as relative to a lawful purpose. Notwithstanding the obvious possibility for administrative harassment, mere breadth or generality is therefore not a valid defense in response to an agency's subpoena.

RULES AND ORDERS

As noted earlier, administrative agencies engage in two kinds of activities—quasi-judicial and quasi-legislative. When an agency functions as a court, the label normally appended to its act is "order." When it performs the function of a legislature, its act normally is called a "rule." The distinction is important because the function the agency performs dictates the procedure it is required to follow. When it issues an order, formal, triallike procedures are required under the federal Administrative Procedure Act. When it issues a rule, on the other hand, although formal, triallike procedures might still be followed, a much more informal procedure is permissible. If the agency makes a rule informally, only three procedural requirements must be met: the agency must give notice that it is considering the adoption of a certain rule; it must give interested persons an opportunity to comment through the submission of written arguments, views, or data; and, if it decides to issue the rule, it must set forth a concise statement of the rule's basis and purpose.

Because an administrative agency is a creature of the legislature, it cannot engage in substantive rule making, whether formal or informal, without statutory authorization. That authority may be implicit; the grant of rule-making power need not be expressly spelled out in the enabling legislation. Agencies traditionally exercise broader latitude when it comes to promulgating housekeeping, interpretative, or procedural rules. The notion of "inherent" authority to promulgate substantive rules—those affecting individual rights and obligations—would fly in the face of the concept of delegated powers.

One reason that the courts have insisted upon express or implied authorization to issue rules is that a rule has the force and effect of a statute. Violation can result in civil or criminal liability. For reasons that are not entirely clear, the Supreme Court has not required administrative agencies to follow their own rules, at least where those rules are not required by the Constitution or by law. Similarly, even though agency action beyond its lawful power results in detrimental reliance by a private party, the agency may deny its authority in an action against it by that party. For example, a woman who had been erroneously told by an official of the Social Security Administration that she was ineligible for certain benefits and who as a consequence failed to file a timely application could not, in an action against the agency, plead reliance upon its erroneous representation. The rationale is that because any agency's rules have the force and effect of law and because a person is held responsible for knowing the law, persons who deal with an agency are responsible for knowing its rules—provided they are published in the Federal Register.

As noted earlier, the Administrative Procedure Act provides for two kinds of rule making, formal and informal. Agencies have been accorded wide latitude in selecting between the two, and they have generally preferred the more flexible, informal approach—an approach seemingly favored by the Supreme Court as well. The Court has held that the federal judiciary may not impose procedural requirements on agency rule making beyond those imposed by statute. In *United States* v. *Florida East Coast Railway* (1973), although the statute allowed promulgation of the rule only "after hearing," the Court held that this provision did not require formal rule-making procedures; use of the words "on the record"—the verbatim language of the act—are necessary to trigger the requirement of formal rule making (which includes a trial-type hearing). Various forms of "hybrid" procedures do exist, but these are provided explicitly by statute in enabling legislation referring expressly to certain agencies (for instance, the Food, Drug, and Cosmetic Act of 1938), and in the absence of such a statutory directive, agencies retain the discretion to choose between the formal and informal rule-making processes.

Not surprisingly, therefore, the courts also have accorded administrative agencies broad discretion to choose whether to act by rule or by order. The procedural requirements that the agency must observe will depend on how it chooses to act. This issue of interchangeability takes two forms. First, an agency may set a new policy in an adjudicatory proceeding, as can courts. Because of the apparent unfairness involved in basing liability on a previously unannounced rule, some have charged that agencies should be permitted to make new policy only by rule. The courts have rejected this argument. Even though it is able to promulgate a new principle in advance through the rule-making power, an agency is not precluded from announcing that new principle in an order. Courts, the rationale goes, do it all the time, and an agency exercising quasi-judicial authority ought not be precluded from doing it. The argument has some merit, but it must be noted that courts have no quasi-legislative authority pursuant to which informed views might be solicited and notice given in advance of a change of the law. Even though the Administrative Procedure Act's requirements for notice-and-comment rule making have not been fulfilled, an agency may announce a new principle in an adjudicatory decision and thereby overturn long-standing precedent. A new principle first promulgated in this manner will be binding only if it is applied in that particular case.

Second, the courts have said that an agency is required to issue a rule even where issuance of a rule would affect individual rights or obligations of a sort normally decided upon in an adjudicatory proceeding. A rule may affect individual rights and obligations in much the same way as an order. Even though the law required an adjudicatory hearing prior to the revocation of certain pilot licenses, for example, the Federal Aviation Administration was nonetheless permitted to issue a rule resulting in ineligibility for a significant number of licensed pilots.

AVAILABILITY OF JUDICIAL REVIEW OF AGENCY ACTION

Agency officials, no less than legislative or executive officials, are subject to the rule of law. Indeed, their power is conferred by law; in the absence of enabling legislation, they would be without authority to carry out their duties, and the scope of an agency's authority can extend only to those activities that Congress has by statute permitted it to perform. It would make little sense to hold that the limits of an agency's authority may be set by Congress but that an agency is immune from judicially imposed checks when it exceeds those limits. Few principles are more fundamental to Anglo-Saxon jurisprudence than the principle that a recipient of power may not define the scope of his power. Similarly, even though an agency acts within its charter, a particular action may be so infected with procedural irregularity that the fairness of the outcome is tainted. For reasons such as these, agency action has consistently been subject to judicial review.

This is not to say that every agency action is subject to the same scrutiny by the judiciary. The courts have developed a number of doctrines aimed at upholding the rule of law without undermining the reasons for establishing administrative agencies. To subject every agency action to judicial review when initiated by any plaintiff, however far removed from the effects of that action, would obviously result in a tremendous duplication of efforts and increased cost and delay to all involved. A substantial body of law has thus arisen concerning the availability of judicial review.

To a large extent (indeed, some argue, to a complete extent), the availability of judicial review is dictated by Congress. The agency action that is reviewable, the court in which it must be reviewed, the form in which review must take place, available remedies as well as time limits—all may be controlled by Congress. If Congress provides for judicial review, review is available solely pursuant to the pertinent statutory terms, which must be followed exactly. If Congress is silent concerning the availability of review, the courts will construe that silence as a legislative intent not to preclude judicial review and will rely upon remedies they themselves have developed.

The question whether review is available is more difficult where a statute directs that no review be available or where a statute is ambiguous but the legislative intent clearly indicates that no review be available. In such circumstances, the availability of review will depend upon whether the matter at issue is viewed as a privilege or as a preexisting right.

If the matter at issue is a privilege, the courts appear willing to give effect to statutes precluding review. Such statutes govern a variety of governmental benefit programs, such as those administered by the Veterans Administration. In such instances, the theory is that the privilege is in essence a gift; because the recipient has no preexisting right to such gratuities, he must take them subject to whatever condition (such as no judicial review) the government has attached. Where a preexisting right is involved, the courts strain to ignore statutory indications of an intent to preclude review and will avoid a literal reading of a statute that might otherwise be interpreted as denying the judiciary's role as final arbiter.

The power of Congress to immunize an agency action from judicial review is not free from doubt. In *Ortwein* v. *Schwab* (1973), the Supreme Court held that Oregon's $25 appellate court filing fee did not violate the due process clause of the Fourteenth Amendment. Some commentators believe that the Court did not directly address the question in that case, the Court's reasoning being that the mere imposition of a filing fee did not cut off appellate review altogether. The argument seems tenuous, however; whatever the measure of review that was available for other, more affluent litigants, the Court assumed that judicial review was not available for the litigant in *Ortwein* because of his financial status. Moreover, Justices William O. Douglas and Thurgood Marshall, in dissent, both argued that the majority held that Oregon could constitutionally commit to an administrative agency the unreviewable authority to restrict preexisting rights. Such a holding by the majority would seem incompatible with the duty of the courts to decide what the law is.

STANDING TO SUE

Even if review is available, the person seeking relief might not be the proper one to do so: he may lack standing to sue. The Court, in resolving this issue, has long focused on the extent of the injury suffered by the person seeking relief. The requirement of standing traces to the mandate of Article III that the judicial branch can act only on cases and controversies. A person who invokes the Court's authority must show, first, that "he personally has suffered some actual or threatened injury as a result of the putatively illegal conduct of the defendant" and, second, that the injury "fairly can be traced to the challenged action and is likely to be redressed by a favorable decision" (*Valley Forge Christian College* v. *Americans United for the Separation of Church and State*, 1982). Underlying these requirements is a concern that the Court not engage in the issuance of advisory opinions. Insistence upon the concrete factual context presented by parties who have suffered injury in fact, economic or otherwise, assures a setting, the Court has frequently argued, in which issues will not be decided in the abstract.

In *Valley Forge*, the Court held that the plaintiff lacked standing to claim that the gift by the government through the Department of Health, Education, and Welfare (HEW) of the hospital to a church-affiliated college violated the establishment clause. Justice William H. Rehnquist, writing for the majority, found that the plaintiff did not have standing. The complaint was directed not at "a congressional action, but a decision by HEW." The logic of *Valley Forge* is dubious, turning as it does upon the existence of an administrative middleman: Congress itself would clearly have been prohibited from doing what it authorized HEW to do. The case suggests that certain constitutional violations are immune from judicial scrutiny. Reasonable steps must surely be taken to reduce the judiciary's burgeoning case load, but it is not clear how *Valley Forge* can be reconciled with the responsibility of the courts to guard against constitutional violations.

RIPENESS

The requirement that an action be ripe for review flows from concerns similar to those which foster the requirement that the complainant have standing. Courts are strongly disinclined to become involved in resolving disputes that are still hypothetical or conjectural. The basic rationale of the ripeness doctrine, the Court has said, is "to prevent the courts, through avoidance of premature adjudication, from entangling themselves in abstract disagreements over administrative policies, and also to protect the agencies from judicial interference until an administrative decision has been formalized and its effects felt in a concrete way by the challenging parties" (*Abbott Laboratories* v. *Gardner*, 1967). Accordingly, in determining whether an issue is ripe, the Court focuses on two considerations: the fitness of the issues for judicial decision and the hardship to the parties of withholding court consideration.

Fitness of the issues for adjudication turns on whether the process of administrative decision-making has reached a stage where "judicial review will not disrupt the orderly process of adjudication and whether rights or obligations have been determined or legal consequences will flow from the agency action" (*Port of Boston Marine Terminal* v. *Rederiaktiebolaget Transatlantic*, 1970). Hardship to the parties that would result from judicial abstention was the reason that the Court declined to withhold consideration of the controversy in *Abbott Laboratories*, an action challenging certain labeling regulations promulgated by the commissioner of food and drugs on the ground that those regulations exceeded his statutory authority. Although no action had been taken to enforce the regulations, the Court found that Abbott Laboratories was nonetheless faced with an unacceptable dilemma: incur the costs of changing its promotional material and labeling or follow its past labeling policy and risk prosecution.

The formality of the agency action is not determinative of the ripeness issue. Internal agency communications and directives, interpretive rulings, policy statements, and even press releases all have been reviewed by the courts. These decisions show that the potential hardship or dilemma to the claimant that would result from delayed consideration of the agency action, rather than finality, is the primary consideration in the doctrine of ripeness.

PRIMARY JURISDICTION

Where both a court and an agency have initial jurisdiction to hear a case, should a court nevertheless insist that the plaintiff first seek relief from the administrative agency? The doctrine of primary jurisdiction deals with this issue. This doctrine requires that courts allow agencies the "first bite at the apple" if such judicial abstention would promote uniformity in the consideration of certain types of administration questions or would bring into play the expert and specialized knowledge of the administrative agency. Because the Court has believed that certain agencies are better equipped to handle, at least at the outset, particularly complicated factual questions more familiar to those agencies, it has held that such issues are within the agency's primary jurisdiction. The Court has required that claimant first go to an administrative tribunal for the resolution of such issues even if the tribunal cannot grant the claimant the relief he requests.

One notable case introduced doubts about the continuing vitality of the doctrine of primary jurisdiction. In *Nader* v. *Allegheny Airlines, Inc.* (1976), Allegheny overbooked Nader's flight and subsequently "bumped" him. Nader sued the airline, claiming that Allegheny's failure to disclose the overbooking practice was a fraudulent misrepresentation. Allegheny defended by arguing that primary jurisdiction lay in the Civil Aeronautics Board, which had the power to declare certain airline practices "deceptive." Because Nader was found to have retained a common-law action in fraud, the Court concluded that it was competent to decide the common-law question, so that no need for agency expertise existed. Nader was therefore allowed to proceed immediately to court.

It is unclear whether the *Nader* decision indicates that the Court is becoming disillusioned with the doctrine of primary jurisdiction because of the expense and time involved in its application or whether *Nader* represents a situation

where the doctrine does not apply at all. This uncertainty arises in part from the fact that the Court based its decision in *Nader* on what it believed Congress intended when it passed the Federal Aviation Act of 1958, rather than on a full discussion of the merits of the doctrine. The case-by-case determination that has characterized the application of the doctrine of primary jurisdiction will thus most likely persist.

EXHAUSTION OF ADMINISTRATIVE REMEDIES

The doctrine requiring exhaustion of administrative remedies is like the doctrine of primary jurisdiction in that it, too, is directed at precluding courts from impinging on the role of administrative agencies in resolving disputes. Unlike the doctrine of primary jurisdiction, however, the doctrine of exhaustion of remedies applies only where an agency has exclusive original jurisdiction to resolve the matter. The issue of exhaustion arises because the claimant who is affected by an agency action might want to go straight to court to get relief rather than to a higher authority within the agency itself. The exhaustion doctrine provides that in most situations, all administrative remedies must be exhausted before judicial relief can be sought. The rationale of the exhaustion requirement—the need to prevent premature judicial interference in agency decision-making—is one that on occasion gives way to stronger, countervailing interests. The exhaustion requirement has thus been held to be subject to a number of exceptions. It has not been held applicable where administrative remedies are inadequate; where undue delay has been encountered (by virtue, for example, of agency personnel shortages or burdensome case loads); where exhaustion of administrative remedies would be futile because the agency determination would almost surely be against the litigant; where the agency is biased to a level of threatening the litigant with a violation of due process rights; where the agency's action has a chilling effect on First Amendment rights; and where the statute in question is unconstitutional on its face (a situation in which the administrative process can contribute nothing, in contrast to a situation where a statute is allegedly unconstitutional as applied, for in the latter instance exhaustion is required so as to avoid causing the courts to decide an issue in a factual vacuum).

A difficult question is whether exhaustion should be required where the litigant claims that the agency has no jurisdiction over him or his business. The argument clearly can be made that causing the litigant to exhaust remedies in an agency that is without jurisdiction to hear the matter in question imposes an onerous burden: the litigant is compelled to spend time and money exhausting administrative procedures that are meaningless and that ultimately may be adjudicated void. Nonetheless, the Supreme Court has held that here, too, administrative remedies must be exhausted. The plaintiff in such circumstances, the Court reasoned, has not yet suffered any legal injury, and resort to the judiciary would disrupt the orderly process of administrative business. Moreover, whether the agency in question has jurisdiction often depends upon the facts of the case. Because an agency may have greater expertise with these factual questions than does a court, it may be desirable to have the agency act first, even if the agency is found in the end to lack jurisdiction. In this way, the courts get the benefit of the agency's superior ability to find the facts. Most states, however, have declined to require exhaustion where the jurisdiction of an agency is challenged.

FORMS OF REVIEW ACTION

There are several ways in which an individual might challenge the legality of an administrative agency's action. First, the individual might seek to set up the invalidity of the agency action in an enforcement proceeding. This is a legal proceeding in which an agency seeks to have its orders made legally binding by a court. Normally, the exhaustion requirement is enforced rigorously at such proceedings; even though an agency action may be alleged to fall beyond the scope of its authority, if Congress required that a jurisdictional challenge be made before the agency and it was not, lack of jurisdiction cannot be set up as a defense in a civil enforcement proceeding. Where administrative remedies have been exhausted, however, the courts will not enforce an agency order found to be beyond its jurisdiction. The exhaustion doctrine is applied less rigor-

ously in criminal enforcement proceedings, at least where no statutory provision governs review procedures. In *Estep* v. *United States* (1946), the defendant, indicted for draft evasion, was allowed to challenge the validity of the induction notice at his prosecution, even though he arguably could have raised the issue before the Selective Service Board. Where review is governed by an applicable statute, however, and a specific adequate administrative remedy is provided, failure to exhaust that remedy might preclude invocation of the invalidity of the agency proceeding as a defense even in a criminal enforcement proceeding.

Second, rather than waiting until the agency seeks judicial enforcement against the individual, he might go directly to court to have the agency's action overturned. If a statute specifies the form of review action to be had, normally only that form is available, and it must be strictly followed. If no statutory provision governs review, however, the person must rely upon nonstatutory remedies developed and traditionally employed by the courts under common law. This usually means seeking an injunction in a federal district court, which orders the administrative agency to perform or not to perform a certain act. Injunctive relief in this context frequently is sought along with a declaratory judgment that the challenged action or inaction is illegal.

Third, the aggrieved person might bring an action for unintended infliction of harm, a tort action, against either a specific public official or a governmental entity. Each such action faces possible claims of immunity. In *Barr* v. *Matteo* (1959) the Court held that federal officials acting within the course of their employment enjoyed absolute immunity from tort liability in actions not charging violations of constitutional rights. With respect to allegations of constitutional violations, the Court held in *Butz* v. *Economou* (1978) that only a limited immunity obtains; that is, government officials are not immune from liability if they knew or reasonably should have known that their action violated constitutional rights. Even when constitutional rights are at stake, absolute immunity continues to apply to judges, prosecutors, and administrative hearing and prosecutorial officials.

Actions brought against governmental entities traditionally were barred by the doctrine of sovereign immunity, a doctrine apparently deriving from the principle that the law can provide no relief against the maker of the law (the legislature). Federal claims to sovereign immunity were in part set aside by the enactment of the Federal Tort Claims Act in 1946. The government's consent to be sued, however, remained subject to important exceptions. One such exception relates to the performance of discretionary functions where immunity is required to avoid interference with governmental decision-making processes. It now appears that the Court will limit the discretionary function exception to those activities that involve the selection of governmental ends rather than the means chosen to achieve those ends.

SCOPE OF JUDICIAL REVIEW

Once a court has determined that review is appropriate, how extensively it may examine the action of the administrative agency depends upon whether the agency finding in question concerns a finding of fact or a finding of law. If a finding of fact is based upon a record compiled pursuant to a formal agency hearing, a reviewing court may set it aside only if the finding is unsupported by substantial evidence. In making this determination, the court must look at the whole record, weighing evidence that supports the agency finding as well as that which does not. In practical application, it appears that the "substantial evidence" test comes down to little more than an inquiry into the reasonableness of the agency's action. Similarly, although an "arbitrary and capricious" standard is applied where no record is involved and although arguably this standard requires greater deference to the agency action, in practical application it seems that here, too, the test is one of reasonableness. The standard for reviewing findings of fact is thus fairly deferential; although a reviewing court is not precluded from scrutinizing an agency's finding of fact, it may not substitute its own independent judgment. In contrast, an "independent judgment" standard is applied pursuant to the so-called doctrine of full review, which requires an inquiry into the rightness of an agency's finding of fact where a constitutional question involving violations of personal rights is raised.

With respect to findings of law made by an administrative agency, courts show no deference. The reason is that the agencies are seen to have no special expertise with respect to legal matters, which are the traditional province of the courts. Accordingly, something in the nature of full review is exercised here; courts will substitute their own independent judgment for that of administrative agencies when it comes to findings of law.

The question that has bedeviled both courts and commentators is the measure of deference required with respect to "mixed questions of law and fact." Such a category, in addition to those covering questions of law and of fact, includes many questions that intertwine factual and legal issues. Some argue that such a category is unnecessary, because every question can logically be divided into its factual and legal components. For example, the court could first decide what A or B did, and then whether this particular conduct constituted negligence or gave rise to a contract. Similarly, when the question involves the application of statutory language, the first question would be what conduct occurred, and the second whether that conduct fits within the language of the statute. The administrative agency's finding on the first issue would then be regarded as a finding of fact, subject to an inquiry into its reasonableness by a reviewing court, whereas the second finding would be regarded as a finding of law, allowing the substitution of the court's independent judgment.

Notwithstanding the apparent logic of such an approach, it is not the one that the courts have adopted. The approach followed in the overwhelming majority of cases is that set forth in *Gray* v. *Powell* (1941), a case involving the application of a statutory term to given facts. The Court applied the reasonableness test, effectively the same standard applied to findings of fact. In other cases, however, such as *National Labor Relations Board* v. *Highland Park Co.* (1951), the Court has applied a far less deferential standard to cases involving the application of statutory terms, effectively substituting its own judgment for that of the administrative agencies. How these two lines of cases can be reconciled is a subject on which commentators disagree. It is important to observe that the Court will always decide what review of agency applications of statutory terms is appropriate; in the end the test applied by the Court will normally be one of reasonableness.

DUE PROCESS LIMITATIONS ON AGENCY ACTION

The discretion of an agency to affect individual rights and obligations without conducting a trial-type proceeding is subject to one overarching constitutional constraint: the due process clause. An individual does not have a constitutional right to be heard in connection with administrative action affecting a large number of people (*Bi-metallic Investment Co.* v. *Colorado State Board of Equalization,* 1915). If, however, a relatively small number of people is concerned and they are exceptionally affected in each case upon individual grounds, there is a due process right to be heard. The former case, it has been suggested, involves the finding of "legislative facts," similar to those facts a legislature uses to make policy decisions. No right to be heard obtains with respect to such legislative proceedings, so it is thought unnecessary in connection with quasi-legislative proceedings as well. On the other hand, where "adjudicative facts" are found, such as those about the parties and their particular activities, businesses, or properties, a formal hearing is required because the agency is acting in a quasi-judicial function.

As a general rule, therefore, where a person is "singled out"—where agency action applies to an individual rather than to a class—the agency is thought to be acting in the nature of a court, and formal triallike procedures are required, although a number of exceptions to this rule exist. A formal hearing generally is not required in connection with inspections, tests, elections, certain emergency situations (involving, for example, public health and safety), or at any specific stage of an agency proceeding—as long as the requisite hearing is held before the final action becomes effective.

It was once the rule that so-called privilege cases also constituted an exception to the due process requirement—that is, where a benefit or gratuity was claimed to which no preexisting right existed, an individual had no right to be heard. Government need not grant such privi-

leges at all, the theory went, so that when it did, it might do so subject to whatever conditions it prescribed. The courts gradually began to move away from this rigid approach, looking to the weight of the private interest asserted (suspension of a driver's license, for example, deprived an individual of an important interest essential to his livelihood). The courts now look not to the weight of the interest asserted but rather to whether it falls within the category of life, liberty, or property, representing something to which the complainant possesses an "entitlement." This is determined by looking to the contract or statute under which the claim is asserted. If the interest sought to be protected falls within the category of life, liberty, or property by virtue of applicable law or contract, some process is due the complainant. Precisely what process is due and what elements the procedures must comprise is a question resolved on a case-by-case basis.

Moreover, although some process may be due, its elements may be minimal. In *Goss* v. *Lopez* (1975), for example, the Court held that, generally, before a student is temporarily suspended from public school, due process requires that the student be given oral or written notice of the charges against him and, if he denies them, an explanation of the evidence the authorities have and an opportunity to present his side of the story. The Court held, however, that "there need be no delay between the time 'notice' is given and the time of the hearing" and that "the hearing may occur almost immediately following the misconduct." A different conclusion obtains where the action is taken for academic rather than disciplinary reasons. In *Board of Curators of University of Missouri* v. *Horowitz* (1978) the decision to dismiss the student rested on the academic judgment of school officials. The Court decided that the procedures employed by the school to decide whether to drop Horowitz from the medical school were all the procedures to which Horowitz had a due process right.

Finally, there are some reasons upon which the government may not act. It may not deny a benefit to a person on a basis that infringes constitutionally protected interests—especially his interest in freedom of speech. In *Perry* v. *Sindermann* (1972), a case involving the nonrenewal of the contract of a state college teacher who had not received a hearing, the Court held that "lack of a contractual or tenure right to re-employment, taken alone," does not defeat an individual's claim that due process rights have been violated.

CONCLUSION

Perhaps more than any other body of law, administrative law mirrors the efforts of the American legal system to keep pace with a rapidly evolving, high-technology society without abandoning certain fundamental principles. Those principles include the responsibility vested in elected officials to formulate public policy, the supremacy of an independent judiciary, and, above all, the primacy of the individual over every organ of the state. The success of administrative lawyers in reconciling those principles with the competing needs of societal efficiency and convenience will have much to do with the success of the American constitutional system in adapting to the new realities of a postindustrial age.

CASES

Abbott Laboratories v. Gardner, 387 U.S. 137 (1967)
Atlas Roofing Co. v. Occupational Safety and Health Review Commission, 430 U.S. 442 (1977)
Barr v. Matteo, 360 U.S. 564 (1959)
Bi-metallic Investment Co. v. Colorado State Board of Equalization, 239 U.S. 441 (1915)
Board of Curators of University of Missouri v. Horowitz, 435 U.S. 78 (1978)
Buckley v. Valeo, 424 U.S. 1 (1976)
Butz v. Economou, 438 U.S. 478 (1978)

Crowell v. Benson, 285 U.S. 22 (1932)
Endicott Johnson Corp. v. Perkins, 317 U.S. 501 (1943)
Estep v. United States, 327 U.S. 114 (1946)
Federal Trade Commission v. American Tobacco Co., 264 U.S. 298 (1924)
Goss v. Lopez, 419 U.S. 565 (1975)
Gray v. Powell, 314 U.S. 402 (1941)
Humphrey's Executor v. United States, 295 U.S. 602 (1935)
Immigration and Naturalization Service v. Chadha, 103 S.Ct. 2764 (1983)
Marchetti v. United States, 390 U.S. 39 (1968)
Myers v. United States, 272 U.S. 52 (1926)
Nader v. Allegheny Airlines, Inc., 426 U.S. 290 (1976)
National Labor Relations Board v. Highland Park Co., 341 U.S. 322 (1951)
Ortwein v. Schwab, 410 U.S. 656 (1973)
Panama Refining Co. v. A. D. Ryan, 293 U.S. 388 (1935)
Perry v. Sindermann, 408 U.S. 593 (1972)
Port of Boston Marine Terminal v. Rederiaktiebolaget Transatlantic, 400 U.S. 62 (1970)
Schechter Poultry Corp. v. United States, 295 U.S. 495 (1935)
Shapiro v. United States, 335 U.S. 1 (1948)
United States v. Florida East Coast Railway, 410 U.S. 224 (1973)
Valley Forge Christian College v. Americans United for the Separation of Church and State, 454 U.S. 464 (1982)
Wiener v. United States, 357 U.S. 349 (1958)

BIBLIOGRAPHY

Kenneth C. Davis, *Administrative Law Text* (1972), and Bernard Schwartz, *Administrative Law* (1976), are comprehensive texts on administrative law, with citations. Bernard Schwartz and H. W. R. Wade, *Legal Control of Government: Administrative Law in Britain and the United States* (1972), is an excellent comparison of the administrative systems of Britain and the United States and the law surrounding them. L. W. Weiss and M. W. Klass, *Case Studies in Regulation: Revolution and Reform* (1981), presents a survey of current problems in the movement to reduce the power of administrative agencies to regulate.
[*See also* ADMINISTRATIVE AGENCIES.]

COMMERCIAL LAW

Jarret C. Oeltjen

A LARGE body of commercial transactions is almost exclusively regulated by a comprehensive statutory scheme known as the Uniform Commercial Code (UCC). The UCC was first released for enactment by the states in 1952 for the purpose of promoting consistency in commercial transactions throughout the United States. It replaced a cornucopia of conflicting common law and outdated statutes. James White and Robert Summers judge the UCC to be the most spectacular success story in the history of American law. To appreciate the significance of the UCC, it is helpful to trace the origin and development of commercial law.

A convenient starting point is thirteenth-century England and the "law merchant." Much of the commercial trade at this time took place at local fairs held pursuant to a royal franchise. With this franchise came the authority to hold court with jurisdiction over the disputes arising from the fair. These informal courts dispensed instant justice. They enforced oral agreements at a time when the common-law courts, courts that enforced customs existing from time immemorial, could only enforce written, sealed agreements. Rules were established, and decisions were made, on the strength of the customs and usages of the merchants, such as the procedure for weighing a duck or establishing a standard measure of coin. These rules became known as the law merchant.

In 1353, faced with an explosion of trade and commerce, England passed the Statute of the Staple. Courts of staple were established in many towns. The mayor was the presiding officer, and the jury was composed of merchants. These courts exercised jurisdiction over matters arising out of the trade of commodities regularly produced in that town. They applied the law merchant rather than common law.

By 1613, with Sir Edward Coke as chief justice of the King's Bench, common-law courts began to assert jurisdiction over commercial disputes. A new form of pleading, an action on the case upon the custom of merchants, was instituted. But a major limitation was that common-law courts refused to take judicial notice of the customs of merchants. This meant that the party seeking relief was obligated to plead and prove the custom anew in each action. This deficiency was cured in the eighteenth century when two common-law judges, Sir John Holt and William Murray, Lord Mansfield, integrated the law merchant into the common law of England.

After the American Revolution, the United States adopted the English common law and the law merchant. But the commercial law that had developed in England did not function well in America, where each state was a sovereign unit enacting its own laws. Mercantile customs peculiar to America meshed uneasily with English common law, and America had not yet adopted a national currency. Interstate commerce added to the confusion and difficulty. Innovative financing techniques that fueled the capitalism machine were frustrated and stifled by uncertainty in the laws governing bills of exchange and promissory notes. Bills of exchange are similar to modern checks, and a promissory note is simply an instrument wherein one party promises to pay another a certain sum of money on specified terms. When an instrument was taken to a different state, it could become subject to regulations specific to that state that were not anticipated at the time and place of the original transaction.

It became increasingly obvious that commercial law needed to be modernized and made uniform. This realization led to the establishment of the National Conference of Commissioners on Uniform State Laws in 1892, composed of judges, professors of law, and lawyers. By 1897 the conference had promulgated the Uniform Negotiable Instruments Law (NIL) to promote and facilitate commerce. The NIL was adopted by all of the states. Encouraged by this success, the conference quickly drafted a series of uniform acts: the Uniform Sales Act (1906), the Uniform Warehouse Receipts Act (1906), the Uniform Bills of Lading Act (1909), the Uniform Stock Transfer Act (1909), the Uniform Conditional Sales Act (1918), and the Uniform Trust Receipts Act (1933). Only the Uniform Warehouse Receipts Act was unanimously adopted by the states; the other acts met with varying degrees of success. But all of these acts form a basis for much of the law codified in the UCC.

Predictably, problems arose under these various acts. Many were drafted by different authors and contained duplicate or inconsistent provisions. Many were enacted piecemeal by the states. Equally important, commercial practices were changing. By 1940, William Schnader, president of the conference, recommended modernizing and integrating these individual uniform acts into one comprehensive uniform code of commercial law. The notion of a comprehensive commercial code was accepted, but it required generous infusions of money and personnel to come to fruition. Much of the necessary funding was donated by the Maurice and Laura Falk Foundation of Pittsburgh. Businesses, financial concerns, and law firms contributed money and technical and clerical services.

In 1944 the National Conference signed an agreement with the American Law Institute (ALI) to undertake jointly the project of drafting the UCC. The ALI, a voluntary organization of judges, law professors, and leading members of the bar, had been formed for the purpose of improving the law. By 1945, work had started in earnest.

The brilliant legal scholar Karl Llewellyn, then a professor of law at Columbia University who was working on a revision of the Uniform Sales Act and was chairman of the Uniform Commercial Acts Section of the National Conference, was appointed chief reporter for the UCC. Llewellyn set the tenor of the UCC and the final product reflects his philosophy. As a legal realist, he believed that legal decisions need not be extrapolated from rigid rules but rather that law should be found in everyday practices, as was the law merchant. He did not believe that legislators should be the mechanism for social reform. The purpose of law was to articulate the realities existing in everyday life. Courts need only ferret out the laws of the current time and place. The UCC reflects this legal realism; it is law *stating* rather than law *making*. It was designed to facilitate constant evolution in line with changing commercial practices.

The UCC was organized into nine basic articles. Each article governed a different aspect of a commercial transaction and had its own reporter. According to Soia Mentschikoff, associate chief reporter for the project, the drafters of these articles looked at real-life problems and attempted to develop the best conceivable solutions. After being subjected to lengthy expert review and general membership approval by both the National Conference and the ALI, the UCC was "finished" in 1951. The official text, published in 1952, includes the provisions of law plus comments drafted by the committees that worked on the UCC. These comments do not carry the weight of law, but they are useful and persuasive aids in the interpretation and construction of the various sections of the UCC. They state the purpose of each UCC provision and cross-reference other relevant sections.

The UCC was almost immediately enacted by the Pennsylvania legislature. Other states watched New York's reaction, as it was a major commercial center. In 1953 the UCC was introduced in the New York legislature, where its passage stalled. It was referred to a committee for hearings and studies; a six-volume report published in 1956 acknowledged the necessity and practicality of the UCC but concluded that further revisions were required. While New York studied the UCC, Pennsylvania monitored its own experience with it. The problems in practical use were surprisingly few. In 1957 and 1958 new official texts that incorporated many of the recommendations were published. Pennsylvania reenacted the UCC, and Massachusetts became the second state to adopt it. Almost every state made minor modifications and amendments to the UCC as it was enacted. As of 1986, forty-nine states, the District of Columbia, and the Virgin Islands had adopted the UCC, and Louisiana, the lone holdout, had adopted Articles 1, 3, 4, 5, 7, and 8. Louisiana is the only state whose legal system is based on French Napoleonic codes rather than on English common law; Articles 2, 6, and 9 did not mesh well with state laws.

In 1961 the UCC sponsors established the Permanent Editorial Board. Its function is to monitor problems with the UCC and changes in commercial practices. As a result of its efforts, new official texts were released in 1962, 1972, and 1978. This comports well with Llewellyn's vision of an evolving code of law that reflects real-life practices, but it has tended to undermine uniformity of the codes from state to state. As modernized official texts are released, they are not quickly adopted by all states. In 1986 roughly one-half of the states still utilized the 1962 version; the other half had adopted the 1972 text, and four states had adopted the 1978 amendments.

The remainder of this essay will focus in turn on the individual articles of the UCC. The discussion is intended as a general overview; there may be variations from state to state.

ARTICLE 1: GENERAL PROVISIONS

The first article contains few substantive rules; rather, it sets the stage for what is to follow. It provides rules of construction and application, and general definitions and principles of interpretation. As section 1-102 declares, the purpose of the UCC is to simplify, clarify, and modernize the law governing commercial transactions and to permit the continued expansion of commercial practices through custom and law. Karl Llewellyn drafted Article 1, and it stands as the clear embodiment of his philosophy.

The UCC was not written to displace individual agreements between parties but rather to foster agreement in a controlled setting. Section 1-102(3) permits parties to vary most provisions of the UCC by agreement, with general contract principles being applicable. It supplies supplemental terms when the terms in the agreement are vague or missing. It indicates how courts can locate applicable standards of conduct. For example, section 1-103 imposes an obligation of good faith and diligence on all parties, a duty

that cannot be disclaimed. Section 1-102(19) defines good faith as honesty in fact in the transaction.

Article 1 also reflects Llewellyn's much discussed open-ended drafting technique. Suppose the UCC requires that an action be taken within a reasonable time. Section 1-204 indicates that what is "reasonable" depends on the nature, purposes, and circumstances of the action. The courts must look to the current common commercial practices to determine what constitutes a reasonable time. Thus, as with the law merchant, real-life experiences provide the answers. In a very real sense, common business practices are elevated to legal standards of conduct; yet the genius of the UCC permits the standards to evolve as practices change. The UCC cannot resolve all questions even in those areas where it is specifically applicable, so it expressly and wisely mandates in section 1-103 that principles of law and equity, including law merchant, contract, principal and agent, fraud, and bankruptcy, shall supplement the UCC unless they are displaced. Section 1-106 emphasizes the notion at the heart of contract law: that the purpose of remedies in a commercial setting is not to punish but to put aggrieved parties in as good a position as if there had been full performance of the agreement.

ARTICLE 2: SALES

Article 2, also drafted by Llewellyn, is one of the most comprehensive in the UCC. It is divided into seven sections and is organized by the sequence of events involved in a typical sale. It represents a modernization of its predecessor—the Uniform Sales Act.

For some purposes the scope of Article 2 extends to all transactions in goods, but its main applicability is to sales of goods; section 2-105 defines goods as all things that are movable at the time they are identified to the contract. Thus, the UCC would not apply to the sale of real estate, but it does apply to the sale, apart from the land, of unharvested crops and of timber to be cut. Questions then arise as to whether a particular transaction is a sale or something else, such as a lease. A difficult question also arises when the contract serves a mixed purpose. Suppose a seller sells and installs hot tubs. The contract provides for supplies and labor. Is this sales-service agreement within the scope of Article 2? There is a split in authority. The majority approach is to look to the dominant purpose of the contract. If it is to make a sale, the UCC would apply to the entire contract.

Agreements for the sale of goods do not necessarily require a written document. If both parties intend to make an agreement for the sale of goods, Article 2 will apply. Simple conduct by the parties is sufficient to show that such an enforceable agreement exists. But, if the sale price is $500 or more, then there must be a written document signed by the party against whom enforcement is sought, and this agreement must also recite the quantity of goods to be sold. This agreement can be quite informal, penciled on a lunch bag.

Article 2 is best explained through example. Suppose the following written agreement: "To Buyer, 50 burglar alarms, signed Seller." This agreement seems too incomplete to be enforceable. What is the price of the alarms? What are the delivery terms? When is payment due? Article 2 mandates a reasonable price based on current commercial practices; the alarms must be delivered in a single lot, at the seller's place of business, and within a reasonable time, and payment is due at the time and place where the buyer receives the goods. Buyers and sellers are free to work out these terms on their own, but failure to provide for these terms will not render the agreement void; the court will plug the gaps with these UCC provisions. Even if the price of the goods exceeds $500 and the agreement is not written as required, in some circumstances it is enforceable, as when the goods have been specially manufactured and are not typically suitable for resale or when the buyer has paid for the goods or otherwise performed part of the agreement.

It may happen that one of the parties fails to live up to an agreement. If there is no performance at all, the aggrieved party will seek to recover the lost advantage. If the buyer refuses to pay for the burglar alarms, the seller may sue for the contract price, or the seller may sell them to a third party and sue the buyer for any difference between that sales price and the contract price. Alternatively, if the seller refuses to perform, the buyer will typically "cover" (that is, buy the goods from a third party) and sue the seller for any losses resulting from the breach.

Specific performance, where a court directs each party to comply with the terms of the agreement, is rarely a proper remedy, because money damages are usually sufficient.

A more typical problem occurs when a seller ships goods, but the buyer is displeased with them. Suppose the alarms are wired with sirens rather than the bells originally specified. Since the alarms fail to conform to the terms agreed upon, the buyer has the right to reject the entire shipment. But the buyer must provide the seller with timely notice that she is going to reject the goods and must first afford the seller the chance to cure any defects that can be corrected. Another option the buyer may exercise is to accept the nonconforming goods on the assumption that the seller will cure any defect. If the seller fails to follow through, the buyer can revoke this acceptance.

Article 2 also establishes several seller's warranties. Suppose the seller states that the alarm will operate properly for at least two years, and during a burglary only three months after installation it fails to work. The buyer can sue the seller for a breach of an express warranty. Any affirmative act or promise made by the seller relating to the alarm that is part of the basis of the bargain creates an express warranty that the alarm will conform to that representation. The seller need not use the term *warranty* or *guarantee* to create such an express warranty. Express warranties can arise through statements on brochures, on labels, and in advertisements. It is, however, often difficult to locate the line that separates an express warranty from mere opinion or puffery.

The failure of the alarm may also violate implied warranties granted by the UCC. First, there is a breach of the implied warranty of merchantability, the warranty that the alarm is fit for the ordinary purpose for which it is used—to scare off burglars and to warn the owners. Second, it may violate the implied warranty of fitness for a particular purpose. This warranty arises when the seller has reason to know the buyer is relying on the seller's judgment to choose an appropriate alarm, and the seller also has reason to know the buyer's particular purpose in purchasing the alarm.

Because the UCC provides for so many warranties, sellers are understandably anxious to limit their liability by excluding or modifying them. Warranties are modifiable by agreement between the parties, subject to a few restrictions. The only certain way to avoid an express warranty is to never create it in the first place. If one clause in a contract makes an express warranty and another clause disclaims all warranties, the express warranty survives. To disclaim the implied warranty of merchantability, the disclaimer must mention merchantability and, if in writing, be conspicuous. To disclaim the warranty of fitness for a particular purpose, the disclaimer must be in writing and be conspicuous. If the product is clearly and conspicuously labeled "as is" or "with all faults," the seller has effectively disclaimed all implied warranties. This returns the buyer to a "let the buyer beware" situation.

Another approach is for the seller to leave all warranties intact, but to limit the remedies available to the buyer in the event of a breach. A buyer's remedies may be limited to an exchange for the goods or to repairs. But these limitations on a buyer's remedies will be unenforceable if they are unconscionable.

Certain warranty provisions and disclaimers permitted by the UCC may be limited by federal law. The Magnuson-Moss Warranty Act, for example, regulates the disclosure of terms and conditions of product warranties made in connection with consumer products. This act does not impose a warranty obligation but regulates any such warranty once it is undertaken. Many of the warranty statements and procedures in department stores are mandated by this act.

ARTICLE 3: COMMERCIAL PAPER

Commercial paper is a term used to describe a method facilitating payments for goods and services. Prior to the use of commercial paper, goods were paid for either with other goods or services, as in the barter system, or with money. Commercial paper includes checks, drafts, bills of exchange, and promissory notes.

Bills of exchange are frequently used to finance international transactions. The concept is relatively simple in practice: a seller transfers goods to a buyer and receives a bill of exchange, which, in essence, is a letter written by one party directing another party to pay a certain sum of money either to any person holding the letter (bearer) or a third party (order). If the transaction is domestic rather than foreign, this letter is called a draft. Bills of exchange and drafts are similar to checks in appearance.

The use of commercial paper dates back at least to twelfth-century England. Bills of exchange and drafts were recognized methods to finance the sale of goods under law merchant and later under common law. Promissory notes met with more judicial resistance. Conceptually, legal rights could not arise without the delivery of some physical token; a mere writing was not sufficient. A person receiving a mere promise of payment could not transfer the benefits expected to be derived from that promise. Finally, in 1704, the Statute of Anne acknowledged promissory notes as being freely transferable and enforceable.

By 1780, bank checks, drafts issued by banks that were the rough equivalent of modern cashier's checks, were commonly used in England. In 1882 the British Parliament adopted the Bills of Exchange Act, which served as the foundation for America's NIL of 1897, drafted by the National Conference. Article 3 of the UCC supersedes the NIL but deviates little from it.

Article 3, like the acts it replaced, was designed to promote the free circulation of commercial paper. It governs all negotiable instruments, including checks, drafts, certificates of deposit, and promissory notes. Any negotiable instrument, to qualify as such, must meet certain criteria: there must be a writing, signed by the maker or drawer, stating an unconditional promise to pay a sum certain at a definite time or on demand, and it must be payable to order or to bearer. A writing that meets all of these criteria is almost as transferable as money; it can be bought, sold, and cashed in.

Although these criteria sound onerous, they are not. Note, for example, the following: "Pay to the order of Joshua one thousand ($10,000) dollars. Signed, X." This simple writing qualifies as a negotiable instrument within the scope of Article 3. Since no time of payment is specified, it is presumed payable on demand. The negotiability is not affected by whether it is antedated, postdated, or even undated. If the words and numbers describing the amount to be paid conflict, as in the above example, then the general rule is applied that words control figures, so that the amount due would be $1,000.

To be liable on an instrument, your signature

must appear on it. An X can be an acceptable signature. Any mark or word intended to authenticate a signature will suffice; the mark can be a thumbprint or a nickname. Once the signer is identified, he is liable. The UCC does not require that this writing be on paper; it can be written on a wall, a watermelon, or the side of a cow. It need not be in ink; crayon, pencil, or even a wood etching will do.

Suppose instead the note stated that X would pay Joshua the value of a fifty-yard-line seat if the Miami Dolphins football team wins the next Super Bowl. This fails to be negotiable for at least two reasons, so Article 3 would not apply. First, the promise to pay is impermissibly conditioned on the Dolphins' victory. To qualify under Article 3, there must be an unconditional promise to pay. Second, the amount to be paid, the value of the seat, does not meet the "sum certain" requirement. The holder of an Article 3 instrument must be able to determine the amount payable from the face of the instrument. In the late twentieth-century economy, where innovative financing appears to be the norm, this requirement raises interesting questions as to whether certain adjustable- or variable-rate notes qualify as negotiable instruments, because it can be difficult to establish from the face of the instrument what amount must be paid.

Mastery of Article 3 terminology can prove to be a challenge. There are two basic types of negotiable instruments—one to which there are two parties and one to which there are three parties. A promissory note is a two-party instrument; it is issued (given) by a maker who promises to pay a payee. When that note is presented to the maker for payment, she is obligated to pay according to its terms. The note represents an obligation to pay a certain sum of money, but it usually states a deferred date of payment. If the payee needs money today but the note is not due to be paid for another year, he can discount (sell) the note to another, who, at the appropriate time, can present the note to the maker for payment.

A check is a three-party instrument. Essentially, a check is a draft (order), drawn (written) by a drawer (depositor), and it directs the drawee (bank) to disburse funds either to the bearer (possessor of the check), the payee (person named on the face of the check), or anyone the payee so orders (as when a payee endorses the

check over to another). If, after presentment of the check to the bank for payment, the bank dishonors (refuses to pay) it and the drawer receives notice of that dishonor, the drawer must pay.

A negotiable instrument, often referred to as paper, changes hands through a process called negotiation. If this is effectively accomplished, certain rights, warranties, and defenses are created. It is essential to distinguish between order and bearer paper. An instrument is payable to bearer when no specific person is designated as payee; for example, "pay to cash," "pay to the bearer or the order of the bearer," and "pay to John Doe or bearer" are all expressions that create bearer paper. Bearer paper is successfully negotiated by simply handing over physical possession of it to a third party. The maker or drawee must pay whoever presents that paper.

Order paper is payable to the order of a specifically designated payee—"pay to the order of Sarah Smith." To be negotiated, order paper must be endorsed by the designated payee, such as Sarah Smith in our example, and then delivered to the third party. If Sarah Smith endorses this check by signing her name, "Sarah Smith," without qualification, the order paper becomes bearer paper. Then, as is the case with all bearer paper, if the instrument is lost or stolen and eventually presented to a bank and the bank pays it, the bank will not be liable for an improper disbursal of funds.

Endorsers often unknowingly subject themselves to liability; by placing their name on the instrument, they become liable for it. The UCC provides that endorsers are liable to one another in the order in which they endorse. This order is presumed to be the sequence in which their signatures appear. But, interestingly enough, there is no requirement in the UCC that endorsements appear in any order or even on the back of a check. In fact, an unspecified signature that appears anywhere on an instrument, front or back, is presumed to be that of an endorser.

To limit unauthorized negotiation, an endorser may use a restrictive endorsement, such as "for deposit only." The bank receiving this check is bound to obey the restrictive order; if it pays out cash instead, the bank is liable for those funds. This restriction applies only to the immediate transferee; subsequent transferees are not affected.

The rights a transferee acquires will depend

on how the instrument was negotiated. When a party takes an instrument for value, in good faith, and without notice of dishonor or that it is overdue, or of any claims against it, that transferee attains a special status called "holder in due course" (HDC). HDC status is valued because such a holder (transferee) takes the instrument free from certain defenses that were available to the original parties to the contract. For example, a maker or drawer cannot refuse to pay an HDC because of nonperformance of a contract, nondelivery of goods, or lack of payment. These "personal defenses" cannot be asserted against an HDC. But certain "real" defenses can still be raised against an HDC, such as infancy (the instrument was signed by a party under eighteen years of age), duress (the instrument was signed at gunpoint), illegality of the underlying transaction, and bankruptcy. If the transferee does not rise to the level of HDC status, all of these are valid defenses against a demand for payment. Because a non-HDC is a subject to both real and personal defenses, he faces greater uncertainty that he will be able to collect on the instrument than does an HDC.

Consider the following situation. A seller sells a refrigerator to a buyer. The buyer signs a promissory note to finance the sale. The seller sells the note to a third party, who becomes an HDC. The seller takes the proceeds and disappears. The refrigerator works for less than three months. If the HDC presents the note for payment, the buyer must pay even though the buyer would have a valid warranty claim against the seller. The Federal Trade Commission has enacted regulations to assist consumers in such situations. Sellers must include in consumer credit contracts, such as the refrigerator note, a notice that the holder of such a contract is subject to all claims that the buyer could assert against the seller of the goods or services. An HDC's rights are thus restricted in consumer transactions.

ARTICLE 4: BANK DEPOSITS AND COLLECTIONS

While Article 3 applies to the creation, transfer, and negotiation of commercial paper, Article 4 establishes the role of banks in depositing, collecting, and paying these instruments. It defines a bank as any person engaged in the business of banking. There are many "types" of banks enumerated in Article 4. For the purposes of this article, banks are "typed" by the function they perform. The provisions of Article 4 can be changed by agreement between the parties; but if the agreement is not reasonable, a court can invalidate it, and a bank's obligation to exercise good faith and reasonable care while discharging its duties cannot be disclaimed, and the damages for such a breach cannot be limited.

Perhaps the simplest way to understand Article 4 is to follow a check through the process. Judy writes Jim a check in the amount of $100. Jim, the payee, goes to the bank and presents the check for payment. This bank, the "depository" bank, has several options. It can pay Jim cash; this constitutes final payment. If Judy's check is "bad," the bank cannot reclaim those funds from Jim unless the presentment warranty was breached, such as an alteration in the amount of the check or the presence of unauthorized signatures. Alternatively, Jim could deposit the check in his account, and the bank would defer payment (that is, "hold" the check). It will then forward the check to Judy's bank, the "payor" bank, to be certain that sufficient funds are on deposit to cover the check.

Because most checks are good, many banks will grant a depositor provisional credit. This means that Jim can withdraw funds against the check even though the sufficiency of Judy's funds has not yet been ascertained. If the check "bounces" because Judy has insufficient funds to cover it, the depository bank can recover those funds from its depositor, Jim. Quite often a depository and payor bank will be the same bank, especially in a small town.

A bank, pursuant to agreement with its customer, has a duty to pay its customer's checks. But a bank can rightfully refuse to honor a check on several grounds. A bank is not obligated to honor Judy's check where to do so would overdraw the account; neither does it have a duty to honor a check more than six months old, but the bank may choose to honor such checks anyway. In addition, a customer has the right to stop payment on a check. The bank may be liable if it ignores the stop-payment order. If Judy wants to stop payment, she must notify the bank in time to allow the bank a reasonable opportunity to act. In most states Judy can simply telephone the bank, but the bank may only be bound for fourteen days unless she confirms this stop-payment order in writing.

There exists a debtor-creditor relationship between a bank and its customer; the customer is the creditor and the bank is the debtor. A bank disburses funds as ordered and may charge against its customer's account any item that is properly payable. Suppose that Judy's signature is forged on the $100 check made out to Jim, and the payor bank cashes the check. It cannot charge this item against her account. This check is not properly payable because the drawer did not sign it. Theoretically, a bank is obligated to recognize the signatures of its customers. But the bank does have a cause of action against the forger who signed the instrument. Even though the forger did not sign his own name, he will be responsible for the amount of the check. If Judy had been negligent—for example, she had left her checkbook on her desk at work alongside a folder containing copies of her signature—her negligence may preclude her recovery of the lost funds.

Suppose Judy's signature is genuine, but the payee, Jim, or a subsequent endorser alters the amount of the check from $100 to $1000. Judy is entitled to have $900 recredited to her account if the bank cashes the check. The check was properly payable only for the amount she originally ordered—$100. What if the defect is instead a forged endorsement? Again, the check is not properly payable, and the funds cannot be charged against Judy's account. The bank's remedy is to proceed against the party who presented the defective check. By proceeding up the chain of transferors, ultimate liability should rest on the wrongdoer. If the wrongdoer cannot be found or is insolvent, the person who dealt with the wrongdoer sustains the loss. This explains why stores are reluctant to accept checks and why they institute elaborate procedures to protect themselves.

Article 4 was written with a "paper" society in mind. But today, electronic fund transfers and automatic teller machines are commonplace. Such innovations are not consistent with Article 4, which does not address questions such as who is liable for an unauthorized withdrawal from an automatic teller machine. There is currently much litigation, with conflicting outcomes. In response to commercial transaction innovations, the National Conference and the ALI are preparing a new payment code that will amend Articles 3 and 4 to include noncash payments such as electronic fund transfers.

Although the UCC has little to say regarding these modern innovations, there have been an increasing number of state and federal regulations regarding them. Probably the most significant is the federal Electronic Fund Transfers Act of 1978, which deals with disclosures of terms and conditions of transfers, error resolution, consumer liability for unauthorized transfers, waiver of rights, and liability of financial institutions. Basically it delineates the consumer's rights.

ARTICLE 5: LETTERS OF CREDIT

Even though most people would probably not recognize one, letters of credit have been in use for centuries. In medieval Europe, travelers fearful of being robbed by highwaymen would deposit their funds with a local merchant who was reliable and had contacts elsewhere. This merchant would write a letter directing a distant merchant to advance funds to the traveler with the understanding he would be reimbursed by the merchant holding the funds. Through this device, the credit-worthiness of the merchant was substituted for that of the unknown traveler. These letters, which became known as traveler's letters of credit, are still in use today but are usually arranged through banks.

Letters of credit have many other uses, the most common of which is to finance both international and domestic sales transactions. For example, a buyer in Maine wants to purchase perfume from a seller in Paris. The buyer does not want to pay in advance; he may not trust the seller to ship the goods. Conversely, the seller may not want to ship in advance of payment. To relieve this stalemate, the buyer can arrange for his local bank to issue a commercial letter of credit running in favor of the seller. This letter of credit contains the bank's promise to pay. The seller can ship the goods knowing that once she has performed, she can present this letter of credit to the issuing bank and be paid. The buyer will have agreed to reimburse the bank for any disbursements of funds; the bank usually charges a fee for these services. The letter of credit works equally well if the seller is a sheep rancher in Montana, and the buyer, a wool merchant in Georgia.

There are at least three parties to a letter of credit, the customer, the issuer, and the beneficiary, but there can be additional parties. The seller in Paris could request a Paris bank to confirm the letter of credit. Upon written confirmation, the Paris bank also becomes liable for payment on the letter of credit. This confirming bank in Paris has a right of reimbursement against the issuing bank, which, in turn, can exercise its rights against the buyer. Article 5 establishes the rights and liabilities of all these parties.

Article 5 functions well on an interstate level, but at the international level a different set of rules may apply. The International Chamber of Commerce, formed in 1919, has developed guidelines for commercial practices in international trade—the Uniform Customs and Practice for Documentary Credits (UCP). Although the UCP does not have the force of law, it is widely recognized and routinely incorporated by reference into letters of credit. Usually Article 5 and the UCP produce the same results, but not always. Alabama, Missouri, and New York have adopted an amendment to help resolve such conflicts. In those states, Article 5 does not apply to a letter of credit if it is subject to the UCP either by express terms or by course of trade.

Letters of credit may appear to be very formal transactions, but this is frequently not the case. A letter of credit can be issued by any person; the issuer need not be a bank. No special phrasing is required, only a writing signed by the issuer. Even a telegram qualifies if it identifies its sender by an appropriate authentication.

Discussions of letters of credit have traditionally focused on sales transactions, but recently standby letters of credit have come into vogue. Standby letters provide the beneficiary with a source of payment in the event of default on financial or performance obligations; they are used in lieu of bonding and other security devices. For example, a National Football League quarterback whose salary may be portioned out in deferred payments could contract to have the club issue a letter of credit running in his favor. Or a landlord who rents very expensive property may demand that the tenant supply a standby letter of credit to protect the landlord in the event the tenant defaults. Note that traditionally the issuer of a letter of credit would expect to pay on that letter and be reimbursed for these payments. But this expectation shifts when using a standby letter of credit; the issuer expects not to pay and is only obligated to pay upon the default of the customer.

ARTICLE 6: BULK TRANSFERS

Bulk-transfers law does not seem to mesh with the general commercial scheme of the UCC. Nevertheless, Article 6, the shortest article in the UCC, fills an important gap. Consider the following: A seller runs a boutique. A creditor lends the seller money to help her through a business slump. A few weeks later the creditor learns the seller has sold her entire inventory to a third party, a "bulk" transfer, and absconded with all of the money.

If this had occurred before the UCC, the creditor might have been out of luck. As far back as sixteenth-century England, the Statute of Elizabeth voided conveyances made with the intent to hinder, defraud, or delay creditors. But if a third party bought the property in good faith, there may well be no fraudulent conveyance to void. Article 6 was enacted to protect creditors from this commonplace type of commercial fraud.

Article 6 is very narrow in scope. It applies to bulk transfers of a major portion of inventory, transfers not ordinarily made in the course of that business. It also applies to transfers of substantial parts of equipment made in connection with a transfer of inventory. What is a major portion of inventory or a substantial part of the equipment? The answer varies between jurisdictions; generally a transfer of more than 50 percent of the inventory qualifies, and transfers of equipment ranging from 10 percent to 70 percent have been ruled substantial.

Notice that the transfer must be one that does not occur in the ordinary course of business. If it is a common commercial practice for boutiques to sell all their remaining inventory at the end of a season, Article 6 may not apply. The article governs enterprises whose principal business is the sale of merchandise from stock. Businesses such as building contracting, service industries, and farming are excluded.

When a bulk transfer does fall within the scope of Article 6, certain duties are imposed on both the transferor-seller and the transferee-buyer. The transferor must provide a list of all creditors, whether their claims are disputed or not. The transferee must prepare a schedule of all property transferred and provide notice to all of the creditors prior to possession of, or payment for, the goods. If a creditor, such as the one in the above hypothetical instance, appears on the list but is not given notice of the bulk transfer, the transfer is ineffective as to him. He can proceed as though the transfer never occurred; he may attach the goods or enjoin their resale as if they were still in the hands of his debtor, the transferor. The creditor usually has only six months to assert any claim.

Failure to comply with Article 6 renders a transfer voidable, not void. This means that an innocent party who subsequently buys the goods from the transferee, in good faith with no notice of the defect, receives good title free of any defects; the creditor cannot proceed against this innocent party.

ARTICLE 7: DOCUMENTS OF TITLE

Article 7 addresses the problems arising out of the storage and shipment of goods and the documents of title representing those goods. The term *documents of title* includes bills of lading, warehouse receipts, dock receipts, orders for delivery, and any other document generally recognized as evidence that the person holding it is entitled to receive, hold, or dispose of the document or the goods it represents.

When a seller takes goods to a carrier to be shipped, the carrier issues a bill of lading; or when a person stores goods in a warehouse, the warehouseman issues a warehouse receipt. The carrier or warehouseman to whom the goods are entrusted is a bailee, and as a holder of goods he is obligated to fulfill certain duties of care regarding the goods and to whom the goods shall be delivered. Essentially, these "receipts" for the goods are documents of title. The holder of these documents of title may subsequently transfer them to a buyer of the goods, who in turn would present the documents to the carrier, or warehouseman, and collect the goods. Article 7 establishes the rights and liabilities of the various parties involved. When shipments are made

through interstate commerce, the Federal Bills of Lading Act governs and preempts any otherwise applicable UCC provisions.

Documents of title may be negotiable or nonnegotiable. One of the duties of the holder of goods—the bailee—is to deliver goods only to the person entitled to them under the document. If a buyer presents a negotiable document of title, the bailee must deliver the goods to the buyer. If the document of title is nonnegotiable, the bailee must deliver the goods only as instructed by the owner or by the document itself; for example, the document may direct the bailee to deliver to a named person.

If a bailee fails to deliver the goods to the appropriate party, the general rule is that the bailee is liable for the value of the undelivered goods. But there are situations where a bailee's failure to deliver goods will be excused. For example, a bailee will not be liable when the goods have been delivered to a person with a title superior to the document holder or when the goods have been destroyed by an "act of God," such as lightning striking a load of highly flammable chemicals.

ARTICLE 8: INVESTMENT SECURITIES

Article 8 governs the issue, transfer, and negotiation of investment securities, such as stocks of intrastate entities. Additionally, the prerequisites for issuance and disclosure requirements of securities are heavily regulated by state blue-sky laws and federal law. Article 8 fulfills a different role. Article 8 functions for investment securities much the same as Article 3 does for commercial paper; it establishes the rights and liabilities of the parties to an investment security.

Prior to 1977, only certificated securities came within the scope of Article 8. For example, John buys a share of stock in Dynamo Corporation. He receives a stock certificate that evidences that share of ownership in Dynamo. To qualify as an investment security under the unamended Article 8, a certificate of a certain form has to be issued. Once issued, John can sell or transfer his ownership rights, often by delivery of the certificate.

Traditionally, shares of stock were represented by certificates. The 1960s witnessed an explosion in trading on the stock exchange, and the mountain of paperwork thus generated almost brought the securities industry to a standstill. Brokerage houses were unable to transfer stock certificates fast enough. Currently, many corporations offer dividend reinvestment programs where the small amounts due a shareholder are frequently reinvested in the corporation. All of this paperwork is expensive and inconvenient. Clearly, a paperless system is needed, allowing the issuer to simply keep an accounting of registered owners and eliminating the use of certificates. The problem with such an accounting notation system, however, is that if there is no certificate, unamended Article 8 will not apply. With no guidance as to the legal rights of the parties, investors are reluctant to venture from the system of paper certificates.

A remedy is available. In the early 1970s the American Bar Association formed a committee to study the paper problem and to recommend solutions. The National Conference considered these recommendations and in 1977 approved an amendment to Article 8. The new version of Article 8 was published in 1978. As of 1986, it had been adopted by only four states; significantly, New York is one of them. The amended Article 8 governs both certificated and uncertificated securities; the new sections closely parallel the former sections that only regulated certificated securities.

ARTICLE 9: SECURED TRANSACTIONS

There is nothing like Article 9 in the history of commercial law. The UCC reporter Grant Gilmore will be forever remembered for his influence on this bold, innovative approach to commercial transactions. Not surprisingly, this article has spawned more case law and statutory amendments than any other article in the UCC. A seller is often willing to sell goods on credit to a buyer only if the seller can be assured she has an enforceable right in some property of the buyer, which right she can exercise to recoup any losses incurred in the event the buyer defaults. Under Article 9, this enforceable right to the debtor's property is called a security interest.

This concept is not new. Prior to the drafting of the UCC, this right was referred to as chattel security, and a number of devices were created to make it legally enforceable.

In addition to the creditor's and debtor's interests in such an arrangement, public policy has long granted special protection to innocent third parties, even though such protection may conflict with the creditor's interest. One such protection is the general requirement that third parties be alerted that a creditor has a claim on certain goods.

One of the earliest forms of chattel security, the pledge, dates back to Roman law. The creditor would take physical possession of the pledge, some personal property such as a jewel or a garden tool, in exchange for a loan. Once the debt was retired, the property, or pledge, was returned. So long as the creditor retained physical possession of the property, his claim was superior to that of any third party. The fact that the debtor lacked physical possession of the property served as notice to all the world of another's claim to that property.

In many instances the pledge was an unsatisfactory form of chattel security. The borrower might be a farmer who needed that tool to harvest the crops to earn the money to retire the debt. The chattel mortgage, modeled after real estate mortgages, evolved as a way for the seller to create a security interest while permitting the borrower to retain use of the property. A formal agreement that created the security interest was drawn up. It was then filed with the county recording office to serve as notice to third parties. But chattel mortgages were often expensive and cumbersome to prepare; and often the chattel was mobile and could be easily carried across county lines to areas where the notice was ineffective.

The next innovation was probably the conditional sale. Property was sold on credit to the buyer. Physical possession of the property was transferred to the buyer, but title was retained by the seller until the property was paid for in full. This "innovation" did not alert third parties to the fact that the buyer had few rights beyond possession. Because the buyer did not have title, the only right she could technically transfer was possession. The danger to the creditor was that courts, in an effort to protect innocent third parties, sometimes found the original transaction was, in effect, a chattel mortgage, and because it was not recorded, the creditor lost any right to recover the chattel from the third party.

Article 9, which replaced these and other confusing devices, provides one coherent, comprehensive scheme to protect a creditor's security interests. Article 9 applies to any transaction that is intended to create a security interest in personal property or fixtures. Within the term *personal property* is included not only goods such as bicycles and eggs but also intangibles such as negotiable instruments, documents of title, investment securities, and leases of personal property. Fixtures are goods that are affixed to real property but not integrated into it. A brick that becomes part of a wall is not a fixture; it is part of the realty. But a brick used as a doorstop is a good. A built-in dishwasher and a furnace are fixtures. Specifically excluded from Article 9 are real estate, tort claims, and wage assignments.

The security agreement, generally required to be in writing, establishes the creditor's (secured party's) right to proceed against the debtor in the event of default of payment or performance. It does not protect a secured party against the rights of most third parties. Consider the following: Sharon lends Justin $1,000 and takes a security interest in Justin's canoe. He then sells the canoe to a third party, squanders the sales proceeds, and defaults on the debt to Sharon. The success of a proceeding by Sharon against the third party to recover the canoe depends on whether or not she, as secured party, "perfected" her security interest.

For an interest to be perfected, not only must there be a security agreement but also the debtor must have some rights in the secured property and must have been given value such as the loan proceeds, and the creditor must give public notice unless such notice is otherwise excused by the provisions of Article 9. If properly perfected, the secured party's claim receives "priority" over most subsequent creditors' claims to the same property.

In the canoe example, suppose that Sharon perfects her security interest in Justin's canoe. Subsequently Kathy also lends Justin $1,000 and perfects her security interest in the same canoe. Justin then abandons the canoe and absconds with all the money. Sharon's claim to an interest in the canoe is senior to Kathy's because Sharon's interest was perfected first. There is only one canoe, and if it is of insufficient value to satisfy both creditors' claims, the creditor who perfected first is entitled to priority; thus, Sharon is entitled to have her claim satisfied first.

There are several ways to satisfy the notice requirement or to be excused from it. In general, the methods are divided along practical and functional lines. Some security interests are "noticed" simply by the creditor taking possession of the collateral. Examples include security interests in pledges, letters of credit, and negotiable instruments. As in the use of the Roman pledge, a debtor not in possession is notice to the world. Usually a creditor files a financing statement at a central location to fulfill the notice requirement. This financing statement need include only the names and addresses of the parties, any required signatures, and a reasonable description of the collateral. The financing statement may be filed at any time during the transaction, but there is no perfection until all of the requisites have been met.

When two creditors extend credit on the security of the same property and the debtor defaults on both obligations, the general rule is that the secured party who perfects first has priority. This means that a creditor must file promptly at the proper location. Generally, fixtures and consumer, agricultural, and other land-related security interests must be filed in the county of the debtor's residence. Security interests in accounts, equipment, and most other collateral must be centrally filed, in most states with the secretary of state. If a creditor is unsure of where to file, most lawyers advise the creditor to file in each of the possible locations.

The main exception to the notice requirement is for the creditor who holds a purchase-money security interest in consumer goods. Assume Jane purchases a stereo on credit from Acme Audio. If Acme enters into the security agreement with Jane and she is given possession of the stereo, then Acme's purchase-money security interest will be perfected without the need of filing or retaining possession. This is referred to as "automatic" perfection. Automatic perfection promotes consumer credit sales by eliminating the need to race to the filing office every day to perfect. It also saves filing fees and reduces what would otherwise be a mountain of paperwork.

But, unless Acme does exercise its optional right to file the security, any third party who purchases the stereo from Jane for their personal use will take the stereo free and clear of Acme's security interest. Thus, an automatically perfected purchase-money security interest will protect a creditor from all competing creditors but not from a third-party consumer purchaser.

Most legal contests arising under Article 9 require a determination of the relative priorities of secured creditors asserting claims against insolvent debtors. Suppose a creditor perfected a security interest in a debtor's boat and the debtor defaults on the obligation. What rights does the creditor have? Article 9 authorizes the creditor to repossess the boat without resort to judicial process, so long as she can do so peacefully. The creditor can tow away the boat if it is sitting in the debtor's front yard, but she cannot break into the garage to get it. The creditor may then dispose of the boat in any "reasonable commercial manner"; usually the creditor will resell it. If the creditor does not receive enough from the resale of the boat to retire the debt, she may proceed against the debtor for any deficiency. Conversely, the creditor must turn over any surplus from the sale to the debtor.

There are many instances in which the protections and priorities that Article 9 provides to creditors may be in conflict with the current trend of consumer-debtor protection. Interestingly, the reporter for Article 9, Grant Gilmore, was subsequently concerned that the UCC, which was drafted with commercial considerations in mind, granted too much protection to secured creditors in a consumer setting. In spite of such problems and considering the novelty of its approach, Article 9 has worked surprisingly well. It has generated international interest and has been cited as the most comprehensive and rational system of security interests in the world today. France, England, Canada, and India are a few of the countries that have studied the statutory scheme established by Article 9. Most have agreed that these principles are logical, adaptable, and possibly exportable.

Although the initial reaction to the introduction of the UCC was at best indifferent, the UCC has gained widespread approval, and it works well despite its shortcomings. It has effectively reduced the uncertainty that previously existed in commercial law because of the numerous jurisdictional variations. The latter half of the twentieth century has witnessed an explosion in use of commercial and consumer credit and a vast increase in the speed and volume of business, travel, and communication. As noted by Homer Kripke, the UCC seems to have arrived just in the nick of time.

BIBLIOGRAPHY

Richard M. Alderman and Richard F. Dole, *A Transactional Guide to the Uniform Commercial Code* (1983), is a clear, comprehensive analysis of the scope and application of each article of the UCC. ALI-ABA Course of Study Materials, *Letters of Credit* (1983). American Bar Association, *Uniform Commercial Code Handbook* (1964). Martin J. Aronstein, Robert Haycock, Jr., and Donald A. Scott, "Article 8 Is Ready," in *Harvard Law Review*, 93 (1980).

Henry J. Bailey, *Brady on Bank Checks* (1979), traces the evolution of financing techniques from the 1700s through late twentieth-century innovations such as NOW accounts. Donald I. Baker and Roland E. Brandel, *The Law of Electronic Fund Transfer Systems* (1979), with suppl. (1984). Charles A. Bane, "From Holt and Mansfield to Story to Llewellyn and Mentschikoff: The Progressive Development of Commercial Law," in *University of Miami Law Review*, 37 (1983), outlines the English origins of American commercial law and the birth of the UCC. William Everett Britton, *Handbook of the Law of Bills and Notes* (1961), discusses the history, functions, and types of negotiable instruments.

Peter F. Coogan, "Article 9—An Agenda for the Next Decade," in *Yale Law Journal*, 87 (1978); and "Security Interests in Investment Securities Under Revised Article 8 of the Uniform Commercial Code," in *Harvard Law Review*, 92 (1979), evaluate the changes initiated by the revised Article 8 on investment securities. Arthur L. Corbin, "A Tribute to Karl Llewellyn," in *Yale Law Journal*, 71 (1961–1962). Richard Danzig, "A Comment on the Jurisprudence of the Uniform Commercial Code," in *Stanford Law Review*, 27 (1975), analyzes the philosophy of law, especially that of Karl Llewellyn, which shaped the underpinnings of the UCC.

David G. Epstein and James A. Martin, *Basic Uniform Commercial Code Teaching Materials* (1977). Grant Gilmore, "The Good Faith Purchase Idea and the Uniform Commercial Code: Confessions of a Repentant Draftsman," in *Georgia Law Review* (1981), examines how Article 9 affects both creditors and purchasers; and *Security Interests in Personal Property* (1965), reviews the history of security interests, explains the role and function of Article 9, and gives insights regarding its application. Ray D. Henson, *Secured Transactions Under the Uniform Commercial Code* (1973).

Homer Kripke, "A Reflective Pause Between UCC Past and UCC Future," in *Ohio State Law Journal*, 43 (1982), evaluates both the past performance and anticipated problems of the UCC. Karl N. Llewellyn, *The Common Law Tradition: Deciding Appeals* (1960), explains the common-law philosophy and illustrates its evolution and application. Soia Mentschikoff,

"Reflections of a Drafter," in *Ohio State Law Journal,* 43 (1982), shares memories, opinions, and anecdotes with other drafters of the UCC. John C. Minahan, "The Eroding Uniformity of the Uniform Commercial Code," in *Kentucky Law Journal,* 65 (1977).

Robert J. Nordstrom, *Handbook on the Law of Sales* (1970), is a comprehensive analysis of the history of the law of sales and the role and applications of Article 2. Norman Penney and Donald I. Baker, *The Law of Electronic Fund Transfer Systems* (1980). William A. Schnader, "A Short History of the Preparation and Enactment of the Uniform Commercial Code," in *University of Miami Law Review,* 22 (1967), is a concise overview of the drafting and passage of the UCC. Edward E.

Symons, Jr., and James J. White, *Banking Law: Teaching Materials* (1984).

E. Hunter Taylor, Jr., "Uniformity of Commercial Law and State-by-State Enactment: A Confluence of Contradictions," in *Hastings Law Journal,* 30 (1978), examines the erosion of the uniformity of the UCC due to the nonuniform amendments by the amending states. James J. White and Robert S. Summers, *Handbook of the Law Under the Uniform Commercial Code* (1972), is a popular book that gives a thoughtful and comprehensive analysis of the various provisions and applications of the UCC.

[*See also* COMMON LAW AND COMMON LAW LEGAL SYSTEMS *and* PROPERTY LAW.]

CONTRACTS

Joseph P. Tomain

WE experience contracts law daily. Some contractual arrangements are more formal than others and sometimes we are more conscious of our contractual obligations than at other times. Insurance policies, apartment leases, car sales, even ordering food in a restaurant are all contractual events. We are also familiar with the social practice of promising. Through promises we create new relationships binding ourselves to others, usually with expectations for mutual advantage. Some promises bind us morally, others bind us legally. These legally binding promises are contracts. To fully appreciate how contracts law operates, we must become conscious of our experiences of promising and contracting in the lay sense. As persons acting in the world, the legal regime we create and operate should reflect our needs and desires. Translated, this claim means contracts law emanates, at least in part, from our daily lives and experiences. Contracts law is a paradigmatic example of how law, as an ordered rules system, responds to human needs and desires. Sometimes the response is successful, sometimes it fails. The achievements of law are measured by the quality of law's responsiveness. This essay is guided by a belief in the ability of law to respond, reflect, and satisfy several human aspirations.

THEORETICAL BASES

As noted, the central activity behind contracts law is the practice of promising. The initial definition of the Restatement (Second) of Contracts, the major treatise on contracts law, relies on promises: "A contract is a promise or a set of promises for the breach of which the law gives a remedy, or the performance of which the law in some way recognizes as a duty." Put more simply but no less abstractly, contracts are legally enforceable promises. Note the significant role the state plays in contracts law. In the simplest contract, two persons agree to an exchange. The state lends its enforcement power if and when one person breaks the contract. The role of the state in the enforcement and regulation of private agreements cannot be underestimated. Not only do parties to an agreement order their future conduct but the state also influences that relationship through contracts law. Implicit in the statement about legal enforceability and in the formal definition is the assertion that not all promises are legally enforceable. Before categorizing promises into sets of enforceability and nonenforceability, we must examine the social practice of promising.

Much of contracts law is common sense. Most of us, in the manner of well-socialized persons, have no difficulty understanding what it means to make a promise. We can distinguish bluffs and jokes ("I'll sell you the Brooklyn Bridge") from commitments and obligations ("I'll sell you my book for $5"). Still, a large area of uncertainty surrounds the act of promising. Even when bargainers are certain they intend to be obligated or bound to each other, uncertainty may surround the details or terms of the bargain. Parties may be unclear about when or what performance is due or about the quality of the goods or services. These are examples of uncertainty.

The law of contracts occupies the gray area of ambiguity and establishes a system of rules and principles designed to ascertain both when someone is legally obligated to another and the extent and consequence of that legal obligation. The body of doctrine we somewhat arbitrarily call contracts law is not held together by an over-

259

arching unitary theme. Instead, contracts law is motivated by competing, sometimes conflicting, values. In large part, the values shaping contracts doctrine reflect the requirements of particular types of contractual transactions. Contracts between merchants, for example, are interpreted with a set of contracts rules and principles greatly influenced by economic norms. Other transactions are influenced more by moral prescriptions. Through the rough and imperfect process of categorization, law attempts to serve various interests and mediate conflicting norms. Next, promissory transactions of different types will be discussed to demonstrate both the values underlying contracts law and the explicit interests contracts law attempts to protect.

Nonenforceable Promises. The category of nonenforceable promises illustrates why certain promises are enforced at all. By refracting contracts law through a prism of nonenforceability, the reasons, justifications, and motivations behind the law of contracts can be illuminated. The refractory technique also sharpens the distinction between law and morality. The division between morals and law is hardly discrete. While some theorists hold that we should only obey laws that are moral, and other theorists hold that law and morals should be completely distinct, all theorists recognize the fuzzy overlap between the two value systems. Nevertheless, statements in this essay about the enforceability or nonenforceability of promises refer to legal, not to moral, enforceability.

1. Promises to make gifts. When Aunt promises Niece to pay her law school tuition, is Aunt legally obligated to do so? The statement "I promise to pay for your law school education" can be interpreted reasonably to mean Aunt wishes to obligate herself. However, without more than this expressed intention, Aunt is not legally bound. Our society does not hold everyone to every promissory statement they make. Although it is logically possible to have a society in which all promissory statements are legally binding, it is not the society we have. There is no profound reason why the legal system differentiates between gift promises and others. Instead, "policy" reasons for not enforcing donative promises are usually proffered. Policy reasons are essentially rhetorical arguments offered in support of a particular rule or interpretation of law. By exploring the policy arguments behind not enforcing gift or donative promises, we will uncover two of the three foundational principles of contracts law.

Ask yourself, should all of your promises to make gifts be enforced by the state through its courts? The answer to the question is no, and the first reason is that generally the promisee (the individual to whom the promise is made) suffers little or no injury if the promisor reneges. If the promisor was really serious, the gift would have satisfied the legal requirement of delivery. A gift is binding once delivery or a symbol of delivery is made. The rationale for nonenforceability continues on the note that no one is really much worse off. The promisor retains the freedom or autonomy of changing her mind, and recognizing this, the promisee does not rely on the promise. Aunt may run into financial difficulties when the time comes for Niece to go to law school and she may want to avoid the obligation, or Niece may find another way of paying for law school.

Where there is no reliance by the promisee, then the promise to make a gift is not legally enforceable and the promisor can change her mind without incurring legal liability. Except for a small degree of disappointment, the promisee is left unharmed. So far the discussion of donative promises has been peculiarly narrow. There has been no assertion that people should or should not keep promises as a moral proposition. Simply, the law does not go so far as to force people to keep all promises. Instead, as a matter of policy, the law does not enforce donative promises, because of the small degree of harm hypothesized. The law assumes there is or should be little or no reliance or creation of expectations requiring protection. These statements about reliance and expectation are not empirical. Instead, common sense is relied upon to assess the degree of harm. Further, common sense and experience reveal that the social practice of promising has certain self-enforcing provisions. Reliance and expectation are protected through custom. If you fail to send a birthday gift to a friend, chances are your birthday will go unnoticed too. Such a custom helps mitigate harm caused by disappointed expectation or undue reliance.

The rationalization that no one is harmed by gift promises is inapplicable once the promisee relies on the promise. If the hypothesis about the *de minimis* (small) harm caused by failure to enforce gift promises is wrong, then contracts law has a corrective rule. If Niece changes her position by applying to law school or forgoes other opportunities by turning down a research fellowship, her change of position, her reliance, dramatically affects the transaction. No longer is the gift promise without legal consequence, the promisee has been put in a disadvantageous position. It really does not matter that going to law school may be good for Niece; she has done something she would not have otherwise done because of Aunt's statement. Naturally, the promisee cannot act unreasonably and try to "snap up" an opportunity by acting quickly and trying to bind the promisor. Nevertheless, if the promisee acts reasonably in reliance on a donative promise, then contracts law protects her *reliance interest,* which is one of the foundational principles of contracts law. When Niece enrolls in law school or declines employment in order to go to law school in reasonable reliance on Aunt's promise, she can look to Aunt for recompense if Aunt welches.

The second reason for not enforcing gift promises is that gifts can be seen as "sterile" transactions. If we think of contracts as bargains, exchanges going both ways, we must then realize both bargainers assume they are entering into a mutually advantageous deal. Both parties have increased expectations, and society is bettered by an increase in wealth because both parties experience an increase in utility as a consequence of the exchange between them. The argument against enforcing gift promises is that there is no increase in net social value by a gift being given by A to B because this is simply a zero-sum transaction. B gains what A loses.

Although the description of gift giving as a zero-sum game is clearly not accurate, this is the received idea according to contracts law. There are distributional and allocational consequences of gift giving when wealthy Aunt gives impecunious Niece law school tuition. Gifts are also wealth-creating to the extent that the person receiving a gift has a sense of return obligation. However, gifts are not bargains because only one side of the transaction receives anything, and theoretically, they receive exactly what the promisor gave. Since there is no bargain or rea-

sonable expectation created with donative promises, courts refuse enforcement. Thus, the second foundational principle is the *expectation interest,* which is most clearly seen in the following discussion on bargained-for exchange transactions.

2. Other nonenforceable promises. Donative promises absent reliance constitute one category of promises that do not create contracts. The remainder of the class is composed of void, illusory, illegal, and immoral promises, and promises that contravene public policy. This class of nonenforceable promises is not closed nor are these mutually exclusive categories. A contract for prostitution may be illegal, immoral, and void as violative of public policy. A promise to sell as much wheat as a farmer wishes whenever the farmer wants to sell violates none of the prohibitions in the contract for prostitution yet it is unenforceable because it is illusory.

When a promisor says something similar to "I'd like to give you something in the future but don't rely on it," the first issue to discern is whether the statement is a promise at all. As the Restatement notes, "A promise is a manifestation of intention to act or refrain from acting in a specified way, so made as to justify a promisee in understanding that a commitment has been made." If the statement is read to mean that no commitment was intended, then analysis ends. There is no promise because there is no intent to act or not to act and there is no need to continue to assess whether the statement is a legally binding contractual event. However, if worded more strongly, "I promise to give you $10,000 for your law school education," the statement moves closer to being legally enforceable because it is less vague and more capable of inducing reasonable reliance.

There is a hybrid group of promises that are enforceable at the election or ratification of one of the parties. These are called voidable contracts, such as a contract entered into by a minor or a person lacking the requisite mental capacity. A person lacking mental capacity may choose to ignore or ratify a contract at his or her election. Other contracts are voidable because they fail to satisfy certain formalities, including contracts discharged in bankruptcy, contracts required to be in writing, or contracts sought to be enforced after the statute of limitations has run out.

CONTRACTS

Enforceable Promises. Enforceable promises include what we commonly call "contracts" as well as promissory relationships outside the common understanding. The class of enforceable promises occupies the whole field of contracts law.

1. Bargained-for exchanges. Ordinary contracts are voluntary exchanges of goods or services, usually, but not necessarily, for money between two or more parties of relatively equal bargaining strength. So situated, the bargainers enter into agreements for exchanges, and at least part of the performance is to be rendered in the future. Contracts as bargains typify our common understanding. Most commercial transactions fit this description. The purchase and sale of a car, a house, or a business are examples of bargained-for exchanges. However, the reasoning and theoretical basis behind this common understanding may be less than clear. The very simple, yet deep, answer to why the law honors and encourages bargained-for exchanges is that enforcing exchanges is wealth-creating.

When Carpenter promises to build kitchen cabinets for Home Owner in exchange for a fee, both parties become promisors and promisees committing themselves to performances they were not obligated to do before. Prior to the exchange of promises between them there were no cabinets and now there are; thus, wealth is created. Cabinets are literally, as well as figuratively, created out of contract. Parenthetically, Home Owner may have also created wealth by working extra to earn money to pay Carpenter.

Extend the wealth-creating analogue a bit further and we have created a credit economy as distinct from a barter economy. In a barter economy, parties exchange things contemporaneously with the promises ("I'll trade my rock for your seashell"). In a credit economy, persons bind themselves together today to perform obligations tomorrow. Now the attractiveness of enforcing executory (future) promises should be apparent. Not only are contracts wealth-creating between the parties to the transaction but there is also a multiplier effect. Assume A enters a contract with B to build an office complex. A goes to C for construction money and to D for mortgage money. D sells the commercial paper to E, who may in turn trade the paper for a discounted value. B subcontracts the work to X. X purchases materials from Y and Z. All of these contractual relationships, stemming from the

underlying A-B contract, create wealth. From the A-B contract, a series of expectations are intentionally created, parties can plan for the future, and contracts law protects a series of *expectation interests.*

What motivates parties to enter a bargained-for exchange is the belief that once they enter the contract they are each better off than they were prior to the agreement. This description is a fundamentally utilitarian and economic analysis of contracts. The economic theory of contracts takes a particular view of the world. This view is market-based and motivated by the goals of wealth maximization and economic efficiency. In a market world, people bind themselves to each other for exchanges because doing so is mutually, materially beneficial.

The economic vision sees contracting parties as traders in a marketplace who consistently, knowingly, and voluntarily enter trades to maximize their own economic or material self-interest. This impersonal, commercial world is also a partial world with powerful implications for contracts law. Contracts law, in no small measure, attempts to promote this world and to facilitate commercial transactions by having fairly clear, understandable, certain, and predictable rules. Certain, objective, predictable, and understandable rules foster markets because planning is easier when consequences can be predicted with more accuracy. Further, trading risks are lessened and more risk-averse traders can enter the market.

This formalistic portrait of commercial law is accurate historically. In the Middle Ages, special merchants courts existed and legal rules developed to settle international trade disputes and to accommodate mercantile interests. In the late nineteenth century and early twentieth century, uniform sales laws existed for the express purpose of creating a set of formal contracts rules. A formalized body of rules develop coincidently with rapidly expanding and industrializing economies. A specialized body of rules for commercial transactions exists today in the form of the Uniform Commercial Code (UCC), which has been adopted in forty-nine states. Although the nine articles of the code are devoted to special topics (for example, sales, commercial paper, banking, bulk sales, and secured transactions), the code greatly influences the whole law of contracts because in many instances it is used analogically to resolve contracts disputes not directly covered by its articles.

2. Nonpecuniary trades. Commercial transactions are only part of the world of contracts. People enter contracts for nonpecuniary reasons and enter contracts in nonmarket situations. Examples of nonpecuniary transactions include family arrangements such as antenuptial and separation agreements, some personal-services and unique-goods contracts, and group or long-term arrangements such as collective bargaining agreements and employee benefit packages. Nonpecuniary transactions have economic ramifications (money is a crude common denominator and convenient translator); however, these contracts are often motivated by concerns other than economic efficiency or wealth maximization.

In addition to or in place of material reward, people enter contracts for reasons of participation, solidarity, trust, loyalty, even love. Nonpecuniary trades often occur in the absence of strong viable markets. Competitive markets exist when there are numerous traders with small market shares, price signals and information are relatively accurate and inexpensive, there are substitutes for the commodity being traded, and bargainers have relatively equal bargaining power. Competitive markets often do not exist in nonpecuniary situations because one or more of the market elements is absent.

When Family commissions Artist to paint Grandfather's portrait for presentation on his eightieth birthday, Family will likely rely on Artist's assurances of timely delivery. Further, as the birthday approaches, the market for portraits collapses. Even though Family may have had several artists to choose from initially, after contract performance commences there is no viable market because no substitutes are available. The contract for the portrait, a unique good or service, is an example of a nonmarket transaction with nonpecuniary value. Clearly, the contract price is evidence of economic value. The contract also has nonpecuniary value because the portrait was commissioned for a special occasion. Further, because the Artist rapidly becomes a monopolist as Grandfather's birthday approaches, the Family is foreclosed from bargaining in a competitive market.

What binds parties to nonpecuniary or nonmarket contracts? Put differently, what is the theoretical basis for enforcing these arrangements? In contradistinction to the economic base, these promises are better supported by a moral argument that asserts promises ought to be kept as a way of honoring the dignity of parties to a transaction. People ought to keep their promises because keeping promises is fair or good. This claim focuses on the place, role, and importance of the individual in the contracting process rather than hypothesizing some utilitarian end state to which all traders and transactions must conform. The obvious weakness with the moral justification is that it does not adequately explain why donative promises are not enforced. Neither the moral nor the economic argument stands alone. To some extent they support each other (merchants ought to keep promises, too) and to another extent they offer independent bases. In our contracts jurisprudence, both are necessary, neither one is sufficient.

Even assuming people enter contracts with mixed motivations, contracts law is skewed toward protecting economic interests through market norms. A long-term relationship between a supplier and a distributor, for example, requires a bond of trust as well as economic incentive. Still, the legal rules shaping their contractual relationship are significantly influenced by economic principles and justifications. Consequently, market-based rules are appropriate guides for regulating pecuniary trades. Market-based rules do not offer sufficient justification for or an explanation of nonpecuniary trades.

3. Promissory estoppel. The hallmark of the above two categories is the voluntariness of the exchange. People connect with each other either for mutual material advantage in the case of market exchanges or for nonpecuniary reasons such as loyalty or trust in the examples of nonmarket transactions. In both situations, however, the parties voluntarily intend to be bound to each other. A serious contractual problem occurs when parties are unclear about their intention to be bound. As will be explained in more detail in the next section on the contracting process, sometimes during negotiations one party is left with or given the impression that a contract has been formed when the other has not. In such a situation, the party who believes a contract has been formed can be disadvantaged by relying on a promisor's assurances or can advantage the promisor in some way. If the court finds that the promisee has been disadvantaged, then the court can protect the promisee's *reliance interest* even in the absence of a contract. Similarly, if the promisor is advantaged at the expense of the promisee, a court can force the promisor to disgorge the advantage, return a deposit for example, and restore the promisee to his status quo ante, the place he was in before bargaining began. In this way the promisee's *restitution interest* is protected.

Contracts law attempts to protect and honor three foundational interests: *reliance, expectation,* and *restitution.* The most frequent justifications offered to protect these interests stem from economic theory and moral philosophy. Market contracts are promoted because it is economically wise to do so. Individuals and society materially benefit, and individuals are accorded autonomy in the world. Nonmarket contracts are protected because it is morally good to do so. Again, individuals and society benefit because liberty to contract and create community-regarding arrangements are protected. Both categories of contracts coexist in a political universe committed to honoring the pluralistic desires and needs of individuals who enter contracts and to creating a social climate conducive to encouraging exchanges that morally and economically benefit society. So regarded, contracts law attempts to mediate power conflicts between the one and the many and values conflicts among diverse interests. The foundational interests are thus based upon arguments drawn from economic, moral, and political theory.

THE CONTRACTING PROCESS

There is no unified theory of contracts. Several theoretical bases exist, some predominate. More accurately, one theory predominates some contract situation or some historic period. Nevertheless, there is a more or less identifiable corpus of contracts doctrine, and lawyers, judges, and academics speak to each other about contracts law within a common framework. That framework of rules and theory can be made accessible by exploring contracts law functionally. The contracting process can be broken down into six recognizable stages representing the chronological life of a contract. The chronological continuum drawn below corresponds with the remaining sections of this essay and is in-

tended to depict distinct stages in the contracting process having legal significance.

CONTRACTS CONTINUUM

Assumptions and Definitions. Living in a society that prizes contracts, we are enveloped in a complex set of sociolegal norms surrounding the contracting process. We bring to that process certain assumptions and beliefs. Some are conscious, some exist at lower levels of semiconsciousness or unconsciousness, and others are counterintuitive or simply false. Contracts law attempts to order those assumptions and beliefs. One misconception is that contracts are written documents and that parties dicker over contract terms until each side is mutually satisfied. A negotiated exchange agreement was earlier referred to as an "ordinary contract." The misconception is that ordinary written contracts occupy the whole field of contracts law. They do not. Although ordinary or express written contracts constitute the bulk of the field, they are only one category. Express contracts may also be made orally such as when someone bids at an auction and her bid is accepted by the auctioneer. Therefore, express contracts may be either oral or written. The primary difference between oral and written contracts is that the existence (if not the meaning) of the written agreement is easier to prove than an oral agreement. This difference is not insignificant. However, in most instances the absence of a written agreement is not fatal to enforceability.

Once the category of express contracts is created, its twin, implied contracts, cannot be far behind. Implied contracts fall into two subcategories and here contracts law goes from the familiar to the sticky. Ordering a meal in a restaurant, particularly from a menu without prices, is an example of an "implied-in-fact" contract. A contract to pay the restaurant's price for the meal ordered is created through the act of ordering in response to a request for an order. The parties to the transaction act as if they intend to be bound to each other. Their conduct, rather than their expressed words, creates the contract.

The other type of implied contract is called an "implied-in-law" or quasi-contract. Our normal understanding is that contracts are voluntarily created obligations. From this standpoint, quasi-contracts are not contracts at all. Rather, quasi-contracts are imposed upon parties by courts. Imagine sitting at home and Builder starts working in your backyard. When you ask him what he is doing, he says he is installing a swimming pool. You smile, knowing you did not order the pool, sit comfortably, and watch the installation. After the work is completed, can you resist Builder's lawsuit because you had not expressly entered into a contract for the pool? No. While it is true there is no express contract, and most likely no implied-in-fact contract for the pool, by keeping the benefits of the pool you would be unjustly enriched at the expense of Builder. Through the device of quasi-contract, a court will impose an obligation on you to pay Builder something for the pool. The court will order you to disgorge the unjustly retained benefit as a way of protecting the *restitution interest* of Builder.

Contracting can be viewed as a communications process. The practical significance of the communications concept is obvious but nonetheless significant. Contracting is a social not a subjective exercise. An individual cannot privately will himself into a legal obligation; he must communicate his desires to another. The deepest desires of parties to a contract are irrelevant for interpreting and understanding the nature of the agreement unless those desires are somehow outwardly manifested. There are two competing theories about when a contract comes into existence. The first, the will theory, attempts to protect the subjective desires of the parties. According to the will theory there is no contract until the minds of the parties meet. The second, the objective theory, requires complete outward manifestation by the parties of their desires. Alone, both theories are incomplete and a historical tension between the "will" theory and the "objective" theory pervades the contracting process. A rigid objectivist interpretation would preclude contract formation when one party says, "I'll sell you my cow," and the other party accepts, saying, "I'll buy your cow," in a situation where both parties intended the sale of a horse, because the outward manifestations are inconsistent with the subject matter of the contract. At the subjective extreme, anytime an unsatisfied party says she never "really intended to enter an agreement," a contract could not be formed. Clearly, neither theory works in the extreme. The objectivist theory precludes contract formation with even the slightest slip in communications. The will theory provides a dissatisfied party with a broad avenue of excuse. Currently, the law attempts some reconciliation of the two theories. The formation and terms of a contract must be somehow outwardly manifested, and what the parties meant or intended is relevant to explain the outward manifestations.

The contracting process starts as soon as possible parties to a contract begin communicating. People can begin talking and consciously discuss the possibility of contractually binding themselves to each other without making a legal commitment. Asking a salesperson at Tiffany's about the brilliance and cost of a four-carat diamond does not obligate you to buy it. Yet, such conversation may be a prelude to a lawful commitment. Thus, the first stage in the process is *negotiation*. During this period people may or may not become bound to each other. In other words, legal obligation may or may not attach during negotiations.

As the parties move toward agreement (and legal commitment), a contract goes through the *formation* stage. Not surprisingly, the rules during this period are more formalistic. In part, the rules serve as sign and ritual to indicate when the magic moment of contractual obligation attaches to conversation. After formation, *performance* begins. Take a simple, discrete transaction. For example, I order a book from a bookstore to be delivered on 1 December in exchange for payment of $20. Ascertaining what performance is due and when it is due is relatively easy. In simple, discrete transactions there is either performance or breach. In more complicated, long-term situations, sometimes referred to as relational contracts, performance and breach are not so neatly divided. The relationship of the parties may be a series of minor and major disagreements about contractual obligations. During the performance stage, the parties attempt to ascertain what performance is due, what is excused, which imperfections to tolerate, and whether failure to perform releases one party or both parties from further obligations.

Breach is the next stage in the process. If a party does not do what was promised, then breach has occurred and the breaching party is liable to the nonbreaching party. However, all breaches do not terminate the contract or release the nonbreaching party from further obligations.

Finally, if an unexcused breach occurs, the nonbreaching party is entitled to a *remedy,* the last stage in the process. Perhaps not so curiously, most practicing lawyers examine remedies first. Before lawyers reconstruct the story of the contracting process, they must assess the types and likelihood of relief available from a court. An exercise in legal analysis is purely academic if relief is unavailable and law does not function well at such a rarefied level of abstraction. Instead, law works best when it works in the world. With this functional perspective in mind, we will proceed chronologically through the contracting process.

Negotiation. Negotiation is as varied a topic as contracts law itself. Much of a lawyer's time is spent negotiating. In fact, negotiations engage much of everyone's time. All negotiations share an attribute. Negotiations are preliminary to commitment. Not all negotiations lead to contractual commitment. Further, all contracts do not require sophisticated bargaining. When negotiations occur, they are preliminary to contractual obligation and what is said or done during the negotiations period may affect the interpretation of the resulting agreement.

The simple case is the contract entered or rejected without haggling. If I offer to sell you my puppy for $25 and you accept, then we have a contract. If you walk away, we have no contract. If you counter and offer $20, we have begun to negotiate and no contract will be formed until we agree on a price. Determining whether a contract exists turns on how clearly parties manifest their intentions. The outward manifestation of intention to be bound is the central force behind the attachment of legal obligation during the negotiating process. If speakers manifest an intent to be bound, then they are contractually bound. If they manifest an intent not to be bound, then they are not bound. There is no need for a complicated system of legal rules to discern the consequences in these simple cases. Instead, a system of rules and principles is needed for complex or ambiguous cases such as the sale of a business during which negotiations go through various stages and contract documents go through several drafts.

Determining when parties are legally bound during protracted negotiations presents two questions. First, have the parties manifested an intent to be bound? Second, to what are they bound? A negative or an indeterminate answer to either question precludes the formation of a contract.

During the negotiation process it is not unusual for parties to act ambiguously toward each other. This can happen in several ways. One party can mistakenly believe a contract exists. Or one party may intentionally induce another party to act as if a contract were formed. In both cases, one party relies on the existence of a contract that the other denies. The disadvantaged party may seek judicial protection. Sometimes parties mutually and intentionally act ambiguously. Both parties can intentionally "agree to agree." Whether a contract has been formed in this situation is an open question. Parties may "agree in principle" and act ambiguously about either whether they intended to enter a contract or what are the precise terms of the proposed agreement. Because of ambiguities surrounding contract terms and contract formation, a court may not be able to enforce an agreement to agree.

If parties clearly intend to wait until the contract is more formally drafted before they are bound, then there is no contract. If the parties envision the final draft as a "mere memorialization" of what they have already agreed upon, then a contract exists even without the final draft. The answer as to whether a contract or no contract exists depends on how a decision-maker assesses the parties, their relationship, the context of the conversation, the setting, the stuff bargained over, and other indicia shedding light on intent.

Assuming the parties intend to be bound, then to what are they bound when terms are unclear? Too many open questions about contract terms can make the contract unenforceable. Without more information, a promise by one builder to another to sell fill dirt cannot be enforced because price, quantity, and delivery terms, among others, are unknown. Contracts with ambiguous terms can be resolved in one of three ways. First, a contract can be found. The propensity is to favor the formation of contracts. The court can supply the missing terms or otherwise clarify ambiguities. In commercial transactions all contract terms except quantity can be approximated. Questions about such items as price, delivery, and payment can be resolved by referring to reasonable commercial practices or the Uniform Commercial Code. Second, a court may find no contract because the ambiguities cannot be reasonably resolved. The parties then go their separate ways. Such a finding, however, is not as neat as it sounds. The party wishing to be bound may find himself disadvantaged by either relying to his detriment and incurring costs or enriching the other party with an advance payment or delivery, for example. The disadvantaged party may then have a claim for reliance or restitution. Thus, the third response is that a court can either impose a quasi-contract forcing the disgorgement of any unjust enrichment and thus protect one party's restitution interest, or protect a party's detrimental reliance losses.

Therefore, at some point during negotiations, legal liability may attach in one of two ways. The parties may intentionally and expressly agree to be bound. Or, even when the formal rules are not strictly followed, legal liability may attach to protect persons who have reasonably relied on the statements and assurances of another, or anything wrongly obtained or unjustly held can be ordered returned.

As a matter of doctrinal housekeeping, during the negotiation stage there are two important legal rules at work. First, pursuant to the Statute of Frauds, certain types of contracts must be in writing before they are enforceable. The Statute, first enacted in England in 1677, is subject to many exceptions. Written contracts are on safer ground than oral contracts because they are easier to prove and they may be subject to the Statute. Second, there is a countervailing danger in reducing an agreement to writing. This danger is embodied in the Parol Evidence Rule, which holds that once a writing is intended to be the final embodiment of the negotiations of the parties then prior oral or written communications and contemporaneous oral communications cannot be used to vary, alter, or contradict the final writing. Therefore, the oral assurances or "guarantees" by a salesman about a used car having a perfectly sound transmission made while signing the final document may not be part of the contract. If the transmission falls out before the car has left the lot the customer may not be protected by the oral "guarantee." The Parol

Evidence Rule is also open to numerous exceptions yet it does require care in drafting a contract.

Formation. During the formation stage we encounter the most elaborate rules and rituals of the contracting process. Offer and acceptance rules during the nineteenth century and much of the twentieth century were extremely technical. The modus operandi behind contracts law during this formalistic period was to create a set of certain and predictable rules so parties could know how to behave during the contracting process. Objectivity, certainty, predictability, and uniformity were the attributes of a good contracts rule. They are also the characteristics of a fast-paced market economy of the sort rapidly industrializing nations need to facilitate commercial transactions. Commercial transactions are made easier and more profitable if parties can plan and rely on those plans. Technical offer and acceptance rules were an attempt to cast norms of ordinary commercial communications into a concrete set of prescriptions. Not surprisingly, rigid rules also fostered litigation and confusion. Communications between people are inherently imperfect. We hear what we want to hear and read situations most favorably to our side. Consequently, when market shifts occur, contract parties interpret their situations differently. Market traders want more formal rules as long as markets remain stable. During periods of instability, contractual flexibility is desired, at least by the party who misread market signals.

During the more formalistic period of contracts law, lawsuits regarding offer and acceptance rules turned on rather arcane issues such as when and how the initial communication was made (the offer) and on the response to the communication (the acceptance). Cases discuss the legal propriety of sending an offer by mail and an acceptance by telegraph. During this period contracts law attempted to organize a coherent set of rules to deal with obvious imperfections in normal communications. One attempt at shoring up imperfections in communications was to require symmetry between the offer and the acceptance. Before a contract was formed the offeree had to accept the offer precisely as made. This symmetry between offer and acceptance became known as the mirror-image rule. The rule failed miserably. Traders naturally realized that perfect symmetry was a fearful symmetry. Rarely does an acceptance exactly mirror an offer, and a slight alteration would preclude contract formation. The mirror-image rule had the undesirable effect of allowing one party to a contract to renege halfway through performance when the market was unfavorable and escape liability by successfully arguing that the acceptance was not perfectly symmetrical with the offer. Such formalism was too unconnected with the realities of the marketplace and with the needs and desires of traders. In the marketplace, communications are not so inflexible. Modern contracts law has tried to accommodate this imperfection. If parties act as though they are or want to be bound, then they are bound and differences in terms are resolved by the Uniform Commercial Code or the courts.

The conceptual and ideological bulwark of the formation stage is the doctrine of consideration. Loosely defined, consideration is a bargained-for exchange. Consideration is a quid pro quo where parties exchange goods or services between themselves. Recall the discussion about the wealth-creating nature of exchange transactions. When bargainers exchange goods or services, total social utility is enhanced. The exchange in value is called consideration. Consideration functions as a contractual talisman. The presence of consideration is indicative of the parties' intent to be bound and therefore of the existence of a contract. An exchange of promises supported by consideration constitutes an enforceable contract.

To further encourage exchange transactions, with a reverential tip of the hat to the sacred principle of freedom of contract, courts frequently say that they never assess the adequacy of consideration or the value of the exchange. Courts will never rewrite (re-right) a contract in which one party makes a bad deal unless, of course, the court wants to. This little bit of sarcasm has more than sanctimony to commend it. The closed eye approach of courts to consideration was never absolute. Courts prefer to give parties a great deal of discretion and do not reevaluate the deal in an effort to avoid second-guessing the value of the contract. However, courts do look to the adequacy of the consideration as probative of other infirmities in the contracting process. The amateur who buys a Stradivarius for $225,000 from a cagey violin dealer only to learn it is a $300 copy will argue

that something more is going on than an inequality in consideration. Gross disparity in the value of the contract may trigger an inquiry into fraud, misrepresentation, undue influence, duress, unconscionability, or inequality in bargaining power. Courts can then step into the contracting process either to realign bargaining strengths or to repair injuries.

In fuzzy situations when parties negotiate and tentatively act on the negotiations but are unclear on the extent or existence of a legal commitment, contracts law resorts to assessing the reasonableness of the reliance. The doctrine of promissory estoppel is captured in Restatement (Second) of Contracts section 90: "A promise which the promisor should reasonably expect to induce action or forbearance on the part of the promisee or a third person and which does induce such action or forbearance is binding if injustice can be avoided only by enforcement of the promise. The remedy granted for breach may be limited as justice requires."

The doctrine serves as both a departure from and a supplement to the doctrine of consideration. First, section 90 sustains an independent cause of action. This means that in the right circumstances (that is, satisfaction of each of the above elements) an injured party can sue without proving the existence of a contract. During the negotiation process, for example, if one party consistently and in good faith relies on the assurances of another that a contract is forthcoming, and no agreement is reached, the injured party can recoup losses without a contract. Second, section 90 acts as a substitute for consideration. This means a contract can be formed without the explicit bargained-for exchange required by the doctrine of consideration. Good-faith reliance can satisfy the consideration requirement. The significance of this apparently artificial distinction between section 90 as an independent cause of action and section 90 as a substitute for consideration is revealed in the last sentence of the rule. How one treats the doctrine (as an independent cause of action or as a substitute) has important remedial consequences. If section 90 functions as a substitute, then a contract may be found and the injured party may be awarded the benefit of her bargain. The court will assess the relationship between the parties as if a contract were formed and the *expectation interest* is protected. Otherwise, the court may award an injured party her costs in reliance or order a return of benefits conferred—for example, a deposit given back. Promissory estoppel opens up the scope of contracts law by eliding the market-based doctrine of consideration into a broader sweep by encompassing *reliance* and *restitution* as well as *expectation*.

Performance. Determining whether a simple, discrete contract has been performed or not is a relatively easy matter; either the promised performance is rendered or it is not. If the promised performance does not occur, then the contract has been breached. Likewise, injuries or consequences flowing from the breach of simple contracts are readily identifiable. Long-term relational contracts, however, are more complicated affairs. During performance, it is not unusual to find one or both of the parties dissatisfied in various degrees. Each failure to render the promised performance is a breach. Some breaches give the nonbreaching party a right to assert a remedy; other breaches are excused and the nonbreaching party has no recourse. The consequences of breach will be discussed in the next section. Here we will discuss the most litigated area of contracts law: determining what performance is due and what performance is excused.

Contracting parties are not particularly well known for their prescience even when lawyers are involved during the negotiating and the drafting stages. Most contracts are entered into without the aid of lawyers. Sometimes lawyers draft standardized agreements to be used by their clients in a variety of situations. The use of form or pad contracts, sometimes referred to as contracts of adhesion, presents a variety of problems because one form is drafted for various transactions that are not individually negotiated events. On rare occasions lawyers draft agreements to fit specific situations. Major equipment leases, collective bargaining agreements, sales of businesses, construction contracts—the list of usually negotiated contracts continues.

Even with the existence of a written negotiated document drafted with a lawyer's talent, problems develop. Frequently, the parties are imprecise about what they write into the contract. This imprecision may be caused by unawareness, neglect, conscious evasion, or intentional ambiguity. Lawyers, because they must translate the needs and desires of their clients into writing, add another layer of ambiguity. To this multilevel process, add communications between self-interested parties and the result is a contract document that is a less-than-perfect embodiment of the wills of the parties. Ambiguities abound. If there were no ambiguity, there would be no need for a legal system with contracts rules to determine a contracting party's legal rights, duties, powers, and obligations. The process of determining the meaning of this bundle of legal relations is called interpretation.

During performance most contractual disagreements center on problems of interpretation. Interpretation can be simply defined as explaining the meaning of the symbols (words) of the contract. This is no easy task and there are several possible answers to the question, What does the contract mean? Conflicting interpretations always exist when a dispute develops. The problem comes in choosing one meaning over another or in imposing a meaning. Do we give more weight to the meaning attached to the document by the expert or novice or drafter or nondrafter? Does the contract have meaning independent of the meanings attached by the parties? Does the decision-maker's meaning govern interpretation?

Contracts law has established an elaborate set of interpretive strategies. Although there is no single formula, an approximate ordering of interpretive rules attempts to explain both the text and context (and sometimes subtext) of the contractual relationship between the parties. The first step in contract interpretation is to examine the text, especially the particularly troublesome language of the contract. If interpreting a single phrase does not resolve the ambiguity, then the contract document or documents will be read as a whole. If meaning is plain to the objective observer (usually the judge), then the interpretive inquiry ends. If the meaning is unclear (nearly always at least one party will disagree with the decision-maker's interpretation), then we move beyond the text in an effort to find out what these parties "really" meant—what they intended. At this point the objective and will theories of contracts merge. To understand the meaning of the outward manifestations of the parties (to understand the contract), questions about the parties' intent must be asked.

The decision-maker can look back to the negotiation process for help in understanding the meaning of the contract. What was said during negotiations aids interpretation and helps explain the contract. Who the parties are, what they were contracting for, and under what circumstances help explain intent. Next, how the parties dealt with each other during the course of performance of the disputed contract may uncover meaning. So far all inquiries about meaning have centered on the parties and the particular contract. Further away from the disputed event, the history of dealing between the parties on other contracts can be examined. Finally, the customs and usages of the trade or industry may help clarify meaning.

If there is one central question that ties the interpretation process together it is, How did or should the parties allocate risk? Most contractual disputes deal with partially executory contracts. Executory contracts, contracts where performance remains due, essentially allocate risk now against future contingencies. Viewed from a perspective of risk allocation, the interpretive inquiry may yield a reasonably definite or, at least, workable answer. If it does not, the court has the power of implication. The court can put terms into the contract.

Legion cases note the judiciary's reluctance to "rewrite" or "remake" a contract for parties. Nevertheless, the inherent ambiguities in the contracting process and the adversary system's pressing need to resolve disputes on matters having apparently no true or objectively correct answer compels courts to imply terms into a contract. Because disputes involve ambiguities and there is no scientific way to find a "true" solution, the second-best method is to have a disinterested decision-maker evaluate the evidence and judge accordingly. The last step in the search for contractual meaning is known as construction. The judge construes or gives legal effect to the contract as interpreted.

Interpretation, implication, and construction are the processes used to ascertain meaning, particularly determining what performance is due.

Even if the parties are certain about what performance is due, the obligated party may be excused from performance. Contracting parties thus have neat alternative arguments when they wish to avoid contractual obligations. First, they can assert they have no obligation to render the performance the other party says is due. Second, they can assert that even if once obligated they

have been excused from further performance. Excuse is a fertile area of litigation and is linked to interpretation and performance. A party seeks to be excused from performance because the risks have become too high. I am using *risk* in two senses. Either the costs of compliance outweigh the expected benefits or lost opportunities (opportunity costs) outweigh prospective gains. State intervention into the privately ordered relationship of contracting parties is most pronounced in the area of excuse. Effectively, the court tells one party they need no longer perform and tells the other party they can no longer expect performance.

There is some historical ordering to the range of available excuses. If contracts are viewed objectively, then parties must be held to what they objectively agreed to do. What happens, however, if the subject matter of the contract cannot be delivered? For example, a theater owner agrees to lease a theater for a week but the theater is destroyed by fire. Is this contract now impossible to perform? Courts held impossibility to be an excusing condition but were reluctant to go much beyond objective impossibility or acts of God. This reluctance stemmed from the antipathy toward rewriting the contract for the parties.

This hard-line approach gave way to less rigid doctrines such as frustration of purpose. The lessee who rented a room to view the king's coronation procession was excused from paying for the room when the coronation was canceled due to the king's surgery. Naturally, the hotelier argued the room was available and the risk of no coronation passed to the lessee. The courts held otherwise under the theory that the express purpose of the contract was to view the coronation as opposed to merely renting a room. This opens up the contracting process to subjective testimony. The doctrine of frustration of purpose requires an evaluative assessment of the purposes and risks of the contract.

Another area of excuse is commercial impracticability made most famous with the *Suez Canal* and *Uranium Litigation* cases. The closing of the Suez Canal and the alleged existence of an international uranium cartel made performance prohibitively expensive but not impossible, nor was the purpose of the contract frustrated. Can or should sophisticated parties to complex commercial agreements be excused from performance when things (the market) do not turn out as expected? The answer is, Yes, but rarely. Merchants enter contracts to allocate risk. Whenever the market changes drastically, one of the parties will be dissatisfied. One party suffers a wipeout, the other enjoys a windfall. Courts remain wary of adjusting windfalls and wipeouts unless there is clear evidence that certain risks were neither assumed nor allocated. In the language of the Uniform Commercial Code and the Restatement, failure to perform is not a breach if performance has been made impracticable by the occurrence of a contingency, the nonoccurrence of which was a basic assumption of the contract. In less-stilted language, the party asserting the excuse of commercial impracticability must prove that performance became commercially impracticable because of unforeseen supervening circumstances not within the contemplation of the parties.

Generally, market shifts that disadvantage one party will not provide grounds for excuse due to impracticability. The market is the benchmark in commercial contracts. When contracts are made in relatively competitive markets, courts will not upset voluntarily allocated risks. However, when the market is so imperfect that traders cannot bargain as freely or as voluntarily as they might desire, the law affords another ground for excuse —unconscionability. Market imperfections are due to the monopolistic or the oligopolistic nature of the industry and sometimes due to the structure of a firm. When one party to a contract exercises an excessive amount of power allowing that party to skew contract terms or prices in his favor, the disadvantaged party may not have had the opportunity to exercise meaningful choice. A consumer who "bargains" with a car salesman has little or no opportunity to restructure the manufacturer's warranty. The consumer is usually in a take-it-or-leave-it position and any "bargaining" centers on only a few terms such as price. The absence of meaningful choice or the presence of unfair surprise may result in an unconscionable contract or in unconscionable terms. Courts need not enforce contracts or portions of contracts found unconscionable. Defining unconscionability is no easy task. A contract may be procedurally unconscionable when one party occupies a superior bargaining position empowering them to include unfair terms. A contract term may be substantively oppressive

when it shocks the conscience of the court, such as when a door-to-door salesman sells a $300 English-language encyclopedia to non-English-speaking buyers for $1200. In such instances enforcement can be and has been denied.

Breach. Once it is determined that a party must perform and performance is not excused, then any failure to perform is a breach of contract. All breaches do not terminate the contract by relieving the nonbreaching party from further obligation to perform. If Construction Contractor fails to place the proper molding in a custom-designed house, he has breached the contract. However, Home Owner is not excused from paying for the home. Rather, Contractor has substantially performed and any nonperformance is offset by a deduction for damages. Home Owner is liable for the contract price minus an allowance for the cost of the molding.

If the breach is material, if Contractor's workmanship is so poor as to significantly alter the nature of the promised performance, then this breach excuses Home Owner's further performance. The custom-designed house with leaks, misplaced walls, and noticeable cracks in the foundation does not have to be taken and paid for by Home Owner. Although any breach of contract entitles the nonbreaching party to some remedy, all breaches do not excuse further performance.

Contracts may be breached during performance, after one side has fully performed, or even before any performance is rendered. In the last situation, the breach is called anticipatory repudiation. The nonbreaching party has the option of pursuing a remedy at the time of breach or the nonbreacher may wait for the time of performance. To some extent the nonbreaching party can wait for more favorable market conditions or wait and attempt to revive the contract. In any case, the nonbreaching party has a duty to not allow damages to accumulate unreasonably. If Coal Producer breaches a contract before performance is due, Distributor cannot sit back and watch damages rise with market prices while other coal is available. Instead, Distributor has an obligation to purchase substitute coal elsewhere and may charge the difference to Producer. This duty to mitigate is part of the ethos of contracts law that accepts breach as a normally occurring act, as long as the nonbreacher is compensated and damages are minimized.

Remedies. With the topic of remedies we come full circle. Remedies define the types of relief available from courts. For the practicing lawyer, this is the starting place for analysis. For the academic lawyer, the threads of the three foundational principles clearly appear and tie in with the theoretical bases of contracts. Contracts remedies can be arranged in a hierarchy described throughout this section. Legal remedies are divided into three broad classifications—law, equity, and restitution—and each is motivated by a particular insight about what a contracts remedy should accomplish.

1. Damages: A remedy at law. The most frequent remedy at law is damages. Damages are monetary awards designed to compensate the nonbreaching party for harms caused by breach. Compensation is intended to make the injured party whole and is distinguished from punitive damages, which are designed to punish or deter undesirable conduct. The simple idea of compensation is central to jurisprudential thinking about contracts remedies. The direct effect of discouraging punitive damages awards is to empower a party to breach a contract. Parties to a contract have the power to breach either to minimize losses or to enter into better deals.

What lies behind the compensation principle? Oliver Wendell Holmes, Jr.'s famous aphorism about contracts is, "The duty to keep a contract at common law means a prediction that you must pay damages if you do not keep it—and nothing else." Parties to a contract have the power to breach and can legitimately do so as long as they pay the requisite damages. This tilt toward allowing a party to breach and pay sets up the situation known as the theory of efficient breach. Assume A has a contract with B to sell books for $10 each and B plans on reselling the books for $12. The law of damages allows A to breach its contract, and economic theory posits that A will and should do so whenever A receives another offer for anything more than $12. C, for example, may offer to buy the books from A for $15. Given this skeletal set of facts, everyone is happy: A sells the books to C for $15 and makes a profit of $3, pays B the expected profit of $2, and C gets the books. Not only are the parties satisfied, the theory continues, but society is better off because wealth has been created, there is another trader (C) in the market, and the goods have risen to their highest value. Under this economically based

theory each party's expectation interest is secured.

There are two angles to the compensation principle. First, courts attempt to protect contract benefits for the nonbreaching party by awarding expectancy damages for breach. The injured party will be awarded an amount of money necessary to give her the benefit of her bargain or put her in her postcontract position. Put another way, a damages award attempts to put an injured party in the position she would have occupied if the contract had been fully performed. Thus, the injured party is made whole through compensation by receiving the advantages she expected from the contract.

There is one important reservation, however. Sometimes expectancy damages cannot be calculated with a reasonable degree of certainty. If Movie Studio breaches a contract with Actress, Actress will not be able to sue for lost profits on the prospective film because these profits would be too speculative, given the unpredictable nature of the industry. The best courts can do in such situations is to make Actress whole, by compensating her for her losses in reliance. Compensation for these losses, for example, monies spent in preparation for production or for having forgone other employment opportunities, puts Actress into her precontract position. Clearly, reliance costs are of secondary interest when the contract is expected to make a profit. In losing contract situations, it would be profitable to seek reliance damages as opposed to expectancy damages. Reliance damages are also compensatory but measure losses from a different angle. Actress is put into the position she would have occupied if the contract had never been entered.

2. Specific performance: A remedy in equity. In the book contract hypothetical, is B really satisfied? After all, B wanted the books. Should a court order A to perform the original contract? In some situations a court will order A to deliver the books to B. This order is the equitable remedy of specific performance. Indeed, if the books were rare, a court would order A to specifically perform. Still, the remedial scheme favors money compensation over specific performance under the theory that money is adequate substitutional relief. If the books are easily replaceable, B can use money to purchase substitute goods in the marketplace. Therefore, before an injured party can receive specific performance, he must allege and prove that damages (the remedy at law) are inadequate, that substitutional monetary relief puts him in a less advantageous position than performance of the contract does. In this way, the legal system balances the economic and moral bases of contracts. Contracting parties can breach and pay, thus satisfying the utilitarian goal of enriching society. However, if the contract is of the sort that substitutional redress does not make the injured party whole, then the breacher will be ordered to perform, thus satisfying the moral notion that people ought to honor their promises instead of treating people as means to utilitarian ends. In this fashion, the legal system mediates competing normative interests.

3. Restitution. The above remedies focus on the plight of the injured party when a contract is breached by fashioning a form of relief designed to compensate the injured party for losses suffered. Restitution is motivated by another concern. The swimming pool hypothetical is an example of when restitution is appropriate. When Builder mistakenly installs a pool on your property and you could have done something to stop him, technically there is no express contract. There may well be no implied-in-fact contract either. However, a court would be justified in imposing an implied-in-law contract in favor of Builder, even given Builder's mistake. What relief is due Builder? Most contract damages awards are measured by the nonbreaching party's injuries or losses. With restitution, the focus shifts from the Builder's injuries to your gains.

Under the theory of unjust enrichment you may not appropriate an advantage that it would be unfair for you to keep. Several measures of unjust enrichment are available in this situation. You may be responsible for the reasonable market value of the pool or the reasonable market value of Builder's goods and services or the increased market value of the property. The choice of a particular measure turns on culpability, and courts engage in a process of balancing the equities between parties. If instead of watching Builder install the pool, you were away from your home, you may be charged with paying the lowest measurement or no restitution damages. Liability and amount turn on whether it is just for you to keep a benefit at the expense of Builder.

The remedy of restitution attempts to treat parties fairly.

4. Rescission and reformation. Where parties have mistakenly entered into a contractual relationship, contracts law affords another form of relief. If the parties' minds never met regarding the subject matter of the contract, the court will rescind the purported agreement. The classic case involves a contract for the sale of cotton to arrive on a ship called the *Peerless.* There were two ships named *Peerless* and each party had the other ship in mind. The court rescinded (canceled) the contract by refusing to enforce it. Another example of mistake occurs when the agreed-upon document does not conform to the intentions of the party. Vendor and Vendee can enter into a contract for the sale of land after they walk the property and agree on the dimensions of the lot. After they have agreed on the terms of sale, the parties may write the wrong dimensions into the deed by mistake. In this situation, a court will order reformation and the document will be rewritten in conformity with the parties' bargain.

CONCLUSION

Contracts law is a rich discipline. Most contracts involve commercial transactions, and contracts rules and principles derive from, and are influenced by, market interests. Economic theory helps explain and order these arrangements. However, contracts law is not limited to market-based transactions. Different interests arising from nonmarket situations require protection. The earlier discussion of nonpecuniary liability suggests a theory about contracts law in nonmarket transactions. People enter contractual relationships with their families and friends, and may find themselves in specialized relationships where market-based theories assume secondary importance at best. Of what economic moment is it, for example, to the rank-and-file of a labor union, who because of institutional and structural restraints are part of a collective bargaining agreement they had little or no meaningful participation in formulating? Of what efficiency significance is it when clients contract with lawyers or patients with physicians? What is the wealth-maximizing interest of a health insurance policyholder who receives the insurance as part of a benefits package in an employment agreement? Where is the market and what are the exchange values of antenuptial agreements?

Because of superior knowledge and specialized expertise or because of bargaining advantage many parties to contracts are bargaining not for direct pecuniary gain—they are bargaining for nonpecuniary satisfactions such as the right to participate in decision-making, the opportunity to express themselves, the chance to exercise their voice in matters affecting them as individuals rather than as economic units. People enter these relationships because of trust, loyalty, love, solidarity, community, and other reasons. Moral theory helps us understand and empathize with parties so situated. It is accurate to recognize the artificiality of the market-nonmarket dichotomy and realize people (even commercial traders) enter contracts with mixed motivations. Still, the market-nonmarket dichotomy is a useful way to explain and order the legal subsystem we call contracts law.

We live in a heavily market-oriented society, and contracts law is, and should be, responsive to that world. We also live in a society in which the institution of the promise has deep meaning for reasons independent of short-term pecuniary gains at the heart of market analyses. The expansion of contracts law to nonmarket transactions suggests a move away from a contracts-law ideology embodying an idealized version of a nineteenth-century market economy valuing objective, certain, and predictable rules that are economically useful. The movement supplements that vision with rules sensitive and responsive to the noneconomic needs and expectations in exchanged promises. This picture loosens a too-rigid rules system geared to market transactions. It favors a rules system prizing individual interests of parties, respecting their dignity as persons in an imperfect world, honoring their liberty to participate in unbalanced bargaining situations, requiring their responsibility for broken promises, and recognizing their interdependence.

Contracts law is supported on three bases. The market side encourages trades because wealth is created and, theoretically, efficiency is maximized. Our material well-being is thus protected. At the same time, we see that contracts law can respond to other values. The moral argument is that promises ought to be enforced because enforcement advances individual goals of trust, liberty, and responsibility, and social goals are advanced because individuals are encouraged to collaborate to further mutual interest, thereby fostering a sense of community. The economic and moral arguments are supported on a political base committed to respecting pluralist interests. The political base tolerates a certain degree of uncertainty and flexibility in law and thus encourages discourse about values. The political base is self-conscious in its rejection of a unified theory of contracts and embraces the opportunity to reconstruct a more responsible and responsive contracts law. Consequently, contracts law draws upon economic, moral, and political theory in an attempt to protect the expectancy, reliance, and restitution interests of persons engaged in exchanging promises.

CASES

American Trading & Products Corp. v. Shell International Marine, 453 Fuller 939 (2nd Cir. 1972) [Suez Canal Case]

Raffles v. Wickelhaus, 2 H.&C. 906, 159 Eng. Rep. 375 (Ex. 1864) [Peerless Case]

In re Westinghouse Electric Corp., 517 F. Supp. 440 (E.D. Va. 1981) [Uranium Litigation Case]

BIBLIOGRAPHY

Economics. Charles J. Goetz, *Cases and Materials on Law and Economics* (1984), is a general overview of law and economics with a contracts bibliography at 523–528. Anthony I. Kronman and Richard A. Posner, *The Economics of Contract Law* (1974), covers the whole continuum of the contracting process. A. Mitchell Polinsky, *An Introduction to Law and Economics* (1983), is an excellent introductory text that applies economic principles to contracts law in chapters 5 and 8.

History. Patrick S. Atiyah, *The Rise and Fall of Freedom of Contract* (1979), traces the concept of freedom of contract as it developed in English law. Grant Gilmore, *The Death of Contract* (1974), is an elegant essay arguing that contract law is merging with tort law. Morton J. Horwitz, *The Transformation of American Law 1780–1860* (1977), argues that law is historically contingent. Karl Llewellyn, *Bramble Bush* (1951) and *The Common Law Tradition: Deciding Appeals* (1960), are two works presenting contracts law in the tradition of realist jurisprudence.

Moral philosophy. Patrick S. Atiyah, *Promises, Morals and Law* (1981), and Charles Fried, *Contract as Promise: A Theory of*

Contractual Obligation (1981), explore the moral basis of contracts, offering a counterpoint to the economic basis. Morris R. Cohen, "The Basis of Contract," in *Harvard Law Review*, 46 (1933), is a classic of contracts jurisprudence in the realist tradition.

Politics. David Kairys, ed., *The Politics of Law: A Progressive Critique* (1982), contains an essay in which Peter Gabel and Jay Feinman argue that contracts law is politically and ideologically motivated. Duncan Kennedy, "Form and Substance in Private Law Adjudication," in *Harvard Law Review*, 89 (1976), is the seminal contribution about contracts law and one of the initial articles in the contemporary jurisprudential movement known as critical legal studies. Roberto M. Unger, "The Critical Legal Studies Movement," in *Harvard Law Review*, 96 (1983), uses contracts law as an example of how law can be used to transform society and fits this discussion into a broader framework for social change.

Standard references. American Law Institute, *Restatement (Second) of the Law of Contracts* (1981) and *Restatement of the Law of Restitution* (1936), are unofficial sources of law that attempt to codify a substantive area; and *Uniform Commercial Code Official Text* (1972), adopted by every state except Louisiana and intended to guide commercial transactions, serves as a useful analogy for all contracts. John D. Calamari and Joseph M. Perillo, *Contracts* (1977); Arthur L. Corbin, *Contracts* (1952); E. Allan Farnsworth, *Contracts* (1982); James J. White and Robert S. Summers, *Handbook of the Law Under the Uniform Commercial Code,* 2nd ed. (1980); and Samuel Williston, *A Treatise on the Law of Contracts* (1936), are standard reference works in the field.

Law review articles about contracts law doctrine are too numerous to mention. Listed here are some recent expositions and some classic articles. Melvin Eisenberg, "The Bargain Principle and Its Limits," in *Harvard Law Review*, 95 (1982), and "The Responsive Model of Contract Law," in *Stanford Law Review*, 36 (1984), offer a reconceptualization of contracts law, presenting a modern doctrinal look at the subject. E. A. Farnsworth, "Legal Remedies for Breach of Contract," in *Columbia Law Review*, 70 (1970), examines the connecting principles of contracts remedies. Lon Fuller and William Perdue, "The Reliance Interest in Contract Damages," in *Yale Law Journal*, 46 (1936), changed the way lawyers and scholars assess contractual relationships. Friedrich Kessler, "Contracts of Adhesion: Some Thoughts About Freedom of Contract," in *Columbia Law Review*, 43 (1943); and Todd Rakoff, "Contracts of Adhesion: An Essay in Reconstruction," in *Harvard Law Review*, 96 (1983), explain that a contract of adhesion, such as an insurance policy, is one in which parties do not bargain over every term and that, consequently, contracts law must provide a set of rules and principles to govern the non-bargained-for aspects of a contractual relationship. Alan Schwartz, "The Case for Specific Performance," in *Yale Law Journal*, 89 (1979); and Thomas Ulen, "The Efficiency of Specific Performance: Toward a United Theory of Contract Remedies," in *Michigan Law Review*, 83 (1985), both argue for a more expansive use of the remedy of specific performance, not just the usual money remedy.

[*See also* COMMERCIAL LAW.]

CORPORATIONS AND THE LAW

Donald J. Polden

THE American corporation can usefully be viewed as being successfully promoted by a series of incentives and constraints imposed by law. Indeed, it is this harmonious relationship between business interests and legal principles that has forged the corporation as the single greatest instrument for the achievement of economic goals.

Two principal legal constraints—one internal and the other external—that have been created by the courts and legislatures have shaped the incentives and objectives of corporate existence. The internal aspects of corporate structure—the formation, operation, and, indeed, the legal existence of the corporation—are governed by rules of contract, and these rules constrain the contracting parties to conform their behavior to the contractual principles. For example, the relationship between the corporation and the state, which is represented by the articles of incorporation and the certificate of incorporation, is a type of contract. Similarly, the articles of incorporation and the corporate bylaws, which are prepared by the incorporating parties, contain the compacts and rules between the various members of the corporation.

The law has also provided a series of external constraints in the form of government regulation of the corporation and its operation. The federal antitrust and securities laws are two prime, although certainly not exclusive, examples of regulatory oversight that limit the conduct of the corporation. Indeed, as will be discussed in greater detail below, both the growth of federal regulatory intrusion and the "federalization" of corporate law have at times forced rigid conformity to national standards of business ethics and appropriate corporate action.

Finally, the law has enshrined the notion of the corporation as an instrument of social and economic policy. It has been viewed as a mechanism for the advancement of capitalistic democracy and as a device for providing gainful employment or for generating a profit for investors. Obviously, these views are not mutually exclusive; the development of modern theories of the corporation permit the maintenance of corporations for many different reasons.

This basic construct of constraints and objectives will be explored in the following pages to demonstrate how law has shaped the modern corporation and defined its role in American society. It should be noted, however, that at some times and in some circumstances, it appears that economic and social forces have forced the law of corporations to conform to those broader movements, but those situations do not obviate the major premise that law has moved to create the corporation as we know it.

THE CORPORATION AS CONTRACT

In its clearest form, the corporation can be perceived as the manifestation of a series of contracts or agreements. Those contracts represent agreements between various interested parties themselves and between the parties and the state, and they govern the formative and ongoing relationships between the parties and the state. To the extent that the law enforces the agreements, it permits the parties to achieve their expectations in a manner consistent with the public good.

This section examines the historical foundations and current expression of the corporation's relationship with its constituent members and the state. Then, applying the convenient notion that the community of a corporation can be visualized as a series of interrelated agreements, the basic legal principles of corporate structure and behavior are set forth.

Two major controversies have marked the history of corporations. First, the status of the corporation in society has been an issue since the early days of English common law, and the debate was carried over to American law. Second, controversy has existed on the permissible powers of the corporation and the ability of the state to limit the conduct of the corporation.

At early English common law a corporate charter could be obtained only from the crown and was considered a concession of the sovereign. Permissible corporate purposes were limited to certain public objectives, such as colonizing a territory or maintaining a public thoroughfare, and the limitations on appropriate corporate activity were attributable to fears that the corporation, an artificial entity, would fail to act responsibly to the public or to the sovereign. This skepticism about corporations and the role they could fulfill in society was imported into the United States, and as a result, early American corporations were limited in their powers to performing public and quasi-public activities such as operating hospitals, churches, and canals and turnpikes. Furthermore, the creation of a corporation required an act of the state legislature, and the enabling legislation often placed severe limitations on permissible corporate activities, methods of gathering capital, and the duration of the corporation. As in English law, the American corporation was viewed as a special concession from the state for the limited purpose of accomplishing specific quasi-public objectives.

In the early 1800s a different thinking about corporations began to emerge, and the corporation was increasingly perceived not as a concession from the state but, rather, as an arrangement between private persons as a method of conducting their business. In part, this new perception of the corporation was spawned by the United States Supreme Court's decision in *Dartmouth College* v. *Woodward* (1819), in which the Court held that a corporate charter was a form of contract and thus could not be subsequently modified by the state. The decision was read as a limit on the state's ability to exercise power over corporations that it chartered. Although the Court's opinion does not support such a broad reading, it is clear that the decision gave legal impetus to the movement to recognize greater corporate powers.

Social and economic forces also played instrumental roles in changing perceptions of corporation powers. Since the state legislatures were the sole source of charters, graft and favoritism in granting charters were rampant, and growing public dissatisfaction with the legislative process led to changes. Further, in 1869 the Supreme Court in *Paul* v. *Virginia* held that a state cannot exclude a foreign corporation from conducting interstate activities, although the state may exclude foreign corporations from conducting business solely within the state. The Court's holding in *Paul* and other pressures caused competition among the states to liberalize chartering requirements because of the lucrative incorporation fees and taxes that could be collected by the state of incorporation. The competition among the states for corporate charters, according to the memorable dissent of Justice Louis D. Brandeis in *Louis K. Liggett Co.* v. *Lee,* (1933), leads to a "race . . . not of diligence but of laxity" in the promulgation of state incorporation statutes.

These factors culminated in a view of the corporation as essentially an agreement between private parties desiring to do business together. Nevertheless, the corporation continued to be seen as receiving its legal status from the state, and states continued to grant charters, establish limitations on the conduct of corporate business, and revoke charters for unlawful activities. Today, most state corporation statutes continue to provide that a corporation comes into legal existence only by the filing of a charter or articles of incorporation, the acceptance by the state of the articles, and the issuance of a certificate of incorporation.

At one time, the states also prescribed appropriate corporate activity by limiting the activities that a corporation could engage in and by penalizing the corporation or its managers if those powers or purposes were exceeded. The doctrine of *ultra vires*, which means "beyond the corporation's powers," was frequently invoked to escape uncompleted contracts between the corporation and third parties where the subject of

277

the contract was outside the corporation's powers or purposes. For example, some states prohibited corporations from engaging in certain businesses and required that a corporation specify exactly what its business purpose was in the articles. Similarly, some states limited the powers that a corporation could exercise. The courts would void any acts of a corporation that were beyond the stated purpose of the corporation or the accepted corporate powers.

In time, the ultra vires doctrine fell into disuse, largely because it provoked irrational interruptions in otherwise predictable commercial transactions and interfered with business expectations. It was considered unfair to permit a corporation to receive the benefits of a contract with an outside party but then deny any obligation under the contract because, unbeknown to the third party, the corporation did not have power to engage in the transaction. In any event, modern statutory provisions have abrogated or sharply curtailed the ultra vires doctrine and have given corporations broad statutory powers.

The legal status of the corporation is another issue that long generated controversy. One view held that a corporation is an aggregate of individuals who themselves hold rights (such as the ability to sue or the right to own and convey land) and owe duties to the public but that the corporation, as an artificial entity, is incapable of holding rights or owing duties. The opposing view was that the corporation is itself a legal entity and, as such, holds rights, which it could legally enforce, and owes duties to society, the breach of which can be enforced against the corporation.

This controversy is largely of historical interest today as the corporation is generally recognized as possessing most legal rights and owing the legal duties as individual persons. State corporation laws have largely defined the attributes of corporate legal existence. However, this debate has contemporary relevance to the issue of who runs the corporation—the shareholders or the officers—and to the issue of whether a corporation owes any responsibility to society to engage in socially responsible activity. Very real questions concerning corporate governance and the corporation's role as a social, and not just an economic, institution are addressed in subsequent sections. The debate over the status of the corporation as a legal entity is more than a philosophical exercise and focuses attention on issues of the relationship to each other of the parties within the corporation.

EXPECTATIONS AND THE STRUCTURE OF THE CORPORATION

Corporations constitute a method of doing business, and they have been successful in part because they permit individuals to arrange and achieve their expectations. Corporate law has been instrumental in establishing the corporation as a vehicle for negotiating individual expectations and has promoted the corporate form of business by enforcing those expectations to an extent consistent with law and notions of fairness.

Corporation Size and Individual Expectations. Before we can discuss the impact of corporate structure on the expression and achievement of private expectations, we must draw an important distinction between "closely held corporations" and "public corporations," a distinction predicated on the number of the corporation's owners and one with significant legal implications. Closely held firms are usually owned and operated by a small number of people (usually up to thirty stockholders) who are often related or have a hand in managing corporate affairs. By contrast, stock in public corporations is held by hundreds of individual, corporate, and institutional investors, and the corporation is run by professional managers. Since the 1960s the law has increasingly recognized this distinction and has begun to treat close corporations differently from public corporations in a number of ways. The reason for the disparity in treatment is the radically different set of expectations held by shareholders in these two types of corporations.

Shareholder expectations tend to fall into three major categories: those related to control of the assets and management of the firm, those regarding allocation of risk and return, and those about the duration of the firm's existence. Simply stated, control in the corporation means the ability to make decisions governing the employment of the firm's assets, its profitability, its personnel, and its relationship to the outside world. Decisions involving firm risk may also encompass the source and nature of capital committed for use by the corporation; the likelihood and amount of return on investment in capital; access to dividends, salary, and bonuses; and the cost associated with changing one's involvement with the corporation or exiting the corporation.

The expectations of parties in close corporations are often significantly different from those of members of publicly held corporations. Shareholders in large corporations seldom have any interest in managing the corporation (unless, of course, they have very large holdings of stock) and are primarily interested in dividends paid and the growth in value of the stock. The shares of stock are readily marketable, usually on national stock exchanges, at market prices, and professional managers, specialized in training, operate the corporation. In close corporations, on the other hand, there is frequently a greater expectation by shareholders that they will manage the corporation and receive a return on their investment of capital and labor in the form of salary, bonuses, or benefits. The stock seldom has a discernible market value and is therefore not transferable, and for purposes of retaining corporate control, the shareholders often limit the transferability of the stock.

Shareholder Expectations and the Structure of the Corporation. The foregoing discussion of the fundamental nomenclature among corporations and the differing expectations among the participants in those corporations provides a useful framework for examining the structure of the corporation and how the law has accommodated that structure to meet participant expectations. The corporation's structure can be understood by visualizing the corporation as a pyramid; the shareholders form the base, the officers and employees comprise the top, and the board of directors are in the middle.

Under the conventional theory of corporation law, the shareholders are the owners of the corporation; they have invested capital in the form of stock purchases to fund the corporation's activities. However, their power in the corporation is limited; they have the right to elect directors at regular intervals specified in the articles and to vote on fundamental changes, such as mergers or the sale of the corporation's assets. The duty to control the corporation lies with the board of directors. Under the Model Business Corporation Act, all corporate powers must "be exercised by or under the authority of, and the business and affairs of the corporation managed

under the direction of, its board of directors." One of the board's major responsibilities is the hiring, retention, and dismissal of officers, who, under prevailing norms, can be dismissed with or without cause or reason by the board of directors. Under the statutory provisions, therefore, although the shareholders are the owners of the corporation, the directors are empowered to govern the corporation and may hire employees to run the day-to-day affairs of the corporation.

Statutory provisions in many states impose high duties of fairness, honesty, and competency on directors and officers. Section 8.30 of the Model Business Corporation Act, which has been adopted in some form by many state legislatures, provides that officers and directors must act "(1) in good faith; (2) with the care an ordinarily prudent person in a like position would exercise under similar circumstances; and (3) in a manner he reasonably believes to be in the best interests of the corporation." The statutory norms do, however, permit officers and directors, in discharging their duties, to rely on information, reports, and opinions prepared by officers, employees, legal counsel, accountants, and committees of the corporation where there is a reasonable basis for the belief that the information or statements are reliable.

The foregoing description of the structure of the corporation, which has been referred to as the "received legal model" by Melvin A. Eisenberg, does not necessarily depict how corporations actually function in society or explain how the courts treat legal issues concerning the structural relationships of parties within the corporation. In short, the received legal model is accurate as a generalization of how corporations are arranged, how they operate in society, and how the law perceives the relationships of corporate actors; it does not, however, accurately depict the reality of corporation existence.

The disparity between the received legal model and reality can be observed by examining close corporations and public corporations. In the close corporation, the formalities of corporate structure are usually not adhered to and the day-to-day and significant decisions are made by the owners of the business. In such corporations, there is a merging of ownership and control, and the corporate actors do not conduct corporate affairs in the manner contemplated by the statutory scheme. For example, the corporation statutes establish elaborate procedures and requirements for holding meetings, voting, and other decision-making processes. However, close corporations tend to be run informally, without structured decision-making meetings or formal voting.

Public corporations also depart from the conventional theory of corporate structure. In public corporations, there is a separation of ownership and control, and the effective management of the corporation lies in the hands of officers and employees rather than the board of directors. There are several reasons for this. Shareholders in the public corporation tend to be more interested in return on their investment than in directing the corporation. Significant blocks of stock are often held by such institutional investors as insurance companies, pension funds, and mutual funds, and those shareholders are not interested in managing a corporation. Nor do the directors in public corporations always reflect the makeup or attitudes of the shareholder constituency, and often no one on the board represents the "average" shareholder. Directors of large American corporations tend to be officers of the corporation who also serve on the board; outsiders, such as bankers or legal counsel; or holders of large blocks of stock.

Furthermore, management in the public corporation controls the effective decision-making processes and procedures of the board and, through that control, is able to shift corporate decision-making from the board of directors to management. The officers of the corporation frequently arrange the time and places for meetings of the board of directors and establish the agenda for the meetings. Officers also prepare the information that is assembled for, and distributed at, board meetings. Management also frequently prepares the slate of nominees for election as directors of the corporation, and to incur the displeasure of management might mean that a director will not be asked to serve again.

Public corporations have been subject to great criticism for many years as a result of the significant yet unchecked power that rests in the hands of managers, not shareholders. Some commentators have argued that it is undemocratic for the true owners of the corporation—the shareholders—to have little or no control over the corporation, and others have criticized the failure of these corporations to conform to the statutory norms, which impose the duty of corporate management on the directors rather than on the officers. In publicly held corporations, however, many shareholders do not expect to participate in the management of the corporation.

There is a parallel issue in the close corporation, and that problem has been the subject of much litigation. That difficulty concerns compliance with statutory norms for the responsibility of directors. Shareholders in close corporations have attempted to bind one another by contract concerning how they will act as shareholders and directors. In a classic case, *McQuade* v. *Stoneham* (1934), three shareholders agreed to elect one another as directors and, as directors, to elect each other as officers of the corporation. When one shareholder-director refused to cast his votes for another shareholder who wished to be an officer, the ousted shareholder sued. The court held that while shareholders can contract with each other to constrain their conduct as shareholders, it was impermissible for shareholders to agree to limit or constrain their behavior as directors. The court reasoned that it was permissible for shareholders to limit their rights as shareholders but that their attempt to limit the powers and duties of the board of directors contravened the statutory norms because their agreements as shareholders might "sterilize" the board of directors.

Subsequent cases have recognized that shareholders, particularly in close corporations, have legitimate expectations that may be actualized by permitting shareholder agreements. Thus, the Illinois Supreme Court in *Galler* v. *Galler* (1964) upheld the validity of several provisions in a shareholder agreement that dictated action by the corporation's board. Generally, the courts have permitted shareholder agreements that bind the board of directors if there is no complaining minority shareholder who might be harmed by the agreement, there is no fraud on creditors or other outsiders, and the provision does not directly violate any prohibitory statutory provision.

Since the 1970s, the statutory norms have been changing to reflect the differentness of the close corporation and the flexibility needed to permit its shareholders to accommodate their expectations. Several states have passed special corporation statutes that deal only with the close corporation. The Model Business Corporation Act was amended in 1984 to provide that any corporation "having 50 or fewer shareholders may dispense with or limit the authority of a board of directors by describing in its articles of incorporation who will perform some or all of the duties of a board." These statutory changes reflect the prevailing thinking that special recognition is necessary for the close corporation and that an essential attribute of such corporations is that the statutory norms must be flexible in order to permit accomplishment of the parties' expectations.

The Statutory Scheme and Shareholder Risk. There are several important areas in which the statutory norms in many states permit the parties entering into a corporate form of business to structure their relationships to permit achievement of their wishes. The corporation, as noted above, is a capital-formation tool and permits an individual seeking earnings on investments to limit or control the risk of loss. The corporation is a popular capital-attraction device because it allows control over investors' risk in two ways—through the concept of limited liability and through the flexibility permitted under statute in composing the corporation's capital structure.

Shareholders are limited in their liability to the capital they contribute to the corporation. This is unlike partnerships, in which each partner is liable for all debts and liabilities of the partnership, irrespective of his or her agreement with the other partners to limit individual liability. Of course, a corporation may itself be exposed to unlimited liability, but a shareholder cannot be forced to pay in excess of his or her capital contributions for the purchase of stock or for subscriptions for the purchase of stock.

A notable exception to the rule of no personal liability involves the concept of "piercing the corporate veil." Piercing the corporate veil occurs when a court permits a contract or tort claimant to recover against a shareholder for a contractual obligation of the corporation to the claimant or a tortious injury for which the corporation is liable. These situations usually arise when the corporation is insolvent and the court must decide whether the innocent third party or the shareholder should bear the loss. In cases involving a contractual obligation, a third party may pierce the corporate veil only in limited circumstances, such as when the shareholder has misrepresented the integrity of the corporation's financial condition or has managed the corporation so that all profits were immediately siphoned off and the corporation was always insolvent or when the third person is misled into believing that he or she is dealing with a solvent corporation. Generally, however, courts will assume that persons dealing with corporations are on notice of any inability by the corporation to pay its debts or fulfill its contracts and will not impose liability on shareholders. Courts are more likely to impose personal liability on shareholders when an innocent person is injured by the activity of the corporation or its agents. However, the general rule of limited shareholder liability will be relaxed if the corporation is grossly undercapitalized, was not properly and completely incorporated, was operated to siphon off profits to shareholders, or was engaged in an ultrahazardous activity, such as blasting. These situations, then, expose shareholders to risks greater than expected, but the exposure of shareholders in such cases to unlimited liability is necessary for reasons of public policy; the public will lose confidence in corporations generally if they are used as shams to avoid their obligations.

The other method by which corporations can be used by investors to limit their risk of loss pertains to the various types of capital instruments. These instruments, which are usually called "stock" or "shares," are a type of equity capital, as distinguished from instruments of debt. A corporation may be capitalized by debt capital and equity capital. Debt capital consists of loans secured by collateral of the corporation or the personal guarantees of the organizers or by bonds or debentures, which are long-term debt instruments that may or may not be secured by the property of the corporation. For a corporation to remain solvent, it must pay its debts, including making interest payments on bonds. That is not necesarily true for equity capital. A firm's equity is a representation of the investment in the company made by its shareholders or owners.

There are essentially two types of stock used by American corporations, common stock and preferred stock, and each type of stock has several important attributes. Common stock is the typical investment device used by corporations and possesses the flexibility that is often necessary in beginning firms. Preferred stock has a preference over common in the distribution of dividends and the distribution of surplus following a liquidation of the corporation's assets. Dividends on preferred stock are usually expressed in a dollar amount or as a percentage of the face value of the stock, and preferred shareholders must be paid dividends before the board of directors may pay dividends to common shareholders. Preferred stock represents a method by which equity investors in a corporation can limit their exposure to risk by gaining a preference over other equity investors with respect to return on investment and preference in liquidation. There are other possible features to preferred stock, such as convertibility into common stock at some established rate, letting the preferred participate with common stock after payment of the preferred stock dividend, and permitting the preferred stock dividends to cumulate, which means that the corporation must make up all arrearages in preferred dividends before any dividends may be payed on common stock.

The concept of limited liability and the statutory capital-formation devices give shareholders the ability to limit their financial exposure in the event of bad times or insolvency. The use of stock, however, has another importance to the shareholder, particularly in the close corporation, because it is the instrument by which the stockholder exercises the degree of control or power in the corporation; that is, shares of stock can extend voting power to the shareholder.

Voting Power. Another area in which the corporation laws permit great flexibility to the shareholders in designing their corporate relationships is voting rights. Voting to elect directors and on fundamental changes is perhaps the most important power that shareholders possess under modern corporation law, and that power is expressed in the extent of their voting power. Shareholder agreements may affect voting in corporations, especially closely held corporations, by permitting shareholders to pool their votes. In a vote-pooling agreement, shareholders agree to vote their shares in a certain manner, usually for each other, in elections to the board of directors. Such agreements, as previously noted, are routinely upheld by the courts unless the shareholder agreement "sterilizes" the board of directors. However, stock-pooling agreements must establish a method of enforcing the agreements, or the parties may be left without a remedy to ensure that their agreement is adhered to by all parties. One method of ensuring that the terms of the agreement are followed is to create a proxy, by which the legal right to vote the shares of stock is given to a third party, usually with instructions as to how the stock must be voted. The creation of a proxy to vote the stock avoids the difficult problems of enforcing the provisions of agreements when people change their minds. Some courts will enforce a voting agreement if the objectives are clear and the court can compel the parties to adhere to the agreement's terms.

A similar instrument for aggregating voting power is the voting trust, wherein the legal title to the shares of stock is vested with trustees, who receive the shares of stock, register the shareholders' names with the corporation, and issue to the shareholders trust certificates. A voting trust differs from a pooling agreement, wherein the shareholder does not give up title to the stock, while in a trust, shareholders do transfer legal title to the shareholders' trust and receive trust certificates. Voting trust beneficiaries (formerly the shareholders) continue to receive the dividends as before, and they may share in any liquidation surplus as if they were shareholders; however, the sole power to vote the stock lies in the trustees, subject to their fiduciary duties to serve in the best interests of the beneficiaries. Under most state statutory schemes, a voting trust may not extend beyond ten years and the trust agreement must be in writing.

For many years a debate raged over another issue: the two methods of voting stock, straight or cumulative, and whether it was a legitimate exercise of state power to limit the corporation's ability to select the method. To demonstrate the effects of each type of voting on shareholder participation on the board of directors, let us take a simple example. Suppose XYZ Corporation has two shareholders, A and B, who own 60 and 40 shares, respectively, of the corporation's stock; that the corporation has three directors on the board; and that each shareholder nominates three candidates for the board. Under straight voting, A would elect all three directors because she would vote her 60 shares for each of her candidates for the board, while B would vote his 40 shares for each of his candidates. Under cumulative voting, on the other hand, B would be able to elect one director because each shareholder would be entitled to spread his votes (which are the number of shares times the number of director positions available) among all of his candidates. The candidates do not run for specific places on the board, but, rather, the three highest vote-getters would be elected. Thus, in our example, A would have 180 votes and B would have 120 votes, and by placing all 120 votes on one candidate, B would be able to elect one director; A would, of course, take the other two directorships by placing 90 votes on each of her top two candidates.

The reason for constitutional and statutory prohibitions on straight-voting provisions is simply the belief that minority interests (that is, shareholders with less than a majority of shares) should be represented on the board of directors, at least when their ownership interest in the corporation reaches a certain level. It has been argued that it is healthy for a corporation to have representation on the board from many sources and that minority-interest representation on the board will serve as a check on management. Others argue that minority representation on the board will turn the board into a battleground rather than a deliberative decision-making group and that such a representative may use his position to leak confidential information to other minority shareholders or act as a toehold for an attempt to take over the corporation.

As a general matter, however, most states leave it to the organizers of the corporation or subsequent shareholders and directors to decide if cumulative voting is advisable for their corporation. One thing, however, is quite clear: cumulative voting is much more important in closely held corporations than in public corporations. In public corporations, the presence of a minority-interest representative may amount to a nuisance; in a close corporation, a minority shareholder may be deprived of a reasonable expectancy that she would exercise some control in the corporation, maintain a source of information on the operations of the corporation, and obtain a source of income from acting as an officer and employee in the corporation. On the other hand, even with cumulative voting rights—whether imposed by state law or by the articles of incorporation—there are a number of ways that majority shareholders can avoid the effects of cumulative voting. For example, nonvoting stock may be issued instead of voting stock and the size of the board can be reduced to prevent minority shareholders from gaining any representation on the board. Finally, the board can be "classified" or the terms of directors "staggered" so that fewer directors will be elected annually and the effect of cumulative voting will be greatly reduced.

Limitations on Stock Transferability. One final aspect of stock ownership must be considered, and that is the prevalence of share transfer restrictions. There are many reasons, particularly in close corporations, for the shareholders to restrict the transferability of the stock. In the close corporation, it is not uncommon for the articles to limit transferability of stock by requiring that offers to sell the stock must first be addressed to the corporation and/or other shareholders or by mandating that only the corporation or other shareholders may purchase the stock. These stock transfer restrictions, which are usually called "buy/sell agreements" or "options to purchase," permit the stock of a close corporation to stay in family hands, limit the ability of shareholders' spouses to gain possession of the stock in marriage-dissolution proceedings, and maintain ownership proportionality among existing shareholders.

In publicly held corporations, share transfer restrictions are used principally to prevent stock transfers that would violate federal securities laws. The restrictions in these situations prohibit all such sales. While such share transfer restrictions are obviously important to the issuing corporation and the shareholders involved, the normative issues concerning restrictions on transferability are not significant.

Share transfer restrictions were greatly disfavored at common law, but the courts and state legislatures have begun to recognize the usefulness of restrictive provisions, particularly in the close corporation. The restriction must be conspicuously noted on the stock certificate, must be reasonably drawn in terms of scope and duration, and, according to some courts, must be for a legitimate purpose. Options to purchase and buy/sell agreements provide the most troublesome issues when the shares of stock that are purchased by the corporation or the other shareholders must be valued. "Book value," which is simply the value at which the shares are carried on the books of the corporation, may not adequately reflect the value of the stock at the time of the transfer. However, market value is often impossible to calculate on close-corporation stock. The courts have tended to approve share transfer restrictions if an appraisal is done to calculate the option or sales price or if the agreed-upon method of determining the price is reasonable and fair under the circumstances.

The preceding discussion has examined certain essential attributes of the relationship between the structure of the corporation and the ability of the participants in the corporation to achieve their expectations. Certain fundamental matters such as voting rights, limitations on risk of loss, and the right to control and manage the corporation were considered in the contexts of the closely held and the publicly held corporations. The next section examines issues of conduct of corporate actors and again confronts the role of law in shaping appropriate conduct to achieve the actors' expectations and to protect shareholders.

STANDARDS OF CONDUCT WITHIN THE CORPORATION

Both federal and state law have articulated and amplified norms for officers and directors of the corporation. The courts and legislatures have developed safeguards against incompetent and dishonest corporate officers and directors. Corporate directors, because of their overall responsibility to manage the corporation, have a greater duty of care and honesty than officers, and managing officers are usually held to a higher degree of care than other employees. Similarly, shareholders are not generally considered to owe any duties to other shareholders, although some courts have recognized a duty of fairness owed by a majority and controlling shareholder to minority shareholders.

The duties owed by officers and directors to the corporation fall into three broad categories: a duty of due care, a duty of loyalty, and a duty to exercise sound business judgment when acting for the corporation. Although these duties have traditionally been expressed as tenets of state law, to some degree they have been incorporated into federal law and applied by the federal courts in securities law cases.

Duty of Due Care. Directors and officers must act competently on behalf of the corporation, but they are permitted to make honest mistakes of judgment and avoid reprisals by shareholders or other directors. The courts have tended to avoid second-guessing directors and have generally found a lack of due care only where the officer or director was engaged in self-dealing, fraud, or other dishonest conduct in addition to the negligent performance of his duties.

One issue of recurring interest is whether a director can be found to have breached the duty of due care by failing to act as a director—that is, by avoiding statutory responsibilities to manage the corporation. The courts have not imposed liability on a director for failure to direct affirmatively the affairs of the corporation, in part because some directors merely serve nominally as directors and have neither the interest nor the ability to manage the corporation actively.

Duty of Loyalty. Directors and officers must act loyally to the corporation and cannot take action that will benefit them at the expense of the corporation. The two major forms of corporate disloyalty are self-dealing by a director or officer and usurpation of a corporate opportunity. The courts, applying both common-law principles and the statutory proscriptions on directorial disloyalty, have prohibited both kinds of disloyalty.

Conflicts of interest arise in many circumstances; for example, a director who is also an officer in the corporation might participate on the board's action in setting his or her salary or might purchase property from the corporation or lend the corporation money. These transactions create the possibility of unfair activities by the director. On the other hand, some of these transactions may be beneficial to the corporation —for example, where the corporation cannot obtain a loan from any other source.

The courts have tended to approach self-dealing transactions by placing on the implicated director the burden of showing that the transaction was fair to the corporation, and they will examine whether the transaction was intrinsically fair to other shareholders and the corporation. When the transaction is unfair to the corporation and there is reason to believe that the director engaged in fraud or misrepresentation or was wasting corporate assets, the transaction will be voided by the court. When, however, the director can demonstrate that the transaction did not involve fraud, misrepresentation, or a waste of corporate assets, the transaction will be upheld if the director obtains approval or ratification of the transaction from a majority of the shareholders or a disinterested majority of the board of directors. In either event, the implicated director must make full disclosure of all relevant facts to the board or shareholders.

A director's duty of loyalty to the corporation prohibits usurpation of opportunities that come to the director because of a position on the board. Thus, a director may not take a secret profit on corporate business, personally take a profit from a business opportunity that came to the corporation, or compete with the corporation. On the other hand, when the corporation is unable or unwilling to take advantage of some opportunities, there may be a question as to whether a director or officer is flatly prohibited from taking an opportunity that the corporation is not pursuing.

The courts, in determining whether an opportunity was a corporate one, will generally look to whether it is near or in the corporation's line of business and whether it is unfair for the director to take advantage of the opportunity under the circumstances. Some courts look to whether the corporation could reasonably have expected to acquire an interest in the property or opportunity such that it should be protected against usurpation by an insider. Under either standard, it is important to examine a number of factors, including whether the opportunity was in fact offered to the corporation, whether it was rejected by the corporation, whether the director learned of the opportunity because of a position with the corporation, and whether the insider used corporate facilities to take advantage of the opportunity.

As with allegations of self-dealing by corporate insiders, the courts are inclined to examine claimed usurpations of a corporate opportunity in a close corporation differently than in a publicly held corporation. Given the informality of employment relationships in close corporations, it may be well within the parties' expectations for directors and officers to personally take some opportunities that arguably come to them by way of their involvement with the corporation. In one instance, a plaintiff, a one-third shareholder and director of a realty company, was not permitted to maintain an action against the other two shareholder-directors when they purchased property for themselves and resold it for a profit, since the plaintiff knew that the two defendants engaged in personal real estate transactions and there was no understanding that all three directors would only buy and sell property for the corporation (*Burg* v. *Horn*, 1967). In publicly held corporations the courts more closely scrutinize allegations of a director competing against the corporation or taking opportunities that come to the corporation.

Duty of Sound Business Judgment. A director is expected to exercise reasonable judgment in managing the corporation, and the courts generally presume that a director has exercised such judgment when performing corporate activity. Viewed another way, the courts are reluctant to interfere with the exercise of a director's judgment, even when hindsight reveals it to be erroneous, unless it can be shown that the director was disloyal, dishonest, or incompetent. This judicial attitude stems in part from the related beliefs that judges are not businesspersons and should not presume to impose their concepts of wise management on the corporation and that judicial power to protect the corporation and minority shareholders is limited to clear breaches of fiduciary duties and not to allegations of mismanagement. Unlike the fiduciary duties of loyalty and honesty, the business-judgment concept imposes an obligation on complaining shareholders to demonstrate that the implicated director or officer was not acting with the best interests of the corporation in mind and requires proof that the director or officer acted unreasonably.

Fiduciary Duties to Shareholders. As a general proposition, shareholders do not owe duties to other shareholders. However, the courts have recognized a few instances in which majority shareholders, because of their control over the machinery of the corporation, owe fiduciary duties to minority shareholders. Thus, courts have voided transactions in which a majority shareholder has sold control of the corporation to a third party who is known to be a "looter." Basically, a looter is an individual or corporation that acquires control of a corporation for the purpose of stripping away a valuable asset and leaving the acquired corporation valueless. Similarly, the courts have imposed a duty on majority shareholders and insiders (officers and directors) not to trade their shares of stock on the basis of information that they have acquired because of their position in the corporation and that is not available to minority shareholders.

Fiduciary Duties in the Close Corporation. Special duties of insiders and shareholders have been found in close corporations, where shareholders may have a reasonable expectation of continued positions on the board of directors or employment. These expectations are reasonable in the close corporation because employment may be the only method of receiving a return on investment, because election to the board or as an officer may be the only way to exercise some control, and because the corporation stock is not marketable or transferable. In those situations, a shareholder may be "frozen out" of the corporation's decision-making without any way to sell his stock or vote himself a position and salary. The courts have recently begun recognizing the duties of shareholders in close corporations to treat fairly their fellow shareholders and have examined the parties' expectations on forming the corporation.

Judicial recognition of fiduciary duties owed by insiders and shareholders to the corporation and other shareholders has been a major force in moving corporation law to a greater recognition of individual motivations for doing business as a corporation. Moreover, judicial protection of investors' expectations has clearly been instrumental in advancing the role of corporations in society. The recognition of fiduciary obligations has occurred as a part of increased judicial and statutory involvement in the conduct of the corporation, and the next section addresses the enhanced role of government in corporate affairs.

GOVERNMENT REGULATION AND FEDERAL JURISDICTION

Since the 1930s there has been a significant growth in the role of federal and state regulatory agencies and in the degree of federal jurisdiction over the conduct of the corporation. This increased federal oversight has had a substantial impact on the corporate way of life in many ways. Thus, while corporate officials have always owed certain minimum duties under state incorporation laws, the advent of regulatory oversight by federal administrative agencies and the threat of

private damage actions for failure to comply with federal statutes has introduced a speculative quality to doing business.

Several reasons account for the growth of regulatory oversight of corporations and the increased power of federal courts over the conduct of the corporation. First, since the New Deal there has been increased reliance on administrative agencies to perform judicial and quasi-judicial functions. Similarly, as reformers have become increasingly aware of imperfections in markets and industries and have swayed public opinion in the direction of making substantial improvements, the political response has often been to create an agency to eliminate the imperfections, make improvements, or monitor the industry or market. Second, corporations were natural targets for this regulatory zeal, since corporate form is the prevalent method of doing any interstate business. Third, federal courts were thought to be the most appropriate forum for adjudicating disputes between the agencies and private parties and the best-qualified body for exercising jurisdiction over transactions and activity in interstate commerce. There was some feeling that state courts would be more susceptible to local pressure than federal courts.

Scope of Regulation. Since the New Deal the scope of regulation of corporate conduct has dramatically increased, although there is some indication of growing pressures to reverse government oversight of corporate action. This section will briefly describe the pervasiveness of government regulation, and the next section will discuss the most comprehensive and intrusive form of corporate regulation, the federal securities laws.

It has been argued that today virtually every aspect of corporate existence and activity is regulated to some degree by the federal government. Since 1890, the federal antitrust laws have prohibited corporations (and other individuals and business entities) from engaging in conspiracies, agreements, and contracts that restrain trade and conduct that monopolizes a market or constitutes an attempt to monopolize a market. Common forms of restraints on trade are price-fixing agreements, boycotts, and market allocations.

The Environmental Protection Agency (EPA), under its enabling legislation and federal antipollution acts, has delimited the types and amounts of pollutants that firms can dispose of in the water and air. More recently, federal toxic-waste legislation has exposed corporations to staggering potential liability for generating or storing toxic substances. All of these environmental statutes grant substantial rule-making power to the EPA to monitor actions that may degrade the environment and to take preventive measures.

Federal labor laws and workplace statutes regulate the hours and wages of covered workers, the terms and procedures of collective-bargaining arrangements, and occupational safety requirements. The states often have supplementary statutory schemes covering the workplace, including worker's compensation and unemployment statutes, workplace safety rules, and the like. These regulatory structures and myriad others impose significant constraints on the marketplace conduct of the corporation, although it has been frequently argued that these legal constraints have improved the social and economic performance of the firm.

Federal Securities Laws. Perhaps the most significant form of governmental regulation of corporations is through securities laws. The Securities and Exchange Commission (SEC) exerts a pervasive form of control over the fundamental relationship between a corporation's management and its shareholders. In 1933 and 1934, Congress concluded that the economic woes of the Great Depression were in large part attributable to poor supervision of securities markets and financially irresponsible practices by corporations and securities traders. The response was two seemingly unrelated pieces of legislation, the Securities Act of 1933 and the Securities Exchange Act of 1934, which were aimed at essentially four regulatory objectives. These laws required registration of issuers of securities and of issues or distributions of securities. In requiring registration of certain corporations and significant distributions of securities, Congress hoped to monitor more effectively interstate securities markets. The substantive requirements of the acts were designed to get maximum disclosure of information concerning the issuer, the issue of securities, and the market for the issuance into the hands of prospective and actual investors. These laws were also intended to prevent and redress fraudulent and deceptive practices in markets for securities.

Simultaneously, Congress created the SEC to make operational the laws and gave the SEC great rule-making and enforcement powers. The legislative creation of the SEC gave some bite to the other provisions of the law. The extent to which the SEC and the securities laws have achieved those objectives is the subject of great controversy, but it is enough to state that the operation of the securities laws has had a substantial impact on American corporations.

The Securities Act of 1933 requires that any firm that intends to issue securities publicly must register the issuance with the SEC, and the act prohibits all selling efforts prior to the filing of a registration statement. The purpose of the registration requirement is to ensure that investors are provided with relevant information—which is drafted into a prospectus from the material set out in the registration statement—prior to the time that the new issue of securities is marketed to the public.

The Securities Exchange Act of 1934 operates to require registration of security sales by certain publicly held firms that have in excess of $1 million in assets and five hundred or more shareholders in any one class of stock. Thus, unlike the 1933 act, which had required registration of any public issue, the 1934 act requires the registration of any issuance by a public issuer. However, like the 1933 act, the policy of the 1934 act is to encourage informed decisions by potential investors.

Perhaps the most controversial provisions of the 1934 act are the antifraud sections—14(a), 16(b), and 10(b)—which have been augmented by extensive rule making by the SEC and are either very broad in application or strike at the core of corporate management's relationship with shareholders. Section 14(a) makes it unlawful to use the mails, telephone, or other methods of interstate communication for the wrongful or fraudulent solicitation of proxies. It also requires the disclosure of full information on the operations of the company, proposed corporate action, and changes proposed by shareholders. The section also requires that where appropriate, shareholder proposals for corporate action shall be included in proxy solicitation materials sent by management. The impact of this section and its implementing rules has been controversial when shareholders with small share holdings requested the inclusion of materials in proxy solicitation requests that were critical of management's position on social issues and proposed changes in the corporation's position on those issues. The issues include the corporation's employment practices concerning minorities and women, consumer safety efforts, and development and manufacture of military weapons, among others. This controversy focused attention on the issue of whether the proxy machinery and, indeed, the corporate boardroom were properly instruments of social change.

Section 16(b) directly addresses the problem of insider trading. Insider trading involves situations where an officer, director, or significant shareholder purchases or sells stock in the corporation and questions on the motivation for the transaction are presented. More specifically, it may be a breach of an officer's or director's fiduciary and legal duties to sell or purchase on the basis of information received in his or her capacity as an officer or director. Section 16(b) prohibits the taking of any short-swing profits (that is, profits on stock held for six months or less) by officers, directors, or 10 percent shareholders. Any such profits are automatically recoverable by the corporation, and the provision is intended to serve as a deterrent to insiders' trading based on information received because of a position in the corporation.

Finally, Section 10(b) has proven the most potent and controversial antifraud provision. The section is quite simple and prohibits the use of any manipulative, deceptive, or fraudulent statement of material fact or the failure to state a material fact that is necessary in order to make the statements accurate and not misleading. The range of the statute is very broad and reaches statements made, or omissions that should not have been made, in connection with the sale or purchase of any security. The section has, however, engendered a great deal of litigation involving insider trading, blatantly fraudulent schemes, and even ordinary corporate mismanagement, and the United States Supreme Court has begun to impose more narrowly drawn restrictions on Section 10(b) actions. For example, in *Ernst & Ernst* v. *Hochfelder* (1976) the Court held that a plaintiff must allege and prove that the defendant intended to mislead or defraud the plaintiff and that allegations of mere negligence by the defendant are insufficient to support a Section 10(b) claim. Until those cases were

decided, the substantive law of Section 10(b), which provides for exclusively federal jurisdiction, had almost entirely replaced state laws dealing with the purchase and sale of stock. The antifraud provisions of Section 10(b) were construed early on to be applicable to all firms or individuals that attempted to buy or sell a security in interstate commerce; there was no requirement that the sale or purchase be part of an issuance subject to the registration provision of either the 1933 act or 1934 act. Therefore, the reach of Section 10(b) extended to any sale or purchase of securities in interstate commerce and to interstate activities (for example, telephone calls or the use of the mails) to sell or purchase any security.

The Supreme Court has tightened the scope of Section 10(b) jurisdiction by requiring that a private-party plaintiff bringing an action must allege and prove that the defendant consciously and intentionally schemed to deceive, manipulate, or defraud the plaintiff. Moreover, the Court has held that Section 10(b) was not intended to reach allegations of corporation mismanagement (*Santa Fe Industries, Inc.* v. *Green*, 1977). If corporate management discloses the terms of a transaction, such as a merger, to the shareholders, Section 10(b) cannot now be used to reach the unfairness of the transaction; such unfairness must be addressed by the state courts.

The criticism of the SEC's regulation of corporations and, indeed, of the federal securities laws is directed to the information-disclosure objectives of those laws. Critics have contended that governmental regulation imposes high costs on taxpayers and firms marketing securities, does not get relevant information into the hands of investors, and unduly interferes with the efficient operation of markets for securities. The core of the criticism lies in the notion that some information that must be disclosed by law is not helpful or relevant to investment decision-making by investors and is not comprehensible to the average investor. Moreover, according to the critics, most investment in publicly traded securities is done by investment firms, banks, and other sophisticated investors who have little or no use for the historical information required by the statutes. Those investors make decisions based upon projections of future growth or value of the stock and have research departments and access to inside information for making their investment decisions. Therefore, the required information is not understood by small investors and is useless to institutional investors, and the regulatory and compliance costs do not reap any anticipated benefits.

The modern American corporation, particularly the large corporation, is not the only entity that has felt the effects of governmental regulation. However, because so much of the regulatory efforts are aimed at accomplishing social good in the workplace and because the large corporation is engaged in interstate commerce, corporations have been particularly affected by federal regulations. Nevertheless, despite controversy, regulation and federal involvement in corporate activities have played a significant part in the operation and condition of many corporations.

THE OBJECTIVES OF THE MODERN CORPORATION

A final perspective on the corporation and its relationship to the law of corporations concerns the controversial issue of the contemporary objectives and purposes of the corporation. A consideration of this perspective requires an evaluation of the social, political, and economic purposes to which corporations may be applied. In his classic book *Concept of the Corporation,* Peter F. Drucker described the modern American corporation as an institution that integrates social and economic objectives and argued that it is impossible to analyze the importance of the corporation as an instrument of national social and economic policy without recognizing the relationships between those objectives or functions. Although Drucker's concept has normative as well as descriptive elements, it serves as a useful and accepted model for understanding the role of the corporation.

At the root of any concept of the corporation is the traditional notion that the corporation exists to make profits on the production and sale of goods and services. Classical economic theory explains that individuals strive to maximize their wealth or well-being, and when this theory is applied to the firm, a voluntary association of individuals, the objective becomes the maximization of profits. This view of the firm, however, fails to answer two fundamental issues: first, for whom profits are maximized—the entity or the individuals—and, second, whether the firm can legitimately pursue other objectives.

Drucker also described the role of the corporation in social and societal terms and argued that the corporation has functions other than the mere pursuit of profits. As a social institution, the corporation serves human needs by permitting its employees to organize their lives around the accomplishment of economic activity, drawing personal satisfaction from the rendition of labor. Similarly, communities draw strength and integrity from the firms employing their citizens and providing a cohesive element for social and economic activities. Experiences with plant closings in small towns and the deindustrialization of previously prosperous communities confirm the close relationship between industrial and commercial activity and those communities.

Drucker's concept of the corporation argues for a greater degree of cooperation between management and labor and would require a fundamentally different perspective on the employment relationship than exists under current labor law. However, it is undeniable that the modern corporation is a cooperative venture between labor and management. A related issue of current significance involves filling positions on the board of directors with employees and labor-union officials. By the 1980s some corporations had found it necessary to include labor representatives on the board of directors as a part of wage concessions by unions, and those experiences, along with similar, although more routine, practices in European countries, have generated sharp differences of opinion.

Some critics of these so-called codeterminalism experiments have argued that the corporate boardroom is not the appropriate forum for labor-management confrontations, that the policies of the labor laws will be eroded, and that the inherent adversarial nature of labor and management may lead to the leaking of sensitive information by union board-members. Proponents of codeterminalism have responded that labor-management relations need not be built on confrontation and that a cooperative and participative relationship in managing the corporation—which is the duty of the board of directors—will advance the interests of both groups.

These issues of interest-group participation on the board of directors are not confined to labor-union representatives and codeterminalism experiments. There have been frequent attempts to get public-interest or special-interest representatives on the board of directors of corporations that are believed to be in need of guidance on issues of social responsibility. Leading examples include efforts to get consumer-protection advocates, minority and women representatives, consumers, and others on the board of corporations that were considered to be insensitive to social (and perhaps even legal) issues such as sex and race discrimination, product safety, and utility service to the poor and elderly. Again, the controversy revolves around various perceptions of the proper role of the board of directors and the social role of the modern corporation.

The issue of social responsibility becomes more complex when corporate gifts and charitable contributions are made by the corporation. There are many persons who believe that a corporation has the responsibility to support and advance charitable and philanthropic causes. However, others have expressed the belief that if a corporate manager wants to donate to a favorite charity, he or she should do so out of salary or personal earnings, not out of corporate earnings, which represent a fund to pay a return on shareholder investments. Of course, charitable contributions have been treated as a legitimate deduction for corporations, which reduces the after-tax financial effect of the donation; such contributions are the economic life stream of many religious, educational, and public-service groups.

The courts have fashioned some general principles for resolving claims that the management of a corporation committed waste by making a contribution or gift to a charity and that it was a breach of the managers' fiduciary duties to refrain from wasting corporate assets. Important considerations here are whether the corporation is closely held or publicly held and whether the corporate official making the gift is also a majority shareholder. In a close corporation, where a majority shareholder causes a donation to be made to a pet charity, the courts have tended to uphold the gift as long as it is reasonable in amount and does not exceed the maximum deduction under the federal tax laws. In the case of donations by publicly held corporations, the courts have tended to examine whether any cor-

porate benefit was achieved as a result of the donation. A special case involves donations and contributions by public utility companies in which ratepayers will compensate through utility rates the payment of company expenses. The courts have frequently held that contributions by utility companies must come out of profits available for distribution to shareholders and may not be charged to ratepayers.

This tension between shareholder expectations and the legal right to control and manage the corporation is most apparent in the publicly held corporation and underscores the most significant development in the past century—the growth of managerialism. As suggested above, the separation of ownership and control of the modern public corporation precipitated a class of professional managers who generally had a small share in the ownership of the corporation. The legal norms, which grant them substantial control over the management of the corporation, and the rise of shareholder disinterest in exercising managerial power in the corporation combined to divorce ownership and control. The rise in managerialism has created difficulties in policy-making within the corporation and has resulted in the frequent criticism that large corporations are interested solely in profitability and disinterested in accomplishing social objectives. Managers have obvious difficulties in generating any consensus among shareholders as to proper social policies to be pursued by the corporation and instead tend to pursue profits and market growth. Proposals to restore power to shareholders, such as disinterested directors or public-advocate representatives on the board, have been met with disinterest by shareholders, and it appears that until some political consensus is reached on the role of the corporation this dilemma will remain unresolved.

A final issue concerning the modern corporation and public attitudes toward its role is the size of American firms and the relationship between bigness and economic, social, and political policy. American public policy has traditionally expressed great concern over market performance and the exercise of economic and political power by large firms. Equally disconcerting was a trend in some industries toward greater concentration of economic power—measured in market share or assets—in the hands of a few firms. The political and economic concerns expressed in the antitrust laws were related to the ability of large firms or powerful aggregations of firms in some industries to obtain monopoly profits, restrict the output of socially desired goods, and channel the profits and economic power into political persuasion.

It is hotly debated whether the antitrust laws have been successful in limiting monopolies and deconcentrating important industries. The merger laws were rewritten in the 1950s to thwart trends toward concentration in markets, but the mid-1970s saw the beginning of an unprecedented wave of mergers among competitors and firms in vertically related markets. Some of this seeming indifference was due to new thinking about the probable economic harm that a large firm is actually capable of inflicting and, more basically, to changing public attitudes toward large firms and concentrated industries. Public economic opinion appeared more interested in sharpening American industry's ability to compete internationally and to reindustrializing the manufacturing sector; the fears of the disappearance of the small businessman and the economic mayhem of the robber barons, which exerted a pervasive influence on political policy for many years, were replaced by these other concerns during that period.

CONCLUSION

The American corporation is difficult to describe in general terms; it comes in many sizes and serves many purposes. However, it is possible to make the observation that the law has served to advance both the public acceptance and social and economic utility of the corporation. The law of corporations has shaped the operation of the corporation to permit fulfillment of individual investors' expectations and has constrained the conduct of the corporation to protect the public. It has also challenged the corporation to achieve a role in society that better not only the participants within the corporation but the society in which it functions.

CASES

Burg v. Horn, 380 F.2d 897 (2nd Cir. 1967)
Dartmouth College v. Woodward, 4 Wheaton 518 (1819)
Ernst & Ernst v. Hochfelder, 425 U.S. 185 (1976)
Galler v. Galler, 32 Ill. 2d 16, 203 N.E.2d 577 (1964)
Louis K. Liggett Co. v. Lee, 288 U.S. 517 (1933)
McQuade v. Stoneham, 263 N.Y. 323, 189 N.E. 234 (1934)
Paul v. Virginia, 8 Wallace 168 (1869)
Santa Fe Industries, Inc. v. Green, 430 U.S. 462 (1977)

BIBLIOGRAPHY

Adolf A. Berle and Gardiner C. Means, *The Modern Corporation and Private Property* (1932), is a classic formulation of the legal and economic roles of the corporation in society. John P. Davis, *Corporations* (1905), is a thorough explication of the historical foundations for the modern American corporation. Peter F. Drucker, *Concept of the Corporation,* rev. ed. (1972), is a classic treatment of the economic and social roles of the large corporation as developed through a case study of General Motors. Melvin A. Eisenberg, *The Structure of the Corporation: A Legal Analysis* (1976), is a thoughtful analysis of the dynamics of the corporation and the effect of legal roles on those relationships.

Robert W. Hamilton, *The Law of Corporations in a Nutshell* (1980), provides a general overview of corporate law written principally for law students. Richard W. Jennings and Richard M. Buxbaum, *Corporations: Cases and Materials,* 5th ed., (1979), is a detailed casebook used in American law schools. William A. Klein and John C. Coffee, Jr., *Business Organization and Finance: Legal and Economic Principles,* 2nd ed. (1986), reviews the legal and economic factors at work in intracorporate relationships. Wilbert E. Moore, *The Conduct of the Corporation* (1962), takes a well-recognized look at the roles that corporations should play in American society. Christopher D. Stone, *Where the Law Ends: The Social Control of Corporate Behavior* (1975), offers a lawyer's view of the ethical and moral constraints on, and obligations of, corporations.
[See also ADMINISTRATIVE AGENCIES; ADMINISTRATIVE LAW; CHASE AND WAITE COURTS AND ERAS; COMMERCE CLAUSE; COMMERCIAL LAW; CONTRACTS; FULLER COURT AND ERA; LABOR LAW; and WHITE AND TAFT COURTS AND ERAS.]

CRIMINAL LAW

David Robinson, Jr.

Criminal law defines crimes and punishments. It differs from civil law in that it is not primarily concerned with compensating the victim of a crime or even with obtaining court orders that specific conduct be avoided in the future. Instead, it punishes, or threatens to punish, persons who violate its proscriptions. Thus, a criminal case is brought in the name of the governmental unit whose law has allegedly been violated. The plaintiff may be the United States, a state, or a municipality. A single wrongful act, such as an assault on an individual, may result in both a criminal proceeding brought, for example, by a state and a civil action for compensation brought by the individual victim.

Criminal law may be contrasted with that component of civil law which provides compulsory measures with respect to the mentally ill and the mentally deficient. An individual may be involuntarily confined in a state hospital or other mental health facility for an indefinite period of time upon a determination that he meets the criteria for civil commitment—most commonly, that he is mentally ill or deficient and dangerous to himself or to others. It may be intuitively concluded that the distinction between criminal and civil confinement is clear; however, the concepts of mental illness and dangerousness are vague, and they may be attached to individuals whose behavior is deemed socially unacceptable and who are believed likely to continue to be so, absent intervention and perhaps treatment by institutions maintained by the state. These concerns are shared by both the criminal justice and the mental health systems. In contrast to civil confinement, a criminal conviction must be predicated on a finding of a violation of a previously defined proscribed criminal act. Unless such a finding is made, the defendant cannot be punished or sentenced to confinement by a court

exercising criminal law jurisdiction. The imposition of sentence by such a court constitutes, in part, an expression of social condemnation of the defendant for having committed the offense. No such judgment is made by a court ordering the commitment of a mentally ill person. At the same time, mental health and criminal proceedings do have overlapping social control functions. Both are greatly concerned with reducing the incidence of behavior that society regards as maladaptive, harmful, offensive, or otherwise socially undesirable. A number of the most interesting and difficult problems of criminal and mental health law are encountered in the search for an optimal division of labor between the two systems. Deciding who should be subjected to a mental health proceeding, who should be prosecuted for a criminal offense (assuming the commission of a criminal act and any other prerequisite of criminal liability), and who should be referred for voluntary treatment or simply left alone are common and often vexatious questions facing prosecutors, administrators of mental health care systems, and judges. It is only the beginning of understanding to recognize that the "bad" and the "sick" are often overlapping, not separate, categories.

A related problem of classification and social response relates to the significance of immaturity. All American states have special statutes dealing with juvenile offenders. People under a designated age (such as eighteen) are ordinarily not subjected to criminal charges or punishment in adult penal institutions. Instead, the juvenile justice system may be invoked. The model of civil commitment of the mentally ill or deficient has been adapted for the young, although the prerequisite of a finding that the defendant has committed what would otherwise be a crime is commonly retained. The result is a hybrid system, generally less punitive- and more treatment-oriented than the criminal justice process but retaining many of its characteristics, including stigmatization. Many states also have additional hybrid systems for special classes of social deviants, such as repetitive sexual offenders and chronic alcoholics.

CLASSIFICATION OF CRIMES

Statutes Versus Ordinances. State legislation authorizes cities and towns to enact municipal ordinances. Frequently the violation of such ordinances is said to be civil rather than criminal, although functionally the nature of the charge and the required proof may be identical under both systems. For example, petit larceny, if committed within a city, would violate both a municipal ordinance and a statute of the state in which the city is located. An offender could be prosecuted in either jurisdiction, and if convicted, he could be confined in the city or (upon state charges) county jail. Municipal ordinances do not frequently cover the most serious crimes, which are left to state or federal proscription.

Felonies and Misdemeanors. It is common to categorize criminal offenses as either felonies or misdemeanors. Felonies are normally punishable by confinement in state or federal prisons, or even by death. Misdemeanors generally carry only potential confinement in a jail—that is, an institution maintained by a county or a municipality. Felonies carry longer possible terms. Often state statutes utilize both distinctions: misdemeanants can be sentenced upon conviction to a term that may not exceed one year and that must be served in a jail and not in a prison. In some jurisdictions there is an additional separate category for petty offenses that carry little if any possible confinement. For example, the federal Comprehensive Crime Control Act of 1984, in addition to establishing five classes of felonies and three classes of misdemeanors, adds the category of "infraction," which may result in confinement for a period of not more than five days. While the prison and jail populations of the United States are not inconsiderable, the crime rate is also high, and the majority of persons convicted of felonies and misdemeanors are not sentenced to confinement unless they are repetitive offenders or unless they have been convicted of offenses of particular gravity, such as murder.

Common-Law and Statutory Crimes. Another frequent distinction in the classification of criminal offenses is between common-law crimes and statutory crimes. The former are offenses created by courts during the centuries in which English and American courts developed the law of crimes in their jurisdictions. The primary role in the evolution of the criminal law has long since passed from the courts to the legislatures, and American criminal law is today almost exclusively statutory. While some states still recognize common-law crimes (or, rarely, even recognize the authority of their courts to recognize new common-law crimes), criminal prosecution in the United States is usually based on a statute that defines the offense charged. In many American jurisdictions, including the federal system, all criminal prosecutions must be based on statutorily proscribed violations. Nevertheless, the common law of crimes continues to be influential in the interpretation of statutes that fail to completely define offenses as well as defenses to statutory prosecutions.

THE FUNCTIONS OF CRIMINAL LAW

There is continuing disagreement as to the proper functions of criminal law, although both retributive and utilitarian goals are commonly held to be objectives. Retribution is predicated on the view that justice requires punishment, regardless of the consequences of that punishment on the prevention of other crimes. Kant vividly expressed this position when he wrote in *The Metaphysics of Morals,*

> Even if a civil society were to dissolve itself by common agreement of all its members (for example, if the people inhabiting an island decided to separate and disperse themselves around the world), the last murderer remaining in prison must first be executed, so that everyone will duly receive what his actions are worth and so that the bloodguilt thereof will not be fixed on the people because they failed to insist on carrying out the punishment; for if they fail to do so, they may be regarded as accomplices in this public violation of legal justice.
>
> (p. 102)

The utilitarian view of criminal sanctions finds its rationale in crime prevention or deterrence, including the deterrence of persons other than the one punished. For example, federal officials do not have sufficient resources to bring criminal proceedings against the great majority of persons who are believed to have committed violations of the federal statutes proscribing attempting to evade federal taxes, as would be required by a pure retributive theory. Instead, a small percentage of violators are charged, primarily to induce an adequate level of compliance by the general taxpaying population. Deterrence is thus attributable in part to taxpayers' fear that they may be prosecuted and punished if they violate a criminal statute and in part to an educational effect. The public is clearly informed of the prohibition, and social norms are reinforced. Such deterrence is sometimes called general prevention or general deterrence, referring to the inhibitory effect of the sanction on persons other than the one punished.

An additional way in which the criminal law system seeks to reduce the incidence of crime is by incapacitating offenders. Individuals who are confined in jails and prisons (or who are executed) cannot easily commit crimes in the general population while they are thus isolated. Such punishment is especially applicable to recidivists (repeat offenders) and persons who have manifested their dangerousness by committing particularly grave offenses. A number of American jurisdictions have adopted career-offender programs, which are designed to concentrate prosecutorial and correctional institution resources on recidivists in the belief that their incapacitation can have a large effect upon the crime rate. In addition, many jurisdictions have special statutes providing for enhanced punishment of repetitive offenders ("habitual criminals").

A major problem of the restraint theory of criminal sanctions is the cost of imprisoning offenders. In the United States the costs of building and maintaining prisons and jails are quite substantial, although there is wide variation from jurisdiction to jurisdiction. In some other countries, such as the Soviet Union, work camps rather than prisons are the norm, and the economic costs of implementing an isolation strategy are far less.

In the mid-twentieth century, many commentators held that the primary purpose of criminal sanctions ought to be the rehabilitation of offenders. This view has been largely repudiated,

not because of any widespread belief that reform is an inappropriate ideal but because data suggest that we lack the ability to reform an adequate number of offenders by penal programs (Martinson). This does not mean that no individuals sentenced for a criminal offense can be rehabilitated but rather that the ability to reform offenders through social measures is so limited, in most applications, that a general justification of penal rehabilitation becomes difficult. Rehabilitation may occur not only where the desire to violate criminal law is sufficiently reduced to limit criminal behavior but also through intimidation of the offender as a result of the application of criminal sanctions (special deterrence).

THE ELEMENTS OF A CRIME

For a crime to have been committed, there must have been a wrongful act (*actus reus*) or omission to act. In addition, there must ordinarily have been a wrongful state of mind (*mens rea*). The act and state of mind must be in concurrence, in that the latter must cause the former. Furthermore, some crimes, such as murder, require that the act have caused a result, such as the death of the victim.

Criminal liability requires that the actor have engaged in conduct forbidden by law. Usually this will be affirmative conduct, such as shooting a gun or forging a bank check. On occasion (though this is atypical) an omission will suffice. Here the violation is of a legal duty to act. The duty to act may arise out of a relationship, such as the parental duty to support a dependent child. It may be based on contract, such as that of a physician to care for a patient. It may be based upon statute, such as the duty to file income tax returns. It may arise out of a voluntary undertaking to aid another; for example, if a man puts an incapacitated injured person in his car, he must take the person to a hospital rather than leave him isolated in the vehicle. However, Anglo-American law does not impose a general duty to aid others, even when this can be done at no cost and with little effort and the need is great.

Ordinarily, then, a positive act is required, as the Supreme Court held in *Powell* v. *Texas* (1968). In large part, this requirement is attributable to the belief that a mere desire to commit a prohibited act should not result in the imposition of a penalty. Nearly everyone has such desires but usually succeeds in restraining them. Even if a fixed criminal intention could be established without proof of criminal conduct, manifestation of a resulting social danger is insufficient to justify the imposition of a penalty when only such a desire can be proven. For example, the Supreme Court ruled in *Robinson* v. *California* (1962) that it is unconstitutional for a state to attach criminal penalties for mere addiction to the use of narcotics. But when an addict commits proscribed acts, such as purchasing drugs or even voluntarily possessing them, he subjects himself to the possibility of criminal conviction.

In addition to a criminal act, most crimes require a wrongful state of mind. The required mental element varies from crime to crime and even within a single crime with respect to various subsidiary elements. Furthermore, judges and legislatures have added to the complexity and confusion by utilizing imprecise and quite variable terminology to describe what is required. Probably the most useful effort to bring order and comprehensibility to this area of criminal law is that of the American Law Institute, whose Model Penal Code, dating from 1962, was drafted to serve as a model for legislatures seeking to modernize and rationalize their criminal statutes. The Model Penal Code has been highly successful in this endeavor; it has served as a guide, to a greater or lesser degree, for comprehensive criminal law reform in the states, a majority of which have revised their criminal codes in recent years.

After setting forth the requirement of a criminal act or omission, the Model Penal Code turns to criminal intent, which it calls ''culpability'' (Section 2.02). Four levels of culpability are defined for use in later sections of the code, which establish specific criminal offenses: ''purposely,'' ''knowingly,'' ''recklessly,'' and ''negligently.'' The distinction between ''purposely'' and ''knowingly'' is somewhat narrow. A person committing a homicide, for example, kills purposely if it is his conscious desire to cause the death of the victim; he acts knowingly if he is aware that it is practically certain that his conduct will cause the death. Thus, an arsonist who sets fire to a crowded hotel without desire to take human life but believing that lives will be lost acts knowingly; if he consciously desires to kill,

he acts purposely. Most criminal proscriptions do not distinguish between purposeful and knowing acts with respect to liability. Indeed, less precise statutes often use the term *intentionally* to cover both.

In both reckless and negligent situations, a result may be unintentional and yet still result in criminal liability for certain offenses. If the person setting fire to the hotel merely acted to build a bonfire in the middle of his room in order to prepare his dinner and was not aware that human death would be practically certain to result, his killing of other people would at the most be reckless; otherwise, it would be negligent. The distinction would depend on whether he was aware that there was a substantial risk that death would result. If, however unreasonably, he was unaware of the risk of death, his conduct would be negligent rather than reckless. In many states he would therefore be guilty of manslaughter rather than murder, which commonly can be committed purposely, knowingly, or recklessly, but not negligently.

Occasionally, crimes may be committed without culpability, although this is uncommon and much criticized by academic commentators when the offense is other than a petty one. Nevertheless, criminal statutes sometimes proscribe conduct without proof of fault. Examples are statutes of most states that, even when fornication between adults is not a crime, make it an offense for an adult male to have consensual sexual intercourse with an underage female. Since even a reasonable belief that the female was of the age of consent usually is treated as no defense, the crime is one of strict liability with respect to that element of the offense. Other examples are statutes proscribing the sale of unwholesome, mislabeled, or adulterated food or drugs, where good faith of the seller is often immaterial. In the area of minor offenses (which may or may not be technically classified as crimes), strict liability is quite common, as when, because of a defective speedometer, a motorist speeds while reasonably believing that he is driving within the speed limit.

A distinction should be noted between situations of strict liability and those in which the actor erroneously believes that his conduct is not forbidden by law. For example, if a man knowingly has sexual relations with a sixteen-year-old girl in the belief that the legal age of consent in the state is sixteen when in fact the legislature has set it at eighteen, no defense will be recognized, even in the minority of states that would grant a defense upon a showing of a reasonable mistake of the fact of the girl's age. Sometimes it is said that reasonable mistake of fact, when the facts as the actor believed them to be would not constitute a crime, is a defense, whereas mistake of law is never a defense. Such a statement is imprecise, given the areas of strict liability that still remain in American criminal law. However, a mistake of fact that is inconsistent with a required element of a particular crime is exculpatory. This follows from the requirement of culpability. For example, if I take another's raincoat believing it to be my own, I am not guilty of larceny, not because of some special defense of mistake of fact but because the crime of larceny requires that I know that the property that I take does not belong to me. Although it can generally be said that ignorance of the criminal law is no defense, occasionally a crime will be so defined as to require knowledge of the duty imposed by the statute in order for prosecution to occur. Some criminal tax statutes, for example, require this; however, such a requirement is uncommon.

In addition to requiring proof of a criminal act and criminal intent, some crimes are defined so as to require a result that is causally related to the act. Thus, if I shoot at my enemy and miss him, I cannot be convicted of murder, because murder is defined so as to require an actual killing. Furthermore, an adequate causal relationship between the act and the result must also be shown. No liability will occur if my shooting did not in fact result in my enemy's death, as would be the case if he died of a heart attack that was not caused by my shot. In addition, the causal relationship must be sufficiently close to justify the imposition of legal liability. If I slightly wound my enemy, who then goes to a hospital where he is strangled to death by a maniac, it would be held that my conduct is insufficiently proximately related to the victim's death to make me responsible for murder.

COMPLICITY

The discussion and examples thus far have assumed that only one person is involved in a hypothetical crime. Often this is not the case, and criminal liability may depend upon the notion of complicity. If A and B decide to rob a bank, and A enters the bank and robs it while B waits outside in a getaway car, A is clearly liable for the robbery. Under the law of complicity, B is also regarded as a robber. This is because he was purposely and sufficiently present at the robbery and assisted in it. Even if B merely plans the robbery or encourages A to commit it without being present, B will still be liable for robbery under the law of complicity. In contrast, if A commits a robbery without B's knowledge and, upon learning of the crime, B hides A from the police to prevent A's arrest or prosecution, B will not be liable for the robbery but will be treated as an accessory after the fact or an obstructor of justice, both being lesser offenses than robbery.

ATTEMPTED CRIME

In the discussion of the requirements of a criminal act, it was noted that an individual is not liable for mere thoughts or even criminal plans. If an individual begins to act upon his plans, liability for an attempted crime may result. The first question is whether the action has gone far enough toward completion to justify holding the actor for an attempted crime. If A, planning to murder B, buys a gun for that purpose but is arrested before traveling to B's city, A will traditionally not be liable for attempted murder, because his conduct is insufficiently closely related to the consummation of homicide. If, on the other hand, A goes to within shooting distance of B and fires his gun but misses, all jurisdictions would say that A has gone far enough to be charged with attempt. There are many possible intermediate situations between the two cases posed. Various courts, legislators, and commentators have proposed a number of tests to resolve the question of at what point short of consummation of the objective offense attempt liability should be charged. The actual cases are often in considerable conflict.

A second issue in the law of attempts concerns the intent requirement. Many jurisdictions have required that the actor have a true purpose of committing the crime. For example, where a hunter fired his rifle at a lantern in a distant tent, intending to shoot out the light but narrowly avoided killing an occupant of the tent, it was held that although had a homicide occurred, it would be murder (since murder can be committed recklessly), no attempted murder had been committed, since recklessness is not enough for an attempt. Some modern codes do hold, in contrast, that recklessness will suffice for such an offense to be deemed an attempted crime.

A third issue is that of impossibility of completing the objective offense. It is traditionally said that the result depends upon whether the impossibility is factual or legal. The former is no defense, but not the latter. The actual cases indicate no clear delineation between what is regarded as factual and what is regarded as legal. If the failure to consummate the offense is due to inadequate instrumentalities or other means (such as the misfiring of a gun), the impossibility of completion will be classified as factual, and no defense will be found. If, however, the failure is to understand the nature of the objective, the cases are in conflict. If A, intending to murder his enemy B, enters B's bedroom and, seeing a form under the covers, stabs it with a knife but actually stabs only some pillows (B having created a false target), some courts would hold that legal impossibility precludes a finding of attempted murder, but others would call this factual impossibility. The distinction depends upon the perspective from which the case is analyzed. Most traditional courts would view the facts from an omniscient standpoint and conclude that A succeeded in stabbing the pillows and that is not a crime. This is classically what is meant by legal impossibility. The more modern view, supported by the Model Penal Code (Section 5.01), is to view the facts from the standpoint of the belief of the actor. What he intended to do was not to stab a pillow but to stab his victim. He has manifested his dangerousness by acting on his intent and should be treated accordingly.

A fourth issue is the severity of punishment for an attempt. At common law all attempts were misdemeanors. Under contemporary statutes, attempts to commit felonies are usually punishable in the felony range, often with a maximum of half the possible penalty for successful completion of the objective offense. Some statutes provide the same punishment as for the objective offense, even though retributive and deterrent concerns are less pressing, on the grounds that the actor has manifested dangerousness similar to that of the convicted offender.

CONSPIRACY

At traditional Anglo-American common law, conspiracy is a misdemeanor consisting of an agreement of two or more persons to commit a crime or a lawful act by unlawful (although not necessarily criminal) means. Under contemporary statutes the crime of conspiracy is commonly limited to agreements to commit a crime, and the penalty is often raised to the felony range if the criminal objective is itself a felony. It is unnecessary for the agreement to be formal; often it is simply tacit, inferred from cooperative action in a criminal venture. Current statutes often also require the commission of an overt act (other than simply an agreement) in furtherance of the criminal venture.

The crime of conspiracy is an inchoate crime, permitting intervention by law enforcement forces before the crime has been committed or even before it has progressed far enough to constitute an attempt. Conspiracy law is in part a response to the greater danger posed by a group of offenders, as compared to an individual. It also facilitates enhanced punishment for criminal groups, as the general view is that they may be punished both for the conspiracy and for any substantive offenses that they may have committed. In some jurisdictions, including the federal courts, a charge of conspiracy facilitates joint trials of defendants, thus saving prosecutorial and court time. In the opinion of many observers, joint trials also enable conviction of marginal defendants—those marginally implicated in the scheme—on the theory that the jury will conclude that birds of a feather have been flocked together. There are a number of other procedural prosecutive advantages to a conspiracy charge as well.

Although some commentators have criticized the law of conspiracy in terms of its vagueness and the difficulty that individual defendants in complex trials experience in defending themselves effectively (La Fave and Scott), conspiracy charges form an important component of the prosecution of organized criminal groups, particularly in the federal courts. Indeed, Congress has acted to expand conspiracy law by adding specialized statutes, such as the Racketeer-Influenced and Corrupt Organizations Act (RICO), which carries particularly heavy possible penalties upon conviction.

DEFENSES

If the criminal act, culpability, and any other element that may be required by the definition of a specific crime have been shown, the question of potential defenses arises. Some defenses are set forth in the statute or decisions that define an offense. An example is reasonable mistake of age of the victim of a statutory rape, which is a defense in a minority of states. Other defenses are generally applicable. The following are among the most commonly raised.

Immaturity. Youth affords a defense to children who might otherwise face criminal charges. At common law a child under seven years of age could not be found guilty of a crime, and there was a presumption (which could be rebutted) of incapacity of a child between the ages of seven and fourteen to form criminal intent. At fourteen, the child was treated as adult. Today the treatment of immaturity varies substantially from state to state; the primary considerations are age, the nature of the offense, and official discretion. A common approach is to select an age, such as eighteen, at which a child will be treated as an adult. Prior to that age, offenses will be subject to prosecution under the juvenile delinquency laws, which are regarded as technically noncriminal but may result in a loss of liberty in special facilities. Crimes of particular severity, such as murder, may still be subject to criminal prosecution if the defendant is above a minimum age, such as sixteen. Some states also require the juvenile court to waive jurisdiction to proceed under the delinquency laws in such situations as an additional safeguard against overuse of adult procedures, sanctions, and facilities against juveniles.

Intoxication. Individuals who commit crimes are frequently intoxicated. Yet voluntary intoxication is not in itself a defense to a crime, even when it is likely that the actor would not have committed the crime had he been sober. Recognizing intoxication as a defense would protect a large number of offenders from criminal convic-

tion. However, it is common to recognize a defense if the intoxication negates an element of the offense, normally a mental element. If an intoxicated woman, for example, believes that another's umbrella is her own and carries it off, she cannot be held liable for larceny in most states, as her intoxication negates the existence of an intent to steal.

It is most commonly held that for crimes that can be committed recklessly (such as crimes of homicide), intoxication will not serve as a defense, even though the normally required awareness of homicidal risk is negated by intoxication. Although this view is inconsistent with the normal requirements of culpability, it avoids litigation of a difficult issue (the degree of an intoxicated defendant's awareness of a risk), and it is thought (for example, by the authors of the Model Penal Code) to rarely result in injustice in actual cases. Crimes that can be committed negligently are also not subject to a culpability defense of intoxication, because the standard of behavior is that of the reasonable sober person, not of the inebriated one.

Insanity. Mental abnormality may provide a defense to a criminal charge in the great majority of states and in the federal system. There is great variation as to what will suffice to establish this defense. The traditional Anglo-American test is set forth in *M'Naghten's Case* (1843). The defendant was a Scottish political activist who attempted to shoot the British prime minister but in fact killed another person. The House of Lords, in defining the defense, said,

> To establish a defence on the ground of insanity, it must be clearly proved that at the time of committing of the act, the party accused was labouring under such a defect of reason, from disease of the mind, as not to know the nature and quality of the act he was doing; or, if he did know it, that he did not know he was doing what was wrong.

M'Naghten is commonly regarded as a cognition test, as it is directed to what the actor knew at the time of the criminal act. Many American jurisdictions have added a volition test, exculpating a defendant where he knew what he was doing and that it was wrong but, because of mental disease, his actions were deemed beyond his control. This is sometimes called the "irresistible impulse'' addition to the *M'Naghten* test. Since its formulation frequently does not require that the abnormality be characterized by sudden impulse as opposed to brooding and reflection, it is more appropriate to term it a "control" or "volition" test.

Many American jurisdictions have moved from *M'Naghten* and its volitional modification to the proposal of the Model Penal Code (Section 4.01), which provides in part, "A person is not responsible for criminal conduct if at the time of such conduct as a result of mental disease or defect he lacks substantial capacity either to appreciate the criminality of his conduct or to conform his conduct to the requirements of law." This is a somewhat broadened version of the traditional cognition-plus-volition tests. Nevertheless, it has been subjected to a substantial body of contemporary criticism aimed at its vagueness and the breadth of its possible application. The latter criticism was given impetus by the acquittal, on grounds of insanity, of John W. Hinckley, Jr., who was charged with the attempted assassination of President Ronald Reagan. In 1984, Congress narrowed the federal defense by eliminating its volitional component, shifting the burden of persuasion on the issue from the government to the defense and requiring that the defense produce clear and convincing evidence that the defendant acted as a result of severe mental disease or defect. A very small number of states have abolished the insanity defense except to the extent that mental abnormality may be relevant if it negates the criminal intent required by the offense charged.

Two additional matters must be mentioned to put the insanity defense into context. First, the grossly mentally ill or deficient are unlikely to stand trial for their criminal acts, as they usually are found incompetent to understand the proceedings against them and to participate in their defense. Trials of such persons are deemed to be essentially trials in their absence, and they are therefore prohibited as unfair. If it is believed that an incompetent defendant may become competent to assist in his defense after a relatively brief period of treatment, the criminal trial may be suspended in order that this may occur. If it appears that the defendant will be indefinitely incapacitated, the civil commitment process is commonly invoked if the defendant is thought to be dangerous.

Second, a successful invocation of the insanity defense usually initiates a process of commitment of the defendant to a mental health facility if he is thought to still be mentally ill or defective and also dangerous. The possibility of commitment following successful invocation of the insanity defense is undoubtedly a major factor in the infrequency of its use in the defense of criminal cases unless the crime charged is a grave one.

Diminished Capacity. In a number of American states, evidence of mental abnormality may be used to negate the existence of the intent required to commit an offense. The phrase "diminished capacity" has been commonly used to designate this defense, which usually results if it is successful in conviction for a lesser offense rather than acquittal.

Necessity and Duress. A person may face the alternative of violating the literal language of a criminal statute or experiencing a greater harm or evil (*Regina* v. *Dudley and Stephens,* 1884). For example, a prisoner in a jail that catches fire may commit what would otherwise be punishable as an escape, or a person may kill another in order to save yet other lives. In such situations, the defendant may raise the defense of necessity to a criminal charge. Although such cases are infrequent, a number of courts have indicated a willingness to accept such a defense where it can be adequately proven. American courts have been notably unsympathetic to defenses in which economic necessity is claimed, as when a defendant maintains that he was forced to steal because of lack of food or other necessities of life. The rejection of such a defense may be explained by the usual availability of acceptable alternatives to the offense, such as making use of public or charitable food services. Another reason for the rejection of the defense in such contexts is a reluctance to legalize aggressive acts of self-help or even to litigate the question of whether better alternatives were available. A similar attitude has been taken toward claims of pharmacological necessity in cases in which narcotics addicts are charged with possession of a prohibited drug.

Where the evil that the defendant had sought to avoid is a threat by a person to harm the defendant unless he commits what would otherwise be a criminal offense, the defense is usually labeled "duress" or "coercion" rather than "necessity," although generally similar principles apply.

Entrapment. Some crimes do not ordinarily have victims who are likely to complain to the authorities, and the police may attempt to create situations in which the commission of such offenses can be observed by undercover law enforcement officers or by other persons allied with them. In narcotics law enforcement work, for example, plainclothes police or others who work with them (often narcotics addicts themselves) attempt to buy drugs from persons believed to be narcotics sellers. If the suspects sell the drugs and are charged with a criminal offense, they may seek to defend themselves on grounds of entrapment.

In general, there are two theories of the entrapment defense that are accepted by American courts. Under the most commonly followed view, the defendant must establish that the intent to commit the crime originated with the police or the person acting as a police agent rather than with the defendant and that the defendant was not otherwise predisposed to commit the offense. This is sometimes referred to as the "origin of intent" standard of the entrapment defense. Although it is sometimes thought to be justified on the theory that the legislature that created the offense did not intend to apply it to situations of police instigation, its primary rationale is probably to be found in a reluctance to permit criminally disposed persons to escape punishment by blaming the police for their apprehension. If a defendant raises the entrapment defense in a jurisdiction in which the origin-of-intent standard is followed, his predisposition to commit the alleged crime is placed before the jury that tries the case. The prosecution may respond with evidence that the defendant committed prior crimes of a sort similar to the crime with which he is now being charged. Such evidence is ordinarily kept from the jury in the absence of an entrapment defense, as the law of evidence in general precludes the prosecution from putting on evidence of the defendant's bad character unless the defendant raises his character as an issue—for example, by claiming entrapment—and may be highly disadvantageous to the defendant.

A minority of states have adopted a broader entrapment defense, making it available if the conduct of the law enforcement officials creates a substantial risk that the alleged offense would be committed by one who is not predisposed to commit it. This is sometimes called the "police misconduct" standard of entrapment. It focuses on the disposition of a hypothetical person rather than the defendant. It also focuses on the behavior of the police rather than the accused. Some courts have been inclined to sustain defenses under this standard when they strongly disapprove of police behavior, regardless of whether any innocent person might be thought likely to accept inducements of the sort offered. Under the police-misconduct theory, the entrapment defense does not permit a prosecution rebuttal showing that the defendant has committed other crimes similar to the ones charged; his personal predisposition is regarded as irrelevant. Furthermore, the defense is decided by the judge rather than by a jury. Under all standards of entrapment, the person instigating the offense must be a law enforcement official or an individual acting in cooperation with a law enforcement official. Inducement by a private citizen will not suffice.

Self-Defense and Defense of Others. The use of such force as reasonably appears necessary for self-protection against imminent unlawful violence by another is justified under criminal law. The harm that the defendant has sought to prevent must be an immediate, not a future, harm. Even deadly force may be justified under this principle, providing the harm threatened is itself great or deadly. Thus, for example, deadly force is not justified to prevent a simple assault or the theft of property.

Under common law the use of force to prevent an unlawful arrest was allowed. The contemporary view is that in such situations persons should yield to police officers and challenge the legality of their arrests later in court, if necessary, rather than respond with physical resistance.

Some states require that a person retreat, if he knows that he can safely do so, before resorting to deadly force; but most permit an individual faced with the threat of deadly attack to simply stand his ground, even to the point of resorting to deadly responsive force if it then becomes necessary. The view of states requiring retreat, where feasible, is that deadly force in such situations is not necessary and therefore not justified. The contrary view is predicated on the notion that a person who is subjected to deadly threat may, in accordance with popular mores, rightfully choose to stand his ground rather than retreat, even if this results in eventual death to the initial wrongdoer. Another defense of the majority view would be that persons who yield to the urge to stand their ground in the face of unlawful attack do not present the sort of social danger that justifies criminal conviction. Such considerations are controlling where the actor uses less than deadly force, it being agreed that there is no duty to retreat under such circumstances. The conflict in legal decisions exists only when deadly force is used. Furthermore, even in jurisdictions following the retreat rule, a person is not required to retreat from his home or place of business.

In general, individuals have a right to use force, even deadly force if necessary, to protect someone who is the victim of an unlawful assault. Historically, this privilege arose out of a right to protect personal property and was extended only when a special relationship existed between the person claiming the privilege and the person defended (such as husband and wife, parent and child, master and servant), but the modern tendency is to abandon any such limitation.

Defense of Property. An individual may use reasonable force to protect personal property in his or her possession. Deadly force is not authorized under this privilege, as the interest in property is believed to be outweighed by the interest in life. Other privileges may be implicated at the time of defense of property. The use of moderate force, for example, may give rise to a broader privilege of self-defense if the person threatening the property responds to its defense with deadly force.

Crime Prevention. Reasonable force may be used to prevent the commission of a felony or a misdemeanor amounting to a breach of the peace. At common law even deadly force could be used to prevent the commission of a felony. Today the tendency is to restrict the permissible use of deadly force to felonies that would result in death or great bodily harm if consummated.

Arrest. Reasonable force is justified if it is immediately necessary to effect a lawful arrest. Traditionally, even deadly force was regarded as permissible if necessary to arrest an individual reasonably believed to be a felon. In 1985, however, the Supreme Court in *Tennessee* v. *Garner* held that the Constitution prohibits police officers from using deadly force against fleeing felons unless the officers have probable cause to believe that the suspect poses a significant threat of death or serious physical injury to themselves or others. Traditionally, a private citizen had a similar but somewhat narrower right to use force to make a citizen's arrest of an offender; the trend in recent statutes is to restrict such actions somewhat in favor of requiring reliance on the police, unless the private person acts in response to a police request for assistance.

Consent. Consent of the victim is not a defense to the commission of a crime unless it negates an element of the offense. Thus, because the crime of rape is commonly defined to include sexual intercourse without consent, valid consent negates an element of the crime that the prosecution is required to prove to obtain a conviction. Similarly, consent of a participant in a sporting event, such as football, precludes prosecution for batteries that are within the range of reasonably foreseeable conduct in such games. In contrast, consent by the victim in a sale of narcotics does not constitute a defense, because the crime is not defined so as to require the lack of consent of the purchaser.

Similarly, condonation (forgiveness) by the victim after an offense is completed is no defense to its commission, although the police and prosecution sometimes decline to proceed with criminal charges in such cases as a matter of discretion, in part because of anticipated difficulty in obtaining the victim's cooperation in the prosecution.

TYPES AND EXAMPLES OF SUBSTANTIVE CRIMES

Varying statutory developments, which began with attempts at codification and then modifications of the common law of crimes, continue to occur. With the widespread replacement of American common law with statutory offenses in various jurisdictions, the difficult task of attempting a brief but comprehensive overview of substantive criminal law has become nearly impossible. Nonetheless, a summary of important types of specific crimes, along with some individual examples, may be given.

Crimes Against the Person. At common law, there were only two homicide offenses, murder and manslaughter. Many contemporary criminal codes have added a third offense, negligent homicide. Although at common law and under many statutes the distinction between murder and manslaughter is said to turn on whether the killing was done with "malice aforethought," this phrase is not applied literally. It is rather a summary of a number of culpability alternatives that distinguish the most blameworthy homicides from the rest.

The malice-aforethought requirement is commonly met when the purpose of the actor is to kill or cause great bodily injury (or when he knows that death or great bodily harm will result) and he acts without justification, excuse, or legally mitigating circumstances. A second form of murder, sometimes referred to as "depraved heart" murder, occurs when the actor kills in a manner evidencing extreme recklessness but without an intent to kill (that is, without true purpose or even knowledge that death will ensue). The label comes from old cases in which judges spoke of conduct "evincing a depraved heart, devoid of social duty, and fatally bent on mischief." An example would be that of a workman on top of a building who, in spite of knowing that people are below on the ground, nevertheless throws a heavy object from the roof without checking to be sure that no one is in danger of being struck by it, and thereby kills someone. The tendency of modern codifications is to require recklessness (actual awareness of the risk) rather than gross negligence for this type of unintentional homicide to be classified as murder. A third category of murder includes homicides caused by the commission of a felony. For example, if during the course of an armed robbery the robber's gun accidentally fires and the victim is killed, this act is murder, even though the robber did not intend the result. Although this felony-murder rule has been the subject of spirited criticism for generations because it aggravates the punishment for a small percentage of felonies for reasons not tied closely to their culpability, it continues to be the law in most American states. Its scope, however, is greatly narrowed in many of them, and it has been abolished in England, where it was first introduced.

In 1794, to restrict the use of the death penalty, Pennsylvania passed a statute that divided murder into two degrees and retained the possibility of capital punishment only for first-degree murders. Pennsylvania provided that willful, deliberate, and premeditated murders, together with murders committed in the perpetration or attempted perpetration of arson, rape, robbery, or burglary, were first-degree murders, whereas all other murders were murder in the second degree. Many other states followed this pattern.

Unlawful homicide, which is not murder, is traditionally treated as manslaughter, which may be committed either voluntarily (with intent to kill) or involuntarily (without intent to kill). The common-law distinction between murder and manslaughter has been strongly influential in present statutory differentiations. If the killing results from adequate provocation creating a passionate response in the actor and if there is insufficient time for a reasonable person to recover self-control, the crime is manslaughter rather than murder. An example is the killing of a spouse found in the act of adultery. This represents mitigation, not justification, for such homicides. Involuntary manslaughter involves an unintentional killing under circumstances in which the actor is less culpable than in a depraved-heart murder. In many states gross negligence will suffice for a conviction of involuntary manslaughter, as when a motorist kills while driving under the influence of alcohol or while driving at greatly excessive speed. Because juries are reluctant to convict motorists of manslaughter, many legislatures have created a separate and lesser vehicular offense of negligent homicide. The Model Penal Code (Section 210.4) restricts manslaughter to reckless conduct while expanding the statutory offense of negligent homicide beyond the vehicular situation to encompass all grossly negligent, but not reckless, homicides. The distinction is between disregarding a known grave risk of death or great bodily harm (recklessness) and disregarding a similar risk of which the actor should have been, but was not, aware (gross negligence).

Rape at common law is sexual intercourse with a female other than the actor's spouse without her consent. The lack of consent may be established by proof of force, intimidation, incapacity of the victim to give consent, or fraud as to the nature of the act that is being committed. The consent standard is often difficult to apply in practice. Some states require a showing that the victim resisted to the utmost, whereas others have taken the view that such resistance need not be shown, especially where it may have endangered the victim. Some recent statutory revisions have broadened the offense by abandoning the requirement of a male defendant and a female victim, permitting prosecution where the victim is married to the defendant and attempting to shift the focus of inquiry from the resistance of the victim to the compulsion of the defendant. At common law a female cannot be convicted for committing a rape personally, although she may be held liable if she aids a male in a rape.

Assault and Battery. At common law any unlawful harmful or offensive contact with another person constituted a battery. An assault was simply an attempted battery. Some jurisdictions, concerned that at common law pointing a gun known to be unloaded at another person would not qualify as an assault, have expanded the offense to include putting the victim in fear of immediate harmful or offensive contact. Both assault and battery continue to be ordinarily punishable in the misdemeanor range unless aggravating factors, such as the use of a weapon or greatly harmful force, are present.

Crimes Against the Habitation. Burglary at common law is the breaking and entering into the dwelling of another person in the nighttime with intent to commit a felony. By judicial interpretation and statutory modifications the offense has been greatly enlarged so as to include any unprivileged entry into any building (or even vehicle) with intent to commit any crime. Some critics of the scope of the crime of burglary, especially in its expanded form, have sought to abolish it as a separate crime and to replace it with a broadened general law of attempts that would permit punishment when the criminal object is too far from consummation to be reached by traditional attempt law. The notion of a separate crime of burglary with heavy penalties is deeply embedded in American law, however, and the Model Penal Code (Section 221.1) suggests that the crime persist in somewhat restricted form.

Arson. Common-law arson was defined as the malicious burning of a dwelling or related structure of another. The offense was greatly broadened by statute in many states, often to include separate degrees of arson so as to punish burning of other types of buildings and property and to permit punishment for burning one's own property in order to collect insurance. The broadened definition of the crime extended the protection afforded by statute beyond the security of the person to include a wider protection of property interests.

Crimes Relating to Property. Common-law larceny is the taking away of another's personal property from his possession without his consent, with intent to steal. By statute and judicial decision, the law of theft expanded beyond larceny to include situations in which the thief already has lawful possession or custody of the victim's property (embezzlement, larceny by employee, larceny by bailee) or where the thief obtains such property by deception (larceny by trick, false pretenses).

Many of the distinctions between these offenses are explainable only in historical terms and have no present criminological significance. As technical and economic developments have made the possibilities for acquisitive offenses more varied, criminal law has expanded to meet these new situations. For example, many automobiles are taken without intent to deprive the owner of their use permanently and therefore without the element of intent traditionally required for the crime of larceny. "Joy-riding" statutes have accordingly been widely adopted. Another example is credit card transactions, which create a question as to who is defrauded—the rightful holder of the card, the merchant accepting the card for payment, or the bank or other issuer of the card. Special statutes again have often been enacted. The approach of the Model Penal Code (Section 223.1) is to create a single consolidated offense called "theft" while still attempting to define with care the conduct and intent that is criminal. A majority of states have chosen this path. However, even the drafters of the Model Penal Code thought it desirable to supplement the general theft statute with specific additional provisions directed at the fraudulent use of bank checks, credit cards, and records (Article 224).

Robbery, like arson, may be considered primarily a crime against persons, although it has significant associations with theft as well. It is traditionally defined as larceny from the person by means of force or intimidation. Today, the felony of robbery has commonly been divided into offenses of differing severity, depending on whether the robber was armed.

Morals Offenses. Adultery and fornication were

punished by the English church, not by common law. While a number of American states passed statutes defining these crimes and variants of them, often requiring open cohabitation, they have been largely unenforced. The Model Penal Code does not include these offenses, on the grounds that they are commonly ignored, subject to arbitrary and discriminatory use, and an inappropriate use of the criminal sanction. Sodomy was originally defined as anal intercourse but is usually expanded to include oral-genital contacts as well. Although initially an ecclesiastical offense, it became the subject of prohibitory legislation in the majority of states. The Model Penal Code (Section 213.2) takes the position that deviate sexual intercourse between adults should not be the subject of penal proscription in the absence of a showing of force or other imposition similar to that required for the crime of rape. A number of states, but by no means all, have followed this path.

Statutory rape (carnal knowledge) is sexual intercourse with a female below the age of consent, which is varyingly placed by different states between ten and eighteen years. Sometimes the penalty is the same as for forcible rape. Some statutes require the male to be significantly older than the female, and many make the crime sex-neutral, although actual prosecution of adult females for having sexual relations with under-age boys is quite rare.

Crimes Involving Drugs. Although various drugs have been used throughout recorded history, scientific developments, such as the chemical extraction of active components of naturally occurring drugs and the synthesis and production of a large number of additional drugs, have created an acute drug-abuse problem in the present century. By 1900 only a few states had begun to regulate trade in opium, morphine, heroin, and cocaine. Within a few years the situation changed radically, and antinarcotics legislation was passed in every state and by the federal government.

The pattern of overlapping state and federal criminal laws and enforcement efforts has continued to the present, with the statutes becoming more sophisticated to deal with new scientific developments. Under federal law the Comprehensive Drug-Abuse Prevention and Control Act, known as the Controlled Substances Act, creates five categories for classification of drugs, depending on their potential for abuse and addiction and their medical value. A large number of individual drugs are placed in these categories, resulting in differing penalties upon conviction of unauthorized manufacture, distribution, sale, or possession. Most states have adopted the Uniform Controlled Substances Act (1972), which is patterned on the federal legislation and permits the states to prosecute similar offenses. A few states do not punish the private possession of small quantities of marijuana for personal use.

CASES

M'Naghten's Case, 10 Cl. & F. 200 (1843)
Powell v. Texas, 392 U.S. 514 (1968)
Regina v. Dudley and Stephens, 14 Q.B.D. 273 (1884)
Robinson v. California, 370 U.S. 660 (1962)
Tennessee v. Garner, 105 S.Ct. 1694 (1985)

BIBLIOGRAPHY

The American Law Institute's Model Penal Code represents the greatest modern effort to analyze and rationalize American criminal law. This undertaking was immense, beginning with preliminary papers, the establishment of distinguished groups of reporters (leaders) and advisers, the publishing of tentative drafts numbers 1–13 (1953–1961) with extensive and helpful Comments, and the approval of a final "proposed official draft" (1962). The institute published a revised set of commentaries covering a portion of the code as *Model Penal Code and Commentaries, Part II,* in 1981.

George P. Fletcher, *Rethinking Criminal Law* (1978), is a thoughtful effort to analyze, both theoretically and comparatively, many basic issues of criminal law and makes extensive use of British and continental material. Abraham S. Goldstein, *The Insanity Defense* (1967), is a distinguished attempt to deal with a subject area that raises many of the root problems of criminal law. Jerome Hall, *General Principles of Criminal Law,* 2nd ed. (1960), remains one of the most ambitious discussions of a number of issues of criminal law theory.

Sanford H. Kadish, Stephen J. Schulhofer, and Monrad G. Paulsen, *Criminal Law and Its Processes,* 4th ed. (1983), a comprehensive collection of excerpts of cases, articles, and books, together with notes by the authors, is both a leading teaching book for law students and a rich resource for other students and scholars. Immanuel Kant, *The Metaphysical Elements of Justice: Part I of "The Metaphysics of Morals,"* John Ladd, trans. (1965), is the philosopher's major statement on law. Wayne R. La Fave and Austin W. Scott, Jr., *Criminal Law,* 2nd ed. (1986), is the finest contemporary American textbook on criminal law. Peter W. Low, John C. Jeffries, Jr., and Richard J. Bonnie, *Criminal Law: Cases and Materials,* 2nd ed. (1986), is a work designed primarily for law students but constituting a valuable additional source of information for others as well, with notes by the authors that are extensive and of high quality. Robert Martinson, "What Works? Questions and Answers About Prison Reform," in *Public Interest*, 35 (1974), is a leading article on rehabilitation data, summarizing numerous studies.

National Commission on Reform of Federal Criminal Laws, *Working Papers*, 2 vols. (1970), is an extensive collection of analyses, proposals, and commentaries prepared as part of the commission's process of formulating a comprehensive revision of federal criminal statutes, and the work of the commission culminated in the publication of its *Final Report* (1971). Herbert L. Packer, *The Limits of the Criminal Sanction*

(1968), is a classic statement by a distinguished legal scholar about many of the basic problems of criminal law. Rollin M. Perkins and Ronald N. Boyce, *Criminal Law*, 3rd ed. (1982), is a comprehensive summary of Anglo-American criminal law, with an emphasis on historical materials and the elements of specific crimes. Herbert Wechsler, "The Challenge of a Model Penal Code," in *Harvard Law Review*, 65 (1952), is a statement of the bases and scope of the Model Penal Code, written at the outset of that undertaking, of which Wechsler was the principal architect. Glanville Williams, *Criminal Law: The General Part*, 2nd ed. (1961), is an insightful treatise by an eminent English scholar.

[*See also* CRIMINAL PROCEDURE *and* JUVENILE LAW.]

FAMILY LAW

Frances Olsen

Family law has traditionally been thought to involve the formation of families, the rights and duties of family members to each other, the relationship of outsiders to family members, and what happens when a family dissolves. Laws relating to certain intimate relationships, including long-term homosexual or heterosexual partnerships between unmarried persons, are also sometimes considered to be part of the field known as family law. Even though laws related to the financing of family groups, aging, health, pensions, and the like are often predicated on the family, these laws are not generally considered part of family law.

American family law has changed enormously during the past two centuries, both to reflect changes in family roles and to respond to ever-increasing demands for equality for women and for children. During the second half of the twentieth century, the laws relating to family matters have begun to provide tools for creating more egalitarian family relations, and the law serves less often to penalize individuals who try to structure their intimate lives on the basis of mutual respect and equality. Although this development is a marked improvement over the role law used to play in reinforcing family hierarchy, much remains to be done. Family relations continue to be unequal and often oppressive. While family law is sometimes an instrument of reform, it can also undermine reform efforts. For example, the law can perpetuate hierarchy by making family inequality appear to be inevitable, to be the fault of private individuals, or to be the free choice of individual family members. In this manner, family law tends to mask the injustices that occur and thereby to legitimate the status quo. Thus, the changes in family law during the past two centuries have served sometimes to equalize family relations, sometimes to legitimate the status quo, and sometimes to do a little of both at the same time.

GETTING MARRIED

Traditionally, marriage has marked the beginning of a new family. Legally, marriage is a civil contract entered into voluntarily by two people who thereafter bear to one another the legal relationship of wife and husband.

In the United States, entry into marriage is regulated by state law, subject to federal constitutional requirements and limitations. Most states require the couple to obtain a marriage license and go through certain formalities, including a blood test for venereal disease, often a few days waiting period, and usually a marriage ceremony of some kind. All states provide that either a civil or religious officer may perform the ceremony. A few states recognize marriages entered into without a license or other formalities, provided the couple has the legal capacity to marry. When such a so-called common-law marriage is recognized, it will be valid for all purposes and can be ended only by death or divorce, just like a valid ceremonial marriage.

Ordinarily, every state will recognize a marriage that is legally entered into elsewhere; usually a husband and wife can safely travel throughout the United States without finding their marital status suddenly questioned. The same would not be true of a man from a country recognizing polygamy who brought two wives to the United States or of a person who brought a child bride. States would justify their refusal to recognize such marriages (although they might provide financial protection to the woman) by citing a strong public policy against bigamy and against child marriage. In rare cases a state may refuse to recognize a marriage from another state; for example, when teenagers below the age of consent get married in a neighboring state with a lower age of consent, their home state will sometimes refuse to recognize their marriage. Thus, although a marriage that would be valid where performed will usually be valid everywhere, in a few instances such a marriage might be subject to annulment in the parties' home state. Finally, some people who are not married will be treated as though they are married or will be treated somewhat as husbands and wives are treated, in order to serve the interests of fairness or public policy.

Who and How. Each state specifies who may get married and under what circumstances their marriage will be binding. All states require that marriages be between one man and one woman, neither of whom is married to anyone else. Also, the couple must not be closely related by blood, such as sister-brother, mother-son, or father-daughter. Most states forbid all aunt-nephew or uncle-niece marriages; many forbid first cousins to marry; and some forbid marriages between people who are related, not by blood, but by marriage. For example, a man may not be allowed to marry his son's widow or former wife. Young children are not allowed to marry or to be married to anyone by their parents. All the above marriages are forbidden by state policy, regardless of the intention or desire of the parties.

Other marriage requirements are designed to protect one or both parties and may be waived by the interested parties. For example, the marriage must be freely consented to, not coerced or fraudulently induced. The parties must be sane, somewhat sober, and intend to get married. Young teenagers are usually not allowed to marry, and older teenagers may need parental approval or a court order before they are allowed to get married.

Marriage requirements are enforced in at least three different ways. First, laws may direct public officials to refuse to grant a marriage license to people who may not legally marry one another. Similarly, the law may forbid anyone to perform a marriage ceremony if the marriage would violate the state's marriage requirements, and the law may penalize a person who knowingly officiates at an unauthorized marriage. Second, state law may enforce marriage requirements by providing that marriages entered against strong public policy are null and void. For example, if either of the parties to a marriage is already married to someone else, the second marriage is bigamous and void. A third way the state may enforce marriage requirements is by specifying that certain parties may annul a marriage if marriage requirements were not met. For example, if a child marries underage, the child or parents of the child are generally allowed to obtain an annulment.

Marriages that do not violate a strong public policy are usually considered voidable but not void; the marriages are valid until they are annulled. If a marriage is considered voidable, the parties or someone acting on behalf of the parties must move to annul the marriage or it will remain good. For example, suppose a minor who is old enough to understand the significance of marriage but too young legally to marry manages to obtain a marriage license and go through a marriage ceremony. The marriage is voidable, not void, and it becomes a valid, binding marriage if it is ratified after the underage party comes of age—that is, if the couple continues to live together as husband and wife.

Ceremonial Marriage. The most common method for getting married is to obtain a marriage license and go through a marriage ceremony, either civil or religious. Most states require a couple to have blood tests before marriage to screen for venereal diseases. All states designate certain civil and religious officials who may perform marriages. Ordinarily both parties must be present at the marriage, but sometimes a proxy is allowed. For example, if one party cannot enter the United States or cannot leave his or her native country until the marriage has taken place, a marriage by proxy may be allowed and the newly created marriage relationship may facilitate emigration or immigration.

A ceremonial marriage does not have to be consummated in order to be valid. The couple is still legally married even if they never engage in sexual intercourse. As a practical matter, however, courts will more readily annul unconsummated marriages, whether for presumed impotency, fraud, or other reasons.

Minor irregularities in the marriage ceremony or failure to perform other formal requirements, such as recording the license, do not invalidate the marriage. Especially when the marriage has continued for a period of time, courts are reluctant to grant an annulment even for more serious ceremonial flaws. For example, courts have upheld marriages performed by unauthorized people when the couple was unaware of the deception and did not discover it until they had lived together as wife and husband.

Common-Law Marriage. In theory, a common-law marriage is formed when there has been no formal marriage ceremony but all the requirements of marriage have been met, including a "present agreement" to be married—that is, an agreement to be married now, not an engagement to be married sometime in the future. Once widely recognized, common-law marriage is now limited to just over a dozen states. If a common-law marriage is validly entered into, the couple is considered legally married for all purposes; like any other marriage, a common-law marriage continues until it is ended by death or divorce. In theory, a common-law marriage, once entered into in a state where common-law marriage is permitted, will be recognized in all other states, just as ceremonial marriages are generally recognized across state lines. Thus, a brief visit by a cohabiting couple to a state that recognizes common-law marriage may result in a common-law marriage.

In practice, the doctrine of common-law marriage has often been used to enable courts to treat a couple as married when it would seem unfair to treat them as not married, regardless of the true intention of the parties. For example, if a couple had lived together many years without ever getting married and if one partner died without leaving a will, a court might well find a common-law marriage so that it could justify allowing the surviving partner to inherit. In many such cases the surviving party would be coached by his or her lawyer regarding discrete perjury. Evidentiary questions become very important. States commonly require that the couple shall live together, be known in the community as husband and wife, and do nothing inconsistent with being married.

Some court decisions have refused to find a common-law marriage when the couple began living together without any clear intention to be married at the time, even if over the years they came to regard one another, and to be regarded in the community, as husband and wife. Other decisions have found a common-law marriage even when the couple believed they could not legally marry (for example, because one had a prior existing marriage) if the couple continued to live together after the impediment was removed (for example, by the death of the prior spouse), even if the parties were unaware of the removal of the impediment.

"Marriage" by Estoppel or Presumption. In some cases a couple will be treated as married even though a marriage between them is void. In order to prevent injustice, courts will sometimes estop a party from asserting the marriage's invalidity (that is, simply refuse to allow the party to do so). More commonly, courts will engage in presumptions that have the effect of validating invalid marriages. For example, if a person has been married more than once, courts presume that the latest marriage is valid rather than bigamous and that the prior marriages ended by death or divorce. This presumption is commonly invoked when a prior wife shows up after the husband's death and claims that there was no divorce. In such a case the second wife will prevail unless the first can prove that the husband never obtained a divorce, a difficult and sometimes impossible task. A bigamous marriage would then be treated as valid.

Nonmarriage. In some cases courts will grant one or another party some of the incidents of marriage without holding that a couple is married. In some states a party who falsely but innocently believed he or she was legally married will be characterized as a "putative spouse" and given the property interests that a spouse in the same position would enjoy. Depending upon the circumstances, either or both parties to an invalid marriage may have believed the marriage valid and thus qualify as a putative spouse. In such cases, property rights and rights and obligations of spousal support are affected, but the couple is not legally married.

The legal treatment afforded couples who live together without getting married has changed a great deal since the early 1960s. At one time, such relationships were condemned as immoral or "meretricious," and courts would refuse to enforce the property arrangements or other agreements made by the couple. This policy often had the effect of penalizing women, because property was more often held in the men's names. Thus, courts would claim to be leaving the parties to a meretricious relationship where they found them but in fact were often benefiting men at the expense of women. Instead of discouraging all meretricious relationships, courts thereby encouraged some men not to get married, perhaps as much as they encouraged women to get married.

Over the years, courts slowly changed their policies and allowed for more-equitable property dispositions in individual cases. In 1976, California led the way toward granting unmarried couples property rights somewhat similar to those of married couples: in *Marvin* v. *Marvin* the California Supreme Court ruled that an otherwise valid contract between unmarried partners in a relationship would be enforceable and that the court, even in the absence of an agreement between the parties, could order the payment of money from one member of the couple to the other in cases in which it seemed fair to do so. A judge who concurred in part and dissented in part questioned whether the court's decision might not place meretricious spouses in a better position than lawful spouses. Some commentators and judges have expressed concern that the *Marvin* case would encourage nonmarital cohabitation. A few states have refused to follow California's lead in *Marvin,* but most states have begun treating unmarried partners somewhat more like married people in order to avoid injustice.

BECOMING A PARENT

A person becomes a natural parent by giving birth or by impregnating a woman who then gives birth. A person who is not the natural parent can become a legal parent by adoption or by being married to someone who gives birth.

Every child has two natural parents who will usually also be the child's legal parents. A man other than the natural father may become the legal father; for example, a man who consents to the artificial insemination of his wife is the legal father of the child. Finally, either or both natural parents may be replaced by an adoptive parent.

Legitimacy and Illegitimacy. In the late eighteenth century, a child born to an unmarried woman was illegitimate; a child born to a married woman (or within three hundred days of divorce or her husband's death) was legitimate, with little regard to whether her husband was the one who had impregnated her. "Lord Mansfield's Rule" (originating in England in 1777) severely restricted the ability of a man to "bastardize" a child born to his wife; unless the husband could not possibly be the father, he was conclusively presumed to be.

In more recent years, several important changes have taken place. The categories of "legitimate" and "illegitimate" have been softened or even abolished, and many children who would previously have been called illegitimate are now labeled legitimate—for example, children born of void marriages. Illegitimate children and unwed fathers have been granted a number of constitutional rights, and courts are more willing to examine the question of biological parentage of children born to married women.

Historically, the treatment of illegitimate children and their mothers was quite harsh, but the treatment afforded them has been steadily improving. As recently as 1950, the only way to obtain child support from the father of an illegitimate child was through a quasi-criminal paternity proceeding. Unmarried mothers or pregnant women could name a putative father who would be arrested and, if proven to be the biological father, could be ordered to pay medical costs of the pregnancy and delivery and child-support payments. The mother had to prove by clear and convincing evidence, however, that the putative father was the only person who could have impregnated her. Perhaps the best insight into a woman's reluctance to bring a paternity suit under these circumstances comes from a comparison with rape cases. Defense lawyers who attempt to slander the victim's reputation to raise doubt regarding consent would certainly not scruple to abuse a woman in a paternity suit in which her sexual behavior with third parties was actually directly relevant. Moreover, it was not uncommon for the defendant father's friends to perjure themselves and claim to have had sexual intercourse with the woman. Neither parent would find a paternity suit a pleasant prospect. Encouraged, perhaps, by the explicit or implicit threat of such a suit, putative fathers would sometimes agree voluntarily to support their illegitimate children. At one time, many courts allowed such contracts to bar the mother from bringing a paternity action.

Early reforms provided for the "legitimation" of illegitimate children, either by the subsequent intermarriage of their parents or, in some states, by formal declarations by their fathers. Fathers could also "acknowledge" illegitimate children and grant them some rights without going so far as to legitimate the children.

Over the years, paternity proceedings began to lose their criminal and punitive character and became more clearly civil actions designed to give children status and to recover money. Increasingly courts refused to allow a paternity contract to bar a child or its mother from suing the father. Improved blood tests enabled more-certain identification of a child's biological father.

As of 1986, sixteen states had adopted the Uniform Parentage Act, which in theory eliminates altogether the concepts of legitimacy and illegitimacy. The act deals with the "parent and child relationship" and provides that the relationship extend equally to every child and every parent, regardless of the parents' marital status. In practice, however, a child who does not have a "presumed father" under the act may simply be an illegitimate child by another name.

Although most states have not gone quite so far as to eliminate the concept of illegitimacy, they have softened the distinction between legitimate and illegitimate children and have made it easier for children to be labeled legitimate. For example, many states now categorize as legitimate a child born of a void or voidable marriage, and in a few states a child born of a cohabiting couple is legitimate. If a man accepts the child into his home and holds the child out to be his own, the child will be legitimated in some states.

Augmenting these changes in state law, the United States Supreme Court has placed constitutional limitations upon the distinctions that may be made between legitimate and illegitimate children and between the parents of legitimate and illegitimate children. Discrimination is generally not allowed with respect to social security benefits or wrongful-death actions. Certain relatively minor discrimination with respect to social security and discrimination regarding immigration, inheritance, and permission for adoption is permissible. The Court has also held that insofar as legitimate children are entitled to support, an illegitimate child has a constitutional right to support from his or her father (*Gomez* v. *Perez*, 1973).

Years ago, the mother's husband would be considered the father of her child, with all rights and obligations, unless the husband could meet a heavy, sometimes impossible burden of proof that extrinsic facts demonstrated that he could not have been the father of the child—for example, that he was "beyond the seas" when the child was conceived. Increasingly, the husband is allowed to demonstrate that he is not the natural father and thereby to escape liability. In cases in which the husband wants to be treated as the legal father, although he may not be the natural father, he may well be allowed to do so. In general, if the mother agrees with her husband, the natural father is not allowed to prove legally his biological relationship, nor is he allowed to assert any parental rights over the child. Some questions can be raised regarding the constitutionality of such state policies, but they have been upheld in California (*Michelle W.* v. *Ronald W.*, 1985) and Massachusetts (*P. B. C.* v. *D. H.*, 1985).

Rights and Duties of Unwed Fathers. Until the 1972 Supreme Court case of *Stanley* v. *Illinois*, it had been generally assumed that men who fathered illegitimate children had the duty to support their children but had only very limited rights over them. In *Stanley*, the Court declared that an unwed father who had lived on and off with his children and their mother could not be deprived of his parental rights after the death of their mother unless the state demonstrated his unfitness. Unwed fathers, like divorced fathers, have a duty to support their children and sometimes have a right to visitation and to be considered for custody.

Courts debated for some years whether the *Stanley* case meant that all unwed fathers had a veto power over the adoption of their illegitimate children. After some vacillation, the Court decided that unwed fathers had rights but that these rights were limited when fathers had not established a relationship with their children and were not seeking custody of the children (*Quilloin* v. *Walcott*, 1978). Further, in the 1983 case of *Lehr* v. *Robertson*, the Court upheld a New York State scheme that conditioned the father's right to notice of an adoption proceeding upon the father's filing a document with a registry claiming his paternity of the child.

Under many state laws, including the Uniform Parentage Act, an unwed father may have no opportunity to assert or prove his paternity if the mother was married at the time of the child's conception or birth and the husband and the mother both wish for the husband to be the child's legal father. Although such a policy may seem justified in terms of protecting the interests of the child and the privacy of the married couple, it is not completely clear that it will be held constitutional whenever an appropriate test case comes before the Court. From the point of view of the unwed father, his rights regarding the child would be completely extinguished by the unilateral acts of the mother and her husband; the unwed father has no power to protect his interests. From the mother's perspective, such a rule may seem not to go far enough. It may seem unfair that the unwed father's rights will not be cut off unless the mother has a husband who claims paternity. The only way she can ensure that the man who impregnated her cannot use his rights over the child to force continued unwelcomed contact is to enlist the aid of another man. If the natural father's rights will be extinguished for the sake of a husband, the mother may consider it unfair that they will not be extinguished to protect the privacy of the mother and child.

Adoption. Adoption is a purely statutory procedure that is not much over a century old in America. The first modern adoption law was enacted in Massachusetts in 1851. Prior to the enactment of such laws, de facto adoptions would take place without a formal agreement or by a written agreement of dubious enforceability. Apprenticeship laws were also used; some apprenticeships were really like modern adoptions rather than the employment or education agreements that they seemed to be. The foster or quasi-adoptive parents would sometimes but not always be protected against the risk of parents changing their minds.

An 1811 case from New York illustrates some of the problems that arose in these early quasi adoptions. *In re McDowle* involved two boys, aged six and eight, whom their widowed father had "apprenticed" to Shakers. After a couple of years the father remarried and tried to get his sons back. The father argued successfully that the apprenticeship agreements were invalid because they failed to meet certain technical requirements. Nevertheless, when it became clear that the boys wanted to remain with the Shakers, the judge allowed them to do so.

Modern adoption laws are intended to serve the best interests of the adopted child and are designed to promote stability in adoptive relationships. They frequently specify that the court shall grant an adoption if the judge finds that the adoption will promote the child's interests. The child's wishes should be consulted if the child is old enough, and children over a certain age are frequently given a veto power over their own adoptions.

Although some early laws gave adopted children less status than natural children—for example, they had fewer inheritance rights—the clear trend has been toward treating an adopted child just like a natural child. Adoption records are usually sealed, and new birth certificates are issued that conceal or partially conceal the adoption. Efforts by adopted children to unseal these records to enable them to trace their natural parents have met with mixed success. Usually there must be a strong medical need to trace genetic background before courts will unseal adoption records. This reluctance would seem to be based on vague notions of the "integrity" of adoptions and serious concerns about the natural parents' privacy. The child's interest in finding his or her parents for psychological reasons or curiosity has not been granted much weight.

Ordinarily an adoption may take place only if all previous parental ties to the child have been legally severed or are severed as part of the adoption procedure. The exception is stepparent adoption. If one parent has died or lost parental rights and the other parent remarries, the new spouse may adopt the child. If a child has continuing legal ties to both natural parents, however, there cannot be a stepparent adoption, even if all parties desire it. Although there is no logical reason a child should not be able to have more than two legal parents, courts do not yet allow a child to be adopted unless previous parental ties have been severed. Moreover, an adoption by two people is allowed only if the two people are married to each other. It is possible that these rules will change as society becomes more accustomed to divorced couples sharing parenting responsibilities. In cases of divorce and remarriage, the child might be more secure if both stepparents were allowed to adopt the child.

The most serious threat to the stability of an adoptive relationship arises from improper terminations of the parental rights of the natural parents. In some cases in which a parent changes his or her mind, consent to give a child up for adoption was coerced, or proper notice was not given, courts have reversed adoptions. Such cases can be quite disruptive, since court delays and appeals may mean the child has lived with adoptive parents for several years before a final decision transfers the child to a natural parent, who is then a stranger to the child.

RIGHTS AND DUTIES WITHIN A FAMILY

At one time, the husband's rights and duties with respect to his wife were much like the father's rights and duties with respect to his children. As head of the household, the husband and father had a duty to support the dependent members of his family and was responsible for many of their actions. He was responsible for the wife's torts, though usually not the children's. He had a right to the services of his wife and children and to their obedience. He was given title to most property owned at the time of marriage or subsequently received by the wife. A legal wrong to his wife was a wrong to him, and he could sue the wrongdoers. Because he usually was physically the strongest, owned all the property, and had greatest access to community influence and resources, the head of the household rarely had to call upon the state to support his power and authority over the other family members. When the head of the family did call upon the state for assistance in asserting control over his family, the state usually responded.

Courts allowed lawsuits against third parties who offered assistance to runaway wives or children, and some judges permitted fathers to use the children to keep the mother home. On occasion, judges would order young children into the custody of their fathers for the specific and admitted purpose of coercing unhappy mothers to return to live with the fathers, as in *People* v. *Mercein* (1839).

Much of this law has changed during the last two centuries. The husband-father retains considerable power in most families, but the law's reinforcement of this power has become more subtle. The wife and husband are legally equal, as a formal matter; and their rights and duties with respect to one another are now more distinct from the rights and duties between parents and children.

Rights and Duties Between Husband and Wife. The property relations between husband and wife are governed by one of two systems—community property or common-law property. As of 1986, nine states had community property—California, Texas, Washington, Louisiana, Nevada, New Mexico, Arizona, Idaho, and Wisconsin—and the other forty-one states and the District of Columbia had common-law property. A couple's property relations are governed by whichever system their state uses, unless the couple enters into a legally enforceable contract to change these relations.

Until the middle of the nineteenth century, the common-law property system provided that the husband was given title to all personal property to which the wife held legal title at the time of marriage and control over her real property. Trust devices enabled certain wealthy families to provide an "equitable estate" for their daughters that the daughters could keep and control after marriage. Common-law property laws, however, made most women economically dependent upon their husbands: married women could not own property, enter contracts, sue, or be sued. The married women's property acts, which were mainly enacted between 1839 and 1860, changed these rules so that wives could keep their own property and act in the business world. Women continued, however, to be legally obligated to keep house for their husbands without remuneration. Moreover, salaried work for women was difficult to get and poorly paid. Thus, despite the married women's property acts, most women remained economically dependent upon their husbands.

The concept of community property derived from France and Spain and became part of the law in California, Texas, and Louisiana as part of their French and Spanish heritages. The six other community-property states adopted the system after they became dissatisfied with common-law property. In a community-property system the earnings of both spouses are legally shared by each other. The "community" owns all the income, as well as profits made on community property (and, in Texas, profits on separate property as well). Until recent years, the husband was designated the manager of the community property. All states except Texas changed this provision during the 1970s to make the husband and wife equal managers of all the community property; Texas law makes each spouse the manager of his or her earnings unless the earnings are commingled, in which case either spouse may manage them. In 1981 the United States Supreme Court declared unconstitutional a Louisiana provision that had allowed husbands, but not wives, to transfer community property without their spouse's consent (*Kirchberg* v. *Feenstra*).

It is a fair generalization to say that common-law property is based on the ideals of independence and autonomy while community property is based on the ideals of partnership and sharing. However, both systems offer some protection to dependent spouses, and neither system really challenges the husband's economic superiority that exists in most marriages. In the common-law system, the old property rights of dower (life estate to widow of one-third of all real property owned by husband anytime during marriage) and curtesy (life interest to surviving husband in all of wife's real property) and the more modern forced-share provision (allowing surviving spouse to ignore testator's will and take a fixed percentage of the spouse's estate at death) prevent one spouse from disinheriting the other. In the community-property system, the non-wage-earning spouse may be treated legally as an equal partner in some ways, but his or her access to the community assets can often be effectively limited by the wage earner.

At one time, a husband and wife were not allowed to enter enforceable contracts with each other. After the enactment of the married women's property acts, this policy began to change. There are now many circumstances under which married partners may enter enforceable contracts. Usually such contracts will affect property interests or financial dealings. Contracts concerning the everyday functioning of their relationship—who will do what work, how they shall treat one another, how often they will have sexual relations, and the like—are generally not enforceable by the courts. Similarly, contracts involving the care, support, or welfare of the children are usually unenforceable. As a matter of public policy, courts ordinarily retain the power to evaluate for themselves whether the parents' determination is good for the child and to enforce the contract only if it seems best for the child.

In modern times the rights and duties of husband and wife are for the most part formally equal. In theory, each must support the other and neither may abuse the other. One exception is that a number of states still allow husbands to rape their wives without legal redress; and in Alabama, Illinois, and South Dakota, until a divorce is final, husbands may rape their wives even if they are legally separated and living apart.

Rights and Duties Between Parents and Children. Parents have extensive legal authority over their children. They name children, determine where and how they shall live, and how they shall be brought up. Except in cases of child neglect, child abuse, or divorce, parents' power over their minor children is seldom questioned. In rare cases, children are allowed to assert legal independence—for example, in such matters as birth control and abortion. In general, however, parents have extensive legal control over their children.

Many parents find more difficulty asserting practical control over their children as the children reach adolescence. In extreme cases, parents may have their children committed to a mental hospital or incarcerated by the state, but most parents are reluctant to resort to such measures. Economic control is more commonly used as a fallback for parents, but some children have jobs and thus an independent source of financial support. Although parents are legally obligated to support their children, this obligation is largely unenforceable by the child on an intact marriage. Where children have tried to force their parents to support them, the parents have been allowed to demonstrate that the child forfeited the right to support by disobeying the parents.

RELATIONSHIP OF OUTSIDERS TO FAMILY MEMBERS

For much of the past two centuries, one person's rights and obligations toward another would be significantly affected by whether the person belonged to a family. The male head of family could monitor the relations of his wife and children. Harboring a runaway wife could get a person into trouble, contracts with married women were as unenforceable as contracts with children, and a sexual relationship outside marriage could subject a man to financial penalties as well as criminal prosecution. Alienation of affections was an actionable tort, and the head of the family could sue anyone who deprived him of the services of his wife or children. A married woman who formed a close or sexual relationship outside of marriage could be deprived of her children, divorced, and left penniless or be subjected to physical abuse with· relatively little consequence to the "wronged" husband.

Most of these laws have changed. Married women may enter contracts, and in some circumstances, children may. Adultery is illegal in a few states; but the laws are rarely enforced, and most states have abolished the old civil cause of action that used to be available to the husband. On the other hand, husbands can still divorce wives and leave them in poverty, and most wife-beating goes unprosecuted. The law continues, in fact, to permit what it used to directly authorize.

At the present time, one person's rights and obligations toward another are often, though not always, unaffected by the other person's status as a member of a family. A parent may act for his or her child in certain matters in which the child is disabled or partially disabled from acting on his own; such action on behalf of the child may influence the rights and obligations of third parties. For example, a doctor could be in serious trouble if she performed nonemergency surgery on a ten-year-old patient without the parents' consent. If a person negligently injures or kills another person, certain relatives of that person may bring a wrongful-death action against the tort-feasor or sue for loss of consortium (the company, affection, and services of a spouse). Creditors may be able to recover from the spouse or parents for debts incurred by the other spouse or a child for the necessaries of life. Finally, under a special rule known as the family-car doctrine, accident victims may be able to recover from the parents of a child responsible for the accident if the child was driving for what the courts refer to as a "family purpose."

DISSOLVING FAMILY RELATIONS

Family relations may be dissolved in a number of ways. The husband-wife relationship may end by annulment, death, or divorce. The parent-child relationship may end by death or termination of parental rights. For many purposes, the parent-child relationship is said to be ended when the child comes of age (once twenty-one for boys and eighteen for girls, now usually eigh-

teen for both sexes) or is earlier emancipated—usually by getting married but also just by successfully asserting independence.

Annulling a Marriage. In theory, a marriage can be annulled only if it was void or voidable at the time it was entered into. In practice, annulment has sometimes been used as an alternative to divorce. For example, marriages have been annulled for fraud in cases in which the wife was pregnant by another man, whether or not she knew of her pregnancy. New York, which for many years had a very restricted or conservative law of divorce, developed a very liberal annulment law. In one case, *Kober* v. *Kober* (1965), a wife was granted an annulment for fraud when the husband turned out to be rabidly anti-Semitic.

Ordinarily, annulment depends upon the law of the state in which the marriage was celebrated. An exception, noted earlier, is that states may apply their own marriage requirements and annul a marriage that a couple entered elsewhere in an attempt to evade the requirements of their own state.

The effect of an annulment is either to declare that the marriage was void or to find the marriage voidable and to annul it. An annulment used to operate ab initio; that is, the marriage was said to be voided from the beginning, as though it had never existed. At one time, children born within a marriage that was later annulled would become illegitimate. Some courts regretted this harsh result but argued that it followed as a matter of necessity from the logic of the rule that an annulment voided a marriage ab initio. Similarly, courts once regularly refused to divide property or award alimony if a marriage was ended by annulment. Although these rules may seem acceptable when a marriage is annulled shortly after it is celebrated, they led to many injustices when courts annulled long-term relationships.

One response to such injustice was for courts simply to refuse to annul marriages that had continued for many years. In cases such as nonage, impotency, fraud, coercion, or insanity, it was easy for courts to find ratification (that is, to find that the couple continued to cohabit after the innocent party reached the age of consent; learned of the impotence, fraud, or insanity; or became free of coercion) and refuse to annul the marriage. If the marriage were void for reasons such as bigamy or incest, courts were more inclined to grant an annulment, even after many years. In such cases, the annulment would be said to operate just like a declaratory judgment announcing the voidness of the marriage. In theory, the children would have been illegitimate in any event, even without the annulment.

A second response to the perceived injustice of annulment was for courts to treat annulment more like divorce. Many states provided that the children of annulled marriages would be considered legitimate, and some states provided for property division and alimony after an annulment. These reforms occurred shortly before the advent of "no-fault" divorce made annulment law less important by making divorce an easier response to an unhappy marriage. When divorce is easier to obtain, fewer parties seek annulment.

Getting a Divorce. The earliest divorces in England were granted through special bills to Parliament and were generally available only to wealthy men. The ecclesiastical courts enjoyed exclusive jurisdiction over English divorce until an 1857 reform bill transferred divorce jurisdiction to the civil court system. In the American colonies, especially those in New England, divorce was easier to obtain than in England. Legislative divorces were not uncommon in colonial and postcolonial times, and a significant American innovation was the enactment of general divorce laws that empowered the courts to grant divorces. The grounds were often quite limited, such as adultery. The grounds were also sexist: a woman's single act of adultery was a ground for divorce in states in which a man's adultery would provide grounds only if it were repeated and flagrant; a man could sometimes be divorced for refusing to support his wife; a woman could sometimes be divorced for refusing to keep house for her husband or for failing to follow him to wherever he chose to live. Desertion and extreme cruelty were sometimes grounds for legal separation but not grounds for divorce; increasingly they were also made grounds for divorce. A divorce would be granted to the "innocent" party when his or her spouse engaged in serious marital misconduct. Defenses to a divorce action included connivance (the spouse's enticement or encouragement to commit the wrong), condonation (the spouse's forgiveness), collusion (the spouses' cooperation in trying to

obtain a divorce), and recrimination (the fault of both spouses, which prevented either from obtaining a divorce). Over the years, the legal grounds for divorce generally increased and many courts granted divorces on perfunctory proof. Until the 1970s, however, divorce continued in theory to be based on fault.

Beginning in the 1970s, state after state enacted no-fault divorce laws, which provide for ending unhappy marriages without finding either party at fault and without having to find marital misconduct by either spouse. The only requirements are that the marriage relationship be broken down, seemingly beyond recovery, and, in many states, that the parties live separate and apart for a period of time. The effect has been that almost anyone who can afford the lawyer's fees can obtain a divorce, and it has simplified divorce law enormously.

Prior to no-fault divorce, complicated jurisdictional issues arose that continue to be important today. In theory, a person may obtain a divorce only in the state where the person or his or her spouse lives. The spouse must be notified of the action, if possible, but he or she does not have to be present in court.

Before most states enacted no-fault divorce, many people used to go to Nevada or Florida to obtain divorces. These states and some others came to be known as divorce mills. The courts would grant easy divorces to people who visited the state for a few weeks or months and were willing to assert, often falsely, that they had made the state their (more or less permanent) home.

Complicated rules developed about whether other states should recognize these divorces. If both husband and wife appeared in the divorce action or if one party appeared and the other agreed to the court's jurisdiction, the divorce could not be challenged later. If the wife had been subjected to the divorcing court's jurisdiction, she would not be able to bring a later action for a property division and could modify support payments only if some amount had been granted. If one party did not appear and was not subject to the court's personal jurisdiction, then the divorce could be challenged by any interested person except the one who obtained the divorce. Upon challenge, the question would be whether the one who obtained the divorce really had made the state that granted the divorce his or her home. If the state was the party's home—

technically "domicile"—then the divorce was good; if not, the divorce was invalid.

To make matters more complicated, even if the divorce were good and thus ended the status of marriage, in many states it may not affect property and support. As discussed below, a wife who had not been subjected to the court's jurisdiction could still bring a proceeding in her home state for support and property division.

Financial Consequences of Divorce. Upon the dissolution of marriage, courts will ordinarily divide the property obtained during the marriage between the spouses and will sometimes order alimony (also referred to as "maintenance" or "spousal support"). These decisions will often be affected by the court's decision regarding custody and support of children, but technically the issues are largely separate. Property division and spousal support are often settled by the parties in a separation agreement, which may be incorporated into the divorce decree and made enforceable by the court, and sometimes couples agree about these matters before marriage in what is known as an antenuptial contract. Antenuptial contracts and separation agreements will usually be enforced by the courts, unless they seem substantially unfair and one spouse appears to have pressured or deceived the other. Many states, however, refuse to enforce antenuptial agreements that attempt to limit alimony upon divorce, and courts scrutinize such marital contracts more closely than they scrutinize other contracts. Separation agreements are frequently the form in which divorcing couples confirm an out-of-court settlement.

The major issues that arise regarding the financial consequences of divorce are jurisdiction, what constitutes property, what factors affect the appropriate division of the property, what purposes can and should be served by granting or denying spousal support, what factors during the marriage and after the divorce should affect the amount and duration of spousal support, and how property awards should be enforced.

A court must have personal jurisdiction over the parties in order to divide their property or order spousal support payments. A court granting a bilateral divorce (where both spouses are before the court or subjected to its personal jurisdiction) may determine issues relating to property, and often, unless the court does divide property and award support, the spouse with title keeps the property and the parties are barred from raising the issue of support in a later proceeding. A court granting an ex parte divorce (where only one party is before the court and the other has not been subjected to the personal jurisdiction of the court) may not decide issues relating to property rights of the spouse who is not present before the court. Usually when there has been an ex parte divorce, the parties will be allowed to seek a property division and spousal support in another court that does have personal jurisdiction over the parties. In some states, however, such a procedure is not allowed, especially if the person asking for the property adjudication is the same party who brought the ex parte divorce proceeding.

Courts differ regarding what property they will consider subject to division. In community-property states, the community property is subject to division, as is quasi-community property (property that would be community property except that it was obtained in a common-law-property state) in California and Texas. In a common-law-property state, property obtained during the marriage and sometimes inheritances and property owned before the marriage are subject to division. Recent decisions have held that pensions and other forms of deferred salary are property. Professional degrees or professional licenses have generally not been considered property, nor has the augmented earning power they represent, and the spouse's only remedy has been to collect some of the contribution she has already made toward the other spouse's education, as in *In re Sullivan* (1984). Various plans have been devised, however, for repaying the community for the cost of professional education or for replenishing the pool of community property to be divided. The view of professional degrees as individual property, however, may be giving way, for the New York Court of Appeals held that a medical degree was marital property and could be divided in a divorce proceeding (*O'Brien* v. *O'Brien,* 1985).

Community-property states divide the community property either equally or "equitably" (fairly) upon divorce. Some common-law-property states make almost the same division of what they sometimes refer to as "marital property." At one time, however, common-law-property states considered an award of one-third of the property to the wife (or non-wage-earner) and two-thirds to the husband (or wage-earner) to be a good rule of thumb. However unfair this attitude now appears, it seems to have had some continuing effect on courts' decisions dividing property.

Alimony developed out of the earlier practice of requiring a husband to pay maintenance to his wife if she was justified in living separately from him. Although such payments may have had a punitive element or been used to punish a husband who wronged his wife, they were primarily an economic necessity. The law transferred all the wife's property to the husband upon marriage, so she would not be receiving income from the property. Nor were the employment opportunities available to women promising. Moreover, if there were young children who would be living with the mother, child support, if ordered, would usually not include an amount to pay her for caring for the children or an amount to support her while she cared for them. Thus, although such support could be considered a cost of raising children, American courts considered it alimony or maintenance, not child support.

When state laws provided for granting divorces, they often specified that courts could award alimony payments, similar to the maintenance payments during a separation. Ordinarily alimony would not be allowed if the wife were the party found to be at fault in the marital breakup. This provision could of course leave the wife in an extremely difficult economic condition where she was found to be at fault. Because alimony was granted only when the husband, not the wife, was at fault, it came to be seen by some as a form of penalty to the husband. In any event, the alimony payments would cease if the wife remarried or if she died.

Modern alimony provisions are designed to ease the transition out of marriage and to prevent unjust disruption caused by the couple's prior division of labor. The Supreme Court ruled in *Orr* v. *Orr* (1979) that alimony or maintenance must be available on a gender-neutral basis: if legislation permits courts to order ex-husbands to pay alimony, courts must also be allowed to order ex-wives to pay. Most alimony payments are temporary or "rehabilitative," but because of the difficulty older women who have spent their lives working in the home encounter obtaining work in the marketplace, permanent

alimony is still sometimes allowed. Alimony is controversial because even though it is now technically gender-neutral, alimony still seems to be based on women's dependency; yet, great injustices can result to women who have been made dependent if alimony is not allowed. Moreover, both rehabilitative and permanent alimony payment orders are notoriously violated.

In theory, alimony and property awards should be at least as easily enforced as any other money judgment. Actually, alimony should be even easier to enforce because, as a court order, the alimony award is enforceable by contempt of court. When alimony is not paid, the defaulting payer can be found in contempt of court and jailed until he or she pays. In practice, fewer than half of all alimony obligations are ever paid.

Child Custody and Visitation. In the nineteenth century, courts and commentators debated whether child custody should be decided with primary reference to the rights of the father, the rights of the spouse who was not at fault in the marital breakup, or the best interests of the child. By the beginning of the twentieth century, essentially all courts had decided that as between parents, child custody should be determined with reference to the best interest of the child. When a custody dispute is between a parent or parents and a third party, however, it will usually be decided with primary reference to the rights of the parent or parents. Ordinarily a child will be put in the custody of a third party only if the parents are found unfit or if the third party has acted as a parent to the child for a considerable period of time with the permission or acquiescence of the parents.

When courts adopted the "best interests of the child" test, they generally placed children in the custody of mothers. Appellate court cases frequently identify the mother as the nurturing parent and choose the nurturing parent over the parent identified as more powerful, the father. A frequent exception was older boys, whose best interests courts would find to be served by being placed with their father, who could finance their education and give them a start on their careers. These court preferences became known as the tender-years doctrine. The doctrine provided that a child of tender years was ordinarily better off with the mother and that an older child, especially a boy, was ordinarily better off with the father. The second half of the doctrine was never as important as the first half, since many courts tended to allow older children to choose which parent they wished to live with. In some cases, courts held that young children would be placed with their mothers unless the mothers were unfit.

Although most children of divorce continue to be placed in the mother's custody, the tender-years doctrine as such has been all but abolished. A few courts have replaced the tender-years doctrine with a preference in favor of whichever parent has been the child's primary caretaker, and most courts consider a parent's ability to nuture the child to be an important element in the best-interest test. Many courts favor continuity of custody and are reluctant to order the child who has been living with one parent into the custody of the other parent. Generally, however, the best-interest test is applied in a highly individualized case-by-case manner.

Traditionally, the mother has been given custody and the father given visitation rights, but this tradition is beginning to change. Increasingly, parents are being awarded joint legal custody and the father's visitation right is treated as part-time physical custody. Also, in well-publicized cases, usually involving fairly wealthy parents, the children will be placed in joint physical custody and split their lives between two houses and families. A complex debate has arisen regarding the effects of joint custody on children and on the relationship between husbands and wives.

The most controversial cases are those in which courts have awarded joint custody to fathers who played little or no parenting role prior to the marital breakup. Women complain that such awards do not serve the interests of children, because the fathers do not take proper care of the children, and that the practice legitimates the fathers' earlier neglect. Moreover, these women claim that some fathers are more interested in using custody to control or punish their ex-wives than in forming a relationship with their children and that others use their wives fear of joint custody to coerce favorable financial settlements. By contrast, some people argue that joint custody is proper in such cases. It is important for children to know they have a father and to have contact with him, and better late than never. Proponents assert that joint custody encourages fathers to accept responsibility for children and allows the mother time away from her children.

Child Support At common law, parents were not obliged to support their children; soon fathers were legally obligated to support their children, and now both parents are. This support obligation becomes important and enforceable primarily in those cases in which a parent is living separately from his or her child. The most common case of this arrangement is upon divorce, when the child lives with one parent and the other parent is ordered to pay child support. Courts determine the amount of support—often following an agreement reached between the parents, sometimes ad hoc and sometimes using a standardized scale promulgated by courts in some states.

An increasingly important aspect of child-support law involves illegitimate children entitled to support from their fathers. Increasingly also, welfare agencies are forcing needy mothers to assign child-support rights against the father to the agency. The dream of reducing welfare roles without undergoing the work of real social change has been pursued through efforts to enforce the child-support obligations of unwed fathers. Because a great amount of the poverty problem falls on mothers and their children, policymakers hoped to reduce poverty by making fathers pay for their children. Welfare agencies thus get into the business of enforcing or trying to enforce child-support payments, and the federal government has begun taking a more active role in enforcing child support. Despite these effects, child support often goes unpaid, and in California the average father living separately from his children spends more money on his car than on his children.

Termination of Parental Rights. Courts will terminate parental rights to protect children. Sometimes this power has been abused, and impoverished, defenseless children have been separated from parents whose chief fault appeared to be their failure to be sufficiently middle-class. At other times, children have been left in abusive families where they have suffered permanent psychological and physical damage or even death. To avoid these two opposite dangers, agencies have developed forms of protective intervention short of removing the child from the home, and courts have developed procedural and substantive protections. Parents have a right to notice and a hearing before their children can be taken away, and proof by clear and convincing evidence is required before parental rights may be severed.

If a child is neglected or abused, the child may be taken away from its parents. Usually state officials will take the child out of the parents' custody, appoint a guardian, and place the child in foster care. At this point, the parents have roughly the same rights that a noncustodial parent has after a divorce. The child continues to have a right to support from its parents, and no one may adopt the child without the parents' consent. Whenever the parents can convince the court that they can provide suitable care for the child, the court will return the child to their custody.

Especially in the case of young, adoptive children, state officials may try to sever all parental ties. This option requires a further court hearing at which the state must establish its case by clear and convincing evidence. If all parental ties are severed, the parents lose all rights to the child and no longer have to support it. The child can be adopted and become part of a new family.

Family law reflects social relations in society at the same time that it helps to shape those relations. The changes that have taken place in family law have often served to improve relations, but they have also served to reduce pressure for reform by offering a comforting image of progress. Like other areas of law, family law is a growing body of material. We can expect that changes will continue and that some of the changes will be beneficial, some will probably not be so, and many will likely have little or no effect.

CASES

Gomez v. Perez, 409 U.S. 535 (1973)

Kirchberg v. Feenstra, 450 U.S. 455 (1981)

Kober v. Kober, 16 N.Y.2d 191, 211 N.E.2d 817 (1965)

Lehr v. Robertson, 463 U.S. 248 (1983)

In re McDowle, 8 Johnson 253 (N.Y. Sup. Ct. 1811)

Marvin v. Marvin, 18 Cal. 3d 660, 134 Cal. Rptr. 815, 557 P.2d 106 (1976)

Michelle W. v. Ronald W., 39 Cal. 3d 354, 703 P.2d 88, 216 Cal. Rptr. 748 (1985)

O'Brien v. O'Brien, 66 N.Y.2d 576, 489 N.E.2d 712 (1985)

Orr v. Orr, 440 U.S. 268 (1979)

People v. Mercein, 8 Paige 47 (N.Y. 1839), rev'd, 25 Wendell 63 (N.Y. Sup. Ct.), rev'd, 25 Wendell 83 (N.Y. 1840)

Quilloin v. Walcott, 434 U.S. 246 (1978)

P.B.C. v. D.H., 396 Mass. 68, 483 N.E.2d 1094 (1985)

Stanley v. Illinois, 405 U.S. 645 (1972)

In re Sullivan, 37 Cal. 3d 762, 691 P.2d 1020, 209 Cal. Rptr. 354 (1984)

BIBLIOGRAPHY

Robert Burt, "The Constitution of the Family," in *Supreme Court Review* 329 (1979), attracted considerable attention when it came out and remains a classic. David L. Chambers, *Making Fathers Pay* (1979), is the classic book on child support enforcement; and "Rethinking the Substantive Rules for Custody Disputes in Divorce," in *Michigan Law Review*, 83 (1984), proposes controversial changes in child custody law and reviews a good deal of the recent literature. Homer Clark, *The Law of Domestic Relations in the United States* (1968), is an excellent general treatise on family law. Look for an updated version in 1987. "Developments in the Law—The Constitution and the Family," in *Harvard Law Review*, 93 (1980), examines the influence of the United States Constitution upon family law until 1980 and makes some predictions about likely future developments.

Mary Ann Glendon, *State, Law, and Family: Family Law in Transition in the United States and Western Europe* (1977), presents a very interesting international perspective on family law. Joseph Goldstein, Anna Freud, and Albert Solnit, *Beyond the Best Interests of the Child* (1973), is an interesting book that draws heavily upon child psychology and seems to have had an enormous influence on how courts and commentators think about child custody decisions. Martha Minow, "Beyond State Intervention in the Family: For Baby Jane Doe," in *University of Michigan Journal of Law Reform*, 18 (1985), is an intelligent examination of the public debate over laws regulating the care given to or withdrawn from severely handicapped newborns; and "'Forming Underneath Everything That Grows': Toward a History of Family Law," in *Wisconsin Law Review*, (1985), is a pioneering effort to forge a new concept of family law history.

Robert Mnookin, "Child-Custody Adjudication: Judicial Functions in the Face of Indeterminancy," in *Law and Contemporary Problems*, 39 (1975), is a thoughtful examination of the indeterminancy of the best-interest-of-the-child test. Robert Mnookin and Lewis Kornhauser, "Bargaining in the Shadow of the Law: The Case of Divorce," in *Yale Law Journal*, 88 (1979), is a study of the influence of law upon divorce negotiations. Frances Olsen, "The Family and the Market: A Study of Ideology and Legal Reform," in *Harvard Law Review*, 96 (1983), introduces the conceptual framework of the family/market dichotomy to examine the strengths, weaknesses, and possibilities for legal reform; "The Politics of Family Law," in *Journal of Law and Inequality*, 12 (1984), explores the political nature of family law through a brief historical sketch and an examination of the tender-years doctrine in child custody law; and "The Myth of State Intervention in the

Family," in *Michigan Journal of Law Reform,* 18 (1985), criticizes popular uses and misuses of the notion of state intervention.

William Reppy, Jr. and Cynthia Samuel, *Community Property in the United States* (1982), is a good and understandable description of how American community property systems work. Sally Sharp, "Fairness Standards and Separation Agreements: A Word of Caution on Contractual Freedom," in *University of Pennsylvania Law Review,* 132 (1984), is a sensible and thoughtful examination of the laws relating to separation agreements. Lenore Weitzman, "The Economics of Divorce: Social and Economic Consequences of Property, Alimony, and Child Support Awards," in *University of California at Los Angeles Law Review,* 28 (1981).

[*See also* JUVENILE LAW.]

INTERNATIONAL ECONOMIC LAW

Dan Fenno Henderson

INTERNATIONAL economic law is a new field, dating from the end of World War II. It has as yet no precise definition. Still, its core was from the beginning the General Agreement on Tariffs and Trade (GATT, 1948) and the Bretton Woods Conference arrangements for the International Monetary Fund (IMF, 1945) and the World Bank (1945). But where to draw the line between politics and economics in international affairs has become a major problem in defining the coverage of international economic law; another problem is the tendency in international institutions for law, policy, and diplomacy to overlap.

This profile deals first with the institutions and the public international law of international economic affairs; and second with the regulation of private law regimes supporting the multitude of transnational transactions between private enterprises that make up the bulk of free-world trade and investment.

We first sketch the changing political context for global economic affairs, and then deal with the difficulties of definition. Next the post–World War II development of international economic law is traced in two phases: the Bretton Woods era (1945–1970) and the era of the New International Economic Order (NIEO), including the increased participation of new nations through the United Nations Assembly since 1970.

Attention then turns to the structure of the leading international economic institutions: first the core Bretton Woods organs dominated by the advanced nations (IMF, GATT, and World Bank) and the Organization for Economic Co-operation and Development (OECD); and the later United Nations organs dominated by votes of the new nations (UNCTAD, UNIDO, the UNCTC, and others). The important movement mainly within these United Nations agencies to draft codes of conduct to regulate the international conduct of multinational enterprises is also traced up to the mid-1980s.

In the second part (on transnational transactions), the elements of the private international law system (in common-law terms the choice-of-law rules) are explained, especially techniques for designating which of two or more national private laws, both potentially applicable, will govern specific trade and investment transactions across national borders so that the private parties will have a single ascertainable law to control their dealings.

To some degree most all national economies are now mixed, neither wholly free enterprise, nor completely without a private sector. Still, the private sectors in the Soviet bloc and some other socialist nations have little to do with foreign trade and investment. So part two hereafter pertains largely to the nations with relatively free-market economies, wherein foreign transactions are conducted in the main by private enterprise. State trading regimes are still of minor importance to free-world trade; they have different cost accounting, bartering, and other bureaucratic methods of economic interfacing, which are largely public administration with dispute resolution handled by arbitration, which accords only a minor role to private law.

THE POLITICAL CONTEXT

The major global political divisions have traditionally been given geographic labels: the East-West schism and the North-South dialogue. Regional (or continental) groupings are also an important part of the overall environment of international economic law, both within and outside the United Nations. The European Economic Community (EEC) is the prime example of a regional legal regime with concrete economic law in place.

Since World War II, the term *East-West* has become a euphemism for the standoff between the free world and Communism, with its state planning and trading systems. Historically, the East-West terminology had referred to the Orient-Occident dichotomy. Now, the term reflects an anachronistic Eurocentric outlook from which Russia is "east" of, say, London or Paris. Given that the Soviet Union is more than Russia and that the Soviet Union and the United States are now both European and Pacific powers, the term *East-West* is losing its cogency, as Soviet confrontations with China and Japan surely shift the focus of future conflict to Asia, even for Americans with a Western vision. Many have suggested that the twenty-first century will be the "Asian century," with major influences on international economic law; thus viewed, colonial East-West terminology becomes even more inept.

For the system of international economic law, the possibility of finding common ground in East-West economic relations, except in state-to-state trading, is still much more limited than the system's role in mixed or market economies of the free world. This is because the Soviet (Eastern) bloc of nations, having centrally planned economies, has given the state power to own and administer most productive facilities and thus limits the scope of private law, which encourages the creativity of private transactions. Also, the state generally controls distribution of (or rations out) products; all is public administration, with little room for private autonomy, private contracting, and choice in the marketplace. Public law predominates, and there is little need for private law of property, contracts, and so on. The role of law in a free-market economy and the role of law in a planned economy are so vastly different that the East-West international economic law regime has remained as constricted as the economic intercourse it serves, even though in the free world as well as the Soviet bloc most economies have a large public sector and are best characterized as "mixed economies."

In the developed free-market economies, the West has come to focus cooperative efforts in the autonomous Organization for Economic Coop-

eration and Development (OECD), made up of the following twenty-four members: Australia, Austria, Belgium, Canada, Denmark, Finland, France, West Germany, Greece, Iceland, Ireland, Italy, Japan, Luxembourg, the Netherlands, New Zealand, Norway, Portugal, Spain, Sweden, Switzerland, Turkey, the United Kingdom, and the United States (Yugoslavia has special status). With one vote per nation in the United Nations General Assembly, this is, needless to say, a small voting bloc.

The "North-South dialogue" is a label for the political division, accentuated from the 1970s onward, between the developed (advanced or industrialized) nations designated "North" and the developing nations of the "South," mostly nonaligned in terms of the East-West context. Politics in the United Nations for this same period have made the General Assembly a forum for the North-South dialogue, the basic tone of which is statist with less market orientation.

East-West and North-South politics necessarily constrain the efficacy of the original post–World War II international economic law and limit its coverage by sheer inability to bring disparate interests within a single effective legal regime until legal reforms do in fact occur. There are, however, several meaningful regional divisions of the world that produce positive effects in the form of complementary international economic law regimes, addressing shared concerns of nations within each region. Regional economic law is, on balance, a salutary force in the free-world economy, but it also on occasion produces frictions in the broader global arena that must be borne in mind (such as the 1985 complaint brought by the United States to GATT against the EEC's agricultural export subsidies). Also, growing interdependence within the free world seems to require coordination, even of domestic national policies, in order to assume a "level playing field" for the proper interplay of market forces.

Before we leave the subject of global divisions, it will perhaps be useful to reflect upon an even broader issue sometimes argued as a constraint on the further growth of law in international economic relations. What are the limitations (or optimal role) of law in a turbulent world of sporadic warring and massive political schisms? The question has been put in these terms: Where do we draw the line between political activity beyond law, on the one hand, and economic activity regulated by law (even judicialized in the International Court of Justice or regional or national courts), on the other? Much as a world under law may be a desirable ideal, those who would limit legal coverage of some international affairs at this stage of world political maturity argue that only a few countries have legal cultures and independent courts capable of achieving the rule of law, at least at the level of concrete performance as opposed to rhetoric. Not all nations have courts effective enough to enforce law against illegal government action at the behest of their citizenry. Among the 170 nations of the world, only a few afford meaningful choices of more than one political party at the polls. So it is argued that for rule-of-law nations to commit national interests to supranational rules and tribunals only serves to bind such nations without giving them actual reciprocal benefits.

The issue cannot be addressed at large or usefully debated except in terms of balances between specific nations and issues. Although the idea of world law remains highly important, enthusiasm for the spread of the rule of law may blind well-meaning proponents to the dangers of entrapment in political tribunals dominated by opponents not committed to (or yet competent in) legal processes that ensure the free functioning of market mechanisms. Such is the environment in which much of the argument surrounding international economic law in the 1980s is taking place.

EVOLUTION OF LAW AND INSTITUTIONS SINCE WORLD WAR II

Two phases in the history of international economic law since World War II can be distinguished if we take a broad view of its coverage. The first, between 1945 and the mid-1960s, is the Bretton Woods era, during which the United States was a predominant force in the economy of the so-called free world and market orientation underlay its centerpieces, the IMF and the GATT. In the free world, European and Japanese reconstruction after World War II was a goal in which the International Bank for Reconstruction and Development (IBRB), commonly known as the World Bank, was to play a major

role. The bank's name implied development, but its developmental function in the Third World at that time was a narrow one—generally, to finance projects that were considered sound in bankers' terms. "Underdeveloped nations," as they were then called, were to progress in the wake of the improved economic thrust produced by recovery of the industrialized countries. No special design encompassed planned economies, and the Soviet bloc did not participate. But rumors of Soviet reconsideration of IMF and GATT participation made the news in mid-1986.

In the second phase, beginning as early perhaps as the founding of the United Nations Conference on Trade and Development (UNCTAD) in 1964 and continuing into the 1980s, the emphasis in the United Nations and in the nonaligned Third World forums (especially the Group of 77, now about 110) shifted to development economics with strong political overtones. At the outset, therefore, it is essential to look beyond the one-world ideal of the United Nations to the reality of the political divisions that now condition the efficacy of international economic law. Any long-range plans for an international economic law that might some day shape an all-encompassing world economy must deal day to day with these practical divisions. And interdependence of the advanced nations is causing growing friction, which requires reassessment and change in the Bretton Woods system.

THE BRETTON WOODS ERA

Besides its primary peacekeeping and political functions centered in the Security Council, the United Nations coordinates various global economic activities through its Economic and Social Council of fifty-four elective member nations. As mentioned above, the major thrust of the General Assembly has also become the economic development of the poorer nations, which constitute the great majority of a voting membership that has tripled from 50 to over 170 nations since 1945. These global developments are as much political as economic and as yet have produced little binding law. Allied sometimes with the Soviet bloc, this movement urging economic development of poorer nations is often more supportive of state socialism than of mixed or market economies promoted by the developed nations in GATT, the IMF, and the OECD. The result has been the launching of the Declaration on the Establishment of a New International Economic Order (NIEO) and Action Programme (1974), which is essentially a movement to change international economic law to accommodate world changes since Bretton Woods. Triggered by breakdowns within the Bretton Woods system in 1971, the upward surge of oil-cartel prices (and the conviction of developing nations that resource controls and cartels would leverage their future), Mideast hostilities, and increasing debt burdens for many developing nations, the NIEO has become a political expression of the numerical dominance of the developing nations seeking distributive reform in the United Nations General Assembly on a one-nation, one-vote basis. These nations' demands have been articulated through the Group of 77 or other groupings both within and outside the United Nations.

In its extreme majoritarian form, the NIEO will doubtless continue to meet resistance from the developed nations. Nonetheless, much of the NIEO vision is shared as an ideal by the developed nations as well, and as a political movement, the NIEO sets the tone and changes the environment in which international economic regulations will operate and adjust in the future.

In 1975, the General Assembly adopted the Charter of Economic Rights and Duties of States. Although 120 nations voted for the charter, there were significant abstentions, and 6 nations (Belgium, Denmark, West Germany, Luxembourg, the United Kingdom, and the United States) voted against it.

More important to market economies are several of the specialized agencies or autonomous affiliates of the United Nations, which have key roles in regulating money and trade practices in the free-world economy. These agencies are not part of the United Nations, but they often work together under coordination of the United Nations Economic and Social Council. By far the most important in the regulation of world trade and investment are the IMF, GATT, and the World Bank. Also, the United Nations Conference on Trade and Development (UNCTAD) and the United Nations Commission on International Trade Law (UNCITRAL) are newer permanent commissions within the United Nations.

UNCTAD projects are developmental and Third World–oriented, whereas UNCITRAL works for legal uniformity of private law of interest to transnational business. A host of other agencies within and outside the United Nations, both operational and advisory, governmental and private, contribute to the structuring of the world economy. Brief descriptions of the key agencies follow.

International Monetary Fund. The IMF now has over 130 member nations and is headquartered in Washington, D.C. It grew out of the Bretton Woods Conference, and its Articles of Agreement came into force in late 1945. The purpose of the IMF is to promote international monetary cooperation and the expansion of international trade. It aims at currency-exchange stability and orderly arrangements for foreign-exchange payments between its 130-odd members. It seeks to prevent competitive exchange depreciations; it facilitates a multilateral system of payments or currency transactions between nations; and it works to eliminate foreign-exchange restrictions detrimental to trade.

In 1969 the IMF established a kind of monetary unit of its own, the special drawing right (SDR), with which members may purchase other currencies. The SDR value is based on a weighted mix of sixteen currencies so that the value tends to be relatively free from fluctuations of exchange rates. Amendments to the Articles effective in 1978 have tended to reduce the role of gold in the international monetary system and to expand the use of SDRs as credits to nations with balance-of-payments problems.

The IMF also consults with governments and offers "extended facilities" (loans) to meet balance-of-payments deficits of nations in difficulty. It also performs valuable surveillance of domestic policies in times of balance-of-payments stringency for troubled members. In sum, the IMF is the central monetary agency supervising and facilitating currency exchange and balance of payments to minimize restrictions in the flow of money, goods, and services in the free-world economy.

One effect of the IMF Articles of Agreement is legally significant for individual transactions. The articles obligate member nations to not enforce, through their courts, payment by individuals for transactions that are in violation of another member's valid exchange restrictions.

General Agreement on Tariffs and Trade. GATT is a multilateral treaty that came into force in 1948. Since 1968 its staff has jointly operated the International Trade Centre in Geneva with UNCTAD. With over ninety nations, and another thirty-one nations de facto members (including the United States) adhering to the treaty, its principles control over 80 percent of world trade.

GATT lays down a code of conduct for international trade. Its basic principles are that (1) trade should be conducted on a basis of nondiscrimination; (2) protection to domestic industry may be accorded only by customs tariffs, not by quantitative import quotas or other devices; (3) tariffs should be reduced by multilateral negotiations, and members should be bound not to raise them again later; and (4) members should consult to overcome trade problems. A special chapter in GATT deals with the special trade problems of developing nations.

In the "Kennedy Round" (1967), GATT reduced tariffs 30 percent on about $40 billion in trade. The Tokyo Round (1973) addressed the tough issues of nontariff barriers and subsidized exports as well as tariffs, and in the interest of economic development for developing nations, it commenced the preferences for developing nations' trade. Interested developing nations have supported commodity agreements (on wheat, sugar, and other commodities) that seek control of prices; they also oppose in some ways the most-favored-nation principle, in order to seek preferences to aid their development.

World Bank. The World Bank, headquartered in Washington, D.C., and created at the Bretton Woods Conference, was officially organized in 1945. It actually includes three institutions: the International Bank for Reconstruction and Development (IBRD), the International Development Association (IDA), and the International Finance Corporation (IFC). They all have the common purpose of channeling finances to developing countries to raise their productivity and increase international trade.

The IBRD not only finances infrastructure projects but attempts increasingly to promote the peoples' mass participation in development to enhance their productivity. To this end the IBRD has always rendered technical assistance on a large scale. It works closely with the United Nations Development Programme (UNDP),

often as the implementing agency for UNDP projects. Recently, as an adjustment to the changing world, the IBRD has been drawn into the new role of assisting in the refinancing of Third World debts.

IDA, founded in 1960, has the same officers and staff as the IBRD. It concentrates on development in very poor countries—some fifty nations with a per capita gross national product (GNP) of less than $781 (1983 dollars). In practice, however, we are told that loans are made only to nations with a per capita GNP of $400 or less. Its loan terms are soft (for example, fifty-year periods with service fees only and no interest, and ten-year grace periods on principal repayment).

The IFC started as an auxiliary in 1956 to encourage private-sector development in developing countries. Its special field is risk capital for private enterprise engaged in projects deemed helpful to economic development.

The OECD should also be mentioned here as a research and regulatory body for the advanced market economies. The OECD has regular meetings of its representatives, and though its codes are not legally enforced in the strict sense, they are recommendations that its members are committed to follow. An important example is the Code of Liberalisation of Capital Movements (1982 version).

DEVELOPMENTS SINCE 1970

The foregoing original core of post–World War II international economic institutions with market orientations still has the key regulatory role in the world of the 1980s. Since 1945, however, the IMF, GATT, and the World Bank have all made some adaptations to the demands of the developing world, and there is a consensus that further change is needed.

The IMF has developed its "extended facility" and consulting role to assist countries with severe balance-of-payments difficulties. GATT has, since the Tokyo Round, instituted a generalized system of preferences for developing countries, and the World Bank is moving toward a larger role in servicing and rescheduling the debts of distressed debtor nations. From the 1970s onward, these movements within the framework of the original, market-oriented Bretton Woods arrangements were not satisfying the demands of the many developing nations whose voices in the IMF, GATT, and the World Bank are still weak. Those dissatisfactions are increasingly expressed in the United Nations General Assembly, where the Third World has a majority voice. Other agencies expressing this dissatisfaction are UNCTAD, the United Nations Commission on Transnational Corporations (UNTNC), and the United Nations Industrial Development Commission (UNIDO), to mention the most prominent. In each of these organs the developing nations have voting and staffing dominance, and their stance is increasingly to denounce the old economic order, as constructed by the Western industrial nations for their own benefit at the expense of developing nations. Brief descriptions of these agencies follow.

United Nations Conference on Trade and Development. UNCTAD was created in 1964 at Geneva as a permanent organ of the United Nations. It had 159 members by 1984. Its main purpose is to promote international trade as a means of accelerating development. UNCTAD formulates policy on international trade and initiates action for the adoption of multilateral trade treaties. It also acts as a center to harmonize the trade and development policies of governments and regional economic groups. UNCTAD is organized into seven committees: Commodities, Manufactures, Invisibles and Trade Financing, Shipping, Preferences, Transfer of Technology, and Economic Cooperation among Developing Countries. It has been holding conferences about every four years to promote its projects.

Besides international commodity agreements sponsored primarily by developing nations, UNCTAD has already initiated two controversial projects to create codes of conduct: the Code of Conduct on the Transfer of Technology and the Code of Conduct for Liner Conferences (1974). Together with the Code of Conduct for Transnational Corporations, sponsored by the UNTNC, a standing body of the United Nations Economic and Social Council, these codes, though not "hard" law (except, among those nations that ratified it, the Liner Code), tend to shape needed debate in the world arena. As noted, UNCTAD has come to voice the aspirations of, and pursue an agenda for, the developing countries within the United Nations system, and in a sense, it therefore contrasts with the OECD, which speaks

from outside the United Nations for the economic programs of the twenty-four developed countries that make up its membership.

UNCTAD and GATT jointly operate the International Trade Centre in Geneva. The Centre disseminates information on trade opportunities and trains personnel for developing countries in export promotion, among other activities.

United Nations Commission on Transnational Corporations. The UNTNC was established by the United Nations Economic and Social Council in 1974 with forty-eight members. Its highest priority was the formulation of the Code of Conduct for Transnational Corporations, and it held its first meeting in 1975. To gather information and conduct research, the council also established in 1975 the Centre on Transnational Corporations, to deal with the impact of transnational corporations (TNCs) on balance of payments, particularly of developing countries; corrupt practices; the effects of investments by TNCs on investment and production of domestic enterprises; and the effects of TNCs on employment. The UNTNC has also asked the Centre to explore the impact of TNCs on such vital sectors as banking, insurance, shipping, food, and pharmaceutical industries. The Centre reported in 1978 that only about 25 percent of TNC direct investment of $287 billion was in developing countries, suggesting that TNCs were not fulfilling the needs of developing nations. The United States shuns the Centre, saying that it discriminates by excluding government corporations of socialist countries from its inquiries.

The Code of Conduct of Transnational Corporations is discussed below with the several other codes of conduct, which have become the symbol of the NIEO.

United Nations Industrial Development Organization. Headquartered in Vienna, UNIDO was established in 1967 and was transformed into a specialized agency by resolution of the United Nations General Assembly in 1975 with eighty members ratifying its constitution as of 1982. It renders technical assistance to developing countries and supports their industrial development with research and studies. At its second conference, at Lima (1975), UNIDO set an objective of increasing the developing countries' share of world industrial production from 7 percent to 25 percent by the year 2000. UNIDO has been exploring the possibilities of mutual assistance between developing countries by promoting so-called South-South trade and economic cooperation.

The two clusters of agencies—the IMF, GATT, the World Bank, and the OECD, dominated by the developed nations, and UNCTAD, the UNTNC, and UNIDO, dominated by the developing nations—have their own philosophies and agendas, yet they have found much common ground in the 1980s. The stridency of debates in the prior decade subsided with the weakening of the Organization of Petroleum-Exporting Countries (OPEC) and the onset of a worldwide recession in 1981. Both groups have recognized their interdependence, and both have realized that changes in the world wrought by decolonization since World War II and the consequent increase and differing circumstances of new nations in the world have rendered the Bretton Woods system in many respects inadequate. Much of the NIEO movement has also been generally recognized as unrealistic. Probably the present core institutions (the IMF, GATT, and the World Bank) will furnish the base from which many necessary adaptations to the changed world will be made, stimulated by debate in the newer forums of UNCTAD, the UNTNC, and UNIDO, as well as in the General Assembly.

Other agencies with narrower functions have an important impact on the international economic system. Examples are the International Labor Organization (ILO), the International Atomic Energy Agency (IAEA), the Food and Agriculture Organization (FAO), and the World Intellectual Property Organization (WIPO). Because of the importance of reliability and cost of transport in international trade, the International Civil Aviation Organization (ICAO) and the International Maritime Organization (IMO, formerly IMCO) are also important to the world economy. Many other intergovernmental agencies could be mentioned, as well as important nongovernmental organizations in various international fields, such as the International Chamber of Commerce (ICC) and the International Confederation of Free Trade Unions (ICFTU).

The prolonged United Nations Conferences on the Law of the Sea involved worldwide participation and produced a monumental convention now open for ratification. Predictions are that it will be ratified by a sufficient number of nations to become international law within a few years.

While the content of the convention is wide-ranging, some of its provisions are related to economic concerns. The United States is not a signatory, but the convention will probably have some legal significance in the future for signatories and nonsignatories alike.

NEW CODES OF CONDUCT OF THE 1970S

Out of the movement for the NIEO came a succession of so-called codes of conduct sponsored by the Third World and drafted by UNCTAD, the UNTNC, and other agencies. None of these codes will soon have actual justiciable legal effects, except the Liner Code (effective 6 October 1983). Nor are the codes likely to be adopted in the future as binding codes by both the developed and developing nations. The term *guidelines,* used by the OECD, seems better to reflect their functions than does the term *codes.*

Some major codes of conduct that have found their way into drafts thus far are the following, with their sponsoring agencies and dates:

UNTNC: Code of Conduct on Transnational Corporations (1984 draft)

UNCTAD: Code of Conduct on the Transfer of Technology (1983 draft)
Code of Conduct for Liner Conferences (effective 1983, without United States ratification)
Set of Multilaterally Agreed Equitable Principles and Rules for the Control of Restrictive Business Practices (adopted by the General Assembly, 1980)

ILO: Tripartite Declaration of Principles Concerning Multinational Enterprises and Social Policy (approved 1977 after United States withdrawal from the ILO; the United States has since rejoined)

OECD: Guidelines for Multinational Enterprises (1976)

It is important to emphasize the differences in the binding character and enforcement mechanisms of the initial Bretton Woods system sponsored by the advanced, mixed, or market economies, on the one hand, and the declarations and codes of conduct sponsored since the 1970s by the Third World (and sometimes the socialist bloc) in UNCTAD, the UNTNC, and other organs affiliated with the United Nations, on the other hand. The latter do not make law. Over time and with usage, however, they have perhaps the potential of becoming "hard" international customary law. As Hans Baade wrote,

> It is realized that the practice of international organizations, and of states within international organizations, is not (or not as yet) the full equivalent of "hard," customary international law directly based on state practice. . . . The adoption even of codes of conduct expressly declared to be unenforceable internationally is not without substantial legal consequences, and the follow-up mechanisms in existence or at advanced stages of elaboration strongly suggest the eventual emergence of a pertinent body of "hard" decisional law.
>
> (p. 413)

The hallmarks of the Bretton Woods system are its initial efficacy and its enforceability. But it has been also narrow in both outlook and participation, conceived as it was by the United States and a few other advanced countries with a preference for market forces and in a world of only 50 nations. By the 1970s, in a world of 170 nations, the Bretton Woods system began to draw severe criticisms from developing nations, sometimes supported (in rhetoric at least) by the Soviet bloc.

Over the period 1970–1985 the Third World agenda accelerated and has produced a significant body of guidelines or codes of conduct on a variety of subjects. While most of these codes are not law, they have the potential to ripen over time (after appropriate changes and uses) into practices and, ultimately, customary international law. True, this process may produce a changing content and will take some time, but what we have to date, in the form of the concrete codes listed, is significant. It symbolizes a new movement, if not an entirely new international economic order. This movement will surely change international economic law in some degree over time, as it has already in some commodity agreements, the IMF extended facility, and the GATT "generalized preference" in trade with developing nations. These changes have occurred, and will continue to occur, with a consensus because both the advanced market economies and the developing planned economies have accepted interdependence and the need for ongoing institutional adjustments.

PRIVATE BUSINESS AND TRANSNATIONAL TRANSACTIONS

Compared to the law of nations or the law of international organizations, the relevant international economic law is more complex in transactions between market economies, and for the private enterprises structuring an export-import sales agreement, or a foreign joint venture to build a bridge abroad, or a patent-licensing contract with a foreign licensee.

The Bretton Woods system, as it has evolved, is still the public law framework used for private transactions between free enterprises from different countries. The "soft" law (one or more of the codes of conduct) may also have some impact on one or both parties, as may the practice of bureaucrats encountered, if not as mandatory law, then as norms accepted by their government or themselves in exercising discretion.

But in addition, there will be treaty law, often bilateral, which applies specifically to business between any two countries. The most important species of bilateral treaties includes bilateral tax treaties and bilateral treaties of friendship, commerce, and navigation (FCN). In 1986 there were forty-seven bilateral FCN treaties in effect between the United States and other nations, about twenty of them new since 1945, but none since 1967. These treaties have played a central role in American commercial relations with trading partners abroad. After World War II they were regarded as a key diplomatic device with which not only to modernize the terms of American intercourse with other nations but also to encourage private sector contributions to the reconstruction of war-torn advanced nations and to the development of decolonized new nations. In the early postwar days, the assumption underlying FCN treaties was that direct investment was beneficial to both home and host countries, a view that was accepted generally on both sides. Host developing countries have since found that attitude simplistic and have placed many unilateral conditions on direct investment from abroad.

The purpose of an FCN treaty is specifically to

provide a framework for business transactions in and between private businesses of the two nations that are parties to the treaty. The terms are tailored to govern day-to-day business. Such terms normally cover the rights of entry for business and residence, the protection of individuals and businesses, and various rights and duties of individuals, including practice of the professions, acquisition of property, patents and other industrial property, taxation, remittance to the home country of earnings and capital, competition policy, nationalization of property, access to courts, trade duties and restrictions, shipping, and arbitration.

Also on a bilateral basis are the important treaties for avoidance of double taxation. Transnational transactions invite taxation on both sides of a bilateral exchange. The double-taxation treaties provide criteria for determining which country should impose a tax. The FCN and tax treaties are only two of the most important types of bilateral treaties, which supplement the growing framework of public international law built up by multilateral conventions and regulations of international agencies to encourage and regulate private business transactions.

Most transactions occur in a bilateral context, and American business has more trade and investment with Japan than with any other overseas nation and vice versa. So, a business deal between the United States and Japan can serve well as an example to explain the framework of bilateral international business law. In one respect, however, American-Japanese business is a simpler model for private transactions than that of any European nation with the United States because the EEC adds a growing layer of regional public international law—law that must be considered before getting to the national layer of regulation on both sides.

What then, in addition to the public international law, are the components of the legal order relevant to American-Japanese transactions? In broadest terms, they are the Japanese legal system and the American legal system (federal and state) bridged by public international law and ultimately simplified at the private law level by private international law rules (or choice-of-law rules), which determine which of the two national laws, both potentially applicable, shall apply.

Let us assume that an American firm is exporting a product to Japan. Both countries may have their own applicable public national law—that is, regulatory prohibitions and procedures relevant to exports, in the case of the United States, and to imports, in the case of Japan. The choice-of-law rules do not apply to this kind of national public law; domestic courts nearly always apply their own and only their own public regulations. Japan, on the import side, prohibits (as of 1986) the import of apples, restricts plywood or leather-goods imports, and places testing requirements on many drugs and other products before they are allowed to enter; Japan also collects tariffs as taxes at the border before issuing entry permits. The United States has its own set of export prohibitions. In the case of these national statutes (public laws), the regulations of both countries will be applied administratively to the business transaction as the exported goods move out of the United States and enter Japan, although, as noted, in case of litigation, Japanese courts would normally not enforce American public law and vice versa. There are rare exceptions in international economic law. One such exception where foreign public law is enforced is the foreign-exchange licensing of the payment in dollars if the Japanese restriction complies with the IMF. In that case, each country must enforce the exchange laws of the other (IMF Article VIII, section 2(b)).

Also important are other basic business regulations of the United States and Japan that are not confined to the foregoing mechanisms for handling goods and payment. These include antitrust laws, protection of sensitive government technology, shipping policies, antidumping laws, and, of course, the income tax laws, among many other statutes that may apply to specific goods. At the time of contracting for the export sale, each negotiating party must understand these laws because of the possibilities of shaping the transaction (by, say, fixing the place of contracting, payment, or delivery) so as to assure that the law of the country most beneficial to the party will apply. The incidence and rates of taxes, for instance, may differ between the two national taxes, and the transaction can perhaps be shaped and planned so that the tax law with the lower rate will apply. The possibilities depend on the case and the treaty against double taxation, which provides the criteria for determining which nation may tax.

But there remains another important layer of law yet to be considered. This is the private law (contracts, torts, sales, property, agency, corporate, and the like) of both countries. Japan's private law is based in civil law, whereas that of the United States is founded in common law. Thus, in the private-law field, subtle comparative-law issues inhere in American-Japanese transactions, which can only be noted in passing. Moreover, there is no American law as such. Rather, the relevant private law (for example, contract law) in the United States is that of the particular state involved, or perhaps of federal law (as in the case of shipping).

The critical importance of the private law to the system of international economic law is that in market economies, it is the law that governs the business relationships between traders and investors in all of the multitude of transactions. In turn, these transactions, in the aggregate, are the foreign trade and investment between countries. These private traders, not officials, conduct the foreign trade of market economies and in doing so must rely upon a specific private law order. To the extent that the private law system is clear and efficient, economic intercourse between nations will be enhanced.

But the critical point in the American-Japanese example for businesspeople is that the rules of Japanese private law may differ from the law of their state. Where there are differences in the two countries' private law rules for contracts, the sales contract will potentially have two legal meanings unless one or the other of the two national rules is eliminated at the time of contracting, perhaps by an agreement on a governing-law clause—that is, a clause that specifies which of the two laws will govern the enforceability of the contract. This choice of law by agreement of the parties cannot, of course, be done intelligently without knowing the content of both Japanese and various American state rules to determine which best supports the parties' understanding.

Suppose the parties make no choice of American or Japanese contract law to govern their agreement. In such a case, each country has a special body of law called conflicts law, which supplies choice-of-law rules for the purpose of selecting the law governing the contract (either the law of Japan, or that of an American state). These choice-of-law rules, too, may differ between the United States and Japan so that, for example, Japan's rule might choose American law, and the state's rule might choose Japanese law.

These choice-of-law rules specify, in certain factual situations, which of the two nations' private laws will be applied by a court. For example, one such choice-of-law rule says: the validity of a contract shall be governed by the law of the place where the contract is signed.

So, actually, the choice-of-law rules will function on one of two levels. The first level is called the "principle of party autonomy," which means that the choice-of-law rule is that the parties may choose by agreement one of the two national laws as the governing law. If the parties in our example of the export contract agree that California law governs, the courts in Japan will nearly always apply the California private law as the governing law chosen by the parties; likewise, in the United States the trend is also to apply the national law chosen by the parties, although the common-law tradition was against such enforcement until after World War II, and some states remain less reliable than others in enforcing governing-law clauses.

If the Japanese law is agreed upon, the parties should also agree on a forum (choice-of-court) clause in the contract; that is, they may want to agree to litigate only in Japan because a Japanese court can apply Japanese law more easily than an American court through translated texts. Japan and most American states will normally enforce a forum clause (even if the choice is a foreign court) by dismissing a suit in breach of the clause. A contract should therefore also include a choice-of-court clause, choosing a court likely to enforce the two choices (law and court) of the parties.

The second level at which choice-of-law rules may operate arises when the contract between the parties is silent on choice-of-law issues. The problem with such contracts, which rely on the general choice-of-law rule of the forum state to choose the governing law, rather than the agreement of the parties, is that the decision as to which (Japanese or American) law applies under the choice-of-law rules may remain unpredictable until a case is filed and the court speaks, because the choice-of-law rules themselves may be ambiguous. Or, even if the rules of both countries are reasonably clear in the situation we are considering, the Japanese rule may clearly designate one country's law (say, its own) and the American rule may clearly choose the opposite law (also, here, its own). This is the case, for example, where a contract is made by mail. Japan might apply the law of the country from which the offer to buy was sent (Japan), whereas in some circumstances California might apply the law where the contract was made (concluded), which would often be where the acceptance was posted (California). These rules would thus clearly reach opposite results, so that the parties would know which law governs (and thus what their contract means legally) only after one of the parties has decided which court to sue in. This is too late for clarity of contractual meaning. Indeed, because of differences in the law concerning jurisdiction of the two countries, jurisdiction over a case may often be obtained in the courts of both countries. A contract without a choice made by the parties in the contract would always speak with two voices on issues on which the substantive law of the two countries to be chosen differs and would create different obligations enforceable in the two courts. Such differences in the substantive contract laws of the two countries are in fact quite common. The resulting confused legal regime is of little use to the party trying to understand its legal duties at the stage of performance.

Howsoever infrequently the juxtaposition of differing choice-of-law rules, jurisdictional rules, and the underlying substantive law may fall in such a way as to produce the kind of distressing double-talk demonstrated above (from the parties' viewpoint), still it serves to highlight the usefulness of the unification of private law between trading countries.

THE UNIFICATION OF PRIVATE LAW

To address this problem, several international agencies have attempted to unify key areas of private law so that some or all nations will enact and be bound by the same law in transnational transactions such as contracts and sales. These efforts are the topic of the concluding discussion.

The United Nations General Assembly created the United Nations Commission on In-

ternational Trade Law (UNCITRAL) in Vienna in 1966. UNCITRAL complements the work of two older bodies with long experience and accomplishments in the effort to unify private international law. They are the Hague Conference on Private International Law and the Rome International Institute for the Unification of Private Law. They are described briefly below.

UNCITRAL's role is primarily to promote uniformity in the private law governing transactions between individuals from different nations. UNCITRAL also encourages cooperation in other legal matters among existing international organizations active in trade. It prepares conventions and models of uniform laws and promotes their adoption by the legislatures of all countries. It also promotes the use of uniform terminology and interpretation in trade law, and it trains and assists developing countries in trade-law matters.

UNCITRAL sponsored the Draft Convention on the International Sale of Goods in 1972. Its Convention on the Limitation Period in the International Sale of Goods was adopted in 1974 by a conference convened by the General Assembly. The limitation period is set at four years, and the convention will come into effect six months after ten states ratify it, an event that had not occurred as of 1986.

UNCITRAL also adopted arbitration rules in 1976, which were then recommended for use in international commerce by the General Assembly. The rules are a model for optional use of arbitration bodies; they deal with the organization of new arbitral tribunals, their proceedings, and the awards they make. The UNCITRAL rules will add to the efforts of regional arbitration groups as well as those of the International Chamber of Commerce headquartered in Paris and the IBRD's International Centre for the Settlement of Investment Disputes (ICSID). National private bodies (such as the American Arbitration Association) are also working to extend arbitral tribunals around the world for resolution of commercial disputes.

A serious legal issue may be raised as to the theoretical, as well as practical, relationship that should be maintained between arbitration and litigation in world trade. It has been argued that arbitration, while efficacious in dispute settlement, is not so reliable in enforcing uniform law. Hence, the argument goes, balance must be struck so that arbitral tribunals will not jeopardize uncompromisable legal rights.

The Hague Conference. The Hague Conference on Private International Law dates from 1893 and has twenty-five member states, including the United States (since 1963). It also has some eighteen new conventions in various phases of review, aimed at unifying specific areas of law. The efforts of the Hague Conference is confined to so-called conflicts of law: "to work for the progressive unification of the rules of private international law"—in our term, rules of choice of law (Article 1 of its statute).

Rome International Institute for the Unification of Private Law. The institute, known as Unidroit, is an intergovernmental organization created in 1926 at Rome by the Italian government. It has forty-two members, including the United States (since 1962). Unidroit has concentrated on drafting rules of substantive private law in areas ripe for unification. Conflicts of law and jurisdictional rules are left to the Hague Conference. Unidroit has also avoided fields that are the preserves of specialist agencies: air law (ICAO), maritime law (IMCO), and labor law (ILO). Unidroit's recent successes have centered on international sales law and transport law.

Together, the Hague Conference, Unidroit, and UNCITRAL have not only at last brought both common-law and civil-law nations into the work of unification, but they have also made some progress in transport, sales, conflicts, and arbitration. A new body of model private law that is uniform and therefore international is continuing to accumulate for commercial matters. All that remains in these instances is to have nations each enact these model laws in their legislatures. Progress has also been made by United Nations conventions in aid of transnational litigation—for example, in service of process on foreign defendants and in enforcement of foreign arbitral awards.

To sum up the several strata of international economic law from the perspective of two parties buying and selling across national boundaries: there is first the multilateral treaties of public international law (IMF, GATT); second, there are the bilateral treaties (FCN; double taxation); third, there are national regulatory laws on both sides; fourth, there is the party autonomy principle allowing the parties to choose the governing law; fifth, there are private international law rules (choice-of-law rules) of both countries, which both may be relevant until suit is filed, because filing may occur in either country; and finally, there is the private law (contracts, sales) of one of the countries, applied in accordance with the choice-of-law rules. The advantage of the movement to make the private law and the private international law uniform is to assure that the ambiguity of the choice-of-law rules can be avoided; also the parties can avoid the necessity to know diverse private law (such as the rules of contract) of two countries.

BIBLIOGRAPHY

Hans Baade, "Codes of Conduct for Multinational Enterprises: An Introductory Survey," in Norbert Horn, ed., *Legal Problems of Codes of Conduct for Multinational Enterprises*, vol. 1 in the Studies in Transnational Economic Law series (1980), is a summary of the work of several international organizations on codes of conduct. Jagdish Bhagwati and John G. Ruggie, eds., *Power, Passions and Purpose: Prospects for North-South Negotiations* (1984), presents several perspectives on international economic law in transition and in the context of North-South interaction. Kenneth W. Dam, *The Rules of the Game* (1982), offers a lucid perspective on the role of law in monetary affairs since the nineteenth century, including the post–World War II IMF experience. Norbert Horn and Clive Schmitthoff, eds., *The Transnational Law of International Commercial Transactions*, vol. 2 in the Studies in Transnational Economic Law series (1982), gives a more detailed treatment of transactional law. Thomas Hovet, Jr. and Erica Hovet, eds., *A Chronology and Fact Book of the United Nations, 1941–1985*, 7th ed. (1986), is extremely useful for events, dates, documents, and lists relating to the United Nations; besides a chronology of United Nations events from 1945–1985, there is a documents section that includes the United Nations Charter and a section providing up-to-date lists of memberships in various agencies.

John H. Jackson and William Davey, *Legal Problems of International Economic Relations*, 2nd ed. (1986), is a law school course book with many valuable materials arranged in terms of layers of law (international and national) and by problem areas, not an overview to be read as an introduction. John H. Jackson, Jean-Victor Louis, and Mitsuo Matsushita, *Implementing the Tokyo Round* (1984), provides essays on American, Japanese, and EEC actions required by the GATT negotiations in Tokyo (1973–1979) and shows the intertwining of international and national law required for effectiveness of free-world trade policies. L. Judas, "The UNCTAD Liner Code," in *Journal of Maritime Law and Commerce*, 16 (1985), shows the legal problems arising after the liner code came into effect in 1983. John M. Kline, *International Codes and Multinational Business* (1985), is a useful survey and assessment of the significance of the code of conduct movement. Andreas F. Lowenfeld, *International Economic Law*, 6 vols. (1984), deals with the international monetary system in vol. 4.

E. McGovern, *International Trade Regulation: GATT, the United States and the European Community* (1982), is an integrated survey of international trade law and supporting EEC and American regulations. Seymour J. Rubin and Gary C. Hufbauer, eds., *Emerging Standards of International Trade and Investment* (1984), is a collection of views on the several codes of conduct. W. Surrey and D. Wallace, Jr., eds., *A Lawyer's Guide to International Business Transactions*, Parts 1–4 (1980), offers a voluminous treatment.

United Nations, *Everyone's United Nations*, 9th ed. (1979), is a compact reference book on the United Nations and its family of organizations; and *Yearbook of the United Nations* (1981), is a useful source of annual reports on recent events, work, and changes within the United Nations and its affiliate agencies, but there is a lag of about three years before the yearbooks are published.

G. J. H. van Hoof, *Rethinking the Sources of International Law* (1983), provides a summary and reanalysis of sources of international law including the "soft law" approach. V. Van Themaat, *The Changing Structure of International Economic Law* (1981), gives a synoptic history and theory of the economic legal order as it exists, as well as proposals for the future and a thoughtful overview. Donald T. Wilson, *International Business Transactions in a Nutshell* (1984), provides a simple introduction to the law of transnational transactions.

[*See also* CIVIL LAW SYSTEMS; COMMON LAW AND COMMON-LAW LEGAL SYSTEMS; INTERNATIONAL HUMAN RIGHTS LAW; *and* INTERNATIONAL LAW AND ORGANIZATIONS.]

INTERNATIONAL

HUMAN RIGHTS LAW

Roger S. Clark

As with any vast subject, it is necessary to be selective. Accordingly, this discussion will concentrate on four areas: a brief history of international human rights efforts until 1945; the work of the United Nations since 1945 (the bulk of the discussion); regional efforts, particularly in Europe and the Americas; and the United States' role internationally and the impact of international human rights law on United States domestic law.

HUMAN RIGHTS EFFORTS TO 1945

The development of a distinctive body of international human rights law and the organizational structure that goes with it is largely a phenomenon of the period since World War II. It can be viewed in large measure as a reaction to that cataclysm. Its antecedents go back at least to the formation in Britain in 1787 of the Anti-Slavery Society, which was devoted to the abolition of slavery at the global level. Similar lofty sentiments motivated the work of Jean Henri Dunant, which led to the adoption in 1864 of the first of the Geneva (Red Cross) Conventions, treaties dealing with the protection of victims in time of war. Efforts such as these were essentially ad hoc and aimed at a particular problem in a relatively narrow area. They did not lead to the creation of an international organizational structure that would maintain continuing supervision of state activities. (Even the International Committee of the Red Cross, which supervises the Red Cross Conventions, is essentially a Swiss rather than an international organization.) Indeed, the first permanent organizational efforts to deal with human rights at the international level were the mandates and minorities' protection arrange-ments undertaken by the League of Nations and the creation of the International Labor Organization (ILO). The League and the ILO were both established by the 1919 peace treaty, the Treaty of Versailles.

Article 22 of the "Covenant," the League's constituent document, provided that in certain colonies detached from Germany and Turkey during the war the new administering powers should operate according to the principle that the well-being of the peoples of those territories should "form a sacred trust of civilization." In order to fulfill this trust, the administering authorities owed certain obligations to the League, which were supervised, in a rough-and-ready way, by a body of experts, the Permanent Mandates Commission. Analogous procedures found their way into the United Nations (UN) Charter and generated an enormous amount of UN human rights activity.

As part of the peace settlement, obligations to respect minority rights were also undertaken by (or imposed upon) many of the new European states that emerged following the war. Again, procedures were created to enforce these obligations, but they were not notably successful. This kind of guarantee of group rights was not repeated in the UN Charter, which, aside from its important references to the principle of the self-determination of peoples, proceeds primarily on the basis that human rights are rights of the individual rather than of the collective.

The ILO was created to set international standards for the protection of workers and to collect and disseminate knowledge on the world's labor problems. Underlying its creation was the notion that there could be no real peace without social and economic justice for the workers of the world. A system of standards has been developed by the organization for such areas as working conditions, social security, and trade union rights. Of particular significance are the enforcement mechanisms that have been developed. Not only are there procedures for dealing with complaints of violation of standards in particular cases, but there is also a structure that devotes expert attention to examining the reports from governments on how they are giving effect to ILO standards in general. This expert examination, and the strong persuasive forces for compliance that it generates, have had a significant impact on the securing of both formal and de facto compliance with ILO standards. The ILO survived World War II to enter into a relationship with the UN as a specialized agency of that organization. Its experience with the examination of governmental reports has been of particular significance in shaping parts of the UN's own program.

THE WORK OF THE UN SINCE 1945

Some of the smaller countries represented at the San Francisco Conference wished to include in the approved UN Charter a bill of rights. By this means, they argued, future sources of conflict might be diverted at their source. Their efforts were not entirely successful, but the Charter (in particular Articles 1, 13, and 55) does contain several references to the "promotion" of human rights and fundamental freedoms for all, without distinction as to race, sex, language, or religion, as one of the goals of the organization. In Article 56 members of the UN pledge themselves to take joint and separate action in cooperation with the organization to achieve that promotion. The notion of "promotion" was deliberately chosen to suggest a weaker obligation of states than might have been the case if a strong word like "protect" had been used. Nevertheless, the organization's founders expected that the organization would work actively at the drafting of various international instruments, both to give more detailed content to the generalities of the Charter and to devise enforcement and supervision procedures to encourage states to abide by their obligations.

The drafters "balanced" their human rights provisions with Article 2, paragraph 7, which represents the invariable refuge of states called to task by the UN for their human rights sins. It provides that nothing contained in the Charter shall authorize the UN to intervene in matters that are essentially within the domestic jurisdiction of any state or to require states to submit such matters for settlement under the Charter. A proviso (relevant to action taken by the organization against the former Southern Rhodesia and against South Africa) says that the principle of Article 2, paragraph 7 shall not prejudice enforcement measures taken under Chapter VII of the Charter, that is, action with respect to threats to the peace, breaches of the peace, and acts of aggression. As inevitably as the domestic-jurisdiction argument is made by those accused of violations in UN forums, it is just as inevitably overridden by proponents of action. Depending upon the states concerned and the issue before the organ involved, application of the paragraph is generally avoided by varieties of one or more of these arguments: (a) human rights, because of their inclusion in the Charter and in general international law, are no longer "essentially within the domestic jurisdiction of any state"; (b) the specific action proposed in the UN, such as putting the matter on the agenda, making a study, or adopting a recommendation, does not amount to "intervention," which is said to have a technical meaning of "dictatorial interference," that is, some kind of force; (c) in any event, the provision has no application where "massive" or "systematic" violations are concerned, especially those likely to affect the maintenance of international peace and security. In practice "domestic jurisdiction" does not inhibit UN action where the political will to act is present.

Various organs of the UN are particularly concerned with human rights. At the top of the hierarchy is the General Assembly, which acts mainly through a committee of the whole called the Third Committee. Beneath the General Assembly is the Economic and Social Council (ECOSOC), which consists of fifty-four members of the UN elected by the General Assembly. Below that is the Commission on Human Rights (forty-three members) and the Commission on the Status of Women (thirty-two members). The Commission on Human Rights, which is where the bulk of the UN's human rights work takes place, is aided by the Subcommission on Prevention of Discrimination and Protection of Minorities, composed of twenty-six "experts." While the experts are in fact nominated and elected by governments, they serve in their personal capacity and tend to behave in a less political and more independent fashion than the representatives of governments at the commission, ECOSOC, and the General Assembly. The commission and subcommission have various working groups such as those on communications (discussed below), enforced or involuntary disappearances, slavery, and the rights of indigenous populations.

In the first twenty years of its life, the UN devoted most of its energies in the human rights area to giving concrete content to the Charter generalities by elaborating various detailed "instruments." The instruments are of two kinds, treaties and resolutions (usually of the UN General Assembly). Treaties such as those in the list below are clearly intended to impose obligations under international law on those states which become parties to them. When first adopted, resolutions of the kind contained below have perhaps no more than some kind of moral force; but over time they tend to develop into rules and principles of customary international law. In recent years, while this activity has continued, more attention has been paid to means of "supervising" the performance of states or to "enforcing" the rules contained in the instruments. The following is a compilation of the main instruments.

TREATIES

Convention on the Prevention and Punishment of the Crime of Genocide (1948)

Convention for the Suppression of Traffic in Persons and of the Exploitation of the Prostitution of Others (1949)

Convention Relating to the Status of Refugees (1951)

Convention on the Political Rights of Women (1952)

Convention on the International Right of Correction (1952)

Protocol Amending the Slavery Convention (1953)

Convention Relating to the Status of Stateless Persons (1954)

Supplementary Convention on the Abolition of Slavery, the Slave Trade, and Institutions and Practices Similar to Slavery (1956)

Convention on the Nationality of Married Women (1957)

Convention Relating to the Reduction of Statelessness (1961)

Convention on Consent to Marriage, Minimum Age for Marriage and Registration of Marriages (1962)

International Convention on the Elimination of All Forms of Racial Discrimination (1965)

International Covenant on Economic, Social and Cultural Rights (1966)

International Covenant on Civil and Political Rights (1966)

Optional Protocol to the International Covenant on Civil and Political Rights (1966)

Protocol Relating to the Status of Refugees (1967)

Convention on the Non-Applicability of Statutory Limitations to War Crimes and Crimes against Humanity (1968)

International Convention on the Suppression and Punishment of the Crime of Apartheid (1973)

Convention on the Elimination of All Forms of Discrimination Against Women (1979)

Convention Against the Taking of Hostages (1979)

Convention Against Torture and Other Cruel, Inhuman or Degrading Treatment or Punishment (1984)

RESOLUTIONS

Universal Declaration of Human Rights (1948)

Standard Minimum Rules for the Treatment of Prisoners (1957, amended 1977)

Declaration of the Rights of the Child (1959)

Declaration on the Granting of Independence to Colonial Countries and Peoples (1960)

Permanent Sovereignty over Natural Resources (1962)

Declaration on the Promotion Among Youth of the Ideals of Peace, Mutual Respect and Understanding Between Peoples (1965)

Declaration on the Elimination of Discrimination Against Women (1967)

Declaration on Territorial Asylum (1967)

Declaration on Social Progress and Development (1969)

Declaration on Principles of International Law Concerning Friendly Relations and Cooperation Among States in Accordance with the Charter of the United Nations (1970)

Declaration on the Rights of Mentally Retarded Persons (1971)

Principles of International Cooperation in the Detection, Arrest, Extradition and Punishment of Persons Guilty of War Crimes and Crimes Against Humanity (1973)

Declaration on the Establishment of a New International Economic Order (1974)

Programme of Action on the Establishment of a New International Economic Order (1974)

Charter of Economic Rights and Duties of States (1974)

Declaration on the Protection of Women and Children in Emergency and Armed Conflict (1974)

Universal Declaration on the Eradication of Hunger and Malnutrition (1974)

Declaration on the Use of Scientific and Technological Progress in the Interests of Peace and for the Benefit of Mankind (1975)

Declaration on the Rights of Disabled Persons (1975)

Code of Conduct for Law Enforcement Officials (1979)

Declaration on the Elimination of All Forms of Intolerance and of Discrimination Based on Religion or Belief (1981)

Declaration on the Participation of Women in Promoting International Peace and Co-operation (1982)

Principles of Medical Ethics (1982)

The philosophical forces at work in the drafting of the instruments are interesting. It is common in the treaties and resolutions to refer to "inalienable" rights, which suggests some natural law underpinning the rights in question. In practice, however, the recognition of a particular right takes on more of a positive law approach: a consensus is slowly and perhaps painfully achieved within a set of highly political UN organs, a process that also permits the gradual evolution of new rights and potentially the erosion of old ones.

MAJOR UN INSTRUMENTS

It is difficult to single out for special treatment a handful of the treaties and resolutions listed above. Nevertheless, it is hoped that an examination of some of the major documents will give the reader a good feel for the whole program.

Universal Declaration of Human Rights. The crowning jewel of the UN's efforts is the Universal Declaration of Human Rights, adopted by the General Assembly on 10 December 1948 by a vote of forty-eight to none with eight abstentions (Belorussian SSR, Czechoslovakia, Poland, Saudi Arabia, Ukrainian SSR, USSR, Union of South Africa, and Yugoslavia). Included in the Declaration are not only the traditional or "first-generation" rights such as equality before the law, freedom from arbitrary arrest, detention and exile, the presumption of innocence, and freedom of speech, religion and assembly, but also "second-generation" economic, social, and cultural rights such as the right to social security, the right to work, the right to decent housing and health care, and the right to education. (In recent years writers on international human rights law have noted the emergence of controversial "third-generation" rights not included in the Declaration that are sometimes called "solidarity rights," such as the right to peace, the right to disarmament, the right to development, and the right to a safe and healthy environment.)

Many of those who drafted the Declaration were at pains to insist during the drafting process that the instrument did not constitute binding international law. Its preamble in fact describes the Declaration as "a common standard of achievement for all peoples and all nations." Whatever may have been its status in 1948, many scholars (such as Louis B. Sohn) have argued that it is part of the corpus of international law either as an authoritative interpretation of the Charter, as part of the body of customary law, or as evidence of general principles of law. It has had enormous significance in the work of the UN and in the efforts of nongovernmental human rights "do-good" organizations such as Amnesty International or the International League for Human Rights to persuade states to comply with its lofty standards. Its principles and its very words have found their way into the constitutions of many nations.

Covenants and Optional Protocol. With the ink dry on the Declaration, work began on what eventually became two International Covenants on Human Rights, one on Civil and Political Rights and one on Economic, Social and Cultural Rights, as well as on the Optional Protocol to the Covenant on Civil and Political Rights. The covenants spelled out in greater detail and in more "legal" language most of the rights contained in the Universal Declaration. The Optional Protocol allowed for the enforcement of the Covenant on Civil and Political Rights by means of a complaints procedure. As treaties these instruments were intended to impose legal obligations on the states that ratified them. Initially, there was to be only one covenant, just as there was only one declaration. Two main arguments were made for splitting the material in two. One was that different kinds of rights require different kinds of supervisory mechanisms. While some kinds of complaint procedures by individuals or states might be helpful in the case of civil and political rights, they would be inappropriate in the case of, say, the right to health care. The second argument was that the nature of the rights was different in a way that affects the nature of the legal obligation a state may be expected to accept. Civil and political rights can be guaranteed immediately; economic, social, and cultural rights are by their nature programmatic —they are to be achieved gradually as resources permit. This second argument is in fact enshrined in Article 2 of the Covenant on Economic, Social, and Cultural Rights, which has no counterpart in that on Civil and Political Rights. Article 2 obligates each state party to "take steps, individually and through international assistance and cooperation, especially economic and technical, to the maximum of its available resources, with a view to achieving progressively the full realization of the rights recognized in the present Covenant."

In spite of the division into two, the covenants did not have a speedy journey through the General Assembly. It was not until 1966 that they, along with the Optional Protocol, were finally approved by the Assembly and opened for ratification by states. In 1976 the covenants and the Optional Protocol at last came into force. In November 1985 there were eighty-five parties to the Covenant on Economic, Social, and Cultural Rights, eighty-three parties to the Covenant on Civil and Political Rights, and thirty-six parties to the Optional Protocol.

A number of factors explain this slow progress. Early postwar euphoria for the UN was replaced by the cold war. Responding to domestic pressures, United States Secretary of State John Foster Dulles announced in 1953 that the United States, a leader in the drafting effort to that point, would not become a party to the covenants. Many of the colonial powers were outraged by the decision taken in 1952 at the insistence of Third World members to include as identical first articles of both covenants a strong assertion of the right to self-determination. Nevertheless, the controversial Article 1 survived in the final version of both treaties.

The Covenant on Economic, Social, and Cultural Rights includes a weak supervisory regime under which parties to it agree to submit to the secretary general of the UN reports on the measures that they have adopted and the progress made in achieving the rights contained therein. The secretary general refers the reports to the UN's Economic and Social Council, where a committee makes a perfunctory examination of them. The best that may be said of this is that the system has potential.

The Covenant on Civil and Political Rights sets up an eighteen-member Human Rights Committee composed of nationals of states parties to the covenant who are "of high moral character and recognized competence in the field of human rights" and who serve in their personal capacity. The committee (which is not to be confused with the Human Rights Commission discussed above) is elected by the states that are parties to the covenant. Its main function is to examine reports that are made on a regular basis by these states. Some of the questioning of states about their performance has taken place at a high level of sophistication, and there is some hope that the procedure is developing into a rigorous tool for the promotion and even the protection of the rights concerned. The committee has developed into a worthy counterpart to the ILO Committee of Experts, which provided the model for it.

If a state voluntarily accepts its jurisdiction, the committee is empowered to examine complaints by another state that has made a similar acceptance to the effect that the first state is not fulfilling its obligations. States are reluctant to rattle the skeletons in other states' closets for fear that their own may be rattled in turn, and no such complaints have yet been made. Of great significance, however, has been the work of the committee under the procedure of the Optional Protocol. States parties to the protocol (who must first be parties to the covenant) accept the jurisdiction of the committee to receive and consider "communications" (UN jargon for complaints or petitions) from individuals subject to their jurisdiction who claim to be victims of a violation by the party concerned of any of the rights set forth in the covenant. Complainants must have exhausted their legal remedies in the state concerned and may then write to the committee. At what is known as the "admissibility" stage, the committee may reject the communication out of hand on the basis that it is anonymous, an abuse of the right of submission, or incompatible with the provisions of the covenant. If the complaint survives this stage, the committee must send it to the state concerned for its comments. The comments are in turn relayed to the complainant, and then the committee forwards what the protocol calls its "views" to the state and the individual concerned. This procedure is not exactly like that of a court, and no oral proceedings take place. Nevertheless, the end result is a written statement not unlike the judgment of a court. An impressive body of decisions is being built up which adds significantly to the law laid down in the covenant itself.

The Race Convention. The International Convention on the Elimination of All Forms of Racial Discrimination was adopted and opened for signature by the General Assembly on 21 December 1965. Significantly, this was a year before the covenants were finally adopted. The momentum given to the human rights program by developing countries' support for this instrument helped give the final push for approval of the covenants. The convention came into force quickly for a treaty of this kind, on 4 January 1969. With 124

parties in November 1985, it is the most widely ratified of the UN human rights treaties.

Discrimination on the basis of race is one of the most difficult issues of the twentieth century. Japan had created a dilemma for the Western powers when it tried unsuccessfully to have a proscription of racial discrimination included in the covenant of the League of Nations. The UN Charter speaks of human rights for all without distinction as to race, sex, language, or religion —race being placed prominently at the head of the list. Since the very first meetings of the General Assembly, the racial problems of South Africa (which led to that country's abstention in the voting on the Universal Declaration) have had a prominent place on the agenda of that body and of the other human rights organs. Interest in the matter of race was heightened with the influx of newly independent members of the UN in the early 1960s.

Racial discrimination is defined in the convention as "any distinction, exclusion, restriction or preference based on race, color, descent, or national or ethnic origin which has the purpose or effect of nullifying or impairing the recognition, enjoyment or exercise, on an equal footing, of human rights and fundamental freedoms in the political, economic, social, cultural or any other field of public life." Parties to the convention condemn racial discrimination and undertake to eliminate it and to promote understanding among all races. An interesting feature of the convention is that it permits what is often known in the United States as affirmative action, provided that such measures do not lead to the maintenance of separate rights for different racial groups and are not continued after the objectives for which they were taken have been achieved.

The Genocide Convention. Inclusion of the promotion of human rights as one of the purposes of the UN was in large measure a response to the Holocaust. It is not surprising that the Convention on the Prevention and Punishment of the Crime of Genocide was the first UN human rights treaty. It was approved by the General Assembly and opened for signature and ratification on 9 December 1948, the day before the adoption of the Universal Declaration.

The term genocide had been coined in 1944 by Raphael Lemkin to "signify a coordinated plan of different actions aimed at the destruction of essential foundations of life of national groups." Under the rubric of "crimes against humanity," this general concept had been included in the Charter of the International Military Tribunal, which set up the Nuremberg trials of the major German war criminals. Although the term genocide was not used in the charter of the tribunal, it was used several times in the course of the proceedings by the prosecutors. Resolution 96(I) adopted at the General Assembly's first session in 1946 affirmed that genocide is a "crime under international law which the civilized world condemns." According to the resolution, genocide is the denial of the right of existence of entire human groups, as homicide is the denial of the right to live of individual human beings. According to the General Assembly, "many instances of such crimes of genocide have occurred when racial, religious, political and other groups have been destroyed, entirely or in part." The drafting of the convention permitted some mischief to be wrought. While the parties to the convention confirm once again that genocide, whether committed in time of peace or in time of war, is a crime under international law that they undertake to prevent and punish, the definition of genocide is not as broad as might be expected. Article II of the convention provides that

> in the present Convention, genocide means any of the following acts committed with intent to destroy, in whole or in part, a national, ethnical, racial or religious group, as such:
>
> (a) Killing members of the group;
>
> (b) Causing serious bodily or mental harm to members of the group;
>
> (c) Deliberately inflicting on the group conditions of life calculated to bring about its physical destruction in whole or in part;
>
> (d) Imposing measures intended to prevent births within the group;
>
> (e) Forcibly transferring children of the group to another group.

The listing of the kinds of groups protected against liquidation coupled with the use of the words "as such" leaves open the possibility, understood by the drafters of the convention, that widespread killings on political grounds may not be covered by the definition. Thus, political killings in Germany that came within the notion of crimes against humanity may not be within the treaty; the Gulag Archipelago was peopled in significant part with ethnic Russians and stands outside the definition; the killings of ethnic Khmers in Democratic Kampuchea under Pol Pot, as opposed to some of the killings of minority groups, are arguably not genocide, no matter how horrible they may have been. It can be argued that such activities are contrary to the Nuremberg principles and to general human rights law, but it is unfortunate that there should be any question about whether they come within the category of the most heinous international crimes for which the term genocide was devised.

As of late 1986, almost one hundred states had become parties to the Genocide Convention. In that year, the United States Senate gave its advice and consent to the convention, but at year's end, ratification had not been completed, because the necessary implementing legislation had not been passed. The American attitudes that led to the delay in acting on the convention are discussed below.

SUPERVISION AND ENFORCEMENT

Lawyers in the Anglo-American tradition tend to see as the essence of law how breaches of the law are treated, how law is enforced. They regard as the primary technique for enforcement a court acting in response to a complaint that some violation has taken place. Clauses providing for reference to the International Court of Justice for disputes among states concerning the application of the provisions of the treaty in question appear in a number of the human rights treaties, such as the Genocide Convention, the refugee treaties, and (with some escape clauses) the 1979 Convention on the Elimination of All Forms of Discrimination Against Women. None of these provisions has ever resulted in the referral of an actual case to the International Court, for the same reasons that other kinds of state-against-state complaints are unpopular. None of the treaties permits individuals to proceed in the Court against states, but there are some procedures, such as those under the Optional Protocol to the Covenant on Civil and Political Rights, which do permit individual complaints, albeit not to a court. Much more common in the treaties are reporting provisions such as those contained in the covenants and the Race Convention, which were discussed above.

One further complaint procedure requires mention here. It is the procedure for dealing with "gross violations," which the organization carries out pursuant to its general powers under the Charter rather than pursuant to one of the later treaties.

Early in its life the Commission on Human Rights and the Economic and Social Council decided that neither the commission nor any other body had power to act on the thousands of complaints alleging violations of human rights which were being received each year by the UN. The Economic and Social Council finally pulled back from this position in its Resolution 1503 (XLVIII) of 1970. This resolution enables some action to be taken on some of these communications. The Subcommission on Prevention of Discrimination and Protection of Minorities is empowered by the resolution to appoint a working group of its members to meet in private session and bring to the attention of the subcommission those communications "which appear to reveal a consistent pattern of gross and reliably attested violations of human rights and fundamental freedoms." The subcommission, also meeting in private, may in turn refer any such communications to the Commission on Human Rights. The commission (which also operates first through a working group and in private) after examining any situation referred to it by the subcommission can determine (a) that the situation be given a "thorough study" and a report and recommendation be submitted to the Economic and Social Council, or (b) that the situation should be the "subject of an investigation by an ad hoc committee to be appointed by the Commission which shall be undertaken only with the express consent of the State concerned and shall be conducted in constant cooperation with the State and under conditions determined by agreement with it." Communications may originate from a person or group of persons claiming to be victims of gross violations, from any person or group of persons who have direct and reliable knowledge of those violations, or from nongovernmental organizations acting, in the quaint words of the resolution, "in good faith in accordance with recognized principles of human rights, not resorting to politically motivated

stands contrary to the provisions of the Charter of the United Nations and having direct and reliable knowledge of such violations." This is hardly an individual complaint procedure, and in fact most of the handful of communications that have made their way from the subcommission to the commission have been brought by significant international nongovernmental organizations. Unlike the procedure under the Optional Protocol where the complainant is consulted at each step of the way, the author of a "1503 complaint," as it is known, theoretically loses complete control over the process once the complaint is filed. But this has not stopped the organizations making the complaints from going to Geneva or New York to attend meetings of the commission and subcommission and lobbying informally, feeding information to members of the UN bodies and generally trying to drum up support for their cases. The UN organs are not like courts, where such behavior would be inappropriate. They are highly political bodies, and the only way to get them to function is to use the techniques normally used to make sure that political bodies function.

It is easy to become impatient in dealing with the UN organs exercising enforcement and supervision procedures, but it is important to remember that they all began to exercise those functions only as recently as the early 1970s, and they are still gaining experience and building momentum.

REGIONAL MEASURES

A human rights program within the UN must run the gauntlet of all the difficulties, conceptual and practical, of doing anything at the global level. Getting the agreement of some 160 states is a daunting task indeed. It is often argued that more progress is likely to be made in what is still relatively virgin territory by operating at the regional level, where common features of history and geography will encourage cooperation. There is something to this argument, as practical experience in Europe and the Americas would seem to demonstrate. As applied to other regions (the ASEAN countries, for example), such efforts are less likely to succeed. We turn to an examination of the two existing regional systems and a new one contemplated for Africa.

In force since 1953, the European Convention on Human Rights and Fundamental Freedoms contains the most sophisticated operative treaty system for the protection of human rights. It functions among the states that are members of the Council of Europe. Given those states' long tradition of the rule of law, it is not surprising that the institutions set up under the convention contain many of the features of a court structure. Two bodies are created by the convention, a Commission of Human Rights and a Court of Human Rights.

The European Commission has jurisdiction to hear complaints by one state that another is in breach of the convention and, if the state in question accepts the right of individual petition (most of them do), complaints by individuals or groups claiming to be victims of violations. The commission acts in part like a court and in part like a conciliation commission. It endeavors to find the facts and the law and to effect a friendly settlement of the matter on the basis of respect for human rights as contained in the convention. If no settlement is reached, it draws up its report, which is sent to the Committee of Ministers, the main political body of the Council of Europe. At this point either the commission or any states involved (but not individual complainants) may bring the matter to the European Court of Human Rights if the state alleged to have engaged in the violations accepts the jurisdiction of the Court. The Court then has formal hearings and renders its judgment. If the case is not referred to the Court, the Committee of Ministers will endeavor to take action on the basis of the commission's report. The commission and the court have developed an extensive body of case law that has had a significant impact on the protection of human rights in Europe.

In May 1948, seven months before the UN's adoption of the Universal Declaration of Human Rights, the member states of the Organization of American States (OAS) agreed to the American Declaration of the Rights and Duties of Man. Like the Universal Declaration, this is a nontreaty instrument. It covers essentially the same field as the Universal Declaration, encompassing both civil and political and economic, social, and cultural rights. As the title indicates, it emphasizes somewhat more than does the Universal Declaration duties to others, to the family, and to the state.

In 1960 the OAS established a Human Rights Commission. Its task was to promote the rights contained in the American declaration. Among other powers, the commission was given the power to examine complaints ("denunciations" in OAS parlance) alleging breaches of the provisions of the declaration most closely associated with danger to life and liberty. This arrangement was largely superseded in 1978 with the entry into force of the American Convention on Human Rights, which had been agreed upon in 1969. The American Convention protects mostly civil and political rights, although it has one general provision concerning the progressive development of economic, social, and cultural rights. It establishes two organs, the Inter-American Commission on Human Rights and the Inter-American Court of Human Rights, which function in roles fairly similar to their European counterparts. The main differences are that (a) in the American Convention individual complaints are automatically permitted against any states that become parties to the convention, whereas in Europe a specific acceptance must be made; and (b) the American Commission operates in a much more informal manner than the European one. The pre-1978 arrangements have not been entirely superseded because a few members of the OAS, most notably the United States, had not as of 1986 become parties to the convention. For them the commission continues to exercise the powers of the old commission in respect to the declaration. It is not possible, however, for a case involving a state that is not a party to the convention to proceed on to the court.

In June 1981 the Assembly of Heads of State and Government of the Organization of African Unity (OAU) adopted the African Charter of Human and Peoples' Rights. The charter needs ratification by half of the members of the OAU before it comes into force, and it is still well short of that. In addition to recognizing basic civil and political rights, the charter contains guarantees to economic, social, and cultural rights such as the right to work, to health, and to education. All "peoples" are said to have the right to equality, to self-determination, and to freely dispose of their wealth and natural resources. States parties also undertake to eliminate all forms of foreign economic exploitation, particularly that practiced by international monopolies. There is also a promise of "third-generation" rights to peace and to a "general satisfactory environment" that is favorable to development. Individuals are said to have duties to their families, to society, to the state, to other legally recognized communities, and to the international community. The commission that will be established to promote the rights contained in the charter has power to consider state-against-state complaints concerning violations and some kinds of individual complaints, although the charter contains many ambiguities on this point.

THE UNITED STATES AND INTERNATIONAL PROGRAMS

International Level. In the early stages of the UN program, the United States was actively involved in a leadership role in the drafting of the human rights instruments. Eleanor Roosevelt occupied the chair in the Commission on Human Rights when the Universal Declaration was being drafted. Civil and political rights were always part of the American tradition, and economic, social, and cultural rights, which were ultimately to fall into disrepute in the United States, were at the heart of Franklin D. Roosevelt's Four Freedoms speech of 1941. President Harry S. Truman duly forwarded the Genocide Convention to the Senate for its advice and consent in 1949, but that body took no action on it for thirty-seven years. The convention in fact became something of a watershed in American attitudes toward the UN human rights program. It was seen as creating a dangerous precedent for the intrusion of the treaty-making power into areas that were not a fit subject for treaties and that would, moreover, upset the delicate federal-state balance. Fears were expressed that this was the thin end of a massive wedge that would lead—via the covenants that were then being drafted—to some form of pernicious creeping socialism, with Uncle Sam footing the bill. The American Bar Association (ABA), through its inaptly named Committee on Peace and Law Through the United Nations, vigorously opposed ratification with such arguments. It was not until 1976 that the ABA finally reversed its stand. Although the Senate Foreign Affairs Committee recommended the convention to the full Senate several times during the 1970s, no final action was forthcoming until 1986, following President Ronald Reagan's 1984 call for the Senate's advice and consent. As has been mentioned, the secretary of state announced in 1953 that his administration

did not intend the United States to become a party to the covenants then being drafted. The moment that was lost in 1953 for the whole human rights program has never been regained. Presidents Kennedy and Johnson spoke of a new approach, but the only significant results of their efforts were the ratification in 1967 of the Supplementary Slavery Convention and in 1968 of the Protocol to the 1951 Convention Relating to the Status of Refugees (which effectively also meant ratification of the 1951 convention). The only UN human rights treaties that have been ratified since then are the 1952 Convention on the Political Rights of Women, ratified in 1976, and the 1979 Convention Against the Taking of Hostages, ratified in 1984. In 1978 President Jimmy Carter, who had made the international protection of human rights a strong point of policy, sought the Senate's advice and consent to ratify the two covenants, the International Convention on the Elimination of All Forms of Racial Discrimination, and the American Convention on Human Rights. As of 1986 none of these has received the imprimatur of the Senate, and any action on them in the near future appears unlikely.

Domestic Level. In *The Paquete Habana* (1900), an important case arising out of the seizure of Cuban fishing boats during the Spanish-American War, the Supreme Court affirmed that international law, both treaty law and customary law, is part of the domestic law of the United States and must be "ascertained and applied" by the courts where appropriate. "For this purpose," the Court said, "where there is no treaty, and no controlling executive or legislative act or judicial decision, resort must be had to the customs and usages of civilized nations." Moreover, Article VI, paragraph 2 of the Constitution gives treaties equal status with federal statutes as the "supreme law of the land." In practice, the courts have not taken the language of the Constitution literally but have drawn a distinction between self-executing treaties (which become the law of the land without further action by Congress) and non-self-executing ones (which do not). The distinction can be elusive. It is clear that a treaty that requires the appropriation of money (such as the UN Charter) or the creation of a criminal offense (such as the Genocide Convention) will be treated as requiring legislative execution. Vague, general language may be treated as non-self-executing, but not necessarily. The matter is extremely important for human rights treaties. If a treaty is self-executing, it follows that individuals might acquire rights or obligations pursuant to it that could be directly enforced in the courts. If it is not, then any rights acquired through American ratification will be enforceable (if at all) only on the international plane. Opponents of international human rights programs tend to regard the possibility of the treaties being self-executing as anathema. When President Carter sent the various treaties to the Senate in 1978, he endeavored to forestall the problem by including with the proposed statement of ratification a "declaration" to the effect that the treaties were not self-executing.

Execution or nonexecution is only part of the story, as indeed is ratification or nonratification. A treaty that is non-self-executing, an unratified treaty, a nontreaty instrument, and custom can all provide standards to which a court might look to give concrete meaning to such general parameters as the due process and equal protection clauses of the federal Constitution or their counterparts in state constitutions. Because the United States is not a party to any of the major human rights treaties, the question of their execution is moot. In the early years of the UN, however, efforts were made in a number of cases to apply the human rights provisions of the UN Charter itself, either as a self-executing law or as standards for constitutional interpretation. In *Oyama* v. *California* (1948) the United States Supreme Court struck down, as violative of the equal protection clause of the Fourteenth Amendment to the Constitution, certain procedural provisions of the California Alien Land Law that effectively discriminated against American citizens of Japanese descent. Four judges concurring in the result noted Articles 55 and 56 of the Charter as a separate ground for their decision, apparently accepting that they were self-executing. In *Namba* v. *McCourt* (1949) the Supreme Court of Oregon struck down the substance of an Alien Land Law under the equal protection clause of the Fourteenth Amendment, using the Charter provisions to infuse the clause with meaning.

Oyama was the high-water mark for the Charter in the federal courts. *Shelley* v. *Kraemer* (1948) concerned the enforcement of racially restrictive covenants attached to real estate. The international issues were squarely presented to the Supreme Court in several briefs, most notably one filed on behalf of the American Association for the United Nations. But the Court chose to pass over the Charter arguments in complete silence as it struck down such covenants on the basis that state court enforcement of them constituted state action that violated the equal protection clause of the Fourteenth Amendment. It is not known why the members of the Court who had embraced the Charter in *Oyama* did not persist, but the brush-off continued and the great civil rights litigation of the 1950s and 1960s proceeded without reference to the Charter.

At the state level, *Namba* was overshadowed by the decision of the Supreme Court of California in *Sei Fujii* v. *State* (1952). The California District Court of Appeals had struck down the substance of the California Alien Land Law on the basis of the Charter and (arguably) the Universal Declaration. The Supreme Court, holding that the law contravened the equal protection clause, went on to hold that the Charter provisions were non-self-executing, apparently on the ground that they were too vague. Yet it is hard to believe that the equal protection of the laws clause of the federal Constitution is any less vague. The Court even declined to take the middle ground, occupied by the Oregon court in *Namba,* of using the Charter to illuminate the equal protection clause.

The Supreme Court of California is a leader among the nation's state courts, and its decision in *Sei Fujii* was regarded as gospel for a couple of decades. It is only in the past few years that serious arguments based upon UN and OAS materials have again begun appearing in civil rights cases. A much-discussed example of this is *Filartiga* v. *Pena-Irala* (1980). Dr. Joel Filartiga and his daughter Dolly claimed that Pena-Irala, a former police inspector general of Paraguay, had under color of state authority tortured their son and brother, Joelito, to death. Pena-Irala was discovered in New York, and proceedings were commenced in federal district court. The suit was for wrongful death and asserted that the acts in question had been "committed in violation of the law of nations." This was designed to bring the case, for jurisdictional purposes, within section 1350 of Title 28 of the United States Code, which provides that "the district courts shall have original jurisdiction of any civil action by an alien for a tort only, committed in violation of the law of nations or a treaty of the United States." The United States Court of Appeals for the Second Circuit held that torture was a tort contrary to the law of nations and that accordingly there was jurisdiction in the district court. In its reasoning, the Court seemed to accept that Articles 55 and 56 of the Charter are not self-executing, so that no treaty obligation was involved. It relied, however, upon the Charter, the Universal Declaration, the 1975 Declaration by the General Assembly on the Protection of All Persons from Being Subjected to Torture, the American Convention, the European Convention, the Covenant on Civil and Political Rights, and constitutional prohibitions in the laws of some fifty-five countries for the proposition that torture was condemned by international custom. Meanwhile, Pena-Irala, who had overstayed his visa, was deported in spite of the Filartigas' efforts to keep him in the country. The trial judge entered a default judgment when Pena-Irala did not appear personally or by counsel in subsequent proceedings. The court made an award of $200,000 for compensation plus $5 million in punitive damages in the case of the father and $175,000 for compensation plus $5 million in punitive damages in the case of the sister. In addition, $10,364 in costs were awarded. It is unlikely that the money will ever be collected, but the vindication of rights involved appears to be of tremendous cathartic significance to the plaintiffs.

In addition to demonstrating that human rights arguments could at last be taken seriously in the courts, the *Filartiga* case gave some promise that American courts might on occasion be useful forums for litigating human rights violations that occurred elsewhere. This promise was not fulfilled in *Tel-Oren* v. *Libyan Arab Republic* (1984). Survivors and representatives of persons murdered in an attack on a civilian bus in Israel sued Libya, the Palestine Liberation Organization (PLO), and organizations allegedly associated with them in the United States, asserting their joint responsibility for the attack. It was clear that Libya was immune from suit under the doctrine of sovereign immunity and that its connection with the organizations other than the PLO was tenuous. Thus, the most important question was whether the PLO was amenable to suit in United States federal court. The trial judge dismissed the action on the basis that the district court had no jurisdiction over the subject matter and that the claim was in any event barred by the applicable statute of limitations. Jurisdic-

tion was lacking, in the trial court's view, both because it was not established that the same consensus had been reached for terrorism as was the case for torture, namely, that it was contrary to international law, and because even if terrorism were contrary to international law, a private right of action was not conferred by international law as a remedy for breach of such rules of international law.

Each of the three judges who heard the appeal to the District of Columbia circuit court agreed that the action should be dismissed, but their reasoning differed widely, and the case represents a primer for all the difficulties that still face an effort to litigate breaches of human rights law in the domestic courts. Judge Edwards approved strongly of the reasoning in *Filartiga* but saw it as crucial to that decision that Pena-Irala was acting in his capacity as a state official—even if what he did was theoretically illegal under Paraguayan law. In Judge Edwards's view, international law does not impose the same responsibility or liability on nonstate actors, such as the PLO, as it does on states and persons acting under color of state law. Judge Edwards also took the same position as the trial judge that terrorism has not yet become condemned by international law in the same way that torture has. He thus agreed to the dismissal of the action. He did not, however, agree with the trial judge's opinion that it would be necessary for international law to confer a right of action. In his view the question of what kind of remedy is provided in domestic law for breaches of international law is left by international law to the state concerned. Given the array of legal systems in the world, a consensus would be virtually impossible to reach, especially on the technical aspects of such an action. Requiring such a consensus would effectively nullify such statutes as Section 1350, which provided the potential jurisdictional basis in federal court. Judge Bork was critical of the *Filartiga* decision because it did not address the question whether international law created a cause of action that the parties could enforce in a "municipal" (that is, noninternational) court. He insisted also that because of its politically sensitive nature the *Tel-Oren* case was not a proper one for federal court adjudication unless there was a clear grant of a cause of action somewhere in the international material. Because he could find no support in international law for a right of action, he agreed that the case should be dismissed. Judge Robb, the third judge, did not believe that the case was a suitable one at all for a court. He believed that it was a political matter and nonjusticiable.

Tel-Oren probably shows the outer limits of the use of international human rights law in United States courts. The scholarly nature of the opinions by Judges Edwards and Bork attests, however, to the serious way in which the subject is again being considered. International human rights law has been taught in a careful and professional way in many American law schools since the mid-1970s, and one can be certain that there will be many more attempts to weave it into the fabric of the American judicial system in coming years.

CASES

Filartiga v. Pena-Irala, 630 F.2d 876 2nd Cir. (1980)
Filartiga v. Pena-Irala, 577 F.Supp. 860 E.D.N.Y. (1984)
Namba v. McCourt, 185 Or. 579, 204 P.2d. 569 (1949)
Oyama v. California, 332 U.S. 633 (1948)
The Paquete Habana, 175 U.S. 677 (1900)
Sei Fujii v. State, 38 Cal. 2d 718, 242 P.2d 617 (1952)
Shelley v. Kraemer, 334 U.S. 1 (1948)
Tel-Oren v. Libyan Arab Republic, 726 F.2d 774 D.C. Cir. (1984)

BIBLIOGRAPHY

Ian Brownlie, *Basic Documents of Human Rights* (1981), contains many documents and some useful references. David P. Forsythe, *Human Rights and World Politics* (1983), is one of the best introductory texts. Hurst Hannum, ed., *Guide to International Human Rights Practice* (1984), is an excellent how-to book for the activist who wants to make best use of international and domestic procedures for the promotion and protection of human rights. *Human Rights Internet Reporter,* based in Washington, D.C., is an indispensible tool for keeping current in the field. James Avery Joyce, *Human Rights: International Documents* (1978), gives valuable selections of source material.

Hersh Lauterpacht, *International Law and Human Rights* (1950), is a classic study by one of the leading international law scholars of our century. Raphael Lemkin, *Axis Rule in Occupied Europe* (1944), is a classic from the originator of the term *genocide.* Richard B. Lillich and Frank C. Newman, *International Human Rights: Problems of Law and Policy* (1979), gives good teaching materials widely used in law schools. Bert Lockwood, Jr., "The United Nations Charter and United States Civil Rights Litigation: 1946–1955," in *Iowa Law Review* (1984), provides a thorough study of early efforts to make use of international human rights materials in United States courts.

Myres S. McDougal, Harold D. Lasswell, and Lung-chu Chen, *Human Rights and World Public Order: The Basic Policies of an International Law of Human Dignity* (1980), offers a "policy science" approach to the subject crammed full of useful references. A. Glenn Mower, Jr., *The United States, the United Nations and Human Rights: The Eleanor Roosevelt and Jimmy Carter Eras* (1979), is a good introductory text that emphasizes policy issues.

Adamantia Pollis and Peter Schwab, eds., *Human Rights: Cultural and Ideological Perspectives* (1979), selects a useful collection of addresses and essays widely used in political science courses. Louis B. Sohn and Thomas Buergenthal, *International Protection of Human Rights* (1973), gives an absolute mine of source material and references in an indispensable research tool.

Vernon Van Dyke, *Human Rights, the United States and World Community* (1970), is a very stimulating introductory text. Karel Vasak, ed., *The International Dimensions of Human Rights* (1982), collects very interesting essays along with a good bibliography and a chart of parties to human rights treaties.

[*See also* EQUAL PROTECTION CLAUSE.]

JUVENILE LAW

Victor L. Streib

FUNDAMENTAL to the American judicial system is the premise that "children have a very special place in life which law should reflect" (*May* v. *Anderson,* 1953). Children are significantly different from adults in many important ways and simply cannot be shuttled mindlessly into adult legal processes. Law has reflected the unique nature of childhood in many ways, both for children who are offenders and for children who are victims.

This essay on juvenile law focuses primarily upon the juvenile justice system. The system has responsibility for protecting children and the general public from harm while observing a very intricate network of legal rights and procedures for those involved.

The juvenile justice system appears in many different guises to those who come into contact with it. Children arrested for misbehavior and brought before a stern judge may perceive the system as being the same as the punitive adult criminal justice system but on a smaller scale. For parents who bring their errant children to the juvenile court as a last resort, the system may appear to be the superparent who can discipline even the most exasperating teenager. For others who are drawn into it as complainants, witnesses, and consultants, the system may appear to be dominated by law and lawyers to the exclusion of logic and rationality. Each observation is warranted, for the juvenile justice system is all of those things, and more. This essay provides a range of information about this perplexing sociolegal system.

HISTORY AND PHILOSOPHY OF JUVENILE JUSTICE

The first formal juvenile court was created in Chicago in 1899, but even before that, children had received special treatment under the law. Because of their immaturity, children under seven could not be convicted of crimes under English and American criminal law. Children between seven and fourteen years of age could not be convicted unless the government proved that they had an adult's ability to have criminal intent. Even when a child was convicted in criminal court, his sentence commonly was less severe than that which an adult would have received.

Early juvenile institutions were exemplified by the New York House of Refuge (established 1825) and the Chicago Reform School (1855). These and similar later institutions were founded to avoid harsh criminal penalties for child offenders and to provide conventionally approved moral, ethical, political, and social values and role models for deprived, unfortunate children. The juvenile court was a product of social and political movements from the 1890s through the early 1900s. Some have characterized those movements as progressive child-welfare movements reaching out to rescue children from the harsh criminal justice system (Besharov). Others have suggested that these movements were simply looking for mechanisms to impose middle-class values upon poor and powerless children (Platt). Whatever the motives for its creation, the juvenile court idea took root and spread throughout the country. By 1912, about half of the states had juvenile justice legislation; by 1925, all but two states had juvenile courts. The juvenile court concept remains strong today, with about thirty-five hundred courts presently hearing juvenile cases in the United States (Fox).

Until 1967, the juvenile justice system operated under a concept of law and justice fundamentally different from other American judicial systems. Instead of reacting to violations of law or providing a forum for resolution of legal disputes, the socialized juvenile justice system attempted to intervene before serious violations of law occurred. This approach involved predicting the future behavior of a child rather than deliberating over evidence of a child's past criminal acts. It was designed to offer approximately the same care, custody, and discipline that a loving parent would offer to a child.

The socialized juvenile justice system adapted the medical treatment model applied to troubled children: "early identification, diagnosis, prescription of treatment, implementation of therapy, and cure or rehabilitation under aftercare supervision" (Faust and Brantingham). The emphasis was not upon punishment but upon rescue. Acting in the capacity of a foster parent, the state might well expect almost absolute obedience to its parental admonitions. The concept of the child having extensive rights to effectively challenge such foster guidance and care was foreign to the system. Parents have, within very wide guidelines, total, unchallengeable authority to force the child to do what the parents see as best for the child. Thus, when a special legal system was being established to act in behalf of parents, it is not surprising that a similar unchallengeable authority was given to it.

The socialized juvenile justice system was functionally much like the present constitutionalized system except for the legal procedures required by *In re Gault* (1967) and its progeny. All of the basic functions were performed in the socialized system that are performed in the constitutionalized one, albeit in a much more informal and perfunctory manner. The socialized system simply left presentation of the child's side of the case to the same police officer or probation officer responsible for presentation of the state's side of the case.

The socialized system split from the comparatively legalistic criminal justice system in 1899 and spent perhaps the first thirty or forty years of its life trying to match its rhetoric with action. It progressively became more socialized in that it tried new and individualized treatment techniques to react to delinquency. The constitutionalized system also offered more rhetoric than action during the first few years of its life; it has only more recently become what could be called truly legalistic or constitutionalized.

The constitutionalized era of the juvenile justice system began in 1967, the year the Supreme Court decided *In re Gault.* After *Gault,* all juvenile courts were required to follow certain constitutional guidelines. Some juvenile courts had followed such legalistic guidelines before 1967, and the constitutionalization of the system had been anticipated in 1966 by the Supreme Court in *Kent* v. *United States:*

> While there can be no doubt of the original laudable purpose of juvenile courts, studies and critiques in recent years raise serious questions as to whether actual performance measures well enough against theoretical purpose to make tolerable the immunity of the process from the reach of constitutional guaranties applicable to adults. . . . There is evidence, in fact, that there may be grounds for concern that the child receives the worst of both worlds: that he gets neither the protections accorded to adults nor the solicitous care and regenerative treatment postulated for children.

Within a few years of *Gault,* the Supreme Court had decided other major cases dealing with the juvenile justice system. *In re Winship* (1970) held that proof beyond a reasonable doubt in delinquency cases is among the essentials of due process and fair treatment required by *Gault.*

In *Kent, Gault,* and *Winship,* the Supreme Court revised fundamental premises of the juvenile justice system. No longer were juvenile court judges permitted to ignore constitutionally mandated procedures in order to do what they thought best for the child. The Court concluded that the system was incapable of matching action with rhetoric, largely because of the significant gap between social scientists' aspirations and knowledge, on the one hand, and the apparent lack of funding and personnel to implement the available knowledge, on the other.

These procedural requirements had a profound effect upon the operant philosophy and ambience of the juvenile court process. Assurance of representation by an attorney meant that the hearings were converted from informal conferences into adversarial contests quite similar to a criminal trial. Proof requirements meant an increased focus upon the elements of the offenses charged and a correspondingly decreased emphasis upon the child.

However, in *McKeiver* v. *Pennsylvania* (1971), the Court held that trial by jury in the juvenile adjudicatory hearing is not a constitutional requirement. In *McKeiver* there seems to be a re-kindling of faith in the ability of the juvenile justice system to achieve its goals. The current Court is making an effort to establish a middle ground between the parental and the constitutional modes of juvenile justice. This perspective was used by the Supreme Court in *Schall* v. *Martin* (1984): "We have tried, therefore, to strike a balance—to respect the 'informality' and 'flexibility' that characterize juvenile proceedings—and yet to ensure that such proceedings comport with the 'fundamental fairness' demanded by the Due Process Clause.''

The philosophical premises of the original juvenile courts have not been immune from political and social pressures. The blind faith placed in juvenile court judges always to do the best for the child has come under criticism (Streib, 1978). The notion of coerced treatment came more and more to be equated with punishment, despite official disclaimers to the contrary (Forer). Individualized treatment for each child came to be seen as rife with abuse of discretion and as resulting in grossly unequal handling of similar children and similar offenses (Fox, 1981).

The juvenile justice system of the 1980s retains the essence of its earlier self but in the context of constitutional limitations. Its procedures have been brought into line with criminal court procedures, and the focus is somewhat more on punishment and prevention than solely on the treatment of errant children. More serious juvenile offenders are being shunted out of juvenile court to criminal court, and very minor offenders are being handled informally outside of juvenile court. However, the juvenile court continues to process the broad midsection of juvenile offenders and to view them in a more parental, clinical manner than the adult criminal court does.

CHILDREN AS OFFENDERS

The concept of children as offenders encompasses the instances in which persons under the juvenile court age limit (usually age eighteen) commit acts that harm or threaten to harm the persons and/or property of others or, in some cases, of themselves. Most of these acts would be crimes, but they are not treated as such solely because the actors are still children. Children as offenders are to be distinguished from children who are victims either of the acts of others or of circumstances in general. Children as victims are discussed later. This essay surveys various delinquent acts and status offenses, including several defenses recognized by juvenile courts. Traffic offenses and serious criminal offenses are also considered here.

Traffic Offenses. Originally, juvenile court laws in many states treated traffic offenses no differently from other juvenile offenses. The inclusion of traffic offenses within juvenile court jurisdiction has come under considerable criticism. One reason is the widely held view that a typical, routine traffic offense does not necessitate major juvenile court intervention to effect rehabilitative treatment of young drivers. The other reason is the work load that the heavy volume of traffic cases involving sixteen- and seventeen-year-old drivers creates, preventing juvenile courts from providing each child with personalized, individual attention.

The current trend is to relegate less-serious traffic offenses to traffic court. The teenaged driver is treated just as an adult driver would be. More-serious traffic offenses, such as reckless homicide, tend to remain in juvenile court and are processed as regular delinquency cases. Some jurisdictions allow the trial proceedings to be held in either the juvenile court or the traffic court, but the Supreme Court has made it clear that trials in both courts for the same offense would be unconstitutional (*Breed* v. *Jones*, 1975).

Status Offenses. This category of juvenile offenses is labeled differently from state to state but tends to include the same kind of acts and statuses. Other labels often used are *persons in need of supervision* (PINS), *children in need of supervision* (ChINS), *wayward children, undisciplined children,* and *unruly children.* All of these cover a range of noncriminal behaviors by children and may account for up to one-half of the total work load of juvenile courts (McCarthy and Carr). Behaviors included as status offenses are failure of a child to subject himself to the reasonable control of his parents, teachers, guardian, or custodian, by reason of being wayward or habitually disobedient; habitual truancy from home or school; and deportment that injures or endangers the health or morals of the child or others.

Status offenses are comparatively vague, broad, all-encompassing behaviors that could easily be interpreted to include the behavior, at some time, of every child. As a result, juvenile courts have essentially unchecked power to find almost any child to be a status offender. The juvenile courts also have power to order almost the same dispositions for status offenders as for delinquents. Thus, status-offender jurisdiction remains broad and sweeping as compared to the comparatively narrow delinquency jurisdiction.

Delinquency Offenses. An act of delinquency is defined generally as a violation of a state or local criminal law. That is, it is an act that would be a crime if committed by an adult. The elements of the offense are proven in the same manner as they would be for an adult in criminal court, with the only significant difference being the age of the defendant-respondent.

Some states have limited this broad definition of delinquency by excluding the most serious and/or the most minor criminal offenses. Such jurisdictions will exclude, for example, any criminal offense punishable by death or life imprisonment. At the other end of the scale, some jurisdictions exclude such minor crimes as traffic offenses and fish and game law violations. Children violating such laws are handled directly by a misdemeanor court with jurisdiction over those offenses.

Several states include as acts of delinquency the violation of a federal law or of another state's law even though such acts may not be violations of the subject's state law. A few states continue the now largely outmoded policy of including under delinquency such conduct as truancy, disobedience, and running away, which today most commonly constitute the separate category of status offenses.

Some acts of delinquency are law violations that apply only to children. Violations of curfew laws by minors is the most common example, but others include possession of air guns or drinking alcohol. While these acts of delinquency are violations of state law, they obviously are not acts that would be crimes if committed by adults.

Serious Criminal Offenses. Some states, such as Louisiana, expressly exclude certain offenses from juvenile court jurisdiction and place them within criminal court jurisdiction, regardless of the age of the offender. Such offenses include murder, manslaughter, rape, robbery, burglary, and kidnapping. Other states, such as North Carolina, place all cases in criminal court if the offender could receive the death penalty and is age fourteen or older.

If the child is prosecuted in criminal court for a serious criminal offense, the case proceeds essentially as it would for an adult. The child receives all of the rights and protections of adult criminal defendants but also faces all of the adult criminal sentences. Except for the special substantive law defenses described in the next section, the youth of the defendant is ignored.

Exclusion of serious criminal offenses from juvenile court jurisdiction appears to be, for these offenses, a rejection of rehabilitation and an embracing of retribution and deterrence. The retribution premise underlying harsh criminal penalties is that the community is always outraged by serious offenses, regardless of the age of the offender, and feels the need to express its social and moral condemnation through severe punishment of the offender.

The deterrence premise assumes that such severe punishments will deter everyone, including children, from committing serious offenses. Infliction of a severe punishment upon a particular child will convince that child never to repeat that offense. Retribution and deterrence are the primary foundations of criminal sanctions for adults and, in some cases, are also imposed upon persons under the juvenile court age limit.

JURISDICTIONAL AND SUBSTANTIVE LAW DEFENSES

Many state statutes and several model statutes require a court determination that a child needs treatment before that court can go on to find either an act of delinquency or a status offense. This is not the right to treatment that is part of juvenile court disposition but a much earlier determination of the child's need for treatment even before the court takes control of the matter.

This requirement stems from the treatment orientation of the juvenile court, the premise being that the juvenile court should not concern itself with children who do not need treatment. Thus comes the requirement that a need for treatment be found before the juvenile court may act. This preliminary finding of a need for treatment has been more of a rhetorical ideal than a practical bar to juvenile court action.

Closely related to the need-for-treatment consideration is the defense of insanity as it has been developed in adult criminal court. Legal insanity at the time of the crime is generally accepted as a defense to conviction of an adult crime. The result is that the adult criminal court must find the person not guilty and turn the case over to a civil commitment process for the dangerously mentally ill. If that civil process finds the person still to be dangerously mentally ill, the person will be committed to a hospital for the criminally insane.

In juvenile court, the same reasoning seems applicable if the issue is whether the juvenile knew what he or she was doing at the time of the delinquent acts. However, use of the insanity defense in juvenile court has been sporadic and nonuniform across the states and, in several cases, has been rejected so as to support juvenile court attempts to help the child.

Minimum- and maximum-age limitations also are critical to juvenile court jurisdiction and authority. Since juvenile courts handle children and not adults, an age line must be drawn between childhood and adulthood. For more than two-thirds of the states, the maximum age is established as eighteen. Juvenile court has jurisdiction only over those persons who were under the age of eighteen at the time their offense was committed.

The minimum-age limit is not so clearly established. Under early English common law and modern American criminal law, children under the age of seven always were excluded from criminal court jurisdiction, and children under fourteen were excluded unless the prosecution could prove they were mature enough to have adult criminal intent. Some states, such as California, have imposed this principle upon juvenile courts.

Most states have not addressed the minimum-age question but simply as a matter of practice do not process cases with very young children. However, one study has verified that surprisingly young children, even those aged seven to nine, are being handled occasionally by juvenile courts (Sametz).

JUVENILE COURT JURISDICTION AND PROCEDURES

When children within the age limits of juvenile court jurisdiction commit acts of delin-

quency or status offenses, the juvenile justice system usually has the authority to process them accordingly. However, most such juvenile offenses never come to the attention of the system and thus no legal procedures ensue. It is the rare adult who never committed any offenses as a child, even minor shoplifting, disobedience to parents, jaywalking, skipping classes at school, or drinking beer. However, very few were reported to the police or the juvenile court for these common adolescent behaviors. Thus, the initial premise is that most delinquent and status offenses never come to the attention of the juvenile justice system. For those that do, a fairly detailed and complex process is followed.

Precourt and Extracourt Procedures. It is not unusual for juveniles and their parents voluntarily to contact the police juvenile officer or the juvenile probation officer without an arrest or a request to appear. In these cases they are seeking help, which they believe those agencies can provide. Most often the family is referred to other social service agencies for the assistance they request. In some cases official court action is deemed necessary. If so, the process will continue in juvenile court, and the juveniles will have waived any right to object to the means by which they came to the court's attention.

Before considering the procedures by which a juvenile may be taken into custody, forcibly if necessary, it should be noted that in a majority of cases in which the police could make an arrest they instead divert the would-be cases to handling by informal means. That is, they have sufficient legal grounds to arrest a juvenile but nevertheless decide that such an arrest would not be the best way to handle the youth's misbehavior. In lieu of an arrest, the police will give the juvenile an oral reprimand, send him home, perhaps issue him a warning notice of some sort, or just tell him to get help from various community agencies. This informal adjustment of juvenile cases has always been very common in most jurisdictions.

In a more-serious case or one involving a child who has committed past offenses or who is particularly uncooperative with police, the child may be taken into police custody. The primary legal requirement that must be met before the child can be taken into custody is probable cause that an offense has been committed and that this particular child committed the offense. Probable cause is a level of evidence or certainty that would lead a reasonable person to believe that the child committed the offense.

The arrest of a child is not significantly different from the arrest of an adult. Considerable physical force can be used to effect the arrest, up to and including deadly force if absolutely necessary, although this is rare. Along with the arrest there is a wide variety of police investigative activities necessary to gather evidence for use in the case being prepared against the juvenile. This may involve, for example, search of the child's person, home, car, or school locker. These searches usually require probable cause to believe that seizable items exist in those places, with the concept of probable cause being at a level of certainty similar to that of probable cause for arrest.

Some searches and seizures do not require independent probable cause. If the child is arrested, the police have the authority automatically to search the child at the time of the arrest. Searches of the child's room in the parent's home can be effected by gaining the consent of the parents, even if it is over the objection of the child. Searches of school lockers can be conducted by school officials who have master keys and, thus, access to all school property.

Police questioning of a juvenile is controlled generally by the Constitution. While not perfectly clear, it would seem that the police must give the required warnings prior to custodial questioning, which include the right to remain silent and the right to have an attorney present during questioning (*Fare* v. *Michael C.,* 1979). Some states prohibit questioning of children if their parents are not present. Others require that the child first consult with an attorney before being allowed to make any statement.

Juvenile courts have been quite reluctant to allow police to photograph juvenile detainees or to fingerprint them, but this is being relaxed somewhat. As for lineup identification procedures, the juvenile will have a right to counsel present at the lineup only if it occurs at a stage after the juvenile has been formally charged with an offense. The right to counsel does not apply to situations in which the juvenile and the victim or witness are brought together in an early confrontation for identification purposes.

Local laws most frequently require the police to contact the child's parents and a juvenile probation officer promptly if the child has been taken into custody. In the majority of cases, the parents come to the police station or the juvenile center and pick up their child after promising to bring the child to subsequent meetings and hearings with juvenile court personnel. Juveniles usually do not have the adult right to post bail; the juvenile's release to parents is thought to suffice.

If there are no parents to take the child, if the child's parents refuse to take the child, or if the situation is so serious that release seems inappropriate, the child may be detained pending further proceedings. The initial decision to do this is made on the spot by a juvenile probation officer, but soon thereafter a detention hearing is held before the juvenile court judge.

The decision to detain the child usually stems from a belief that the child would not appear for subsequent hearings or that the child will commit more offenses after release. The belief that defendants would not appear for subsequent proceedings is a historically accepted reason for denying pretrial release to juveniles or bail to adults. In addition, the policy of denying pretrial release to juveniles to prevent interim offenses was approved as constitutionally acceptable by the Supreme Court in *Schall.* Such pretrial detention of juveniles is permitted in almost all states today.

Initiation of Juvenile Court Jurisdiction. The foregoing description of police procedures presumed that the subject is under the juvenile court age but that a juvenile court case had not yet been formally initiated. If the police decide to process the case, it is referred to the juvenile court. Usually the next step is the intake hearing, conducted by the juvenile probation officer on behalf of the juvenile court judge.

The intake hearing is the first stage of the juvenile court process; here potential cases are screened for appropriateness for further, more formal action. Typically, the juvenile probation officer meets with the child and parents to discuss the police charges. The child is asked to give his or her side of the story, and all try to determine whether or not formal court action will be necessary to resolve the matter.

Many, if not most, cases are diverted from formal court action at this juncture and sent off to various community agencies for informal counseling and treatment. However, court officials retain the right and power to reactivate the case and send it on to juvenile court should the informal diversion prove ineffective or should the child refuse to cooperate.

An informal juvenile justice system exists parallel to, and often in competition with, the formal one. The informal system involves numerous social service agencies, which serve the young people of a community but are not necessarily a regular part of the formal system. Such agencies receive referrals from formal juvenile agencies and include youth service bureaus, drug-abuse counselors, community mental health clinics, and regular probation officers acting in an unofficial capacity in supervising a child under "informal probation."

The informal juvenile justice system performs all the same functions and tasks as the formal system but does so in a much less restricted, legalistic, and procedurally defined fashion. For example, the decision as to the truth of an allegation is not made by a judge in a courtroom after a hearing but is made by a probation officer or other counselor in a closed conference after a brief discussion. The choice of the most appropriate disposition for the child is made in a similar fashion. Often the formal system serves as a backstop for the informal system, allowing system agents to threaten taking the case through the formal system if the child does not cooperate for the informal one.

If the case is not diverted at the intake hearing, the probation officer initiates a formal juvenile court petition under the authority of the juvenile court judge. This juvenile petition establishes a formal prosecution of the juvenile in a court of law.

In delinquency cases, the juvenile petition alleges that the child violated certain specific laws on a certain date in a certain place in a certain manner. Status-offender petitions are somewhat less specific but also allege the violation that is the basis of the case. It is these allegations that become the focus of the subsequent adjudication hearing in juvenile court, so accuracy and provability are crucial to the progress of the case.

Trying Juveniles in Adult Criminal Court. Even though the children committing the offenses are chronologically under the age limit for juvenile court, several means exist by which their cases could be processed in adult criminal court rather than in juvenile court. The consequences of a change to adult criminal court are enormous.

While juvenile court is limited to ordering probation or perhaps institutionalization until the child is age twenty-one, the criminal court has the full range of criminal sentences available to it even for young teenage offenders, including long terms in prison and even the death penalty. In fact, since the Republic was founded, 275 juveniles have been executed, and as of March 1986, there were 32 juveniles on death row, including 4 who were only fifteen at the time of their crimes.

Some states have always excluded some very serious law violations from juvenile court jurisdiction. In these instances the case against the child is filed directly in adult court.

An alternative method by which the case could be filed directly in adult criminal court is illustrated by those few states that give the prosecuting attorney the discretion to file cases either in juvenile court or in adult criminal court. When, for example, a child commits a very serious criminal act, such as murder or rape, it is left up to the local prosecuting attorney whether to prepare a juvenile petition alleging an act of delinquency or a criminal charge alleging a crime.

The first alternative for direct filing is mandated by the state legislature that enacted the statute requiring certain cases to be always handled by adult criminal court, regardless of the characteristics of the child offender. The second alternative for direct filing leaves that decision to the prosecutor to make on a case-by-case basis. Neither leaves much leverage in the hands of the child or attorney or gives the juvenile court the ability to receive a case it thinks is appropriate for juvenile jurisdiction.

The juvenile court may also waive its jurisdiction over the case and transfer the case to adult court. This process begins with the filing of a juvenile court petition as previously described. For cases involving very serious offenses by juveniles who are very near the maximum juvenile court age and have a record of past offenses, the prosecutor may file a motion in juvenile court to transfer the case to adult criminal court.

The first case in which the Supreme Court directly considered juvenile justice issues involved this waiver and transfer process. In *Kent,* the Court required that juvenile courts considering transfer of juvenile cases to criminal court must hold a hearing, determine the facts of the case, give reasons for any decision to transfer, and allow the juvenile's attorney free access to reports and other evidence being considered. This procedure ensures that a fairly thorough consideration will be made before any juvenile case is waived to criminal court.

Juvenile Court Adjudication Procedures. In juvenile court a trial is referred to as an adjudication hearing. A full hearing may not actually be held in many cases because the prosecutor and the defense attorney commonly plea-bargain a consent agreement in which the child admits the offenses in return for a more desirable disposition. While plea bargaining is not as pervasive in juvenile justice as it is in criminal justice, it still is an important means by which a large number of juvenile cases are handled.

If the adjudication hearing is held, it is quite similar in procedure to the criminal court trial. The prosecutor presents the evidence for the state tending to prove that the juvenile committed the offenses alleged in the petition, and the defense counters with evidence tending to cast doubt on that evidence. Prior to 1967 this hearing was quite informal and seldom involved legal evidence or lawyers. In 1967, however, the Supreme Court imposed the requirements of constitutional due process upon the juvenile court's adjudication hearing *(In re Gault).* These constitutional requirements include the right to counsel for the juvenile, the right to notice of the charges and hearings, the right to confront and cross-examine opposing witnesses, and the right to remain silent and not to testify against oneself.

These basic procedural rights were bolstered in 1970 when the Supreme Court decided that delinquency cases must be proven beyond a reasonable doubt by the state, the same level of proof required in adult criminal cases *(In re Winship).* Since the general rules of evidence from criminal court also are followed in juvenile court, these juvenile adjudication hearings are now almost indistinguishable from criminal trials.

The one key difference for juvenile cases is that the Constitution does not require that they be decided by juries *(McKeiver).* Thus, in almost all states the adjudication hearing is presented to the juvenile court judge alone, who returns the verdict and decides upon the proper sentence or disposition. Also, juvenile hearings are almost always closed to the public.

Evidence is presented at adjudication hearings much as it is at any trial. The prosecutor will normally call witnesses and present physical evidence, and the defense attorney will cross-examine the witnesses and challenge the evidence. The roles then switch, with defense attorneys presenting their case and prosecutors doing the challenging.

At the conclusion of the adjudicatory hearing, the juvenile court judge decides whether or not the state has proven its case. If the case has been proven, the court finds the child to be either a delinquent or a status offender. If the case has not been proven, the judge releases the child from any custody and stops further proceedings. While the terminology is different from the criminal court's "guilty" and "not guilty," the functional results are the same.

Juvenile Court Disposition Procedures. If the child has been adjudicated to be a delinquent or a status offender, then the juvenile justice process moves into the sentencing, or dispositional, stage. During the period between the adjudication hearing and the disposition hearing, the probation officers prepare a social history or presentence report. This report documents the child's family environment, school record, past offenses, or problems known to the court, and similar information. If community or state resources permit, the child may undergo various psychological tests and evaluations to determine amenability to various modes of treatment. This information is put into the social history report, which then serves as the most important item of evidence relied upon by the judge at the disposition hearing.

The disposition hearing is typically scheduled a few days or weeks after the adjudication hearing in order to give all concerned ample time to gather evidence concerning the most appropriate disposition for the child. In addition to the probation officer's social history report and disposition recommendation, the juvenile court considers evidence and disposition recommendations presented by the juvenile's attorney, the parents, and anyone else knowledgeable about the child.

The juvenile court is not permitted to choose a juvenile disposition designed to punish the child for wrongdoing; it may only treat and rehabilitate children, not punish them. Therefore, in choosing the best disposition for a particular child, the court must shun the pressure from some sources to "get tough" with juveniles and punish them for what often are very serious offenses against people and their property. This treatment-not-punishment limitation continues to be a source of misunderstanding for the general public and many critics.

The dispositional alternatives available to the juvenile court judge in delinquency and status-offender cases are some form of probation and some form of institutionalization. Generally, younger juveniles with minimal previous offenses who have not committed very serious offenses tend to be placed on probation, while institutions are reserved for older juveniles with several past offenses and those who have committed more-serious offenses.

JUVENILE CORRECTIONS

The primary reason for the existence of the juvenile justice system is to treat and rehabilitate young offenders before they progress into an adult life of crime. Given this premise, the correctional stage of the system is the key to its success. Unfortunately, the correction of juvenile misbehavior is a very complex and difficult task, success in which is all too rare (Murphy).

Probation and Community Placements. If placed on probation, the juvenile remains under the general supervision of the juvenile court through its probation officers. Beyond this universal condition of probation, the other conditions of various forms of probation are tailored to fit each case. The most common form of juvenile probation is to require the juvenile to report to the probation officer regularly for counseling sessions and otherwise to live at home in much the same living situation as before the court proceedings. The juvenile continues to attend the same school, hold the same job, and so forth. The other conditions of probation, such as not leaving town without court permission or being at home even earlier than the curfew laws require, are only minor nuisances for the child. Moreover, given the heavy case loads of most probation officers, the supervision the juvenile receives while on probation may well be minimal.

A common variation of probation is the requirement that the child live somewhere else within the community other than at the parental home. The new location may be the home of a relative or family friend, or an independent group foster home or shelter care facility. This provision works to break up the juvenile's previous living pattern that led to the difficulties, in that it may mean living in another part of town and going to a different school. However, the common theme of probation is maintained, since the child remains in the community and is essentially free to carry on life without severe disruptions.

If juveniles do well under the conditions of probation, they are released from probation after a period of time, and juvenile court authority ends. However, should the child violate one or more of the conditions of probation, probation may be modified or even revoked by the juvenile court judge at a subsequent hearing. Revocation of probation means that the child is committed to an institution.

Institutionalization. Another choice open to the judge at the disposition hearing and at the probation revocation hearing is to commit the child to the care and custody of a juvenile institution. This requires the juvenile court to terminate its authority over the child and transfer the child to the authority of the juvenile corrections personnel who operate the state institutions.

Most states have only one juvenile institution, so juvenile courts have only one option. While there may be one institution for boys and one for girls and/or one for delinquents and one for status offenders, the choice is still limited to one institution for a particular child. In other, more populous states (for example, California and Texas), juvenile courts commit the child to the control of a central juvenile correctional authority, which in turn determines what institution is best for that child.

Juveniles typically are committed to institutions until they reach the age of twenty-one unless released sooner by the institution. This means several years of potential confinement for the child between fourteen and sixteen. However, very few children actually are kept in these institutions for more than a year or two. As in adult prisons, children are often released early on parole, often called juvenile aftercare.

The conditions of juvenile aftercare are similar to those of probation in that the child returns to live in his community, often with parents or with relatives, and attend his former school. He is supervised generally by a parole-aftercare officer. If he does well on this status, it is terminated after a year or so.

If a child violates the conditions of aftercare, he can be brought back to the institution to resume serving the time of the original commitment there. This aftercare revocation procedure is controlled by institution personnel and not by the juvenile court judge, but they still must provide a fair process for the child in making this decision to revoke.

CHILDREN AS VICTIMS

The above descriptions of substantive offenses and the legal procedures that follow such offenses focused upon acts committed by children that are seen as harmful to the child or to others. This section concerns children as victims of acts by others or of circumstances in general.

The substantive law of child victimization defines three primary categories. While the labels and categories vary from state to state, they are commonly referred to as dependent children, neglected children, and abused children.

The classic dependent child is the hapless orphan, left homeless and parentless, clearly needing intervention by the state to provide surrogate parental custody. Other dependent children may not be orphans but nevertheless are clearly without sufficient parental care. These include cases in which the child's parent or guardian suffers debilitating physical illness or is mentally retarded or psychotic. Such cases commonly result in long-term hospitalization of the parent-guardian, leaving the child without proper parental custody for what could be months or years.

Child neglect also includes children who are without proper parental care and custody, but in neglect cases the parents are typically quite capable of providing proper care but refuse to do so. The child's needs are the same, but the parents' culpability is the significant difference between neglect and dependency. Examples of neglect cases include families in which the parents have sufficient income but choose to spend it on themselves rather than on the needs of their children.

Child abuse includes the most serious offenses against children and may involve severe injury, rape, and even death for the child. While this may be seen as simply an aggravated form of child neglect, child abuse typically involves willfully injuring a child. The essence of the definition of child abuse involves physical injury by other than accidental means that causes a substantial risk of death or serious injury.

Legal Processes. Generally, cases of dependency, neglect, and abuse are handled by the local welfare department, often in cooperation with the local juvenile or family court. If the welfare department cannot intervene successfully and correct the problem informally, then the next step is to involve the juvenile court by seeking a dependency, neglect, or abuse petition. The most serious child-abuse cases, such as murder, may be referred to criminal court.

Dependency cases usually come to the attention of the welfare department and/or the court because of a family's request for assistance. Since no culpability is being alleged concerning the child or any member of the family, only the possible embarrassment of being dependent upon public support would deter such self-reporting. In some cases, a child is found by the police under circumstances suggesting a status offense, such as a curfew violation, but the case is reported as a dependent-child case because this sort of assistance is what is really needed.

Child neglect and abuse are seen as quite serious by legal authorities, and all states require reporting of known or suspected child abuse. Persons who routinely become aware of such cases because of their occupations, such as physicians, nurses, and teachers, are required to report such cases or suffer civil or criminal penalties for failure to report. Other persons are permitted to make such reports; some states require everyone to report cases.

Reports are usually made to child welfare or protection agencies or to law enforcement agencies. Persons making such reports, whether voluntarily or as required by law, are protected from subsequent lawsuits by embarrassed and angry parents. The conditions required to be reported include any intentional physical or mental injury, sexual abuse or exploitation by anyone, and neglect by persons responsible for the child's welfare. Such persons include parents and guardians as well as private and public institutional personnel who abuse children in their care. All reports are to be investigated promptly.

Procedural rights in neglect and abuse cases have lagged behind those in delinquency and status-offender cases, but the trend is toward requiring more formality in proceedings and more rights for the child and adults involved in the case. The right to attorneys, paid for by the state if necessary, to represent all parties is becoming fairly common. Similarly accorded is the right to notice of the precise allegations made and the time, place, and topic of hearings to be held concerning the case.

Neglect and abuse hearings have become more adversarial than they were in the past and have most of the characteristics of a delinquency hearing or a criminal trial. The legal rules of evidence apply, and the accused parents or guardians have full rights to present their case to the court. The party alleging the neglect or abuse, usually the state, has the burden of proving the case by at least a preponderance of the evidence in ordinary cases.

Most cases result in a somewhat informal court-ordered agreement protecting the children from harm while requiring the parents to accept assistance with their problems. The most severe action the court may take is to terminate the parental rights of the mistreated child's parents, leaving the child available for adoption and custody by others. Such cases involving termination of parental rights must be proven by clear and convincing evidence (*Lassiter* v. *Department of Social Services of Durham County*, 1981; *Santosky* v. *Kramer*, 1982). However, in *Lassiter* the Supreme Court did not require that an attorney be appointed to represent poor parents in all termination proceedings but left that to be determined on a case-by-case basis.

Child abuse and neglect cases can also end up in adult criminal court. Intentionally injuring a child is the crime of assault and battery, and premeditatedly killing a child is no less murder simply because the victim is so young. Thus, many states permit criminal charges to be brought in these cases and the neglectful and abusive parents to endure criminal punishment.

ent. The current pressure on the juvenile justice system that seems destined to continue and perhaps increase in intensity is the demand that it become more punitive. This pressure directly counters the system's fundamental premise, which expressly limits the system to treatment and rehabilitation of juvenile offenders. Indeed, the sociopolitical climate is reversing itself, since the original impetus for starting the juvenile justice system in the early 1900s was to remove children from the harsh, punitive criminal justice system.

One increasingly popular means is to transfer more cases from juvenile to criminal court and to increase the discretion given to prosecutors to file cases directly in criminal court. This taps the punitive function of the criminal court without compromising the treatment premise of the juvenile court. This alternative is being used most frequently for the older, violent juvenile offender.

The other trend that seems significant is the effort to remove status offenders from the formal juvenile court process and to handle these cases through some form of informal community mediation and/or arbitration forum. This frees the juvenile court to follow its comparatively strict and formal legal process with delinquency offenders while permitting the less legalistic, family support mechanisms to assist in correcting the problems of the disobedient or truant child.

Finally, it seems clear that the juvenile court and the rest of the juvenile justice system will continue to exist much as it has since *Gault*. It will continue to be one of the most innovative social experiments for handling children's misbehavior and will undoubtedly register at least as many failures as successes. It most certainly has its shortcomings, but it seems clearly better than any other alternative currently available.

FUTURE TRENDS

The ebb and flow of political and social currents that, in part, gave birth to the field of juvenile law have continued to work changes on it. The only certainty for the future of juvenile law is that changes will continue, and the directions of some of these changes are becoming appar-

CASES

Breed v. Jones, 421 U.S. 519 (1975)
Fare v. Michael C., 442 U.S. 707 (1979)
In re Gault, 387 U.S. 1 (1967)
Kent v. United States, 383 U.S. 541 (1966)
Lassiter v. Department of Social Services of Durham County, 452 U.S. 18 (1981)
May v. Anderson, 345 U.S. 528 (1953)

McKeiver v. Pennsylvania, 403 U.S. 528 (1971)
Santosky v. Kramer, 455 U.S. 745 (1982)
Schall v. Martin, 467 U.S. 253 (1984)
In re Winship, 397 U.S. 358 (1970)

BIBLIOGRAPHY

Douglas J. Besharov, *Juvenile Justice Advocacy: Practice in a Unique Court* (1974), surveys the practical needs and issues that arise for lawyers representing juveniles. P. F. Cromwell, Jr.; G. G. Killinger; R. C. Sarri; and H. M. Solomon, eds., *Introduction to Juvenile Delinquency* (1978), is an excellent comprehensive reader for beginning courses in juvenile delinquency and juvenile justice. Samuel M. Davis, *Rights of Juveniles: The Juvenile Justice System* (1984), is the leading treatise covering every aspect of the law of juvenile justice. Edward Eldefonso, *Law Enforcement and the Youthful Offender,* 3rd ed. (1978), covers the development of youthful misbehavior and the problems it presents to law enforcement.

Frederic L. Faust and Paul J. Brantingham, eds., *Juvenile Justice Philosophy* (1974), includes articles on the philosophy and practice of juvenile justice. Lois G. Forer, *"No One Will Lissen": How Our Legal System Brutalizes the Youthful Poor* (1970), is a disturbing compilation of horror stories by an experienced judge in juvenile court. Sanford J. Fox, "Juvenile Justice Reform: An Historical Perspective," in *Stanford Law Review,* 22 (1970), is an exceptionally perceptive history of the development of juvenile justice systems; *Cases and Materials on Modern Juvenile Justice,* 2nd ed. (1981), is a law-school casebook authored by the most prominent scholar in juvenile law; and *The Law of Juvenile Courts in a Nutshell,* 2nd ed. (1984), clearly summarizes legal and political issues in juvenile justice.

Thomas A. Johnson, *Introduction to the Juvenile Justice System* (1975), focuses primarily upon the processes of juvenile justice. Francis B. McCarthy and James G. Carr, *Juvenile Law and Its Processes* (1980), covers the legal processes for children as offenders and as victims. Patrick T. Murphy, *Our Kindly Parent —The State: The Juvenile Justice System and How It Works* (1974), simply lays out various problems in the juvenile justice system. Anthony M. Platt, *The Child Savers: The Invention of Delinquency* (1969), is an incisive and compelling study of the political and social movements that gave rise to the juvenile justice system.

Lynn Sametz, "Revamping the Adolescent's Justice System to Serve the Needs of the Very Young Offender," in *Juvenile and Family Court Journal,* 34 (1983), describes and analyzes what happens to seven- to ten-year-olds when they are processed by juvenile courts. Larry J. Siegel and Joseph J. Senna, *Juvenile Delinquency* (1981), is a leading and thoroughly reliable undergraduate textbook on delinquency and the juvenile justice process. Victor L. Streib, *Juvenile Justice in America* (1978), is a detailed systems analysis of the juvenile justice system concluding with thirty specific recommendations for changes to the system; "The Juvenile Justice System and Children's Lawyers: Should Juvenile Defense Lawyers Be Replaced with Children's Lawyers?" in *Juvenile and Family Court Journal,* 31 (1980), details the various functions of juvenile lawyers throughout the juvenile justice process; and "Death Penalty for Children: The American Experience with Capital Punishment for Crimes Committed While Under Age Eighteen," in *Oklahoma Law Review,* 36 (1983), describes and analyzes the legal, sociological, and philosophical issues involved in capital punishment for children's crimes. Robert C. Trojanowicz, *Juvenile Delinquency: Concepts and Controls* (1978), focuses primarily upon the causes and cures for delinquency and child neglect.

[*See also* CRIMINAL JUSTICE SYSTEM *and* PLEA BARGAINING.]

LABOR LAW

Abe F. Levy
Lewis N. Levy

L<small>ABOR</small> law is that body of statutory law enacted by Congress, the various state legislatures, decisions of the courts (both federal and state), and the various administrative agencies that deals with the relationships between employers and trade unions or labor organizations.

The complex structures and relationships created by the employment process have from the earliest days logically led working people to conclude that their contractual power as individuals could not compare with the power exerted by employers acting either singly or in concert. From the beginnings of the United States (and in England even before the American Revolution), workers have sought to combine so as to strengthen themselves against the greater power of their employers, to balance that with their own, and to exert greater economic pressure on their employers to improve their wages and working conditions. This struggle for power has led directly to the development of the entire body of labor law in the United States.

ORIGINS OF AMERICAN LABOR LAW

As with other areas of common law, the roots of American labor law go back to British practices. The Statute of Labourers, adopted in 1562 during the reign of Elizabeth I, represented the first attempt by the English Parliament to create a comprehensive labor code. The Statute of Labourers made it illegal for workers to join together to assert their collective power in order to secure better conditions of employment for themselves. The English courts developed over the following years the legal concept that workers thus combining were thereby engaged in a "common-law conspiracy," a criminal act.

It naturally happened that the early American courts, harking back to their common-law roots, followed the English precedent. The first recorded strike in America seems to have been a strike by bakers in New York City in 1741. All such efforts by employees were met by very strict legal opposition in the form of criminal indictments for criminal conspiracy, enforced by the courts. Throughout the rest of the eighteenth and well into the nineteenth century, courts held that the mere joining together of laborers to improve the conditions under which they labored was subject to criminal conspiracy doctrines.

The first case to bring the notion of conspiracy into American labor law was the Philadelphia cordwainers' case, *Commonwealth* v. *Pullis* (1806). That case arose when the cordwainers (leatherworkers) in Philadelphia attempted to withhold services from their employers until certain wage concessions were granted. Such an act, according to the court, amounted to a criminal conspiracy and restraint on trade. The court held that the workmen who engaged in such actions were in effect restraining the ability of fellow workmen freely to enter the workplace and that any combining of laborers was an intolerable impediment to employers' ability freely to set wages, terms, and conditions of employment. The decision resulted in a stiff criminal sentence for the indicted workers.

American labor law used this conspiracy approach to organized labor activity throughout the first half of the nineteenth century. In 1842 the watershed case of *Commonwealth* v. *Hunt* was decided by the Massachusetts Supreme Judicial Court. The issue in *Hunt* was whether workmen could join a society or association whose bylaws prohibited its members from working with nonmembers and required members to pay dues,

359

threatening discharge from employment if the dues were not tendered. In *Hunt,* an employee was discharged when he failed to pay his dues to such an association, and the employer, who was compelled to fire that employee after a strike, turned the matter over to the district attorney for prosecution under the state's criminal conspiracy law.

The trial court held that such an association violated the criminal conspiracy statutes of Massachusetts, but the Massachusetts Supreme Judicial Court reversed that holding and, in so doing, recognized for the first time that working people should have the right to unite in organizations designed to improve the conditions of their labor. As Congress was a long way from acting on the question of national regulation of labor, the *Hunt* case represented a significant step toward state recognition of workers' ability to organize themselves.

American legal principles of the nineteenth century, as applied to labor disputes, distinguished between acts of forbearance, on the one hand, and those of action, such as strikes and boycotts, on the other. Most courts held that forbearance, or the withholding of services, was lawful. However, picketing and boycotts were usually held to be unlawful. Therefore, the ultimate question of whether workers could combine to better their lot turned upon the degree to which such activity impinged upon other workers' rights to work under such conditions and wages as they chose to accept. This principle found its roots in the notion that "freedom" forbade any organized source from interfering with individual action. Gradually this precept gave way to a new formula: what one individual may rightfully do, he or she may do in combination with others.

By 1880, most states recognized the legality of efforts to improve wages, terms, and conditions of employment. However, this tilt toward the recognition of unions did not result in the wholesale organization of skilled or industrial workers. This was due, in large part, to the abundance of cheap labor, which employers could easily hire to replace those workers who went on strike for better conditions.

The shift away from the conspiracy doctrine led to a new legal trend that was effectively an attempt to control and defeat unionization: the use of the labor injunction to inhibit, forestall,

and quash organized labor. The courts turned away from examining the goals of collective action and began to consider whether the means employed by labor were lawful. The most famous and emulated decision concerning the use of injunctions in labor disputes was *In re Debs* (1895). That decision by the Supreme Court upheld the use of injunctions to stop strikes and, to most observers and commentators, granted wide latitude to federal district courts in formulating and granting injunctive relief to employers whose businesses were subject to strikes and other union activities. In *Debs,·* the federal government requested and obtained an injunction prohibiting the American Railway Union from striking any railroads that used cars manufactured by the Pullman Car Company. The *Debs* Court reasoned that the powers that allow a court to protect property from irreparable damage extended to protecting an employer's freedom to hire workers, sell goods, and generally run a business in a proper manner.

Some courts continued to question the purpose of the union's activity. Essentially, this allowed the judge reviewing the injunction application to make his own determination, based upon his own social and political views, as to whether the ends of the strike were lawful. This approach led to the invocation of the "blanket injunction," which in effect prohibited anyone from furthering or abetting a labor controversy then before a court. The all-inclusive nature of these blanket-type injunctions issued by the courts had the effect of making unlawful certain acts that were in and of themselves lawful. Many of these injunctions were vague and indefinite as to what precise acts or conduct were prohibited under their terms. Blanket injunctions also had two side effects: they generated a public feeling that strikers became lawbreakers when they violated the terms of the injunction, and they discouraged the workers involved in a strike, who naturally became fearful of arrest or other court-ordered punishment.

By 1917 the use of the injunction, already pervasive, was extended to enforce the "yellow-dog" contract, an agreement between an employee and employer that the employee would not join a union. In *Hitchman Coal and Coke Co.* v. *Mitchell* (1917) the United States Supreme Court held that federal courts had the power to enforce such agreements. This ruling allowed employers to force their employees to sign such agreements and, if a union made organizational inroads in a workplace, to apply for an order requiring employees who had signed a yellow-dog contract to either renounce the union or withdraw from their employment. The union could also be ordered to cease interfering with this contract between the worker and the employer by attempting to organize a union. It was not until 1932, in fact, that employer access to federal courts for injunctive relief was curtailed by the Norris–La Guardia Anti-injunction Act.

At the same time that the injunction was developing as a potent weapon against labor organizational drives, the courts began to use "antitrust" doctrines against attempts to organize labor. In 1890, Congress enacted the Sherman Antitrust Act, which prohibited "every contract, combination, . . . or conspiracy, in restraint of trade or commerce among the several States." Since the act did not specifically exclude unions from its provisions, it was soon extended to encompass and prohibit organizational attempts by workers. Several early lower-court decisions applied the act to any strike that involved the nation's railroads. In 1908 the Supreme Court decided the antitrust question in a landmark decision, *Loewe* v. *Lawlor* (otherwise known as the *Danbury Hatters* case). The hatters' union had attempted to organize its employer's plant in Danbury, Connecticut. Because of organizational problems, the union resorted to indirect economic pressure by declaring a nationwide boycott against products of the Danbury plant. The Supreme Court extended the prohibitions of the Sherman Act to labor-union activity, holding that the boycott had the effect of restraining trade, was a combination prohibited by the Sherman Act, and so was unconstitutional. Further damage was done to the union movement by the Court's holding that both the union and its individual officers were responsible for damages incurred as a result of Sherman Act violations.

In 1914, Congress enacted the Clayton Antitrust Act in response to political pressures brought by the trade union movement. The Clayton Act was intended by Congress to protect organized labor from the reach of the Sherman Act. Section 6 of the Clayton Act provided

> that the labor of a human being is not a commodity or article of commerce. Nothing contained in the anti-trust laws shall be construed to forbid the existence and operation of labor, agricultural, or horticultural organizations, . . . or to forbid or restrain individual members of such organizations from lawfully carrying out the legitimate objects thereof; nor shall such organizations, or the members thereof, be held or construed to be illegal combinations or conspiracies in restraint of trade, under the anti-trust laws.

The Supreme Court had its first opportunity to rule on the Clayton Act as it applied to labor union activity in *Duplex Printing Press Co.* v. *Deering* (1921). The International Association of Machinists attempted to organize Duplex through a boycott of its products. The Court held that the Clayton Act did not exempt unions or their members and officers from liability under the Sherman Act if the means invoked by the union resulted in an illegal combination or conspiracy to restrain trade as defined by the antitrust laws. The Court did not read the Clayton Act as depriving federal courts of jurisdiction over Sherman Act claims against unions.

Throughout the first third of the twentieth century, then, the Supreme Court continued to extend application of the Sherman Act to the labor movement. In *Coronado Coal Co.* v. *United Mine Workers of America* (1925) the Supreme Court declared that strikes were not themselves subject to the restraints of the Sherman Act. On the other hand, the Court did rule that where the object of a strike is to keep certain products out of the flow of commerce, the Sherman Act did apply, and a damaged employer could bring suit for treble damages as provided for in the act.

Prior to the New Deal era, the labor law of the United States was decidedly proemployer. Although the law recognized the legality of workers' desires to organize into trade unions, this right was severely restricted by the courts, the states, and the federal government. But with the coming of the New Deal, this trend abruptly changed.

FEDERAL REGULATION OF LABOR-MANAGEMENT RELATIONS

By 1930, labor-management relations law consisted of a vague body of federal case law and state restrictions upon labor's ability to engage in organizing. Organized labor and its allies saw the need for governmental action to change the status quo. The Great Depression was the catalyst necessary for organized labor to achieve desired clout at both federal and state levels. In 1930 the Democrats gained control of Congress and passed, over President Herbert Hoover's veto, the Norris–La Guardia Anti-injunction Act (1932). This legislation effectively stripped federal courts of equity jurisdiction—and hence the ability to issue injunctions—in labor disputes.

In one of its most significant provisions the Norris–La Guardia Act declared it the public policy of the United States that employees must have freedom to organize for the purpose of collective bargaining to better the terms and conditions of their employment. A major victory for organized labor was the section of the Norris–La Guardia Act that specifically outlawed the enforceability in federal courts of yellow-dog contracts. Other sections of the act prohibited injunctions unless the party seeking the order had exhausted every feasible avenue of dispute resolution, including arbitration, or unless violence had occurred and the appropriate officials were unable to control it.

The Norris–La Guardia Act did not provide labor with any new weapons. Although it did free labor from the heavy hand of the federal judiciary, it did not completely divest federal courts of jurisdiction over suits for injunctions in labor disputes. As will be seen, the power of federal courts to issue injunctions in labor disputes has remained very much alive.

In 1932 a sweeping defeat for the Republican party brought into office President Franklin D. Roosevelt and his team. One of the first programs undertaken by the Roosevelt administration was the passage of the National Industrial Recovery Act in 1933. Section 7(a) of the act contained a federal governmental endorsement of employees' right to organize and to bargain collectively through representatives of their own choice. To facilitate implementation of Section 7(a), President Roosevelt set up the National Labor Board. Created in August 1933, the National Labor Board attempted to mediate labor disputes throughout the country and to guarantee workers the protections accorded them under Section 7(a). However, in *Schechter Poultry Corp.* v. *United States* (1935), the Supreme Court declared the act unconstitutional. Thus, federal protection of employees' rights to organize came effectively and abruptly to an end.

National Labor Relations Act. In response to the *Schechter* decision, Congress in 1935 passed the National Labor Relations Act, popularly known as the Wagner Act. The fundamental aim of the act was to promote industrial stability and to remedy the perceived inequality of the powers of the employer and the individual unorganized worker. By protecting the right to unionize and by providing the support of the federal government in the exercise of that right, the act created a method by which employees could choose, in a democratic and fair election method, to be represented by a union in collective bargaining. Section 1 of the act stated that it was the public policy of the United States to promote and encourage the practice of collective bargaining and the exercise by workers of their full freedom of association and organization for mutual aid and protection.

The heart of the Wagner Act is contained in Sections 7, 8, 9, and 10. Section 7 declared that employees who came under the coverage of the act had the right to organize, to join labor organizations, to bargain collectively through elected representatives, and to engage in concerted activities for mutual aid or protection. Section 8 enumerated "unfair labor practices" that employers were prohibited from committing and that the newly created National Labor Relations Board (NLRB) was empowered to redress. Section 9 of the act gave the NLRB authority to conduct elections in which workers chose their collective-bargaining representatives. The board also had the power to certify a labor organization as the majority collective-bargaining representative for a group of employees after a union won such an election, and the law compelled the employer to bargain with that union "in good faith" over conditions of employment and wages. Section 10 of the act gave the NLRB the ability to enforce its orders against employers found guilty of committing unfair labor practices by petitioning the circuit courts of appeal for judicial enforcement of its decisions.

The Wagner Act constituted a milestone in federal regulation of labor-management relations because it both recognized employees' rights to join labor organizations for the purpose of collective bargaining and accorded the administrative agency in charge of overseeing the law a method for enforcing its decisions.

The first Supreme Court case to arise under the act was *National Labor Relations Board* v. *Jones and Laughlin Steel Corp.* (1937), in which a challenge to the constitutionality of the Wagner Act was mounted. The Supreme Court upheld the Wagner Act as an appropriate exercise by Congress of its powers enumerated in the commerce clause of the Constitution. The Court also endorsed the principle of extending the act's jurisdiction to the manufacturing sector. From that point on, the act was applied to almost every aspect of commerce in the United States.

In the years between 1935 and 1947, unions experienced tremendous growth in membership and power. Most major manufacturing and mining industries were thoroughly unionized, and the earnings and conditions of employment of workers in those industries changed dramatically for the better. By 1947, membership in unions had mushroomed to 15 million and continued to grow.

Amendments to the Wagner Act. The Wagner Act has not remained unchanged throughout the years. Congress has amended provisions of the act to meet what it has seen as prevalent national policy concerns. The first such amendment took place after the Republican party won control of both houses of Congress in the 1946 elections, the first in which it had done so since the 1928 elections. The Republicans immediately made it their first order of business to pass the Labor-Management Relations Act, best known as the Taft-Hartley Act, over President Harry S. Truman's veto. This act was to have a long-term regressive effect on the trade union movement.

The Taft-Hartley Act, as Congress indicated in its policy statement, was intended to restore the government to a "neutral position in labor disputes." Whereas under the Wagner Act only employers could commit unfair labor practices against the rights of workers, the Taft-Hartley amendments now added unfair labor practices that unions were prohibited from committing. These included restraining or coercing employees in the exercise of their rights guaranteed pursuant to Section 7 of the Wagner Act, coercing employers with regard to choosing an agent for collective bargaining, bargaining in bad faith,

carrying out secondary strikes and boycotts, imposing excessive or discriminatory shop or initiation fees, and "featherbedding."

The Taft-Hartley Act included several additional provisions. For example, Congress specifically granted to employers freedom to express their views concerning union organization if such expressions were not made in conjunction with promises of benefit or threats of reprisal. Section 7 was amended to allow employees the right to refrain from collective-bargaining activities. A new provision permitted states to pass "right-to-work" legislation, which prohibited compulsory union membership as a condition of continued employment. Section 9 of the Wagner Act was amended to provide that employers could call for representation elections to determine whether a specific union represented a majority of its employees. Employer contributions to employee organizations were forbidden unless made under very specific circumstances. Various reporting and disclosure requirements for unions were provided. The 1947 amendments established the office of the general counsel of the NLRB, who was empowered to determine whether complaints of unfair labor practices should issue. This function had until then been performed by the board itself. The Taft-Hartley Act also rejuvenated the labor injunction by providing for its use in cases of secondary boycott by unions.

The Taft-Hartley Act was amended in 1959. These amendments are collectively known as the Landrum-Griffin Act or the Labor-Management Reporting and Disclosure Act. In response to certain evils that Congress discovered following extensive investigatory hearings between 1955 and 1959, the Landrum-Griffin Act was enacted to sever what were then perceived to be organized-crime connections with organized labor. Improprieties in intraunion elections, rampant graft by union officials, and the deprivation of fundamental membership rights of members were corrected by the act, which created a "bill of rights" for every union member. As with the Taft-Hartley amendments, the Landrum-Griffin Act required unions and employers to file with the secretary of labor reports on membership, compensation paid to officers, and operating expenses incurred by the reporting organization. It also set forth specific election procedures and placed financial responsibilities upon the officers of unions.

The Landrum-Griffin amendments also affected the substantive purview of the Taft-Hartley Act. First, Section 8(b)(4) of the Taft-Hartley Act was amended to include within the definition of unlawful secondary boycotts such occurrences as interunion jurisdictional disputes or disagreements. The same section was also amended to allow unions to publicize their disputes and to request the public to cease doing business with the employer who is the subject of a primary dispute.

The 1959 amendments also prohibited "hot cargo" contracts (agreements not to deal in nonunion goods or services) except in the garment and construction industries. "Recognitional picketing" for more than thirty days against an employer with whom the picketing union did not have an agreement and for which the union had not petitioned for an election (pursuant to the rules and regulations to the NLRB) was declared an unfair labor practice. Finally, the amendments made it an unfair labor practice for unions and employers to enter into "sweetheart" agreements when the union did not represent a majority of the employees in a bargaining unit.

In 1972, Congress changed the National Labor Relations Act as it applied to health-care establishments. Pursuant to the health-care amendments, unions and employers in the health-care industry are subject to certain requirements and restrictions because of the necessity of maintaining health services for the public with as few strikes as possible.

INTERPRETATION OF THE TAFT-HARTLEY ACT

After the *Jones and Laughlin* decision, the NLRB and the courts struggled to develop a comprehensive federal scheme for the regulation of labor-management relations. This struggle has encompassed the effort to define precisely the acts that result in the commission of unfair labor practices and to develop a general body of federal labor-management relations law.

Unfair Management Practices. Under the provisions of Section 8(a)(1) of the Taft-Hartley Act, an employer commits an unfair labor practice when it restrains, interferes with, or coerces employees in the exercise of their Section 7 rights. The most typical violations occur during representational campaigns and include employer surveillance of employees or union adherents, employer refusal to allow the union access to the employees, and antiunion campaign rhetoric used by the employer.

Before determining whether an employer's conduct has violated the law, the NLRB makes an initial inquiry to establish whether the affected employees were engaged in concerted activity. This usually entails a determination as to whether the acts of an employee or employees are designed for the mutual aid and benefit of fellow employees. If the employees' conduct meets this test, such conduct is afforded full protection of the act.

Once the NLRB or a court decides that the affected employees were engaged in concerted activity, it will examine the alleged unfair labor practice. With respect to Section 8(a)(1), the board and the courts invoke the "totality of the circumstances" test. Under this test, antiunion statements by employers are considered lawful if they do not constitute a promise of benefit or threat of reprisal with respect to unionization. The employer's motive is not a factor; the board will look to see whether the statements and actions of the employer tend, in fact, to interfere with the free exercise of employees' rights under the act.

With respect to surveillance and interrogation of employees, the board also uses the totality-of-the-circumstances test. The key element is whether the conduct of the employer, in ordering surveillance or interrogation of an employee, had the effect of restraining or coercing the employee's rights under the act. Until recently, the board followed a per se rule that held unlawful all attempts by employers to interrogate their employees about their union sympathies in the absence of guarantees against reprisals. However, the decision of the board in *Rossmore House* (1984) adopted the totality-of-the-circumstances test for such violations.

A major area of rulings revolves around the impact of employers' "no access" and "no solicitation" rules on union organizational and election campaigns. An early decision by the Supreme Court, *Republic Aviation Corp.* v. *National Labor Relations Board* (1945), adopted the legal presumption that if an employer's rules prohibit union solicitation by employees outside of working time, whether on or off the employer's property, such a rule "is an unreasonable impediment to self-organization and therefore discriminatory in the absence of evidence that special circumstances make the rule necessary." In *TRW, Inc.* (1979) the board held that a no-solicitation rule that did not clarify the definition of *working time* or *working hours* was invalid unless the employer specifically informed the employees that the rule did not apply to break time, lunch periods, or other such nonwork periods.

With respect to union access to an employer's premises, both the NLRB and the courts have developed a balancing test to determine whether union organizers have the right to enter an employer's premises. The first major decision was *National Labor Relations Board* v. *Babcock and Wilcox* (1956). The Supreme Court held that employers can prohibit nonemployee union organizers from entering their premises if the union, through reasonable efforts, can reach employees through other available channels of communication and if the rule is not enforced discriminatorily (that is, all nonemployees are barred from soliciting on the property). This test requires a determination as to whether the union attempting the organizational drive has access to other reasonable channels of communication with employees.

Section 8(a)(2) of the Taft-Hartley Act states that it is an unfair labor practice for an employer to "dominate or interfere with the formation or administration of any labor organization or contribute financial or other support to it." To find a violation under this section, the NLRB must first determine whether the organization involved is a labor organization. Under current practice, the board usually finds that an employer has potential power to dominate a union when it pays employees for attending the organization's meetings, the employer's supervisory personnel attend the organization's meetings, the employer has control over the organization's membership, and the employer gives financial or other assistance to the organization.

Section 8(a)(3) of the Taft-Hartley Act provides that an employer may not discriminate against an employee in regard to hire or tenure of employment with the purpose of encouraging or discouraging membership in any labor organization. This section does not prohibit discrimination in employment; it merely prohibits those acts which tend to discourage or encourage membership in labor organizations. Provisions of this section allow unions and employers to enter into a "union shop" agreement, which requires membership in the union representing the employer's employees if these employees have not voted to ban the arrangement or if the state in which the business is located has a right-to-work law.

The Supreme Court has outlined the specific test that the NLRB should use to determine Section 8(a)(3) violations. Under this test, the Court distinguishes between conduct that has a slight adverse effect on employees' rights and conduct that is "inherently destructive" of collective activity. Under current law, where an employer's conduct is "inherently destructive" of Section 7 rights, the board assumes an 8(a)(3) violation; the burden of proof then shifts to the employer to articulate some overriding and substantial business justification for performing the act in question. If the employer comes forth with such evidence, the burden then shifts to the general counsel to demonstrate evidence showing that the employer had antiunion motives. (Of course, the phrases "inherently destructive" and "legitimate or substantial business justifications" are ambiguous for both the NLRB and the courts.)

One major area of continuing dispute involves employers' decisions to replace striking or locked-out employees and whether those employees are entitled to reinstatement. Under current law, an employer may replace strikers or locked-out employees so long as after cessation of the strike or lockout those workers are offered reinstatement when openings occur. However, employers are not required to offer reinstatement to employees who engage in unprotected activity such as picket-line violence or "wildcat" (unauthorized) work stoppages.

Prior to finding a violation of Section 8(a)(3), the board must first find that the employer had knowledge of the employee's union or concerted activity. Knowledge of union or concerted activity is often inferred from the circumstances of the case. When the employer's knowledge is demonstrated from the facts, it must then be proven that the employer had a discriminatory motive or unlawful intent in the conduct at issue;

in turn, the employer may attempt a "legitimate business justification" defense.

Section 8(a)(4) makes it unlawful for an employer to "discharge or otherwise discriminate against an employee because he has filed charges or given testimony" under the act. The NLRB and courts have applied this section with rather striking consistency to the extent that any discipline of, or discrimination against, an employee whom the employer knows has filed charges or testified before the board is considered a violation of the act. However, the protections of the section do not extend to employees who have filed false or malicious charges with the board. The section also applies to employers who discharge employees for refusing to give false testimony at board proceedings and who condition continued employment or reinstatement of an employee upon a withdrawal of board charges filed by that employee.

Good-faith bargaining, as required by the act, envisions both the process of negotiation, with each side intending to reach a final and binding agreement, and, once that agreement is executed, the reasonable operation and interpretation of the collective-bargaining agreement. The NLRB has developed two approaches to determine whether an employer's tactics in bargaining for an agreement or in the operation of that agreement amount to unfair labor practice. However, the task of defining what really is good-faith bargaining is not an easy one, and the board has recognized that the concept of good faith fluctuates from party to party and depends upon the attitudes displayed at the bargaining table.

Once a union is certified as the collective-bargaining representative of a group of employees, the employer of those workers must then meet and bargain in good faith with the union. Time, notice elements, and terms of bargaining are governed by Section 8(d) of the act. A certified collective-bargaining representative has the right to negotiate rates of pay, wages, hours of employment, or other conditions of employment. Other issues may be discussed if they are not illegal under the act or other federal statutes.

The two-tier approach to Section 8(a)(5) violations is built around the concept of whether the employer commits a per se violation or whether under the totality of circumstances a violation has occurred. Both tests hinge on a determination of whether the employer, and in some instances the parties, have entered the bargaining process with an honest desire or intent to reach an agreement. Bargaining positions that constitute per se violations of the act usually entail some type of refusal or failure to negotiate or an insistence upon midcontract changes relating to mandatory subjects; failure to meet with appointed bargaining representatives; refusal to execute collective-bargaining agreements; or insistence upon nonmandatory subjects to the point of impasse.

The totality-of-circumstances test takes into account many of the same factors as the guidelines for violations under other sections. With this test, the board looks for such indications of bad-faith bargaining as arbitrary delay, dilatory tactics, conduct indicating that an employer wishes to set its wages unilaterally, unwillingness to grant concessions, or a failure to supply information necessary to efficiently and intelligently bargain. If, after weighing all factors in consideration, the board arrives at the conclusion that the employer has not entered the bargaining process with good-faith intent to reach agreement, it will find a violation on the part of the employer.

Good-faith bargaining does not require that the parties reach agreement; it merely requires them to engage in good-faith discussions with the intention of reaching an agreement. If, after the parties have engaged in good-faith negotiations, irreconcilable differences remain, the law recognizes an impasse. Once the impasse is reached, any duty of the parties to bargain is suspended until such time as their positions are modified to allow them to return to the bargaining table. Because a precise definition of impasse is nearly impossible to articulate, the board adopts the totality-of-circumstances test to determine whether, after exhaustion of good-faith bargaining sessions, the parties have indeed reached the point of impasse.

When an impasse occurs, each party usually resorts to economic pressures to modify the position of the other. The board and the courts agree that the parties may resort to economic pressure, even during bargaining, if that pressure is used with a good-faith intent to reach an agreement and is not applied for some unlawful purpose.

There are instances that excuse the employer's duty to bargain with the union—for example, if the employer has a good-faith doubt as to the continued majority status of the union. If the employer's position is sustained by the board, upon a finding that the union no longer enjoys a majority status the employer is free to unilaterally set terms, wages, and conditions of employment.

Unfair Union Practices. Section 8(b)(1)(A) of the Taft-Hartley Act prohibits unions from coercing employees in the exercise of their Section 7 rights and from restraining or coercing employers in their selection of bargaining representatives. The union violates the act if its conduct adversely affects the employer-employee relationship or is for some unlawful purpose. Violations usually occur where unions fine members for crossing picket lines after they have resigned from the union; fine or discipline members for refusing to engage in unlawful or unprotected activity; fine or discipline members for filing charges alleging unfair labor practices; use fraud or violence to intimidate members; or levy unreasonable and outrageous fines against members.

Section 8(b)(1)(b) protects the rights of employers, not employees, to choose their own collective-bargaining representatives. This usually applies to instances where the union refuses to deal with an employer's supervisor or other managerial personnel. This section operates to prohibit a union from coercing, intimidating, or forcing an employer to change, by way of demotion, promotion, or transfer, the supervisory or managerial personnel in charge of direct bargaining with the union.

Section 8(b)(2) prohibits union attempts to force employers to discriminate against an employee because of that employee's exercise of his or her Section 7 rights. Typically, violations under this section arise when the union attempts to force an employer to discipline or discharge an employee who is not a member of the union or who has fallen into disfavor with the leadership of the union. Other examples of violations are a union's insistence on the dismissal of workers who have not paid union initiation fees or not joined the union where no union shop agreement exists or where a union operates its hiring hall in a manner that discriminates against nonmembers.

The NLRB has used Section 8(b)(2) to develop the "duty of fair representation" concept, which requires unions to represent in a fair, non-discriminatory, and nonarbitrary manner the interests of their members. This duty of fair representation requires unions to process and review fairly all grievances and problems that their members may encounter. If the union acts in an arbitrary or capricious manner by refusing to process a grievance or deal with a member, it violates the duty of fair representation.

Section 8(b)(3) prohibits a union from engaging in bad-faith bargaining. The same per se and totality-of-circumstances tests apply to unions as to employers.

Section 8(b)(4) generally prohibits unions from engaging in secondary boycotts or pressure to coerce neutral employers to act in a certain fashion. A secondary boycott occurs if a union attempts to persuade the public, other employers, or employees—often through picketing—not to do business with a firm that has business relations with a company that is involved in a labor dispute with the union. The NLRB and the courts have developed several tests and doctrines to determine when and where picketing can occur and what factors cause such picketing to fall under the secondary boycott provisions of the act.

The first and most difficult task confronted by the board and the courts was to define what conduct actually constitutes either "secondary" or "primary" activity. Once again, the board and courts developed a totality-of-the-circumstances test to determine whether the union conduct involved had the prohibited motive of enmeshing others in a dispute. Currently, the board and courts look to the nature of the work in dispute, the location of the picketing, and the surrounding facts and circumstances to ascertain whether the union's conduct is proscribed by Section 8(b)(4). Indeed, the most important factor in determining whether a violation of this section has occurred is the action of the union. The provisions of the act do not prohibit a union from appealing to the discretion of consumers and neutrals not to do business with a primary employer, so long as those requests are not made in a threatening, coercive manner.

The board and the courts have also developed criteria concerning the propriety of the site where picketing takes place. The major problem faced in this area was whether the union could follow a primary employer's workers or products in furtherance of the labor dispute. In an effort to accommodate both the union's interest in picketing a primary employer and the congressional proscription against enmeshing neutral employers in labor disputes, the board formulated what is now known as the *Moore Dry Dock* (1949) doctrine.

Under *Moore Dry Dock,* a union may picket a multiemployer job site where it has a dispute with one or more employers only if the struck employer is present at the job site and is engaged in normal business operations, the picketing is limited to a distance as close as possible to the struck employer, and the picketing is clearly not aimed at any "neutral" employers.

BARGAINING UNITS

Section 9 of the Taft-Hartley Act empowers the NLRB to conduct investigations into, and order elections concerning, employee representation in appropriate bargaining units. To initiate the representational process, a petition for election is filed by the union or by the employer with the NLRB. Once the petition is filed, an investigation is commenced to determine whether there is an appropriate showing of interest in the petition, whether the petition affects interstate commerce, what the appropriate unit for the election is, and whether there are any statutory or other bars to an election.

Sufficient interest in an election petition is established when either an employer is presented with a demand for recognition or the petitioning union demonstrates that it has at least 30 percent support from the bargaining-unit employees. The board then determines whether the petition affects interstate commerce.

The determination of whether the election petition covers an appropriate unit is a more difficult task. A number of tests have evolved to determine the appropriateness of bargaining units. Essentially, the tests look toward whether the employees within the unit are part of a community of interest. The board has broad discretion in determining the most appropriate unit. It looks to considerations such as the bargaining history of the industry in question; the similarity of duties, interests, and working conditions of the employees; the desires of the employees; and the extent and type of union organization of the employees in the affected industry. (Cer-

tain employees, such as professionals, guards, and health-care employees, are governed by separate rules concerning bargaining-unit determination.)

The NLRB then investigates whether there are any statutory or other bars to the election petition. The board may not entertain a representation petition filed less than one year subsequent to a previous petition in the same unit. The board will also refuse to entertain, up to a maximum of three years, a petition where a valid collective-bargaining agreement covers the employees in the requested unit. Under current policy, the board will also refuse to entertain the petition if it comes within an unreasonable time subsequent to a voluntary recognition of a labor organization by an employer; if charges of unfair labor practice, which might affect the outcome of the election in the unit, are filed contemporaneously with, or subsequent to, the petition; or if the union involved disclaims any interest in representing the employees of the unit.

After determining that an election is appropriate, the NLRB will set a time, date, and place for the election. The election is held by secret ballot and is conducted not less than twenty, but not more than thirty, days from the date of the order for an election. Prior to holding the election, the employer is required to prepare a list of eligible voters, with their addresses, and file it with the NLRB, which forwards the list to the union. After the election is conducted, the board then certifies the results, depending upon the wishes expressed by a majority of the voters.

Preelection campaigning by both unions and employers has generated much case law by the board and the courts relating to what practices, statements, and acts are proper during an election campaign. The board will certify the results of elections only if the voting has taken place in an atmosphere without coercion and under conditions as nearly ideal as possible for employees freely to determine their desires. Under this doctrine, statements, threats, and acts of coercion or intimidation justify the setting aside of election results. If the board determines that, because of pervasive unfair labor practices and a coercive atmosphere, a free and unfettered election is impossible, it is empowered to order the subject employer to bargain with the union as the collective-bargaining representative of the employees.

An employer may seek court review of a unit

determination by the board only after it refuses to bargain with a union that was certified pursuant to an election. Such review usually takes place in the context of a Section 8(a)(5) allegation against the employer for its refusal to bargain with the newly certified union.

OTHER LABOR LAWS

We have examined the body of federal law that regulates and defines the relationships between employees and employers in private industry engaged in interstate commerce, and unions representing such employees. Since the passage of the Wagner Act in 1935, there has been extensive development of a body of law concerning the rights of employees not covered by the act to engage in collective bargaining.

The federal government has passed several laws to deal with its own employees. Federal policy toward organizations of federal employees dates back to 1883 when the Pendleton Act, commonly known as the Civil Service Act, was passed by Congress, which retained for itself the authority to regulate wages, hours, and other terms and conditions of the employment of federal workers. Thereafter, many attempts on the part of these employees to gain the right to self-organization were not successful. The current framework within which collective bargaining is structured in agencies under the executive branch of government has evolved from Executive Order 10988, issued by President John F. Kennedy in January 1962, which in turn was revised by President Richard Nixon in 1969 by Executive Order 11491, entitled "Labor-Management Relations in the Federal Service," and President Gerald Ford's further amendment in February 1975 by Executive Order 11838.

Under these various executive orders, federal employees gained the right to engage in collective bargaining and to be represented by unions of their own chosen in representation elections. With this extension of collective-bargaining rights to federal employees, their unions have prospered and shown substantial growth. There is, however, one very important difference: federal employees are denied the right to strike.

The Postal Reorganization Act of 1970 removed postal employees from coverage under the executive orders and gave them collective-bargaining rights comparable to those governing private-industry employees. The NLRB was authorized to determine the appropriateness of bargaining units, supervise representation elections, and enforce unfair-practice provisions, which were very similar to ones contained in the National Labor Relations Act applicable to employees in private industry. However, the Postal Reorganization Act still continues to prohibit strikes by postal employees.

State and local governments have developed differing statutes to extend to their employees various forms of collective-bargaining rights. The development of these state and local statutes has resulted in the representation of more than 3 million state and local government workers by unions in collective bargaining. Most of the statutes prohibit strikes by public employees, but some do not. The California Supreme Court, for instance, ruled in 1985 that public employees (except safety employees such as firemen and policemen) do have the right to strike (*County Sanitation District No. 2* v. *Los Angeles County Employees Assn.*).

The right of public employees of local and state governments to join unions was upheld when a federal court of appeals unanimously ruled in *State, County and Municipal Employees* v. *Woodward* (1969) that a public employee discharged because of union membership had the right to seek an injunction and to sue for damages those public officials who discharged him because of union activities. The *Woodward* court stated that the right to belong to a union is a right protected by the right of association provided by the First and Fourteenth Amendments.

Generally, laws governing public-employee labor relations authorize collective bargaining between the governmental entity and the union representing a majority of the employees in appropriate bargaining units. Bargaining has developed along the same lines as in private industry, dealing with fundamental issues of compensation benefits and working conditions.

CONCLUSION

Labor law is constantly changing to meet the needs of the times. Yet the basic and fundamental principle now clearly established and protected by law—that employees have the right to join together for the purpose of engaging in collective bargaining with their employers so as to reach agreement on conditions of employment —is no longer at issue.

More than 20 million American employees are represented by labor organizations in collective bargaining with their employers. These collective-bargaining relationships have resulted in the standardization and legitimation of wage structures that enable the worker and his or her family to lead a decent life. The concepts of health and hospitalization insurance, pensions, seniority, vacations, and other benefits have all evolved from collective bargaining. Holiday pay, vacation pay, sick leave, and other collective-bargaining provisions, all dealing with the conditions of employment, have resulted in a structure in which the American worker is treated with dignity.

CASES

Commonwealth v. Hunt, 4 Met. 111 (1842)

Commonwealth v. Pullis, Phila. Mayor's Court (1806)

Coronado Coal Co. v. United Mine Workers of America, 268 U.S. 295 (1925)

County Sanitation District No. 2 v. Los Angeles County Employees Assn., 38 C.3d 564 (1985)

In re Debs, 158 U.S. 564 (1895)

Duplex Printing Press Co. v. Deering, 254 U.S. 443 (1921)

Hitchman Coal and Coke Co. v. Mitchell, 245 U.S. 229 (1917)

Loewe v. Lawlor, 208 U.S. 274 (1908)

Moore Dry Dock Co., 81 NLRB 1108 (1949)

National Labor Relations Board v. Babcock and Wilcox, 351 U.S. 105 (1956)

National Labor Relations Board v. Jones and Laughlin Steel Corp., 301 U.S. 1 (1937)

Republic Aviation Corp. v. National Labor Relations Board, 324 U.S. 793 (1945)

Rossmore House, 269 NLRB No. 198 (1984)

Schechter Poultry Corp. v. United States, 295 U.S. 495 (1935)

State, County and Municipal Employees v. Woodward, 406 F.2d 137 (8th Cir., 1969)

TRW, Inc., 245 NLRB No. 149 (1979)

BIBLIOGRAPHY

Derek C. Bok, "The Regulation of Campaign Tactics in Representation Elections Under the National Labor Relations Act," in *Harvard Law Review*, 78, no. 1 (1964), reviews such things as the no-solicitation rules, access to employer premises, and prohibited conduct, as they relate to organizational campaigns. Stephen J. Butler, "Labor Law, Injunctions, Boycotts, and Strikes: Section IV of The Norris–La Guardia Act Bars Federal Court Injunction Against Strike Not over an Arbitrable Grievance," in *Cincinnati Law Review*, 49 (1956), challenges the then-accepted belief that the act completely prohibited any type of federal injunctive relief other than the specific exceptions contained in the Labor-Management Relations Act. Archibald Cox, "Rights Under a Labor Agreement," in *Harvard Law Review*, 69 (1956), reviews, in general terms, the rights accorded individuals under a collective-bargaining agreement and how individuals may enforce their rights; and "The Rule of Law in Preserving Union Democracy," *ibid.*, 72 (1959), argues for strong regulations pertaining to internal union elections.

Frank Elkouri and Edna Asper Elkouri, *How Arbitration Works* (1973), is an excellent review of all sorts of arbitrations involving various types of disputes. Marten S. Estey, Philip Taft, and Martin Wagner, eds., *Regulating Union Government* (1964), reviews the impact of the Labor-Management Reporting and Disclosure Act on internal union politics. Felix Frankfurter and Nathan Greene, *The Labor Injunction* (1930), reviews in depth the pervasiveness of the use of the injunction by employers to thwart organizational drives by the labor movement. Arthur Lenhoff, "A Century of American Unionism," in *Boston University Law Review,* 22, no. 3 (1942), contrasts the development of American unions with that of European unions.

Frank W. McCulloch, *The National Labor Relations Board* (1974), reviews the procedures of the NLRB and its operation within the context of labor-management relations. Jean T. McKelvey, *The Changing Law of Fair Representation* (1985), reviews the circumstances under which a union may be liable to one of its members for failing to represent the member's interests in a nonarbitrary and noncapricious manner. Bernard D. Meltzer, *Labor Law: Cases, Materials, and Problems* (1977), is a widely used text. Harry A. Millis and Emily C. Brown, *From the Wagner Act to Taft-Hartley* (1950), reviews the economic and social considerations that prompted Congress to amend the National Labor Relations Act to include union unfair labor practice. Charles J. Morris, ed., *The Developing Labor Law* (1983), reviews the entire scope of labor relations and is highly recommended as a general source for understanding the issues and rules that exist in labor relations.

Stephen I. Schlossberg and Judith A. Scott, *Organizing the Law* (1983), discusses the law as it pertains to organizational campaigns by unions. Joseph Shister, Benjamin Aaron, and Clyde Summers, eds., *Public Policy and Collective Bargaining* (1962), argues that parties who enter collective-bargaining agreements should fashion those agreements to serve general public policies to improve society and the economy. Benjamin J. Taylor and Fred Whitney, *Labor Relations Law* (1979), is another basic textbook. Ralph K. Winter, "Labor Injunctions and Judge-Made Labor Law: The Contemporary Rule of Norris–La Guardia," in *Yale Law Review,* 70 (1960), discusses the act and Court-imposed exceptions to the rule against federal injunctions. E. E. Witte, "Early American Labor Cases," *ibid.*, 35 (1926), analyzes the development of early American labor law through the court systems.

[*See also* COMMERCE CLAUSE; CORPORATIONS AND THE LAW; EQUITY AND EQUITABLE REMEDIES; HUGHES COURT AND ERA; *and* STONE AND VINSON COURTS AND ERAS.]

LAW AND THE MEDIA

M. Ethan Katsh

Our age is noteworthy for the development of television and computers, media that transmit information over vast distances at electronic speed. The introduction of a new communications technology into a society is a historically rare event, with far-reaching consequences for the culture. Recent studies, for example, have shown that the introduction of writing into ancient Greece and the development of printing by movable type in Europe caused permanent and large-scale societal changes. As Marshall McLuhan once noted, when "a new technology comes into a social milieu it cannot cease to permeate that milieu until every institution is saturated."

The relationship between law and media is complicated, frequently misunderstood, and rapidly changing. Law is a powerful force that may be used to try to resist or to channel the impact of the new technology. The aims of regulation will not be accomplished if the qualities of the new media are not clearly understood. Unfortunately, as we shall see below, in the 1980s the regulation of the new media suffers from a dual handicap: there is confusion both about the special qualities of the new media and about the purposes of regulation.

For television, we are still in an early stage of reacting to conflicts and problems that are perceived to be associated with that medium. For computers, we are in an even earlier phase, one in which many of the conflicts that will challenge courts and legislators in years to come have not yet even surfaced. For both media, the response of the legal system is being shaped by two conflicting traditions. First, there is a constitutional provision protecting free speech and press, which suggests that any danger posed by a communications medium is less serious than the damage caused by regulation. The First Amendment is a force that questions the wisdom of interfering with, and regulating, the media. Second, the United States is the most legalistic nation on earth, generally choosing law to resolve conflicts rather than relying on some other mechanism of control. The pressure to deal with problems associated with the new media has led to a regulatory model that has often sidestepped the First Amendment. As we examine the current regulatory model and the nature of the new media, it is important to ascertain which of these traditions is likely to prevail.

Much of this essay is devoted to an analysis of the first fifty years of legal involvement with the new media, a period characterized by the rise of broadcasting technology and the development of a regulatory model for it. During this era, the regulatory approach seems to have been a more powerful influence than the traditions of the First Amendment. The next fifty years, however, may be different. The law is dealing with a moving target, and the current rapid development of new technologies will leave the existing framework for regulation largely obsolete. As this occurs, important choices will be faced about the nature of new laws relating to the media and about what underlying principles should be applied to them.

THE CONSTITUTION AND THE NEW MEDIA

The starting point in any discussion of law and the media in the United States is the First Amendment to the Constitution, which states that "Congress shall make no law . . . abridging the freedom of speech, or of the press." This

371

amendment expresses a policy and a goal—that free communication is fundamental to a democratic society and that it should not be interfered with by the government. It does not, however, define the meaning or the boundaries of that freedom. Supreme Court Justices Hugo L. Black and William O. Douglas believed that the amendment guaranteed absolute protection and that any interference with speech or press was unconstitutional. The prevailing interpretation of the amendment, however, is that a variety of limits on both the circumstances and the content of expression are permissible. The end result of the many decisions in this area is that not only is there no absolute protection provided by the First Amendment but some media are considered by the Court to be less deserving of the benefits of the First Amendment than are others. All media, then, are not created equal. The basic First Amendment question is whether there should be differences in the legal approaches to the old and the new media. Both the courts and Congress have examined the new modes of communication, but neither the cases nor the statutes reveal great depth of understanding. Ithiel de Sola Pool wrote that

> the law has rested on a perception of technology that is sometimes accurate, often innaccurate, and which changes slowly as technology changes fast. . . . Initially, because it is new and a full scientific mastery of the options is not yet at hand, the invention comes into use in a rather clumsy form. Technical laymen, such as judges, perceive the new technology in that early, clumsy form, which then becomes their image of its nature, possibilities, and use. This perception is an incubus on later understanding.
>
> (p. 7)

The courts have asserted that the new media have a First Amendment interest. Yet, they have also tolerated regulation that would not be acceptable if applied to the print media. The Supreme Court, in several cases, has insisted that "differences in the characteristics of new media justify differences in the First Amendment standards applied to them" (*Red Lion Broadcasting Co.* v. *Federal Communications Commission*, 1969). In a case sustaining a Trenton, New Jersey, ordinance banning sound trucks, Justice Robert H.

Jackson wrote, "The moving picture screen, the radio, the newspaper, the handbill, the sound truck and the street corner orator have differing natures, values, abuses and dangers. Each, in my view, is a law unto itself" (*Kovacs* v. *Cooper,* 1949). In allowing the Federal Communications Commission (FCC) to regulate an "indecent" but not obscene radio broadcast, Justice John Paul Stevens wrote, "We have long recognized that each medium of expression presents special First Amendment problems. And of all forms of communication, it is broadcasting that has received the most limited First Amendment protection" (*Federal Communications Commission* v. *Pacifica Foundation,* 1978).

As a result of Supreme Court decisions in the twentieth century, there is no medium of expression that enjoys absolute protection from government interference. This fact is noted in almost every case in which regulation of broadcasting is at issue and provides the basis for those decisions that allow for broadcast regulation. The First Amendment may be considered an entity that allows varying degrees of protection for different media. But should slight interference with one medium justify large-scale regulation of another? The following overview of speech, print, and broadcast regulation is intended to provide the basis for comparisons between these media and for an assessment of whether different regulatory models are justified.

SPEECH

Speech is the oldest and least-regulated medium. The Supreme Court has ruled that there are some instances in which the content and circumstances of speech may be interfered with. Some categories of speech, such as "fighting words" and obscenity, are outside the coverage of the First Amendment. Narrow regulations concerning the "time, place and manner" of public speaking can be imposed when reasonable and necessary. The Court has had some difficulty developing an acceptable standard for justifying restrictions. It seems fair to conclude, nevertheless, that cases allowing interference with speech are unusual and are exceptions to the general rule, which is that free speech is a highly protected and rarely interfered with activity. Cases involving abridgment of speech are well known and historically important, in part because they are unusual and infrequent.

PRINT

Print is both a technology and an industry. It is a form of expression that is approximately five hundred years old, and its history suggests that one should be wary of predicting the future legal status of a medium of communication on the basis of a society's initial response to that medium.

The invention by Johann Gutenberg in the mid-1400s of a method of printing by movable type quickly brought about legal challenges by those in power who perceived the printing press as a potential threat. Ithiel de Sola Pool noted,

> Before printing, there had been no elaborate system of censorship and control over scribes. There did not have to be. The scribes were scattered, working on single manuscripts in monasteries. Moreover, single manuscripts rarely caused a general scandal or major controversy. There was little motive for central control, and control would have been impractical. But after printing, Pope Alexander VI issued a bull in 1501 against the unlicensed printing of books. (p. 14)

In 1529, Henry VIII banned certain books that were odious to him or to the clergy who advised him.

Other laws that developed as a response to printing involved copyright. The concept of copyright did not exist in the age of scribes and manuscripts; the doctrine was specifically designed for the medium of print. This medium created a new and profitable enterprise, and the new doctrine was used to protect the economic interests of printers and authors.

Copyright was also a useful tool for those in power, because as a ban on unrestricted publication, it is a form of censorship. Indeed, the early grants of exclusive printing rights were intended to protect the state and church from unwanted publications. About England in the sixteenth and seventeenth centuries, Plucknett wrote,

> The legitimate book trade, like other trades in the middle ages, was put under the regulation of a city company, the stationers, while enforcement lay with the Privy Council, the Star Chamber, and (for theological matters) the High Commission, who took the view that all printing, however innocent, was a crime unless the work had been previously licensed. Conversely, the government would sometimes give monopoly rights of printing works which it considered meritorious or useful, and in this way the beginnings of copyright appear. (p. 499)

The English copyright laws were part of a regulatory approach to print that also included taxation, licensing, and libel. Enforcement was not altogether successful, and the regulatory approach was eventually abandoned. It is interesting to consider these early responses in England to the perceived threat of the new medium of print.

Modern court cases involving print most often focus either on the act of publishing or on the newsgathering activities of journalists. Publication is the print equivalent of the individual act of speaking and, like speech, enjoys broad First Amendment protection. Indeed, it is probably more difficult to enjoin publication of printed matter than it is to restrain a public speaker. The proof needed to show irreparable harm, which is required to restrain publication, is unlikely to be available except in the rarest instances.

Newsgathering activities of journalists have a much lower status and do not even enjoy general First Amendment protection. Observers have noted that there is no constitutional right to access to government information.

BROADCASTING

The regulation of television in the United States is based on a model that was originally constructed for radio, which was developed in the late nineteenth century. The first broadcasting law was the Wireless Ship Act of 1910, which required all United States passenger ships to have a radio on board. It was hoped that rescues at sea would be aided by calls for help on the radio. In 1912 the military persuaded Congress to pass a statute requiring all radio transmitters to have a license, and the secretary of commerce was given responsibility to administer the act. World War I accelerated the development of radio, and in 1921 the first commercial broadcast stations were established. The Radio Act of 1912 had required radio operators to obtain a license, but the secretary of commerce was not given any authority to refuse anyone a license.

By the mid-1920s the proliferation of stations had reached the point where there were more stations than available frequencies. In 1923, Secretary of Commerce Herbert Hoover decided to reject a license application, but his decision was overturned by the courts (*Hoover* v. *Intercity Radio Co.*). In 1926 he attempted to impose restrictions on the frequency, power, and hours of operation of a station, but he was again thwarted by the courts (*United States* v. *Zenith Radio Corp.*). Hoover had been urging Congress since the early 1920s to amend the Radio Act of 1912 in order to solve the problem, but without success. Several years later, in *National Broadcasting Co.* v. *United States* (1943), a landmark decision upholding the constitutionality of the Communications Act of 1934, Justice Felix Frankfurter described the situation that Hoover had sought to remedy:

> From July, 1926, to February 23, 1927, when Congress enacted the Radio Act of 1927, almost 200 new stations went on the air. These new stations used any frequencies they desired, regardless of the interference thereby caused to others. Existing stations changed to other frequencies and increased their power and hours of operation at will. The result was confusion and chaos. With everybody on the air, nobody could be heard.

The Radio Act of 1927, passed at the urging of President Calvin Coolidge, created a five-member Federal Radio Commission to issue licenses and to assign hours of operation, wavelengths, and levels of operating power. The new regulations issued by the commission caused about 150 of the 732 existing broadcast stations to lose their licenses. In 1934 the Federal Radio Commission was merged into the FCC, which was established by the Communications Act of 1934. This act has been amended frequently since its passage, and legislation has been introduced to replace it; but it remains the

cornerstone of communications policy in the United States.

The FCC is composed of five commissioners, each appointed for a seven-year term by the president, with the approval of the Senate. Not more than three members may be from the same political party, and the chairperson is selected by the president. The FCC has jurisdiction over the telephone and telegraph industries as well as broadcasting. The telephone and telegraph companies were designated common carriers, meaning that they cannot refuse business from customers willing to pay their rates. Broadcasters, however, were to be regulated and subject to licensing requirements and were not to be treated as common carriers. In areas of business that were not subject to FCC regulation, they were to be free to operate like other private companies. Thus, as will be described in more detail later, the Communications Act of 1934 struck a balance between nonregulation and complete government ownership of both airwaves and facilities. As a result, the airwaves are considered public property, authority to use this resource is given to licensees, and some regulation is allowed over broadcasting practices of the licensee.

LICENSING AND PROGRAM CONTENT

The heart of broadcasting regulation is the licensing process. As a result of a 1981 change in the Communications Act, licenses run for a term of five years instead of three. During this period of time, the licensee is given exclusive control over the use of a particular frequency in a particular area. Although the original impetus for the Communications Act and for licensing was to reduce chaos on the airwaves and allow listeners to receive a clear signal, the licensing process has been used to foster other goals as well. As licenses were distributed and later expired, competitors for licenses challenged the original licensee. As a result, the FCC tried to develop standards for choosing which applicant would best secure the "public convenience, interest, or necessity."

The Communications Act and FCC regulations impose some legal qualifications on applicants. Restrictions exist, for example, for aliens and for those whose licenses were previously revoked for antitrust violations. The most important restriction on applicants concerns large media corporations. The commission has issued rules barring the same person or corporation from owning two licenses in the same area and prohibiting a newspaper owner from acquiring a license in the same area. The commission felt that "diversification of control is a public good in a free society, and is additionally desirable where a government licensing system limits access by the public to the use of radio and television facilities."

Applicants for licenses must satisfy the FCC that they have the equipment and expertise to meet the standards for transmitting a quality signal and that they have adequate financial resources to operate the station for one year, even if no advertising revenues are realized. Applicants must persuade the FCC that they are of good moral character and that the granting of a license will be in the public interest. These are the kinds of issues that are difficult to quantify, and as a result, in evaluating competing applicants, the FCC has also been able to enter the area of programming and content. For example, applicants must ascertain the economic, ethnic, and social composition of their communities and propose programming to satisfy community interests and problems.

While the above criteria may seem reasonable to some and unreasonable to others, it is clear that they have not created a smooth and easily workable process. This is particularly apparent in renewal proceedings where the license holder, having made a substantial investment in the past and already possessing a lucrative license, is competing with an applicant who may be promising higher-quality programming or have some other attribute that is lacking in the current holder. Whether or not the current holder should receive preference has been a matter of controversy at various times in the history of the commission. Attempts to identify how much preference should be given to the licensee have not been very successful.

The number of revocations or nonrenewals is fairly low. Between 1970 and 1978, for example, there were only sixty-four such cases among thousands of licensees. The most common grounds were misrepresentation to the commis-

sion, fraudulent billing practices, and departure from promised programming. According to one study, "the Commission seldom took a license because of a single transgression . . . [and] even major violations of the FCC's rules may be excused or lead to sanctions short of the 'death penalty' if the licensee accepts responsibility" (Weiss, Ostroff, and Clift, 76). Usually, a series of charges was required.

In order to restrict the FCC from involving itself deeply in program content, Section 326 of the Communications Act states, "Nothing in this Act shall be understood or construed to give the Commission the power of censorship over the radio communications or signals transmitted by any radio station, and no regulation or condition shall be promulgated or fixed by the Commission which shall interfere with the right of free speech by means of radio communication." Nevertheless, the act of licensing and the other forms of FCC regulation can be considered to be a form of censorship and would certainly be unconstitutional if applied to a newspaper or magazine. The meaning of this section of the act, however, has only been interpreted to keep the FCC from directly reviewing broadcasts in advance.

A 1968 case indicates that current licensees run few risks of losing their license solely because of the content of their broadcasts. In *Anti-Defamation League of B'nai B'rith* v. *Federal Communications Commission*, a petition was filed contesting renewal of a license for a station that had broadcast programs that "made offensive comments concerning persons of the Jewish faith, equating Judaism with Socialism and Socialism with Communism." The FCC granted the renewal, stating,

> The Commission has long held that its function is not to judge the merit, wisdom or accuracy of any broadcast discussion or commentary but to insure that all viewpoints are given fair and equal opportunity for expression and that controverted allegations are balanced by the presentation of opposing viewpoints. Any other position would stifle discussion and destroy broadcasting as a medium of free speech. To require every licensee to defend his decision to present any controversial program that has been complained of in a license renewal hearing would cause most—if not all—licensees to re-

fuse to broadcast any program that was potentially controversial or offensive to any substantial group. More often that [sic] not this would operate to deprive the public of the opportunity to hear unpopular or unorthodox views.

The greater sensitivity to First Amendment considerations does not necessarily mean that licensees are completely unregulated. Obscene speech is prohibited. As a result of a case involving the comedian George Carlin's use of seven "dirty" words in a monologue, "indecent speech" may be grounds for punishment *(Pacifica)*. More important, the licensing process probably acts as a force against the creation of great diversity. The power given to the FCC to "review the content of completed broadcasts in the performance of its regulatory duties" and to "take note of past program content when considering a licensee's renewal application" *(Pacifica)* may have the kind of "chilling effect" that the courts would quickly recognize if it involved a different medium.

THE FAIRNESS DOCTRINE AND THE EQUAL-TIME RULE

While licensing's influence on programming may be indirect, the FCC has issued several regulations that directly affect the control of the broadcaster over what is communicated on the air. The two main examples of this are the fairness doctrine and the equal-time rule.

The fairness doctrine was developed by the FCC and is not part of the Communications Act. It has been in effect since 1949, but it came under attack during the 1970s and faces an uncertain future. The doctrine actually consists of two obligations imposed on broadcasters, each of which is designed to give all opinions on public issues fair coverage.

The first duty requires broadcasters to give adequate and fair coverage to public issues and to air opposing views. In 1974 the commission stated that "(1) the broadcaster must devote a reasonable percentage of time to the coverage of public issues; and (2) his coverage of these issues must be fair in the sense that it provides an opportunity for the presentation of contrasting points of view." At the time of license renewal, the station must supply evidence that it has met

its obligation to provide comprehensive coverage of important community issues. When litigation has occurred involving the fairness doctrine, it has generally concerned the question of whether once one side of an issue has been presented, the opposing side must be presented as well.

The most publicized aspect of the fairness doctrine consists of "personal attack" rules. Whenever an individual is attacked on the air, that person must be given time to reply. These rules were challenged on First Amendment grounds in *Red Lion* (1969). In that case, Justice Byron R. White reaffirmed that the scarcity of broadcast frequencies justified federal regulation of broadcasting and that the fairness doctrine was not inconsistent with the First Amendment. White rejected as speculative the argument that "if political editorials or personal attacks will trigger an obligation in broadcasters to afford the opportunity for expression to speakers who need not pay for time and whose views are unpalatable to the licensees, then broadcasters will be irresistibly forced to self-censorship and their coverage of controversial public issues will be eliminated or at least rendered wholly ineffective."

Section 315 of the Communications Act copied a provision of the Radio Act of 1927 that states,

> If any licensee shall permit any person who is a legally qualified candidate for any public office to use a broadcasting station, he shall afford equal opportunities to all other such candidates for that office in the use of such broadcasting station . . . *Provided,* That such licensee shall have no power of censorship over the material broadcast under the provisions of this paragraph. No obligation is hereby imposed upon any licensee to allow the use of its station by any such candidate.

In 1959, Congress amended the act so that appearances on news programs would not trigger the rule. In 1975 the commission changed its previous policy and ruled that political debates are not covered by Section 315 if they are controlled by someone other than a candidate or broadcaster and if they are legitimate news events.

While the fairness doctrine and the equal-time rule are intended to improve access to the broadcast media, it is not necessarily clear that this is their long-term effect. It is possible that the rules will indirectly deter some kinds of broadcasting. It is also interesting that access rights, which the courts have considered to be consistent with the First Amendment for broadcasting, have been ruled to be a violation of the amendment for the print media. In 1972, Pat Tornillo, the director of the Classroom Teachers Association in Dade County, Florida, and a candidate for the state legislature, was attacked in several editorials in the *Miami Herald.* Tornillo's request for space to reply was denied, even though Florida had a state statute that required newspapers to grant such requests. When the case reached the Supreme Court in 1973, the Florida statute was declared to be unconstitutional. Chief Justice Burger wrote in *Miami Herald Publishing Co.* v. *Tornillo* (1974),

> Even if a newspaper would face no additional costs to comply with a compulsory access law and would not be forced to forgo publication of news or opinion by the inclusion of a reply, the Florida statute fails to clear the barriers of the First Amendment because of its intrusion into the function of editors. A newspaper is more than a passive receptacle or conduit for news, comment, and advertising. The choice of material to go into a newspaper, and the decisions made as to limitations on the size and content of the paper, and treatment of public issues and public officials—whether fair or unfair—constitute the exercise of editorial control and judgment. It has yet to be demonstrated how governmental regulation of this crucial process can be exercised consistent with First Amendment guarantees of a free press as they have evolved to this time.

To the surprise of many commentators, the *Red Lion* decision is not even mentioned in *Tornillo.*

CABLE TELEVISION

While the FCC had been struggling with radio in the 1930s and with television in the 1940s and 1950s, it was suddenly faced with the issue of cable television in the 1960s. Cable television, in which signals are transmitted into the home via a wire rather than through the air, was first used in the 1950s to provide service to communities that had difficulty receiving television signals through the air. In such places, a large antenna could be constructed that could receive broadcast signals, and these signals would be transmitted through cables to homes in the areas. In the 1960s cable systems began operating in areas that already had broadcast television. What had been a supplement to broadcast television was becoming a competitor for local stations, who faced the possibility of a reduction in audience size.

Originally, the FCC refused to become involved in cable regulation. The commission has jurisdiction over broadcasting and common carriers, and cable television was neither of these. The FCC thus felt that it had no more responsibility to get involved with the competitive threat of cable than it would with other rivals to broadcasting, such as movie theaters or book publishers.

By 1965 the FCC had changed its mind and decided that cable came within its jurisdiction. It issued rules requiring cable systems to carry local stations and prohibiting the importation of distant stations carrying the same network programming as the local station. When these regulations were challenged in court, the Supreme Court ruled that the FCC had jurisdiction over cable in areas "reasonably ancillary to the effective performance of the Commission's various responsibilities for the regulation of television broadcasting" (*United States* v. *Southwestern Cable Co.,* 1968).

During the 1970s, the FCC greatly increased its regulation of cable. It imposed equal-time requirements and the fairness doctrine on programs originated by cable systems. It also required cable companies with more than thirty-five hundred subscribers to originate programming. When this requirement was challenged in court, the Supreme Court ruled in favor of the FCC, with Justice William J. Brennan, Jr., declaring that "the cablecasting requirement thus applied is plainly supported by substantial evidence that it will promote the public interest" (*United States* v. *Midwest Video Corp.,* 1972).

This decision seemed to give the FCC broad powers over cable. In 1976 the commission ordered that all cable operators with more than thirty-five hundred subscribers develop a twenty-channel capacity by 1986; that four channels had to be available for use by public, educational, local government, and leased-access users; that equipment must be made available for users of the public-access channel; and that no charge may be assessed for the use of this channel. The Midwest Video Corporation again brought suit and this time prevailed (*Federal Communications Commission* v. *Midwest Video Corp.*, 1979). Justice White accepted Midwest's argument that "the regulations wrest a considerable degree of editorial control from the cable operator and in effect compel the cable system to provide a kind of common-carrier service." This is prohibited by the Communications Act, which states that "a person engaged in . . . broadcasting shall not . . . be deemed a common carrier."

The history of cable regulation illustrates the difficulty of trying to impose regulations on a newly emerging technology that is not very well understood. The period of active regulation (from the mid-1960s to the mid-1970s) was followed in the next few years by various acts of deregulation. In 1980 the commission repealed two restrictions that had protected broadcasting and limited the growth of cable. First, restrictions on the number of distant signals that could be imported were eliminated. Second, it was no longer unlawful for a cable system to import a program for which a local station had purchased exclusive rights.

The cable industry has benefited from more recent Court rulings and administrative agency rulings. In addition, cable operators have benefited from how the copyright act has been applied to them. In the mid-1960s United Artists Television brought suit against Fortnightly, a cable operator in two West Virginia towns, for copyright infringement, based on Fortnightly's retransmission of several copyrighted movies. Although an earlier case had held that a hotel that retransmitted a radio program to rooms through a wire was violating the Copyright Act, the Supreme Court reached an opposite result in *Fortnightly Corp.* v. *United Artists Television* (1968). The Court held that what the cable system was doing did not constitute a "performance" of the kind prohibited by the act. Justice Potter Stewart wrote that "essentially, a CATV system no more than enhances the viewer's capacity to receive the broadcaster's signals; it provides a well-located antenna with an efficient connection to the viewer's television set." The cable system, therefore, was perceived by the Court to be more like a viewer than a broadcaster, and Stewart

concluded that "broadcasters perform. Viewers do not perform."

The *Fortnightly* decision, which was reaffirmed in 1974 in *Teleprompter Corp.* v. *Columbia Broadcasting System,* placed cable in the enviable position of being able to benefit from copyrighted works without paying royalties to the owners of the copyright. The *Teleprompter* decision spurred Congress into completing a revision of the copyright laws that it had begun almost twenty years earlier. The new bill, which was enacted in 1976 and took effect in 1978, imposed copyright liability on cable operators but still left them in a more enviable position than their competitors in broadcasting. Rather than having to negotiate with every copyright owner before using a work, the new copyright law gave cable operators a "compulsory license" to use copyrighted works without first securing permission. In exchange, the cable operators have to pay a fee set by the Copyright Royalty Tribunal. Programming of local stations and network shows from distant stations may still be carried on the cable systems without operators paying any royalty fees, because Congress felt that no damage was being caused to the copyright owner.

A review of such cases, statutes, and administrative regulations concerning speech, print, and broadcasting suggests that there are different legal approaches at work. For broadcasting, there is a regulatory model, which largely determines who may use the medium and for what purpose. There is an administrative structure and process that grants permission to use the airwaves but can also revoke this permission. There is a stated purpose to this regulation—to protect the "public interest"—but there are few standards for determining whether this goal is being achieved.

For speech and print, there is no continuing process of regulation. There are limits to what may be said or printed, and the boundaries of free speech or press are contained in many court decisions. There is no absolute protection for these media, and there is self-regulation both by individuals and by the print media, which limits the diversity of views presented. For speech and print, the relevant law is the First Amendment, whereas for broadcasting, the Communications Act or the body of FCC regulations may be more relevant. The First Amendment, unlike the Communications Act, contains no stated purpose or goal. Many scholars and jurists have attempted to explain the benefits provided by the First Amendment, but there is still no single, generally accepted theory of why the protection it provides is needed. The value of the First Amendment is accepted on faith. Publishers and speakers do not have to show that they are fulfilling any kind of social purpose in order to continue their activities. In most instances, the legal machinery of government can be forgotten by publishers and speakers. This is not the case for broadcasters.

COMMON CARRIERS

The regulatory models for broadcasting and for print and speech are not the only legal approaches that have been developed in the United States. There is one more model that should be of interest to persons interested in law and media—the common carrier. The FCC is responsible not only for radio and television but also for telephone and telegraph communication. Yet, the last two industries are treated very differently from the others. Telephone and telegraph companies are treated as "common carriers," entities that have different rights and obligations from broadcasters.

Common carriers are licensed by government and receive benefits from government, but their essential attribute is that they are not allowed to discriminate in deciding to whom they provide service. They are often monopolies, and their monopoly status may derive from government permission to put wires on public lands or to use public facilities. The Communications Act of 1934 defines the telegraph and telephone industries as common carriers. As a result, the rates for these industries are regulated, whereas broadcasting advertising rates may not be.

The law of the telegraph was originally modeled after railroad law. Although the telegraph was used for communication, it was too costly to use as a medium of political expression or debate. The courts therefore did not see the telegraph as having any First Amendment significance. When the telephone was invented, the model applied to it was the telegraph model, not that of the printing press. First Amendment considerations generally were not considered by the courts. As Ithiel de Sola Pool has noted, "The issue simply did not arise. The telephone was seen as a successor to the telegraph, the tele-

graph in turn was seen as a common carrier like the railroad; and so that was the law applied. The phone was not seen as a successor to the printing press" (p. 103).

Discussions of First Amendment implications have generally been absent from cases involving the telephone, because this instrument was not considered to be an instrument of political value. It has been perceived to be more important for business and commerce than for public affairs. Inadvertently, however, the common-carrier model may protect speech more than the broadcasting sections of the Communications Act, which explicitly prohibit censorship. The term *common carriage* means that access to the mode of communication is guaranteed, perhaps even at subsidized rates. Whereas the right to communicate may be more protected for print, the actual ability to communicate may be most available through common carriage.

The common-carrier model is important to understand because it is likely to appear to be a more and more reasonable form of television regulation in the future. More television in the future will be brought into our homes via cable and less via broadcasting. The first twenty years of cable regulation were governed by the model of television and by the legal precedents of television. Yet, the primary justification for regulation of television, scarcity of space on the frequency spectrum, is not an issue for cable. The common-carrier model has been rejected for cable mainly for economic reasons. It was felt that cable systems would not be built if control over the cable channels were removed from the cable owner. What is ultimately to be feared, however, is the power of the cable operator, if he is allowed to control all programming on all of the channels. Cable has the potential to foster more diversity and communication than print, but the problem is that all "publishers" must use the same facility. Since the cable operator may also be a publisher and originate some programming, there is an incentive to prevent access to the cable for competitors. Dealing with this problem will be a major issue during the next decade.

NEW MEDIA AND REGULATION

Is the coming decade to be the beginning of a new freedom for electronic media? This seems to be the direction of current legal change, but it is important to be constantly aware of the two most important forces affecting change. The first of these is the nature of the new media. The second is how the public perceives the effects of the new media.

Current movement toward deregulation is largely the result of recognition that technological change has made the broadcasting model of regulation obsolete and in most respects unworkable. The broadcasting model has generally been justified on the presumed scarcity of space on the frequency spectrum. Respected Supreme Court justices have repeatedly stated that there was no choice but to have such a system and that licensing was necessary to prevent the chaos that existed in the early 1920s. Rarely have the justices' understanding of reality been so wrong.

The broadcast spectrum actually presented no unique problem of scarcity. All goods are scarce when more people want them than are able to have them. Certainly, the spectrum has abundant space when compared to choice real estate in New York City. The difference between Park Avenue and the broadcast spectrum is that we recognize property rights in land, but not in a broadcast frequency. The licensing model was not an inevitable outcome but a choice. One rejected alternative was complete governmental ownership of all broadcasting facilities, as exists in many European countries. Another option was common-carrier status for allotted frequencies. A third alternative was to create property rights in the spectrum and to allow the market to operate as it usually does with valuable resources. All of these choices would have eliminated the chaotic use of radio frequencies in the 1920s.

The licensing model that was developed was both a function of the technology of the time and also of the fears that existed concerning the "new medium" of the 1920s. Licensing could work because the technology of broadcasting and the way it was used allowed effective enforcement of the regulations. Content and programming could be evaluated because the broadcasters could be easily identified and the number of broadcasters was fairly limited.

An equally important cause of the choice of the broadcasting model was anxiety about the effects of the new technology. The chaos on the airwaves made obvious the need for some action, and "spectrum scarcity" provided a useful justification in the courts, but fears of the new medium may explain more accurately why the print model was not accepted. In 1924, Secretary of Commerce Hoover stated,

> Radio has passed from the field of an adventure to that of a public utility. Nor among the utilities is there one whose activities may yet come more closely to the life of each and every one of our citizens, nor which holds out greater possibilities of future influence, nor which is of more potential public concern. Here is an agency that has reached deep into the family life. We can protect the home by preventing the entry of printed matter destructive to its ideals but we must double guard the radio.
>
> (quoted in Pool, 119–120)

Similarly, President Coolidge noted that "in this new instrument of science there is an opportunity for greater license even than in the use of print, for while parents may exclude corrupting literature from the home, radio reaches directly to our children" (quoted in Pool, 120).

History suggests that any new medium will engender some fear and anxiety. Early English regulation of the printing press, for example, resulted from great anxiety about the possible abuses of the press. Speech and press attained their current protected status only after time allowed society to become familiar with them.

The nature of the new media is such that the scarcity rationale cannot be relied on by the courts forever. Too many transmitters have entered the arena. Broadcasting and cable are being joined by direct broadcast satellites (DBS), satellite master-antenna systems (SMATV), multipoint distribution services (MDS), low-power television (LPTV), and videotapes and videodiscs. In addition, there is the growing telecommunications use of the microcomputer, which can raise each individual to the status of a publisher. Computers will allow for the sharing of information among much larger numbers of individuals in ways that are not now possible. New networks of communication will be created with information obtained by citizens being communicated to other citizens. Unlike broadcasting, which is a mostly hierarchical form of communication, microcomputers allow communication horizontally, to other individuals or groups with similar interests.

The difficulties of licensing in such an environment make the problems faced by the early Federal Radio Commission look trivial. Deregulation will inevitably have considerable appeal under such circumstances. Yet, it is important to remember that deregulation of media is not the same as granting First Amendment protection. Deregulation implies that regulation is lawful, although possibly misguided. The First Amendment assumes that except in rare instances regulation is impermissible.

The difficulty of using traditional means to deal with public fears will lead to debates on a variety of issues as to the wisdom of regulatory proposals. Recent years have seen attempts to deal with national-security and privacy issues related to the new media. Legal doctrines associated with print, such as copyright, will inevitably change. Initial attempts in these areas may be repressive, but long-term control over the content of communication carried by the new media is unlikely. The newest media have more in common with the telephone and Xerox machine than with George Orwell's "Big Brother." Regulation of the content of communication when such media are used will prove to be as difficult as trying to correct or stop a rumor. Until society has adjusted to the new media, however, such attempts will occur and provide both a high level of public debate and the basis for working out the applicability of the First Amendment to a changed society.

CASES

Anti-Defamation League of B'nai B'rith v. Federal Communications Commission, 403 F.2d 169 (D.C. Cir. 1968)

Chandler v. Florida, 449 U.S. 560 (1981)

Federal Communications Commission v. Midwest Video Corp., 440 U.S. 689 (1979)

Federal Communications Commission v. Pacifica Foundation, 438 U.S. 726 (1978)

Federal Radio Commission v. Nelson Bros. Bond and Mortgage Co., 289 U.S. 266 (1933)

Fortnightly Corp. v. United Artists Television, 392 U.S. 390 (1968)

Frontier Broadcasting Co. v. Collier, 24 F.C.C. 251 (1958)

Hoover v. Intercity Radio Co., 286 F. 1003 (Ct. App. D.C. 1923)

Kovacs v. Cooper, 336 U.S. 77 (1949)

Miami Herald Publishing Co. v. Tornillo, 418 U.S. 241 (1974)

National Broadcasting Co. v. United States, 319 U.S. 190 (1943)

Red Lion Broadcasting Co. v. Federal Communications Commission, 395 U.S. 367 (1969)

Teleprompter Corp. v. Columbia Broadcasting System, 415 U.S. 394 (1974)

United States v. Midwest Video Corp., 406 U.S. 649 (1972)

United States v. Southwestern Cable Co., 392 U.S. 157 (1968)

United States v. Zenith Radio Corp., 12 F.2d 614 (E.D. Ill. 1926)

BIBLIOGRAPHY

Erik Barnouw, *A History of Broadcasting in the United States*, 3 vols. (1966), is a comprehensive history of television. Daniel Brenner and William Rivers, eds., *Free But Regulated* (1982), is a collection of essays about important media law issues. Zechariah Chafee, *Free Speech in the United States* (1941), explores the historical meaning of the First Amendment. Elizabeth Eisenstein, *The Printing Press as an Agent of Change* (1979), analyzes the impact of the invention of printing on European society. Thomas I. Emerson, *The System of Freedom of Expression* (1970) and *Toward a General Theory of the First Amendment* (1963), presents a theory on the scope and purpose of legal protection of expression.

Fred Friendly, *The Good Guys, The Bad Guys and the First Amendment* (1975), discusses the *Red Lion* case and the history of the fairness doctrine. Eric A. Havelock, *Preface to Plato* (1963), discusses the influence of writing on the society of ancient Greece. Starr Hiltz and Murray Turoff, *The Network Nation* (1978), examines media influence. Harold Innis, *The Bias of Communication* (1951) and *Empire and Communications* (1950), explains the media theories of Innis, McLuhan's colleague and mentor.

Frank J. Kahn, *Documents of American Broadcasting* (1968), contains important historical source material about broadcasting. M. Ethan Katsh, "Communications Revolutions and Legal Revolutions," in *Nova Law Journal*, 8 (1984), explores the nature of the new media and their influence on legal doctrines, institutions, and values. Philip B. Kurland, James Mercurio, and George H. Shapiro, *Cablespeech* (1983), argues for full First Amendment protection for cable television. Leonard Levy, *Emergence of a Free Press* (1985), argues that the framers of the Constitution did not have a comprehensive theory of the relationship between free expression and democratic government. Marshall McLuhan, *Understanding Media* (1964) and *The Gutenberg Galaxi* (1962), explains his theories of the influence of media on society. Alexander Meiklejohn, *Free Speech and its Relation to Self-Government* (1948), argues that self-governance is the most important facet of the First Amendment.

New York University School of Law, *Law and Television of the Eighties* (1983), is a symposium on a variety of legal issues concerning the future of television. Lyman R. Patterson, *Copyright in Historical Perspective* (1968), explains the original reasons for copyright protection. Theodore F. Plucknett, *A Concise History of the Common Law* (1956), is a fine introduction to its subject. Ithiel de Sola Pool, *Technologies of Freedom* (1983), is an important scholarly analysis of the influence of the new media on First Amendment values. Steven Simmons, *The Fairness Doctrine and the Media* (1978), is a scholarly treatment of the history and operation of the fairness doctrine. Potter Stewart, "Or of the Press," in *Hastings Law Journal,* 26 (1976), argues that the media are entitled to special constitutional protection in addition to rights provided by the speech clause.

United States Senate, *Print and Electronic Media: The Case for First Amendment Parity* (1983), a report submitted to the Senate Committee on Commerce, Science, and Transportation, argues that there is no longer a spectrum scarcity problem, which would justify differential treatment of print and new

media. United States Senate Committee on Commerce, Science, and Transportation, *Hearings on Freedom of Expression* (1982), contains testimony on expanding First Amendment rights of broadcasters. Frederic Weiss, David Ostroff, and Charles Clift III, "Station License Revocations and Denial of Renewal, 1970–1978," in *Journal of Broadcasting,* 24 (1980), examines the reasons for, and frequency of, license-renewal denials.

[*See also* ADMINISTRATIVE AGENCIES; ADMINISTRATIVE LAW; FREE SPEECH AND EXPRESSION; *and* PRIVACY.]

MILITARY LAW

Edward F. Sherman

M ILITARY law provides the legal mechanism for controlling the conduct of military personnel. The objective of any criminal law system —and the court-martial is essentially a criminal law system that replaces the civilian courts within the military—is to provide a fair and impartial forum for determination of guilt or innocence. The court-martial also serves the purpose of enforcing good order and discipline and of assuring compliance with the unique requirements and regimen of military life.

HISTORICAL ANTECEDENTS TO AMERICAN MILITARY LAW

Modern military justice traces its roots back to the Roman period. The Romans developed a regularized system of military law with rules, originally customary but ultimately codified, that identified the kinds of conduct prohibited and the penalties to be inflicted. Commanders had broad discretion in matters of discipline and punishment, but they could not personally administer discipline in all cases. Thus, punishment was usually administered by lower-ranking officers or by tribunes—military officers who sat in councils and conducted military trials. These councils were the forerunner of the modern court-martial.

With the rise of a professional military class of knights in the Middle Ages, formal laws of war evolved, aimed not only at maintaining internal discipline but also at ensuring compliance with standards for the conduct of hostilities. The English Court of Chivalry, presided over by the chief military officers in the Curia Regis of the crown, administered regulations called Articles of War, which were issued by the commander in chief. Military officers, serving as constables and marshals, heard cases in accordance with the Articles, which were called councils of war and, by the seventeenth century, courts-martial.

By the end of the sixteenth century, detailed codes had been promulgated on the Continent. In 1621, King Gustavus Adolphus II of Sweden developed a code of military justice that served as a model for other countries. Containing 167 articles, it provided not only a catalog of military offenses with prescribed punishments but also a procedural framework for the formalization of punishment.

Gustavus' code provided for a hierarchy of courts-martial—a high court presided over by the general or his field marshal and lower courts in each regiment. Previously punishment by lower-level commanders had been essentially a matter of command fiat with little formality or regulation. The British developed lower-level regimental courts in 1647, and since that time, the hierarchical model of courts convened by various levels of commanders to try offenses of descending orders of seriousness has been a feature of Western military justice.

Gustavus' articles displayed a strict view of how a soldier should behave. One series of articles was aimed at overcoming fear on the battlefield by threatening even more certain and severe punishments: the first to run or fail to defend would be put to death by his comrades; a unit's retiring before coming "to dint of sword" with the enemy would result in every tenth man being hanged and the rest "condemned to carry all the filth out of the Leaguer, until such time as they performe some exploit that is worthy to procure their pardon." Religious offenses such as idolatry, blasphemy, derision or scorn, swearing, neglect of prayers, and failure to keep the Sabbath were subject to a range of punishments from fines to banishment. Next came offenses related to duty to the king and military superiors. Striking an officer was punishable by loss of a hand and, if the officer were hurt, by death.

The distrust of ferment and the fear of disorder among the troops were at the foundation of a number of articles. Mutiny was a capital offense. Among the serious offenses triable by the high court were giving "dishonorable speeches against our Majesty," having "a spite of malice against us or our Country," and speaking "disgracefully, either of our owne Generall's person or endeavours" or of his under-officers. Soldiers had no "liberty to hold any meeting amongst themselves," and if they did so without leave of their captain, both they and any inferior officers in company with them would suffer death.

Gustavus' code was translated into English in 1639 and influenced the structure and language of articles issued by various British commanders and the crown. By the end of the seventeenth century, the right of the crown to try offenses by court-martial, in war and peace and at home or abroad, was firmly established, and the British Articles of War became a model for other European countries.

The British articles incorporated a number of religious offenses, including missing or behaving irreverently at divine service, using an unlawful oath or execration, profaning a place of worship, or offering violence to a chaplain. The prohibition of traitorous or disrespectful words against the monarch was expanded to the whole royal family, and contempt or disrespect toward the general or "words tending to his Hurt or Dishonour" were also proscribed. The problem offenses of a standing army that spent much of its time in garrison—desertion, drunkenness, fighting, improper conduct in quarters, false musters and returns—constituted the greater part of the code.

Few procedural formalities were prescribed in the British articles. Witnesses were to be examined under oath, but rules of evidence were lax. The accused was not provided a lawyer, and even if he could afford to hire one, the lawyer could only sit with him but not examine witnesses or address the court. When the court deliberated, votes were taken, beginning with the youngest

court member, presumably to prevent influence on younger members by higher-ranking members. Contrary to the requirement of jury unanimity at common law, a simple majority was sufficient, with a two-thirds concurrence required in capital cases.

AMERICAN ARTICLES OF WAR

The eighteenth-century British Articles of War provided a balance between command discretion and procedural regularity that served the needs of the growing British Empire. They were adopted almost verbatim by the Continental Congress in 1775.

One deviation from the British practice in the American Articles of War was a limitation on the number of lashes imposed by a court-martial, to thirty-nine. The British had no limit on the number of lashes, and the average number awarded in British general courts-martial during the American Revolution was more than seven hundred. Flogging was not popular in the colonies and was viewed by many as a symbol of the tyranny they opposed. Nevertheless, in September 1776, upon the importuning of Judge Advocate General William Tudor and General George Washington, Congress increased the permissible number of lashes to one hundred. Washington still thought this insufficient, but Congress refused his further requests to increase the limit to five hundred. Washington, a humane commander for his time, nevertheless shared the prevalent military attitude of the day that men could only be made to bear the danger of battle and the unpleasantness of military life by threats of severe punishment.

The First Congress in 1789 adopted the same articles of war that had governed the Continental army. They were amended slightly in 1806. The 1806 articles governed the army without substantial change until 1874 and provided a structure not substantially altered until the passage of the Uniform Code of Military Justice (UCMJ) in 1950. The Articles for the Government of the Navy became the naval counterpart to the Articles of War, differing somewhat in terminology, offenses, and procedures.

There were two kinds of courts-martial: the general court-martial, convened by a high-level commander for serious offenses, and a regimental court-martial (later called a special court-martial), convened by the commander of a regiment (about one thousand men) for less serious offenses. Garrison courts-martial (subsequently called summary courts-martial) developed later, permitting commanders below the regimental level to convene a court with even more limited punishments. The overriding characteristic of the system continued to be the breadth of control exercised by the commander who convened the court. Unlike a civilian trial, where different functions were performed by independent persons, the commander alone determined whether there was sufficient evidence to prosecute, selected court members and counsel from his subordinates, and reviewed the decision.

The court-martial was a distinctively military hearing, with few of the trappings of a civilian trial. The court members sat at a long table at the front of the room with the president—the highest-ranking member—as presiding officer. Rules of military courtesy, such as saluting and respect for prerogatives of rank, were strictly observed. There was no judge. The judge advocate, who sat directly in front of the court's table, filled the multiple roles of legal adviser to the court, administrator, prosecutor, and informal adviser to the accused. Trials could also be held in the field, with a box or a drum as a desk—hence the term *drumhead justice.* The trial was a simple, relatively nonlegalistic proceeding. Ordinarily, none of the participants were lawyers. The British rule that a defendant could not be actively represented by counsel, even if he provided his own, was accepted in American court-martial practice by the early nineteenth century.

All offenses listed in the Articles of War were of a military nature because civilian crimes like murder, rape, and larceny could only be tried in a civilian court. However, an act constituting a civilian offense could be the basis for court-martial under the two "general articles" that forbade conduct "prejudicial to good order and military discipline" and conduct "unbecoming an officer and a gentleman." Wide latitude was given to the court-martial to define the content of conduct "prejudicial to good order and military discipline," a provision that came to be called "the Devil's Article" by American sailors because of its malleability of interpretation in the hands of a commander.

Some of the archaic wording of military offenses was updated in the Articles of War of 1874, and some weeding out of anachronistic procedures and language was accomplished in further amendments made in 1913 and 1916. A significant development toward more legalized court-martial procedures was the adoption of a new *Manual for Courts-Martial* in 1917. It contained a new, fifty-page chapter on evidence, which reflected an approach consistent with progressive civilian jurisdictions. It was written largely by the legal scholar John Wigmore, who had recently been commissioned a major and a judge advocate in the army reserve. Other sections of the new *Manual* also drew on civilian practice in respect of certain aspects of the trial, such as motions, receipt of testimony, introduction of evidence, examination of witnesses, objections, and charges to the court.

Based on substantial criticisms of the harshness of the military justice inflicted on the citizen-soldiers of World War I, amendments to the Articles of War were passed in 1920. They added more judicial procedures—such as a "law member" lawyer to advise the court, a right to an appointed nonlawyer defense counsel, and an appeal to newly created boards of review in the judge advocate general's office. But the command-dominated structure of the court-martial was left intact.

POST–WORLD WAR II REFORMS

A new groundswell of criticism of military justice arose after World War II. More Americans than ever before had experienced military justice firsthand, and it was clear that they did not like it. There were more than 1.7 million courts-martial during the war—some 80 percent for acts that would not have been crimes in civilian life—and one hundred capital executions. Forty-five thousand servicemen were still imprisoned when the war ended, and a clemency board appointed by the secretary of the war in 1945 remitted or reduced the sentence in 85 percent of the confinement cases reviewed.

In 1946 a board headed by General James H. Doolittle was appointed to investigate abuses in relationships between officers and enlisted men. It found that "the largest differential which brought the most criticism in every instance, was in the field of military justice and courts-martial procedure which permitted inequities and injustices to enlisted personnel." It called for a "review of the machinery for administering military justice and the courts-martial procedure with a view to making all military personnel subject to the same types of punishment."

The debate over military justice was carried on in legal journals, bar association meetings, the mass media, and finally Congress. Proposals ranged from modest cutbacks on commanders' powers over the appointment of personnel and the conduct of the trial, to the creation of a court-martial system independent of commanders. The services generally opposed changes in the court-martial structure, conducting an active campaign to counteract public support for limiting command control. A number of prominent generals, including Omar N. Bradley and Dwight D. Eisenhower, defended the traditional structure. The "division of command responsibility and the responsibility for the adjudication of offenses and of accused offenders cannot be as separate as it is in our own democratic government," argued General Eisenhower at a meeting of the New York Lawyers' Club on 17 November 1948. "An army is organized to win victory in war and the organization must be one that will bring success in combat," stated Secretary of War Robert Patterson, and "that means singleness of command and the responsibility of the field commander for everything that goes on in the field."

Changes in military organization had weakened the force of these arguments. The war had seen the redistribution of such functions as logistics and personnel administration among specialized units over which individual commanders had no direct authority. If centralized personnel services that deprived the field commander of his authority over such vital matters as assignments, promotions, and training requisites were acceptable, then, it was argued, limiting the commander's authority over court-martial administration should not cripple his effectiveness. In addition, improved communications and transportation had now removed the isolation of individual units, and it was often feasible to transport an accused for court-martial to a center with legal resources or to bring legal personnel to the unit.

The debate was resolved by a compromise, the Uniform Code of Military Justice passed by Congress in 1950. The UCMJ extended significant new due process rights in courts-martial, some of them, such as a right to warnings prior to interrogation, more favorable than were then provided in civilian courts. It also furthered the judicialization of military justice by bringing procedures, at least in general courts-martial, closer to civilian court procedures. A law officer would now perform many of the functions of a judge; a defendant would be entitled to representation by a legally trained military defense counsel; a pretrial investigation by an officer appointed by the commander convening authority would be held before charges could be referred for trial; an accused enlisted man could elect to be tried by a court composed of one-third enlisted men; and the new civilian Court of Military Appeals (COMA) would have discretionary review powers over certain cases from the intermediate boards of review.

Despite the advances it made in military jurisprudence, the UCMJ failed to change the traditional military structure of the court-martial. It retained the traditional hierarchy of general, special, and summary courts-martial, with many procedural safeguards limited to the general court-martial (for example, holding a formal pretrial investigation, having a legally trained law officer preside, and according the right to a lawyer defense counsel). It made no substantial changes in the wording of military crimes, retaining traditional military offenses phrased in vague terms ("conduct unbecoming an officer and a gentleman") and imposing severe limitations on free-speech rights ("contemptuous words" against various political officials).

The commander continued to control court-martial machinery and to appoint the investigating officer, counsel, and court members. The investigating officer could make recommendations, but the commander could still refer charges to a court-martial over his contrary recommendation. The commander reviewed the findings and sentence, but he could only remit or reduce the sentence. "The basic reform which the court-martial system requires and without which no *real* reform is possible—the elimination of command control from the courts—is conspicuously lacking," complained Arthur E. Farmer, chairman of the War Veterans Bar Association committee, in 1949. "We will still have the same old story of a court and counsel, all of whom are dependent upon the appointing and reviewing authority for their efficiency ratings, their promotions, their duties, and their leaves."

COURT OF MILITARY APPEALS

The UCMJ took effect on 31 May 1951, during the Korean War. Contrary to predictions, manpower disruptions and breakdowns of discipline did not materialize. The most significant change turned out to be the creation of the Court of Military Appeals, composed of three civilian judges appointed to fifteen-year terms by the president. The intent of Congress in creating a civilian court was to bring civilian influence to bear on military law, and the COMA accelerated that process. Although its express powers (limited to reviewing certain categories of court-martial convictions) suggested something less than a "supreme court of the military," it would ultimately come to approximate that description.

One of the interesting chapters of American constitutional history is how the individual-rights sections of the Constitution were read into military law by the COMA and by federal courts acting under an expanded doctrine of judicial review on writs of habeas corpus (which was the only available form of federal court review of courts-martial). Historians disagree over the intent of the Founding Fathers to apply the Bill of Rights to courts-martial. As the military became more professional in the early nineteenth century, the view that it was a separate society outside the reach of the Bill of Rights took root in judicial thinking. This culminated in an 1858 Supreme Court decision that military courts were administrative, not judicial, bodies (*Dynes* v. *Hoover*), and in the statement of Chief Justice Salmon P. Chase eight years later that "the power of Congress, in the government of the land and naval forces and of the militia, is not at all affected by the fifth or any other amendment" (*Ex parte Milligan*). This judicial development was reinforced by the publication of Colonel Winthrop's influential treatise on military law in 1886, which stated as absolute doctrine that the Bill of Rights is not applicable to courts-martial, because of their administrative nature.

In its precedent-setting 1953 decision in *Burns* v. *Wilson* (which expanded federal court habeas corpus review of courts-martial to encompass claims of denial of constitutional rights), the Su-

preme Court asserted that "military courts, like the state courts, have the same responsibilities as do the federal courts to protect a person from a violation of his constitutional rights." Chief Judge Robert E. Quinn of the newly created COMA interpreted this as meaning that constitutional guaranties apply to courts-martial, although a majority of that court initially held to the position that service personnel are only entitled to "military due process" (defined as those rights, derived from the UCMJ rather than from the Constitution, requisite to fundamental fairness under the military system). The COMA failed to devise satisfactory standards for application of this doctrine and, after a decade of fitful attempts to apply it, abandoned it in 1960, stating that "the protections of the Bill of Rights, except those which are expressly or by necessary implication inapplicable, are available to members of our armed forces" (*United States* v. *Jacoby*).

The principle that constitutional rights are available unless expressly or by necessary implication inapplicable reflects competing policies that must be reconciled on a case-by-case basis. The willingness of the COMA to scrutinize claims of military necessity as a justification for procedures that do not satisfy constitutional standards has varied with the personnel on the court. The first three appointees in 1951—Robert E. Quinn, a former Rhode Island governor; George W. Latimer, a Utah Supreme Court judge; and Paul W. Brosman, a former dean of Tulane Law School—had all served in the military. During its first five years, the court took a cautious, nonactivist approach to military law, gradually establishing a comprehensive body of precedents but refusing to extend its role much beyond elementary applications of the UCMJ.

The COMA embarked on a more activist course after the appointment in 1956 of Homer Ferguson, a former Michigan prosecutor, United States senator, and ambassador to the Philippines. Ferguson had never been in the military and had little prior exposure to military law. Over the next dozen years, the court began to chip away at traditional court-martial practices that conflicted with constitutional standards. As the Warren Court was remaking civilian criminal law procedures according to more exacting constitutional standards, the COMA increasingly looked to it for precedential guidance. By the late 1960s, the COMA had assimilated into military law many constitutional limitations relating to such matters as search and seizure, interrogation and self-incrimination, detention and arraignment, and speedy trial.

Personnel changes in a court of only three members often affected its prevailing judicial philosophy. Rapid turnover in court personnel in the 1970s kept the alignments in constant flux. A brief activist phase in the late 1970s led to further rejection of some traditional military practices as contrary to the Constitution. However, taking its cue from the Supreme Court's increasingly deferential view of distinctive military practices, the COMA in the 1980s dealt more regularly with the nuts and bolts of military law than with sweeping constitutional issues.

MILITARY JUSTICE ACT OF 1968

By 1968 a number of proposals for change in the UCMJ had gained the support of key members of the military and congressional reformers, resulting in the passage of the Military Justice Act of 1968. The 1968 act did not alter the basic command structure of the UCMJ but contributed to the further civilianization of court-martial functions by converting the law officer into a military judge with powers roughly equivalent to those of the federal judiciary and placing him under the command of the judge advocate general rather than of the local commander. The boards of review were changed into "Courts of Military Review," still constituted under the judge advocate general, but divided into panels. The right to a legally trained defense counsel was extended to special courts-martial, and court-martial convictions previously reviewable only by the convening authority could now be reviewed on request by the judge advocate general.

The reforms of the Military Justice Act of 1968 came at the time when, because of the Vietnam War, public attention was again focused on defects in the court-martial system. Faced with problems of increased absence without leave (AWOL) and desertion, racial violence, drug abuse, graft, political dissent, and war crimes, the military justice system was sorely challenged. Although court-martial rates rose astronomically, the military justice system was curiously impotent to deter the conduct charged. The services relied increasingly upon less-than-honorable administrative discharges, rather than court-martial, in dealing with AWOL, although these procedures also came under attack for their paucity of due process.

Further attempts to bring military practice closer to its civilian counterpart have largely failed. Bills introduced in the 1970s to remove commanders' control over court-martial appointments and machinery and to adopt civilian procedures in such matters as pretrial hearings and investigation, bail, and discovery died in congressional committees. Most of the services did establish defense counsel sections independent of the commander convening authority, and military judges moved to asserting broad authority over the general administration of pending courts-martial and to wearing robes in most of the services. Nevertheless, military judges still lack a fixed term of office and thus can be removed at any time by superiors.

The Military Justice Act of 1983 made a few procedural changes that the military requested: allowing convening authorities to delegate certain court-martial powers (such as excusing court members and detailing military judge and counsel), authorizing the government to appeal certain rulings of the military judge, permitting the accused to waive appellate review, and authorizing, for the first time, direct review of a narrow category of courts-martial by the Supreme Court on writ of certiorari. However, the right to appellate review is still restricted to certain levels of sentence (such as a punitive discharge or a year's confinement), and thus many court-martial convictions are not reviewed by anyone outside the chain of command.

Developments in military law in the 1980s reflected the general retrenchment in the country regarding the rights of those accused of crimes. The Military Rules of Evidence, issued by executive order in 1980, generally followed the format and standards of the Federal Rules of Evidence but retained some distinctive military approaches and chose less protective rights in some areas, such as self-incrimination and search and seizure, than are provided under civilian constitutional precedents. A new *Manual for Courts-Martial* was issued in 1984, also under executive authority. It updated and regularized a number of aspects of court-martial procedures but also took a more prosecutorial approach to such matters as speedy trial, pretrial restraint and confinement, pretrial investigations, and immunity.

THE FIRST AMENDMENT AND THE MILITARY

The question of whether service members are entitled to free-speech rights has often been raised in American history, but until the mid-twentieth century it was generally answered in the negative. The first modern free-speech case was decided by the COMA in *United States* v. *Vorhees* (1954). It upheld censorship regulations as applied to a book by a lieutenant colonel about the Korean War containing passages critical of General Douglas MacArthur. The court recognized the applicability of the First Amendment to the military but said that it was limited by the requirements of military necessity.

The Vietnam War brought a rash of military free-speech cases. The first arose in 1965 when a second lieutenant, Henry W. Howe, Jr., carried a sign reading, with misspellings, "End Johnson's Facist Agression in Vietnam" and "Let's Have More Than a Choice Between Petty Ignorant Facists in 1968" in a peaceful offpost rally. Although off duty and in civilian clothes, he was convicted in a general court-martial of two traditional military crimes applying only to officers, "conduct unbecoming an officer and a gentleman" (Article 133) and using "contemptuous words against the President" (Article 88). He was sentenced to two years at hard labor, forfeiture of pay and allowances, and dismissal.

The Army Board of Review upheld the conviction on a rationale that Howe's conduct endangered the military's subordinate-superior structure by criticizing the commander in chief. This was inconsistent with the Supreme Court's 1968 decision in *Pickering* v. *Board of Education,* which held that a public employee's criticism of a remote employer is protected speech. Given that Howe's speech was expressed in a traditional First Amendment forum (a public rally) and was in the nature of political hyperbole generally allowed in American society, the result could only be justified if military officers' rights to participate in public policy debates are not protected under the First Amendment.

The COMA affirmed, relying on a different rationale. Although the First Amendment applies to the military, it said, the right to free speech is not an absolute, and Howe's speech constituted a "clear and present danger" to discipline in the armed forces when a war was going on (*United States* v. *Howe,* 1967). It relied principally on the Supreme Court's 1951 decision in *Dennis* v. *United States,* which upheld the conviction of Communist party leaders under the Smith Act. However, *Dennis* was modified by a 1957 decision, *Yates* v. *United States,* which reversed the convictions of Communist party members, holding that mere advocacy or teaching of violent overthrow of the government is constitutionally protected and that speech can only be punishable if it is reasonably and ordinarily calculated to incite persons to prohibited action. The Court's 1969 decision in *Brandenberg* v. *Ohio* reiterated that advocacy, even if angry and threatening in tone, is protected speech in the absence of immediate incitement to unlawful conduct. It is difficult to imagine how Howe's participation in the peace rally could meet the *Brandenberg* test, for there was no evidence that he was recognizable as an army officer or that the words on the sign were calculated to incite others to unlawful action.

The COMA returned to First Amendment issues in a 1970 decision involving two black marines, George Daniels and William Harvey, who were court-martialed for making statements at an informal "bull session" that Vietnam was a white man's war and black men should not fight there. Their speech had resulted in some fifteen black marines requesting mast (a procedure for presenting grievances) to talk to the commander about their opposition to going to Vietnam. There were no other incidents, breaches of discipline, or disobedience of orders. Daniels was convicted of the civilian Smith Act offense of attempting to cause insubordination, disloyalty, and refusal of duty in the armed forces, while Harvey was convicted of making "disloyal statements." They received ten-year and six-year sentences, respectively.

The COMA reversed the convictions in *United States* v. *Daniels,* because the court members had not been instructed that his statements must be found to have had a natural tendency to lead to disloyalty, disobedience, or refusal of duty, and in *United States* v. *Harvey* (1971), because the court had not been instructed that Harvey's statements must be found to have been disloyal to the United States and not merely to the Marine Corps. Thus, the COMA limited military prosecutions under the Smith Act to cases where the speech posed a clear and present danger in terms of its tendency to incite others and limited the offense of "disloyal statements" to speech found disloyal to the United States itself.

The COMA again addressed the scope of the First Amendment in the military in a 1972 decision, *United States* v. *Priest*. Seaman Priest, who worked in the Pentagon, edited and published while off duty an underground newspaper called *OM* that was left around the Pentagon and handed out to service members. Printed in red, white, and blue, it offered Priest's opinions about the military and the war, interspersed with cartoons, drawings, poems, and quotations ranging from Goethe to General William Westmoreland. It was full of statements like "Today's Pigs Are Tomorrow's Bacon," "Smash the State. Power to the People," and "Bomb America, Make Coca-Cola Someplace Else."

The COMA upheld Priest's conviction for "disloyal statements," finding that "taken in its entirety, each issue is a call to violent revolution against our Government as an institution because of its role in the Vietnam War." It observed that "comparable statements by civilians must amount to more than mere advocacy and be directed to 'inciting or producing imminent lawless action and likely to produce such action,'" but found this standard unsuitable for the military. It conceded that there was no real risk of revolutionary violence resulting from Priest's bombastic statements but stressed their possible effect on good order and discipline.

Again this constituted a very different view of the clear-and-present-danger test that protects civilian speech under the First Amendment. It assumed, without proof in the individual case, a causal link between statement and disobedience and gave no weight to the positive effects that allowing a free exchange of ideas in the marketplace can have upon morale and in effecting beneficial changes in policies.

The COMA's distinctive treatment of the clear-and-present-danger test coincided with the Supreme Court's acceptance of the separate-society view of the military. In 1973 the Supreme Court upheld the conviction of Captain Howard

Levy, a medical officer who had criticized the war in the presence of other servicemen and stated that he would refuse to go to Vietnam if ordered to do so. Levy challenged as unconstitutionally vague and overbroad the general articles under which he was convicted ("conduct unbecoming an officer and a gentleman"; "disorders and neglects to the prejudice of good order and discipline"; and "conduct of a nature to bring discredit upon the armed forces"). Justice William Rehnquist, writing for a 5–3 majority in *Parker* v. *Levy* (1974), found that there was sufficient elaboration in the *Manual*, military cases, and custom to give a service member notice of what was criminal. He also held that military offenses may sweep more broadly regarding speech than is permissible under civilian statutes because "the military is, by necessity, a specialized society separate from civilian society."

Both the historical support for, and conclusions from, the separate-society rationale are subject to question. Military organization theory today recognizes a gradual convergence of military and civilian social structures. Leadership manuals emphasize "consultative" and "participative" management, rather than unquestioned obedience to authority. Although the military has more exacting demands regarding discipline and obedience, it does not differ materially from police, firefighters, and prison guards who also work in life-endangering situations but whose free-speech rights are not similarly restricted.

The difficult question is whether the military is so distinctive that it must at all times (for example, even in noncombat, barracks situations) deny critical speech rights and protective constitutional procedures. The Vietnam War speech cases challenged that assumption but failed to persuade the courts. The *Levy* case was followed by a series of Supreme Court cases holding that lesser First Amendment standards as to such matters as giving political speeches and distributing literature on post are justified by the separate-society rationale.

THE SCOPE OF COURT-MARTIAL JURISDICTION

A recurring issue in American military law has been the scope of court-martial jurisdiction. The original American Articles of War applied only to soldiers and only included typically military offenses. There was a modest expansion of court-martial jurisdiction during the Civil War, adding common-law felonies (such as murder and rape) committed by soldiers in "time of war" and, in 1916, adding common-law felonies by soldiers in peacetime outside the United States. The UCMJ for the first time established a comprehensive military criminal law system empowered to try service members for both military and civilian offenses committed at any place and under any circumstances. In addition, court-martial jurisdiction was extended to a large collection of civilians, including anyone "serving with or accompanying" an armed force in the field "in time of war"; anyone "serving with, employed by, or accompanying" the armed forces outside the United States; and anyone who, although discharged, was charged with committing, while subject to the UCMJ, an offense punishable by at least five years of confinement.

In 1955 the Supreme Court began chipping away at this expansive military jurisdiction. *Toth* v. *Quarles* declared unconstitutional the UCMJ provision that allowed the court-martial of discharged service members for serious crimes committed while on active duty. Justice Hugo L. Black, writing for the Court, found that fundamental constitutional rights provided in a criminal trial in a federal court—such as a jury chosen at random from peers and independent judges protected by life tenure—are not available in a court-martial. "Conceding to military personnel that high degree of honesty and sense of justice which nearly all of them undoubtedly have," he wrote, "it still remains true that military tribunals have not been and probably never can be constituted in such way that they can have the same kind of qualifications that the Constitution has deemed essential to fair trials of civilians in federal courts." *Toth* also invoked the principle that extensive military court jurisdiction upsets the balance in civil-military relations intended by the Constitution to limit military influence to a narrow sphere of strictly military matters.

After *Toth* the Supreme Court eliminated court-martial jurisdiction over persons "accompanying" the armed forces outside the United States as applied to civilian dependents and employees of the military overseas during peacetime (*Reid* v. *Covert,* 1957). During the Vietnam War, the military court-martialed a number of civilian employees. However, courts overturned such convictions for lack of jurisdiction, stating that to avoid unconstitutionality, the UCMJ article had to be interpreted narrowly so as not to reach such civilian employees abroad, in a war not formally declared by Congress.

In 1969 the *Toth* line of cases reached a high point in imposing constitutional limitations on court-martial jurisdiction. In *O'Callahan* v. *Parker,* the Supreme Court held that mere "status" as an active-duty service member is not sufficient to allow court-martial jurisdiction and that courts-martial may only exercise jurisdiction over servicemen's offenses that are "service-connected." Specifically, it found no court-martial jurisdiction to try a sergeant for housebreaking, assault, and attempted rape in a hotel in Honolulu while he was off duty and in civilian clothes. Justice William O. Douglas' 6–3 majority opinion observed that while a court-martial system "less favorable to defendants" may be necessary when "special needs of the military" are at stake, "history teaches that expansion of military discipline beyond its proper domain carries with it a threat to liberty."

O'Callahan left unclear what would constitute "service-connection," but a 1971 opinion, *Relford* v. *Commandant,* listed twelve factors said to indicate lack of service-connection, such as commission of the crime away from the military installation, a lack of connection with military duties, and absence of a military victim or violation of military property. In decisions in the early 1970s, the COMA took an expansive view of service-connection. It found an offpost offense always to be service-connected if perpetrated against other servicemen or if military affiliation or rank was used in its commission, and it carved out exceptions to *O'Callahan* for "petty offenses," "offenses committed overseas," and offpost marijuana and drug offenses. However, a number of these claims of jurisdiction led to contrary federal court precedents finding no military jurisdiction.

Offpost drug offenses were the most hotly debated issue of court-martial jurisdiction. COMA precedents shifted back and forth on the issue as personnel changed on the court in the 1970s, but in *United States* v. *Trottier* (1980), the court upheld court-martial jurisdiction over sale of marijuana and LSD to an air force drug agent posing as an airman in an offpost apartment. Chief Judge Everett wrote for the majority that drug abuse in the military was of crisis proportions and "as military equipment has become more sophisticated, there is the concomitant increased risk that an operator will be unable to handle the complicated weapons system with which he is entrusted and upon which his safety and that of others may depend." The court viewed jurisdiction over drug offenses as a proper exercise of "war powers" to interdict drug commerce affecting military installations and also found that a number of *Relford* factors were present, such as connection with military duties and threat to a military post. Since *Trottier*, the COMA has rejected automatic jurisdiction over drug cases, instead requiring an ad hoc *Relford* analysis to show that the particular case is service-connected.

THE FUTURE OF AMERICAN MILITARY LAW

American military justice is a complex system of courts, boards, and administrative bodies. It governs more than two million active-duty armed forces and Coast Guard members, one million reservists when on active duty for training, ten thousand service academy cadets and midshipmen, and retired service members entitled to pay, a constituency larger than one-third of the states. At the height of the Vietnam War, more than one hundred thousand courts-martial were being held each year, a figure down to about thirty thousand by 1985, but increased by large numbers of nonjudicial punishment hearings, discharge boards, and other quasi-judicial proceedings. There are some five thousand full-time military lawyers serving in the judge advocate general's corps of the services and many more civilian lawyers and paralegals engaged in various aspects of military law within the defense establishment.

Public interest in military justice rises with wars and recedes in other times. It is perhaps not surprising to find that military justice, when made an issue, often gives rise to polar positions. The countervailing values of defense of the nation and respect for fairness and civil liberties are both central to a democratic society.

History shows that the natural fear of tampering with an institution burdened with the protection of the nation breeds caution. Thus, the great movement for more civilianized procedures and expansion of individual rights in the three decades after the passage of the UCMJ has been followed by a cautious retrenchment. But an institution with the influence, power, and impact that the military has on American society also raises concerns when its internal system of justice fails to conform to societal values. Military justice is thus likely to continue to trouble American society with its unique procedures and extensive controls over the individual.

CASES

Brandenberg v. Ohio, 395 U.S. 444 (1969)
Burns v. Wilson, 346 U.S. 137 (1953)
Dennis v. United States, 341 U.S. 494 (1951)
Dynes v. Hoover, 20 Howard 65 (1858)
Latney v. Ignatius, 416 F. 2d 821 (1969)
Ex parte Milligan, 4 Wallace 2 (1866)
O'Callahan v. Parker, 395 U.S. 258 (1969)
Parker v. Levy, 417 U.S. 733 (1974)
Pickering v. Board of Education, 391 U.S. 563 (1968)
Reid v. Covert, 354 U.S. 1 (1957)
Relford v. Commandant, 401 U.S. 355 (1971)
Toth v. Quarles, 350 U.S. 11 (1955)
United States v. Daniels, 19 U.S.C.M.A. 529, 42 C.M.R. 131 (1970)
United States v. Harvey, 19 U.S.C.M.A. 539, 42 C.M.R. 141 (1971)
United States v. Howe, 17 U.S.C.M.A. 165, 37 C.M.R. 429 (1967)
United States v. Jacoby, 11 U.S.C.M.A. 438, 29 C.M.R. 244 (1960)
United States v. Priest, 21 U.S.C.M.A. 564, 45 C.M.R. 338 (1972)
United States v. Trottier, 9 M.N. 337 C.M.A. (1980)
United States v. Vorhees, 4 U.S.C.M.A. 509, 16 C.M.R. 83 (1954)
Yates v. United States, 354 U.S. 298 (1957)

BIBLIOGRAPHY

Joseph W. Bishop, Jr., *Justice Under Fire: A Study of Military Law* (1974), is an account of the controversial issues of contemporary military justice, from a promilitary position. James Finn, ed., *Conscience and Command: Justice and Discipline in the Military* (1971), contains a series of articles on Vietnam War military justice issues, some by participants in key cases, from a critical position. William T. Generous, Jr., *Swords and Scales: The Development of the Uniform Code of Military Justice* (1973), is a comprehensive history of the UCMJ and its first twenty years, by a historian. Homer E. Moyer, Jr., *Justice and the Military* (1972), is the first modern treatise on military law, covering the principal issues of the time.

Peter J. Rowe and Christopher J. Whelan, eds., *Military Intervention in Democratic Societies: Law, Policy, and Practice in Great Britain and the United States* (1985), is a collection of essays by military-law scholars from different disciplines, focusing on the role of the military in civil disorders and strikes. David A. Schlueter, *Military Criminal Justice: Practice and Procedure* (1982), examines court-martial practice and is directed at practitioners. Charles A. Shanor and Timothy P. Terrell, *Military Law in a Nutshell* (1980), provides an overview of military law.

Robert Sherrill, *Military Justice Is to Justice as Military Music Is to Music* (1970), is a readable and muckraking attack on military justice from the Vietnam War era. William Winthrop, *Military Law and Precedents,* 2nd ed. (1920), is regarded as the classic nineteenth-century and pre-UCMJ military-law treatise. Adam Yarmolinsky, *The Military Establishment: Its Impacts on American Society* (1971), offers a wide-ranging overview of the role of the military in American society, with a focus on legal and structural issues. Donald Zillman, Albert P. Blaustein, Edward F. Sherman, et al., *The Military in American Society* (1978), is a comprehensive text that includes cases and materials on military law with a focus on contemporary issues.

[*See also* CERTIORARI *and* FREE SPEECH AND EXPRESSION.]

PROPERTY LAW

William G. Coskran

PROPERTY law deals with the relationships between two or more parties, a characteristic it shares with most other areas of the law. The distinguishing characteristic of property law is its focus on the relationships that pertain to "objects." Thus, the concept of property law has three components: parties, objects, and relationships.

AN ILLUSTRATIVE FABLE

Let us see how this works in a fable. Suppose that Springview is a large hill that contains a natural-water spring. There is a house on top of the hill. Suppose, further, that Jack and Jill bought Springview. They borrowed money from Buckalot Bank to pay the seller. The Buckalot Bank wanted some protection in case Jack and Jill failed to repay the loan. Buckalot made them sign an agreement (called a mortgage) that authorized the bank to have Springview sold to get the money for repayment of the loan if Jack and Jill failed to pay. Ned Nabor owned land next to Springview. Nabor entered into an agreement (called an easement deed or agreement) with Jack and Jill. It allowed Nabor to run a driveway from his land, across Springview, to the highway. Jack and Jill formed a corporation, called Bucket-Co, to operate a bottled-water supply business. To raise money for its operations, Bucket-Co sold shares of stock in the corporation to Jack, Jill, and Fred Friend. Jack and Jill entered into an agreement (called a lease) with Bucket-Co. According to the agreement, Jack and Jill gave Bucket-Co the right to possess Springview for thirty years and to take water from the spring. Bucket-Co agreed to pay rent to Jack and Jill for the same thirty years.

One day, while Jack and Jill were at Springview to fetch the rent, Jack had a nasty fall down the hill. He died from the injuries. Jill also took a tumble, but she survived her injuries. Jack left a document (called a will) with instructions for giving away his property after his death. It said that his real property should go to Reliable Trust Company. Reliable was directed to manage the property, pay expenses, and spend the profits to take care of Mother Jacquie. Upon the death of Mother Jacquie, Reliable was directed to give the property to Baby Brother Bob. The same document also said that Jack's personal property should be given directly to Sister Sally. The state of Wonder passed an environmental protection statute that prohibited any further water removal from Springview. The house on Springview burned down after being struck by lightning.

This soap opera of events contains examples of parties, objects, and relationships, the three components of property law.

THE PARTIES TO A PROPERTY LAW TRANSACTION

Parties may be individuals. Our fable involves several individuals: Jack, Jill, Ned Nabor, Fred Friend, Mother Jacquie, Baby Brother Bob, and Sister Sally. Parties may also be organizations, such as corporations or government bodies, which are considered to have a legal existence that is separate from the individuals in the organization. Buckalot Bank, Bucket-Co, and Reliable Trust Company are examples of corporations. The state of Wonder is an example of a government entity. Even though Jack, Jill, and Fred Friend were the only stockholders of Bucket-Co, the company had its own separate existence in the eyes of the law. Even though all of our individuals are residents of, voters in, and perhaps officeholders of the state of Wonder, the state has a separate legal existence.

OBJECTS AND PROPERTY LAW

Objects may be divided into three categories: real property, tangible personal property, and intangible personal property. Real property includes land, space above the land for some distance, and growing objects and improvements on the land. Springview and the trees and house on it are examples of real property. Tangible personal property includes movable physical objects. For example, Jack owned an antique bucket collection, hill-climbing boots, and a crown safety helmet. These are examples of tangible personal property.

The term *fixture* is used to identify an object that has changed its category from tangible personal property to real property. The hot-water heater in the house and the pumping equipment for the spring at Springview are examples. These objects started out as movable personal property in a warehouse or storeroom. They were then installed on Springview with the apparent intent that they be adapted for use as part of the real property for their working lives. At this point they became fixtures and classified as real property for most purposes. It is the parties' intent of relatively permanent use as part of the real property that distinguishes fixtures from the objects that remain tangible personal property. The furniture in the house and the water barrels at the spring on Springview remain in the tangible personal property category.

Real property and tangible personal property have physical substance. They can be seen, touched, and, in some cases, heard and smelled. The squeaky water pump and the fragrant rosebushes on Springview catch the attention of our senses. However, intangible personal property is a more illusive category and concept. It is difficult to think of intangible property separate from the physical items or the observable effects associated with it. This problem is not unique to the law, and a common example from physics may help to illustrate the point. We know that electricity exists, yet it is difficult for most of us to have a clear concept of it. We generally think

of electricity in terms of the observable effects, such as a lighted lamp or a running motor. We also think of it in terms of the physical items associated with it, such as switches, meters, and wires. A child asks us for an explanation of electricity flowing through a wire. We most commonly reach for the example of water running through a pipe, because it is easier to grasp the physical characteristics of water.

Jack the tripper, at the time of his death, owned shares of stock in Bucket-Co and had a savings account at Buckalot Bank. These are examples of intangible personal property. Jack received a piece of paper called a stock certificate from Bucket-Co. He received a little booklet called a passbook from Buckalot Bank. But the piece of paper is not the stock, and the booklet is not the savings account; rather, they are the physical evidence of the shares and the account. They are merely the items of tangible personal property that verify the ownership of the intangible personal property. The shares themselves are a composite of rights and duties in the relationship between the corporation and the shareholder. For example, Jack's stock entitled him to receive a portion of the business profits, entitled him to vote for directors to run the corporation, and may have obligated him to contribute additional money to the corporation under limited circumstances. The savings account is basically Jack's right to receive from the bank a certain amount of money. Generally, it would be the amount equal to what he gave the bank, plus the agreed interest, minus any agreed charges.

There are many different types of intangible personal property, and there are even subcategories, such as intellectual property. When a person receives a patent for a product or a copyright for a story, it is recognition that his idea has reached the point that it is a legally protected property interest. There will be tangible evidence of the idea: a written description and model of the product, or a manuscript of the story. However, it is the idea that the law will protect and that is considered to be intangible personal property.

The categories of real property and tangible personal property have had a rather peaceful existence for many years. Their meaning and content have remained quite definite and clear. There has been a gradual but undramatic change over the years in the concept of a fixture. The early approach was to focus on the permanent manner of attachment of the object to the land or building. Today, the focus is on the intent of the parties. The manner of attachment is just one of the ways that intent can be shown. Even with this change, there is no dispute over the categorization of the tangible object as property. The dispute has been over the point at which that property changes from personal to real.

If an object exists and has physical substance, there are no major social policies or values involved in designating it as property. These policies and values come into play when we decide the rules that govern the relationships between parties with respect to the object. This degree of certainty and detachment from policies and values is not true of the intangible personal property category. Here the focus is on the word *property*. Consider the difference between the following two questions: Should we classify this property as real or tangible personal? Should we classify this intangible as property? In the first question, we assume that the physical object is property, and we move right to the question of the type of property. In the second question, we inquire whether the intangible is property at all.

THE NATURE OF PROPERTY

This is an appropriate point to consider what property is. An easy but ambiguous answer is, It depends. The various theories and definitions of property could easily fill a volume. The various views typically deal with the same basic factors: parties, relationships, and objects. They differ primarily in the emphasis placed on particular factors. Suppose we both see an elephant for the first time. You see it by looking back as you run from the charging animal. I see it by turning to look just after the animal has run by, trampling my food supply into a wafer-thin mess. Our concepts of elephant are likely to differ because of a difference in vantage point.

Although an analysis of the varied views of property is fascinating, a couple of simple approaches here must suffice. One is to think of objects such as land, furniture, and stock as property. This is how most people, including most lawyers, commonly use the word. This usage has the virtue of familiarity and simplicity. However, when used in this sense, we must keep

in mind that the object may be intangible, without physical substance, such as the stock. Another approach is to focus on the relationship between the parties and think of property as the position in the relationship that is given recognition and protection of the law. This approach has the virtue of flexibility for dealing with more complex issues and analyses. We will follow a simple usage. *Property* will refer to objects. The legally protected position in the relationship between the parties will be referred to as an *interest in property* or *property interest*.

INTANGIBLE PERSONAL PROPERTY

When thinking about intangible personal property, it is most difficult to separate the object from the relationship. It is also difficult here to separate property from social policies and values. Several court decisions in recent years have dealt with the question of whether certain intangibles should be categorized as property. A decision to treat a particular intangible as property seems to be a policy decision that it should be given the same legal recognition, treatment, and protection that we give to property.

The area of constitutional protections contains some excellent examples. The Fifth Amendment to the Constitution of the United States provides in part, "No person shall . . . be deprived of life, liberty, or property, without due process of law." The Fourteenth Amendment provides in part, "Nor shall any State deprive any person of life, liberty, or property, without due process of law." The Fifth Amendment also provides in part, "Nor shall private property be taken for public use, without just compensation." The government cannot deprive you of your property without due process of law, and if your property is taken for a public use, you must be given just compensation. If an intangible is involved, the availability of these protections depends on categorizing it as property.

The term *due process* refers to fair and reasonable treatment. *Just compensation* refers to the price you would receive for the property if it were sold in the marketplace. The development of concepts of intangible personal property in this area of constitutional protection is quite important. Here are some examples.

In *Goldberg* v. *Kelly* (1970) the Supreme Court

of the United States considered whether the continued entitlement to welfare benefits is a property right protected by the Constitution. New York administered a welfare program that provided financial aid to families with dependent children. Administrators of the program were allowed to terminate benefits when they decided recipients were no longer qualified. The recipients were not given an opportunity for a hearing to challenge the decision before payments were terminated. The former recipients were entitled to a hearing for reinstatement of the benefits after termination. Recipients argued that the lack of a prior opportunity to see and present evidence concerning continuing eligibility was a denial of due process of law. There were two issues before the Court. First, whether the entitlement to continued benefits is protected by the Constitution, and, second, what procedures for terminating benefits are required in order to comply with the fairness requirements of due process of law. Unless the first question were answered affirmatively, there would have been no need for the court to consider the second question.

The Court concentrated on the substantial importance of the entitlement in coming to a decision that it was protected under the Fourteenth Amendment. It is interesting that the Court did not spend time trying to define the word *property*. It concentrated on the significance of the entitlement as a right, based on statute, of the individual in the society. A footnote mentions that it may be more realistic to treat welfare payments as property rather than a gift. The Court in *Goldberg* integrated social policies and values into the decision to treat an intangible as property. Consider this statement by the Court:

> Thus the crucial factor in this context . . . is that termination of aid pending resolution of a controversy over eligibility may deprive an *eligible* recipient of the very means by which to live while he waits. Since he lacks independent resources, his situation becomes immediately desperate. His need to concentrate upon finding the means for daily subsistence, in turn, adversely affects his ability to seek redress from the welfare bureaucracy.

Once the decision was made to extend constitutional protection to the intangible right, the Court moved on to consider the details of a fair procedure for terminating that right.

Does a college or university teacher have a property right to continued employment? Suppose that the educational institution terminates the employment or refuses to renew it. If there is a property right, there are due process protections under the Constitution. These may include a requirement for the institution to show a reasonable basis for the decision at a fair hearing. Two 1972 Supreme Court decisions differed in results but agreed in principle that the benefit of continued employment could be considered to be intangible property. In *Board of Regents* v. *Roth,* the Court decided not to give property protection to a probationary teacher hired on a specific one-year contract. In *Perry* v. *Sindermann* the Court gave property protection to a teacher with several years of teaching employment on annual contracts in the state college system.

Both cases agree on protecting the security of intangible property interests that a person has acquired in specific benefits. They agree that although the property interests may take many forms, they arise from mutual expectations based on rules or understandings. An abstract need or desire for the benefit is insufficient. The facts in the *Roth* case were insufficient to show mutual expectations and understandings of continued employment. The facts in the *Perry* case were sufficient. The Court in *Roth* made an interesting comment that indicates the component of values in property law: "It is a purpose of the ancient institution of property to protect those claims upon which people rely in their daily lives, reliance that must not be arbitrarily undermined." There is a sense of stability that the Court seeks to identify and protect.

Can we consider information to be property? The Supreme Court considered this issue in the case of *Ruckelshaus* v. *Monsanto Co.* (1984). Monsanto Company invents, produces, and sells pesticides, among other products. A federal statute regulates the sale and use of pesticides and requires the pesticides to be registered by the Environmental Protection Agency (EPA). The statute was adopted because of concern over risks to humans and the environment from pesticides. An applicant for registration is required to submit detailed information about the content and effects of the pesticide to the EPA. The agency is authorized, under certain conditions, to disclose the information to other applicants (including competitors) and to the public.

Monsanto claimed that the collection and disclosure of its information pursuant to the statute was a taking of its property without just compensation. The company filed suit against the administrator of the EPA, asserting a violation of Fifth Amendment protection. Monsanto argued that the information should be treated as property for the purposes of constitutional protection. It showed that the information was the product of many years of expensive experimentation, testing, and development. The company maintained strict security procedures to keep the information secret, particularly from its competitors. There was evidence that it typically requires $5 million to $15 million annually for several years to develop a pesticide for commercial use. Development might take between fourteen and twenty-two years. The average company screens twenty thousand prospects for every pesticide it finally markets.

The Court concluded that information called trade secrets could be considered to be property within the meaning of the Fifth Amendment. The opinion states that trade secrets have many of the characteristics of tangible forms of property. Also, the Court pointed out that this treatment of trade secrets is consistent with the idea that property includes more than real property and tangible personal property. It includes the results of labor and invention. When it was decided that the trade secrets were protected property under the Fifth Amendment, the Court then considered whether the statutory procedures amounted to a taking for public use without just compensation.

Sports fans are not neglected in the contests about intangible property. In *Regents of the University of Minnesota* v. *National Collegiate Athletic Association* (1976), a federal trial-court judge decided that the opportunity to play intercollegiate basketball was a property right. Players could not be suspended from the team without the due process requirement of a fair hearing. The judge emphasized the importance of team participation to the student-athlete. Such participation develops concepts of winning, losing, and exerting best efforts. It is an important part of the educational experience, and education is a necessary ingredient of economic success in life. Also, in some cases, it might lead to a rewarding professional basketball career.

The Raiders football organization has been engaged in courtroom battles that make their stadium battles look tame. One of these concerned the nature of intangible personal property. The Raiders organization is a partnership that owns a professional football team as a franchise member of the National Football League. The team played in Oakland, California, for several years. In 1980, negotiations for the team's use of the local stadium broke down. The Raiders decided to move to a new home field in Los Angeles. The city of Oakland expected the move to seriously harm local finances and pride. It blitzed the Raiders in an effort to block the move, bringing an eminent domain action to take over the football team. Oakland has the power of government to take private property for a public use (eminent domain power), subject to the obligation to pay just compensation. The Raiders argued that the team franchise is a network of intangible contract rights, not property subject to eminent domain. In *City of Oakland* v. *Oakland Raiders* (1982) the members of the 1982 California Supreme Court recognized the franchise as intangible personal property. It pointed out that the eminent domain power covered intangible personal property too. The nature of an intangible as property was just one issue in a series of issues to be decided.

It is important whether a particular object or interest is categorized as real property, tangible personal property, or intangible personal property. Something more than conversational rectitude is involved. Rules of law are developed to deal with the relationships between parties. The relationships pertain to certain objects or interests. It is logical that the different characteristics of the objects should be considered in the development of the rules. Jack, the unfortunate character in our fable of Springview, had all three types of property. He owned a real property interest in Springview. He owned the tangible personal property antique bucket collection, hill-climbing boots, and crown safety helmet. He also owned the intangible personal property stock in Bucket-Co and the savings account at Buckalot Bank. Surely we would expect the rules that governed Jack's relationship with other parties to take into account the significant differences in the characteristics of these items.

RELATIONSHIPS BETWEEN PARTIES AND PROPERTY LAW

The action of property law takes place in the relationships between the parties. This is the area where the rules of property law are developed, tested, and applied. Rules arise only when two or more parties assert some power over a tangible or intangible object. Until that occurs, there is no need to deal with the rules of property law. If you somehow lived alone on an undiscovered island, you would not be concerned over rules about property and the concept of ownership. The rules define the rights and obligations arising from the relationship between the parties.

The web of relationships in the Springview fable provides several examples of typical problems. Payments on the loan from Buckalot Bank to Jack and Jill became delinquent after Jack's fatal fall. Buckalot claims it can force a sale of Springview and take the proceeds for repayment of its loan. Jill claims she can protect her interest in Springview by paying only one-half of the loan balance. Bucket-Co claims that a buyer at the forced sale should honor the lease from Jack and Jill to the corporation. Ned Nabor claims that the buyer must permit his continued use of the driveway easement. Reliable Trust Company, Mother Jacquie, Baby Brother Bob, and Sister Sally want the bank to hold off until their interests can be straightened out. Mother Jacquie wants to sell Springview and use the money to travel with a troupe of senior citizen skydivers. Baby Brother Bob, now forty years old, demands that the Reliable Trust Company stop Mother Jacquie. Bob claims that a sale now will jeopardize his right to the appreciated value of Springview when Mother Jacquie dies.

Jill refuses to pay any attention to Reliable Trust Company, Mother Jacquie, or Baby Brother Bob. She claims that she became the sole owner of Springview when Jack died because Jack's will could not give his interest to anyone else. Sister Sally claims the valuable pump equipment at the spring is hers. She relies on Jack's will, which gave his personal property

to her. Mother Jacquie and Baby Brother Bob claim it is part of the real property given to them by Jack's will.

Bucket-Co disagrees. It claims that the corporation can remove the equipment and keep it because the corporation paid for and installed the equipment on the land. Ned has fenced in the driveway easement across Springview. Bucket-Co objects because the fence blocks its use of the driveway. Fred Friend, the new president of Bucket-Co, claims that the corporation is excused from further rent payments because the house on Springview burned down, and the state of Wonder has shut off the water source. Jill claims the use of the land was the purpose of the lease, so the existence of the old house was immaterial. She also claims that the state of Wonder cannot enforce a statute that deprives Springview of the economic value for water extraction. The governor of Wonder, recently elected in a flood of votes from conservationists, asserts the legitimate power of the state to protect trees and shrubs from the danger of drought. These are but a few of the situations where rules are developed to provide stable property relationships between the parties.

The fable of Springview demonstrates that many parties may simultaneously have an interest in the same object. Ownership of real property is not a single, indivisible interest. It is a composite of many interests. Compare the ownership of Springview, in a neighborhood with other properties, to a deck of cards in a box with other decks. We might view the ownership of Springview or the deck as a single unit among the other single units in the neighborhood or the box. On the other hand, we could look at the ownership of Springview or the deck as a composite of interrelated components with different characteristics. Value to the holder depends on the characteristics of the particular component or combination of components being held. The cards, or interests, may be divided among several parties or be held by the same person.

DIVIDING PROPERTY INTERESTS

Interests in property may be divided in a variety of ways. We can observe the effects of physical division in our communities. The apartment or house in which you live is most likely on land that formerly was just a small part of a large parcel. Springview was originally part of a huge parcel of land owned by the government. Many years ago the government divided this parcel into several large farm sites and transferred each site to a different farmer. The expansion of a nearby town made the farmland more valuable for other uses. Frank Farmer sold part of his farmland to Dorothy Developer. Dorothy planned a residential community, which she named Totoville in honor of her former dog. She divided the land into one hundred lots, built houses, and sold each house lot to a different family. Frank sold another part, called Springview, to Jack and Jill.

Physical Divisions. A physical division may also take place in the vertical area above or below the surface of the land. On each lot, Dorothy Developer built a single one-story house, with a little room left over for a small yard. Suppose she had wanted to provide a large parklike recreation area for the residents of Totoville. There would not be enough room for it if she builds separate housing units on separate lots, and she needs to sell one hundred housing units to make the project economically feasible. She could have built a tall building containing one hundred housing units. This would have left substantial open space for the private park. Each buyer would get sole ownership of a particular cubicle of space in the building as the housing unit. Each buyer would also get a partial interest in the building and land, in common with the other ninety-nine buyers. The word *condominium* is typically used to refer to the combined sole ownership of the housing unit cubicle and the common ownership of the land and buildings.

The division of land above and below the land provides for more-varied and more-intense uses as land space becomes scarce. Here is a fascinating example. An old, small restaurant located on a corner at a major intersection in downtown Los Angeles has been open twenty-four hours a day since 1924. Loyal fans have considered it sufficiently unique to have it designated a historic landmark. A real-property development division of a major life insurance company proposes to build a project covering almost the entire block in which the old restaurant is located. The project will include a thirty-six-story office building and a plaza with retail stores and restaurants.

The owner of the old restaurant wants to save it from a demolition crew. He sells the land around the restaurant and the airspace above it to the development company. He retains the restaurant and land below it. Picture the thirty-six stories of polished granite and bronze glazing rising above the humble, 1924-vintage, single-story restaurant. What a creative blend of our need for historical perspective and modern progress!

An additional physical division may take place below the ground. The building will require a multilevel parking area, and presumably, most or all of it will be below ground level. It is conceivable that the restaurant owner could sell the land below a certain level under the restaurant. The development company could then use this subsurface area for parking, subject to the obligation to support the land and restaurant above. The restaurant owner would then end up owning a slice of land and space sandwiched between the airspace and subsurface owned by the development company.

The physical division of real property above and below the land surface raises a couple of interesting questions. Suppose you buy a piece of land, and there has not been any previous division above or below the surface of the land. How far below the surface do you own? How far above the surface do you own? Two Kentucky judges took different approaches in answering those questions in *Edwards* v. *Sims* (1929). There was a dispute over the ownership of the Great Onyx Cave in Kentucky. Lee claimed ownership of any part of the cave extending under his land, and he wanted the court to order a survey. Edwards, the owner of the land containing the mouth of the cave, objected to the survey and Lee's claim of ownership.

Judge Stanley referred to an old legal maxim to resolve the dispute in favor of Lee: *Cujus est solum, ejus est usque ad coelum ad infernos* ("To whomsoever the soil belongs, he owns also to the sky and to the depths"). This rule views the physical extent of real property like a wedge or a piece of pie. It starts at a point in the core of the earth and expands upward into space. Under this view, any portion of the cave beneath Lee's land —that is, in his piece of pie—would belong to him. This is a simple rule that was developed during simple times to resolve simple disputes. It developed before man took so freely to the sky above and the earth below. The question arises whether the rule is still suitable in governing more complex relationships in modern times. Consider the irony of massive claims of trespass as a space shuttle circles the earth, slicing through billions of pie wedges.

Judge Logan dissented in *Edwards* and rejected the old maxim as unrealistic and untrue. He believed that Edwards should own the cave even if part extended under Lee's land. The clarity and eloquence of Logan's words deserve note:

> The rule should be that he who owns the surface is the owner of everything that may be taken from the earth and used for his profit or happiness. Anything which he may take is thereby subjected to his dominion, and it may be well said that it belongs to him. . . .
>
> A cave or cavern should belong absolutely to him who owns its entrance, and this ownership should extend even to its utmost reaches if he has explored and connected these reaches with the entrance. . . .
>
> It is well enough to hang to our theories and ideas, but when there is an effort to apply old principles to present-day conditions, and they will not fit, then it becomes necessary for a readjustment, and principles and facts as they exist in this age must be made conformable. . . . Man had no dominion over the air until recently, and, prior to his conquering the air, no one had any occasion to question the claim of the surface owner that the air above him was subject to his dominion. Naturally the air above him should be subject to his dominion in so far as the use of the space is necessary for his proper enjoyment of the surface, but further than that he has no right in it separate from that of the public at large. The true principle should be announced to the effect that a man who owns the surface, without reservation, owns not only the land itself, but everything upon, above, or under it which he may use for his profit or pleasure, and which he may subject to his dominion and control. But further than this his ownership cannot extend.

The approach taken by Judge Stanley is a simple spatial test. The approach taken by Judge Logan is a more complex test, with factors that will vary from one situation to another. Logan looked at factors such as dominion and control, ability to use for profit or pleasure, and freedom from unreasonable interference. The majority followed the old spatial rule. The different approaches of the two judges have a significance far beyond the issue of the vertical scope of ownership. They demonstrate a tension between the needs for stability of tradition and flexibility of new solutions. The rules governing relationships between parties should be stable so that the parties can plan their conduct with known consequences. On the other hand, the rules should be sufficiently flexible to adapt to the changing needs of a developing society. There are only a few rules that are sufficiently basic to warrant the permanence of stone tablets.

Temporal Divisions. Property interests can be divided into durational segments of time as well as physical segments of area. Each interest has a particular duration. Some interests are considered to be perpetual. If the interest has this longest duration characteristic, it is called a fee simple absolute. Frank Farmer had a fee simple absolute interest in Springview, and he transferred it to Jack and Jill. Generally, the duration of the interest has no relationship to the life duration of the party owning it. When Jack died, his interest in Springview lived on and was transferred (subject to a possible exception mentioned later). However, the duration of the interest may be made identical to the owner's life. Mother Jacquie was given an interest in Springview by Jack's will. The interest, appropriately called a life estate, lasts only as long as she lasts. The length and termination date of a life estate are uncertain. An interest can be created with a specific termination date and duration, such as the thirty-year lease from Jack and Jill to Bucket-Co. A blend of certainty and uncertainty can be found in the month-to-month tenancies used in many apartment rentals. It is certain to last at least one month, and it will be automatically renewed for monthly intervals until one of the parties terminates the relationship.

The perpetual duration of an interest can be divided into a sequence of shorter time segments. These divided, sequential segments of time can be owned by different parties. When Jack and Jill leased their interests in Springview to Bucket-Co, a division of time resulted. Bucket-Co received an interest characterized by the right to possession of Springview for thirty years. Jack and Jill retained an interest characterized by the right to get possession at the end of the thirty years and keep it forever thereafter. This retained interest also included the entitlement to rent during the thirty years. When the lease became effective, Jack, Jill, and Bucket-Co simultaneously had interests in Springview. However, the right to possession pursuant to the interests was sequential. Bucket-Co was given a present interest entitling it to present possession. Jack and Jill retained a present interest entitling them to future possession, after the lease ends.

Jack's will presents another example of a temporal division of property. Assuming for now that his interest did not end at his death, Jack's will made an additional time division of his interest in Springview. The first time segment was given to Mother Jacquie, and the subsequent time segment was given to Baby Brother Bob. The life estate interest owned by Mother Jacquie entitles her to a portion of the rent, shared with Jill, produced by the lease. If the thirty-year lease term expires before Mother Jacquie does, she will be entitled to share possession of Springview with Jill. When Mother Jacquie dies, the life estate interest will end and Baby Brother Bob's interest will then become productive for him. If the lease is still in effect at that time, he will share the rent with Jill. If the lease is over, he can share possession of Springview with Jill.

Look at the web of relationships pertaining to Springview that has arisen just as a result of this time division of property interests. Formerly, Frank Farmer was the sole owner of a fee simple absolute, the perpetual duration interest in Springview. Now, Jill, Bucket-Co, Mother Jacquie, and Baby Brother Bob all have interests in Springview, and each interest has different characteristics.

Concurrent Property Interests. In the previous examples, we focused on dividing the time into successive segments. An interest may also be divided so that possession is shared by parties during the same time segment. When Frank Farmer conveyed his fee simple absolute interest in Springview to Jack and Jill, the two became co-owners of the fee simple absolute. This simultaneous sharing of the same time segment in the same property by two or more parties is referred to as concurrent interests. There are different types of concurrent ownership. Some of the rules governing the relationships between the concurrent owners are the same regardless of the particular type of concurrent ownership. Other rules vary according to the type involved.

This can be seen in a comparison between two common forms of concurrent ownership, a tenancy in common and a joint tenancy. Suppose that before Jack died, Jack and Jill owned their concurrent interests either as tenants in common or as joint tenants. They were each entitled to a share of the benefits of rent from Springview, the amount of each share of profits being proportionate to the amount of the respective share of the concurrent ownership, presumably one-half each; likewise, they were obligated to perform obligations, such as payment of property taxes, in the same proportion. Their relationship of property interests created a mutual obligation of trust and fairness with respect to Springview. Neither could take unfair advantage of the other in dealing with the property. Either one of them was free to make a lifetime transfer of his or her interest to another party. These are general rules characteristic of both the tenancy in common and joint tenancy.

A significant difference between the two would come into play at Jack's death. If Jack and Jill are tenants in common at Jack's death, his interest would continue and be transferred by his will to Reliable Trust Company, Mother Jacquie, and Baby Brother Bob. Together, they would hold a one-half interest received from Jack and would share with Jill, who would retain her one-half interest. If Jack and Jill are joint tenants, Jack's interest would end at his death. The concurrent ownership would end, and Jill, as the surviving joint tenant, would have the interest all to herself. This is called the right of survivorship. Since Jack was powerless to transfer his joint tenancy interest at his death, Jill would not have to share with Reliable Trust Company, Mother Jacquie, or Baby Brother Bob. The desire either to have or to avoid the right of survivorship is the foremost factor in choosing between a tenancy in common and a joint tenancy.

There is an important practical consideration involved with a joint tenancy. In most states that recognize a joint tenancy relationship, it is possible for one of the joint tenants to convert the joint tenancy into a tenancy in common and thereby destroy the right of survivorship. The traditional rule allows this to be done without the consent or knowledge of the other joint tenant. This can frustrate the reasonable expectations of the surviving concurrent owner who neither participated in nor knew about the termination of the right of survivorship.

Suppose that Jack and Jill originally took their interests in Springview as joint tenants. Suppose further that Jack later became disenchanted with the relationship. He could then have followed a simple procedure for terminating the joint tenancy and converted the relationship into a tenancy in common without telling Jill. When Jack died, Jill would have discovered for the first time that the right of survivorship in their relationship had been terminated. The result is that Jill, to her surprise, would have to share with Reliable Trust Company, Mother Jacquie, and Baby Brother Bob. The question arises whether a secret termination of the right of survivorship is consistent with the mutual obligation of trust and fairness required in the concurrent ownership relationship. This is a situation where that which is legal and that which is fair are not aligned. It seems that a requirement of notice to the other party would be a reasonable compromise. The extremes are total freedom to make a secret termination and total prohibition against termination without mutual consent.

Marriage and Property Interests. Jack and Jill might have been married. The marriage relationship has some type of impact on the property relationships of the spouses in every state. There are a variety of ways in which the marital status of an owner can be given recognition in terms of property interests. Several states deal with the situation by following a system of concurrent ownership called community property. This system considers the husband and wife to be a community unit. Their labor and skills during marriage produce as a cooperative venture for their marital community rather than just for the individual dollar producer. If the source of particular property can be traced to a spouse's skills or labor after marriage, the property is owned by both spouses equally in the community-property form of concurrent ownership. This results in rules governing three significant stages of the marital and property relationships: use and disposition of the property during the marriage, division of the property at divorce or dissolution of the marriage, and disposition of the property at the death of one of the spouses. If Springview had been the community property of Jack and Jill at the time of Jack's death, generally Jack would have had the power to transfer a one-half interest by will. The other one-half would remain with Jill. If Jack had not transferred his one-half to others by will, it would have passed to Jill as his surviving spouse.

The community-property system can present difficult issues when the blissful dreams of a personal relationship end. Suppose that Jack was a well-known and highly paid actor in fantasy films. Suppose further that he and Jill lived together somewhat like husband and wife but without marriage. After about six years, Jack and Jill had differences and terminated their personal relationship. During the time they were living together, Jack earned considerable money, which went into his intangible personal property savings account. Jill claimed a share of the property accumulated during their relationship. The California Supreme Court that decided the case of *Marvin* v. *Marvin* (1976) would not treat the relationship as a marriage and would not treat the property accumulated during the relationship as community property. The court would only allow Jill to share if she could prove that she and Jack had made an express or implied contractual agreement to share accumulations during the relationship.

Suppose that instead of being a successful actor living with Jill without marriage, Jack was a college student who met and married Jill, also a college student. Jack went on to medical school, internship, and residency. Jill worked most of the time to support the family. Shortly before Doc Jack opened a private practice, they separated and ultimately ended their marriage. Jack claimed that his antique hickory bucket collection was acquired before the marriage and therefore was his separate personal property. Jill asserted that the medical education and the enhanced earning capacity connected with it constituted the greatest asset of the marriage. She claimed a share of the benefits. Jack denied Jill's claim. Is a professional education acquired during marriage considered property? If so, is it community property of both spouses, or is it separate property of the degreed spouse, acquired with community contributions? If the education is not property, the issue becomes whether the supporting spouse is nevertheless entitled to economic recognition of contributions to the student spouse's achievement. Even if we answer these questions in favor of the supporting spouse, how do we come up with a specific dollar amount? Professional-school students and their spouses (and surely some brides and grooms to be) had racing pulses while watching the progress of a similar dispute in California, *In re Sullivan* (1984).

Before the state supreme court could examine the challenging questions, the state legislature adopted a statutory remedy, effective 1 January 1985. The statute provides for a reimbursement of community contributions to a spouse's education or training when they substantially enhance that spouse's earning capacity.

Other Complex Property Relationships. We have seen property interests physically divided, horizontally and vertically. We have also seen divisions into successive and shared rights to possession. There is still more flexibility for creating multiple relationships regarding a single piece of property. The parts played by Buckalot Bank, Ned Nabor, and Reliable Trust Company demonstrate three more forms of divided interests.

Buckalot Bank received a limited interest in Springview for the purpose of securing repayment of its loan to Jack and Jill. Rules governing the relationships arising from a mortgage or other security interest vary between the states. The rules do, however, share a common characteristic. If the debtor's obligations are not performed, the creditor may cause a forced sale of the debtor's interest to provide repayment of the debt.

Jack and Jill gave Ned Nabor the right to use a driveway across a portion of Springview. The purpose of the use was to provide access to and from Ned's adjoining property. Jack and Jill still retained ownership of the possessory interest in the land where the driveway was located. The easement given to Ned is one example of a variety of limited rights to use the property of another for a specific purpose. Other examples are the city or utility-company pipeline and cable easements running through a portion of Springview for water, electricity, gas, telephones, and sewers.

Jack's will directed the transfer of his interest in Springview to Reliable Trust Company. Reliable was instructed to administer the property for the benefit of Mother Jacquie and Baby Brother Bob. This transaction, called a trust, is an example of division into legal and equitable interests. Reliable Trust Company, the trustee, holds a legal interest that includes the power to manage the property. Mother Jacquie and Baby Brother Bob, the beneficiaries, have equitable

interests that entitle them to receive the net benefits from the property. Jack may have chosen this trust form of division because Mother Jacquie and Baby Brother Bob lacked the experience and judgment to look after the property safely. He also may have thought it desirable to have a neutral party making the business decisions affecting the economic value of the different interests of Mother Jacquie and Baby Brother Bob.

THE GOVERNMENT AND PROPERTY INTERESTS

The most basic relationship in property law is the one between the public government, as the governing body of the society, and the private party. Many theories of public versus private ownership have been tried by various societies. There are many more theories that remain untested outside of academic institutions. A nomadic approach would keep the land free from public or private ownership. The land would be open to roaming use by shifting groups. This approach would limit private property to a few humble products and animals from the land taken for personal use. An authoritarian approach would reserve the ownership of most property to the government. Private parties would be allowed temporary and restricted use of property at the will of the government. An anarchic approach would recognize private ownership of the party with sufficient power to obtain and defend possession.

The American solution is a unique blend of innovation and experiences from other countries. We recognize the sovereign power of the government to take private property for public use or to regulate it for a public purpose. However, we protect private property from government action. The Constitution requires just compensation if the interest is taken and reasonableness if the interest is regulated.

The government may only take private property from an unwilling owner for a public use. The concept of public use is both fundamental and elusive. It goes to the very core of expectations of the proper function of government in American society. Hawaii was the lush scene for a dispute testing the limits of public use. The original Polynesian settlers followed a system of landholding that was remarkably similar to that followed by the people of early England. One island high chief controlled all the land but parceled it out to subchiefs for development. They in turn passed it on to lower chiefs who managed those people occupying and working the land. Private ownership was not recognized. Although this system no longer exists in Hawaii, it left a legacy of ownership concentrated in the hands of a few landowners.

Hawaii enacted legislation designed to break up the large holdings. Basically, it provided for a forced sale of properties to the tenants of the properties. Some of the private owners attacked the legislation as a violation of the Constitution, even though compensation was provided. They argued that it was not a public use to take private property from one owner and transfer it to another private owner. In 1984 the Supreme Court upheld the validity of the legislation in *Hawaii Housing Authority* v. *Midkoff.* The Court reaffirmed the requirement of a public purpose but recognized the broad discretion given to a legislature in adopting socioeconomic legislation. If the taking is rationally related to a conceivable public purpose, the Court will not debate the wisdom of the taking. The Court pointed to the efforts of Hawaiians to remedy the perceived social and economic evils of a land oligopoly and found this to be a permissible public use.

The required payment of just compensation applies when the property interest is taken. However, the government can reasonably regulate property interests without payment of compensation. This regulatory power, often referred to as the police power, is limited to a reasonable exercise for a public purpose. Zoning is a good example. In *Village of Euclid* v. *Ambler Realty Co.* (1926) the Supreme Court declared a comprehensive zoning plan to be a reasonable use of the police power. Generally, the government's exercise of the power to take, requiring compensation, and the power to regulate, not requiring compensation, are clearly distinguishable. However, in some situations there can be a spirited debate over the proper dividing line between regulation and taking.

The state of Wonder restricted deportation of water from Springview. This was an exercise of the regulatory power for the public purpose of preserving the water table for the benefit of the community environment. Suppose the state restricted use of Springview so that it could not be built upon and could not be used for any purpose that would interfere with a totally passive natural state of the land. State officials might assert this was a creative and economical way to accomplish public goals by regulation. Owners of Springview would counter that the regulation goes beyond the reasonable exercise of the police power and has the practical effect of taking the property for public open space.

Justice Oliver Wendell Holmes recognized that regulation which goes too far can amount to a taking of property interests. He also recognized the temptation to use regulation, a less costly alternative for achieving a public purpose. In *Pennsylvania Coal Co.* v. *Mahon* (1922) he said, "When this seemingly absolute protection [against a taking without just compensation] is found to be qualified by the police power, the natural tendency of human nature is to extend the qualification more and more until at last private property disappears. But that cannot be accomplished in this way under the Constitution of the United States." Some might argue that the worthiness of a public goal may justify an uncompensated taking by regulation. Justice Holmes would admonish them as follows: "We are in danger of forgetting that a strong public desire to improve the public condition is not enough to warrant achieving the desire by a shorter cut than the constitutional way of paying for the change."

The American system provides for a fair blend in the relationship between public and private parties. Private property interests are subordinate to the common good of the community. Membership in the community carries the expectation of reasonable regulation. If the action of government amounts to taking a property interest for the benefit of the community, the cost of achieving that benefit is shared by the community members by payment of just compensation.

CONCLUSION

A fair, orderly, and predictable system of relationships is important for the conduct of property affairs. Rules define the rights and obligations arising in the particular relationship between parties. The goal is to provide a clear set of expectations to govern the conduct of the parties in that relationship. The rules contained in express writings or shared understandings provide stability in the relationship and an orderly process for resolving the differences. In most cases, the parties voluntarily conform to these expectations. When a party refuses to comply, the system of laws provides an enforcement mechanism.

America's rules of property law are a product of its unique blend of history, economics, religion, sociology, politics, and other factors. As conditions in the country change, the rules are again tested to see if they continue to function in a manner consistent with its values and goals. This results in a continuing process of pruning and growth.

CASES

Board of Regents v. Roth, 408 U.S. 564 (1972)
City of Oakland v. Oakland Raiders, 32 Cal. 3d 60, 646 P.2d 835, 183 Cal. Rptr. 673 (1982)
Edwards v. Sims, 232 Ky. 791, 24 S.W.2d 619 (1929)
Goldberg v. Kelly, 397 U.S. 254 (1970)
Hawaii Housing Authority v. Midkoff, 463 U.S. 1323 (1984)
Marvin v. Marvin, 18 Cal.3d 660, 557 P.2d 106, 134 Cal. Rptr. 815 (1976)
Pennsylvania Coal Co. v. Mahon, 260 U.S. 393 (1922)
Perry v. Sindermann, 408 U.S. 593 (1972)
Regents of the University of Minnesota v. National Collegiate Athletic Association, 422 F. Supp. 1158 (1976)
Ruckelshaus v. Monsanto Co., 467 U.S. 986 (1984)
In re Sullivan, 37 Cal.3d 762, 691 P.2d 1020, 209 Cal. Rptr. 354 (1984)
Village of Euclid v. Ambler Realty Co., 272 U.S. 365 (1926)

BIBLIOGRAPHY

Richard F. Babcock, *The Zoning Game* (1966), examines the goals, processes, and participants in government regulation of property uses. Ralph E. Boyer, *Survey of the Law of Property* (1981); Olin L. Browder, Jr., Roger Cunningham, and Allan Smith, *Basic Property Law* (1984); John E. Cribbet, *Principles of the Law of Property* (1975); Roger Cunningham et al., *The Law of Property* (1984); and Richard R. Powell and Patrick J. Rohan, *Powell on Real Property* (1968), all provide a general discussion of the background, nature, and application of various property rules.

Cornelius J. Moynihan, *Introduction to the Law of Real Property* (1962), analyzes the creation and transfer of basic property interests, emphasizing historical documents. *Restatement of the Law, Property* (1936–1944), is a collection of rules relating to a variety of property topics, with comments and examples. *Restatement, Second, Property (Donative Transfers)* (1983), is a collection of rules relating to property interests used primarily in family estate planning, with comments and examples. *Restatement, Second, Property (Landlord and Tenant)* (1977), is a collection of rules relating to the relationship between landlord and tenant, with comments and examples.

[*See also* CORPORATIONS AND THE LAW *and* DUE PROCESS OF LAW.]

TAX LAW

Stephen C. Halpern

T HIS brief review focuses on federal personal income tax law. The federal personal income tax, both practically and philosophically, raises central issues about the American governmental system. Practically, the federal income tax provides the fiscal foundation that sustains the operations of the United States government. Philosophically, the law governing the federal income tax raises profound questions about the fairness, wisdom, and legitimacy of the rules determining the share of an individual's "income" that is taken under the law to support the federal governmental enterprise.

These practical and philosophical issues raise complex questions of politics, economics, and ethics. It is through the law of personal income tax that American society tries to determine what is the most effective and equitable method of distributing the burden of paying for the costs of national government. As a corollary, these questions invite analysis of the comparative benefits that the national governmental system bestows on different categories of taxpayers. In this sense, tax law poses perhaps the oldest and most fundamental of cost-benefit analyses. It addresses, quite literally and concretely, the price that the citizenry pays for the benefit of civil government. Decades ago Harold Lasswell defined politics as "who gets what, when, where and how." Seen in this light, the federal income tax law sits squarely at the intersection of American law and politics.

The discussion of the income tax is divided into four parts. The first deals with how income is defined, the second with how the tax concept of "basis" is defined, the third with income taxes associated with gift giving, and the fourth with the notion of income splitting.

THE DEFINITION OF INCOME

Section 61 of the Internal Revenue Code of 1954 defines gross income as "all income from whatever source derived." In view of this skimpy and tautological definition of income, it has historically been left to the courts to flesh out the meaning of income. That has proven to be extremely important as the definition of income is basic to the entire system. By determining what kinds of economic advancements and transactions fall within the definition of income, the amount and nature of the earnings subject to the income tax are computed.

The student of income tax law quickly learns that the cases defining the scope of Section 61 define income to include a wide range of things. The two major cases, *Commissioner* v. *Lo Bou* (1956) and *Commissioner* v. *Glenshaw Glass Co.* (1955), establish that Section 61 of the code taxes all "economic gain" that is not specifically excluded in the statute. At least initially, then, the student learns that any economic gain is considered taxable income unless it is an economic gain specifically excluded from the income tax by the Internal Revenue Code. If *Lo Bou* and *Glenshaw Glass* teach that all economic gain is subject to an income tax, then the crucial next question is, What is "economic gain"? In answering that question we must first wrestle with the fundamental tax concept of "realization." The leading case analyzing that concept is *Eisner* v. *Macomber* (1920).

In *Eisner* the issue before the Supreme Court was whether a stock dividend was income. This proved to be a constitutional question in part, because in the Revenue Act of 1916, Congress had specifically provided that the value of a stock

407

dividend was to be considered income for income tax purposes. Mrs. Macomber, the taxpayer in *Eisner,* alleged that the 1916 act violated the constitutional provision requiring that direct taxes be apportioned according to population. The Sixteenth Amendment, ratified in 1913, had authorized congressional taxes on income even where such taxes were not apportioned according to population. Consequently, when the 1916 Revenue Act declared a stock dividend to be income, it raised a constitutional question: Are stock dividends "income" within the meaning of the Sixteenth Amendment and hence exempt from the constitutional requirement of apportionment?

The Supreme Court responded that while the Revenue Act defined a stock dividend as income, such dividends did not constitute income, because when a taxpayer received a stock dividend there was no realization of income. The Court concluded that the 1916 act was unconstitutional because it levied an unapportioned tax on a kind of economic gain—receiving a stock dividend—that should not be considered income for income tax purposes.

The constitutional import of *Eisner* is of no special significance today. By contrast, the requirement it imposed that there be realization of economic gain for gain to be taxed as income is a bedrock principle of income taxation. The realization issue arose in *Eisner* not in connection with the constitutional question but as an outgrowth of the second fallback position the government argued in the case.

The stock on which the dividend had been issued to Mrs. Macomber had appreciated in value from $100 to $366. The government claimed that because of that appreciation Mrs. Macomber had achieved $266 of gain, which should be subject to an income tax. The government argued that it was using the issuance of the dividend as the occasion to tax the $266 of appreciation in the value of the stock. The Supreme Court rejected that argument, maintaining that the federal income tax reached only realized income. This was an extraordinarily significant legal doctrine, economically and politically.

Ever since *Eisner,* the realization requirement has excluded from the federal income tax all increases in the value of capital. This flatly conflicts with the general gloss given by the courts to Section 61 declaring all economic gain taxable.

The realization requirement means that, for purposes of the federal income tax, the ownership of appreciated property does not constitute economic gain. So much for the need for legal doctrine to square with economic reality.

The exemption from federal income taxes for any increases in the value of capital is the most important exception to the basic rule of Section 61, which defines income as all economic gain. Indeed, this exception to the definition is so large and important as to seriously alter, if not entirely undermine, the original definition itself. In view of *Eisner,* the overarching principle of Section 61 is not that all economic gain is taxed but that all "realized" economic gain is taxed.

In the aftermath of *Eisner* it was established that unrealized increments in the value of capital are not taxable. Courts have determined that the economic benefit produced by the ownership of property that appreciates in value is to be placed in a special category and given extraordinarily advantageous treatment. The tax on that economic gain is, in effect, deferred until the individual taxpayer's investment in the property is terminated. This gives the taxpayer owning appreciating property a tax deferral. The millions of Americans who own homes that appreciate in value each year are familiar with, and take advantage of, this tax-deferral system on the value of what is typically an appreciating but unrealized asset. Moreover, under the so-called step-up provisions of Section 1014 affecting the tax basis of property acquired from a decedent, it is possible to escape entirely any taxation on the appreciation of property held over a period of time.

There are two basic arguments advanced in support of not considering the increased value of an individual's property as taxable economic gain. The first is based on administrative considerations; the second, on equitable ones.

The Evaluation Argument. This objection is premised on the assertion that a proper assessment of the value of capital cannot be made until it is sold. Consequently, it is argued that an accurate determination of the economic gain enjoyed by the taxpayer-owner of appreciating capital cannot be made until the investment ends. If the government taxed individuals on the appreciation of their property each year as of some arbitrary date, the argument goes, everyone would have to assess the value of their homes, cars, jewelry, stock, and other property. Accurately deciding the value of such property and even deciding as a policy matter what kinds of property would be required to be assessed (for example, would the value of rare books or family heirlooms be included) would present administrative encumbrances that would stall and stalemate the tax system.

The Hardship Argument. The rationale behind this objection is that if the government taxed individuals who own valuable appreciating property, such persons might be forced to sell some of that property to pay the tax on it. That result would be unfair and undesirable from a policy perspective. Opposition to taxing people on the appreciation in the value of the family residence would strike most people as oppressive for no other reason than that it would transform what is now a tax boon to millions of taxpayers—home ownership—into a tax disadvantage.

Critics of the hardship and evaluation arguments respond that administering the tax system is already an extraordinarily complex and cumbersome task. Moreover, tax evasion under the current system is already a chronic problem of startling and epidemic proportions. In this context, refraining from taxing appreciating property because it might be difficult to administer such a system is not a compelling reason. First, the government could, without too much difficulty, establish a particular date on which assets had to be officially appraised, and a system—private, public, or a combination of both—for carrying out appraisals. Second, the government could devise a categorization of the items that required appraisal. Such a listing would probably not include all of a taxpayer's property that had changed value during the year.

Policies as to what to include and exclude might be somewhat subjective. Nonetheless, the scope of property to be evaluated for tax purposes could be changed as administrative needs, revenue consequences, and other policy considerations evolved over time. It might be added that in any given year, most taxpayers have a fairly accurate sense as to what is colloquially referred to as their "net worth." Moreover, evaluations of assets for tax purposes already occur in the context of estate taxation.

As to the hardship rationale, here, too, it can be argued that there is no compelling reason to spare owners of valuable, appreciated property the financial hardship that might result from tax-ing the economic gain they have seen from the appreciation of that property. Any taxation is almost by definition a hardship. No taxpayer would see it otherwise.

In the final analysis, the legal doctrine establishing the requirement of realization is an artificial and arbitrary construct that judges have engrafted on to the tax system. There is simply no logical or policy reason that ineluctably supports the definition that has emerged. The realization requirement provides an opportunity to reflect more broadly on the relationship between the judicial and legislative branches and on the role of courts generally.

The Adversarial System and Its Implications. Note the circumstance of Mrs. Macomber. She was an individual taxpayer whose lawyer raised legal and constitutional questions in her behalf to save her money. It is odd that important legal policy decisions should be made in this context—the context of litigation between parties with a particularized dispute to resolve.

In deciding cases like *Eisner,* courts simultaneously seek to accomplish two different, somewhat irreconcilable tasks. They attempt to do justice vis-à-vis the individual litigants to a specific dispute and simultaneously to set a just, fair, and wise policy precedent for all those "similarly situated" who will be affected by the precedent established by the court. Sometimes the need to do justice in the individual case may conflict with the need to deal with the larger policy question reflected in a particular dispute.

Eisner, like any other major policy decision, is significant not for the fate it sealed for the individual litigants but for the general policy rule it advanced. Yet the issues, information, and theories used to resolve the larger policy question derive from the facts of a specific dispute and the arguments advanced by the respective counsel for the litigants in that dispute. In this way, private litigants represented by hired professionals committed to their clients' interests frame the issues, arguments, and range of answers that appellate courts consider in resolving broad policy questions. This might be construed as a strange way to make important national policy decisions under the income tax or any other law.

Donald Horowitz and Arthur S. Miller, among others, have pointed out that the breadth of information and perspective supplied to appellate court judges making national policy decisions is remarkably limited. If this is so, it should be noted that the limited vision and data available to such judges is an artifact of the American adversarial system. In that system disputes framed by lawyers working on behalf of their clients are used as springboards by appellate judges to establish public policy.

The Relationship Between the Judicial and Legislative Branches. That Congress enacts laws and courts interpret them is a commonplace observation about the American system of checks and balances. Yet, what Congress means when it uses certain statutory language in a provision of the code is often hardly an elementary matter.

The so-called intent of Congress with respect to a particular provision, phrase, or word may really be the separate and distinct mental impressions and intentions of as many as 535 members of Congress who voted on the language and formed their individual perceptions and understandings as to what the words mean. In any collective body the meaning of language contained in rules passed by the body is invariably difficult and quite often impossible to discern. This is as true in tax law as in other substantive areas of the law. Hence, ambiguity about the meaning of phrases or provisions in the code, including some critical provisions, inescapably leaves courts free to legislate—to make and actually establish the tax law in the guise of interpreting it.

Yet, the interpretation of statutory language by courts is complicated not merely because different people may understand the same words to mean different things but because language itself suffers certain inherent limitations. However precise, specific, deliberate, careful, and comprehensive a legislator may try to be in drafting tax or other rules, it is inescapable that there will be subjectivity and discretion in interpreting the language in those rules. Hence, even if the proverbial philosopher-king rather than a collective body like Congress wrote the tax code, interpretive choice in construing words would not, and could not, be eliminated.

The nature of the legislative process compounds the problems associated with "interpreting" the law. It depends on negotiation, give-and-take, and a willingness to compromise. Specificity and precision of language may be compromised in order to pass legislation. From the perspective of those seeking to win enactment of laws, it may be very desirable that ambiguous language be employed or that different legislators have different understandings of the same language or words. Such ambiguity and confusion may be needed to win passage of tax or other legislation.

Ambiguity and generality in language may be necessary to camouflage or smooth over deep and irreconcilable differences among legislators and to enhance the likelihood of majority legislative approval. The result of this situation is that courts often have to construe congressional language, which leaves the judiciary with much discretion and power to determine the governing legal rule. The meaning of Section 61 of the Internal Revenue Code is a good example.

We know that Section 61 defines gross income as "all income from whatever source derived." The "realization" requirement was engrafted onto that statutory language by the courts. Such engrafting gives rise to a fundamental legal phenomenon. In the guise of "interpreting the law," judges independently created legal concepts and rules with important consequences. By virtue of the legal system's traditional commitment to precedent, these judge-made legal rules and concepts take on a life and significance of their own. This judicial "freedom to legislate" is at the root of both the unique power of American courts and of the intense political criticism occasionally directed at them.

The thorny problems that attend the interpretation of language are exacerbated by the adversarial legal system. Lawyers, and most emphatically tax lawyers, are paid professionals whose task it is to interpret any possible ambiguity in the code to the advantage of their clients and to press that interpretation in as compelling and persuasive a manner as they can on the Internal Revenue Service (IRS) or a court adjudicating the dispute.

The use and meaning of language is central to the attorney's craft. That skill is perhaps nowhere as important as in interpreting tax statutes. The interested layperson would be well advised, when moved by a momentary pique of curiosity, to obtain a copy of the Internal Revenue Code and the several volumes of accompanying regulations that are promulgated by the IRS and that interpret the code. The complexity, density, and occasional incomprehensibility of the code and regulations will perhaps at first dazzle and challenge the reader, but ultimately cause despair and depression. Yet, in the interpretation of these cumbersome and densely worded rules, the attorney's client has a direct and often substantial pecuniary interest. The client's pecuniary interest will in turn be directly affected by the accuracy of the attorney's interpretation of the language and the persuasiveness with which he can press his construction on the IRS or court.

For lawyer and layman alike, legal language generally is stilted, excessively formalistic, full of unnecessary jargon, and often difficult to follow. Standard leases, wills, and even parking tickets confirm this view. Yet in all of American law the Internal Revenue Code and Regulations rank among the most difficult set of legal rules to decipher.

It is exceedingly difficult for the layperson to develop even the slightest capacity to fathom the "system" even as it applies to a very specific and limited area of the tax law. Lawyers, too, recognize the complexity of tax law. The Internal Revenue Code is the longest law in the world. It consists of six thousand pages of small print. The topical index to the statute in the version printed by the Commerce Clearing House is fifty-five pages in length. The income tax regulations interpreting the law are contained in four volumes covering about ten thousand pages. Tax lawyers often feel a special bond with one another precisely because they share a knowledge and understanding of an intricate, arcane, and convoluted system of very important legal rules. While the work of most general practitioners typically encompasses a wide range of substantive legal work in such areas as matrimonial matters, wills and estates, real estate, corporations, negligence, and contract law, there is greater acknowledged need among members of the bar for specialization and expertise specifically in tax law. It is not uncommon to find tax attorneys who specialize in one small part or provision of the code.

The master's degree in law is an advanced graduate degree in law requiring formal course work beyond the standard three years of law school, typically involving one and one-half to two years of course work. Few practitioners in solo practice or small or large firms hold such a degree. For the most promising young tax attorneys practicing in the largest and most prestigious firms in the major urban centers and engaged in the most sophisticated tax practice, the master's degree is an increasingly important, if not essential, credential. The need for specialization in tax matters even extends to the judiciary, where a special federal tax court exists.

It is significant that the language, length, and complexity of the income tax law requires highly specialized professionals to decipher it. As noted at the outset, income tax law performs a basic practical and philosophical function. It apportions the costs of operating the governmental apparatus among the individual members of the society. The rules governing that apportionment are of basic political and economic import. Yet, a grasp of, and appreciation for, that system of rules is concealed from the body politic—indeed, concealed from all but a handful of experienced tax attorneys.

Many of the observations advanced thus far are illustrated further by exposition of some additional tax concepts.

BASIS IN TAXATION

The amount of federal income tax due in a taxable exchange is determined by taking the amount the taxpayer realized on the exchange and then subtracting his or her basis from that amount. Be there gain or loss, the greater the basis, the greater the benefit to the taxpayer. Where there is gain, a larger basis diminishes the taxable gain; where there is a deductible loss, a larger basis increases the tax deduction. "Basis" is a good thing for the taxpayer to have.

Essentially, Section 1012 of the code establishes that the basis of property shall be its cost, except where otherwise provided in the code. The underlying rationale of the code is that the government will allow the taxpayer to deduct the costs of obtaining income, thus essentially taxing only profit for the year. Consequently, the taxpayer may deduct the costs of obtaining whatever income is attained. In this respect, the income tax is a tax on net income. Most taxpayers, and most especially entrepreneurs, appreciate this feature of the system. Yet, here again, seemingly arbitrary constraints are placed on this principle. The cost of an individual's labor—the costs associated with providing the personal services that produce income—are not applicable to the basic cost of earning a living. In other words, there is no basis in personal services or labor.

In terms of federal income taxation, at least, personal services are deemed to involve no costs to the taxpayer. In practical effect, this means that the laborer-taxpayer is considered to have paid nothing for the ability to labor. Consequently, every penny that is made from personal services is considered 100 percent economic gain. The personal services that one provides by working for a wage are not considered recognizable costs.

BASIS IN GIFTS AND INTER VIVOS TRANSFERS

Section 102 of the code applies to gratuitous transfers both during life and after death. In a gratuitous transfer, a party transfers ownership of an asset without receiving valuable or legal consideration in return. In lay language, in a gratuitous transfer the asset is conveyed by way of gift. Section 102 provides that gross income does not include the value of property acquired by gift, devise, bequest, or inheritance. As we have seen, Section 1012 provides that an individual's tax basis in an asset is the cost of the asset unless the code specifies otherwise. Section 1015 is one of those sections providing otherwise.

Section 1015 establishes the basis of property acquired by inter vivos gifts. An inter vivos gift involves a voluntary transfer of property by a living person. It is to be contrasted with a testamentary gift, which is a transfer taking effect upon the death of the owner of the asset. Under Section 1015 the basis of property acquired by gift is the donor's basis. Sections 102 and 1015 typically apply in family transactions in which gifts are given.

In combination, Sections 102 and 1015 work as tax deferral for life. Under Section 102, it will be recalled, the value of a gift is excluded from the donee's income. Under Section 1015 the donee, or recipient—who, in reality receives the gift for no cost whatsoever—is permitted to assume the basis of the donor. That is to say, the donee is permitted to take as his or her cost of obtaining the asset, the cost incurred by the donor. Consequently, when the donee ends his or her investment in the gift, the donee is permitted to deduct the donor's basis as the donee's

basis and thereby to diminish the taxable gain, which the law recognizes and taxes. Sections 102 and 1015 in combination facilitate the intergenerational transfer of wealth by minimizing the tax costs that attend such transfers.

The policy choice of Congress in Section 102 and Section 1015 of not taxing the donee on gifts and then giving the donee the basis of the donor—the so-called carry-over basis—amounts to taxing the donee on the income of the donor in a deferred way. The donee may ultimately pay for the appreciation in the value of the property while in the donor's hands when the donee ends his or her investment in the property. But this deferral of income taxation in the inter vivos transfer of gifts can lead to a total exclusion of taxation when Section 1014 is combined with Sections 102 and 1015.

The basic provision of Section 1014 is that the basis of property acquired from a decedent is the fair market value of the property at the date of the decedent's death. This so-called stepped-up basis for property acquired from a decedent constitutes a most effective vehicle for the intergenerational transfer of appreciated property with minimal tax consequences. It all works in a remarkably simple manner.

We have seen that under Section 1012 a donee who receives a gift of property in an inter vivos transfer is not taxed on the value of that property and that, under Section 1015, he steps into the donor's shoes and receives the donor's basis in that property. If the donee dies with the property and arranges to transfer it upon death, the basis in that property, under Section 1014, steps up to the fair market value of the asset at the time of the donee's death.

The significance of this treatment of a decedent's property is that all the appreciation on the value of the property while the decedent held it is completely excluded forever from any income taxation. The new owner of the property—the one receiving it upon the death of the decedent—takes ownership of the asset with a tax basis equal to its fair market value at the time of the decedent's death. In turn, the new owner may hold it for life and pass it on to heirs, who also would receive it with a stepped-up basis under Section 1014. It would be hard to overstate the significance of Section 1014 as a congressional tax giveaway to individuals who own appreciated property and who wish to make intergenerational transfers of that property with minimal tax consequences.

Whether we are speaking of real estate or stocks, the appreciation in the value of property under Section 1014 may forever escape income taxation. Marvin Chirelstein, in his standard summary of federal income tax law, makes the following observations about the import of Section 1014:

> With the value of securities and real estate moving ever higher in the decades that followed the end of World War II, the tax-savings conferred on families of wealth by Section 1014 was obviously immense. The Treasury has estimated that the untaxed appreciation passing through estates was between $10 and $12 billion in 1966 alone. . . .
>
> But apart from revenue loss it could also be observed that Section 1014 substantially extended and magnified an existing inequality between taxpayers who were otherwise similarly situated. If taxpayer A earned, say $100,000 a year in cash salary, while taxpayer B "earned" $100,000 in unrealized stock appreciation, A would pay a current tax of some $50,000 while B would pay nothing. The advantage to B of tax-postponement is very considerable, as has been shown, but one tends to accept it as an unavoidable consequence of the realization requirement. If, however, tax postponement was turned into absolute forgiveness—which was the effect of the step-up in basis under Section 1014—the discrimination between A and B became too great to be justified solely on grounds of administrative necessity.

In response to criticisms of Section 1014, Congress, in the Tax Reform Act of 1976, replaced that provision with Section 1023, which provided that property obtained through inheritance "carried over" into the hands of the heirs at the same basis it had in the hands of the decedent. Having presumably decided to end the Section 1014 stepped-up basis at death, Congress then postponed the effective date of the Section 1023 carry-over provision until 1980.

Yet, when the time came for the end to the stepped-up basis to be implemented, Congress changed its mind and reinstated Section 1014. This was accomplished as a result of provisions that were tacked on to the Crude Oil Windfall Profit Tax Act of 1980. The principal purpose of this legislation, the largest tax bill in United States history, was to deal with the energy problem. However, under the lead of the Senate Finance Committee, the carry-over provisions in Section 1023 for the basis of property transferred by a decedent was eliminated and the Section 1014 step-up was put back in place. In justifying its decision, the Senate Finance Committee estimated revenue losses far below the figures cited in the above passage from Chirelstein. Nonetheless, the Senate's own estimates produced hardly trivial revenue losses. They estimated that the Section 1014 step-up would reduce revenues by $36 million by 1981, $95 million in 1982, $330 million in 1985, and nearly $1 billion in 1990.

Senator Robert Dole, who along with Senator Robert Byrd led the initial effort to delay implementing Section 1023, explained that the reason for completely eliminating the carry-over provision was that the carry-over basis was too complex and difficult to administer and imposed too harsh a tax result. In 1985 the Senate Finance Committee, by unanimous vote, recommended repealing the carry-over basis. A conference committee also voted to include the repeal, citing only the impact the intended reform would have had in raising the cost of administering estates. When the issue reached the floor of the House and Senate, there was no debate reported in the *Congressional Record* on what was apparently considered a minor issue in the tax bill. The concept of basis has a pervasive impact on income tax law. It is a legal construct that affects and structures economic relationships in powerful ways. Like realization, it has become one of the concepts fundamental to the tax system.

INCOME SPLITTING

The splitting of income is really a variation on the problem of calculating what is income for income tax purposes. Income splitting may be an especially dramatic way to cut back the progressive rate structure by enabling two or more individuals, in effect, to divide a total sum of earnings so that the amount of total income is reduced and, consequently, a lower rate of taxation is applied.

Since 1948, husband-and-wife joint returns have been permitted by statute. As a practical matter, this permits income splitting within the marital relationship. Outside the marital context, the most important kind of income splitting that can be pursued by taxpayers is primarily generational income splitting—that is, splitting income between parents and children. The opportunity for families to split income generationally by assigning income to offspring may be quite useful and financially attractive.

Income splitting is of crucial tax significance because as one increases the tax entities to split income, one increases the extent to which the progressive tax-rate structure is avoided and undercut. In the material that follows, we will examine the various opportunities available to taxpayers to realize such advantages and how courts have contributed to them.

Lucas v. *Earl* (1930) is the cornerstone of the income tax system with regard to income splitting. This is so even though *Lucas* involved a husband and wife trying to split income before the 1948 statute permitting joint returns. In *Lucas,* Justice Oliver Wendell Holmes concluded that under the code the individual who earns the income should pay the income tax on it and be precluded from escaping taxation by what Holmes called "anticipatory arrangements and contracts however skillfully devised." There are two critical elements to the definition of earning that evolved in the wake of *Lucas.* The earner of money has come to be considered the individual who generates the money and actually has the power to receive it.

Commentators and judges have said that *Lucas* established the first principle of the American income tax system. In the area of the assignment of income, it is difficult to exaggerate its importance, for it established the basic guidelines with regard to the assignment of income for working and professional people. *Lucas* established, in effect, that such individuals are taxed on the totality of the income they earn, no matter how many children they have. In sum, it decided that they were stuck at the rate that prevails at the income level at which they earn. They could not syphon off their income to their children and thereby reduce their rate of taxation.

As we have noted, *Lucas* has been read to mean that whoever earns the income and whoever could have gotten the income must pay the tax. In a most unusual and significant line of cases applying the code, however, the courts have interpreted the word *earns* to apply to earnings from personal services and not to earnings from property. Once again the critical importance of judicial interpretation of statutory language is clear. We need to note that the issue in *Lucas* was whether personal services income—the fees that a lawyer generated by his professional labors—could be assigned to a spouse. In that regard, there is a very important refinement of the *Lucas* holding in *Blair* v. *Commissioner* (1937).

In *Blair,* a father had created a trust in his will for his son. That trust called for a payment of all the income from the trust to the son during the son's life. The son, in turn, assigned to his daughter for the rest of his life a certain percentage of the income from the trust. Note that in *Blair,* the taxpayer-son transferred to his daughter a part of his interest in the trust established for him by his father. But the interest that he transferred was measured by the same term or period of time during which he himself was entitled to that interest. That is to say, the period during which his daughter was to receive her share of the interest from the trust was chronologically coterminous with the period of time during which the son was entitled to receive benefits from the trust. The taxpayer-son had a life interest, and he assigned a part of that interest to his daughter for the entire term for which he held the interest. The Court held that under these circumstances the daughter would pay the tax on the income transferred to her.

The rule in *Blair* represents a very important and powerful way for parents to carve out for their children portions of money that the parents have received in trust. If utilized properly, it can ensure that the children will be considered the taxable entities for monies generated by trusts originally established to benefit their parents. In seeking to reconcile its holding with *Lucas,* the *Blair* Court acknowledged that *Lucas* imposed the tax on the individual who earned the money and that *Lucas* also explicitly provided that the tax on those monies could not be escaped by skillful anticipatory avoidance schemes. However, in *Blair,* the Court went on to legislate, by little more than judicial fiat, that the *Lucas* holding applied to compensation for personal services and not necessarily to income generated and derived from other sources.

The Court in *Blair* also noted *Burnet* v. *Leininger* (1932). In *Burnet,* a husband who was a member of a laundry firm assigned part of his future partnership income to his wife. The Court concluded that the wife did not thereby become a member of the firm and that the code specifically taxed the distributive share of each partner in the net income of the firm. The Court therefore concluded that the husband could be taxed on his total distributive share, including the amount assigned to his wife. In *Blair* the Court sought to distinguish the circumstances in *Lucas* and *Burnet* from those in *Blair.* The Court observed that *Lucas* and *Burnet* "are not in point. The tax here [in *Blair*] is not upon earnings which are taxed to the one who earns them. . . . There is here no question of evasion or of giving effect to statutory provisions designed to forestall evasion."

The rationale the Court proffers in *Blair* is altogether unpersuasive on two accounts. First, the language of the code makes no distinction whatsoever between the income tax on earnings from personal services and earnings from property held in trust. To suggest otherwise is to rewrite the code in the guise of statutory explication. To the extent that the *Blair* Court suggests that there is any import in tax law to the distinction, one needs to observe quite simply that it is a distinction created by judicial assertion in the *Blair* case itself. Second, it is scarcely credible for the Court to maintain that in *Blair* there was no attempt to evade the progressive tax rate structure. That is precisely what Mr. Blair's arrangement was intended to do. Why else carve out a portion to his daughter in the peculiar way in which he did?

The upshot of the case law on the splitting of income is quite significant from the practical perspective of the taxpayer. The case law makes plain that taxpayers who make money by the sweat of their brow cannot assign any of their income to the members of their family (save wives through joint returns). However, by contrast, individuals who earn money from real property or stocks may assign such income and thereby effectively lower the rate at which they are taxed. This extraordinary result has been produced solely by judicial interpretation of the code and is the direct result of the Court's holding in *Blair.*

The basic tenets of *Blair* and *Lucas* are directly in conflict in terms of the permissibility of splitting income. Nonetheless, both cases established principles of federal income taxation. *Blair* is important because it established the ability of a person to assign the income from property to a family member who is in a lower tax bracket—something that cannot be done with the income earned through personal services. The critical technical element to recognize is that the proper way of splitting income and avoiding the tax on money earned from property holdings is for the donor to transfer a portion of the donor's interest and to retain no reversion. In a reversion, there is a returning of property to the owner of that property after a grant has expired. In other words, where there is a reversion, property is temporarily granted to another for a specified period of time. When that time has elapsed, the property reverts to the grantor. As the case law has evolved, the courts have held that where a donor transfers out part of his interest from the earnings of property to a member of the family, he may thereby shift the tax burden to the donee so long as the donor does not retain any reversion in the interest he transfers.

What emerges from the *Blair* case, among other things, is a distinction based on how the donor happens to slice the pie—the pie being the economic interest involved. It is a distinction between the donor's slicing the pie in a way in which he retains a reversion and slicing it in a way in which he does not retain a reversion. If the donor transfers out in the latter way, he effectively transfers the tax burden. This distinction has nothing whatsoever to do with economic gain, the concept explicitly noted in the definition of income in Section 61. Indeed, the distinction ignores underlying economic realities by imposing an arbitrary criterion that produces different tax treatment. For example, if a person owns two shares of stock and gives away one share to a son, the son pays the income tax on the dividends of that share under the *Blair* ruling. That is so because the donor has given up his entire interest in that share. In fully giving up one share the donor has retained no reversion. But if the donor owns a commercial office building in New York City and gives his son the right to the income from that piece of property for five years, then the donor continues to pay the tax on the income generated by that property. That is true even though in the latter instance, the donor has transferred an economic interest substantially in excess of the one share of stock in the first illustration.

Helvering v. *Horst* (1940) added yet another wrinkle to the arbitrary distinctions that courts have established regarding income splitting. In the *Horst* case the donor did retain a reversion on his income property. Consequently, under the *Blair* ruling, since the donor retained a reversionary interest, he should have the obligation to pay taxes on the earnings. However, in *Horst* the Court indicated that where a donor transferred substantial portions of his economic interest in the property while nonetheless retaining a reversion, it was appropriate for the donee to be the individual taxed on those earnings. *Horst* suggests that if the donor slices his economic interest in property and yet keeps a reversion, the donor may still be able to transfer the tax to the donee if the donor slices a substantial enough portion of his interest. The Court did not define how much of an interest is sufficient to lift the taxable burden from the donor where the donor retains a reversion.

The basic thrust in splitting income derived from the ownership of property is that the property owner can successfully assign such income and transfer the tax on it. The property owner, however, must do so in the correct manner. The preferable manner is to slice out that property interest to a donee in a nonreversionary way. However, the donor may still be able to shift the tax burden to the donee even if he keeps a reversion, if the donor transfers a substantial enough slice of the total economic interest that he holds in the property.

What all of this technical tax case law means is simple and significant. It means that any individual who derives income from the ownership of property is able to reduce his taxable income by assigning the income produced by the property to members of his family. This represents a powerful and effective means for families of wealth to reduce substantially their income tax obligations and to facilitate the intergenerational transfer of wealth derived from the ownership of property. Such a result would be significant and dramatic in its own right. However, when that possibility is contrasted with the one that applies to individuals who earn their income from wages

or salaries, the situation becomes quite remarkable indeed.

CONCLUSION

In examining the way in which the American tax system defines income, in looking at the rules that apply to the basic tax concept of basis, and in reviewing the case law structuring gift giving and income splitting, we have seen a pattern of legal interpretation and doctrine that produces important tax-law distinctions for Americans. The tax law precludes income taxation on the ownership of appreciating property. The concept of realization accomplished that advantage. In connection with the concept of basis, we have seen that the tax law has been interpreted so as to provide wage earners no basis at all in their own labor and services; consequently, all of the gain earned by the taxpayer's labor is taxable. In connection with gift giving, Section 1014 of the code provides an extraordinarily powerful mechanism by which those who own property may transfer appreciated property intergenerationally without paying taxes on the amount that the property has appreciated. Finally, we have seen that case law permits individuals who earn income from property, but not individuals who earn income from their labors, to assign part of that income to members of their family, thereby effectively reducing their tax rate and obligation.

The fundamentals of American federal income taxation provide fertile soil for the political analyst. Those concerned with the equitable distribution of wealth in America could look to the law of the federal income tax to explore the extent to which the tax system sustains and legitimates economic inequality. It is surprising and unfortunate that very little of such analysis has been undertaken to date. Perhaps the political impact of the federal income tax law has been little explored because tax law mystifies layperson and lawyer alike.

Tax law, like all law, veils the political function it plays. In the tax area, courts have developed a highly technical, apolitical case-law doctrine, which rarely addresses or even acknowledges the political and economic implications of the law of federal income tax. Lasswell's definition of politics as "who gets what, when, where and how" seems manifestly applicable to the law of taxation.

Surely there is no body of American law that has a more direct and significant distributive effect than federal income tax law. Yet the profound distributive impact of the federal income tax structure is shrouded in an arcane system of legal rules that is perhaps the most abstruse, technical, specialized, and conceptually complex body of United States substantive law. Moreover, the courts are reluctant to recognize, let alone analyze, the profound political and economic repercussions of federal income tax law. Because courts rarely move beyond a legal doctrine that seems to develop and apply abstract, apolitical legal conceptualizations, students, practitioners, and certainly laypersons are distracted from any serious consideration of the social ramifications of the federal income tax law. The doctrinal garb in which courts have clothed the income tax system conceals fundamental characteristics of the system worth careful scrutiny.

It is especially ironic that tax law is so veiled from the comprehension of the mass of laypersons. Few people ever have any firsthand exposure to or stake in the prosecution of a criminal or civil matter. Yet each of us is directly and tangibly affected by tax laws and rules in significant ways over the course of our lives. The argument can be made that of all legal rules, tax rules are an especially fitting subject for democratic, majoritarian control and review. They constitute a fundamental ordering of our communal life.

Taxation is at the heart of American politics. It is, and always has been, a subject eliciting deep political passions. So it has been since the time the English had difficulties extracting taxes from the colonies and America's revolutionary leaders asserted that Britain could not lawfully collect any taxes from the colonists. Yet, given the passions that the subject evokes, perhaps it is altogether predictable and politically functional that the law of taxation has evolved into an arcane specialty understood only by a small cadre of lawyers who must devote years of their professional lives to mastering its intricacies.

CASES

Blair v. Commissioner, 300 U.S. 5 (1937)
Burnet v. Leininger, 285 U.S. 136 (1932)
Commissioner v. Glenshaw Glass Co., 348 U.S. 426 (1955)
Commissioner v. Lo Bou, 351 U.S. 243 (1956)
Eisner v. Macomber, 252 U.S. 189 (1920)
Helvering v. Horst, 311 U.S. 112 (1940)
Lucas v. Earl, 281 U.S. 111 (1930)

BIBLIOGRAPHY

Boris I. Bittker and Lawrence M. Stone, *Federal Income Taxation*, 5th ed. (1980), is a standard case-law text containing heavily edited versions of major income tax cases. Marvin A. Chirelstein, *Federal Income Taxation* (1958), is a highly readable introductory commentary on federal income tax law. *Merten's Law of Federal Income Taxation*, regularly updated, is a multivolume reference tool for the tax specialist. Daniel Q. Posin, *Federal Income Taxation* (1983), contains an especially useful first chapter, which reviews the historical and policy foundations of the tax system. *Stanley and Kilcullen's Federal Income Tax Law*, regularly updated, is a standard concise reference text geared to the code and containing commentary on the most important cases, regulations, and rulings dealing with specific sections of the code.
[*See also* ADVERSARY SYSTEM *and* LEGAL REASONING.]

TORTS

Herbert L. Sherman, Jr.

No completely satisfactory definition of *tort* has ever been formulated. However, in general, a tort is a civil wrong other than breach of contract. It is a wrongful act for which a civil action can be brought in court and for which the court will provide a remedy of damages and possibly some other remedies. Torts cover a wide range of miscellaneous wrongs. Excluding certain kinds of causes of action (lawsuits recognized by courts), torts occupy a large residuary field.

A tort differs from a crime. The state prosecutes a criminal to vindicate a public right and to punish the criminal; a tort action is brought by the injured person against the wrongdoer primarily to recover compensation for the injury suffered and also for punitive damages in a few situations in which the wrongdoer's conduct is especially outrageous. Some acts may constitute a tort and a crime, for which both a tort action and a criminal prosecution may be brought. Some acts constitute torts but not crimes; some acts constitute crimes but not torts.

The law of torts is evolving. New tort actions have been recognized by the courts in recent years, and undoubtedly more will be recognized in the future. Tort cases constitute the largest group of civil lawsuits in most United States courts. Tort law is primarily common law, which means that the law is developed on a case-by-case basis by the courts' use of logic and public policy. Nevertheless, in some situations tort law has been affected by statutes adopted by Congress and by state legislatures. The development of tort liability also has been affected by history, morality (even though legal liability does not coincide with moral blame or impolite conduct), the capacity of the respective parties to spread the loss (for example, by price or tax increases or through insurance), the deterrence of future

wrongdoing, and problems of applying a proposed new rule of law.

Because tort law and liability insurance (under which insurance payments must be made only if the insured person who caused harm is legally liable under tort law) have not provided adequate protection to all persons injured in automobile accidents, many states have adopted various forms of no-fault statutes that are applicable to automobile accidents. Under no-fault statutes a victim of an automobile accident ordinarily claims compensation from the victim's own insurance company (without having to prove any tort). But the amounts recoverable under such plans for medical expenses and loss of earnings are often quite limited. Where no-fault benefits have been generous (as in Pennsylvania), the insurance premiums increased dramatically (leading to abolition of the original no-fault statute in that state). Most no-fault statutes continue to permit a tort action to be brought in court only if certain threshold tests are met. The tests are satisfied when serious injuries are sustained by a person. Most no-fault plans do not apply to property damage, but car owners may purchase collision insurance to cover damage to their cars even where no tort is involved.

Three broad, fundamental bases of tort liability are (1) intentional harms to persons, land, and personal property; (2) negligence; and (3) strict liability. Specific torts and defenses will be discussed in this article under these broad headings, as well as other topics that deserve special treatment.

INTENTIONAL HARMS TO PERSONS

Examples of intentional torts to persons are battery, assault, false imprisonment, and the intentional infliction of severe mental distress on another by outrageous conduct. An underlying social policy that supports recognition of such tort actions by the courts is the policy of discouraging retaliation by force. The meaning of the word *intent* is important. It is not sufficient to show that a defendant intended to do an act that happened to result in certain consequences. *Intent* is defined in the law as either having the purpose of bringing about a result or knowing that the result is substantially certain to be brought about.

Courts have held that a battery consists of conduct whereby defendant intentionally causes a harmful or offensive contact with another person. Thus, if A tells B that he is going to hit him and in fact A swings at B, striking B with his fist, A has committed a battery on B. Intent must be distinguished from motive. If A deliberately kills B because A honestly believes that the country will benefit from B's death, A has committed a battery, even if the jury believes that A had a good motive. If A shoots at B with the intent of killing B but the bullet strikes C who suddenly appears on the scene, A is liable to C for a battery, under the doctrine of transferred intent. A harmful contact is not necessary for a battery; an offensive contact, such as the flicking of a glove in the plaintiff's face, satisfies the contact requirement. It is sufficient if the contact is with the other person's clothing or anything held in a hand, such as a cane.

If A tells B that he is going to hit him and A swings at B, thereby causing B to be put in apprehension of an immediate harmful or offensive contact even though in fact A does not hit B, then A has committed an assault, but not a battery, on B. Under tort law a person may be liable for an assault without being liable for a battery, or liable for a battery without being liable for an assault, or liable for both. A typical judicial view is that an assault is an act which is intended to put another person in reasonable apprehension of an immediate battery and which succeeds in causing an apprehension of such battery. The necessary intent is the same for assault as for battery. However, although a harmful or offensive contact must be proved for a battery, no contact is necessary for an assault. But the plaintiff must suffer the necessary apprehension for an assault, whereas no such apprehension must be suffered by the plaintiff for a battery action. Courts have said that words in themselves, no matter how threatening, do not constitute an assault, that the actor must be in a position to carry out the threat immediately, and that he must take some affirmative action to do so. Thus, A's threat by telephone to B on Wednesday to kill B on Saturday with A's gun is not an assault. However, A might be liable under a tort of intentional infliction of severe emotional distress.

False arrest is treated by some courts as one kind of false imprisonment. If a person is arrested (taken into custody) without proper legal authority, the false arrest is a false imprisonment. Courts have held a defendant liable for false imprisonment where the defendant intends to confine another person and the defendant's conduct results in confinement of the other person. The confinement may arise out of an intentional breach of a duty to release the other person from a confined area. Confinement for this tort action may consist of restraint of a person in a moving area, such as a truck moving on a highway. There is no confinement if there is a reasonable avenue of escape, but confinement exists even when the victim submits to it if the submission is obtained by duress. Some authorities take the position that a legal action for false imprisonment should be unsuccessful unless the victim who is confined is aware of the confinement or is harmed by it. On the other hand, some scholars and some judicial opinions adopt the view that an action for false imprisonment should extend to a situation where the plaintiff who is intentionally confined by the defendant is not conscious of confinement and is not harmed by it. Although false imprisonment is an intentional tort, the plaintiff does not have to prove that the defendant acted with malice.

Since the 1960s most courts have recognized a new tort of intentionally or recklessly (not merely negligently) causing severe emotional distress (not merely humiliation or mental anguish) by extreme and outrageous conduct (not merely insulting remarks). Prior reluctance of the courts to recognize such an independent tort action was based on the difficulty of proving and measuring damages for mental distress, on the fear of fraudulent claims, and on the fear of a flood of lawsuits if such a cause of action were recognized. Under this theory, recovery would be allowed if a defendant's automobile struck a young boy, the defendant hid the boy's body in his garage and later buried it in a field, and more than two months later the partially decomposed body of the boy was found. The parents of the boy would be allowed to recover damages from the defendant for their severe emotional distress. But recovery under this theory was denied where a caterer, in breach of contract, charged the plaintiff's guests for checking their coats at the plaintiff's wedding anniversary party. Moreover, the law does not permit recovery of damages for all insults and rude conduct. There are some exceptions—for example, where a bus driver uses grossly insulting language to a passenger—but in general, freedom of speech permits a person to express an unflattering opinion about another and even to use profane language to the other.

INTENTIONAL TORTS TO PROPERTY

Interference with personal property embraces the tort of trespass to chattels and the tort of conversion; interference with land embraces the tort of trespass to land and the tort of nuisance.

A person may be liable for trespass to a chattel by intentionally taking the chattel (personal property that is movable, such as furniture or an automobile) of another or by using or otherwise interfering with a chattel in the possession of another. Most courts have held that this tort action cannot be maintained unless the chattel has sustained actual damage or there has been a loss of use of the chattel as a result of the defendant's conduct. The tort of trespass to a chattel applies to an interference with a chattel (for instance, beating another's dog or damaging another's fishing net) that is not sufficiently serious an interference as to justify application of the law of conversion. The difference is important in terms of the measure of damages. In an action for trespass to a chattel, the chattel's possessor may recover for the harm to the chattel or for a substantial loss of use of it. In an action for conversion the successful plaintiff may recover the full value of the chattel.

Conversion is another intentional tort. Courts have defined this tort as an act of dominion (control) wrongfully exerted over the personal property of another in denial of, or inconsistent with, the owner's rights therein. Various factors—such as the defendant's intent, the defendant's good or bad faith, or the extent of harm to the chattel —are considered by the courts in determining whether the defendant may in all fairness be required to pay the plaintiff the full value of the chattel. Courts also have held that conversion may be based on destruction, alteration, or misdelivery of a chattel, or on refusal, on demand, to surrender a chattel to another entitled to possession of it. In general, a mistake is no defense to an action either for trespass to chattels or for conversion. If A buys a stolen bicycle from B, honestly and reasonably believing that the bicycle is owned by B despite the fact that the bicycle is owned by C, then A and B are liable to C for conversion. Under sales law, A would be able to obtain legal relief from B. If B obtained a sale of the bicycle from C by fraud, and then sold the bicycle to A, who was in good faith without notice of B's fraud, A would not be liable to C for conversion, because A would have obtained the title to the bicycle, which B obtained when he purchased the bicycle from C. In this case, C would have an action for fraud against B.

The tort of trespass to land involves trespass to realty, which means land, including the buildings or improvements on it. Although the term *trespass* has been used with different meanings, the preferable view concerning liability for trespass to land is that a defendant must intentionally have entered the land in the plaintiff's possession or caused something to enter the land or must intentionally have remained on the land or failed to remove something from the land that he had a duty to remove. The courts have held that if the defendant engages in such conduct without any privilege to do so, the individual is liable even though he may not have caused any harm to the land. The utility and reasonableness of the defendant's conduct are not relevant to an action for trespass to land unless a defense of privilege is relevant. A person trespasses on land merely by intentionally walking on the land or throwing a stone on it without any privilege to do so. The intent required for this tort is simply an intent to enter or remain on the land. No intent to trespass is required. A mistaken belief, even if reasonable, by the defendant that he is entitled to possession of the land or that he has consent or a privilege to be on the land is no defense.

Cases have held that a trespasser is liable for harm to the land, to a house on the land, to the possessor, and to the possessor's family and chattels even though the trespasser is not negligent. Moreover, a person may be liable not only for trespass on the surface of the land but also for trespass beneath the surface of the earth (for example, by installing foundation stones encroaching upon neighboring premises) and for trespass in the air space above the surface (for example, by shooting a bullet across the land even though the bullet does not fall on the land). Flights by aircraft across the land are governed by special considerations.

A tort action of private nuisance must be distinguished from a public nuisance, which involves an unreasonable interference with a common right of the general public and for which a citizen normally has no right to legal relief unless he suffers some special damage. Section 822 of the Restatement of Torts (2d), adopted by many courts, provides that a person is liable for a private nuisance, which involves an invasion of another's interest in the private use and enjoyment of land, if "the invasion is either (a) intentional and unreasonable, or (b) unintentional and otherwise actionable under the rules controlling liability for negligent or reckless conduct, or for abnormally dangerous conditions or activities." In contrast with trespass to land, a private-nuisance action based on an intentional interference with the use and enjoyment of land will be successful only if the interference is substantial and unreasonable. An intentional invasion is deemed to be unreasonable if the gravity of the harm outweighs the social utility of the defendant's conduct or if the harm caused is serious and the financial burden of compensating for the harm would not be too great. A court may grant relief in damages but, balancing the equities, refuse to issue an injunction to stop the activity, as in a case involving noise from an airport.

Nuisance actions may be based on a wide variety of conduct (such as those resulting in factory odors, flooding, barking dogs, or stored explosives). Courts have held that the purchase of land after a nuisance has come into existence is not by itself enough to bar a nuisance action, but it is a factor in determining whether there is a nuisance. If the existence of a nuisance is established, there are three possible remedies—damages, injunction, or self-help. But the self-help remedy of removing the alleged nuisance is risky, because an honest belief by the actor that the removal is justified is no defense to a criminal prosecution or a civil action for damages.

DEFENSES TO INTENTIONAL TORTS

Consent usually bars recovery for intentional interferences with the person or property, since consent negates the existence of a tort. Consent may be manifested by words ("It's OK"), by action (holding up an arm to be vaccinated), and by silence where a reasonable person would vocally object. Consent also may be inferred from custom in the community, such as a custom of allowing persons to fish on a lake.

Consent, which is given in fact, may not be effective to bar a tort action if consent is given under duress, if it is given under a mistake and the mistake is known to the other person or is induced by the other person's misrepresentation, or if the person consenting does not have the capacity to consent (for example, if the person were underage). But consent is effective to bar many tort actions even though the consent is to engage in conduct that is a crime. (For instance, a woman has no battery action against a doctor if she consents to a criminal abortion and the operation is skillfully performed by the doctor.) Where two parties mutually consent to engage in a fight that constitutes a breach of the peace, the courts do not agree on whether each has a tort action against the other, although each is guilty of a crime. If conduct is made criminal by statute to protect a limited class of individuals from their inability to appreciate the consequences of their conduct, consent to the criminal conduct by a member of that class does not bar a tort action. (For example, if a statute makes it rape to have sexual intercourse with a girl under the age of sixteen even with her consent, then A, a girl who is under sixteen, has an action for battery against B when B has sexual intercourse with A with her consent.)

In an emergency a person often may act as if consent existed. (For example, B, a surgeon, is protected from liability by implied consent when the surgeon performs an operation on A, who is unconscious and who needs the operation immediately to save his life.) Such a situation arises when it is necessary to take action before there is opportunity to obtain consent from the other person (or from one empowered to consent for him) and the actor has no reason to believe that the other would refuse consent. Even if a person has consented to a contact, a tort action may be maintained for force that exceeds the consent.

(For instance, A and B agree to engage in a fistfight, but B slashes A with a knife.) Where a patient consents to an operation but the surgeon has not informed the patient of the nature of the operation or the consequences, many courts hold that the consent is not an "informed consent" and thus is not a defense to an action for battery. Courts do not agree on whether the proper test is what a reasonable doctor would disclose or what a reasonable patient would expect to be told.

The law recognizes numerous privileges as defenses that will defeat intentional tort actions. Illustrative of these privileges are the privilege of self-defense, the privilege to defend third persons, the privilege to defend a person's own land or chattels, the privilege of using force to enter or reenter land, the privilege to recapture a chattel, the privilege of detention of a shoplifter, the privilege to arrest, the privilege to prevent a crime, the privilege to discipline children, and privileges to utilize the property of another in order to save a person's life or property. The law, however, imposes many detailed qualifications on the right to exercise these privileges.

NEGLIGENCE

Negligence gives rise to more torts cases than any other tort. The word *negligence* is sometimes used to refer to one element of a cause of action for negligence and sometimes to an entire cause of action for negligence. In order to determine the sense in which the word is used at any given time, it is necessary to consider its context. The elements of a cause of action for negligence are as follows: (1) a duty to exercise reasonable care (a duty not to be negligent); (2) negligence (a failure to conform to the required standard of care, thus breaching the duty); (3) proximate cause or legal cause (a reasonably close causal connection between the conduct and the resulting injury involving both cause in fact and legal limitations on liability); and (4) actual harm.

If a defendant has no duty to exercise reasonable care, obviously the defendant cannot be held liable for failure to do so. Since in most states a person has no legal duty to exercise reasonable care to render aid to another person merely because it is clear that the other seriously needs help, there is no liability in such a situation. In most cases, however, a person does have a legal duty to exercise reasonable care, and a breach of duty occurs if he is negligent. Negligence is conduct (not a state of mind) that falls below a standard established by law for the protection of others against unreasonable risk of harm.

Normally, the standard of conduct to which the actor must conform to avoid being negligent is that of a hypothetical "reasonable man" under like circumstances, sometimes described as a "person of ordinary prudence." This reasonable-person standard combines both objective and subjective elements. For adults the standard for minimum mental capacity is objective. It is not sufficient that the actor did the best that he knew how to do. Mental deficiency, including insanity, does not relieve an actor from liability for conduct that does not conform to the standard of the reasonable man. The standard is an objective one for a minimum amount of knowledge and intelligence. (For example, lack of knowledge of the danger of driving with bald tires is no excuse.) If in fact a person has knowledge or skill superior to that of the ordinary person, they must be used. A medical doctor must use reasonable care in light of her superior knowledge, skill, and training, but she is entitled to be judged according to the school of medical thought that she professes to follow. Usually expert testimony is required to show negligence by a doctor.

Physical disabilities are distinguishable from mental capacity. The standard man is deemed to have the physical attributes of the actor. Thus, a blind person must act as a reasonable blind person would act. An allowance in the standard is also made for children: a child must act as a reasonable person of like age, intelligence, and experience would act. Children normally are liable for their own torts, but a few courts have held that a child under seven years of age is incapable of negligence. In many states, if a child engages in an adult activity, such as driving a car, the child is held to the adult standard of care. In applying the adult standard of care the actor (of any age) is not required in an emergency to conform to the standard of conduct normally applied when there is no emergency.

Many courts have held that a common carrier (such as a bus company) must exercise the "highest degree of care" to protect passengers. Some courts use degrees of negligence in connection with bailments where goods (for example, a book or a bicycle) are delivered by one person (a bailor) to another person (a bailee) to be held for a specific purpose and returned when that purpose is ended. Where the bailment is solely for the benefit of the bailee, the bailee is liable for slight negligence. Where the bailment is solely for the benefit of the bailor, the bailee is liable only for gross negligence. Where the bailment is for mutual benefit, the bailee is liable for ordinary negligence.

"Reckless, wanton, and willful conduct" refers to still a higher form of misconduct. Use of these terms is commonly found in guest statutes, which provide that a driver of an automobile is liable to a social guest only for a higher form of misconduct than ordinary negligence. The usual meaning of recklessness is that the actor has done an unreasonable act in disregard of an obviously great danger so that it is highly probable that harm will result.

Various kinds of evidence are relevant to the issue of the proper standard of care. Custom in the community does not establish the standard of care, but evidence of custom is admissible in court to be considered in determining negligence. Similarly, evidence of a defendant's own customary safety rule may be used against him to show that he had knowledge of a certain risk. Stronger evidence of the proper standard of conduct may be found in a statute as well as in municipal ordinances and administrative regulations.

The question of the effect of violation of a statute on tort liability requires consideration of various types of statutes. A few statutes expressly provide that violation of the statute gives rise to civil liability. Most statutes, however, simply provide for a criminal penalty if the statute is violated, thus suggesting that perhaps violation of the statute should be viewed as irrelevant to tort liability. In fact, violation of some kinds of statutes (for instance, a statute requiring registration of automobiles) is often held to be irrelevant to tort liability, although a criminal penalty may be imposed. But the prevailing view is that an unexcused violation of many kinds of safety statutes is negligence in itself (negligence per se). In contrast, some courts hold that the unexcused violation of a safety statute or of a municipal ordinance or administrative regulation is simply evidence of negligence for the jury's consideration. A court also may recognize an excuse, such as an emergency, for violation of a statute. Violation of a few types of exceptional statutes gives rise to strict liability in tort because of the purpose of such statutes (such as one prohibiting the employment of child labor). Since the purpose of such a statute is to protect a specific class of persons from their inability to protect themselves, the usual defenses to negligence will not prevail in this situation.

In order for violation of a statute to be relevant to a common-law tort action, it must be proved that (1) the violation has a proper causal relationship to the resulting harm, (2) the injured person is within the class of persons that the statute is intended to protect, and (3) the resulting harm is the type of harm that the statute is designed to prevent. Although violation of a statute frequently is viewed as negligence per se, compliance with a statute does not prove nonnegligence per se. Because safety statutes usually are interpreted as establishing minimum standards of conduct, the circumstances may show that even greater precautions should have been taken.

The types of evidence just discussed bear not only on the question of what is the proper standard of conduct but also on proof of negligence. Relevant to the latter question is the doctrine of *res ipsa loquitur* ("the thing speaks for itself"), a doctrine that deals with circumstantial evidence. Many courts have said that the doctrine applies under the following conditions: (1) the accident or event is of a kind that ordinarily does not occur in the absence of negligence, (2) the cause of the accident was within the exclusive control of the defendant, and (3) the harm was not due to any voluntary action or contribution of the plaintiff. The first requirement deals with a balance of probabilities, while the latter two are designed to rule out causes for the harm other than the defendant's conduct. The real significance of applying this doctrine to such cases as bricks falling from the defendant's premises or the explosion of a boiler under the defendant's control is that it gives rise to an inference of negligence, according to most courts. This permits the plaintiff to avoid a dismissal of the case, as there is sufficient evidence to go to the jury.

Although everybody agrees that the defendant's negligence must have a proper causal connection with the plaintiff's harm to establish liability, scholars and the courts do not agree on the meaning of proximate cause. The term is used in many different senses by courts, without adequate explanation. In any event, the plaintiff must establish causation in fact. Many courts use the "but for" test for determining factual causation: the defendant's conduct is a cause of the harm if the harm would not have occurred but for the defendant's conduct. This is a rule of exclusion in the sense that cause in fact is not established if the harm could have occurred without the defendant's conduct. The "but for" test does not operate fairly if two causes concur to bring about a single result and either alone would have brought about the same result (for example, when two pillars support a roof and the roof will fall regardless of whether both pillars collapse or just one does). Thus, courts have developed the "substantial factor" test as a test of factual causation: the defendant's conduct is a cause of the plaintiff's harm if the conduct was a substantial factor in bringing it about even though another cause also contributed substantially to the result.

Even though the defendant's negligence is a cause in fact of the plaintiff's harm, other rules limit liability. One conflict among the courts revolves around whether a negligent defendant should be liable only for foreseeable harm or whether a negligent defendant should be liable for all consequences directly caused by him. Probably the most famous case in tort law, which deals with one aspect of this problem, is *Palsgraf* v. *Long Island Railroad* (1928). In that case the defendant railroad's employees, in helping a passenger to board a train, knocked a package from the passenger's arms. The package, which contained fireworks, fell on the rails and exploded, and the concussion caused some scales (many feet away on the railroad platform) to fall on the plaintiff. The jury found that the railroad's employees were negligent. However, although harm to the passenger boarding the train and harm to the package could reasonably have been foreseen, no harm to the plaintiff could reasonably have been foreseen. Judge Benjamin Cardozo (later a justice of the United States Supreme Court), writing for the majority of the New York Court of Appeals, held that the defendant was not liable to the plaintiff because

there was no negligence to the plaintiff; that is, she was not within the class of persons to whom harm reasonably could have been foreseen to come. The dissent argued that everybody owes a duty to the world at large not to be negligent. Even though Section 281 of the Restatement of Torts (2d) has adopted Cardozo's view in *Palsgraf*, scholars continue to debate this case. A majority of the small number of courts that have dealt with this issue have adopted Cardozo's view.

Palsgraf involved an unforeseeable plaintiff. Another issue is whether a negligent defendant should be liable for a type of harm that was not reasonably to be foreseen. Adopting an intermediate position between conflicting judicial views, the Restatement, in Section 435, excuses a defendant from liability for consequences that, even in hindsight, appear to be "highly extraordinary." But Section 461 of the Restatement and the courts distinguish the situation in which a negligent defendant causes much greater harm to a victim because of the victim's unforeseeable physical condition. If the defendant negligently strikes the plaintiff lightly on his abnormally thin skull and causes great harm, the defendant is liable for the full amount of the harm because the tortfeasor (the wrongdoer) takes his victims as he finds them.

A negligent defendant's potential liability may be cut off by an intervening cause or force if it is viewed as a superseding cause. An intervening cause by itself does not cut off a negligent defendant's liability. An intervening cause that is foreseeable is within the scope of the original risk created by the defendant. The same is true when the intervening act is a normal consequence of the situation created by the defendant. Regardless of whether the intervening act is innocent, negligent, intentionally tortious (wrongful), or criminal, the defendant is nonetheless liable for the harm if the likelihood that a third person will act in that manner is one of the hazards that makes the defendant negligent.

An example of an *intervening negligent act* would be when the defendant, a tavern operator, negligently serves intoxicating beverages to a visibly intoxicated patron who then negligently drives his car and strikes the plaintiff. The negligent intervening act of the patron does not cut off the liability of the defendant to the plaintiff. On the other hand, the defendant is not liable for the results of abnormal forces of nature, unforeseeable acts of animals, and highly extraordinary conduct of adults, which have been viewed by the courts as superseding causes.

SPECIAL PROBLEMS IN NEGLIGENCE LAW

The following topics warrant separate treatment: prenatal injuries and "wrongful birth," death, joint tortfeasors, emotional distress, duty to render aid, and the liability of owners and occupiers of land.

Only in recent decades have most courts allowed a child to recover for prenatal injuries where injury to the pregnant mother by a negligent defendant caused the child to be born in an injured condition, and many courts have imposed two limitations on recovery: (1) the fetus must have been viable (capable of independent life) at the time of injury, and (2) the child must be born alive (not stillborn). The modern trend is to eliminate the requirement that the child be born alive. Only since 1975 have courts allowed an action for wrongful birth or wrongful life against doctors who have negligently performed a sterilization or abortion procedure or failed to tell the parents that their child might be born deformed. Although most courts have refused to recognize a claim by a child that it should not have been born, many courts have allowed parents to recover their out-of-pocket costs for the wrongful birth of a deformed child and even for the wrongful birth of a healthy but unwanted child.

Two statutes are relevant to death: a survival act and a wrongful-death act. If the defendant injures but has not caused the death of a person and the injured person or the defendant dies before trial, only a survival act is applicable. It provides that most tort actions survive the death of either party. If defendant's act has caused the death of another person, both statutes are applicable. Under a survival act the estate of the deceased has an action for damages that the deceased could have recovered, and under a wrongful-death act near relatives of the deceased may recover damages for benefits they probably would have received had deceased not been killed. However, terms of these statutes vary from state to state.

The term *joint tortfeasors* has been used to refer to two or more persons who have acted in concert (by common understanding) and have wrongfully caused harm to the plaintiff. The term also has been applied to two or more negligent persons acting independently who have caused a single, indivisible harm to the plaintiff. Many courts have held that joint tortfeasors are jointly and individually liable to the plaintiff for the entire harm suffered, but the plaintiff is entitled to be compensated only to the extent of the full amount of the harm. If the plaintiff collects the full amount of the damages from one defendant, that defendant may seek contribution (the fair share of the total amount of the damages) from other defendants under statutes in most states.

Emotional distress cases can be broken down into five categories: (1) Where the defendant negligently causes emotional distress with no accompanying physical harm, most courts usually deny recovery. (2) Where the defendant by extreme and outrageous conduct intentionally or recklessly causes severe emotional distress, most courts allow recovery. (3) Where the defendant negligently causes physical injury and where mental distress, such as pain and suffering, flows from the injury, the courts have long allowed recovery. (4) Where the defendant negligently causes emotional distress that results in physical consequences, most courts since midcentury have allowed recovery. (5) Where the plaintiff's emotional distress resulting in illness is caused not by fear for the plaintiff's own safety but by seeing another person killed (for instance, a mother sees her child killed because of the defendant's negligent conduct), most courts have denied recovery, but a strong minority view is developing. One of the questions this minority faces is where to draw the line in determining who should have a tort action when "close" relatives or friends have suffered emotional distress in such a situation.

Since in most states a person has no legal duty to render aid to a stranger in peril merely because the person knows that the other needs help, an expert swimmer who sees a stranger drowning is not legally required to try to save him. Nor does a person who sees an automobile accident have any legal duty to help an injured stranger. If the law were otherwise, fifty persons who passed an accident would be liable for failure to render aid. Nevertheless, the following special relationships have been deemed to give rise to a legal duty to exercise reasonable care to render aid: common carriers and passengers; innkeepers and guests; possessors of land open to the public and business visitors; employers and employees; hosts and social guests; and schools and pupils. A duty also exists where a person takes another into custody, thus depriving the other of normal opportunities for protection. Where the defendant negligently harms the plaintiff, there is a duty to give reasonable assistance to prevent further harm. On the other hand, where the defendant without fault injures the plaintiff, in the absence of statute the courts do not agree on whether the defendant has a legal duty to render aid. But a Good Samaritan who voluntarily renders aid assumes a duty to exercise reasonable care. This rule has led most states to adopt "Good Samaritan statutes," which provide that a doctor who renders aid in an emergency is not liable for ordinary negligence.

Tort liability for injuries resulting from dangerous conditions and activities on land rests mostly upon the occupier (the possessor) of the land, whether or not the occupier is the owner of the land. Liability of the possessor depends on the duty owed, and the duty owed, according to most courts, turns on a series of distinctions. (Since 1968 a minority of the courts have abolished these distinctions and have held that the duty is simply to exercise reasonable care under the circumstances.) These distinctions involve some basic questions. Was the plaintiff injured off or on the premises? If off the premises, did the injury occur as a result of a natural condition (for which usually there is no liability) or as a result of an artificial condition or an activity (for which there may be liability for negligence)? If the plaintiff is injured on the premises, was the plaintiff on the land as an adult trespasser, an infant trespasser, a licensee (permitted to be on the premises), or an invitee for a business purpose? Was he injured by an activity or by a passive condition? The legal duty differs depending on the category into which the case falls. The least duties are owed to an adult trespasser, while the highest duties are owed to a business invitee and a public invitee (a member of the public invited on land for a purpose for which the land is held open to the public). Liability of the owner-landlord who has leased the premises depends in part on whether the plaintiff was injured on or off the premises. In general, landlords and vendors of land have less responsibility for harm caused as a result of activities or conditions on the land than the occupier of the land. But there are many exceptions under which a landlord may be liable. Also, a statute may impose responsibilities on a landlord.

DEFENSES TO AN ACTION FOR NEGLIGENCE

Historically, contributory negligence (negligence of a plaintiff that creates an unreasonable risk of harm to the plaintiff and that contributes as a legal cause to that harm) is a complete bar to recovery against a negligent defendant who causes harm to the plaintiff. Similarly, the rule of avoidable consequences, which applies after a legal wrong occurs, bars recovery for such further damages as the plaintiff could have avoided by reasonable care. Because of the harshness of the defense of contributory negligence most courts have adopted some form of a doctrine of "last clear chance," under which, in general, a plaintiff who is in helpless peril because of the plaintiff's prior negligence may recover from the defendant who discovers the plaintiff's danger while there is still time to avoid harm to the plaintiff but fails to use reasonable care to avoid such harm.

During the 1970s and early 1980s most states adopted the concept of comparative negligence by statute. Although it is difficult to find any two statutes that are identical in all detail, most states have adopted one of two types of comparative negligence plans: (1) pure comparative negligence, under which a plaintiff's contributory negligence reduces the plaintiff's damages in proportion to the plaintiff's fault, but he is not barred from recovery even if the plaintiff's fault is much greater than the defendant's; or (2) modified comparative negligence, under which a plaintiff's contributory negligence bars the plaintiff's recovery unless the plaintiff's fault is less than the defendant's fault, in which case the plaintiff's contributory negligence simply reduces the plaintiff's damages in proportion to his fault.

Historically under the common law, assumption of risk has been a defense to an action for negligence. Many courts have held that, as a general principle, a plaintiff who voluntarily assumes a risk of harm from the negligent conduct of the defendant cannot recover for such harm. The doctrine applies where a plaintiff expressly or impliedly agrees to take his chances (for instance a spectator at a baseball game usually assumes the risk of being struck by a batted ball), regardless of whether his conduct is reasonable or unreasonable. For this defense to apply, the plaintiff must know of the risk and appreciate its consequences (a subjective standard, unlike the objective standard applied to contributory negligence). Nevertheless, this defense is deemed to be against public policy in some situations, and some states have abolished the doctrine.

A statute of limitations may bar an action for negligence and other actions. The purpose of such a statute is to require a plaintiff to file an action in court (if the plaintiff plans to file an action) before memories fade and witnesses become unavailable, and so that the prospective defendant will not have to face the possibility of a lawsuit indefinitely. The time periods of statutes of limitations differ not only from state to state but also in terms of the type of action (usually two or three years for most tort actions) within a given state. In most instances the statute of limitations starts to run against a negligence action from the date that the injury occurred.

Actions for negligence (and other tort actions) also may be defeated by the immunity of the defendant from tort liability. Governmental immunity of the federal government, the state government, and local government units, as well as the immunity of public officers, may defeat a tort action. Nevertheless, the modern trend is in the direction of limiting the defense of governmental immunity. Commonly the matter is covered by a statute; for example, most tort claims against the federal government are governed by the Federal Tort Claims Act. An immunity of charitable institutions from tort liability, which once existed in most states, has largely been abolished under the modern trend.

VICARIOUS LIABILITY AND IMPUTED CONTRIBUTORY NEGLIGENCE

Under the doctrine of *respondeat superior* a master is liable for the torts of his servant committed in the scope of his employment. This is one form of vicarious liability. For example, if X, employed by Y to drive a truck, negligently injures Z while X is performing his duties for Y, then Y is vicariously liable to Z for the harm even though Y is not personally negligent. In general, contributory negligence is not imputed (attributed) from one person to another to bar recovery from a negligent third party. However, if Z also was negligent in causing the collision with Y's truck in this example, Y is barred from recovery from Z for damage to the truck, even though Y was not personally negligent, because X's contributory negligence is imputed to Y, thereby providing a defense to Z.

A joint enterprise, which is similar to a partnership but exists for a shorter period of time and for a more limited purpose, is another exception. If A and B go on an automobile trip to a common destination for a common business purpose, share expenses and have the right to change the route only by mutual agreement, A and B are engaged in a joint enterprise. If A drives and negligently collides with C, B would be vicariously liable to C for A's tort even though B is a passenger and is not personally negligent. If C also is negligent in causing the collision, B would be barred from recovery from C for injury to B, even though B is not personally negligent, because A's contributory negligence is imputed to B, thereby providing a defense to C. But, contrary to popular belief, parents are generally not vicariously liable under the common law for the torts of their children, although a statute may provide otherwise, and a parent is liable for his or her own personal negligence.

Automobile accident problems have led to the adoption of other examples of vicarious liability. Although normally a bailor is not vicariously liable for a bailee's negligence, some courts have adopted a family-car doctrine under which the owner of a car who permits members of his household to drive it, even for their own pleasure, is vicariously liable for the driver's negligence in causing harm to someone. Another example of vicarious liability is found in some states in a "consent statute," which provides that the owner of a car is vicariously liable for harm caused to other persons by the negligence of anybody (not just a family member) who is using the car with the owner's consent.

STRICT LIABILITY AND PRODUCTS LIABILITY

Strict liability, which involves imposition of liability where a defendant has not intentionally or negligently caused harm to another, is one of the fundamental bases of tort liability. Strict liability is imposed for harm caused by trespassing livestock (cattle, sheep, pigs, horses), but dogs and cats are treated separately. Some states do, however, impose strict liability by statute for harm caused by dogs. Most courts impose strict liability on possessors of wild animals (lions, tigers, monkeys, elephants) for harm resulting from a dangerous propensity characteristic of wild animals of that class, but a public zoo may be held liable only for negligence. Under the common law a possessor of a domestic animal (cattle, dogs, cats) is liable for harm caused by the nontrespassing animal only if the possessor knows of an abnormally dangerous propensity of the animal.

A person who carries on an abnormally dangerous activity (such as blasting in a city) is strictly liable for harm caused by it if the possibility of that kind of harm makes the activity abnormally dangerous. Courts have held that ordinary contributory negligence is not a defense to an action for strict liability, but assumption of risk and trespass by the injured party are possible defenses.

Although lawsuits for physical harm caused by products are still based to some extent on negligence law and on breach of warranty law, such lawsuits are increasingly based on a "402A theory," a form of strict liability. Section 402A of the Restatement of Torts (2d), recognized by almost all states, provides the following:

> (1) One who sells any product in a defective condition unreasonably dangerous to the user or consumer or to his property is subject to liability for physical harm thereby caused to the ultimate user or consumer, or to his property, if

> (a) the seller is engaged in the business of selling such a product, and
> (b) it is expected to and does reach the user or consumer without substantial change in the condition in which it is sold.
> (2) The rule stated in Subsection (1) applies although
> (a) the seller has exercised all possible care in the preparation and sale of his product, and
> (b) the user or consumer has not bought the product from or entered into any contractual relation with the seller.

Under 402A a seller includes a retailer, wholesaler, or manufacturer. Some courts have extended 402A to a rental car agency, which is not a seller. Services are not products and are not covered by 402A. Merely causing harm is not enough, as the product must be defective and unreasonably dangerous. Physical harm, but not mere economic harm, is covered by 402A. Although bystanders are not users or consumers, some courts have extended 402A to bystanders. Comments of the drafters of 402A state that this strict liability is not affected by any disclaimer of liability and that ordinary contributory negligence is no defense, although assumption of risk and misuse of the product may constitute defenses.

DECEIT AND OTHER MISREPRESENTATIONS

Misrepresentations causing financial loss may give rise to legal relief. Although much confusion exists because the word *fraud* has been used by courts to mean many different things, the preferable view is to consider fraud as referring to deceit. Under the traditional view a plaintiff must prove the following in order to maintain a tort action of deceit: (1) a misrepresentation of a material fact, (2) knowledge or belief by the defendant that his statement is false, or conscious ignorance by the defendant of the truth of the statement, (3) intent by the defendant that the plaintiff rely on the misrepresentation, (4) justifiable reliance by the plaintiff, and (5) damage to the plaintiff. Depending on the particular factual situation, there are many possible legal remedies for a misrepresentation in addition to an action for deceit to recover damages. Other potential remedies include a tort action for negligence for damages, a contract action for breach of warranty or use of the misrepresentation as a defense to a contract action by the seller to recover the purchase price, a lawsuit to rescind the sale, and a lawsuit for restitution of the money paid.

Misrepresentation clearly embraces false representations by words or acts, concealment of material facts, half-truths, and nondisclosure where the parties have some relation of trust to each other (for example, principal and agent). But the law is still evolving on the question of whether one is liable for nondisclosure in other situations. Courts often will not grant any legal relief for misrepresentations involving matters of opinion.

The law of misrepresentation is broader than the traditional action of deceit. But actions for negligent misrepresentation and for strict liability based on an innocent misrepresentation do not extend to as many persons as an action for deceit, and the recoverable damages may be more limited.

SLANDER, LIBEL, AND INVASION OF PRIVACY

Slander is oral defamation; libel is written defamation. For the plaintiff to have a legal action for defamation, the defendant must have intentionally or negligently communicated the defamatory statement about the plaintiff to a third person. Defamation is defined as a communication that tends to harm the reputation of another so as to lower that person in the estimation of the community or to deter third persons from dealing with the individual. But courts tend to hold that statements of opinion, even if abusive, do not constitute defamation, and that general statements about large groups (such as "All lawyers are liars") do not warrant legal relief unless special circumstances indicate that the reference is to a particular member of the group.

An action for slander will be unsuccessful unless the plaintiff proves actual damage or unless the plaintiff proves slander per se. The four types of slander per se are statements that impute to the plaintiff (1) commission of a serious crime, (2) a loathsome disease, (3) conduct or characteristics inconsistent with his business or trade, or (4) unchastity, if the plaintiff is a female. Whether equal-rights amendments to state constitutions will require abolition of the fourth category or extension of this category to males is not yet known. Under the common law many courts have held that in libel cases, unlike slander cases, damage is presumed, at least where the libel is clear on the face of the written communication.

Starting in 1964, however, the Supreme Court has decided many cases that have revised the law of libel, at least as applied to the press and broadcasting media (magazines, newspapers, radio, and television broadcasters). Under *New York Times* v. *Sullivan* (1964, involving false statements about a racial incident in Alabama) and other cases, such defendants are not liable to a public official or public figure for a defamatory falsehood relating to his official conduct unless the statement was made with knowledge that it was false or with reckless disregard of whether it was false. In *Gertz* v. *Welch* (1974, involving a falsehood about an attorney) the Court held that so long as the states do not impose liability without fault, they may define for themselves the appropriate standard of liability (for example, negligence) for a publisher or broadcaster who publishes defamatory falsehoods about a private individual. Other rulings of the Court have dealt with types of damages that may be recovered in these situations.

In most states truth is a complete defense to an action for defamation. Recovery also may be barred by the absolute privileges of (1) the judge, witnesses, attorneys, and litigants at a judicial proceeding, (2) federal and state legislators, and (3) federal and state government executives. When the defense of absolute privilege is applicable, it means that the defendant is not liable even if the defendant makes a clearly defamatory statement about another person. Thus, the defendant does not have to feel restrained by a fear of liability. A defendant's malice will not defeat such an absolute privilege, which is designed to encourage fearless management of the government. Other bars to recovery are absolute immunity for communications between spouses, and consent. Numerous types of qualified privileges (such as statements by an agent to a principal) are defenses, but they can be defeated by showing malice or other abuse by the defendant.

The courts have recognized an action for invasion of privacy, which actually involves four different torts: unreasonable intrusion upon the seclusion of another, appropriation of another's name or likeness, unreasonable publicity about another's private life, and publicity unreasonably placing another in a false light. But the Supreme Court has held that no recovery in false-light cases is possible unless statements are made with knowledge of their falsity or reckless disregard of the truth, and the Court has held, in a case involving rape, that no legal relief can be granted for publication of truthful information contained in public records open for public inspection.

TORTS AND FAMILY RELATIONSHIPS

Family relationships present special problems in tort law. Courts disagree over whether a husband and wife should be immune from tort liability for personal injury when one spouse sues the other, and over whether a minor child who is dependent on his or her parents and the parents themselves should be immune from such suits when a child or parent sues the other. Courts supporting immunity have relied on the danger of fraud and the possible disruption of family harmony if such suits are permitted, but the modern trend is to eliminate these immunities with some exceptions.

Three torts involving interference with the family are loss of consortium, alienation of affections, and criminal conversation. Most courts hold that a person who wrongfully causes physical injury to one spouse is liable to the other spouse for loss of consortium (sex, society, affectionate relations, and services). An action for alienation of affections exists for intentional deprivation of one spouse of the affections of the other spouse where the defendant knows of the marriage; however, near relatives have a defense of privilege to advise on marital matters. Criminal conversation is a tort action against a third party who has committed adultery with the plaintiff's spouse. The defendant's ignorance of the existence of the marriage is no defense to this tort. Most courts hold that neither a parent nor a child has an action for alienation of affections of the other. Moreover, because of dangers of

blackmail and extortion a majority of the states have abolished an action for alienation of affections or an action for criminal conversation, or both actions.

Most courts have held that contributory negligence of a spouse bars not only that spouse's action for personal injuries against a negligent defendant but also the other spouse's action for loss of consortium. Similarly, the courts have held that contributory negligence of a child bars not only the child's action for personal injuries against a negligent defendant but also the parent's action to recover for the medical expenses and loss of services of the child.

One final note concerns other miscellaneous torts. Courts permit a tort action for malicious prosecution where a prior criminal proceeding instituted by the current defendant against the current plaintiff was terminated in favor of the accused, there was no probable cause for the proceeding, and the defendant instituted the criminal proceeding with malice (*Russo* v. *State of New York*, 1982). Where the prior proceeding was a civil action instituted without probable cause and with malice, courts disagree on whether a tort action exists in the absence of special injury to the plaintiff. Courts recognize still another tort action of abuse of process, where a lawsuit has perverted legal procedure to accomplish a purpose for which the process was not designed. For example, in *Bull* v. *McCuskey* (1980), a medical doctor recovered from an attorney for an abuse of process because of a prior medical malpractice suit by the attorney against the doctor for the ulterior purpose of coercing a settlement, where the attorney knew that there was no basis for the malpractice claim. Further torts involve commercial operations. Examples of such torts are injurious falsehood (such as a false statement that the plaintiff has gone out of business), intentional interference with contractual relations, slander of title, trade libel, and unfair competition. However, the law recognizes certain privileges and other defenses to such tort actions.

FUTURE DIRECTIONS OF TORT LAW

Until the end of this century, the courts probably will continue, on the whole, to expand liability in tort, at least in those situations where state